THE MACHIAVELLIAN MOMENT

THE MACHIAVELLIAN MOMENT

Florentine Political Thought
and the Atlantic Republican Tradition

J. G. A. Pocock

PRINCETON UNIVERSITY PRESS

Library of Congress Cataloging in Publication Data
will be found on the last printed page of this book

Composed in Linotype Janson and printed
in the UNITED STATES OF AMERICA by Princeton
University Press at Princeton, New Jersey

CONTENTS

THIS BOOK is in two main parts, and the complexity of its theme must be the justification of its length. In the first half—subdivided into Parts One and Two—I attempt a treatment of Florentine thought in the era of Machiavelli, which groups him with his contemporaries and peers—Savonarola, Guicciardini, Giannotti, and others—in a manner not previously attempted in English; and I do this by seeking to situate Florentine republicanism in a context analyzed in the three chapters composing Part One. I here presume that the revival of the republican ideal by civic humanists posed the problem of a society, in which the political nature of man as described by Aristotle was to receive its fulfillment, seeking to exist in the framework of a Christian time-scheme which denied the possibility of any secular fulfillment. Further, I presume that the European intellect of this period was possessed of a limited number of ways of rendering secular time intelligible, which I discuss in the first three chapters and group under the headings of custom, grace, and fortune. The problem of the republic's existence in time had to be dealt with by these means and no others; and it is the way in which the Florentines of the first quarter of the sixteenth century—Machiavelli in particular—stated and explored the problem thus posed which gives their thought its remarkable character.

"The Machiavellian moment" is a phrase to be interpreted in two ways. In the first place, it denotes the moment, and the manner, in which Machiavellian thought made its appearance; and here the reader is asked to remember that this is not a "history of political thought," whatever that might be, in the last years of the Florentine republic, or a history of the political experience of Florentines in that era, designed to "explain" their articulation of the ideas studied. The "moment" in question is selectively and thematically defined. It is asserted that certain enduring patterns in the temporal consciousness of medieval and early modern Europeans led to the presentation of the republic, and the citizen's participation in it, as constituting a problem in historical self-understanding, with which Machiavelli and his contemporaries can be seen both explicitly and implicitly contending. It became crucial in their times and remained so, largely as a result of what they did with it, for two or three centuries afterwards. Their struggle with this problem is presented as historically real, though as one selected aspect of the complex historical reality of their thought; and their "moment" is defined as that in which they confronted the problem grown crucial.

In the second place, "the Machiavellian moment" denotes the problem itself. It is a name for the moment in conceptualized time in which the republic was seen as confronting its own temporal finitude, as attempting to remain morally and politically stable in a stream of irrational events conceived as essentially destructive of all systems of secular stability. In the language which had been developed for the purpose, this was spoken of as the confrontation of "virtue" with "fortune" and "corruption"; and the study of Florentine thought is the study of how Machiavelli and his contemporaries pursued the intimations of these words, in the context of those ways of thinking about time explored in the earlier chapters. In seeking to show that Machiavelli was one of a number of greater and lesser men engrossed in the common pursuit of this problem, I hope also to show that this is an appropriate context in which to study his thought, and that to study it in this way may diminish the amount of magniloquent and unspecific interpretation to which it has been subjected.

It is further affirmed that "the Machiavellian moment" had a continuing history, in the sense that secular political self-consciousness continued to pose problems in historical self-awareness, which form part of the journey of Western thought from the medieval Christian to the modern historical mode. To these continuing problems Machiavelli and his contemporaries, Florentine theory and its image of Venetian practice, left an important paradigmatic legacy: concepts of balanced government, dynamic *virtù*, and the role of arms and property in shaping the civic personality. In the second half of the book—Part Three—I pursue the history of "the Machiavellian moment" into English and American thought of the seventeenth and eighteenth centuries, and seek to show that the English-speaking political tradition has been a bearer of republican and Machiavellian, as well as constitutionalist, Lockean and Burkean, concepts and values. The crucial figure here, it is asserted, is James Harrington, who brought about a synthesis of civic humanist thought with English political and social awareness, and of Machiavelli's theory of arms with a common-law understanding of the importance of freehold property. The first three chapters of Part Three are devoted to a consideration of how a classical republican presentation of politics came to appear appropriate in the otherwise unlikely setting of Civil War England, where the conflict of Tudor monarchism with Puritan religious nationalism and sectarianism ensured the presence of many more competing styles and languages of thought than seems to have been the case in Florence. The steady growth of a neoclassical conception of politics, as in some sort an heir to Puritan millennialism, and its ascendancy in eighteenth-century England and America, is a phenomenon that requires exploration, and this the remainder of the book seeks to provide.

"The Machiavellian moment" in its eighteenth-century form provides the subject of the concluding chapters, whose emphasis is increasingly American. The confrontation of "virtue" with "corruption" is seen to have been a vital problem in social and historical philosophy during that era, and its humanist and Machiavellian vocabulary is shown to have been the vehicle of a basically hostile perception of early modern capitalism, grounded in awareness of the elaborate conventions of public credit rather than of the more direct interchanges of the market. The role of "fortune" was increasingly assumed by the concepts of "credit" and "commerce"; but while this led thinkers to perceive secular time more as dynamic and less as merely disorderly, the antithesis of "virtue" with "corruption"—or "virtue" with "commerce"—continued to operate as the means of expressing the quarrel between value and personality on the one hand, history and society on the other, in its first modern and secular form. This quarrel culminates, so far as the eighteenth century is concerned, with the beginnings of a dialectical perception of history in Europe, and of a utopian perception of global space in America, where an essentially Renaissance awareness of time is seen to have endured into the nineteenth century. What started with Florentine humanists as far back as Leonardo Bruni is affirmed to have played an important role in the shaping of the modern sense of history, and of alienation from history.

The book originated when Norman F. Cantor asked me to write a study of European constitutional thought in the sixteenth and seventeenth centuries for a series he was then editing. It has developed far from his or my original intention during nearly ten years; but I must not neglect to acknowledge his initial encouragement, or the generosity of his then publishers (John Wiley and Sons) in releasing me from obligations which I had formed.

When I seek to name those scholars whose work has meant most to me in writing this study, the presence of Hans Baron looms numinously if controversially (and entirely without his prior knowledge) over the whole scene. Among those whose works and conversations I have more immediately consulted, the names of Felix Gilbert, Donald Weinstein, William J. Bouwsma, John M. Wallace and Gordon S. Wood stand out in a host of others; and closer still to the historian's workshop, J. H. Hexter (Yale), Peter Riesenberg and John M. Murrin (Washington University), Richard E. Flathman (University of Washington), and Quentin Skinner (Cambridge) have read and criticized various sections of the manuscript at various stages. They of course bear no responsibility for its contents. Mr. Skinner even suggested the title, though he is not to be blamed for what I have made of it. I should also like to thank Peter Fuss, Max Okenfuss, and Henry Shapiro, my colleagues in the St. Louis chapter of the Conference for the Study of Political Thought, who endured a great deal at my hands; and my dear wife, who organized the index at a time when we had many other things to do. And the Graduate School and History Department of Washington University have been an unfailing source of material, moral and intellectual support for eight years.

J.G.A. POCOCK
Washington University, St. Louis
November 1973

PART ONE

PARTICULARITY AND TIME

The Conceptual Background

CHAPTER I

THE PROBLEM AND ITS MODES

A) Experience, Usage and Prudence

[1]

A SUSTAINED INTENTION throughout this book will be that of depicting early modern republican theory in the context of an emerging historicism, the product of the ideas and conceptual vocabularies which were available to medieval and Renaissance minds—such as C. S. Lewis called "Old Western"[1]—for the purpose of dealing with particular and contingent events and with time as the dimension of contingent happenings. The republic or Aristotelian polis, as that concept reemerged in the civic humanist thought of the fifteenth century, was at once universal, in the sense that it existed to realize for its citizens all the values which men were capable of realizing in this life, and particular, in the sense that it was finite and located in space and time. It had had a beginning and would consequently have an end; and this rendered crucial both the problem of showing how it had come into being and might maintain its existence, and that of reconciling its end of realizing universal values with the instability and circumstantial disorder of its temporal life. Consequently, a vital component of republican theory—and, once this had come upon the scene, if no earlier, of all political theory—consisted of ideas about time, about the occurrence of contingent events of which time was the dimension, and about the intelligibility of the sequences (it is as yet too soon to say processes) of particular happenings that made up what we should call history. It is this which makes it possible to call republican theory an early form of historicism, though we shall find that many of the connotations of our word "history" were at that time borne by other words and their equivalents in various languages—the words "usage," "providence," and "fortune" among them. Well-developed conceptual vocabularies existed in which the implications of these and other terms were expanded, and these vocabularies to some extent cohered with one

[1] "De Descriptione Temporum," in *Selected Literary Essays* (Cambridge University Press, 1969).

3

another; so that it is possible, and seems not improper, to reconstruct a scheme of ideas within which the sixteenth-century mind sought to articulate the equivalent of a philosophy of history. This, with its many difficulties and frustrations, constituted the conceptual framework within which the doctrine of the *vivere civile*—the ideal of active citizenship in a republic—must struggle to maintain itself; and that struggle is the subject of this book.

The next three chapters therefore consist of an exposition of what appear to have been the chief of these vocabularies, the principal modes of rendering the particular phenomenon, the particular event in time, as far intelligible as possible. The assumption throughout will be that this was difficult: that the late medieval and Renaissance intellect found the particular less intelligible and less rational than the universal; that since the particular was finite, it was local both in space and time, so that time became a dimension of its being and consequently shared in the diminished rationality and intelligibility of the particular. The language employed suggests that this assumption is susceptible of a philosophical explanation. The vocabularies which will be isolated, and around which this book will be organized, will be seen to have been of a sub-philosophical nature and to have offered means of rendering time and the particular intelligible on the assumption that they were less than perfectly rational; and hypotheses will be put forward concerning late medieval philosophy, designed to show why this imperfect rationality may have troubled men's minds.

The following generalizations may be advanced. Medieval philosophy tended to debate whether the sole true objects of rational understanding were not universal categories or propositions which were independent of time and space. The process of arriving at knowledge of them had indeed to be carried out within time and space, but recognition of their truth or reality was grounded upon perceptions independent of either; there was a self-evidence which was timeless and non-circumstantial. Reality of this order consisted of universals, and the activity of reason consisted of the intellect's ascent to recognition of the timeless rationality of universals. The truth of a self-evident proposition was self-contained and did not depend upon contingent recognition of some other proposition, still less upon evidence transitory in time and space; it was in this self-contained quality that timelessness largely consisted. In contrast, the knowledge of particulars was circumstantial, accidental, and temporal. It was based upon the sense-perceptions of the knower's transitory body, and very often upon messages transmitted to his senses by other knowers concerning what their sense-perceptions had permitted them to sense, to know, or to believe. Both for this reason and because propositions concerning particular

4

phenomena had to be constructed by moving through a dimension of contingency, in which one proposition was perpetually dependent upon another, knowledge of particulars was time-bound, just as the phenomena of which it was knowledge, localized by particularity in space and time, were time-bound themselves.

If we use "history" as a name for this time-dimension, we can say that a scholastic "philosophy of history" emphasized its contingent and sub-rational character; but there are several senses in which we can say that the scholastic intellect did not offer a philosophy of history at all. By "history" we normally mean successions of events taking place in time, social and public rather than private and subjective in character, which we try to organize, first into narratives and second into processes; but this was not an objective which the scholastic intellect greatly valued. Narrative, the mere telling of a tale, it followed Aristotle in considering inferior to poetry, as poetry was inferior to philosophy, because it was inferior in bringing to light the universal significances of events; and these were best arrived at by thinking which abandoned the particular event altogether and rose above it to contemplation of universal categories. As for processes and time as the dimension of process, the process of change which the Aristotelian intellect singled out was that by which a thing came to be and then not to be: *physis*, the process by which it fulfilled its end, perfected its form, realized its potential, and then ceased—all of which are extensions of the idea of coming to be and then not to be. All things come to an end in time, but the intelligibility of time was closer to being in the things, since the essential systole and diastole were in the being and not-being of the things, and it was this of which time was the measure. But the being and not-being of a thing is not identical with the replacement of that thing by another thing; it is a closed process whereas the latter is open-ended; and to the extent to which the Aristotelian intellect identified change with *physis*, it tended to adopt a circular concept of process and therefore of time. This had the advantage of rendering time entirely intelligible. If time was to be measured by motion, Aristotle considered,

> regular circular motion is above all else the measure, because the number of this is the best known. Now neither alteration nor increase nor coming into being can be regular, but locomotion can be. This also is why time is thought to be the motion of the sphere, viz. because the other movements are measured by this, and time by this movement.
>
> This also explains the common saying that human affairs form a circle, and that there is a circle in all other things that have a natural

5

movement and coming into being and passing away. This is because all other things are discriminated by time, and end and begin as though conforming to a cycle; for even time itself is thought to be a circle. And this opinion again is held because time is the measure of this kind of locomotion and is itself measured by such. So that to say that the things that come into being form a circle is to say that there is a circle of time; and this is to say that it is measured by the circular movement; for apart from the measure nothing else to be measured is observed; the whole is just a plurality of measures.[2]

It is easy to detect that Aristotle was well aware that to treat time as circular because the sphere was the most perfect figure, and consequently the best measure, was an intellectual convenience and not—what it became for others—an expression of faith in the ultimate intelligibility of the universe; little less easy to see that he understood the difficulty of applying the circular concept to history, that is, to "human affairs." For in human affairs a great diversity of things happen without any predictable order, and we can only say that these form a cycle as a means of saying that the whole variety of human experience forms a single gigantic entity having its own self-fulfilling and self-repetitive *physis*. Post-Aristotelian philosophies existed which were prepared to make this assertion, but we are now warned against overestimating their importance;[3] it was well enough understood that the application of *physis* to human affairs was an intellectual convenience and a metaphor, and it was, after all, Greeks who pioneered the writing of history as what it has so largely remained, an exercise in political ironics—an intelligible story of how men's actions produce results other than those they intended.

But it was one thing to recognize that there were limits to the application of circular *physis* to human history—to treating the succession of one thing to another on the analogy of the succession of the being and not-being of a single thing; quite another, at the philosophical level, to produce any equally satisfactory mode of treating the former succession. The Hellenic intellect wrote history, but it did not make history philosophically intelligible. As for the Christian intellect on these matters, it of course repudiated all ideas of cosmic recurrence;

[2] Aristotle, *Physics*, IV, 223b-224a; trans. R. P. Hardie and R. K. Gaye in W. D. Ross (ed.), *The Works of Aristotle*, VIII (Oxford: The Clarendon Press, 1930).

[3] Robert F. Nisbet, *Social Change and History: Aspects of the Western Theory of Development* (New York: Oxford University Press, 1969); Chester G. Starr, *The Awakening of the Greek Historical Spirit* (New York: Alfred A. Knopf, 1968); *History and Theory*, Beiheft 6, "History and the Concept of Time" (Middletown, Conn.: Wesleyan University Press, 1966).

"the wicked dance in circles";[4] such a vision of things would make the world uncreated and endless. But Christian insistence on a God who had created the world and men at a point in time past and would redeem men and end the world at a point in time future, though of incalculable importance for the development of historical thought, did not of itself render intelligible the succession of particular events and phenomena in time, or ascribe any special importance to time considered as the dimension of that succession. The problem of divine foreknowledge, the problem of how the individual might relate his timebound existence to the immediate presence of a timeless and eternal God, led Augustine and Boethius to postulate the idea of a *nunc-stans* or standpoint in eternity from which God saw every moment in time as simultaneously created and present; but whether the individual affirmed the *nunc-stans* as an act of intellect or of faith, it was evident that he could not share it and that one moment in time could not be known to an intelligence imprisoned in another moment. Nor was such knowledge of any final importance. Movement in fallen man, if effected by his own depraved will and intelligence, was movement away from God and toward further damnation, away from meaning and toward deepening meaninglessness (this movement may be detected in the *Inferno*). Given the promise of an ultimate redemption, historical time could indeed be seen as equally the movement back toward God; but this was effected by a separate sequence of acts of redemptive grace, sharply distinguished from and only mysteriously related to the happenings of history in the secular sense. The footsteps of God might be in history, but history as a whole did not consist of such footsteps; eternity might be in love with the products of time, but time was a passive and inert beloved. Finally, an Aristotelianized Christianity tended to restore the analogy of *physis*; man had lost his form, his true nature, and *reformatio*—the work of grace—was operating to restore him to it. One might debate whether *redemptio* was not something more than *reformatio*: whether the movement consisted of a circular return to the state of the unfallen Adam, or a spiral ascent to a condition higher than that lost by the *felix peccatum*;[5] but in neither case did it consist of the succession of human actions and suffer-

---

[4] Psalms XI: 9; quoted as from St. Augustine in Frank E. Manuel, *Shapes of Philosophical History* (Stanford University Press, 1965), p. 3.

[5] See generally, Gerhart B. Ladner, *The Idea of Reform: Its Impact on Christian Thought and Action in the Age of the Fathers* (Cambridge, Mass.: Harvard University Press, 1959), and for a particular instance of debate, Jesper Rosenmeier, "New England's Perfection: the Image of Adam and the Image of Christ in the Antinomian Crisis, 1634 to 1638," *William and Mary Quarterly*, 3d ser., vol. 27, no. 3 (July 1970).

ings. Secular time—there is an etymological tautology here—was the theater of redemption, but not its dimension. Without redemption, furthermore, it was entropic: the loss of form, the movement from order toward disorder, which might be reversed but could not be meaningfully continued.

Christian thought concerning a succession of particulars therefore tended to consist of a succession of efforts to relate the particulars to universals, carried out by means that might be philosophical or poetical, typological, anagogical, or analogical—there was an impressive, even majestic, array of devices existing to this end—but operated so as to view each particular in its relation to eternity and to pass by the succession of particulars itself as revealing nothing of importance. The eternal order to which particulars were related was not a temporal or a historical order, even when it made history by manifesting itself in time; and history was often—though not always—seen as little more than a series of symbolizations, in which sequential narrative was of little more than expository significance.[6] The dual meaning of words such as "temporal" and "secular" is at this point beginning to appear in its true importance: both connote the ideas of time (tempus, saeculum) and of the nonsacred because noneternal. It is a useful simplification to say that the Christian world-view—while of course containing the seeds of what was to supersede it—was based upon the exclusion from consideration of temporal and secular history, and that the emergence of historical modes of explanation had much to do with the supersession of that world-view by one more temporal and secular.

This book is concerned with some aspects of that process, and it is going to be argued that an important role in generating it was played by consideration of politics. There is a historically resonant vocabulary in which politics is presented as "the art of the possible" and therefore contingent, "the endless adventure"[7] of governing men, the "ship" sailing "a bottomless and boundless sea";[8] and if we think of the domain of contingency as history, "the play of the contingent, the unexpected and the unforeseen,"[9] it will appear that a powerful stimulus to the growth of secular historiography may arise from this view of politics (so that political man may prove to have had his own quarrel with the

[6] For one aspect of this, see William J. Brandt, The Shape of Medieval History: Studies in Modes of Perception (New Haven and London: Yale University Press, 1966).

[7] F. S. Oliver, The Endless Adventure: Personalities and Practical Politics in Eighteenth-Century England (Boston: Houghton Mifflin, 1931).

[8] Michael Oakeshott, Rationalism in Politics and Other Essays (London: Methuen, 1962), p. 127.

[9] H.A.L. Fisher, preface to A History of Europe (Boston: Houghton Mifflin, 1935).

Christian world-view). But it is not from political philosophy, in the premodern sense of that term, that we shall see ideas of secular contingency arising. In what some still like to call "the great tradition" of that philosophy, the political community was seen as a universal phenomenon, something natural to man. Efforts were made to state its idea or form, to relate its principles to those of the universal order of which it formed part, and these tended for obvious reasons to remove it from the domain of particularity and contingency. Yet even within the philosophical tradition it was recognized that political society was, when viewed in the concrete, a secular and consequently a time-bound phenomenon. The province of philosophy was not perhaps extended to include the provision of wholly temporal modes of intelligibility, ways of understanding the time-bound from within secular time; but somewhat outside the philosophical tradition, modes of thought can be detected which were explicitly concerned with problems of political particularity, with what was intellectually possible when the particular political society was viewed as existing in time, when the particular contingency or event was viewed as arising in time, and when the particular society was viewed as a structure for absorbing and responding to the challenges posed by such events and as consisting, institutionally and historically, of the traces of such responses made in past time. An attempt will now be made to expound three such modes of thought and, in so doing, to construct a model which will help to elucidate what happened when the republican ideal posed the problem of the universal's existence in secular particularity.

[II]

Sir John Fortescue (c. 1390-1479), an English lawyer and the kind of amateur of philosophy who helps us understand the ideas of an age by coarsening them slightly, wrote the greatest of his works, the *De Laudibus Legum Anglie* (*In Praise of the Laws of England*) about 1468-1471. At that time he was in exile with the Lancastrian claimants to the English throne, from whom he held the title of Lord Chancellor, but it is of far more significance that he had served before exile as Lord Chief Justice of the King's Bench, the premier office of the English common law. If at a later time it was said of Francis Bacon that "he wrote philosophy like a Lord Chancellor," it could with equal truth be said of Fortescue that—not for the last time in English history—he wrote philosophy like a Lord Chief Justice. The two great legal offices made different demands on the application of intellect to society, and encouraged correspondingly different social philosophies.[10]

[10] See the present writer's studies of Sir Matthew Hale (1609-1676) in *The*

The *De Laudibus*, at all events, is a dialogue on the study of English law between a Prince of Wales and a Lord Chancellor of England, both in exile. The chancellor seeks to persuade the prince that he should study the laws of the country he is to rule, as well as martial exercises; and when the prince objects that English law is known to be of such technicality that professional lawyers immerse themselves for years in its details before presuming to practice it,[11] we encounter a reply that introduces us straightway to the central philosophical problem of our subject. The chancellor replies, in effect, that every branch of study is approached by gaining a grasp of its principles. These are called maxims in mathematics, paradoxes in rhetoric, rules of law (*regula juris*) in civil law, and maxims, once again, in the study of the laws of England. If the prince gains a knowledge of these maxims, he will deserve to be called learned in the laws of England, even though he never applies his knowledge to exact points of legal interpretation, which he will normally leave to his judges, serjeants-at-law, and other professional lawyers. The prince is satisfied by this reply, but it remains to be seen what he has gained by it. For in all that Fortescue says of these maxims, it is evident that, like the axioms, paradoxes, and so forth in other sciences, they are the universal, self-evident, undemonstrable principles on which, according to the basic procedures of Aristotelian philosophy, any system of knowledge must rest. They are acquired directly "by induction through the senses and the memory"; they "are not known by force of argument or by logical demonstrations"; they are not deduced from one another, or from any antecedent premise; "there is no rational ground for principles," but "any principle is its own ground for holding it."[12] In all this, Fortescue is quoting direct from the medieval texts of Aristotle, and we have begun to observe the use of a rigorously deductive philosophy by a mind steeped in the practice of customary law.

In the philosophy which Fortescue is outlining here, all rational knowledge is essentially deductive. Knowledge, of whatever kind, starts with the acceptance of certain basic principles, some of which are the foundations of all knowledge as such, while others distinguish knowledge into its various branches and form the bases of the various sciences which they distinguish. The rational proof of any statement is arrived at by demonstrating that it is the necessary logical conse-

---

Ancient Constitution and the Feudal Law (Cambridge University Press, 1957; New York: W. W. Norton, 1967), pp. 170-81, and *Politics, Language and Time* (New York: Atheneum, 1971; London, Methuen, 1972), pp. 215-22, 262-64.

[11] Sir John Fortescue, *De Laudibus Legum Anglie*, ed. and trans. S. B. Chrimes (Cambridge University Press, 1949), ch. VII, pp. 19-21.

[12] *De Laudibus*, ch. VIII, pp. 20-23.

quence of some principle or combination of principles, and from this it follows (a) that there can be no rational proof of any principle, since nothing which can be deduced from a principle is a principle itself, (b) that any branch of knowledge—mathematics, rhetoric, civil law, English law—consists of knowledge of the relevant set of principles and their deducible consequences. Reason in the strict sense of the term is simply that by which we are enabled to perform deductions from principles; induction is the mental process by which we arrive at knowledge of principles; but that by which we recognize what cannot and need not be proved, namely the truth of principles, is neither reason nor induction—intuition, though not used by Fortescue, is possibly the best word for it.'But if we use "reason" slightly more loosely, to mean that faculty of the mind by which the consequences of principles are detected and validated, we instantly encounter the central difficulty of Fortescue's argument with respect to English law. Principles, inescapably, are universal statements; and from universals we can deduce only universals. Now if English law is to be a rational branch of study, it must consist of certain principles, underived from other principles, and their consequences, which must be true of all English legal situations to which they apply. It is affirmed that English law consists of a series of uniform deductions from certain maxims, with which it is all logically coherent; but what principles (we must now ask) could there be, underived from other principles and intuitively perceived to be self-evident, of which "England" is the subject? "England" must be the name, either of a unique constellation of factors, or of a member of a class of which there are other members. In the former case there could be no body of universals concerning it, since you cannot make universal statements concerning a single unique object; in the latter the principles and universals concerning English law would apply also to the law of other members of the class to which "England" belonged. But the prince in Fortescue's dialogue, when he doubted whether he could study English law, expressed doubt also whether he should study it in preference to civil law, i.e., the law of Rome; and the chancellor undertook to settle both doubts, that is, to convince him that there existed a readily accessible rational science of English law as distinct from the law of other nations. Fortescue's purpose seems entangled in contradiction from the start, and the prince's chance of learning the law by mastering a purely "English" set of principles appears to be foredoomed.

At a rather later point in the *De Laudibus* Fortescue declares it to be a universal truth in the study of law that all human laws are either law of nature, or custom, or statutes.[13] The law of nature consists of

---

[13] *Ibid.*, ch. xv, pp. 36-37.

those self-evident principles of justice, and their universally deducible consequences, which are true and have binding force among all men. Human laws may be simply the translation of the commands of natural law into the formalized commands or rules of a particular kingdom. But there is nothing here which need detain the student of specifically English law, for

> the laws of England, in those points which they sanction by reason of the law of nature, are neither better nor worse in their judgements than are all laws of other nations in like cases. For, as Aristotle said, in the fifth book of the *Ethics, Natural law is that which has the same force among all men.* Wherefore there is no need to discuss it further. But from now on we must examine what are the customs, and also the statutes, of England, and we will first look at the characteristics of those customs.[14]

The universal principles of justice are cognizable by reason and, it should seem, it is they which form the maxims on which the science of jurisprudence is founded; they which the prince may learn by the brief exercise of his own reason, while leaving their detailed application to his professional servants with their long years of specialized study and experience. But there is nothing specifically "English" about knowledge of the law of nature, or of that part of English law which is identical with the law of nature or with the corresponding element in the laws of other nations. To discover what is uniquely English about the laws of England we must turn to what have been described as "custom and statute," the two remaining categories into which all human law must fall. It is in these divisions that the law of England is uniquely English, and the law of any nation uniquely itself.

In agrarian societies which are highly decentralized and traditional, but which a professionally organized class of literate bureaucrats, obedient to a central direction, is trying to bring under control, it is common—at least in the West—to find a distinction between unwritten custom, usage, or tradition, recognized by the king's servants but recognized as being already established by the spontaneous and traditional adoption of society itself, and the written commands, edicts, ukases, or statutes as Fortescue calls them, imposed upon society by order of the king and his literati, whether or not these claim to be digesting or modifying what was previously unwritten tradition. It may be observed that the distinction, though clear, is not absolute; it may be hard to distinguish between a written judgment, recognizing that such has been and is the law by virtue of custom, and a written

---

[14] *Ibid.*, ch. XVI (the whole chapter), pp. 38-39.

decree, ordaining that such is and shall be the law by virtue of the authority of whoever issues the decree. English lawyers sometimes attempted to distinguish on this basis between unwritten law or *lex non scripta*, which might be written down but which claimed no authority but that of custom and tradition, and written law, *lex scripta* or statute, whose authority was that of the author of the writing—normally the king in parliament; but parliament also functioned as a court, whose business was to declare old law (custom) rather than to promulgate new (statute), and in a statute itself the notion of a declaration of custom might survive and render its nature ambiguous.

Fortescue's problem may be resummarized as follows. Customs and statutes together make up the particular laws of any nation. Now if these are to claim rational justification they must be rationally deducible, or at least contain nothing contrary to what is rationally deducible, from the principles of natural justice; but it is not their deducibility or their rationality which gives them their particular character. To understand wherein the laws of England differ from those of Rome or France, we must investigate not their rationality—since therein they are identical with those of other nations—but the ways in which the principles of justice have in them been applied to the special character and circumstances of England. In short, English law contains—as does the law of any nation—an element other than the purely rational, based on the cognition of circumstances and conditions peculiar to England and on the application or adaptation of universal principles to these local and peculiar conditions.

Fortescue's account of this element is found in his seventeenth chapter, which follows immediately, without the interposition of a word, upon the passage last quoted.

> . . . and we will first look at the characteristics of those customs.
>
> [XVII] The kingdom of England was first inhabited by Britons, then ruled by Romans, again by Britons, then possessed by Saxons, who changed its name from Britain to England. Then for a short time the kingdom was conquered by Danes, and again by Saxons, but finally by Normans, whose posterity hold the realm at the present time. And throughout the period of these nations and their kings, the realm has been continuously ruled by the same customs as it is now, customs which, if they had not been the best, some of those kings would have changed for the sake of justice or by the impulse of caprice, and totally abolished them, especially the Romans, who judged almost the whole of the rest of the world by their laws. Similarly, others of these aforesaid kings, who possessed the kingdom of England only by the sword, could, by that power,

have destroyed its laws. Indeed, neither the civil laws of the Romans, so deeply rooted by the usage[15] of so many ages, nor the laws of the Venetians, which are renowned above others for their antiquity—though their island was uninhabited, and Rome unbuilt, at the time of the origins of the Britons—nor the laws of any Christian kingdom, are so rooted in antiquity. Hence there is no gainsaying nor legitimate doubt but that the customs of the English are not only good but the best.

[xviii] It only remains, then, to examine whether or not the statutes of the English are good . . .[16]

and with that, indeed, Fortescue has completed all that he has to say in the *De Laudibus* concerning the grounds for the legitimation of custom. In this chapter, at once very English and very medieval, the particular laws of particular nations are being legitimized by reference, not to reason and the knowledge of universals, but to antiquity and usage. The laws of Rome and Venice are good because they have been for very long periods in continuous use; the laws of England are the best because they have been in use longest, and the testing to which they have been subjected is underlined by consideration of the succession of kings, of various ruling races, who had opportunity to have changed them if they had so desired. But we are told nothing of the process of rational reflection by which these rulers decided that the existing laws were the best, nor—strictly speaking—is it possible that we should be. The essentially deductive process which was reason in Aristotelian philosophy was capable of testing a law only by testing its conformity to the principles of natural justice, and that test, however valuable and necessary, was not the only one. In dealing with the particular laws of particular nations, Fortescue must also ask whether they suit the peculiar character and circumstances of the nation whose life they regulate, and that is what is being tested here. In that context, of course, the laws of England can be "better" than those of Rome or Venice only in the sense that they suit the English better than their equivalents suit the Romans or Venetians. How is such an elusive comparison to be carried out? Since reason is concerned with universals, there must be some other instrument which detects national character and conditions and tests the suitability of national law to these conditions.

Such an instrument there is, and it is called usage or experience; but since it is not reason in the fully reflective and ordered sense of the

[15] The Latin is *"tantorum temporum curriculis . . . in quantum . . . inveterate sunt"* (p. 38), but the word *usus* frequently occurs in Fortescue's text and is rendered by Chrimes as "usage."

[16] *De Laudibus*, ch. xvi, pp. 38-41.

term, it is, though available only to intelligent creatures, unanalytic, uncritical, and inarticulate. It can be, and very often is, unconscious. Men observe usages and customs, or they do not. If the customs are observed, they must be good customs in the sense of well suited to the people who observe them; but the people could not tell you why the customs they observe are good or those they abandon bad, not merely because the people are not philosophers, but because the philosopher himself could not tell you. The philosopher can see only the universal aspects of things; there is no method, no self-critical or self-verifying intellectual procedure, yet evolved for dealing with their particular aspects. Consequently, the goodness of a good custom can be inferred from the fact of its preservation; it can hardly be demonstrated, since demonstration consists in deduction from a universal premise, and no such premise can contain the particular character and circumstances of the people whose custom it is. We cannot give the "reason" why a custom is good or bad; we can only say "there is reason to believe" that it is good (because preserved) or bad (because abandoned). This is what Edmund Burke—a direct heir of this way of thinking—was to call "prescriptive" or "presumptive" reasoning. Because a custom or a particular institution had a "prescriptive" claim—i.e., was already established—there was a "presumption" in its favor; we presumed that it had been found to work well.[17]

The longer it had been in existence, the greater the presumption in its favor. The naivety of Fortescue's argument that English law is best because oldest should by now be becoming intelligible. There can, according to a strictly deductive conception of reasoning, be no rational mode of dealing with particulars, no rational way of proving that a nation has certain characteristics or that its laws suit those characteristics. How then can there be any comparative evaluation of legal systems? The Venetians have testified that their law suits them by retaining it for a very long time; the English have testified to the suitability of their law in exactly the same way. There is no rational—or, in modern terms, scientific—method of selecting and analyzing the peculiar characteristics of the Venetians and the English respectively, detecting and analyzing the peculiar characteristics of their respective laws and evaluating the latter by measuring them against the former. We cannot rationally say that (or why) English law suits the English better than Venetian law suits the Venetians; we have only two sets of presumptions, neither of which can be fully stated or rationally demonstrated. We can, however, have recourse to the last refuge of the social scientist when faced with incommensurables: we can quan-

[17] See, for a theory of presumptive tradition, *Politics, Language and Time*, chs. 6 and 7.

tify. If the laws of England are indeed older than those of Venice and have been longer in continuous usage, then more men, in more years and more situations, have testified silently in their favor; there is a greater weight of experience, a greater weight of presumption, impelling us to believe them satisfactory to the historic society where they obtain, than exists with regard to the laws of Venice. Such is the rationale of the argument from antiquity, with which in this book we shall be much (though indirectly) concerned. It is a direct consequence of the shortcomings of the deductive philosophy.

But the prince of the *De Laudibus* is now seen to have been cheated by his chancellor. He was assured that if he would only learn the principles of English law, he would know enough to understand what his judges and other professional lawyers were doing when they applied these principles to concrete cases. It has turned out, however, that the cognition of concrete cases and the discernment of how principles are to be applied to them is a sharply different intellectual process from the cognition of principles and the deduction of their logical consequences. Indeed, it is scarcely an intellectual process at all; it is a matter of pure trial and error, since the test of a custom's goodness is not its demonstrable rationality, but the simple fact of its having remained in usage. Therefore the learning of a professional lawyer is not to be reduced to a knowledge of principles and their consequences; it is knowledge of what customs have been retained and what the technical, rather than logical, consequences of their retention have been. Customary law is a technical and traditional, rather than a rational structure; and Fortescue is well on the way to the later conception—expressed by Sir Edward Coke, another Chief Justice—of English law as "artificial reason."

> Thus you, prince, would marvel at a lawyer of England if he told you that a brother shall not succeed in a paternal heritage to a brother not born of the same mother, but that rather the heritage shall descend to a sister of the whole blood or shall fall to the lord-in-chief of the fee as his escheat, because you are ignorant of the reason for this law. But the difficulty of such a case does not in the least perturb one learned in the law of England. Wherefore . . . you will realise that if by instruction you will understand those laws of which you are now ignorant, you will love them, since they are the best; and the more you reflect upon them, the more agreeably you will enjoy them. For all that is loved transfers the lover into its own nature by usage, wherefore, said Aristotle, *Use becomes another nature.*[18]

[18] *De Laudibus*, ch. v, pp. 14-17.

16

It will be argued later on that the last sentence is of great importance: that in the concepts of "use" and "second nature" may be found
the beginnings of the historicist doctrine that we become what we do
and so make ourselves. But there was not much for the prince to do
with English law but love it and permit it to transform his nature.
Words like "the reason for this law" and "since they are the best"
consciously beg the question. Such statements were not demonstrable
and consequently were above criticism. The prince was in no position
to criticize the application of law by his judges, unless reason should
tell him that what they were doing was contrary to natural justice.
Except in such rare cases, the reason of the law was prescriptive and
based on antiquity; he could only accept (and, of course, love) the
customs of his kingdom on the presumption that, being ancient, they
were good and, being the oldest in the world, they were also the best.
The judges knew what the usages of the kingdom were, and his knowledge of natural justice and its consequences not only did not tell him
but did not equip him to find out; for the study of customary law was
not a scholastic process of rational deduction but—as Coke was to tell
James I[19]—a matter of lifelong study in the records and working
experience in the courts.

It is very possible that Fortescue's main intention was still to argue
that English law was reasonable, in the sense that it could be shown
to be consonant throughout its structure with deductions performed
from the principles of jurisprudence or the maxims characteristic of
common law itself. But there exists in his thought an inexpugnable
level at which it appeared that English law was not rational, in the
sense that it could never be reconstructed by the performance of any
such deductions. Other forms of intelligence than the philosophical,
which took longer to learn because they were based on experience
rather than study, had been at work in its making; and consequently,
the prince might hope to admire his judges intelligently, but—once
the point was reached at which law had to be considered custom—
admire he must.

Custom is the fruit of experience, operating at the lowest and least
articulate level of intelligence, that of trial and error. Only experience

---

[19] "Then the king said, that he thought the law was founded upon reason, and
that he and others had reason as well as the judges: to which it was answered by
me, that true it was, that God had endowed his Majesty with excellent science,
and great endowments of nature; but his Majesty was not learned in the laws of
his realm of England, and causes which concern the life, or inheritance, or goods,
or fortunes of his subjects are not to be decided by natural reason, but by the
artificial reason and judgment of law, which law is an art which requires long
study and experience before that a man can attain to the knowledge of it": Coke,
Twelfth Reports, Prohibitions del Roy (12 Co. Rep. 65).

can establish it; only experience can know it to be good; and the experience of the mind that recognizes it necessarily rests on the experience of countless other men in past generations, of which the custom itself is the expression. Custom therefore is self-validating; its own existence and its own presumed longevity are the main reasons for presuming it to be good and well suited to the needs and nature of the people, and it peremptorily requires the scrutinizing mind to rest satisfied with the assumptions which it contains about itself. The prince is not equipped to be a critic and reformer of custom for the following reasons: there is no method, other than that of experience itself, by which the intellect can reason from the needs and nature of the people to their customs, or determine scientifically whether the latter are well or ill suited to the former; and since there is only experience, which must be accumulated rather than systematically constructed in the threescore and ten years of a man's lifetime, the prince must recognize that his is the experience of one man only, not to be pitted against that of the myriad men of antiquity which has gone to the making of any single custom, let alone the whole body of the customary law of his realm.

It is therefore hard for Fortescue's prince to legislate, for the reason that there is no scientific method of determining what particular laws will suit particular peoples or particular situations. The only method known to the scholastic mind is that of deductive logic, which deals only with universals; the adjudication of the particular must be left to experience, which for the most part issues in customs, and in the immeasurably slow processes of the formation of custom the prince's intellect has no preeminence. Sometimes, it is true, laws must be promulgated in shorter time than it takes for a custom to crystallize out from the general mass of behavior, and here we reach the third division of legislation according to Fortescue, the category of statute. But here too the dichotomy of reason and experience, and the principle of the quantifiability of experience, operate. Immediately after he has grounded custom upon usage and antiquity, Fortescue says:

> It only remains, then, to examine whether or not the statutes of the English are good. These, indeed, do not emanate from the will of the prince alone, as do the laws in kingdoms which are governed entirely regally, where so often statutes secure the advantage of their maker only, thereby redounding to the loss and undoing of the subjects. . . . But the statutes of England cannot so arise, since they are made not only by the prince's will, but also by the assent of the whole realm, so they cannot be injurious to the people nor fail to secure their advantage. Furthermore, it must be supposed that they

are necessarily replete with prudence and wisdom, since they are promulgated by the prudence not of one counsellor or a hundred only, but of more than three hundred chosen men—of such a number as once the Senate of the Romans was ruled by—as those who know the form of the summons, the order and the procedure of parliament can more clearly describe. And if statutes ordained with such solemnity and care happen not to give full effect to the intention of the makers, they can speedily be revised, and yet not without the assent of the commons and nobles of the realm, in the manner in which they first originated. Thus, prince, all the kinds of the law of England are now plain to you. You will be able to estimate their merits by your own wisdom, and by comparison with other laws; and when you find none in the world so excellent, you will be bound to confess that they are not only good, but as good as you could wish.[20]

The dice are as heavily loaded as ever against the capacity of the prince, as a student of comparative legislation, to arrive at any other conclusion, and as heavily against his ability to function as a legislator or critic of legislation, in respect of statute no less than of custom. Particular laws—this is the key of the matter—can be framed only by experience, by usage in the long run and by prudence in the short; the prince's experience is only that of one man, as against that of his three hundred counselors, of the body of his subjects now living or the unnumbered democracy of the dead of antiquity (the test of quantification makes custom presumptively wiser than statute); and his reason, which tells him only whether custom and statute are in accordance with the principles of natural justice, can after all tell him no more than reason will tell any other *animal rationale* who possesses it. On every score, then, the prince whose authority is above that of any other man cannot legislate effectively without afforcing his reason and experience with the reason and experience of as many other men as possible, and this is never done better than when he joins with the democracy of the dead to respect the usages of antiquity. Here we have come to one of the pillars supporting Fortescue's preference for the prince who rules by law and consent over the prince who rules by his own reason and experience alone. The latter need be no tyrant, but an honest man attempting the impossible and neglecting the help which others can bring him. The whole question, however, deserves to be reviewed in a wider theoretical context.

C. H. McIlwain, in *Constitutionalism Ancient and Modern*,[21] traced

[20] *De Laudibus*, ch. xviii, pp. 40-41.
[21] Ithaca: Cornell University Press, Great Seal Books, 1958, chs. ii and iv.

the philosophical distinction between Fortescue's *regnum regale* and *regnum politicum et regale* back to the parting of the ways followed by Plato when he wrote the *Republic* and by the later Plato and Aristotle after him. In the *Republic*, Plato raised the question whether the city should be ruled by law or by the unfettered wisdom of its ideal ruler, and decided in favor of the unrestricted authority of the philosopher-ruler. He did so on the grounds that a law was only a generalization which must be modified to fit the particular case, or else distort the particular case to make the latter fit it, whereas the philosopher possessed an intuitive grasp of universals which gave him, at one and the same time, an intuitive grasp of the essential character of each particular case. Where a law was like a stiff bar which must be bent to fit each case if it was not to break it, the philosopher's wisdom was fluid; it flowed around each case and embraced all its details. But for this to be true, the relation between universals and particulars must be very different from what it is in Fortescue's medieval Aristotelianism. The doctrine of the *Republic* involves the existence of the Ideas or Forms of Platonic philosophy, those ideal and perfect intellectual objects which constitute the only real world, to one of which every object in the phenomenal world of our senses corresponds, but of which it is only a derivative and imperfect copy. Knowledge of the Forms is not sense-knowledge, nor is it abstracted or generalized from sense-knowledge; it is attained when the intellect is directly illuminated by the Form itself, or by the world of the Forms, as happens to the prisoner in the Myth of the Cave when he escapes from a place where he can see only the shadows of things cast by firelight and emerges into the sunlight where he can see things themselves. Once our intellects have been illuminated by the Forms, we have complete knowledge of all the phenomenal things derived from them, because derivative reality is illuminated by the reality from which it is derived. In this way—but only in this way—the philosopher-ruler can be said to know particular situations and cases better than the general rules of the law can be said to "know" them.

But in the *Statesman* and the *Laws*, McIlwain continued, the later Plato was prepared to consider the possibility of a philosopher-ruler whose knowledge was not knowledge of Forms but consisted in a series of generalizations from experience. Such a ruler should submit his decisions to be disciplined by laws, since these generalizations could be constructed on a wider basis than was possible to his intellect alone. Government of this kind, however, would necessarily be imperfect, since its knowledge would consist of generalizations abstracted from experience, which must be laboriously reconverted into concrete terms to fit each individual case, which in turn might contain elements not allowed for in the original generalization. There must be a discontinuity between abstract and concrete, universal generalization and particular case, in any system of knowledge except that enjoyed by the philosopher of the *Republic*; and it could be argued that the lesser breed of ruling intellect must be doubly disciplined by law, first by the need to submit his individual decisions to the law's general rules, secondly by the necessity to accept some sort of guidance when it came to converting them into particular decisions—for if his only knowledge was of imperfect generalizations, imperfect too must be his understanding of particular cases.

Aristotle, in the *Politics*, developed this line of argument and, discussing whether wisdom or the law should rule, concluded that only if a philosopher should appear whose intelligence was as far above that of men as theirs was above that of beasts should he rule without the discipline of law; a ruler who possessed the same kind of intelligence as his subjects, but raised to its highest attainable level, could not possibly be as wise as the laws.[22] The implication is that Aristotle was ceasing to believe that the Forms were real, or at least were knowable by man. Because our bodies located and limited us in space and time, we could know only what our senses and memory told us and what our intellects then did with the information thus received. Ideas were thus "attained by induction through the senses and memory," as Fortescue summarizes Aristotle as saying; they were abstractions from the data. But the abstractions thus arrived at formed propositions, and some of these propositions were self-evident principles; that is, their truth was instantly and intuitively perceived by the intellect. Now the history of Aristotelian metaphysics shows that it was possible to regard these absolute intellectual propositions as real entities, and even as the only ultimate reality created by God; the phenomenal world appeared as the exemplification, operation, modification, or even degeneration of its principles, which thus came after all to resemble Platonic Forms more closely. But even if ultimate reality was intellectual, it could be known by men—rational animals, but animals all the same—only in the shape of concepts abstracted from sense-data and social communications. Christianity, with its emphasis on the difference between the life of the body and that of the spirit, encouraged the idea that "now I see through a glass darkly, but then face to face"; and in Christian Aristotelianism the direct apprehension of intellectual reality was possible only to angels, those created intelligences who sought knowledge of the Creator's works but, because they were spirits without body, parts,

---

[22] Aristotle, *The Politics*, ed. and trans. Ernest Barker (Oxford: The Clarendon Press, 1946), pp. 134-35 (1284a), 126-27 (1282a-b). All citations hereafter are to this edition.

or passions, were unrestricted in space or time and had no need of sense, memory, or inductive generalization, but knew reality immediately and intuitively. Because their knowledge had not to be filtered through the mesh of particularity, it was said that angels were species, not individuals: universal, not particular beings. Time, then, was the inescapable condition of particular existence.

The philosopher-king of the *Republic* was thus transformed into an angel and exiled from this world to another. In Christian thought, of course, the two worlds interpenetrate; but though the church had the task of maintaining certain of the truths of eternity on earth, it was not expected that angels would come to undertake the burden of rule over earthly societies, and it was therefore remote even to impossibility that any earthly ruler would have the intuitive grasp of reality that would enable or entitle him to dispense with laws. Aristotelian thought, in fact, brings us, even in an Athenian and pre-Christian context, to a philosophy of government not too remote from that of Fortescue. Knowledge is built up by generalization and abstraction from the data, and some of these generalizations are seen to be universal propositions whose truth is self-evident and independent of the inductive process. Such principles become the foundations from which reason can derive further propositions, whose truth can be demonstrated by showing them to be necessary logical consequences of the truth of the first principles. But from abstract universals only abstract universals can be deduced, and if reason is identical with deductive logic, the inductive process cannot be put into reverse. Sooner or later we must face the problem raised by Plato, that of how the generalization can be made to fit the particular, and we must face it without the aid of a Platonic philosopher who has intuitive and perfect knowledge of the particular and its characteristics. What sort of knowledge is possible of the particular? By what intellectual instrument can accommodation of the universal and the particular be carried out?

So far as human government is concerned, Aristotle's answer is plain: common experience. This is the meaning of his famous dictum that the judge of a dinner is not the cook, but the man who has to eat it.[23] At the lowest level of unreflecting human intelligence, you need neither the art of the shoemaker nor the science of the chiropodist to know whether or not your boots hurt you; when the shoemaker and the chiropodist have done their best, you will have to tell them the result of their labors; and if, as is particularly likely to happen in affairs of government, there is no shoemaker or chiropodist to help you, it is theoretically possible—though extremely uneconomic—to go on stitching yourself pairs of boots until, by trial and error which may have

[23] *Ibid.*, p. 126 (1282a).

involved your learning so little from your errors that ultimate success is a matter of pure luck, you hit on a pair which do not hurt you. When wise rulers have generalized about the needs of the people and the circumstances of their lives, and have framed laws as a result of these generalizations, they should leave it to the people to decide whether the laws actually suit their needs and circumstances; for only thus can the gap between idea and reality be bridged. This may be done by calling an assembly of the people and asking them whether they think the law will suit them. No individual may be able to repeat the process of generalization which the rulers have performed, but the sum total of their predictions will probably furnish the rulers with an excellent critique of their law's chances of success. This is the case for governing by consent. But the same result may be achieved by usage, by leaving the people free to decide for themselves whether to observe the law or ignore it. The outcome of their decision will not be a prediction—"We think this law will or will not suit us"—as it will be if you consult an assembly, but rather a verification: "The people have retained the usage, so it suits them; they have abandoned it, so it does not." And the people are quite capable of framing their own customs, without rulers to guide them, simply by falling spontaneously into patterns of behavior which constitute usages. This is the case for governing by custom.

The only objection to legislating by waiting for popular usages to form themselves is that this takes an extremely long time (though, as we have seen, this has compensating advantages; the older a custom, the more reasons for thinking it suits the people, and the fewer for fearing that circumstances may arise in which it does not). It must take a long time, for essentially what we are asking is that one man's experience of particular things be added to another's until a consensus is built up, and that this process be repeated over a time-dimension until the resultant custom can claim the authority of repeated usage and antiquity. But further, this—the slow creation of a custom—is only the most highly developed instance of what all particular legislation, particular acts of government and particular decisions must be. For if reason is concerned only with deduction and universals there is no science or method of dealing with the particular *per se*. Each man must use his own judgment of the particulars he happens to know, and the only way of extending its sphere beyond the merely private is by combining it with other men's judgments of their particular knowledge. Since there is no organized critique of particular judgment—since it is like (though not identical with) an art rather than a science—one of the few criteria by which one judgment can claim *a priori* superiority over another is that of the number of men whose experience has gone to its making. The judgment of three hundred men is by that figure more likely to be the best than that of one man; the judgment of many generations than that of the men now living; the oldest custom than the custom slightly less old. "The individual is foolish," said Burke; "the multitude, for the moment, is foolish; but the species is wise and, given time, as a species it always acts right."[24] He meant, incidentally, the biological, not the scholastic, species.

All such statements are statements concerning probability, since the rightness of a decision can be demonstrated only insofar as it accords with principles, not particulars—except, indeed, that on the "second nature" argument, my customs have become so much a part of my self that they must be right for me. It is another matter to ask if they are right for my external circumstances, as opposed to my personality. But a custom is a particular judgment to which so many men's experience testifies, and which has attained so high a degree of consistency under repeated tests over time, that the probability of its continuing to give satisfaction (given the stability of conditions which it presumes and helps to maintain) is very high indeed. However, a custom is a judgment which it is possible to view in the longest of long runs, and there must be many judgments which have to be made with the concurrence of fewer men's experience. Burke's "individual" and "multitude for the moment" have both to make decisions, although both are "foolish" in the relative sense that the quantity of experience and knowledge of particulars that goes to the making of their decisions is measurably less than is available to the "species given time." The decisions of the "multitude for the moment" are Fortescue's statutes, and the virtue displayed in making them is what he calls "prudence." The "proof"—it is not, of course, a demonstration—of a custom is its antiquity, and "prudence" might be defined as the ability to formulate statutes which will stand the test of time and acquire the authority and antiquity already enjoyed by customs. But prudence is also the virtue displayed by the individual in making his decisions, for in the last analysis it is nothing less than the ability to make such use of one's experience, and that of others, that good results may be expected to follow.

Aquinas defines art as "right reason about things to be made (*factibilium*)," prudence as "right reason about things to be done (*agibilium*)," and some modern translators render *ratio* as "judgment," so as to minimize the difficulty of distinguishing between speculative

[24] Edmund Burke, *Works* (London: George Bell and Sons, Bohn's Libraries edition, 1877), VI, 147; notes for a speech *On a Motion Made in the House of Commons, May 1782, for a Committee to Enquire into the State of the Representation of the Commons in Parliament*. Cf. *Politics, Language and Time*, pp. 226-27.

ratio which proceeds from principles and practical *ratio* which proceeds toward ends.[25] He continues by quoting Cicero as mentioning "three other parts of prudence, namely memory of the past, understanding of the present and foresight of the future," and concludes that these "are not virtues distinct from prudence," but "integral parts or components."[26] Prudence, it should now be evident, was the present and future, where custom was the perfect, tense of experience. In custom, experience judged what had proved good and satisfactory; it judged also what had proved adapted to the particular nature, or "genius," of the people, and this judgment was likely to be self-fulfilling, since use and custom created this "second nature" as well as evaluating it—the past was perfect indeed. In statute experience judged what further experience was likely to confirm, but should in theory do this only where custom could not be shown to have done its work already. When in the course of human events, unstable and fluctuating in time as they were, a contingency arose which was not already integrated into usage, the first steps must be taken toward attending to that integration. Statute was based upon experience and expected the confirmation of further experience; it was therefore a step taken at a moment when a new emergency had arisen a number of times, and experience had accumulated to the point where the process of generalizing it into custom could begin. Experience, in the shape of prudence, performing this generalization, was Janus-faced; it bridged the gap between innovation and memory, statute and custom, present, future, and past.

But what of the very first response to a contingency, the action taken for the first time? In this connection McIlwain was led to establish his famous if controversial distinction between *jurisdictio* (the saying of the law) and *gubernaculum* (the holding of the tiller).[27] He rightly saw that the first response to contingency formed part of prudential theory, but that it could be only indirectly if at all grounded upon experience. Let something happen for the first time. Either it bears no resemblance whatever to any previous occurrence, in which case we have no language for it and no way of dealing with it; or it resembles previous occurrences sufficiently to appear to belong to a class of such occurrences, but presents sufficient characteristics (or combinations of characteristics) of its own to appear what we uneasily term *sui generis* or unique. If characteristics of the latter sort preponderate, it will be inappropriate to summon a council of elders and pool

[25] St. Thomas Aquinas, *Summa Theologica* (Blackfriars: New York and London), vol. 23 (1969), 1a-2ae, question 57, 4 (p. 51).
[26] *Ibid.*, 57, 6 (pp. 57, 61).
[27] McIlwain, *op.cit.* (above, n. 21), pp. 77ff.

their experience; the thing must be dealt with on the basis of its newness, which will almost certainly appear coterminous with the speed with which it comes upon us and demands a response. If time is the dimension of change, velocity is directly proportionate to unfamiliarity.

The unprecedented event, therefore, must be dealt with by one man who did not have time to summon his council; but since it could not be dealt with by experience, dealing with it was unlikely to issue in statutes or general prudential statements by which further events of the same class could be dealt with. They must wait until the emergency has been repeated a number of times and was no longer entirely unprecedented. Given the fluctuations of human affairs, there were occasions when normative judgment and statute were inappropriate; the problem was too new, too unfamiliar, there was not enough time; but given the assumptions which underlay the concept of "experience," the moment when statute would be appropriate would fairly surely come. McIlwain therefore found it possible to arrange the governing powers of a medieval king along a spectrum leading from *jurisdictio* to *gubernaculum*. At one end the decisions of experience had already been made and the monarch had only to say what they had been, to exercise memory to the exclusion of other aspects of prudence; his own experience need make no contribution to custom and he took no initiative of his own. At the various intermediate stages, as unfamiliarity and the required speed of response concurrently increased, more was demanded of prudence by way of inputs to the custom-forming process; the king took advice of fewer counselors, relied more upon his own prudence, but made decisions whose generality, permanence, and binding force as laws correspondingly decreased. Finally, the point was reached where unfamiliarity was total, response must be instantaneous, and there could be only one hand on the tiller; the monarch was absolute in the sense that his decisions were bound neither by custom nor by counsel, but they did not, because they could not, instantly become general laws of conduct. Only repetition and further experience could make them that.

This is to state the *jurisdictio-gubernaculum* sequence in a highly simplified and idealized form, which might indeed have surprised its author; and McIlwain's critics have often asked whether his thesis does not oversimplify the facts of medieval government. Incautiously handled, it tends to produce theory not unlike that found so unsatisfactory in early Stuart England: that there were a royal power limited by law and a royal power not limited by law, with no necessary contradiction between them; and, following Harrington in the seventeenth century[28]

---

[28] *Oceana* (1656): ". . . no other than a wrestling match, wherein the king, as he has been stronger, has thrown the nobility, or the nobility, as they have been

and Hume in the eighteenth,[29] some modern writers have argued that medieval government was both less coherent and, under pre-Tudor conditions, more flexible than this would suggest.[30] But it seems one thing to argue that the various forms of *jurisdictio* and *gubernaculum* were not so far institutionalized as to be clearly distinct, another to argue that the mode of thought which the words convey was not the principal or only scaffolding of theory available to medieval minds thinking about government. Now that we have stated it in a form presenting government as a series of devices for dealing with contingent time, we can see that the structures of which it consists are open-ended, no more to be distinguished from one another than the moments of past, present, and future into which we organize time. It thus becomes less surprising that medieval minds could speak of custom both as established by royal or ministerial action and as existing from uncreated antiquity; that the distinction between statutes as making new law and as declaring old were both apparent and habitually slurred over; that the distinction between the *gubernaculum* uttering an *ad hoc* decision, confined to a single emergency, and the *gubernaculum* establishing a rule possessing some degree of generality and to that degree binding in futurity ("law"), could not be maintained in practice. The Janus-like character of experience, of the present as a moment in time organized solely by sequential memory, accounts in principle for all these things.

We are concerned here somewhat less with what happened in government than with the deficiencies of the conceptual system to which government must appeal. Chief Justice Hengham on his bench knew well enough how to make new statute law by reinterpreting old;[31] but Chief Justice Fortescue in his study could give no theoretical account

---

stronger, have thrown the king. . . . where the laws were so ambiguous that they might be eternally disputed and never reconciled. . . ." John Toland (ed.), *The Oceana and Other Works of James Harrington* (London, 1771), pp. 63, 69.

[29] *History of England* (ed. of 1762), vol. v, ch. 1, p. 14: ". . . the several constituent parts of the gothic governments, which seem to have lain asleep for so many ages, began, every where, to operate and encroach on each other."

[30] Donald W. Hanson, *From Kingdom to Commonwealth: the development of civic consciousness in English political thought* (Cambridge, Mass.: Harvard University Press, 1970). See especially chs. 4-7, for a critique of the McIlwainian tradition.

[31] See Hengham's words to a pleader (Hanson, p. 207): "Do not gloss the statute; we know it better than you, for we made it, and one often sees one statute undo another." Cf. T.F.T. Plucknett, *The Legislation of Edward I* (Oxford: The Clarendon Press, 1949), pp. 72-74. Hanson further (pp. 220-22) seeks to show that Fortescue did not make statute inferior to custom in the sense of being limited by it. But Hanson does not distinguish between the authority of statute and the prudence of its content.

of how this was done which did not reabsorb Hengham and his innovating prudence into the world of experience, custom, and retrospection. And at one end of the spectrum, where the concept of experience failed altogether and the contingency and its response were acknowledged as unique, nothing was left but mystery. With the policy decision we entered the sphere of pure *gubernaculum*, at the furthest remove from that of customary jurisdiction; in it all rulers were acknowledged to be at once absolute and highly insecure. In matters of policy, the king and his counselors must proceed with nothing but their own prudence and experience to guide them. It was their profession to do so; their lives were one long training in it; God, who had laid this task on them, might of his grace assist them to perform it; and they might develop a marvelous skill in the exercise of what was essentially a professional "mystery" or art. It was on their expertise in statecraft, in the *arcana imperii* or secrets of power, in judging the fluctuations of times and seasons, events, circumstances, and human wills, that outstandingly successful rulers, like Philip II of Spain—*El Prudente*—or Elizabeth I of England, based their claim to a mysterious and quasi-divine authority. The sphere in which they operated was that of the inscrutable providence of God, and success in that sphere seemed providential; it argued that they were divinely commissioned to exercise power. But the statecraft of pure policy was detached from either jurisdiction or legislation, for it had nothing to do with the establishment and maintenance of rules of law. It was a mysterious, in a sense an irrational, art of coping with the unique, the contingent, and the unforeseen, at the point where all hope must be abandoned of bringing things under legal control. But where experience could be mobilized in the form of custom or consent, and general rules could be established and interpreted, government became much less an arcane and mysterious art and—subject always to the sharp distinction between reason and experience—much more a rational method or science. On the assumptions used by men like Fortescue, the king's statecraft did not entitle him to be either a judge or a legislator; the demands of government were not the same. He might have the prudence to be a policy-maker, where prudence was at a premium and experience at a discount; he quantitatively lacked the experience to be judge or legislator, as must any one man who did not call on the experience and the prudence of others.

The pure *gubernaculum* was pure mystery; and as long as experience remained the only means of generalizing about particular cases and testing the application of universals to them, *jurisdictio* and legislation by consent must remain the only methods of framing and administering laws that would stand up to intellectual scrutiny. Yet this philosophy of government must fail to cover satisfactorily those situations where *gubernaculum* was involved in *jurisdictio*, where the king was felt to be personally concerned in justice and legislation and charged, by reason of his office, with a responsibility for their proper performance which was not like that of any other man. Argument like Fortescue's tended to strip him of any intellectual capacity commensurate with his office and leave him—as the chancellor of the *De Laudibus* left his prince—a mere respectful spectator of what his judges were doing, no wiser than any other intelligent layman. But no theory of *gubernaculum* seemed able to provide the king with a stable yet unique role in justice and legislation, since it was inherent in the whole philosophy we have been reviewing that the *gubernaculum* was in the last analysis a craft rather than a science, concerned with the unique rather than the recurrent, with the management of policy rather than the establishment of laws. Since the king was charged with this terribly difficult task, he enjoyed an authority analogous with or based upon that of God's providence; since, too, there were points of contact between it and what was done in councils and courts of law, there were moments when the king, face to face with his counselors or his judges, might speak "as the roaring of a lion," with the terrible and quasi-divine authority of *gubernaculum*. Then he might not be gainsaid or resisted; then he might set aside laws, for short intervals, by the same authority. But when it came to decreeing judgment, to promulgating statutes, and particularly to the technicalities of customary jurisprudence, the voice of the lion was stilled and the inconvenient fact reemerged that laws were made by reason and experience, of neither of which had the king more than other men; James I and Coke were face to face again.

What the king had in greater measure than other men was authority, but authority is ceasing at this point to be grounded upon any theory of human knowledge. We may conveniently appeal here to Walter Ullmann's thesis of the "descending" as opposed to the "ascending" power;[32] the ruler's authority might come to him from his share in political intelligence (Fortescue's *politice*) or it might come to him from above (*regaliter*), from God himself conceived as *rex* rather than *lex*, as will rather than reason. Even this Fortescue was disposed to minimize by equating it with the exercise of *lex naturae*, the law of universals perceivable by common human reason; but in particulars the divine authority was unshared to the point where it became a mystery how the king received it, for the precise reason that it was providential. Only God from the *nunc-stans* perceived the full meaning of the

[32] Walter Ullmann, *Principles of Government and Politics in the Middle Ages* (London: Methuen, 1961).

sequence of particular events, and it was easier to conceive of him as willing it. Providence was the name of his will as directing this sequence, at least as that will was perceived by men from inside time; and to them, who had no *nunc-stans*, it was inscrutable and mysterious. As the roaring of a lion, the king spoke with authority that descended to him from God; his authority therefore became inscrutable, mysterious, and not to be resisted. But the gift of authority added nothing to the faculties of his time-bound intelligence; it was a hierocratic rather than a secular phenomenon; and this is why Jean Bodin, like many another theorist of "absolute monarchy," is to be found saying both that as a matter of authority, the king may set aside custom whenever he so wills, and that as a matter of prudence and even wisdom, he should will to do so only on the rarest of occasions.[33] Even the king did not fully bridge the gap between God and man; and it seems to follow that authority left prudence behind it at a point where it left the domain of contingent time as perceived by human memory and entered that of time as shaped by the will and providence of God. But when providence decreed positive laws binding upon men in general, it operated from Sinai rather than Rome or Byzantium; its acts were not those of a human lawgiver. Before the king or the community could fully assert a power of positive legislation, there must be a theory vesting men with the ability to create new orders in the domain of secular history. In discovering why such a theory was still lacking, we have next to turn to a fuller exploration of the conspectus of providential time.

[33] M. J. Tooley (ed. and trans.), *Six Books of the Commonwealth by Jean Bodin*, abridged and translated (Oxford: Basil Blackwell, n.d.), pp. 43-44, 123-28.

CHAPTER II

THE PROBLEM AND ITS MODES

B) Providence, Fortune and Virtue

IT IS A DIALECTICAL PARADOX that while the Christian doctrine of salvation ultimately made the historical vision possible, for centuries it operated to deny that possibility. The Greek and Roman intellects saw little reason to expect anything very new to happen in the human future, and doctrines of cyclical recurrence or the supremacy of chance (*tyche* or *fortuna*) arose and interpenetrated—though we must beware of exaggerating or simplifying their importance—to express this lack of expectation, which sometimes occasioned world-weariness and *angst*.[1] Within these empty-seeming schemes, however, there was room for much acute study of political and military happenings, and the actions of men did not lose interest—rather, perhaps, the reverse—when it was thought that they would some day, in the ordinary or the cosmological course of things, be repeated. The advent of the savior monotheisms, however, reorganized and transformed time by making it an aspect of events whose significance was in eternity. God had covenanted with men, and the covenant would some day be fulfilled; man had been created, he had fallen, God had begun action intended to bring about his redemption, and this process would at a point in time to come be carried to its final completion. All these propositions denoted temporal events; the past or the future tense must be used in stating them; and yet the significance of every one of them was extra-historical in that it denoted a change in the relations between men and that which was outside time altogether. Time was organized around the actions which an eternal agent performed within it; these actions formed a sequence whose meaning appeared in time and gave time meaning; but since the meaning of the actions lay outside time, it followed that time acquired meaning from its relation to the eternal. It might even seem that man entered time at his departure from Eden, and that the sequence of acts which constituted sacred history were

---

[1] See n. 3 to ch. 1, above. On *fortuna* as a goddess and the object of an actual cult, see John Ferguson, *The Religions of the Roman Empire* (Ithaca: Cornell University Press, 1970).

intended to bring time ultimately to an end and consummate its meaning at the moment of transcending and terminating its existence. History, in short, acquired meaning through subordination to eschatology.

The patristic intellect thus came very often to see the individual life as involved in two separately visible time sequences. On the one hand was that formed by the actions and events that had separated men from God and were now leading to their reunion; most of these had occurred at moments in the past, theoretically and often specifically datable in terms of the chronologies of recorded human history, but some were of course expected by believers at moments in the future which could not be reliably dated and which it might not even be legitimate to seek to date. This raised the problem of the eschatological present, of the religious life which was to be led in the interval of expecting the fulfillment of the program of redemption; and once it was accepted that this present might cover many lifetimes and generations, the interval was necessarily filled by the other time-sequence visible to human perceptions. This was what the patristic vocabulary termed the *saeculum*[2] and the modern intellect prefers to call history; human time organized around happenings in the social world, which the Greco-Roman mind saw overwhelmingly as political and military, and the mind of late antiquity, not surprisingly, largely in terms of the rise and fall of empires. The question must now arise of how, or whether, these two independently perceived sequences (or histories "sacred" and "secular") might be related to each other. To civic intelligences—and the Christian minds of late antiquity were very civic—intensely involved in what befell their urban, provincial, and imperial societies, it must seem that happenings in this realm were in some way bound up with God's intentions for the redemption of men; and indeed, in the perpetual struggle to keep a world-renouncing asceticism distinct from a world-denying dualism, it might be dangerous to deny that God was somehow present and concerned in the happenings of secular history and directing them to soterial ends. The *saeculum* was in the drama of salvation; might it not also be of it?

Furthermore, there were—and had been at least from the times when the books of Daniel and Revelations were accepted into the Christian canon—schemes of prophecy, in the sense of utterances acknowledged as inspired and foretelling events which might not yet have occurred; and in these the eschatological completion of the program of redemption and the end of time itself were described in terms suggesting the catastrophe of cities and empires in a drama of human history. It was therefore neither impossible nor illegitimate to believe that "secular"

---

[2] Throughout this chapter I am indebted to R. A. Markus, *Saeculum: History and Society in the Theology of St. Augustine* (Cambridge University Press, 1970).

history had indeed been the subject of prophecy, and that the prophet or interpreter of prophecy might "read" secular events in such a way as to discern the program of redemption in them, and them as part of that program. But the construction of a prophetic key to history was not historiography in any autonomous sense of the term. Insofar as it consisted of the reading and application of prophetic books like the two just mentioned, the language it employed was heavily oracular and symbolic, and the working out of associations and identifications between the events described in prophecy and the events experienced and perceived in the *saeculum* necessitated the construction of a number of secondary vocabularies of symbolization. These proved capable of relating a number of secondary sequences to the prophetic sequences, and the latter consequently ascended from the status of symbol to that of type: the primordial arcane reality capable of being repeatedly typified in a number of independently existing sequences. In this way eschatology retained its primacy over history. Not only was the latter intelligible only as a pattern of the process of redemption, but the latter was capable of being patterned over and over again—the drama capable of being rehearsed many times—in sequences some of which were not those of secular history at all, but of the individual soul's pilgrimage or of abstract nonhistorical occurrences, while historical events themselves might stand in a typical, not a historical, relation to each other. The language of prophecy, in short, constantly tended to retreat from the narrative prose of history into the poetry of a cosmic symbolism; the same patterns were repeated on many levels, instead of unique events succeeding one another in unrepeatable sequences, and the intellect that could deal with the particular only by relating it to the universal took fresh hold in this medium as in that of philosophy.[3]

Nevertheless, the historical event or phenomenon could be related to the eschatological without losing its historical uniqueness, if it could be directly related to the final, unrepeatable and hence unique redemption of all mankind; but it was this procedure which the patristic intellect, in the person of Augustine, was to reject decisively and relegate to the underworld of heterodoxy. The language of Daniel and Revelations, it was discovered, could be used in more than one way to denote structures of membership to which the Christian might belong and which he might visualize as playing a role in eschatological drama. Triumphant Christians in the reigns of Constantine or Theodosius

---

[3] One result could be that the linear sequences of prophecy in the strict sense became merged with cyclical sequences reflecting the repetitions of types. See, e.g., John W. O'Malley, *Giles of Viterbo on Church and Reform; A Study in Renaissance Thought* (Leiden: E. J. Brill, 1968).

might see the Christian empire and its church as constituting a prophesied act of God in history and as pointing directly to some eschatological fulfillment; but militant puritans in Africa saw the need to maintain a church free of compromise with secular authority so clearly that they insisted that salvation was to be had only in a Christian association independent of both empire and its ecclesiastical collaborators.[4] Salvation was in society and history, but in a history yet to come and to be perfected only at the end of time; meanwhile the false church and the secular empire that maintained and falsified it were to be identified among the hostile and diabolic agencies with which the symbolism of the prophetic books abounded. In this apocalyptic separatism—the creation out of eschatology of a counterhistory expected in a future—we have that millennialism or millenarism which Christians in all ages have used to express their rebellions against established churches wielding secular power or being wielded by it.

The response of Augustine—and the tradition which followed him—was to renounce both the imperial and the sectarian versions of apocalypticism and to effect a radical divorce between eschatology and history. The Christian's relation to the finality of redemption consisted in his membership of the *civitas Dei*, a society in communion with God and consequently existing, with him, rather out of time than in occasional descents into it; and since no *civitas terrena* could ever be identical with the *civitas Dei*, salvation was to be found in membership neither of a Christian empire fulfilling God's will in the course of visible history, nor of an apocalyptic antichurch expecting to be the vehicle of his will at history's end. No doubt there would come an end of the redemptive process in time and the Christian might hope to be raised to be of a company of saints on that day; but his salvation was not to be the outcome of a historical process, or of his participation in a pattern of life conceptualized as involving such a process. Civil society and its history indeed existed and were necessary; but they were radically imperfect even to their own ends—the ends of human justice—and certainly did not suffice to redeem man in his relation to God.[5] The acts of redemption were performed by God in time and could be seen as constituting a sacred history; but they were not necessarily performed through or upon the structures of civil society, and consequently man's redemption could not be the result of secular history, or of the apocalyptic antihistory of an antisociety which had fallen into the error

[4] Markus, *op.cit.*, ch. 2, "*Tempora Christiana*: Augustine's Historical Experience," and pp. 110f. See also W.H.C. Frend, *The Donatist Church* (Oxford: The Clarendon Press, 1952).

[5] Markus, chs. 3 and 4, "*Civitas Terrena*: the Secularisation of Roman History" and "*Ordinata est res publica*: the Foundations of Political Authority."

of supposing that it was society and history which needed to be redeemed. But if salvation was for individuals, and individual lives did not span the whole of history, the ends of time were not all located at the end of time. The eschatological vision became, in the Augustinian perspective, a vision of something in part extra-historical. It might seem that the individual's salvation or damnation took place at the hour of his death, the moment of his departure from time into eternity; the historical eschaton, to be expected at the end of time, was rather the resurrection of his body, to complete his joy or suffering in the condition to which he had been adjudged. In Dante, writing after nine centuries of Augustine's influence, it appears that the damnation and perhaps also the salvation, in which the spirits are beheld, are not yet perfected since the resurrection of the body and the end of time are still to come.[6] Purgation may be completed—as Statius moves on to paradise—before that moment comes.

This separation of salvation and society, redemption and history, soul and body, sundered but did not abolish the problem of the eschatological present. It became a problem to account for the state of the soul between the death and resurrection of the body, but a radical heresy to solve this problem by doctrines of mortalism or psychopannychism, which asserted that the being or the experience of the soul were suspended during the remainder of secular time; for this denied the extra-temporal nature of membership in the *civitas Dei* and consequently of that *civitas* itself.[7] Within the *saeculum*, there remained the problem of assigning meaning to the social and historical events experienced by individuals throughout the remembered past and henceforth to the end of time. If these could not be known as possessing any specific eschatological significance, there was no other way of assigning meaning to them; the *saeculum* was nothing other than the dimension of man's fall—his cumulative if not progressive damnation— and the only historical events that had meaning within it were those designed to reverse the consequences of which it consisted. If redemption was not to be seen as operating through social and historical events, these were not to be seen as possessing either sacred or rational significance in the light of which they could be explained. Yet the *saeculum* must not be dismissed as simply meaningless. The events of the redemptive process took place in the same time-series—all that was lacking was the means of relating sacred and secular events—and no part of the Christian universe, not even hell itself, could be seen as without

---

[6] *Inferno*, VI, 100-111; X, 94-108; *Paradiso*, XIV, 10-18, 37-66.

[7] S. H. Williams, *The Radical Reformation* (Philadelphia: The Westminster Press, 1962); Pocock, "Time, History and Eschatology in the Thought of Thomas Hobbes," in *Politics, Language and Time*, ch. 5.

meaning. It could not be denied that God was present and active in secular history; all that was denied was that we could identify secular events with the fulfillment of his purposes. It could not therefore be denied that secular history was directed by God to our ultimate redemption; it could only be denied that we could know, or should seek to know, how this was being done. Since, in the Augustinian perspective, history has not been the subject of prophecy, the problem of living in the historical present is the problem of living with an unrevealed eschatology.

Yet Christian men continued, in one way and another, to be Romans: civic beings, intensely concerned with the events of political history, the civil and military happenings which befell them and of which they from time to time asked God the meaning. Boethius's *De Consolatione Philosophiae* is of course the classic of this branch of literature; it states, in one of the most-read books of Western history, so many of the key themes of the present study that it can usefully be analyzed once again, and the question how far its author's thought was fully Christianized may be passed over in view of the centuries of Christian readership it enjoyed. A Roman aristocrat in the service of a Gothic king, Boethius fell from power, was imprisoned, and in due course put to death; it was presumably during imprisonment that he wrote the work which complains against, and reconciles him to, a fate perhaps worse than he anticipated. The *De Consolatione* is not a work of political philosophy, but it is the philosophy of a political man. Boethius is complaining against the loss of a power he believes he has used for good and the oppressions unjustly inflicted on him by others misusing power. He therefore speaks for all who felt—as it was not un-Augustinian to feel—that men must act in the sphere of the *civitas terrena* even though they must act without illusions; and there are passages which state the ancient ethic commanding a man of virtue to act so that his actions may be the occasion of virtue in others, and which indicate that there are virtues which rust and decay unless expressed in action.[8] But to act in politics is to expose oneself to the insecurities of human power systems, to enter a world of mutability and *peripeteia* whose history is the dimension of political insecurity; and it is of the utmost significance to our subject that the name which Boethius gives to this dimension is Fortune. *Fortuna*—the Latin had become in large part assimilated to the Greek *tyche*—was a word of complex meanings, and in opposing virtue to fortune Boethius was appealing to a long-standing tradition of discourse, which, however, he proceeded to set in a Christian context. In the senatorial ethos of republican and imperial Rome,[9]

[8] *De Consolatione Philosophiae*, I, iv; II, vii; IV, ii.
[9] D. C. Earl, *The Moral and Political Tradition of Rome* (Ithaca: Cornell Uni-

fortuna had rather the meaning of luck than of chance: a man might be lucky (*felix* or *faustus*) in the sense that there was something about his personality that seemed to command favorable circumstances; but the element of chance was acknowledged in the recognition that luck could not be counted upon, and that circumstances could be neither predicted nor controlled. The *baraka*, *mana*, or *charisma* (to use terms from other cultures) of the successful actor thus consisted both in the quality of personality that commanded good fortune and in the quality that dealt effectively and nobly with whatever fortune might send; and the Roman term for this complex characteristic was *virtus*. Virtue and fortune—to Anglicize them—were regularly paired as opposites, and the heroic fortitude that withstood ill fortune passed into the active capacity that remolded circumstances to the actor's advantage and thence into the charismatic *felicitas* that mysteriously commanded good fortune. This opposition was frequently expressed in the image of a sexual relation: a masculine active intelligence was seeking to dominate a feminine passive unpredictability which would submissively reward him for his strength or vindictively betray him for his weakness. *Virtus* could therefore carry many of the connotations of virility, with which it is etymologically linked; *vir* means man.

A term which was originally, and largely remained, part of the ethos of a political and military ruling class, *virtus* became assimilated to the Greek *aretē* and shared its conceptual development. From the meaning of "civic excellence"—some quality respected by other citizens and productive of leadership and authority over them—*aretē* had been refined, by Socrates and Plato, to mean that moral goodness which alone qualified a man for civic capacity, which could even exist without it and render it unnecessary, and which, at the highest levels of Platonic thinking, rendered existence and the universe intelligible and satisfactory. *Aretē* and *virtus* alike came to mean, first, the power by which an individual or group acted effectively in a civic context; next, the essential property which made a personality or element what it was; third, the moral goodness which made a man, in city or cosmos, what he ought to be. This diversity of meanings was carried by "virtue" and its equivalents in various languages down to the end of Old Western thinking; the word is of obvious importance in any book organized around the figure of Machiavelli.

Boethius, whose thought is so strikingly Platonic and neo-Platonist as to render the quality, if not the fact, of his Christianity debatable, opposes *virtus* to *fortuna* in a way which both brings out the diverse

versity Press, 1967); Charles Norris Cochrane, *Christianity and Classical Culture* (New York: Oxford University Press, Galaxy Books, 1957).

Roman, Platonic, and Christian connotations of *virtus* and transmits the use of *fortuna* and the *virtus-fortuna* polarity to subsequent centuries of Augustinian Christianity. That is, as a person in his own dialogue he complains[10] that his senatorial *virtus*, which led him to engage in politics in the hope of doing good, has exposed him to the insecurities of the power struggle, symbolized as *fortuna*. But his complaint is theodical rather than political; he does not ask the reasons for his failure as a politician, but inquires how God, who is perfect virtue, has permitted *virtus* to become *fortuna*'s prey. Augustine would have replied simply that men must expect injustice if they insist upon acting in the fallen city; Boethius, more engaged politically and more Platonic in his thinking, is in search of a perspective from which it can be understood how the heavenly city permits the earthly to exist. But in employing *fortuna* to symbolize the insecurities of the *saeculum*, he is carrying out a powerful synthesis of languages which will perpetuate the Roman and political conception of *virtus* in the very act of rendering it questionable. A benign female figure, Philosophy, now appears and sets about consoling Boethius. Her intention is to explain away Fortune by endowing him with an understanding of history as part of God's purposes, so that the *virtus* he acquires to resist Fortune's malignity will be philosophical and contemplative rather than political and active; but it is in the Athenian tradition that the political is not eliminated by the simple substitution of contemplation for action. To follow Boethius's problem we must bring out some of the significances inherent in the figure so central to his thought.

Fortune is, first of all, the circumstantial insecurity of political life. Her symbol is the wheel, by which men are raised to power and fame and then suddenly cast down by changes they cannot predict or control. It is engagement in the affairs of the *civitas terrena* which commits us to the pursuit of power and so to the insecurities of *fortuna*; but if happenings in the world of power-centered human relationships are of all things the least predictable and those we most desire to predict, the political symbol of *fortuna* is thus able to stand for Plato's phenomenal world, the image created by our senses and appetites, in which we see only particular things succeeding one another and are ignorant of the timeless principles which give them reality. Plato did not make use of the symbol of *tyche* in the *Republic*, but in Boethius's use of *fortuna* we see it to be part of the profoundly political nature of the Western vision that the phenomenal world of sense-illusion is also the political world of the interpersonal city. Time, furthermore, is the dimension of them both: as things seem to succeed one another because we do not see the timeless reality to which they belong, so

[10] *De Consolatione*, I, iv.

the turnings of the wheel are felt to our bitter insecurity because we act in the *civitas terrena*, not the *civitas Dei*. It is now Philosophy's task to convince Boethius that *saeculum* and *fortuna*—the unpredictabilities of power in a world of politics—are aspects of phenomenal and historical unreality, but that a perspective exists from which all is seen to be real.

She does this by setting up the doctrine later known as that of the *nunc-stans* or eternal now.[11] To God who is eternal all moments in time are simultaneously visible; the entire secular pattern is discerned, and decreed, as a whole and problems of succession and prediction do not exist. The historical world is visible in simplicity, unity, and perfection and is directed by God's will and intelligence (which are one) toward the redemption of men, which he can see in its accomplishment. It follows—the central assertion of the *De Consolatione*—that "all fortune is good fortune,"[12] or rather that Fortune is swallowed up in the twin concepts of Providence and Fate. Providence is that perfection of the divine vision in which God sees to (or, to human intellects, foresees) all circumstantial things; Fate is the perfection of the pattern in which he decrees and perceives them.[13] What we sense as *fortuna* is our imperfect experience of the perfection of history. In a later but closely related rhetoric, it became more usual to speak of Providence as the inscrutable course of things directed to our redemption by an intelligence we could not share, and by a further figure as that aspect of the divine intelligence which directed particulars and phenomena while perceiving universals and ideas; and in this rhetoric Fortune could be dealt with by equating her with Providence. A highly Boethian moment in the *Divine Comedy* is that[14] in which Dante and Virgil come upon a battle between spendthrifts and misers in hell, and Virgil explains that both parties are guilty of having contemned the opposite goods brought them by Fortune, a heavenly being who distributes the things of this world in ways inaccessible to human knowledge and is herself, being blessed, inaccessible to human complaints; and to complain against the ways of God is, we already know, to have begun losing *il ben dell'intelletto*, as the damned have lost it altogether.[15] The Providence equated by Boethius with Fate denoted God's timeless perception as it was to God himself; but it became more usual to speak of Providence as Dante here speaks of Fortune, indicating God's knowledge made apparent to us as foreknowledge, an intellect which we must call inscrutable because it directed what we must know as a succession of particulars in time. This there was no way of

11 *Ibid.*, III, xii; IV, vi; V, iii-vi.   12 IV, vii.
13 IV, vi.   14 *Inferno*, VII, 25-99.
15 *Ibid.*, III, 18.

knowing from within time; God knew it from the *nunc-stans*, but it was our business to believe that he knew it, as we could not until time should have an end. The spendthrifts and misers had failed in faith; what Dante here called Fortune could be and usually was termed Providence—Boethius's Fortune seen with the eye of faith that knew her to be good. In a contrary sense, the Fortune of the pagans, the malignant and irrational goddess of the wheel, denoted Providence as seen and experienced by those whom faith had not made whole.

But Boethius in the dialogue is in time, which is why he is subject to Fortune; and Philosophy affords him the intellectual certainty that the *nunc-stans* exists, not the capacity to share its vision. It follows that philosophy is not separate from faith, although Boethius does not develop the concept of a Christian faith in the sense of a personal devotion to his Redeemer. Philosophy is not bringing him a share in the divine vision, but consolation and resignation to his fortune in the certainty that God ordains it to be good and knows it as he cannot know it; and faith is the appropriate name for this spiritual condition. Philosophy and faith, then, are to replace (or reconstitute) *virtus* as the response to *fortuna*; where a pagan and civic virtue found in Fortune the raw material for glorious deeds in war and statesmanship, and fame after death, the Boethian Christian regards it as a test, the occasion which demands and should evoke a life redeemed by philosophic faith and freed from the bitterness of death. If he acts in the secular world, it will be to ensure that his is not "a fugitive and cloistered virtue," to give his faith greater perfection by exposing it to the trials of Fortune. Such, for centuries afterwards, was a proper meaning of the term "Christian virtue," although to Aquinas the *virtutes* were matters of moral practice and moral habit.[16]

It might seem that faith and the *vita contemplativa* had replaced politics and the *vita activa* at the core of the moral life, and there is of course a very great deal of truth in this; though it has to be kept in mind that contemplation is an activity,[17] and the activity most appropriate to life in the *civitas Dei*, that city whose end is knowledge of and communion with God. But the relationships between pagan and Christian virtue, and between virtue and knowledge, are more complex still. Applying an Aristotelian teleology to Roman ideas of *virtus*, it could be held that in acting upon his world through war and statecraft, the practitioner of civic virtue was acting on himself; he was performing his proper business as a citizen and was making himself through action what Aristotle had said man was and should be by nature: a political animal. In this context the relation of *virtus* to *for-*

[16] *Summa*, 1z-2ae, question 55 (Blackfriars ed., vol. 23, 1969).
[17] Aristotle, *Politics*, p. 289 (1325b).

tuna became as the relation of form to matter. Civic action, carried out by *virtus*—the quality of being a man (*vir*)—seized upon the unshaped circumstance thrown up by fortune and shaped it, shaped Fortune herself, into the completed form of what human life should be: citizenship and the city it was lived in. *Virtus* might be thought of as the formative principle that shaped the end, or as the very end itself. The Augustinian Christian finds his end in the *civitas Dei* and in no earthly city— though the fact that unity with God is still thought of in the image of a *civitas* shows that it is still the political definition of man's nature that has to be transcended—and the *virtus* by which he finds it is now the Boethian blend of philosophy and faith, through which he comes to be what by nature he is: a creature formed to know God and to glorify him forever. But Boethian philosophy is still opposed to *fortuna*, the darker side of societal life, and *fortuna* still assails men with circumstance which it is their proper business to shape into human life as it ought to be; their faith integrates suffering into the pattern of the redeemed life.[18] At the same time, the redemptive spirit consists as much in intellect—philosophy—as in belief; and the philosophy of the *nunc-stans* offers means of perceiving the phenomenal and temporal world—now equated with Fortune's domain—in such a light that its transitory and time-bound particulars become intelligible through knowledge of the purposes, ends and universal entities for which they were formed. Men become what they ought to be through certainty of that God who has shaped the world toward what it ought to be. It was when the *civitas Dei* became an eternal community of intellects that the political definition of man's nature seemed finally to have been transcended.

That time was not yet, and might not be till the end of time. While men inhabited time-bound bodies, philosophy could only convince them of the existence of a divine vision, and faith must support them as long as they could not share it. But faith, in this definition, was reposed in the assurance of a timeless vision in which phenomenal things were perceived in the light of the ends to which they were formed; and at the same time faith helped shape men to their end, which was to share in this vision. Since man could achieve his true end only through redemption from the consequences of his Fall, this *formatio* must be thought of as a *reformatio*, a recovery of his true nature which had been lost by Adam; an Aristotelian reformation is a recovery of, or return to, form. But in the Augustinian tradition it was most sharply stated that man's redemption was not possible through philosophy alone, or even through a combination of philosophy and faith; it could come about only through an act of God's grace, which philoso-

---

[18] *De Consolatione*, II, viii; IV, vii.

phy, faith, and virtuous practice might solicit but could never command, and might not even be thought of as meriting. The Aristotelian teleology had thus to be reconciled with the concept of grace—of those acts of God's love which were in the strict sense gratuitous—and if man could recover his true form, which included the perception of things in the light of their true forms, only through grace, it was also necessary that the original creation of things in their natures, essences, or ends, by a God who was that of the Bible and not of Aristotle, be thought of as an act or acts of grace and gratuitous love. Grace thus appeared at the beginning and end of a circular motion of creation and redemption; it created things in their true natures and restored to their natures those creatures which had lapsed from them. Through a Christian *virtus* the individual did what he could to bring himself toward his *reformatio* by grace; but the effects of the Fall were such that there must be discontinuity between virtue and grace, even if one held with Aquinas that *gratia non tollit naturam, sed perficit*. In redemption one would behold things "face to face,"[19] in the true essences to which grace had shaped them, which one could not do even in the movement toward redemption—which, again, only grace had made possible.

But if *fortuna* was the matter of history, then secular history was merely inert matter to be used in a process of *reformatio*; it had no form, and in that sense no end, of its own. Boethius can be situated wholly within the Augustinian tradition; he regards the sequence of events in the sociopolitical world as a series of challenges to faith and philosophy, which the individual overcomes and integrates in the pattern of his redeemed life as a citizen of the heavenly city. All fortune is good fortune only in the sense that every circumstance can be so used; there is meaning and pattern to it—what Boethius terms Fate—only in the sense that God can see the totality of history as the sum of individual redemptions. The sequence of events in the *saeculum* is not to be generalized into a sequence of redemptive meaning. Yet it remained doubtful how far the grand operation by which Augustine had divorced the redemptive process from the rise and fall of empires had been efficacious. The acts designed to bring about redemption had been performed by God in time, in an *aevum* hard to separate from that of the *saeculum*; they were dated by reference to the events of secular history—as in the creed it was daily recalled that Christ had "suffered under Pontius Pilate"; and in the incorrigibly political thinking of Western men it was hard not to see some, perhaps mysterious, significance in such facts as that Daniel had prophesied to the rulers of Babylon, that the Apostle of Patmos at least seemed to be alluding

---

[19] I Corinthians: 13.

to earthly empires, and that the great institutions of Christian society appeared to have something to do with the conversion of the emperor Constantine. Augustine's separation of history from eschatology had rested in the last analysis upon his denial that life in civil society had much to offer to the salvation of the soul. Once the possibility was entertained again that kingdoms and commonwealths, governed by Christians under Christian laws, might achieve a measure of earthly justice, practice of which, at a level sufficiently public to involve one's membership in some kind of *civitas terrena*, might be positively related to one's redemption through grace, the events of public history—the life of the *civitas* extended through time—must be seen as more than mere *fortuna*; or rather, a public *fortuna* must be shown as subject to the operations of grace. The revival of the Aristotelian doctrine that political association was natural to man therefore logically entailed the reunion of political history with eschatology.

In the post-Augustinian world of Boethius political history had appeared as mere Fortune, convertible into Providence only through the eye of faith which knew that the individual's fortunes might become the stuff of his redemption. History (to employ the modern term) had thus only a private meaning. But if the events of public history were to play any kind of redemptive role, the concept of providence must be expanded—as at any moment it could be—to include that of prophecy. The events of prophetic history were, like the creation and the ultimate redemption, the work of grace and gratuitous love; but here grace was seen, not in the creation or reformation of essential being, but in the performance of acts which, being unique and unrepeated, must be in time and, being in time, must be inaccessible to the philosophic intellect. That which performed them must be thought of as providence, since it performed purposive acts which constituted a series of occurrences in time and whose reasons were therefore beyond us; but in performing the acts of prophetic history, it at the same time revealed, by verbal or other means, some part of their significance to men. In accepting these divine messages to be true, men displayed faith of a somewhat different order from that we have so far been considering. Instead of intellectually affirming the existence of a divine intelligence whose perspectives could be described but not shared, faith now acknowledged that certain words or signs had been uttered, certain acts performed, at certain moments in time, and that these had been the acts of God, who had in them revealed certain truths to man. Because to acknowledge this was to make affirmations of historical fact, it was not the work of the philosophic intellect; and when the messages of revelation consisted of statements of what had happened, as that God had been born a man, or promises of acts yet to come, as that he would return at the end of time, they too exceeded the province of philosophy. (It is this dimension of belief that we miss in Boethius.) The faith reposed in prophecy could be thought of as acceptance of authority, and both the authoritative statements themselves and many of the messages which they uttered constituted points in time, in the sequence of prophetic history. And the authoritative utterances were public, not private; they had been made to societies of men—Israel, the church—and had helped to institutionalize them and give them a history. It was this which rendered them important in any attempt to revive political eschatology. Prophecy was the public action of providence; it united the fortune which was converted into providence by faith with the fortune that was the historical dimension of secular societies. In prophetic time one did not merely affirm the timelessness of the *nunc-stans*; one affirmed the imminence of the eschaton. *Hora novissima, tempora pessima sunt; vigilemus.*

Prophetic history, then, served as a means of politicizing grace and re-sacralizing politics. The work of Augustine could be undone at any time that it was found possible to identify moments in the history of civil societies with moments in the eschatological scenario to be derived from the various prophetic books. There remained, of course, the difficulty that prophecy did not, by its nature, deal directly with the problem of the eschatological present; the scenario did not provide for everything which should happen between "now" and the final eschaton, but took as its proper business the depiction of those scenes which should precede the end. And if one had resort to the complexities of typology and suggested that secular history—not to mention other realms of experience—would prefigure the apocalyptic occurrences at many times and in many places, one might find oneself back in a world of timeless archetypes and universals, in which secular history would return to the foot of the ladder of correspondences, as lacking any autonomous significance. If the life of civil society, lived forward in time as a succession of unrepeatable experiences, was to find its meaning in the context of sacred history, it would have to be suggested that in the tract of civil history to be explained, prophecy itself was approaching its unique and unrepeatable end. Clearly, to claim that Florence or England and its history were on the point of becoming the theater of Christ's return and God's final judgments was to expose oneself to charges of extreme *hubris* and blasphemy, as well as to make predictions peculiarly liable to falsification; but the claim was so frequently made that it cannot be dismissed as a mere aberration. In these paragraphs we are concerned to construct a framework in which its recurrence may become intelligible.

Perhaps the best way to explain the frequency of political apocalyptic is to treat it as an index to the ideological tensions between
church and secular society to be found in the later Christian centuries.
The papal church rested upon the Augustinian divorce between eschatology and history; it denied redemptive significance to the structure
and history of any secular society, while claiming itself to act and
exercise authority as a bridge between *civitas Dei* and *saeculum*, a kind
of institutionalization of the *nunc-stans*. So monolithic were these
claims that any secular commonwealth or kingdom desiring to assert
its autonomy was almost obliged to assert that it possessed redemptive
significance and so that redemption was to be attained through its
secular and historical operations. The church for its part was so heavily committed to denial of the redemptive character of history that it
was peculiarly vulnerable to revivals of the prophetic element in Christianity which asserted the historical character of redemption. Medieval
heretics therefore almost invariably had recourse to apocalyptic, if
with no other motive than to assert that redemption was to be found
in the fulfillment of prophecy and not in the institutional operations
of the timelessly based church; and in the prophetic languages they
reactivated, secular rulers found the symbolism needed to give their
operations redemptive significance. Princes and heretics were, within
limits, natural allies; they shared a disposition to undermine the Augustinian monolith by displacing the *nunc-stans* in favor of the eschaton,
the *civitas Dei* in favor of Christ's return to his saints at the end of
history. Persons in both categories therefore made use of the two main
streams of heterodox apocalyptic which ran through the later middle
ages, meeting and mingling but remaining analytically distinguishable:
the millenarian tradition which relied on the Book of Revelations to
expect an overturning of all forms of worldly rule and a reign upon
earth of Christ and his saints, located within the end of historic time;
and the tradition handed down from Joachim of Fiore through the
Spiritual Franciscans, which declared that after an Age of the Father
in which God had ruled through the covenant with Israel, and an Age
of the Son in which Christ ruled through his mystical body the church,
there would come an Age of the Spirit in which God would be manifest in all men so chosen, as now he was incarnate in Christ alone.[20]
It is obvious that both these schemes had revolutionary potentialities,

[20] Norman Cohn, *The Pursuit of the Millennium* (2d ed., New York: Harper
and Row, 1961); Gordon Leff, *Heresy in the Later Middle Ages* (Manchester
University Press, 2 vols., 1967); Marjorie Reeves, *The Influence of Prophecy in
the Later Middle Ages: A Study in Joachism* (Oxford: The Clarendon Press,
1969).

in that they envisaged a rule by illuminated saints not bound by earlier laws and dispensations, whether secular or prophetic; and it happened from time to time that a prince found his heretical allies turning these weapons against his own authority. Nevertheless, the attractions of the prophetic scheme to any prince in conflict with the church were great, and subsequent history suggests that the princes and republics who embraced this ideology were wise in their generation. In the short view, religious individualists, anxious to exile the church from worldly affairs and reconstitute it as a purely spiritual communion, were often glad to subject themselves wholly to the prince of this world in the belief that he could not touch their inner spirituality. In the long view, it is possible to trace the mutation of the expected millennium or Third Age into that indefinite secular future which distinguishes the modern from the premodern sense of history.[21] Apocalyptic, in fact, was a powerful instrument of secularization, a means of drawing the redemptive process back into that dimension of social time from which Augustine had sought to separate it, and of depicting it as the extension or the transformation of existing secular processes. This is why, in studying the period with which this book is concerned, we shall have to bear in mind that political eschatology was a weapon to be employed on behalf of the ruling institutions of secular society as well as one for chiliastic insurgents against those rulers, and that the saint's relation to society was never free from ambiguity.[22]

There is a sense, then, in which apocalyptic helped to open the path toward modern secular historiography; but for the purposes of the present moment in the analysis, which is concerned with the poverty of the modes of historical explanation available in the political thought of late medieval man, what requires to be emphasized is that the main question raised by the appeal to apocalyptic was whether secular political experience was capable of an eschatological dimension, or whether it was not. If it was so capable, emergent crises in secular experience could be rendered intelligible by identification with moments, persons

[21] Ernest Tuveson, *Millennium and Utopia* (Berkeley and Los Angeles: University of California Press, 1949).

[22] William M. Lamont, *Godly Rule: Politics and Religion, 1603-1660* (London: Macmillan, 1969), has been one of those pointing out that the merits of Cohn's *Pursuit of the Millennium* should not permit us to think of millennialism as exclusively an insurgent phenomenon; see also William Haller, *Foxe's Book of Martyrs and the Elect Nation* (London: Jonathan Cape, 1963). Michael Walzer's *The Revolution of the Saints* (Cambridge, Mass.: Harvard University Press, 1965) is a classic study of the saint as alienated from both the ecclesiastical and the social orders; it has, however, become a commonplace of criticism that the two modes of alienation were not necessarily concurrent and that the saint's involvement in secular society was greater and more productive of tensions than Walzer seemed to allow. See below, pp. 336-39

or symbols in one or other of the available eschatological scenarios; if not, not; and that was all the question at issue. We have not yet reached a point which it can be imagined how apocalyptic might contribute, even indirectly, to the enlargement of the modes of explaining the succession of one particular occurrence in secular politics, and so in secular history, to another. We have simply added one more mode of dealing with the secular occurrence to those with which we were previously familiar. The emergency or occurrence we are imagining might be dealt with by the devices of experience and prudence, integrated in usage and custom or responded to by means of statute or policy decision. It might be dealt with by means of faith, integrated in the patterns of the redeemed Christian life of the believing individual who had suffered it as fortune and reconstituted it through the eye of faith as providence. The Christian believer might, somewhat intensifying the activity of his political responses, enlarge his concept of providence to include prophecy, and deal with the emergency by attributing to it an eschatological significance. Lastly—an alternative not much considered hitherto—he might, at the cost of considerable diminution in the vivacity of his faith, treat the emergency simply as the work of Fortune, either because he did not deserve or because he did not believe that Providence was at work on his behalf. The occurrence would then be without essential meaning, the sequence or time-dimension of such occurrences a mere spinning of the wheel. Fortune thus came to symbolize the irrationality of history, the medieval sense of the absurd: history as it must seem to those who lacked faith, history as it must be if God and his providence did not exist. When medieval minds despaired, this symbolism appeared: the crystal spheres revolved perfectly in the heavens, but within the orbit of the moon the consequences of the Fall caused the irrational circularities of Fortune to spin eccentrically[23] and unchecked, and all history was summed up in the

---

[23] On the title page of Robert Recorde's *The Castle of Knowledge* (London, 1556; the first English work of Copernican astronomy), Knowledge appears poising the Sphere of Destiny on an upright staff, Ignorance driving the Wheel of Fortune by a rod attached to the center by a crank-handle. The following verses appear:

Though spitefull Fortune turned her wheele
  To staye the Sphere of Vranye,
Yet dooth this Sphere resist that wheele,
  And fleeyth all fortunes villanye.
Though earthe do honour Fortunes balle,
  And bytells blynde hyr wheele aduaunce,
The heauens to fortune are not thralle,
  These Spheres surmount al fortunes chance.

figure of Hecuba lying beneath the wheel.[24]

Experience, prudence, and the *arcana imperii*; fortune + faith = providence; providence — faith = fortune; providence + prophecy = revealed eschatology; virtue and grace. These formulae constitute the model so far established of an intellectual equipment which lacked means of explicating the succession of particulars in social and political time, so that all responses to such particular occurrences must be found somewhat between the poles of experience and grace. We proceed to test the model by using it to explain the intellectual innovations which occurred when a conscious republicanism imposed, upon minds limited by such an equipment, the added burden of sustaining in time a political structure intensely conscious of its own fragility and instability. How that challenge came to be imposed is the theme of the next chapter.

The sphere's accompanying symbol is the sun, the wheel's the moon. The irregular patches on the moon's face, no less than her after all regular waxing and waning, seem to have gained her the reputation of inconstancy and imperfection. The matter is discussed by Beatrice in *Paradiso*, II, 49-148. For fortune symbolism in general see H. R. Patch, *The Goddess Fortuna in Medieval Literature* (Cambridge, Mass.: Harvard University Press, 1927).

[24] Fortunae rota volvitur
    descendo minoratus
    alter in altum tollitur
    nimis exaltatus.

    Rex sedet in vertice
    caveat ruinam
    nam sub axe legimus
    Hecubam reginam.

Carmina Burana, LXXVII (ed. J. A. Schmeller, Breslau, 1904). (The images of Hecuba and the wheel recur in the Player King's speech in *Hamlet*, II, 2.) Cf. the other "Fortune" songs (I, LXXV, LXXVIA) and the drawing of the Wheel prefixed to the whole collection.

CHAPTER III

THE PROBLEM AND ITS MODES

c) The *Vita Activa* and the *Vivere Civile*

[1]

IT CAN BE ARGUED that the ideal of the citizen implied a totally different conceptualization of the modes of political knowledge and action from that implicit in the scholastic-customary framework which we have so far studied. Within the limits of that framework, the individual employed reason, which disclosed to him the eternal hierarchies of unchanging nature and enjoined him to maintain the cosmic order by maintaining his place in that social and spiritual category to which his individual nature assigned him; he employed experience, which disclosed to him immemorial continuities of traditional behavior and could only counsel him to maintain them; and he employed a blend of prudence and faith on those occasions when the stream of contingent and particular events faced him with a problem so individual that neither reason nor syllogism, experience nor tradition, provided a ready-made answer to it. Only on these occasions, it might be contended, did he behave like a decision-making animal (and even then, not infrequently, more like an apocalyptically guided true believer); for the rest his behavior was that of the inhabitant of what some theorists call a traditional society. To say so much would be to overargue the case; political processes often (some say always) go on within a received and inherited pattern of behavior, and the interpretation of tradition can be a complex and self-conscious political decision. Yet it remains true that a citizen, constantly involved with his fellows in the making of public decisions, must possess an intellectual armory which takes him beyond the perception of hierarchy and tradition, and gives him cause to rely on his and his fellows' power to understand and respond to what is happening to them. A customary community in one corner of an eternal order is not a republic of citizens. If they believe in tradition as the only appropriate response to the challenge of contingent happenings, they will not apply their collective powers of positive decision; if they think of prudence as the response of a few decision-makers to the marginally unique problem, their bias will be toward the acceptance of a monarchical *gubernaculum*; if they think of a universal hierarchy of being as the matrix of all values, they will not be thereby disposed to associate themselves in an independent sovereign body of decision-makers. The citizen must have a theory of knowledge which allows great latitude for public decisions upon public events. To attempt the erection of a civic way of life upon epistemological foundations which allow the recognition only of universal order and particular traditions is to be hampered by certain limitations. It can be argued that the history of Florentine political thought is the history of a striking but partial emancipation from these limitations.

There is evidence that fourteenth-century minds visualized Florentine citizenship in a context of universal order and authority, which could be both hierarchically and apocalyptically expressed. The civic patriotism of Dante (1265-1321) was memorably intense, but he saw the delivery of Florence from faction rule as part of the restoration of Italy to political and spiritual health within a universal empire; and with that part of his mind which held the reformation of mankind to be accomplished by imperial rather than ecclesiastical authority, he envisaged the descent of an emperor from the Alps as both a temporal and a holy event, long prophesied in the context of apocalyptic time, which as we have seen was the time-context created by viewing redemption as a temporal process. There was an affinity between temporal power and apocalyptic prophecy. Considering empire an instrument of salvation, Dante placed Trajan and Justinian not far from Christ, and Brutus and Cassius with Judas in the very bottom of hell. The republic, being a mode of temporal authority, is viewed in the context of empire, and empire in the context of universal salvation apocalyptically conceived. Dante's vision is, in a very high and complex sense, both temporal and hierarchical, but to the extent that it is hierarchical it depicts human perfection, both personal and political, as to be found in occupying one's due place in an eternal order; to the extent that it is apocalyptic, in playing one's revealed or archetypal role in the historical processes of grace. In neither does the emphasis fall on joining with one's fellow citizens to engage in collective secular decisions. The hierarchy is monarchical in form, being determined by authority descending from above, and because the hierarchy of the empire reflects that of the cosmos, it is the manifestation of principles which do not change. Dante's patriotism was Ghibelline and imperialist; it gave his vision of time an apocalyptic but not a historicist dimension; he saw secular rule as the empire in which the eternal order was repeated and restored, not as the republic in which a particular group of men resolved what their particular destiny should be.

In his *Paradiso*, Dante gave an exalted place to Joachim of Fiore,[1] whose teachings, or traditions deriving from them, reappear in connection with that most extraordinary of the precursors of civic humanism, the Roman demagogue Cola di Rienzo (1313-1354). Cola was attempting, by dint of his own charismatic and indeed paranoiac personality, to unify the inhabitants of Rome into something like a commune, but found it necessary in pursuit of this aim to present the fourteenth-century city as identical with the ancient Republic—and himself as its Tribune—and to declare unabated the direct authority of the Roman People over the pope as its elected bishop, the emperor as its elected prince and the whole world as its subject empire. Such claims asserted the republic by implying the continuity of universal empire, and it is not surprising to find that after his first fall from power, Cola spent some time with a community of Joachite hermits in the Abruzzi and emerged as a herald of the Third Age, summoning the emperor to take up his prophesied mission of reforming the church and ruling the world.[2] To him as to Dante, republic, empire, and apocalypse were all of a piece; and though only a powerful charisma can account for Cola himself being taken seriously for long, the content of his claims, whether as Tribune of the Republic or as prophet of the Third Age, did not seem absurd to the best minds of his time. The pioneer of humanism, Francesco Petrarca (1304-1374), saw in Cola's Republic a hopeful augury of the restitution of ancient virtue to Italy and the world, but at the same time saw no inconsistency in hoping that Cola would restore virtue by restoring the republic, hoping that the pope would restore it by returning to Rome from Avignon and hoping that the emperor would restore it by descending from the Alps to set Italy in order. Petrarch, not a committed political man, did not radically distinguish between different forms of rule; it is also significant that in elaborating the image of virtue's restoration, he set no great store by apocalyptic prophecy.[3] The techniques of humanist scholarship, as we shall see, were building up too human an image of ancient virtue, too social an image of the life of man in time, to leave much room for the types and symbols of the prophetic vocabulary. It may be significant too that the people least impressed by the Tribune's rhodomontade seem to have been the Florentines; they felt no need to manufacture a dramatic symbolism for the republic, or clothe it in prophetic

---

[1] *Paradiso*, XII, 139-45. Reeves, *Influence of Prophecy* (ch. 2, n. 20, above).

[2] Iris Origo, *Tribune of Rome* (London: Hogarth Press, 1938).

[3] E. H. Wilkins, *Life of Petrarch* (Chicago University Press, 1961), ch. XII, pp. 63-73; pp. 117-18, 120, 134-35. J. H. Whitfield, *Petrarch and the Renascence* (New York: Russell and Russell, 1965), pp. 35-37.

declamation, because they had it already and could offer—especially in their more disenchanted moments—a singularly realistic account of its workings. Yet it was the Florentines, during the two centuries to come, who were to produce the most incisive articulations of the civic consciousness and its problems; and though these expressions were to owe most to humanist ways of thinking and writing, the apocalyptic mode was far from having uttered its last word in their thoughts.

In the early fifteenth century—to go no farther back—there can be traced in Florentine writings, notably those of Coluccio Salutati (1331-1406) and Leonardo Bruni (1361-1444), what appears to be a decisive break with the way of thinking just outlined. The modern writers who have dealt most fully with this theme are Hans Baron and Eugenio Garin;[4] but their work, while of great and deserved prestige, is still the subject of controversy among scholars and it is necessary to pick our way with caution. There does not seem to be much question that the following changes in the Florentine ideological pattern can be seen taking place. There is, to begin with, a fairly rapid repudiation of a hitherto well-established foundation myth which had insisted that the city of Florence was originally a settlement of Julius Caesar's soldiers, and the substitution of a myth which proclaimed the city a foundation of the Roman republic. In somewhat later work, Bruni is disposed to look even farther back, to consider Florence affiliated to the Etruscan city republics which had flourished before Roman domination of the peninsula, and to suggest that the absorption of these republics by one republic had prepared the way for the latter's absorption into a world tyranny (this, incidentally, was to anticipate a theme of Machiavelli's). That the opposition of republican to Caesarian rule and the equation of the latter with tyranny rather than monarchy were no accidents is demonstrated by an attempt, found at the same time, to rescue the historical figure of Brutus from the depths of infamy into which Dante had cast him.[5] Dante had seen Brutus as a traitor against his superior,

[4] Hans Baron, *The Crisis of the Early Italian Renaissance* (Princeton University Press, 2d ed., 1966); *Humanistic and Political Literature in Florence and Venice at the Beginning of the Quattrocento* (Cambridge, Mass.: Harvard University Press, 1955); *From Petrarch to Leonardo Bruni; Studies in Humanistic and Political Literature* (Chicago University Press, 1968); "Petrarch: His Inner Struggles and the Humanistic Discovery of Man's Nature," in Rowe and Stockdale, eds., *Florilegium Historiale: Essays Presented to Wallace K. Ferguson* (University of Toronto Press, 1971). Eugenio Garin, *Italian Humanism, Philosophy and Civic Life in the Renaissance*, trans. Peter Munz (New York: Harper and Row, 1965). George Holmes, *The Florentine Enlightenment, 1400-1450* (London: Weidenfeld and Nicolson, 1969).

[5] For denunciations of Caesar in Petrarch see Baron, in *Florilegium Historiale* (n. 4, above), pp. 19-20, 37-39.

and since that superior prefigured the emperor, who reigned over the hierarchies of men as did God over the hierarchies of nature, had placed him and Cassius beside Judas who had betrayed God himself. But the subsequent revolution in historical imagery presented Brutus (Cassius has never been so responsive to idealization) as the type of republican citizen and tyrannicide, and condemned Caesar as tyrant and subverter of the republic.[6]

There is more to this than a mere revision of myths. The whole image of human authority and its history to which Florentines were supposed to look was being drastically reconstructed, deprived of its continuity and—in a most important sense—increasingly secularized. In what may be termed the imperialist vision of history, political society was envisaged as the existence among men of the hierarchical order existing in heaven and in nature; its legitimation and its organizing categories were alike timeless, and change could exist in it only as degeneration or recovery. Affiliation with the empire, then, like affiliation with monarchy generally, was affiliation with the timeless. Those who sought, whether from a papalist point of view or one committed to political realism, to emphasize that empire or monarchy were of the *civitas terrena*, might indeed stress their secular character. But in the newer vision, the republic of Florence, stated as a high ideal but existing in the present and in its own past, was affiliated only with other republics and with those moments in past time at which republics had existed. The republic was not timeless, because it did not reflect by simple correspondence the eternal order of nature; it was differently organized, and a mind which accepted republic and citizenship as prime realities might be committed to implicitly separating the political from the natural order. The republic was more political than it was hierarchical; it was so organized as to assert its sovereignty and autonomy, and therefore its individuality and particularity. When the Florentine intellect was prepared to accept loyalty to Florence as a concept separated from the natural order and its eternal values, we have one primary meaning of the widespread Florentine saying about loving one's country more than one's own soul; there was an implied distinction and a conflict. But to assert the particularity of the republic to this extent was to assert that it existed in time, not eternity, and was therefore transitory and doomed to impermanence, for this was the condition of particular being. That the republican ideal accepted the fact of the republic's mortality is symbolized by the choice as hero of the unsuccessful rebel Brutus. The one thing most clearly known about republics was that they came to an end in time, whereas a theocentric universe

[6] Baron, *Crisis* (n. 4, above), ch. 3.

perpetually affirmed monarchy, irrespective of the fate of particular monarchies. It was not even certain that the republic was the consequence of a principle.

To affirm the republic, then, was to break up the timeless continuity of the hierarchic universe into particular moments: those periods of history at which republics had existed and which were worthy of attention, and those at which they had not and which consequently afforded nothing of value or authority to the present. The idea of "renaissance" after an age of barbarism would seem to owe something to a patriotic insistence on confronting the Florentine with the Roman republic and dismissing the intervening centuries of Roman and Germanic empire as an interlude of tyranny as well as barbarism. The particularity and historicity of the republic involved the particularization of history and its secularization: involved, too, the repudiation of great part of it as devoid of value. It is interesting and important, however, that this raised a subsidiary problem in the evaluation of Florentine history itself: that of the place to be assigned to Dante and other glories of Florentine letters, who had accepted the affiliation of republic to empire, denigrated Brutus and exalted Caesar, and done so in the vulgar tongue which rigorous humanists considered one symptom of medieval barbarism. The impulse to exalt the republic by declaring it the revival of antiquity could not pay the price of repudiating major elements of the republic's own past, and Dante and the *volgare* were in due course rehabilitated. But this had to be done by providing explanations of how they could have existed, and done so gloriously, in a time of their own which was neither classical antiquity nor the classicizing present; and the image of the present itself was altered by the acknowledgment that it gloried in, and was descended from, the men of the *trecento* as well as those of antiquity.[7] Thought was approaching the threshold of modern historical explanation, and the central discovery of the historical intellect that "generations are equidistant from eternity"—that each of the phenomena of history existed in its own time, in its own right and in its own way. It was doing so in consequence of a movement of ideas which may be discerned at other moments in other cultures: when an image of past time as continuous and as bearing authority for the present is attacked, and segments of the past are dismissed as possessing no value—this may happen as a result of a classicizing attempt to locate all value in a particular period—it may follow either that the repudiated period reasserts its claim to authority over the present in consequence of some other rela-

[7] Baron, *Crisis*, chs. 13-15. See also David Thompson and Alan F. Nagel (eds.), *The Three Crowns of Florence: Humanist Assessments of Dante, Petrarca and Boccaccio* (New York: Harper and Row, 1972).

tionship to it, or that it becomes necessary to explain how, if the phenomena concerned were without authority or value, they nevertheless existed and were causally linked with both present and past. In these circumstances some relativist mode of explaining the past, as having its own way of existing and its own values or other claims upon our attention, may very well arise.[8] In the case we are studying, the continuity of the past exhibited many of the characteristics of a timeless hierarchical order. It was attacked, and broken up into a sequence of moments possessing positive or negative value, because the existence of a particularized political form was imposed on it as a criterion of value; and a moment (the *trecento*), of negative value according to this scheme, proved to have positive value to the present because of the republic's intense awareness of its own continuity and traditions. Two images of time came into conflict, and the result was historical explanation of the *trecento*; but the whole organization of the timeless into time, and the conflicting evaluations of past time that followed, came about only in consequence of assertion of the republic's individuality and continuity.

Hans Baron, supporting his thesis by a detailed criticism of the chronology of certain key works of Florentine humanism, has argued that all this originated in a political crisis undergone by the citizens about the year 1400. The powerful ruler Giangaleazzo Visconti, whose family possessed a base of great power at Milan, seemed to be building up a system of hegemonies which might have resulted in the formation of a permanent monarchical state in north and central Italy. His power was spreading rapidly in Tuscany; a diplomatic and military separation had developed between Florence and Venice; and in this crisis, Baron argues, the Florentines felt themselves dramatically and traumatically isolated, while standing forth in their own eyes as the last champions of republican liberty in Italy and the known world. It is Baron's thesis[9] that in the two years preceding Giangaleazzo's sudden death in late 1402 and the consequent collapse of his power, the revolution in historical self-affiliation which we have been tracing came about in Florentine thought as part of a crisis in patriotism which was also a crisis in republican self-awareness. Isolated by the Visconti power, the Florentines were intensely aware of themselves as a threatened community; isolated by the growing territorial power of one man, they were aware of themselves as a structure based on republican institutions and values. The language of Milanese propagandists was Caesarian and

[8] For an extended theoretical treatment, see my *Politics, Language and Time*, ch. 8 ("Time, Institutions and Action: An Essay on Traditions and Their Understanding").

[9] *Crisis*, chs. 1-2, 10-11, 16.

imperial, and in reply the Florentine humanists, especially those connected with the diplomatic chancellery of which Salutati and Bruni in turn were heads, took the revolutionary step of repudiating Caesarian symbolism and the imperial tradition altogether, identifying Florence with the republican principle, and polarizing the legitimating past into republican moments and interludes of darkness in the way that has been described.

In association with this revolution in historiographical concepts, Baron finds evidence in writings of this time of a yet more profound crisis in Florentine thought. Since the time of Plato and Aristotle, the question had been intermittently discussed of the relative merits of a life spent in social activity—the *vita activa*—and a life spent in philosophical pursuit of pure knowledge—the *vita contemplativa*. To Athenians, convinced with one part of their minds that only the life of the citizen was truly ethical and human and with another that only the abstract world of unmotivated contemplation was truly intelligible and real, the problem of whether politics and philosophy were not antithetical had been a painful one. The medieval mind had, of course, loaded the debate in favor of contemplation; the philosopher's concerns, like those of the Christian, were not of this world, and even after the Aristotelian revival had rehabilitated belief in rational and social action, the knowledge by which universals were recognized was discontinuous with the prudence by which they were applied in social decisions. The individual of Fortescue, obedient to natural law and custom and politically active only on the rare occasions when statutes were to be made, could scarcely imagine his civic life as in serious rivalry with his philosophic contemplation, if he engaged in the latter at all; and Petrarch had felt able to reproach his ideal Roman, Cicero, with getting himself entangled in disreputable politics and put to an unworthy death when he should have been attending to his proper business as a philosopher.[10] But in later Florentine thinking there is a great deal said in favor of a *vita activa* which is specifically a *vivere civile*—a way of life given over to civic concerns and the (ultimately political) activity of citizenship; and it is plainly possible to correlate a writer's preferred way of life with his allegiance to a political form. The practitioner of the *vita contemplativa* might elect to contemplate the unchanging hierarchies of being and to find his place in an eternal order under a monarch who played in microcosm God's role as guarantor of that order; but the exponent of a *vivere civile* was committed to participation and action in a social structure which made such con-

[10] There is an extensive literature on Petrarch's changing attitudes; see Baron, in *Florilegium Historiale*, and *From Petrarch to Leonardo Bruni* (n. 4, above), chs. 1 and 2.

duct by the individual possible—to citizenship, therefore, in some species of polis, so that at a later date *vivere civile* became a technical term for a broadly based civic constitution. Baron not only finds such a contrast of attitudes implicit and manifest in the writings of Milanese and Florentine publicists during the crisis of 1399-1402; he also aims at explaining by reference to the same series of events what appears to be fluctuating behavior by Florentines with regard to the same polarization of values. Coluccio Salutati, in particular, wavered most remarkably between asserting the values of active citizenship and asserting those of contemplation, withdrawal from the world and acquiescence in monarchical or even tyrannical rule. By a most detailed examination of the texts of Salutati and other writers, Baron endeavors to relate them to the progress of the Viscontian crisis in such a way as to show that a decisive shift in favor of active and participant values occurred during this crucial period.[11] The rediscovery of citizenship, like the revaluation of history, was produced by a sudden intensification of republican self-awareness in the traumatic confrontation with Giangaleazzo.

Baron's thesis has for some years been exposed to the criticisms of scholars, and it may be observed that its most challenged, and challenging, elements are those which concern chronology and motivation, by asserting that a decisive shift in values can be dated to a single period and described as the result of that period's dominant experiences. It is natural that historical criticism has tended to be focused on these assertions; historians are interested in questions of cause and motive, and historians of ideas in the relations between ideas and events, thought and experience, and it is right and proper that they should wish to know whether a major ideological change came about at the moment and for the reasons that Baron says it did. It is also right to remind ourselves that to know the occasion of an intellectual happening is not to know everything about what it was that happened. The present study has been so designed that we are concerned with identifying certain conceptual vocabularies which were available for talking about political systems considered in their particularity, with exploring their limitations and implications and considering how these operated, and with examining the processes by which these conceptual systems, their uses and implications, changed over time. It is therefore not of exclusive importance to us to know whether or not certain changes in Florentine thought came about as part and as result of the events of 1399-1402; we wish no less ardently to know what these conceptual changes were, what further changes they implied and what came about

[11] Baron, *Crisis*, chs. 5 and 7; *From Petrarch to Bruni*, chs. 3 and 4; "Leonardo Bruni," *Past and Present* 36 (1967).

in the world of thought as the consequence of their having occurred. So in the case of a major linguistic breakthrough or revolution in concepts—such as a revaluation of history in association with increased stress on values of civic participation—it is important to know what happened in terms of the implications and consequences of changes in men's conceptual vocabularies, as well as in terms of the occasions and causes of these changes' first occurring.

The term "civic humanism" has become inseparably attached to Baron's thesis, and scholars who wish to challenge the latter are disposed to challenge also either the utility of the term or the importance of the phenomena it denotes. In addition to attacks upon Baron's chronology, it is argued, first, that humanists' concern with the *vita activa* did not significantly arise from their *crise de conscience* as republican citizens; second, that the citizen of the Italian commune did not need the language of the humanists in order to articulate his civic consciousness. Since in the remainder of this book it is proposed to use the term "civic humanism" to denote a certain formulation of republican consciousness and its problems, we have reached a suitable point at which to indicate what will be implicitly claimed whenever the phrase is used, and to what historical postulates its use may commit the writer and the reader. This can conveniently be done by placing alongside Baron's certain other interpretations of the character of humanist political consciousness.

Jerrold Seigel has argued[12] that the origins of the humanists' concern with the *vita activa* lie in their professional and intellectual commitments rather than their civic sensibilities. He points out that humanists were by their social function affiliated with the art of rhetoric, an intellectual pursuit fully as important in Italian culture as philosophy and always seen in the sharpest contrast with it. Philosophy was concerned with the knowledge of universals and the understanding of particulars in their light, and the attitude appropriate in the presence of universals was one of contemplation, not action; philosophy therefore was nonpolitical and a universe seen as composed of universals was inhabited only secondarily by political animals. Rhetoric, on the other hand, was concerned with persuading men to act, to decide, to approve; it was intellect in action and in society, presupposing always the presence of other men to whom the intellect was addressing itself.

[12] Jerrold E. Seigel, *Rhetoric and Philosophy in Renaissance Humanism: the Union of Eloquence and Wisdom, Petrarch to Valla* (Princeton University Press, 1968); "Civic Humanism or Ciceronian Rhetoric?" *Past and Present* 34 (1966), to which Baron's "Leonardo Bruni" is a reply. And see David Robey, "P. P. Vergerio the Elder: Republicanism and Civic Values in the Work of an Early Humanist," *Past and Present* 58 (1973), pp. 3-37.

Political by its nature, it was invariably and necessarily immersed in particular situations, particular decisions, and particular relationships; and being immersed in the particular world, must always face the question whether, once compared with philosophy, it brought knowledge of anything. It is to be observed, however, that rhetoric, occupying a place in Italian thought comparable with that occupied by experience in the thought of Fortescue, is in virtue of its political character far more positive and active; it is forward-looking and persuades men to do things, whereas experience results only in discovery of what they have already done. A world where rhetoric ranks equal with philosophy is a world of face-to-face political decisions; a world where experience and custom occupy its place is one of institutionalized traditions.

Seigel contends that humanist thought in this respect stems from the confrontation between philosophy, whose values were contemplative, and rhetoric, whose values were civic and active: that the achievement of Petrarch was to persuade his admirers and successors to accept this confrontation as a dialectic between rival value systems, neither of which could be given absolute priority over the other; and that it became the characteristic of humanist thought to move back and forth between the civic and contemplative positions, in a way which was inherent in the humanist heritage and need not be directly related to the history of external events. Consequently, he says, Baron both underestimates the extent to which Bruni, as well as Salutati and no less than Petrarch, was prepared to take up the contemplative option, and misunderstands the way in which option for one or other set of values should be explained. To opt for civic values did not mean to commit oneself wholly to republicanism as a political cause, and to opt for contemplative values did not mean to express total disillusionment with the republic. The humanist was ambivalent as between action and contemplation; it was his *métier* as an intellectual to be so, and he could practice it perfectly well within the framework of the republic. Consequently, humanism as a whole did not become "civic" when the republic triumphed, or "contemplative" when it fell on evil days, and the individual's movement between the two preferences need not be explained in terms of his responses to political events. Baron's emphasis on explanation by chronology may therefore be misplaced.

Now all this may very well be; but clearly it does not mean that there was no such thing as civic humanism. Since rhetoric was both civic and active, it was possible for the rhetorician—or the humanist *qua* rhetorician—to provide a language in which to articulate a civic consciousness he might or might not share. The rhetorician and the citizen were alike committed to viewing human life in terms of participation in particular actions and decisions, in particular political relationships between particular men; and we have found in one development of the style of civic humanism a means of expressing this view of life by reconstructing history as the story of republics existing in time. That the affinity ran far deeper than that, and that the whole bias of humanism, whether civic or not, was toward viewing life in terms of particular actions at particular times, is suggested by the study of the humanist spirit to be found in the works of Eugenio Garin.[13] The humanist scholar, he contends, regarded philology rather than philosophy as the path to knowledge, and in a case like that of Lorenzo Valla, this came about because he was a rhetorician; regarding truth as uttered rather than perceived, he became interested in the moments and occasions on which—the contexts in which—the speech-acts embodying it had been performed.[14] The scholastic philosopher confronted with a text of Aristotle engaged in a complex process of abstraction, analysis, and arrangement, in which the text and its context and author might virtually disappear and the all-important step might be the statement of universal principles whose consequences could then be perceived. The humanist's criticism of this procedure—a criticism vehement and often unjust—was that the actual thought of Aristotle, the actual wisdom of Aristotle, was being destroyed and replaced by schematizations, and he set himself to learn what he could from Aristotle himself, from his mind as revealed in his words, from his words as preserved in the document. In point of fact, Aristotle is a poor example; so far was he considered the originator of the scholastic process now under attack that he was denounced and replaced by other authors, and it was some time before humanists, having completed their denunciation of Aristotelianism, returned to the study of Aristotle. But the effect of the humanist technique was to exalt philology, the attempt to find out what the documents actually contained, what the words actually meant, what the philosopher, orator, historian, or poet had

---

[13] Above, n. 4.

[14] Garin, pp. 5-7, 15-17, 50-66, 69-77. For Valla and the role of rhetoric see also Seigel, *Rhetoric and Philosophy*, ch. v; Donald R. Kelley, *The Foundations of Modern Historical Scholarship: Language, Law and History in the French Renaissance* (New York: Columbia University Press, 1970), chs. I and II; the present writer's review essay in *History and Theory* 11, no. 1 (1972), 89-97; Nancy S. Struever, *The Language of History in the Renaissance* (Princeton University Press, 1970). Discussion of civic humanism from a social-political point of view may be found in Lauro Martines, *The Social World of the Florentine Humanists, 1390-1460* (Princeton University Press, 1963) and *Lawyers and Statecraft in Renaissance Florence* (Princeton University Press, 1968), Marvin B. Becker, *Florence in Transition* (2 vols., Baltimore: The Johns Hopkins University Press, 1967-68), and others (see the handbook edited by Anthony Molho, *Social and Economic Foundations of the Italian Renaissance*, New York: John Wiley and Sons, 1969).

actually said.[15] In place of logic it tended to exalt "grammar," which like "philology" itself was a compendious term for the study of past languages, textual criticism, the structure of sentences, and in general the written word as an instrument for conveying meaning. Through grammar and philology, and in a sense only through them, the author's meaning might be known; the auxiliary sciences of language permitted his mind to communicate direct with his reader's.

But the epistemological and, ultimately, the philosophical consequences were drastic. The more it was stressed that an author long dead was speaking to us in the present, and the less we made of any structure of timeless universals through which his voice was mediated, the more conscious we must be of communication across time and of the time-space separating him from us; and the more carefully we facilitated this communication by studying the text and the context in which he had spoken or written, the more conscious we must become of the temporal, social, and historical circumstances in which he had expressed his thought and which, in shaping the language and the content of it, had shaped the thought itself. This intensified historical awareness is clearly stated in the letters which Petrarch addressed to Cicero and Livy, speaking direct from his moment in time to them in theirs— from such and such a year "of the Incarnation of Him of whom you would have heard had you lived a little longer."[16] We may find something similar in the speech of Dante to Virgil—"poet, by the God you did not know, lead on"[17]—but Petrarch does not follow Dante in accompanying Virgil on an extra-historical journey through the regions where individual lives become eternal. Poetry (a close relative of prophecy) is concerned with the universal and the divine, but prose— especially the prose of the historian or the orator—is social and secular. The philological consciousness is very much a consciousness of the mind as expressed, and the world as seen, in prose; the humanist rhetoricians were converting the intellectual life into a conversation between men in time.

A certain affinity between philological and political humanism is beginning to appear. Both isolated certain moments in the human past

---

[15] In the final stage this endeavor was extended to the words of God himself. See George Newton Conklin, *Biblical Criticism and Heresy in Milton* (New York: King's Crown Press, 1949), pp. 1-2, and the dictum of Valla (quoted by Garin, p. 16) that "none of the words of Christ have come to us, for Christ spoke in Hebrew and never wrote down anything."

[16] This is the dating of the letter to Livy, *Fam.*, xxiv, 8, but nearly all his letters to classical authors—at least to philosophers and historians, but not to poets—employ similar language. See Mario E. Cosenza, trans., *Petrarch's Letters to Classical Authors* (Chicago University Press, 1910).

[17] *Inferno*, I, 130.

and endeavored to establish communication between these and moments in the present. Petrarch learned direct from Livy and wrote direct to him; Salutati's and Bruni's Florence learned direct from republican Rome and envisaged itself as Rome's revival. Later in the story, Machiavelli's famous letter to Francesco Vettori describes how he comes home in the evening, puts on formal clothing, and enters into the presence and conversation of the ancients by reading their books.[18] The conversation is meant to restore Machiavelli not only to the understanding of politics, but indirectly to actual civic participation. The idea of direct conversation with antiquity is a key concept in all forms of humanism and may occur in or out of a political context, but there is something ineradicably social and even political about it: the implication that the heights of human experience, under God, are to be found in a meeting of like minds and in their communication and joint conception of propositions, sentiments, and decisions. The conversation with the ancients which results in knowledge is affiliated with the conversation among citizens which results in decision and law. Both take place between particular men, located at particular moments in time—ancient and humanist occupy different moments, the citizens are all at the same point together—and employing the language, while experiencing the problems, appropriate to their several moments (the humanist must be a grammarian, the citizens must speak a common *volgare*). If man as intellectual animal is defined as "humanist," while man as political animal is defined as "citizen," both acts of knowledge and acts of decision assume some of the character of what Fortescue called "statutes"; they are agreed upon by living men, located in time and employing the intellectual resources possessed by beings so located. But such intellectual acts, which occupy a tertiary place in Fortescue, are fixed by both humanists and citizens at the very center of the picture and call for intellectual powers considerably greater than the simple prudence which was the only means of performing them known to Fortescue. The humanist stress on communication was enough to raise the question of how particular men, existing at particular moments, could lay claim to secure knowledge. The answer could not be given in terms of the simple cognition of universals, or the intellectual animal would be thrust back into the universe of the scholastics, the political animal into that of the imperial hierarchies; to give it in terms of the simple accumulation of experience would be similarly fatal to humanist

---

[18] ". . . entro nelle antique corti degli antiqui huomini, dove, da loro ricevuto amorevolmente, mi pasco di quel cibo, che *solum* è mio, et che io nacqui per lui; dove io non mi vergogno parlare con loro, et domandarli della ragione delle loro actioni; et quelli per loro humanità mi rispondono . . . ," Machiavelli, *Lettere*, ed. F. Gaeta (Milan: Feltrinelli, 1961), p. 304.

and citizen alike. Yet an answer must be given somehow, or Petrarch would be unable to read Livy, Florence unable to govern itself. How might a conversation between particulars be capable of organized rationality? The rhetoric of philology, or of politics, might provide the answer; but politics was more than rhetoric.

Humanist attitudes toward the problem of universals were various and exceedingly complex, and by no means the same at Florence as they were, for example, at Padua; but it seems clear that the main lines of thought which emerged were those which neither reverted to straightforward scholastic realism nor adopted the relativistic position that only particulars could be known. Humanist philosophy certainly did not dispense with the idea that there were universal objects of knowledge, awareness of which provided the only true certainty or rationality; but, committed by its adoption of philology to the view that these could be known only through the works of particular men in particular times and places, it sought—often in a reworking of Platonic themes—justification for thinking of universals as somehow immanent in the words and deeds of men, to be known through creative knowledge of and engagement in these. The Renaissance was at its most Platonic[19] in exalting the living relationship of the soul with the universal paradigm or value above the intellect's abstract contemplation of it; history could be praised above philosophy on the grounds that the latter inspired the intellect with the idea of truth, but the former the whole spirit with concrete examples of it. Truth itself became less a system of propositions than a system of relationships to which the inquiring spirit became party by its inquiry. In consequence, participation in the humanist conversation, in one or other of its forms, became in itself the mode of relation to the universal, and the universal could be known and experienced by perpetual engagement in the conversation with particulars. The question was what form the conversation should take, what manner of conversation most fully realized the universal.

To Aristotle it had been a problem whether the highest life for the individual was one of politics and action or one of knowledge and contemplation; and if Florentine humanism acquired from its civic environment a bias toward the political, it absorbed a contrary bias from the mainstream of philosophic tradition. If the universal were thought of primarily as an object of intellectual knowledge, then the preferred form of conversation would be contemplative, a philosophical dialogue with one's contemporaries and the great dead. It is significant, however, that contemplation has itself become social, a matter of dialogue and mind-to-mind relationships rather than of formal deduc-

---

[19] Garin, pp. 9-11, and chs. III and IV.

tion and demonstration, and that the term "politia" (in Greek *politeia*, which to Aristotle had denoted the structure of relationships composing the city) is sometimes employed, as we might speak of the "republic of letters," to describe the community of minds, living and dead, in which it went on. The Athenian polis had been a community of culture as well as of decision-making, and words like "polite," "civil," "urbane" seem to have acquired from the contemplative style of humanism the connotation, which they bear in contrast to their cognate terms "political," "civic," "urban," of a social life which consists in civilized conversation rather than in political decision and action.[20]

Such a contemplative style there was, and it not infrequently appears under the rule of a benevolent prince and patron who could be seen as a philosopher-king—at Milan, in Medicean Florence, at Rome or Urbino. The alternative style took citizenship as its ideal; it therefore flourished in a republican climate and preeminently at Florence, for the atmosphere of Venice, while it encouraged learning in an environment of relative liberty, was too heavily senatorial for passionate asseverations of an ideal of active citizenship. The full reality, however, is markedly more complex than these words would suggest. It can be seen that the ideal of the *vivere civile*, in competition—if competition there was—with the contemplative ideal, was possessed of great strengths and great weaknesses. In the first place it is now apparent that whether as philologist, rhetorician, or republican citizen, the humanist had a profound commitment to participation in human life in concrete and particular detail, whether the emphasis lay on letters and language or on politics and persuasion. The need to make the particular intelligible had given rise to the idea of conversation, the idea that the universal was immanent in participation in the web of life and language, and so the highest values, even those of nonpolitical contemplation, had come to be seen as attainable only through conversation and social association. But it must follow that association was itself a high and necessary good, a prerequisite for attaining the universal, and the entire Athenian and Aristotelian tradition was emphatic that the highest form of human association was political, the community of distribution, decision, and action which Aristotle had seen in the polis. There were therefore the strongest reasons leading the humanist who had identified knowledge with social activity toward identifying himself with the citizen—Seigel is at bottom arguing that civic values were inherent in the humanist's social position rather than his response to external events.

It could be held besides that if knowledge was to be found in conversation, it was a kind of activity. The philosophic basis of the *vivere*

[20] Garin, pp. 38, 87, 158-62.

civile was the conception that it was in action, in the production of works and deeds of all kinds, that the life of man rose to the stature of those universal values which were immanent in it. The active man asserted with the total engagement of his personality what the contemplative man could only know, through the inward eye of his intellect or the dialectics of Platonic conversation and friendship; Garin sees in civic humanism anticipations of Vico's doctrine that we know the world through creating it in history.[21] But if action was to assert the universal, it must be shown that some form of action possessed universality. Here is the peculiar importance of those disputes over the relative primacy of law and medicine, to be found in the writings of Petrarch, Salutati, and others during the fifteenth century.[22] Medicine was on the whole a practical rather than a contemplative art. It could of course claim to be concerned with the universal laws of the natural world, and in a hierarchical society where politics were held to reflect nature could claim to have much to teach the statesman by way of analogy; but in the humanist environment it was made to fight on other ground and was accused, first of a merely mechanical concern with securing individual results in individual cases, and second of being limited to a knowledge of the world of particulars that never rose above it to the knowledge of laws. Plato had accused it of being empirical but never philosophical, and it was in the spirit of the *Republic* that Salutati made personified Medicine confess with lamentations that it was confined to the merely traditional knowledge which came with the simple accumulation of experience.[23] By contrast, the statesman or jurist was concerned with the universal and with that which did not change. Morality was inherent in man and human laws the result of his knowledge of his own nature. Since the political community was the necessary setting for such self-knowledge and the laws that were its issue, the conduct of the affairs of such a community was Plato's architectonic art, the conduct of human activity at the point where it attained universality and itself the highest form of that activity that could be conceived. Salutati was continuing the Athenian tradition of declaring that the political community was self-sufficient and consequently universal; and he presented the activity of ruling such a community not as the lonely rationality of a specialized ruler or monarch, but as a perpetual conversation between citizens engaged in, yet rising above, a multitude of social activities. Here was the active conversation in which human life attained universality in the conduct of particulars.

Yet Salutati was capable of proclaiming the superiority of contem-

---

[21] Garin, p. 55.
[22] Seigel, pp. 37-40; Garin, pp. 24, 31-36.
[23] Garin, pp. 32-33.

plation, of monastic withdrawal and of accepting the rule of a monarch or tyrant;[24] and if we reject Baron's attempt to relate this to the progress of the Viscontian crisis, we shall follow other writers in holding that ambivalence as between civic and contemplative values was inherent in the humanist mind. It would not be surprising if this were so. None of Salutati's praise of statesmanship altogether eliminates the lurking weakness of the civic position. When all was said and done, universals were intellectual realities if they were realities at all; their *esse* was *percipi* and they must be the objects of acts of knowledge. And while universals might be immanent in human laws, human laws were not themselves universals; they were the fruits of particular human decisions (the *recta ratio agibilium*), had reference to particular human situations and existed in particular moments of time. Universals could only be known; decisions and actions could legislate only particulars. The fruits of statesmanship and citizenship might still appear particular and transitory, and the statesman after all little better than the physician. All this could be in the mind of any humanist opting (as so many did at one time and another) for philosophy rather than rhetoric, contemplation rather than action, monarchy and unchanging hierarchy as against citizenship and the risks of action in time. If citizenship could assert only particular decisions and values, it was doomed to transitoriness; and if citizen bodies were only collocations of particular men, they could neither decide nor constitute anything permanent. But here civic values could reassert themselves. There did exist in the Athenian political tradition means of asserting that the republic was a partnership of all men aimed at the realization of all values. If it was this it was a universal entity; but this assertion rested on the theory that it could achieve a distribution of authority such that every citizen's moral nature would be fulfilled. Without such a distribution the republic would be neither universal, just, nor stable, and its citizens could not rely on the support of a cosmic order in the way that a king and his subjects could, since their polity did not claim to mirror the cosmic order as a monarchy did. The theory of the polis and its constitutional structure thus became crucial to the humanist enterprise. The civic humanist must possess a body of constitutional theory which was also a philosophy. It happened that one such was available.

[II]

There are several ways of reading Aristotle's *Politics*, and this greatly complicates the task of assessing its place in Western tradition. Read in conjunction with his main philosophical treatises, it asserts the

---

[24] Baron, *Crisis*, ch. 7.

great theme of natural law; men perceive the values inherent in nature and pursue them in society. When we study its interrelations with the tradition of Augustinian and medieval Christianity, we find it making assertions about the autonomy of reason and the rational direction of politics which are potentially revolutionary because they call in question the extent to which grace and the channels of grace are necessary in the conduct of earthly affairs. But it may also be read as the originator of a body of thought about the citizen and his relation to the republic, and about the republic (or polis) as a community of values; and this is the approach which reveals its importance to humanists and Italian thinkers in search of means of vindicating the universality and stability of the *vivere civile*. There is a tradition of thought on these matters of which the *Politics* formed part, but its role in that tradition is difficult to assess precisely because it is so vast and all-pervasive. The tradition in question may be referred back to Aristotle in nearly every respect, but (leaving aside the fact that certain decisive formulations of its doctrines were made by Plato before him) so many subsequent authors restated parts of it and were influential in their own ways that, especially under Renaissance conditions, it is hard to define with certainty the particular writer exerting authority at a particular point. We are, in short, confronted by the problems of interpreting a tradition of thought; but that tradition (which may almost be termed the tradition of mixed government) is Aristotelian, and the *Politics*, as well as forming the earliest and greatest full exposition of it, makes explicit so many of the implications which it might at one time or another contain that—apart from the enormous direct authority which the book exerted —it is worth rehearsing the theory of citizenship and polity which it contains in order to see what might (and did) result and what importance the theory might (and did) possess for intellects in the problem-situation of civic humanism.

Aristotle taught that every human activity was value-oriented in the sense that it aimed at some theoretically identifiable good; that all value-oriented activity was social in the sense that it was pursued by men in association with one another; and that the polis or republic was the association within which all particular associations pursued their particular ends.[25] Association with others, and participation in the value-oriented direction of that association, formed both a means to an end and an end—or good—in itself;[26] and participation in the association whose end was the good of all particular associations, and the attainment of all particular goods, was in itself a good of a very high, because universal, character. Until the point was reached where the

[25] See *Politics*, Book I, ch. 1, #1 (1252a).
[26] I, xiii, #4-8 (1259b-1260a); III, iv, #10-15 (1277a-b).

choice between action and contemplation had to be faced, the highest conceivable form of human life was that of the citizen who ruled as head of his *oikos* or household, and ruled and was ruled as one of a community of equal heads making decisions which were binding on all. He took part in the determination of the general good, enjoying in his own person the values made attainable by society while contributing by his political activity to the attainment of values by others.[27] Since this activity was concerned with the universal good, it was itself a good of a higher order than the particular goods which the citizen as social animal might enjoy, and in enjoying his own citizenship—his contribution to the good of others, his relationship with others engaged in so contributing—he enjoyed a universal good and became a being in relation with the universal. Citizenship was a universal activity, the polis a universal community.

But all citizens were not identical; they were alike *qua* citizens and universal beings, but they were dissimilar as particular beings; each had his own priorities as regards the particular goods which he might elect to pursue, and each found himself banded in particular categories with those who shared one, some, or all of his priorities. The polis thus faced a problem in allocating priorities, in determining what particular goods should be enjoyed at a particular time by those who had given them priority, and though the determination of this problem was plainly the task of citizenship, Aristotle did not think that the individual as citizen, engaged in the universal activity of pursuing and distributing the common good, should be considered out of relation with the same individual engaged in the particular activity of pursuing and enjoying the particular goods he preferred. Since it was the definition of the citizen that he both ruled and was ruled, the activity of ruling must be coupled with the activity in respect of which he was ruled.[28] Universal and particular met in the same man, and if the citizen assumed a particular social personality as a result of pursuing, enjoying and excelling in the attainment of the particular values he preferred, this must modify his capacity to engage in the universal activity of making decisions aimed at distributing the common good. The problem confronting the polis now became that of distributing the particular exercise of this universal function in a way related to the diversity of social personality which the citizens displayed as a result of their individual value-priorities. Aristotle now turned to consider the categories in which the citizens might be arranged in consequence of this diversity.

These were of two kinds: theoretical and traditional. In principle, they might be as indefinitely numerous as the values which human

27 III, ix (1280a-1281a).
28 III, x (1281a), xii (1282b-1283a), xiii (1283a-1284b).

68

activity aimed at achieving. Since each of these was pursued by men acting in association, it was possible to think of an association of persons aimed at achieving each one of them and, by a natural extension of the concept, of an association of persons who gave that value a priority, who had devoted more energy to pursuing it, who had gone further toward achieving it, and who—to complete the development of the train of ideas—might be thought of as an elite group of persons distinguished by possessing it to a degree above the common. In the ordinary language of the Athens where Aristotle had studied in Plato's Academy, there were established terms which denoted a variety of categories recognized as forming elites of this sort: the good, the wise, the brave, the rich, the wellborn, and so on. But it is important to remember that such elites were in theory as many as the identifiable value-goals which men pursued, and that since every citizen had been defined as possessing his own value-priorities, there was in principle no citizen who did not belong to as many of these elites as he had chosen values for special emphasis.[29] Next Aristotle remarked a widespread traditional habit of distinguishing citizens into two main groups, the "few" and the "many." This was of great practical consequence, since it furnished the basis for distinguishing between those cities which tended to restrict and those which tended to disperse the distribution of political authority as among the citizens—the "oligarchies" and "democracies" of contemporary parlance. It was observable further that though "few" and "many" implied that the criterion of distinction being used was quantitative, the normal uses of language implied something more. The "few" were often described as the "best," "oligarchies" as "aristocracies." If we did not persistently and rigorously ask such questions as "best at what?" this tendency to combine quantitative with qualitative criteria might lead us to fall—as Aristotle himself occasionally fell—into speaking of civic populations as if each could be divided into a minority identifiable as belonging to the various elites and a majority identifiable as belonging to no elite in particular. Aristotle is clear, however, that such a polarization of the "few" and the "many," though it may be useful for talking about the real world in which such distinctions are traditionally recognized, provides an unsatisfactory theoretical basis for differentiating among citizens.[30]

Such a differentiation could only be carried out by the employment of multiple criteria. In the first place there were as many qualitative criteria as there were theoretically or traditionally identifiable values which men might prefer and associate to enjoy, and the individual might respond differently to the application of different criteria. In the

[29] IV, iii, #1-6 (1289b-1290a).
[30] IV, iii, #6-IV, #22 (1290a-1291b); III, vii-viii (1279a-1280a).

second place, there was a criterion which might be employed on those occasions when it was appropriate to treat all citizens as of equal value—to emphasize, for example, that all were engaged in the pursuit of good without differentiating between them on the basis of preference or attainment. Nonqualitative in character, this was the criterion of number,[31] and its employment might have a variety of consequences; it served to distinguish a number of categories and its use might mask a variety of confusions. There were three traditionally recognized categories whose use might be seen to rest on the basis of quantitative distinction—the "one," the "few," and the "many"—and in each case the confusion of quantitative with qualitative criteria might be detected: the one and the few would be thought of as possessing elite characteristics which qualified them to rule, but the many would be thought of as lacking such characteristics, so that a defense of their claim to rule became (as it has remained) a defense of the separation of political authority from elite characteristics of any kind. Though Aristotle knew this confusion of criteria to be unsound, he took the risk of employing the terminology of one, few, and many pretty much as it was employed in ordinary speech. He had good reasons for doing this. In the first place, actual states really were divided into monarchies, aristocracies, and democracies; in the second place, it was to be important to his theory that decision-making groups be thought of as differing in size.

When it came to correlating the distribution of political authority with the diversity of personal qualification, therefore, Aristotle disposed of a theoretically infinite number of criteria which it might seem appropriate to employ. Each of these served to distinguish an elite group, and they were both qualitative and quantitative in character. The problem of constructing a *politeia*—this word, while translatable as "constitution," means the formal distribution of authority to make decisions within a universal decision-making process in which all citizens are participant—became the problem of seeing that every elite group, including that unique elite of the non-elite, "the many" or "all the citizens," was allotted such a role in decision-making that it could contribute as its character best fitted it to the attainment of particular and general goods.[32] This was possible because the process of making a decision was so complex that it could be decomposed into a number of functions and each of these entrusted to a particular group. There were differences between drawing up a list of alternative policies, deciding which of these to adopt, choosing persons to perform one or other of these functions, resolving to confirm any decision made by

[31] III, ix, #1-4 (1280a); III, xii, #67 (1283a); III, xiii, #4 (1283a).
[32] III, viii, #3-8 (1279b-1280a); IV, viii (1293b-1294a).

others—the list could be indefinitely prolonged, and consequently it was theoretically possible to associate an indefinite number of groups with the making of public decisions. Aristotle premised that one could distinguish between different types of decision, or rather of functions in the process of arriving at a decision, and say of them that some required this or that special qualification; that others should be trusted to those affected by the outcome of this or a previous decision; that some should be made by small and others by large groups; that some required complex reasoning by trained minds, while others were best adjudicated by the experience of life shared by all in common.[33] In this way the *politeia* became the paradigm of a society organized in such a manner that any theoretically conceivable group had opportunity to contribute to decisions in the way for which it was best fitted, while any individual citizen might contribute many times over, both as a member of any specialized group for which his attainments might qualify him and as a member of the non-elite *demos*, the citizen body as a whole, to which all belonged. Any value to which a man might give priority, or by which he might be judged and evaluated—even the egalitarian value of not giving priority to particular values or using them to distinguish between men and men—might become one mode of his participation in the determination and distribution of general values. The relation between the pursuit of particular and universal values would thus be established.

Aristotle was well aware that the making of decisions meant power, and that power was exercised over others. Each group in the *politeia*, and each citizen in virtue of his group membership (which might be multiple), was to have power to pursue each group's particular good in such a way as to involve it in the pursuit of other goods by other groups, and since the pursuit of each good was carried on by means of decisions affecting the priorities of other groups, each group like each citizen must be subject to power as well as the exerciser of it. The evil to be avoided was the situation in which any group was able to exercise an unshared power over the whole.[34] Any form of government in which the good of a particular group was treated as identical with the good of the whole was despotic, even though the particular good might be, at least initially, a real good in itself; perverted government consisted essentially in the dictatorship of the particular over the universal, and led toward the corruption of the good which had assumed dictatorial power. Such despotism could in principle be exercised by any group whatever; there might even be a despotism of the good or

[33] IV, ix (1294a-b), xiii-xv (1297a-1300b).
[34] III, vi, #11-vii, #5; viii, #2 (1279a-b).

the wise, if the good which they pursued were less than the good of the whole (and the implementation of this concept might involve permitting the less good and the less wise their due share of power).[35] In classifying good and bad forms of government, however, Aristotle made use of a shorthand composed of terminology at once quantitative and traditional. He accepted the common classification of forms of government according as the one, the few, or the many predominated in the exercise of power, and added the supposition that in each case it might happen that the predominant element ruled with attention to the good of all, or that it identified that good with its own. The threefold classification thus became sixfold: there were monarchy and tyranny, aristocracy and oligarchy, polity (*politeia*) and democracy. It is the last pair that is of the greatest theoretical interest. The polity, as the form of government in which power is shared among all the groups or categories into which the citizens may be divided, is consequently that in which power is least likely to be exercised in the interests of a limited group or coalition. By democracy, on the other hand, Aristotle meant to designate not simply a system of widespread participation in power—for the polity was that and possessed many of the characteristics of democracy in the ordinary sense—but one in which power was widely distributed and yet despotically exercised. In general, this tended to mean a system weighted in favor of the poorer and less privileged, thought of as belonging to no elite group;[36] but another, more formal and precise, meaning of the term would be rule by men not differentiated from each other, a system in which all power was exercised by mechanical, numerical majorities, and only those goods taken into account which could be discerned on the assumption that all men were alike. Such would be a tyranny of numbers and a tyranny of equality, in which the development of individuality was divorced from the exercise of power, what a man was from what part he might play in politics. Aristotle was anticipating features of the modern concept of alienation, and there are elements of his criticism of undiscriminating equality in present-day criticisms of the depersonalizing effects of mass society.

As the antithesis he set up the image of the polity, the system in which individuality and the differences between individuals were taken into account in the distribution of political roles and power. But whether as a pure or as an applied science, there were difficulties in working out the theory of a society in which every conceivable individual and social type had its appropriate role in decision-making. In the first place, though society could be analyzed into many specialized

[35] III, x, #4 (1280a).   [36] III, viii.

groups and the decision-making process into many specialized functions, it was hard to find so close a correspondence between the two series as to permit the inference that every value-oriented group had its own peculiar and appropriate mode of political activity. Here there was a profound, though in many ways a fruitful, ambiguity in Aristotelian theory. On the one hand, the concept of polity was reinforced in its tendency to become congealed in traditional terms, to be abridged and presented as a duality of aristocracy and democracy, of elite and non-elite, of few wise and foolish (or common-sensical) many. On the other we find the important result that the complex blend constituting the polity could be thought of either as a blend of classes and social groups; or as a blend of the moral and intellectual qualities which such groups were held to possess; or as a blend of the numerically differentiated groups into which the polis could be resolved; or as a blend of the different political functions into which the decision-making process could be analyzed; or as any combination of these blends. An aristocracy, for example, could be thought of as a hereditary nobility, as a minority of the exceptionally wise, talented, or ambitious, or as that few which any political system must contain and for which it must provide a special role; and these concepts could be either conjoined or disjuncted. The political function of the few might appear as the exercise of those qualities which only the few possessed, as the performance of those specialized functions to which the qualities of the few were appropriate, or as the performance of functions which it was best to leave to a small number irrespective of their special talents. The looseness of Aristotelian language was also its richness; it was capable of pursuing analysis in many directions, if it was also capable of getting those directions mixed up. At the level of applied science, the difficulty was that a society in which every conceivable type and category had its appropriate political function could not be thought of as institutionalized in any single form. For practical purposes, therefore, it was usually visualized in terms of the shorthand mentioned above, as a blend or balance of the one, the few, and the many, or rather—since monarchy was not an immediate issue for city-state Greeks—of aristocracy and democracy. Each had its particular virtue, its appropriate role and special contribution to the common activity of decision-making; but on this drastically simplified image there operated the multiplicity of concepts inherent in the Aristotelian analysis, encouraging the citizen to conceptualize his political role in a diversity of ways. The polity was both an institutional and a moral structure, and its search for the appropriate institutional form was always an attempt to solve the exceedingly complex problem of reconciling the activities of men who were moral only in their relations with each other.

There were tensions, also, in conceptualizing the individual as citizen and member of this structure. On the one hand, it was his pursuit of particular goods as an individual that made him a citizen; on the other, it was only in his concern for and awareness of the common universal good that his citizenship could persist; and there was always the possibility of conflict between the two. If he became preoccupied with his private goods to the point of subordinating the universal good to them, he might find himself party to the tyranny of some smaller or larger group, and the value inherent in his personal aims was no guarantee that this would not happen. Like the fallen man of Christian theodicy, he could not be saved by his own virtues; but where Augustine would have set the operation of divine grace, the Aristotelian analysis of civic virtue set the political activity of the individual's fellow citizens, ruling and directing him as he them, or—more rigorously—the moral and political laws that governed all of them. But the fundamental ambiguity between particular and universal good remained. The citizen might be thought of as an Athenian, the diversity of whose particular attainments heightened his capacity to act in the public interest, or as a Spartan, sacrificing every particular form of self-development in order to act as a citizen and out of civic solidarity alone. Aristotle had on the whole concluded against the Spartan ideal, whatever might be said of Plato; but in Renaissance Europe, from the fifteenth to the eighteenth centuries, the preponderant voice was in favor of the grim patriots of the Eurotas.[37] Sparta had been stable and a mixture of powers, Athens democratic, unstable, and addicted to persecuting the philosophers she favored. Sparta certainly had had no philosophers at all, but perhaps it was better to have citizens—to pursue the perfection of complete self-identification with the common good. Yet what was the common good if it led to the abnegation of all particular goods? The contradiction continued to defy solution; but the one point never to be lost to sight was that the polity was a relationship between values, and that the good of citizenship—of ruling and being ruled—consisted in a relationship between one's own virtue and that of another. It was in this sense of the mutual and relational character of virtue that only the political animal could be a truly good man.

The theory of the polis—which is, in a certain sense, political theory in its purest original form—was cardinal to the constitutional theory of Italian cities and Italian humanists. It offered a paradigm of how a body politic might be held together when it was conceived, as an Italian commune must be, as a city composed of interacting persons rather than of universal norms and traditional institutions; and its value in this

[37] See Elizabeth Rawson, *The Spartan Tradition in European Thought* (Oxford: The Clarendon Press, 1969).

capacity did not end when it had depicted the polity as a moral community, since a city like Florence, whose normal institutional structure was that of a complex of interlocking assemblies, boards, and committees, could learn much about the theory of such a structure from Aristotelian analysis and Athenian history. To the civic humanists and advocates of the *vivere civile*, it offered the theory which their commitments rendered necessary: one which depicted human social life as a universality of participation rather than a universal for contemplation. Particular men and the particular values they pursued met in citizenship to pursue and enjoy the universal value of acting for the common good and the pursuit of all lesser goods. But the theory was bought at a high price; it imposed high demands and high risks. The polity must be a perfect partnership of all citizens and all values since, if it was less, a part would be ruling in the name of the whole, subjecting particular goods to its own particular goods and moving toward despotism and the corruption of its own values. The citizen must be a perfect citizen since, if he was less, he prevented the polity from attaining perfection and tempted his fellows, who did for him what he should have done for himself, to injustice and corruption. To become the dependent of another was as great a crime as to reduce another to dependence on oneself. The dereliction of one citizen, therefore, reduced the others' chances of attaining and maintaining virtue, since virtue was now politicized; it consisted in a partnership of ruling and being ruled with others who must be as morally autonomous as oneself. In embracing the civic ideal, therefore, the humanist staked his future as a moral person on the political health of his city. He must in a totally non-cynical sense accept the adage that one should love one's country more than one's own soul; there was a sense in which the future of his soul depended on it, for once the justice which was part of Christian virtue was identified with the distributive justice of the polis, salvation became in some degree social, in some degree dependent upon others.

To the Renaissance mind, this problem was bound to present itself as a problem in time. We have seen that the problem of the republic was the problem of maintaining a particular existence, that instability was the characteristic of particularity and time the dimension of instability. In the theory of the polis and the polity, it was possible to recognize the republic as a universal, because a comprehensive and therefore stable, harmonization of particular values; and such a harmonization should in principle—even when it assumed the abridged form of a successful combination of the one, the few, and the many—remain stable and unchanging in time. Yet as against this there was the presumption that the republic, being a work of men's hands, must come to an end in time; there was the unmistakable historical fact that Athens, Sparta, and Rome had all declined and ceased to be; and there were, inherent in the Aristotelian analysis, excellent theoretical reasons why this should be so. Since the range of particular values and of activities, associations, and individuals seeking them was of indefinite extent, it would always be very hard to construct a polity which was not in fact a dictatorship of some particulars over others, and it would be similarly difficult to ensure that the citizen did not prefer his particular values to the common good. If he did this, he sacrificed his civic virtue; but, as we have also seen, it was the predicament of civic virtue that it could only be practiced with one's fellow citizens, and consequently might be lost as surely in consequence of another's dereliction as of one's own. The laws and other imperatives enjoining the virtues of citizenship might be enforced as rigorously as they had been at Sparta, and yet the citizen could not be forever sure of the self-maintained virtue of his fellow, let alone of his own. Corruption (as it came to be called) was an ever-present possibility. If virtue depended on the freely willed actions of other men, on the maintenance of laws seeking to regulate those actions, and on the continuance of the external circumstances which made those laws possible, it in fact depended on a myriad variables—on the polis seen as a myriad particulars as well as on the polis seen as a single universal—and the name of the force directing the variations of particulars was Fortune. Since Boethius, it had been held that though the flux of secular happenings was inscrutable, unpredictable, and to all appearances unjustifiable, nevertheless the Christian might have faith that it was being providentially directed in ways relevant to his salvation and that what appeared mere fortune in fact provided the context in which his active virtue took shape, the matter to the latter's form. The theme was resumed and intensified in the writings of Christian humanists, as their sharpened philological and historical sense made them more acutely aware of the varieties of fortune and the vicissitudes of the social and moral contexts in which men acted. But the politicization of virtue introduced a dramatic change. The operations of fortune were no longer external to one's virtue, but intrinsically part of it; if, that is to say, one's virtue depended on cooperation with others and could be lost by others' failure to cooperate with one, it depended on the maintenance of the polis in a perfection which was perpetually prey to human failures and circumstantial variations. The citizen's virtue was in a special sense hostage to fortune, and it became of urgent moral importance to examine the polis as a structure of particulars seeking to maintain its stability—and its universality—in time.

For reasons which must be presumed to inhere in the character of Athenian temporal consciousness, Aristotle had not been overwhelmingly concerned with the image of time as the dimension of instability, but there existed at least one pre-Christian classic in which this concept was applied to political and constitutional thought. The sixth book of Polybius's *Histories*, though it did not become available in a language other than Greek until the second decade of the sixteenth century, exercised so great an influence on Renaissance ideas about politics in time that it may be considered here as indicative of that age's fundamental conceptual problems. Polybius, a Greek exile of the second century B.C. who witnessed from a vantage point within the Roman governing class Rome's conquest of the central Mediterranean, set himself[38] to explain this unprecedented achievement by a city-state on the supposition that the republic's military success might be related to its internal stability. He was thus led into a lengthy analysis of stability and instability in cities, and to a rephrasing of the theory of polity which was to have a momentous appeal to the Renaissance mind. He took a variation of the sixfold classification used by Aristotle—monarchy, tyranny; aristocracy, oligarchy; democracy, ochlocracy (mobrule or anarchy)—and pronounced it a developmental sequence, the famous *anakuklōsis politeiōn* or cycle of constitutions.[39] That is, he declared (with little warrant from the historical data known to him) that any state, unless prevented, must pass through each of these forms in turn and in the order stated, and from anarchy must return to monarchy and begin the cycle again. The only stable system would be one which had escaped the cycle, or might hope to do so; it would resemble Aristotle's polity in being a blend or balance of the three numerically defined forms of government—monarchy, aristocracy, and democracy.

To Polybius the cycle was a *physis*, a natural cycle of birth, growth, and death through which republics were bound to pass;[40] yet insofar as he offered means of escaping from it, he presented it less as nature than as an undesired and malignant fate and, though in his writings *tyche* and *fortuna* operate rather in the field of external events than in that of internal relations, it is very important to understand how the

---

[38] In Book VI of his *Histories*. See vol. 1 of the 2-vol. ed. of E. S. Shuckburgh's translation, with a new introduction by F. W. Walbank (Bloomington: Indiana University Press, 1962); F. W. Walbank, *A Historical Commentary on Polybius* (Oxford: The Clarendon Press, 1957); K. von Fritz, *The Theory of the Mixed Constitution in Antiquity* (New York: Columbia University Press, 1954) and Robert Denoon Cumming, *Human Nature and History* (The University of Chicago Press, 1969), vol. 1, chs. 4 and 5.

[39] VI, 3-10 (Shuckburgh, pp. 459-66), 57 (pp. 306-307).

[40] Shuckburgh, p. 466; note, however, the dictum (repeated from p. 461) that the Roman constitution is *preeminently* the product of natural causes, meaning perhaps that it was not the result of forethought (p. 467).

cycle might come to appear a special case of the rotation of Fortune's wheel. Each simple form of government had its virtue, and it was this that was bound to degenerate if unchecked by the virtues belonging to the other potential ruling elements. In this idea of the corruption of a good agent by the excess and overbalance of its single good quality, there was something of the Greek tragic concept of *hubris*; something more of the Aristotelian concept that the dictatorship of one good over others was fatal to the ruling good as well as to the ruled. A Roman, however, would recognize *fortuna* as the normal adversary of *virtus*, and would understand that the *virtus* of each part, balancing and integrating the *virtutes* of the others, was what in this case imposed order and glory upon fortune. At the same time, it could be seen that through *politeia*—the constitution, or relation between virtues exercising powers—the *politeuma*, or citizen body, of Aristotle was being organized into *polis*, as matter into its proper form, and held stable against the deforming work of time—which, again, we have seen to be the work of virtue against fortune. But *virtus* was now politicized; not the heroic manhood of a ruling individual, but a partnership of citizens in a polis.

To Renaissance readers, the point must be that each simple virtue must degenerate precisely because it was simple and particular. The problem of the particular was its finitude, its mortality, its instability in time, and once a virtue (itself universal) was embodied in a particular form of government it partook of this general instability. The mortality in time of a system of human justice, moreover, was not simply a matter of *physis*, the natural life and death of living things; it was a moral failure, a repetition of the Fall, and at the same moment another triumph of the power of Fortune. When men sought to erect moral systems in finite and historical shapes, they were placing their virtue at Fortune's mercy. The wheel that raised and threw down kings was an emblem of the vanity of human ambitions; a wheel that raised and threw down republics was an emblem of the vanity of the human pursuit of justice. And the citizen who had committed himself to the active practice of a *vivere civile* must pay a heavy price for the retreat into Boethian faith and contemplation; one no less heavy for the fact that it was often paid.

A world in which justice rode the wheel of Fortune was a frightening prospect, but a certain intelligibility was paradoxically imported by the notion of cyclical recurrence. Fortune, it could be argued, was essentially uncreative and could only shuffle endlessly a pack of cards she had not made. It was implicit in the whole concept of change as irrational that change contained no principle of growth and could produce nothing new; therefore there could be no understanding of growth or of change as history. But in that case Fortune was doomed to repeat her effects. When every possible combination of the cards had been dealt, there was nothing she could do but begin again; to do so was the only recourse, and *ricorso*, like *rivoluzione*, became a term regularly used to indicate that the fortune-process was beginning again from an earlier point—perhaps from the beginning of everything. In the long run, therefore, everything had happened before and would happen again; Fortune's wheel became the image of repetition as well as of unpredictability, and there arose the extremely important and, within limits, heartening consequence that if one knew what had happened before, one could make predictive statements concerning the combinations in which things would happen again. To the extent to which this might be possible, Fortune's world would become more intelligible, less frightening, and even more manageable.

It was a long step to the assumption that the cards would be dealt again in the same order, that events would not only recur but recur in identical sequences and cycles. Polybius made this assumption in company with many of his fellow Stoics, and possibly felt the more able to do so because he had reduced the number of variables to be combined in making the polity from infinity to three.[41] If degeneration was the only agent of change it must be uncreative; the number of variables in the world must be finite; the fewer there were in any department of reality the greater the chance that they would recur in a fixed order, and three is a very small number indeed. It followed further that he might permit himself a considerable degree of optimism as to the chances of constructing a polity of universal form which would escape the cycle of change. If all that was necessary was to construct a mixture or balance of the one, the few, and the many, assigning to each the measure—or kind—of power needed to check the simple and self-corrupting reign of any one of the other two, then it might seem that a universal political harmony was well within man's conceptual and perhaps his practical grasp. And if the causes of change lay in the inherent instability of particulars, and there were only three particulars that needed to be taken into account in the construction of a state, then the causes of change were few and might easily be eliminated; it was within the bounds of possibility that a Polybian mixed constitution might be immune from change and so last forever. One would have left the Wheel and entered the Sphere.

But Polybius did not permit himself this position. As a Stoic he held that nothing in this world was immortal, and he also predicted[42] that the richer and more powerful a commonwealth became, the harder

---

[41] Cf. Cumming, pp. 143-54, for Polybius's difficulties and Walbank's interpretation of them.

[42] Shuckburgh, p. 507.

it would be to maintain the orders and virtues composing it in their proper equilibrium. The pursuit of particular satisfactions would become fiercer, until no system of restraints could contain it. He was not only predicting—so at least it would appear to his readers in later centuries—the disintegration of the Roman republic under the strains and temptations of Mediterranean empire; he was stating that, even— or especially—under the most prosperous of historical conditions, the pursuit of particular goods would prove incompatible with the maintenance of civic virtue. The republic was self-doomed. This to a Christian reader must mean that history could not be prevented from reiterating the story of the Fall, and that not even the republic could replace grace in saving man from its consequences. It was possible to say that fortune (or that nature) would bring corruption and decay to any republic in time, and to mean by this a repetition of the Augustinian doctrine that man's salvation did not lie in politics or in history. Indeed, Polybian theory that raised the possibility of a republic's proving immortal virtually forced the Christian back to Augustine; for if the republic lasted forever, the world must last forever, which it was pagan to assert.

The Christian citizen might still seek to have it, as far as possible, both ways. He might declare that a system of politicized virtue—a perfectly balanced Polybian commonwealth—could last as long as virtue without grace could last in a world ruled by fall and fortune, which might be almost forever. Alternatively, he might declare that the virtuous city, which imposed form and stability upon fortune, was identical with the kingdom of grace, that it would appear and manifest itself when grace was bringing the eschaton to pass, that it embodied and actualized the millennium or the Third Age. But the politicization of grace came remarkably close to the replacement of grace by politics. To such extremes and such heresies might the civic humanist mind be driven by its decision to abandon both the traditional and the timeless modes of politics and to attempt the realization of the universal values of the polis in the particular, finite, and historical form of the republic. Since the republic was neither a customary community nor an aspect of the church militant, it must remain a moment in time—a moment either in the fulfillment of prophecy or in the irrational turning of fortune's wheel—or it must seek means of escaping from the conceptual scheme we have so far outlined. Minds that could be led to make such commitments and take such chances would be toughly and secularly civic minds indeed.

PART TWO

THE REPUBLIC AND ITS FORTUNE

Florentine Political Thought from 1494 to 1530

CHAPTER IV

FROM BRUNI TO SAVONAROLA

Fortune, Venice and Apocalypse

[1]

THE SCHEME OF VALUES and problems outlined in the last chapter was clearly not the sole ethos by which the Florentine citizen articulated his sense of civic patriotism. There were other languages, derived from Roman law and from the practical operation of Florentine institutions, in which this might be done and a set of active and participatory values put into words; and it has understandably been the intention of Riesenberg[1] and others to question whether the concept of "civic humanism" is needed at all to explain the rise of a civic consciousness and its articulation. In civil law and municipal statute, they have shown, the citizen's position was expressed in actual rather than theoretical terms, which did not encounter the problems with which this book is becoming concerned. In the chapters which follow, however, it will be argued that a language for which the term "civic humanism" may appropriately be used can be traced, deriving from the assertion of a republican vision of history, and employed for a variety of purposes among which by far the most important was that of asking whether the *vivere civile* and its values could indeed be held stable in time. This purpose was consciously pursued by the great thinkers of the last years of the Florentine republic, among them Guicciardini who, though trained in both civil and canon law, made remarkably little use of jurisprudence in his studies of civic morality and political institutions; while there is evidence[2] that in the daily delibera-

[1] Peter Riesenberg, "Civism and Roman Law in Fourteenth-century Italian Society," in *Explorations in Economic History*, vol. 7, no. 1-2 (1969), pp. 237-54. See also Lauro Martines (as cited above, ch. III, n. 14).

[2] Felix Gilbert, *Machiavelli and Guicciardini: Politics and History in Sixteenth-Century Florence* (Princeton University Press, 1965), ch. 1: "Florentine Political Institutions, Issues and Ideas at the End of the Fifteenth Century," is a study of the language employed in the *pratiche* and other recorded debates which brings out the extent to which its terminology coincided with that of Machiavelli and Guicciardini. See also his "Florentine Political Assumptions in the Period of Savonarola and Soderini," *Journal of the Warburg and Courtauld Institutes* 20 (1957), 187-214.

tions of Florentine citizens, obsessed by external danger and internal divisions, the language whose history we are tracing was employed. At both practical and theoretical levels, the conceptual vocabulary of "the Machiavellian moment" discharged a function and has a history which can be written. It forms a significant part of the Florentine legacy to subsequent European and Atlantic political perception.

In order to bring out that vocabulary's paradigmatic character, we have located it in two ways: in the context of a model which asserts that there were available only certain limited and specific ways of rendering the sequence of secular phenomena intelligible, and in the context of a history which asserts that, for whatever reasons, Italian city-state humanism made increasing commitments to a scheme of active civic values which necessitated existence first, in a polis and second, in time. The formal dilemma of the humanist republic thus became that it was an attempt to realize a universality of values within a particular, and therefore finite and mortal, political structure. The revival of Aristotelian philosophy carried with it the problem of reconciling the Hellenic view that man was formed to live in a city with the Christian view that man was formed to live in communion with God; but it was only when the republic, in its particularity as Rome or Florence, claimed (for whatever reason) an autonomous history of its own that it began opening new gaps between the two schemes of values. If—it was always a question, never an assumption—republics existed only at certain periods in human history, and these periods were exemplary while the others were not, it was peculiarly clear that the republic, which the values of the *vita activa* insisted was the realization of all human goods in a self-sufficient system of distributive justice, led a life finite in time and space, outside which was an unlegitimated world governed by *fortuna*. It therefore faced a problem in mutability, which could be finally overcome only if the final phase of a republic's existence could be made to coincide with the millennium, end of time, or eschaton; while conversely, if it could finally solve the problem of secular stability and last forever, the Christian time-scheme, the view that man's ends transcended time and the city, and even the presence of God himself in history, might vanish altogether.

At a less exalted level—closer to that on which the actual reconciliation of groups and factions must be attempted—republican theory faced the problem of explaining how a system of distributive justice, once defined as finite in space and time, could maintain its existence in a world where *fortuna* constantly presented threats which, because they were irrational, were always immediate rather than remote. It was never quite enough to say that a system of distributive justice, in which every virtue reinforced every other, should be fortified against every cause of instability. Once the polis was admitted to be finite, it ceased to be truly self-sufficient;[3] it existed within, and was conditioned by, an unstable temporal-spatial world, the domain of *fortuna*, in which some of the conditions necessary to its stability were located so that they could not be relied upon. The justice of the republic might be the form into which civic virtue organized the circumstantial matter of human life; but the triumph of republican virtue over historical fortune could not, within this conceptual scheme, be assured unless grace were at work in history in such a way that the republic in its temporal finitude occupied an eschatological moment.

Custom—the alternative, merely human way of organizing the succession of particulars otherwise known as providence or fortune, and fashioning experience into usage and tradition which constituted the second nature of man—however great its continuing importance, was unlikely to meet the requirements of republican theory. There were several reasons for this. The decision-making structure was more than a community of custom; to the experience of the many must be added the superior reflective capacity of the few, and a partnership of all modes of intelligence and all human virtues must be organized before it could be claimed that civic virtue had triumphed, with or without the aid of grace. Both Christian redemption and the *vivere civile* were concerned with man's first nature or essence, rather than his socially conditioned personality acquired through mere use. That must be transformed if the former was to be fulfilled. And custom, it was obvious, had little if any power over the dangers to the republic arising in the external field.

To the partnership of custom, grace, and prophecy, the resources of Greek and Roman political science added, it is true, a formidable armory of reinforcements. We shall see that the end-product of the Florentine experience was an impressive sociology of liberty, transmitted to the European Enlightenment and the English and American revolutions, which arose in reply to the challenge posed by the republic's commitment to existence in secular history. But of the Florentines certainly, and of the Americans probably, it can be said that they did not fully succeed in solving the problem and showing how a self-sufficiently virtuous republic could exist in the secular time which was a consequence of its own finitude. We aver, then, that it was with this problem—in a double sense that of the "Machiavellian moment"—that Florentine thought grappled at the end of the republican period. It is

---

[3] Cf. Polybius, VI, 57 (Shuckburgh ed., vol. I, p. 506): "In all polities we observe two sources of decay arising from natural causes, the one external, the other internal and self-produced. The external admits of no certain or fixed definition, but the internal follows a definite order."

next incumbent on us to show that the problem and the modes of confronting it did indeed appear to contemporary intelligences in terms of the paradigmatic structures so far outlined.

[II]

We now become concerned with Florentine thought during the century which followed 1434, when Cosimo de' Medici established a sixty-year-long rule by his family, manipulating politics behind a republican facade. After more than two full generations and the masked principalities of four heads of the Medici family, this system collapsed spectacularly in 1494 and was followed by an alternation of equally insecure republican and Medicean regimes, until the family was reestablished as a hereditary and titular dynasty by another Cosimo, later Grand Duke of Tuscany, in 1537. The last quarter of this century—from 1512—is that of the transforming writings of Machiavelli, Guicciardini, and Giannotti, but the whole period can be treated in terms of the working out of the implications and contradictions inherent in civic humanism; and it can also be shown how the thought of the Machiavellian epoch served to convey the Aristotelian-Polybian tradition to future generations and to lands beyond Italy. There is danger, however, that to concentrate on the giants of 1512-1530 may be to forget how many of their themes and values had been stated for them; and before the stage is set for the scenes of 1494, 1512, and 1527-1530, something must be done to depict the expression of the civic humanist outlook by the men of the *quattrocento*.

The premier political thinker, among those who witnessed the idealization of the Florentine republic after 1400 and its decline into the crisis of 1434, is Leonardo Bruni from Arezzo. There were other humanists and humanist writers—once there was a humanist style available for use, the terms could not be identical—who concerned themselves with the values of a *vita activa* and the ways in which a civic *virtus* or *virtù* (the choice between Latin and Volgare could itself be significant) might undergo exposure to, and rise triumphantly above, the insecurities of *fortuna*; but not all of these pushed so far ahead as to analyze the role, in relation to *fortuna*, of *politeia*, the formalized relationship between public roles which constituted the structure of civic virtue when fully developed. They might consider public activity and service to the republic as a mode of *virtus* in which the citizen might or might not seek—while agreeing that he might not refuse— to engage; they might show themselves hesitant between private, familial, mercantile, and fully civic conceptions of the active role;[4] and

---

[4] See generally Holmes, *Florentine Enlightenment*, ch. 5; Garin, *Italian Human-*

a great part of the humanist vocabulary of *virtus* and *fortuna* might come into play before the level of political analysis was reached and the citizen depicted as necessarily involved in decision-making and power-relationships with other citizens in varying patterns of distribution. The vocabulary of citizenship, like the vocabulary of humanism, is complex and multiple. But though Florentine thinkers might many times turn away from the image of the citizen as fully political being, this level of analysis could not be neglected. One might easily find oneself admitting that political engagement was necessary to virtue, and when engagement was seen to have been lost or to have become subject to another's manipulation, something had to be said of what had happened and why.

Bruni's development is therefore important to us, since he was both representative and dominant among those who articulated at a political level, first, the efflorescence of civic humanist ideals before 1430, and second, the increasing consciousness of their problematic character toward and after 1434. There is no full-dress study of his political thought in English to compare with the chapters devoted to him by Hans Baron,[5] and these are to some extent dominated by the chronology of Bruni's earlier writings in relation to the Viscontian crisis of 1400-1402. For his later development, however, the crucial periods of activity seem to be the years from 1415 to 1421, the year 1428, and those from 1439 to Bruni's death in 1444, so that the crisis which brought Cosimo to power in 1434 is not immediately reflected in his productions. In his earlier works—the *Laudatio Florentinae Urbis* and the *Dialogi ad Petrum Paulum Histrum*, written after 1402—and those of his middle chancery period—the first four books of the *Historiarum Populi Florentini* (1415-1421), the *De Militia* of 1421, and the *Oratio Funebris* on Nanni degli Strozzi of 1427-1428—the following scheme of civic values emerges. Active *virtus*, to achieve its highest development in the confrontation with *fortuna*—Bruni on the whole differs from those who pronounced that *fortuna* was only externally and contingently related to *virtus*—requires the fullest participation in the life of the city, and the citizen must be involved in the choice of magistrates and the making of laws and decisions. Florence meets this requirement as a republic of a popular kind, in which most offices are open to most citizens and the individual, if qualified at all, is not further restricted by property or other qualification from joining in

---

ism, chs. II and III, pp. 1-3; also Renée Neu Watkins' introduction to her translation of Alberti's *Della Famiglia* in *The Family in Renaissance Florence* (Columbia: University of South Carolina Press, 1969).

[5] Baron, *Crisis*, chs. 3, 9, 10-12, 15, 17-18. Cf. Holmes, pp. 22-25, 26-28, 94-95, 155-64.

political life on many, including some high, levels of responsibility.[6] Bruni goes on to develop an idealization of Florentine civility along lines consciously modeled on the Funeral Oration of Pericles;[7] the citizen is he who can develop as many forms of human excellence as possible and develop them all in the service of the city, and a constitution like that of Athens—which Florence now follows—was praiseworthy because it encouraged and required this combination of versatility and patriotism from as many individuals as possible. The case for the open society, as Bruni saw it, was that the excellence of one could only flourish when developed in collaboration with the diverse excellences of others; not only was it better for any citizen that there should be many rather than few others, but such civic if not directly political excellences as the arts and letters could flourish only under conditions of liberty. It was also better for any one republic that there should be others than that it should rule the world alone. In the writings of his middle period, Bruni restated the theme that Florence was descended from the Roman republic—in which the temporal and spatial finitude of republics, and their consequent mortality, had been clearly acknowledged—by declaring that there had been many free republics in ancient Etruria (the modern Tuscany) and that their subjugation by the single conquering republic of Rome had been a prime cause of the decay of virtue, in Italy at large and ultimately in Rome herself.[8] Republics needed other republics, because virtue was participatory and relational and required the virtue of others; but what were to be the relations between them?

It may or may not be relative to this problem that Bruni is to be found, in the *De Militia* and the *Oratio Funebris* of seven years later, addressing himself to the idealization of the citizen as warrior and the warrior as citizen. It was already in the civic tradition to do this— Petrarch had noticed as one of the highest manifestations of the Roman triumph of *virtus* over *fortuna* that any army of citizens was prepared *pro libertate tuenda recta fronte mori*[9]—and it was part of the Periclean ethos which Bruni was adapting to express Florentine values that the supreme good, the supreme devotion of one's self to the public good, might be to embody in one's life as many virtues as one man might display and then offer them all to the city in a sacrificial death. But, in

[6] See *Laudatio*, part IV; text in Baron, *From Petrarch to Leonardo Bruni*, pp. 258-63.

[7] Especially in the *Oratio Funebris*; Baron, *Crisis*, pp. 412-30. Bruni is therefore an exception to the general rule of pro-Spartanism enunciated above, ch. III, n. 37.

[8] Baron, *Crisis*, pp. 65, 74, 267-68, 417-18.

[9] Petrarch, *Africa*, quoted by Baron in Rowe and Stockdale, *Florilegium* (ch. 3, n. 4 above), p. 28.

the *De Militia* particularly,[10] Bruni is engaged in advancing several statements more complex still. He seeks to identify with one another an idealization of Christian knighthood, the circumstance that some Florentine citizens are knights as that term was used in *quattrocento* Italy, and the historical memory that the Roman *ordo equestris* was a civic category possessing defined political functions, in such a way that the military function can be considered not merely civic but an essential attribute of citizenship itself. Mercenaries appear as half-hearted because they are ignoble; they fight poorly because they are not part of what they fight for; they lack *virtus* in the field because they lack that *virtus* which can be exercised only in the city. Citizens with arms in their hands, by contrast, can not only be praised as exemplifying Periclean virtue; it can be said that they fight better because they are citizens—from which it is only a step to adding that they are better citizens because they are willing to give the supreme proof of virtue. What happens if the citizen warriors of one virtuous republic meet the citizen warriors of another is not so clear. To suggest that they are engaged in a chivalrous contest of virtue ("I will lay on for Tusculum and lay thou on for Rome") would not satisfy the civic realist (and Tuscan patriot) already aware that republics devoured other republics and suffered loss of virtue, as well as inflicting it, when this occurred.

Subject to this qualification, however, the problem of particularity appeared soluble so long as each individual trod his own path toward universality in association with a diversity of others treading theirs; an *isonomia*—as the Greeks had called a society in which office was widely accessible on an equal footing—tended to realize this ideal. But in Bruni's later writings he recorded his awareness of a change. Cosimo de' Medici assumed power in 1434. By the end of the decade Bruni had completed a Latin translation of Aristotle's *Politics*, and had composed in Greek a treatise *On the Polity of the Florentines*; and here as in the later *Histories* he argued that Florence had become less a popular state than a mixed one, in which there was a clear differentiation between the political functions of the few and the many. It belonged to the former to deliberate and propose policies, to the latter merely to accept or reject, choosing between the alternatives placed before them; and this differentiation had come about in Florentine affairs as the result of historical change, the decision by the many to cease bearing arms in their own defense. As a result, the effective control of policy had fallen into the hands of a few, rich enough to possess the resources out of which mercenaries were paid and disposed to employ statecraft

---

[10] See the translation and commentary of C. C. Bayley, *War and Society in Renaissance Florence* (University of Toronto Press, 1961); Holmes, pp. 156-57.

rather than arms as the instruments of power (*consilio magis quam armis uterentur*).[11] Now the wealthy and the sagacious normally form elite minorities in Aristotelian analysis, and Bruni seems to be recording that political power in Florence is being redistributed on a basis of qualitative fitness. It could well be argued that this was no bad thing, as it approximated the city to the condition of an Aristotelian polity, and to say of a constitution that it was neither wholly aristocratic nor wholly popular, but a mixture of both forms, was normally to praise it. Bruni's language is indeed ambiguous; it was entirely consonant with Aristotelian doctrine to say that power should be functionally distributed, so that the elites should exercise more specialized degrees of responsibility than the non-elite, but there was a tension between this and the no less classical principle that the degrees of responsibility should be as evenly distributed as possible, so that the maximum number of citizens should have opportunity to develop their highest capacities. The Aristotelian analysis was flexible to the point of containing profound contradictions. When Bruni says that the Florentine constitution began to change from the moment when the mass of the citizens ceased to bear arms, he is, says Baron, setting forth "a masterpiece of early-humanistic sociological reasoning."[12] This we may accept; he is paying realistic attention to the question "who decides what, and why?"; and yet the thought is grounded in ethical concern for the development of human capacities and we may detect the same underlying ambiguities. Most contemporaries would have thought it an excellent provision that neither arms nor an equal share of power should be in the hands of those outstanding for neither wealth nor wisdom, and it is not certain that Bruni altogether disagrees. Yet he thinks of arms as the *ultima ratio* whereby the citizen exposes his life in defense of the state and at the same time ensures that the decision to expose it cannot be taken without him; it is the possession of arms which makes a man a full citizen, capable of, and required to display, the multiple versatility and self-development which is the crown (and the prerequisite) of citizenship. To abandon arms to professionals is to abandon the control of policy to those elite groups whom wealth and wisdom may render peculiarly fit to control it; yet it is also to abandon on behalf of the many all aspiration to become equally fit and equally virtuous—a goal which they might have achieved through the exercise of arms. And there remains in force Bruni's earlier doctrine that the full development of citizenship requires that it be exercised by as many as possible. If the number of effective citizens is few, then the number of elite

---

[11] From a Latin translation of the Περὶ τῆς πολιτείας τῶν Φλωρευτινῶν, quoted by Baron, *Crisis*, p. 560.

[12] Baron, *Crisis*, p. 427.

groups governing the city is few also; the number of virtues exercised in government must be few correspondingly, and the danger is present—on Aristotelian and on Polybian principles—that these virtues will be corrupted by the lack of any need to acknowledge the existence of others. If the mixed state is one tending toward elite government, it too may contain the seeds of decay, and Bruni's account of Florence's movement from democracy toward polity is ambiguous in its value judgments. Yet so great was the prestige of the word "polity" that Bruni cannot quite equate the transition with degeneration or the triumph of fortune. That judgment must be made by others, in other terms.

Another writer of the early Medicean period noted the trend toward oligarchy within a structure of supposedly wide participation which characterized the years before as well as after 1434, and it is significant that in his thought can be detected a revision of accepted ideas on the subject of virtue and fortune. This was Giovanni Cavalcanti, the author of two somewhat contrasting studies of the exile and return to power of Cosimo de' Medici.[13] In an analysis of his writings a modern scholar, Claudio Varese, begins[14] by studying a predecessor, Goro Dati—one of the leading figures in Baron's reconstruction of civic humanism—who in his patriotic history of the Viscontian war raises the problem of whether Florence's predominance over her Tuscan neighbors is due to providence, fortune, or some special virtue. Dati replies—displaying once again the "sociological reasoning" of the humanists—that because Florence stands on agriculturally poor ground, her people have become merchants, who travel through the world and learn from observing the ways of other nations; there is, as we might say, an intensification and speeding-up of the process of accumulating experience, and it has put Florence ahead of her neighbors in both wealth and intelligence. It is implicit in this argument that a wide distribution of participant civic rights serves, like the practice of trade and travel, to mobilize more intelligence and virtue in the service of the common good than could ever be achieved by a monarchy or tyranny. But, Dati adds, none of this could have come about but for a special gift of divine grace, which is available to all who seek it through the practice of a just and holy life; if it is not sought, then fortune comes into play and takes away the goods of this world from the undeserving.[15] We are looking here at traditional Christian doctrine, but there is a significant difference between Dati's thought and the Boethian tradition: he is, when all is said and done, talking about policy and success, and though

---

[13] Claudio Varese, *Storia e Politica nella Prosa del Quattrocento* (Turin: Einaudi, 1961), pp. 93-131.

[14] Varese, pp. 65-93.   [15] Varese, pp. 76-77.

he thinks of success as a reward for Christian virtue, he also thinks of it as achieved by reason (*ragione*), the characteristic Florentine term for that quality of the mind by which decisions of policy and statecraft were directed. Fortune now invites the response of the appropriate policy decision, and the purpose of such a decision is to control and guide events, or at least to adapt oneself to them; a political definition with a content other than the Christian humility and resignation recommended by Boethius. That Florence is a republic means that the virtues are effectively mobilized in her service, and among the virtues those of Christian piety occupy the foremost place in Dati's mind. But if piety deserves success, *ragione* achieves it; the knowledge, skill, and resolution by which the appropriate event-controlling decision is taken are also virtues; and we are near the point at which *ragione* and *virtù* are almost interchangeable terms, and virtue confronts the challenge of fortune less as the appropriate Christian than as the appropriate Roman and political response—*virtù* beginning to take on its Machiavellian meaning of the skill and courage by which men are enabled to dominate events and fortune.[16] Along this line of development, of course, it was possible for *virtù* to lose its Christian and even its ethical meaning altogether; but as long as it appeared that *virtù*, in the policy sense, was best practiced by the concurrence of citizens in a republic, it could not lose its association with the social virtues, which were still best described in Christian terms. Should the republic break down, however, much that made human life intelligible and moral might break down with it.

Giovanni Cavalcanti put these words in the mouth of a Florentine urging a mercenary captain to leave the Viscontian service: "Surely you have heard of the great constancy of the Florentines, and what it is to have the love of a republic so constituted. That of your master, though it be very great, yet it is brief; it cannot be more stable than is the life of one man; but the Republic is continuous."[17] The sentiment was something of a humanist commonplace, yet had not lost its exciting and liberating implications. By joining together the energies of many men, the republic achieved virtue and—what was very nearly the same thing—stability; by taking on the technical immortality of a corporation, it ceased to depend upon the virtue of one man (or a finite number of men), which as it was less durable must actually be less in

16 "Ma la forza accompagnata della ragione debbe sempre vincere." Varese, p. 79.

17 "Per certo tu conoscerai la gran costanza de' Fiorentini, e quello che è ad avere l'amore di una cosí fatta repubblica. Quella del tuo signore, posto che ella sia grandissima, ella è piú breve; con ciò che sia cosa che ella non può essere stabile se non quanto è la vita d'un uomo: ma la Repubblica è continua." Cavalcanti, *Istorie fiorentine* (Florence, 1838), III, xxv, quoted by Varese, p. 117.

virtue. We can see very clearly why it was that humanist knowledge, which gave simultaneous access to the whole store of human wisdom, was the mode of knowledge appropriate to a republic: since the latter was a *universitas*, it could not depend on the knowledge and virtue of one or a few men; neither could it depend upon an immemorial continuity of experience, since it was not a customary structure but lived and acted in the present. The continuity of which Cavalcanti wrote was a matter less of antiquity than of immortality. All social virtue was mobilized in it; all human wisdom was made accessible by learning. But Cavalcanti lived to see that the virtue, and the *virtù*, of the Florentine republic had indeed become that of a limited number of persons, and could not maintain itself as such.

He describes how, in the last phases of pre-Medicean rule, there came to be a strange discrepancy between what was said and who was elected in the public assemblies of the republic, and what was determined and how it was determined in the political backrooms where things were actually done. Many were called and few were chosen, he observed; many were called to office and few to real power.[18] The sensation is not an unfamiliar one to students of governing assemblies, but Cavalcanti believed he was witnessing the decline of government by participation. Rule by the citizens themselves, on a footing of absolute or proportionate equality, was being replaced by the government of a courthouse gang, of which the Medicean machine politics that replaced it was only the culmination. To the phenomena he described, later analysts were to give the name of corruption, a term among whose many meanings perhaps the salient one is the replacement by private relationships of those public relationships among citizens by which the republic should be governed; and it is clear that Cavalcanti found the most alarming feature of the process to be the replacement of rationality by something else. He describes an assembly in a time of crisis, to which citizens come and give their views; all is public and seemly, what is said is both rational and virtuous; but there is no connection between what is said and what is ultimately done, and by whom and for what reasons decisions are finally taken cannot easily be found out.[19] Again, most modern readers will know how he felt; but the

[18] ". . . il Comune era piú governato alle cene e negli scrittoi che nel Palagio; e che molti erano eletti agli uffici e pochi al governo." *Istorie fiorentine*, II, 1, p. 29. Cf. Varese, p. 122.

[19] "Dette che ebbero queste ed altre convenevoli parole, molti cittadini salirono alla ringhiera a consigliare: diversi cittadini consigliarono, e diversi consigli vi si disse. E perché io non ero pratico a vedere come si amministravano i fatti della Repubblica, disposi l'animo mio al tutto a portarne alcuna regola di governo con meco; e, per meno fallibile, elessi la regola e l'arte del preclaro cittadino Niccolò da Uzzano, maestro piú reputato e piú dotto. Mentre le preallegate lettere si legge-

important point to an understanding of Cavalcanti and his world is that, to a republican idealist of the period, decisions could not be rational or virtuous unless they were taken with the universal or at least unhampered participation of the qualified citizens. Republics existed to mobilize the intelligence and virtue of all citizens; their stability was dependent on their doing so and if they failed they became governments of a few, whose intelligence and virtue were doomed to decline by their finite and insufficient character. A hidden oligarchy behind a republican facade must lack rationality, because it did not direct the intelligence of all to the good of all; it must lack virtue, because it subjected the good of all to the good as seen by a limited number; it must lack *virtù*, because it did not mobilize the *ragione* and *costanza* of all to deal with the happenings by which it was surrounded. It must prove insufficient in both integrity and durability, and Cavalcanti calls it *tirannesco e non politico*.

Consequently, it must encounter in new and complex forms the problem of *fortuna*. Since it was less than virtuous, it must encounter the temporal flux in its unlegitimated form and, since it lacked *virtù*, without knowing how to control events or adapt oneself to them. It must therefore confront a world irrational because not understood, one in which words (as Thucydides noted in similar circumstances) changed their meaning. We have seen the extraordinary importance which the age attached to the notion of stability, but Cavalcanti, anticipating a theme of Machiavelli's, wrote that in Florence the pursuit of stability had itself become a fault: "I accuse not the mobility of fortune, but the immobility of diverse persons and perverse men in our republic . . . this pertinacity and fixity of nature (*stabilità della condizione*) among our citizens has been the cause of the many misfortunes

---

vano, e la proposta si feceva, e la turba consigliava, il nobile cittadino fortemente dormiva, e niente di quelle cose udiva, non che le intendesse. Consigliati molti e diverse cittadini, chi una cosa e chi un altra, diverse cose e diverse materie vi si disse. Non so se fosse stato tentato o destino, o veramente il sonno avesse il suo corso finito, tutto sonnelente salí alla ringhiera. . . . Detto che ebbe Niccolò questo cosí fatto parere, tutti i consigliatori si accordarano al suo detto. Allora, avendo io tenuto a mente i modi di Niccolò, per me si giudicò che lui, con altri potenti, aveva sopra quelle lettere, nel luogo privato e segreto, accordato e conchiuso che quel consiglio fusse per lui dato, e per gli altri confermato e conchiuso. Allora, per piú essere certo se il mio credere era d'accordo col suo essere, dissi con alcuni de' miei compagni quello che credeva, e com'egli mi pareva che nella Repubblica ne dovesse seguire tirannesco e non politico vivere, che fuori del palagio si amministrasse il governo della Repubblica. La risposta che mi fu data col mio credere fu d'accordo, dicendo che com' io credeva cosí era . . ." (II, I, pp. 28-29).

of the city."[20] It is sinful to remain unchanged in a world rendered changeable by our own inadequacies and excesses; it is to persist in the private value-pursuits which have disordered it. Florentine thought was ambiguous as to whether men of virtue found the world providentially directed or subject to their rational control, but there is no ambiguity in the general assent that when men are not virtuous, the world becomes problematic and even unintelligible. Cavalcanti insists that when we are studying the moral and political lives of men in a disordered or corrupt society, the world around them must be seen as an uncontrolled and enigmatic flux, and the only question is whether we must not add to the notion of fortune the notion of stellar influence. His conclusion is that we cannot do without astrology: the idea of fortune is that of an essentially meaningless and absurd directing power, but the central assertion of astrology is that the erratic affairs of this world may be correlated with the irregular but not wholly random movements of the errant stars. Paradoxically, such a belief restores the possibility of free will; once we have restored a causal order to human and social events, we may shape our own moral courses relative to that order, and Cavalcanti's defense of astrology is that it is necessary if moral judgments, by citizens or historians, are to be possible.[21] All this because he saw politicized virtue to have collapsed. The political ordering of society and the rational ordering of history had become nearly interdependent.

Fortune controlled a chaos of unlegitimated particulars, visualized almost always in terms of events and circumstantial alterations in human affairs—*vicissitudo rerum, la vicissitude des choses humaines.* The world appeared in this guise, as subject to the empire of fortune, increasingly as the republic failed to unite all citizens in *virtù* and *ragione.* But as that failure developed, there came to be another chaos of unlegitimated particulars, that of individual wills, passions, and personalities, no longer joined in the moral union of citizenship. The failure of politicization brought the problem of particulars to the fore once again—when Cavalcanti wrote of *diverse persone e perversi uomini,* diversity and perversity were almost interchangeable terms— and raised the problem of what power operated to make men unlike one another and to shape the course of events as determined by psychological diversity. It is of some significance that Cavalcanti did

---

[20] ". . . non accusando tanto la mobilità della fortuna, quanto la immobilità delle diverse persone e de' perversi uomini della nostra republica. Al tutto dico che questa pertinacia e questa stabilità della condizione de' nostri cittadini è stata la cagione delle tante sventure della nostra republica . . ." (quoted by Varese, p. 110).

[21] Varese, pp. 108-109.

not ascribe to fortune, nor altogether to the stars, the power of endowing men with their personalities and preferences. Between the stars and
men he introduced a symbolic figure with the arresting name of *Fantasia*, who expounds the history of the world, from the Hebrews to
the Greeks and from the Romans to the Florentines, and declares:

> I am Fantasy common to every rational creature . . . there are as
> many different human wills as there are different influences from
> the stars . . . and as wills differ so differ the fantasies and the actions
> of men. And I am the origin and the stay of all my disciples and I
> have over each authority to exert such sovereignty as is granted me
> by all the starry order, by command of the heavenly emperor to
> whom are subject all things transitory and eternal, and from this
> diversity of fantasy proceed all the diversities of character among
> men . . .[22]

Fantasia does not seem to be precisely a creative power shaping men
as they cannot help being; that role is ascribed to the starry influences.
Rather she is a nonrational creative force immanent in men, by which
each is driven to fulfill his own individuality, sharply distinguished
from the universal values fulfilled by and in each individual according
to the thought of Aristotelian Christianity: a self-created uniqueness
of bent, in pursuing which each man acts out his fantasies and determines his individual personality. She has on the one hand something
in common with Erasmus's Folly, but on the other the rhetoric makes
clear that she shares many of the characteristics of Spenser's Mutability
or—more immediately—the traditional *fortuna*. As a force driving particulars toward diversity, subject only to the stars and the Creator, she
is responsible for the course of human history; but exactly the same
role was assigned to fortune, whenever the course of events was not
stabilized and ordered by the successful establishment of republics.
There is a letter of Machiavelli's to the exiled Piero Soderini, in which
we are told that *fantasia* is part of what gives each man his individual

[22] "Io sono fantasia comune a ciascheduna razionale creature. . . . E così sono
differenti voluntà umane quante sono differenti le influenze delle nature nelle
stelle, e perché altra volta fu in Pipo di ser Brunellesco che non fu in Lorenzo di
Bartoluccio et altra fantasia fu nel maestro Gentile che non fu in Giuliano
d'Arrigo [it is significant that these all seem to be the names of artists] e così
come sono differenti le voluntà, così son differenti le fantasie e le azioni negli
uomini. E io sono l'urigine e il sostegno di tutte le mie discepole e ho sopra
catuna autorità di comandare cotale signoria a me conceduta da tutto lo stellato
ordine per comandamento dello imperadore celestiale a cui sono suggette tutte le
cose caduche e sempiterne, e che queste diversità di fantasie procedono tante
diversità d'ingegni negli uomini . . ." (quoted from a manuscript source by
Varese, p. 111).

personality. *Fortuna*, by contrast, gives us our circumstantial fates; and—the thought recurs in *Il Principe*—it is because we find our natures hard to change (Cavalcanti's *stabilità*) that *fortuna* has power over us.[23] *Fantasia* and *fortuna* were concepts necessary to concretize, rather than explain, the course of history when it was not legitimated by political order; but the end of the republic was to establish virtue and reason, and these were seen as utterly incompatible with change. History existed in the absence of the republic, the only order which could legitimize the coexistence of particulars.

Cavalcanti wrote in a context of republican failure, one where virtue had failed to triumph over fortune. He had first seen that failure in the machinations of the cliques which preceded and sought to oppose the accession of Cosimo de' Medici to power. It was open to him either to condemn Cosimo's rule as the culmination of backstairs government, or to praise him as the author of an order which had transcended it. There are signs of ambivalence in his various writings about this matter, and it is perhaps best summarized in his observation that "if I had supposed that human virtues could be immutable and perpetual in this our transient and momentary life, I would have ventured to say that [Cosimo] was a man rather divine than mortal."[24] We may expound his thought as follows. Cosimo rules the city; but unlike the republic, he is not immortal and so cannot mobilize in his person the virtue and reason of all the body politic. His rule will pass, and will not leave behind it a civic life designed to withstand vicissitudes and decay; it is a child of fortune and fantasy, and perhaps a force of evil since it fails to develop virtue and reason in others, a thing possible only through the communion of citizenship which Cosimo frustrates. On the other hand, his system obtains and endures; he has succeeded

---

[23] "Credo che come la natura ha fatto all'uomo diverso volto, cosí gli abbia fatto diverso ingegno et diversa fantasia. Da questo nasce che ciascuno secondo l'ingegno et fantasia sua si governa. . . . Ma perché i tempi et le cose universalmente et particolarmente si mutano spesso, e gli uomini non mutano le loro fantasie né i loro modi di procedere, accade che uno ha un tempo buona fortuna, ed un tempo trista . . . havendo gli uomini prima la vista corta, et non potendo poi comandare alla natura loro, ne segue che la fortuna varia et comanda agli huomini, e tiengli sotto il giogo suo" (*Lettere*, ed. Gaeta, pp. 230-31). See K. R. Minogue, "Theatricality and Politics: Machiavelli's Concept of *Fantasia*," in B. Parekh and R. N. Berki, eds., *The Morality of Politics* (New York: Crane, Russak and Co., 1972), pp. 148-62.

[24] "Cosimo de' Medici, il quale, s'io conoscessi che le virtù negli uomini fossero immutabili e perpetue in questa nostra transitoria e momentanea vita, io avrei ardire di dire che fosse più tosto uomo divino che mortale. . . ." *Istorie*, I, I, quoted by Varese, p. 126. For uses of civic humanist symbolism to exalt Cosimo, see Donald Weinstein, *Savonarola and Florence: Prophecy and Patriotism in the Renaissance* (Princeton University Press, 1970), p. 60, n. 85.

where the republic has failed, and it is just conceivable that he is the restorer of men to citizenship or the creator of an order transcending it. In any case, so far as it is possible to regard him as doing anything which the republic failed to do, he has succeeded where the politicized virtue and reason of society did not succeed. But man is *zōon politikon*; his virtue and reason can flourish only in political associations, and if Cosimo has transcended association by his isolated virtue, it should follow that his virtue is superhuman. This is to equate him with the being adumbrated by Aristotle, as far above political man as man is above the beasts; but Cosimo's methods do not really suggest those of a Platonic philosopher king. From this point the Machiavellian ambiguities may be permitted to run on; if Cosimo's virtue has allowed him to establish an order on the ruins of that in which alone men can be virtuous, it may be that his virtue is *virtù*, outside morality altogether. We shall later study the possibility of a legislator whose virtue preceded the establishment of human civic virtue and was the occasion of it.

Cavalcanti had gone thus far down the road that leads to Machiavelli because, when the republic seemed dissolved into its component particulars, the individual seemed to have lost that community of thought and action with his fellow citizens which the *vita activa* offered him as means of comprehending and controlling both the particulars by which his life was surrounded and his own being as a particular person. The mainly neo-Platonic philosophies which flourished under the government of Lorenzo de' Medici may be read as attempts to restore that harmony and control in a non-civic form.[25] Though they represent a return to the *vita contemplativa*, the contemplation they offer is far from being a monastic meditation on undisturbed universals. The Platonic stress on knowledge as intuition and illumination enables them to reassert the old doctrine that contemplation is a form of action and even creation; man is presented as unique among created beings in his ability to enter into the intellectual essences of all other creatures, so that he identifies himself with them and in return takes them up into his own nature. Hermetic and magic ideas permit it to be said that knowledge and language, articulating into consciousness the correspondences and principles by which all things are held together, make man in his intellectuality (not his *fantasia*) the governor and creator (under God) of all things in creation. Particular natures are universalized in being known by him, and he himself partakes in universality through knowing them. But hermetics are no substitute for politics, if they cannot set up a scheme of relationships between men as equal individuals. The universe of Pico della Miran-

---

[25] For these see Garin, ch. III: "Platonism and the Dignity of Man."

dola's *Oration on the Dignity of Man* is in the last analysis composed of intelligible objects and the intellect that knows them, and although knowledge for Pico has become an Adamic passion of identification and creation, self-identification and self-creation, the relation between citizens cannot really be reduced to the relation between the knower and the known. Citizens are not engaged in knowing (and so creating) the universe and themselves, so much as in managing the relationships between one another's minds, wills, and purposes, and the appropriate quality of mind for this enterprise is not a Platonic *gnosis* so much as an Aristotelian *philia* or Christian *agape*. Magic, the manipulation of objects through knowledge of their natures, is an activity supremely unsuited to a relation between political equals, and to the extent to which it tends to elevate knowledge to the status of action—the magician commands an object simply by speaking its name—it is not even a form of Machiavellian *virtù*. A philosophy which isolated man—always Man, an abstract and solitary universal—in his capacity as knower could envisage the individual as philosopher, or as ruler if ruling were thought of as an intellectual activity, but could not find concepts for a relation between ruling individuals precisely because it thought only of ruling and never of being ruled. The neo-Platonic attempt to reunite knowledge and action failed, therefore, in proportion as it failed to take account of socialized cognition, decision, and action; here was a realm of experience with which it could not deal. It envisaged the life of virtue and reason as an illumined communion with the cosmos, and the stress it laid on the relation between knowledge and action suggests that the cosmos was intended to reconcile man to the loss of the polis. Perhaps this is one reason why Pico and other neo-Platonists were so powerfully drawn to Savonarola, who as we shall see depicted the restored polis as a holy community of justice appearing at an apocalyptic climax of sacred time, so that grace and politics took over from magic and philosophy as restorers of human nature.

In this context constitutional thought—if by that we mean thought about the forms and institutions of joint action between citizens—could assume great moral and even existential importance; it was concerned with the restoration of politicized virtue, without which, there was reason to fear, neither man's nature nor his world could be other than a chaos of unintelligible forces. The theory available to Florentines wishing to consider the relationships between citizens was, as we have seen, Athenian theory mediated through a succession of classical and humanist authors and summarized for working purposes into the paradigms of the one-few-many classification of governmental forms. It was during the period of Medicean ascendancy that the myth of Venetian stability and antiquity assumed the character of a myth of

Venice as an Aristotelian and later a Polybian polity, perfectly stable because it was a perfect balance; and it is significant that this myth was of Florentine as well as of Venetian making. Felix Gilbert has traced its genesis,[26] beginning in the impulse of humanists at Venice—Francesco Barbaro, aided by the Byzantine Giorgios Trapezuntios—to find a classical justification for Venetian government, but evolving soon into a means of characterizing and exploring that government's unique structure. Venice was habitually free from faction and constitutional instability, and could afford to forget many of the historical changes she had in fact undergone, so that a myth of antiquity and changelessness was already traditional and found expression in the epithet *Serenissima* by which the republic chose to be styled. Humanist observers, in search of the principles or classical paradigms which would explain the causes of this stability, fastened on two characteristics of the Venetian constitution, which did not, however, point to identical conclusions. The first of these was the analysis of the ruling powers into a Doge, a Senate, and a Consiglio Maggiore; here, it seemed, was that combination of a one, a few, and a many of which classical theorists spoke. But the other was the long-established limitation of citizenship, in the sense of political participation, to a large yet finite body of ancient families. This seemed to define Venice as an oligarchy or aristocracy; yet it was usual to treat the numerical classification into one, few, and many as equivalent with the social classification into monarchy, aristocracy, and democracy. Was Venice, then, a true mixed government or a true aristocracy? A great deal of the subsequent mythical character assumed by the image of the Most Serene Republic can be attributed to this basic ambivalence of the paradigm, which can in turn be linked with the ambiguities arising from Aristotle's crucial decision to combine different sets of criteria in compressed verbal formulae. Doge, Senate, and Consiglio Maggiore might stand for one, few, and many, for monarchy, aristocracy, and democracy, or for distinguishable political functions which it was appropriate that one/monarchy, few/aristocracy, and many/democracy might undertake; aristocracy might be represented as a pure form of government, as an ingredient in threefold mixed government, or as capable of containing a mixture of one, few, and many within its socially exclusive structure.

It is clear from Gilbert's analysis that the *quattrocento* Venetians had no desire to think of themselves as anything but an aristocracy, though one unusually well balanced and proportioned internally; nor was this view of the case initially challenged by Florentines interested in the

---

[26] "The Venetian Constitution in Florentine Political Thought," in Nicolai Rubinstein (ed.), *Florentine Studies: Politics and Society in Renaissance Florence* (London: Faber and Faber, 1968), pp. 463-500.

constitution of Venice. The Venetian myth's main appeal in Laurentian Florence was to members of the status group known as *ottimati*—those long-established families, rather mercantile than noble in their origins, who could see themselves as a hereditary ruling class or predominant element, distinguished by prudence, experience, and other ruling qualities above the average, and therefore as identifiable with those Aristotelian elites to whom such epithets as "few" or "aristocracy" might justly be applied. *Ottimati*—the term is transferred from the *optimates* or senatorial aristocracy of the Roman republic—who were discontented with the share of responsibility and power allowed them by Medicean political methods were understandably interested in any argument or terminology which emphasized and classified the role of a political aristocracy—a very different thing, by the way, from a feudal or territorial nobility, whether or not the patricians of Venice and Florence at this date were buying lands—and accordingly adopted Venice as the contemporary model of a constitution embodying the classical principles which allowed such an aristocracy its due share of power. In the relations between the Doge and the Venetian aristocracy they saw the relations which ought to, but did not, exist between the head of the house of Medici and the *ottimati* of Florence, and some of them may even have dreamed of a time when a Florentine Doge would be but *primus inter pares* and not necessarily a Medici at all. They had no interest, clearly, in emphasizing—and to emphasize it would be necessary to invent—a democratic element in the constitution of Venice, and yet it is interesting to note how social realities conspired with the paradigm they had chosen to adopt to make them do so. At Florence there really was a *popolo* (whether *grasso* or *minuto*) with a long tradition of active citizenship, which it would be hard to leave out of account in any theoretical or actual distribution of power; and the one-few-many terminology, which both humanist classicism and the tripartite form of the actual Venetian constitution compelled them to employ, required them to talk in terms of a balance between democracy as well as aristocracy and monarchy in the ideal scheme to which they were looking. In the post-Savonarolan era there was to be a hard core of optimate theorists around and after Bernardo Rucellai,[27] who insisted that Venice was an aristocracy, that Florence ought to be no more than an aristocracy, and that this was all they had ever meant; but the intellectual initiative had been taken from them, as much by the inescapable implications of their own language as by anything else.

---

[27] Gilbert, "Bernardo Rucellai and the Orti Oricellari: A Study on the Origin of Modern Political Thought," *Journal of the Warburg and Courtauld Institutes* 12 (1949), 101-31; see *Machiavelli and Guicciardini*, pp. 80-81.

In the long run—at least as viewed in an Anglo-American perspective—the myth of Venice (at its most mythical) was to lie in the assertion that the Venetian commonwealth was an immortally serene, because perfectly balanced, combination of the three elements of monarchy, aristocracy, and democracy. This assertion was to be expressed in the language and assumptions of Polybian theory, but in the *quattrocento* Polybius's sixth book was insufficiently known to be listed among the sources of the Venetian myth, and it is rather to the grand tradition of Athenian philosophy and civic humanism that we should direct our attention.[28] The Florentine *ottimati* who played so large a part in the myth's making can be seen to have invoked ideas and an ideology which went beyond their desires or control, but the fact remains that they saw themselves as citizens and expressed their class interests—if we choose so to put it—in the language of the political community. When what they may have intended as no more than an indication of the relations that should obtain between the one and the few—between Lorenzo or Piero and the *ottimati*—became a paradigm of the relations that should obtain between all parts of the Florentine polity, the ideal of universal citizenship was restored to the Florentine vocabulary in the form of an Aristotelian-Polybian mixture. Yet the circumstances in which this came about—the intellectual tone of the years following 1494—reveal that it could not be done without great political and ideological tensions. The heritage of civic humanism was such that the failure of citizenship compelled the intellect to confront the image of a disordered universe as surely as the failure of "order and degree" did Shakespeare's, and the neo-Platonic philosophies encouraged the thought that the only return to order lay through the union of the intellect with the cosmos, a dramatic restoration of the unity of the intelligible world. The minds that developed the myth of Venice belonged to an alternative tradition, which proposed to restore the world through citizenship and political order, and the image of Venice was merely the vehicle through which they conveyed once more the categories of Aristotelian politics. Yet Venice became a myth, a paradigm exercising compulsive force on the imagination; and—leaving aside the problem of what failure of nerve at Florence it was that compelled thinkers to rely so heavily on the image of a rival city for which they felt no love—the force of the symbol surely lay in its perfection: in the vision it conveyed of a polity in which all particulars were harmonized and whose stability was consequently immortal. If a polity was to restore order to the subjective world, it must be truly universal.

[28] Barbaro and Trapezuntios seem to have modeled their ideal Venice on Plato's *Laws*; Gilbert, "Venetian Constitution," pp. 468-69.

It is intensely interesting that the image of Venice became politically operative at Florence at the moment when the apocalyptic preachings of Savonarola encouraged that city to see herself as holy and elect, the instrument by which God would reform the church and save the world.

In 1494 Medicean rule collapsed at the advent of the French army, and toward the end of the year was set up the constitution which was to symbolize Florentine republicanism for the brief remainder of its political existence—from 1494 to 1512 and from 1527 to 1530. This constitution included a Consiglio Grande, a Signoria, and a Gonfaloniere (who became an official appointed for life in 1502); and contemporary theory insisted on the correspondence between these and the many, few, and one of classical analysis. Further, the admission on a fairly broad scale of nonaristocratic elements into the Consiglio Grande, with the consequent right of election to office in the Signoria, indicated that there was a popular or democratic presence in the constitution—these epithets have of course to be taken in the sense in which they were then used—and that a balance between the social categories of democracy and aristocracy accompanied that between the numerically determined categories of many, few, and one. By the time-honored device of blending the two modes of categorization, the constitution was spoken of as a balance or mixture of democracy, aristocracy, and monarchy, although the *ottimati* by no means dominated the Signoria—the "few" considered in numerical terms—and the exercise of power by one man, even for life, did not constitute him a class or status-group in the sense in which a king and his courtiers might be said to form one. But this was the constitution which was repeatedly and generally said to be modeled on that of Venice—the hall built for meetings of the Consiglio Grande being modeled on that of the Venetian Consiglio Maggiore[29]—and it is to this identification that Venice owed much of her reputation as a uniquely stable blend of democracy, aristocracy, and monarchy. If, however, the myth of Venice owes a great deal to the Florentine constitution of 1494, it is not less true that 1494 marks the capture of the myth by advocates of broadly based mixed government. All the evidence collected by Gilbert goes to suggest that Florentines before 1494 generally saw Venice as an aristocracy. Who then thought Venetian imagery appropriate to the legitimation of a popular-aristocratic mixed government, and why was it that this mode of legitimation was generally accepted as being appropriate? The situation becomes more puzzling when we find the Consiglio Grande, the constitution that went with it and the recommenda-

---

[29] Gilbert, *Machiavelli and Guicciardini*, pp. 9-10.

tion of Venice as the model which that constitution followed, all occurring together in the apocalyptic sermons of Girolamo Savonarola. These often lucid and intellectual addresses reveal to us the eschatological coexisting with the other modes of expounding the affairs of particular political systems, which our model disposes us to expect as crucial in early modern republican thought.

Savonarola[30] had been resident in Florence since 1490 and had developed an increasingly prophetic style of preaching, in which he exhorted his hearers to repentance by foretelling events of a dramatic and terrible nature that should be God's judgment on a corrupt world and prepare the way for its purification. In the climate of the time, this was evocative of a semi-underground strain of chiliastic preaching, whose possibilities were always heretical and subversive; but Savonarola, however responsive to this tradition, showed great determination to remain the orthodox Thomist of his Dominican training. It is, however, remarkable—or at least it appears so to us—to find the apocalyptic mode, which we associate with the irrationalism of the oppressed, exerting such power over the minds of Renaissance Florentines; yet this is a point at which it is easy to construct a false antithesis. The effect of civic humanism, we have seen, was to isolate the community in its present moment of time; apocalyptic history presented time as a series of moments of unique significance, in which any community might find itself called to play a part as momentous as that of Israel or Rome. The attempt to realize the civic community was not far removed, in the thought of the time, from the attempt to realize the holy community and might draw on the same language. Before 1494, however, Savonarola had nothing to say about the political form of the Florentine community—though the Medicean government was understandably uneasy about having a prophet in its midst—and emphasized not that Florence had a unique part to play among the nations, but that God's most terrible judgment was coming upon the city and coming immediately. The fact that it was Florence upon which the doom was to fall must nevertheless have heightened his audience's awareness of their community's unique individuality, and the phrase "at once and swiftly"—*cito et velociter*—which Savonarola repeatedly used with terrific effect, must similarly have heightened sensitivity of the unique importance of the present moment. All this became focused upon the forthcoming expedition of the French king against Naples; Charles

---

[30] A study of the relation of apocalyptic to civic humanism in Savonarola's thought, more subtle and far-reaching than is attempted here, is now available in Weinstein, *Savonarola and Florence*. See the same author's "Savonarola and Machiavelli," in Myron P. Gilmore, ed., *Studies on Machiavelli* (Florence: G. C. Sansoni, 1972).

VIII figured as a *flagellum Dei*, a "king from the north" in the language of Old Testament prophecy, who should punish Italy and purge the church of its corruptions. We may be reminded of the mystical imperialism of Dante or even Cola di Rienzo; but the event was to produce a revolution at Florence which involved Savonarola, irrevocably and as it turned out tragically, in political events and compelled his prophetic vision to take account of the civic ideal. The language of apocalypse had now to blend with the language of political community.

When Charles VIII reached Florence, Medicean rule collapsed in a series of revolutions. Piero de' Medici lost his nerve; the inner ring of influential *ottimati* discovered that they could now bring to an end, by refusing to support, a regime which they found increasingly trying; an attempt, after Piero's abdication, to restore the old republican system by leaving it to the *ottimati* to refurbish the traditional institutions failed in its turn, in the face of an upsurge of political activity on the part of the *popolo*—the non-elite membership of the politically enfranchised classes. These were the circumstances in which there was brought forward and adopted the tripartite constitution based on the Consiglio Grande, and the still obscure decision was taken to recommend this essentially nonaristocratic structure as following the Venetian model. Savonarola played a leading part in recommending and later in guiding this constitution, and the imagery of Venice is to be found in his sermons. It is nevertheless hard to believe that his was the brain that devised the constitution, and the terms in which he recommended it as an imitation of Venice certainly do not suggest that this idea originated with him.[31] In the history of ideology, however, we are concerned less with initiatives, motives, and actions than with languages and the ways in which they are used; and we may study Savonarola's preachings at this juncture—November-December 1494—in order to draw conclusions about the condition of republican ideology at this moment.[32]

The crucial conjuncture was that between Savonarola's apocalyptic utterances and the resurgence of the republican *popolo*: between prophecy and citizenship. He had been convinced that a special divine judgment was in preparation for Florence and the church, and it was possible for this conviction to become belief in a special divine mission for Florence in the world. Whom God chasteneth he loveth; Florence

---

[31] Weinstein, *Savonarola*, pp. 20-23, 150-53; Nicolai Rubinstein, "Politics and Constitution in Florence at the End of the Fifteenth Century," in E. F. Jacob (ed.), *Italian Renaissance Studies* (New York: Barnes and Noble, 1960).

[32] I use the edition of Francesco Cognasso, *Savonarola: Prediche Italiane ai Fiorentini: I, Novembre-Dicembre del 1494* (Perugia and Venice: La Nuova Italia Editrice, 1930).

was to be visited because Florence was elect.[33] He came to believe that the church was to be reformed through a spiritual renewal beginning at Florence—apocalyptic thought identifying spiritual history with the secular community—and more important still, he came to equate this renewal with a restoration of republican citizenship. The precise degree to which his thought moved from the observance of traditional morality to the distribution of political functions is the issue debated between those who dispute how far it continued or departed from medieval norms,[34] but it is of more value to the purposes of this study to notice how Savonarola was able to blend Aristotelian, civic, and apocalyptic language in a single synthesis.

His millennial expectations coincided with the ideological needs of a moment when the republic was to be restored after an eclipse of more than sixty years. Unsophisticated Florentines identified the republic with the traditions of the city and with their patron San Giovanni; San Giovanni was therefore to be restored, just as a short-lived republican regime at Milan in 1447 had taken the name of Sant' Ambrogio, and as at serene Venice San Marco had never ceased to reign.[35] But intellects responsive to a tradition of heretical preaching, and those responsive to the ideals of civic humanism and the torments of its apparent disintegration, might both express in a more sophisticated eschatology the sublime audacity of what they were now attempting. A republic was to be restored; a particular city was to attempt—after earlier failure—to render itself universal in time. Neo-Platonic thought supplied a hermetic vocabulary for such endeavors, but one which did not lend itself to political expression. The language of eschatology, however, described a series of occasions on which human communities had become of universal significance through acts of divine grace. To restore citizenship might be to restore man to his universality; if this could not be done through hermetic wisdom, it might be done through restoration of the *vivere civile* and the *zōon politikon*; but restoration of the active life must be performed by an act in time.

Savonarola's millennialism, however, was obstinately orthodox and Thomist. Though he spoke of a Fifth Age of the church now at hand and came to his ultimate downfall through condemning the pope as

---

[33] Weinstein, *Savonarola, passim*: in particular the discussion, pp. 35-66, of the extent to which a new apocalyptic arose to replace the older Guelfic sense of Florence's divine mission; and the text of the *Compendium Revelationum*—written by Savonarola in 1495 as an account of his history as a prophet—cited in English translation, pp. 68-78; also pp. 168-70.

[34] Weinstein, *Savonarola*, pp. 4-25, surveys the historiographical literature on Savonarola.

[35] Gilbert, "Venetian Constitution," p. 464.

Antichrist,[36] he shared St. Thomas's doctrine that grace fulfilled nature and did not abolish it. There is a form of life which is natural to man, namely the pursuit of values in fellowship and association; the city is that fellowship in which a common good, the good of all, is pursued and men seek others' goods rather than their own.[37] There may therefore be a restoration of the church or the city which is a restoration of the true form to human life. Such a *reformatio* or *rinnovazione* is strictly Aristotelian, an assertion of the primacy of spirit and form over matter, but it must be the work of grace and it must be carried out in time. Since the *prima forma* is the gift of grace, it cannot be renewed without a renewal of grace, and this is for all who will have it by living justly. But things divine—Savonarola makes Noah tell his sons in the Ark—are not subject to time; things temporal are in need of periodic restoration. The church is no exception to this rule,[38] and so can be restored by the establishment of a human *giustizia*, through Florence's becoming what a human community ought to be and naturally is; but this recovery of *prima forma* can come about only through grace operating in time, choosing and proclaiming the moment in Florentine, Italian, and spiritual history and sending to the city the prophetic message of her election. It is for the Florentines to heed the prophet and embrace the moment.

So profoundly mistaken—Savonarola repeatedly insists[39]—is the say-

[36] Weinstein, *Savonarola*, ch. v, is a detailed analysis of Savonarola's millennialism.

[37] For this see especially the sermon of 14 December 1494 (Cognasso, pp. 181-97) and the *Trattato circa il reggimento e governo della citta di Firenze*, composed in 1497, *Edizione Nazionale delle Opere di Girolamo Savonarola*, vol. XI, *Prediche sopra Aggeo con il Trattato . . .*, ed. Luigi Firpo (Rome: Angelo Belardotti, 1955).

[38] Cognasso, pp. 108-10 (7 December 1494): "Si come per el diluvio si rinnovò el mondo, cosí manda Dio queste tribulazioni per rinnovare la chiesa sua con quelli che staranno nell'arca. Ma notate che quelle cose che non sono subiette al tempo non invecchiano, e però non si rinnovano. Dio, li beati ed el cielo non invecchiano, che non sono sottoposti al tempo, ma le cose temporali e composte di elementi mancano ed invecchiano e però hanno bisogno di rinnovazione. Similmente la Chiesa di Dio che fu construtta ed edificata della unione de' fedeli e delle loro buone operazioni, quando quelle mancano, si chiama invecchiata ed ha bisogno di rinnovarsi . . . Or quanto al rinnovare una cosa che sia composta di materia e di forma, dovete notare, secondo l'ordine delle cose naturali, che la rinnovazione sua consiste prima e principalmente nella forma e secundario nella materia. L'uomo è composto di forma e materia, cioè d'anima e di corpo, ed el corpo è fatto per l'anima, però bisogna rinnovarsi prima nell'anima. Adunque vediamo prima la rinnovazione della forma."

[39] Cognasso, pp. 116-17 (7 December 1494), and 186-90 (14 December). The latter are a lengthy and formal refutation of the same dictum, in which it is proved *in extenso* that states can be governed only in perfection of form through grace.

ing (attributed to Cosimo de' Medici) that states cannot be governed with paternosters. In this, clearly enough, he was anticipating Machiavelli's later criticism and meeting it on its own ground. The just city does not exist in the moment of *fortuna* and *ragione*, because it exists in the moment of *grazia* and *rinnovazione*; but an evident corollary is that it must exist in one or the other—there is no third choice. We are now brought, by Savonarola's own use of language, to confront the problem of exactly how far he saw virtue as politicized, the reign of justice as necessitating a high level of general participation in citizenship within a polity. The means existed of making such a transition; if the *prima forma* meant that each must follow the common good rather than his own, the exercise of citizenship was by far the most conscious and institutionalized means of doing this, and polity could well be the form of justice. From this it would follow that the establishment of a republic might be the moment of grace. But it is not easy to maintain that Savonarola ever saw the exercise of citizenship as the paradigm under which the exercise of all the traditional virtues must be brought. What can be established is that he spoke increasingly of *governo e reggimento* as the *forma*, opposed to the *materia*, of the reformed life;[40] that he denounced tyranny[41] and the rule of one man able to subject others to his ends[42] as incompatible with justice, seeming to mean less that the tyrant practised injustice upon others than that he impeded their practice of justice in their own lives; and that when he recommends the adoption of a republic,[43] on the Venetian model,[44] it is in the context of *rinnovazione* and the apocalyptic moment.

At this point it is less clear that Savonarola saw moral reform as pos-

[40] Cf. Weinstein, *Savonarola*, pp. 147, 153-54, 156-58.

[41] See n. 39, above, and Cognasso, p. 212.

[42] Cognasso, pp. 115, 194; 219 (16 December): ". . . t'ho detto e ridico, che tu facci in questo tuo nuovo governo e pigli tale modo di reforma che nessuno cittadino si possa far capo della città, acciò che tu non perda piú quella libertà che Dio t'ha data e restituita. Che male è questo? Anzi quanto è el tuo bene e la tua salute. Io vorrei che voi fussi tutto uno cuore ed una anima e che ciascuno attendesse al ben commune e qual bene che lui avesse dalla città, lo riconoscesse dal commune e dal publico e non da alcuno privato."

[43] *Governo civile* or *reggimento civile* are the terms used in the *Trattato*; cf. Weinstein, *Savonarola*, ch. IX. Such language appears in the later sermons, rather than in those of 1494.

[44] Cognasso, p. 117 (7 December): "E cosí essendo fondati nel timore di Dio, Lui vi darà grazia di trovare buona forma a questo vostro nuovo reggimento, acciò che nessuno possa innalzare el capo, o come fanno e' Veneziani, o come meglio Dio vi inspirerà. Per la qual cosa acciò che Dio vi illumini, vi esorto per tre giorni a fare orazione e digiuni per tutto el populo e poi vi congregate insieme ne' vostri Consigli per pigliare buona forma al vostro governo. E questo basti aver detto quanto alla forma per reformarvi. . . ."

sible only in a republic—though elements of this thought point in that direction—than that he realized that the republic could be legitimized only in the context of a moral reform. But it may be that the best and most revealing index to his underlying feelings about the republican form is to be found in his attitude toward the Florentine character and its history. In the medieval writers who were his guides to Aristotelian politics—St. Thomas and Ptolemy of Lucca[45]—he found it unequivocally stated that monarchy, if the rule of one good man, was the best form of government, but that nevertheless, in the actual world it was necessary to concede to a people the sort of regime best adapted to its particular and local character.[46] He proceeds to argue that tradition and climate (if not, as earlier humanists had declared, the practice of merchandise and travel) have made the Florentines peculiarly habituated to taking part in their own government, and have endowed them with a character peculiarly suited to doing so.[47] If then a *governo civile* or republic is the best form of government for Florence, it is—on the face of it—as a second-best and in consequence of the second nature which the citizens have acquired through usage and custom. But there now comes into play a uniquely Christian mode of thought by which Savonarola is paradoxically enabled to make usage a prerequisite of renewal and rebirth. He repeatedly declares that *consuetudine*[48] is no foundation for spiritual reform. Second nature is a barrier to true realization of one's original nature or *prima forma*; it is an artificial personality which individuals erect around themselves without employing their right reason—as there are musicians so little aware of what they are doing that they can talk to their friends on irrelevant matters while they play[49]—and sometimes use as protective shells so that they can hear the prophet's words without attending to their true import.[50] So powerful a barrier is this that even the reformer must often proceed *pian piano*, like a doctor who sets about curing a disease by slow and careful steps.[51] Yet in these very passages Savonarola makes it clear that he has not suddenly become a cautious pragmatist; it is an agony to proceed *pian piano*, because the burden of the prophetic message becomes greater for the fact that it cannot be spoken all at once.[52] The

---

[45] Weinstein, *Savonarola*, p. 290.   [46] *Ibid.*, pp. 292-93.

[47] Cognasso, pp. 183-84 (14 December); *Trattato*, I, 3 (pp. 446-50), II, 3 (p. 470).

[48] Cognasso, pp. 125 (8 December); 228-31 (17 December).

[49] Savonarola, *Prediche sopra Ezechiele*, ed. Roberto Ridolfi, *Edizione Nazionale*, vols. I-II (Rome: Angelo Belardotti, 1955), I, 90-91.

[50] *Ibid.*, and Cognasso, p. 230.

[51] Cognasso, pp. 125-26, 144, 146, 268, 272.

[52] Cognasso, pp. 144-45 (9 December): "O Firenze, io non ti posso dire . . . O Firenze, se io ti potessi dire ogni cosa . . . Io ho veduto uno infermo piagato

reformation of the artificial personality must be a total rebirth, the old man dying to be born again in the new;[53] the republican traditions of Florence are of little help in the creation of the reign of justice,[54] and the city must change its form through grace and be no longer the city of Florence but the city of God.[55]

But it is Florence which has been chosen to be reborn in this way, and there seems little doubt that the traditional second nature of the citizens is one reason for, or sign of, this election. The old Adam (to use Pauline phraseology) must die and be reborn; but some "old men" are predestined for rebirth above others, and there is no reason why use and tradition should not be among the predetermining forces. The peculiar nature of the Florentines fits them, we are to understand, to be the object of a peculiar act of divine providence and to occupy a peculiar moment in apocalyptic time. It is not humanly intelligible why grace should have chosen to perfect nature in this way and at this moment, but the peculiar or second nature which has been chosen is described in political terms. The nature of the Italians generally, and of the Florentines in particular, is such that they will not endure the rule of masters;[56] but the doctrine of grace perfecting nature must

---

dal capo a' piedi, ed è venuto el medico con vari unguenti per sanarlo ed ha cominciato dal capo e va a poco a poco procedendo. O Firenze, io non possa dire ogni cosa . . . O Firenze, questo infermo è el popolo fiorentino . . . è el Salvatore el quale è venuto per medicarti. O Firenze, credi a me che'l medico è venuto e comincia pian piano, a poco a poco, a medicare diversi membri. El medico grida ed esclama: O Firenze, non si può ogni cosa fare in un tratto. Questo ti sia assai per ora sapere che'l medico è venuto . . ."

[53] Cognasso, pp. 114-15: ". . . cantiamo e rallegriamoci col Signore nostro che fa cose mirabili ed ogni uno si disponga a vita nova, cacciando tutto el vecchio maculato vivere. O Firenze, ora mi volta a te. Se tu vuoi renovarti, O città nova, se tu vuoi esser nuova e se tu hai mutato nuovo stato: bisogna che tu muti nuovi modi e nuovo vivere se tu vuoi durare, e se tu vuoi reggere, e' ti bisogna fare uno nuovo cantico e ricercarsi che tu abbi nuova forma." P. 121: ". . . quelli che saranno al vostro governo non saranno uomini carnali che appetischino cose temporali, ma totalmente uomini spirituali che siano fuori d'ogni appetito di carne e cose temporali." P. 196: "recedant vetera et nova sint omnia; ogni cosa si rinnovi e la forma che si piglierà farà sicuro ognuno, perche si darà ad ognuno quello che è suo e che gli si conviene; e però nessuno debbe temere e tutta la città sara d'ognuno . . . Orsù, oggi si cominci: oggi sia il principio del ben vivere . . .".

[54] Cognasso, pp. 221-22, 231-32.

[55] Cognasso, p. 201: "Così dico io a te, Firenze, egli è tempo ora da edificare di nuovo la casa di Dio e rinnovare la tua città . . . ed io ti dico che Dio vuole che tu la faccia e bisognati rinovare la tua città e rinnovare lo stato, e che la città tua sia la città di Dio e non più città di Firenze, come ella è stata insino adesso; ed ogni cosa consiste nella forma che tu piglierai, e mutata la forma sara mutata la città."

[56] E.g., Trattato, I, 3.

have meant to Savonarola that if it was normal for men to live under the *reggimento* of human masters the masterless life was such that it could be lived solely under grace—as in the Third Age of Joachim, whom he occasionally cites.[57] But we now see the relationship between Savonarola's vision of the polity in which no man is the master over the good of his fellows, and his call to the Florentines to proclaim Christ their King.[58] "Christ," he once declared, "was the form of all governments,"[59] and both the republic and the divine monarchy might be conceived as states of grace and recovery of the *prima forma*. Indeed, the two could be identified; in this way the Thomist insistence on monarchy as the ideal mode of government might be reconciled with the Aristotelian doctrine of the polity. The republic—that state in which each man devoted himself to the common good—was a theocracy; it was the kingdom of grace, and when grace was personified as Christ, it appeared as what Aristotle had indeed intended as the perfect monarchy—the rule of one man who was as far above men as they were above beasts.[60] In this way the second nature of the Florentines prepared the way for its own supersession, for the restoration of man to his true nature as midpoint on the great chain of being, and for the city's occupation of a messianic moment in an Aristotelian *reformatio*. To this exent, Savonarola's thought combined the extremes of custom and grace, the time of secular usage and the moment of apocalyptic redemption.

This is the appropriate point at which to address ourselves to the problem of his use of Venetian imagery. Generally speaking, the tenor of his sermons of 1494—after which allusions to Venice grow few— does not suggest that the Venetian symbol possessed much resonance for him, or his use of it for his hearers. Past experience, he says, will reveal that the Florentines have never enjoyed political institutions capable of stabilizing the city; it will also reveal that the Venetians, without being any better than other people in the sense of more virtuous, have from the beginning enjoyed the priceless gift of stability, and will even indicate the institutional forms by which it has been guaranteed. It is therefore proper for the Florentines to study the constitution of Venice, or that of any other city, and take from it what suits them— such as the pattern of the Consiglio Grande—while rejecting what is unsuited to their special nature and their special needs, such as the

---

[57] Weinstein, *Savonarola*, pp. 146, n. 30, 175-77.

[58] *Prediche sopra Aggeo*, pp. 409-28 (28 December 1494) and Weinstein, pp. 294-95.

[59] Cognasso, p. 119: "Cristo fu la forma di tutti e'reggimenti. . . ." Cf. *Prediche sopra Aggeo*, p. 128.

[60] Aristotle, *Politics*, III, xiii, #13-14; xvii, 2-3, 5-8.

hereditary Dogeship.[61] This is far from mythopoeic language, and one wonders what function the myth of Venice had in the thought of Savonarola, leaving aside the larger question of its role in legitimating the constitution of 1494. What that function could have been is theoretically clear. The republic, perfecting man's nature, might be seen as existing at a moment of apocalyptic grace; the only fully satisfactory alternative was to see it as exempt from time altogether, existing as a Platonic form which no secular change could disturb. The Polybian equilibrium, in which all modes of human knowledge and virtue coexisted in perfect harmony, met this near-utopian requirement, and there is a Platonic component in the "myth of Venice," as we shall see; but no Florentine could with other than a wry mouth declare that Venice was unique in virtue and that his own city was not. To Savonarola it was still more impossible to admit Venice to the center of his picture, since that picture was one of the moment of election and depended on the idea of Florence as a chosen vessel for some divine and apocalyptic transformation of the world. The admission of Venetian stability to any level above that of accident and experience would entail the admission that Venice too was elect and holy like Florence; and apart from any other objection to this, there was the circumstance that the Venetians did not behave as if they had any notion that they were either. It was Florence that was in a mood of messianic excitement in 1494; not Venice, in that year or any other. The myth of Venetian stability might represent it as the outcome of art and contrivance, never of grace. Savonarola therefore stressed the virtues which Florentines should practise to make them worthy of grace and election, rather than the institutional arrangements which they might borrow or copy to make their polity stable; this though the virtues in question are in large measure social and civic, those which conduce to political stability—itself a sign of grace—and which a mixed constitution like that of the Venetian myth, equilibrated so that no one virtue preponderated over the others, was supposed to encourage.

The revolution of 1494, in which Savonarola played a leading role, nevertheless marked a decisive stage in the growth of the image of Venice as a perfect combination of all three forms of government, and the reasons are to be sought in the way political discussion was carried on after Savonarola's failure and death. To restore the republic which Florence had never succeeded in being—to make of Florence a republic more stable than Rome had been—was to do what had never been done before, and the myths of Sparta and Venice, the two republics

---

[61] Cognasso, p. 195: ". . . resecando però qualche cosa di quelle che non sono a proposito, nè el bisogno nostro. Come è quella del duce." Cf. Gilbert, "Venetian Constitution," pp. 478-82.

endowed by literature with extraordinary longevity, were bound to return to the center of the picture. Savonarola had declared that it would be done, but he had also declared that it would not be done without the conjoint aid of nature, grace, and the fulfillment of prophecy, in which the old Florence should be burned away and all made new. So difficult was it to render a particular body stable, or raise it to universality. Machiavelli's famous passage[62] in which he presents Savonarola as the type of "unarmed prophet"—a prophet, moreover, of uncertain authenticity—occurs in the context of a treatment of political innovation as the most difficult thing which men can attempt, and of the different personalities and means by which it has been attempted. We shall understand the issues better if we suppose—what is in any case probable—that Machiavelli was not simply sneering at his predecessor or dismissing him as a fool or a charlatan, but was taking him and his thought as seriously as the age and its predicaments demanded.[63] The air of Florence was heavy with apocalyptic, and Machiavelli could not have been as impervious to it as he may have liked to pretend. Innovation at the highest level, the creation of a just and stable society, had been attempted under the protection of the greatest concepts in Christian thought—nature, grace, prophecy, and renovation; and the attempt had failed, so that it must have been falsely conceived. It was a momentous and authentically terrifying question to inquire what came next. The myth of Venice provided one possible answer, more Platonic and Polybian than Christian, but *esprits forts* would be needed if any sort of virtue was to be set in the room of grace.

[62] Below, pp. 170-72.

[63] The most authoritative discussions of the relation of Savonarola to Machiavelli are those of J. H. Whitfield, "Savonarola and the Purpose of *The Prince*," reprinted in *Discourses on Machiavelli* (Cambridge, England: W. Heffer and Sons, 1969), and Weinstein, *Savonarola* (cited in n. 30 above).

CHAPTER V

THE MEDICEAN RESTORATION

Guicciardini and the Lesser *Ottimati*, 1512-1516

[1]

IT HAS BEEN THE ARGUMENT of this study so far that late medieval thought was limited by an epistemology of the particular event, decision, institution, or tradition, which defined the means which men at that time believed themselves to possess of rendering intelligible secular phenomena as they existed in time. So sharply limited were these means that it was possible to feel that the temporal flux evaded men's conceptual control: that it was under the dominion of an inscrutable power, which manifested itself as providence to men of faith and as fortune to men of none. After the advent of civic humanism, it was possible in addition for the individual to feel that only as citizen, as political animal involved in a *vivere civile* with his fellows, could he fulfill his nature, achieve virtue, and find his world rational; while at the same time it might be that his conceptual means of understanding the particular and controlling the temporal, on which his ability to function as a citizen depended, had not increased to a degree commensurate with the new demands made upon them. The secret of Savonarola—scholastic, prophet, and citizen in that order—seems to be that he felt that the civic life involved a degree of virtue which could only be given by grace, and consequently that it could be achieved only in an eschatological context of prophecies fulfilled and the world renewed. His failure therefore administered a traumatic shock to the ideological structure of Florentine life, one felt by both the simple and the sophisticated.

I was present when this protocol was read [wrote the diarist Landucci of the confession to false prophecy extorted from Savonarola in 1498] and I marvelled, feeling utterly dumbfounded with surprise. My heart was grieved to see such an edifice fall to the ground on account of having been founded on a lie. Florence had been expecting a new Jerusalem, from which would issue just laws and splendour and an example of righteous life, and to see the renovation of the church, the conversion of unbelievers and the consolation of the righteous; and I felt that everything was exactly contrary, and had to resign myself with the thought: *In voluntate tua Domine omnia sunt posita.*[1]

How the more sophisticated might react we shall see when we examine the role of Savonarola in the thought of those who were theorists of civic life. It is already clear, however, that a less pious man than Landucci might feel at Savonarola's downfall that all things were in the hand of Fortune rather than God, and that only the restitution of citizenship could save men from the reign of irrational forces. But if Savonarola had failed to ground citizenship upon prophecy, what other basis might be found? The spread of civic humanism had been accompanied by certain extensions of the accepted range of political knowledge, increasing it somewhat beyond the conceptual apparatus of reason, experience, prudence, and faith with which the tradition represented by Fortescue had confronted the challenge of the particular. In the first place it was now believed that men in the present might hold conversation with the men of antiquity and learn from them direct what they had done in the historical situations confronting them. This belief might result in a naive insistence on the repetitiveness of history, or in an increasing subtlety of historicist awareness; but in either case it seemed to speed up the citizen's acquisition of knowledge and his ability to respond to the exigencies of policy with the appropriate decision. In the second place—and forming part of the wisdom to be learned from antiquity—there was that Aristotelian and Polybian philosophy of citizenship, of which an analysis was conducted in a previous chapter. Its strength as constitutional theory lay precisely in the fact that it was less a comparative study of institutions than a science of virtue. It offered, that is to say, a means of associating the particular virtues of men composing the political society in such a way that they would not be corrupted by their particularity but would become parts of a common pursuit of universal good; and in consequence it offered powerful incentives to consideration both of what types and categories of men, displaying what characteristic virtues and limitations, made up the political society, and of the means by which it was proposed to associate them in a common pursuit. Since this association was to be effected through the distribution of roles in decision-making, the incentive offered here pointed toward analysis of the decision-making process itself, of the roles and functions, institutionalized and otherwise, into which it might be broken down, and of the ways in which these might be distributed among the different moral types composing

[1] Luca Landucci, *A Florentine Diary from 1450 to 1516*, trans. Jarvis (London: J. M. Dent, and New York: E. P. Dutton, 1927), p. 139.

society. The foundations of both Greek and Renaissance political science are in ethical theory coupled with the strategy of decision.

If the Aristotelian categories could be used to help stabilize a republic in Florence, the science of virtue would have succeeded where the prophet Savonarola had failed. It would have helped to reconcile the particular with the universal, to equate political activity with the practice of virtue and to make the flow of political and particular events intelligible and justifiable. The political thought stemming from the restoration of the *vivere civile* in 1494 is therefore profoundly Aristotelian, and consists largely in efforts to define how the essentials of the Aristotelian *politeia* may be established under Florentine conditions. But it has a further dimension which accounts for a great part of its enduring fascination. The alternative to the establishment of citizenship and the republic was the empire of Fortune, that experience of reality in which nothing was stable, legitimate or rational: *questa ci esalta, questa ci disface, senza pietà, senza legge o ragione.*[2] Both the actual history of the Florentines before and after 1494, and the conceptual apparatus which they used in trying to understand it, encouraged their thought to exist in the dialectic between these extremes: between the incorruptible serenity of the republic and the shifting empire of the uncentered wheel. Even before theorists were directly acquainted with Polybius, they were well aware that the aim of political science was to combine particular virtues in one universal good, and that until this was done particular virtues were unstable and liable to self-destruction; nor was it necessary to have read Polybius on the *anakuklōsis* to employ the imagery of wheels and cycles. Their thought was consequently geared to the consideration of virtues as they decayed, political systems as they dissolved, and human experience as it entered the domain of the unstable, the irrational, and the amoral. The stability of the republic, at one extreme, was not more fascinating or more familiar to them than its disruption at the other. In addition, a long-recognized crux of civic humanist thought—the particularity of the republic, its finite extent in space and time, and its consequent non-identity with the laws governing its environment—was brought into high relief by the terror of history after 1494, as Italy became increasingly dominated by non-Italian powers and both Florence and Venice seemed to have lost control over their external relations. If the republic attained serenity internally, might it not lose it if it remained prey to Fortune externally? Could there be so great a difference between the laws governing the politics of internal and external relations? If Aristotelian science provided the means of understanding the former,

---

[2] Machiavelli, *Capitolo di Fortuna*, lines 38-39.

what was the appropriate language for exploring the latter? And if none could be found, must we not have recourse to the rhetoric of Fortune? In 1512, and again in 1527-1530, the inability of the Florentine republic to control what was happening in the power world of Italy coincided with failure to harmonize its internal civic relationships and brought about the collapse of the *vivere civile* and the restoration of Medicean rule—on the second occasion permanently. Each of these failures can be shown—due in part to the presence on the scene of men of genius— to have touched off a complex crisis in thought; and in each crisis it is possible to study what was happening in contemporary minds as they sought to employ the epistemology of the particular, the ethical-political categories of Aristotelian citizenship and the radically new terminology which some thinkers were developing in order to under-stand political behavior at its least legitimated and rational. The era of Machiavelli and Guicciardini shows us thought aimed at the constitu-tion and stabilization of civic bodies in intimate tension with thought aimed at the understanding of rapid and unpredictable change.

[II]

From 1494 to 1512 the constitutional problems of the Florentine republic revolved around the differentiation of functions between dif-fering political groups. In an illuminating analysis, Felix Gilbert has worked out[3] both the institutional structure of this regime and the conceptual vocabulary which was employed by those actually partici-pant in it—not only in works of theory, but in speeches, resolutions, and public documents—and the following conclusions seem to emerge. The crucial step taken after the flight of the Medici in 1494 was the adoption of what was generally described as the Venetian constitution (*il governo veneziano* or *alla viniziana*). This as we have already seen consisted at Florence practically in a Consiglio Grande, a Signoria, and a Gonfaloniere, and ideally in a perfect harmony of the many, the few, and the one, such as Venice was supposed to have achieved. Yet in practice the perceived bias of the 1494 constitution was toward the many. It was universally agreed that its most essential institution was the Consiglio, in which an indefinitely large number (though by no means all) of the citizens had the right to participate, and that the existence of the Consiglio gave the regime the character of a *governo largo*. When it was pointed out that the membership of the Consiglio Maggiore—the analogous institution at Venice—had been confined to a specific number of families by a decree already two centuries old,

---

[3] *Machiavelli and Guicciardini*, chs. 1 and 2.

and that this surely gave Venice the character of a *governo stretto*, the reply most frequently given was that the closing of the Council had merely defined the Venetian citizen body, rather than confining political rights to a limited number among the citizens, and that those excluded from the Council and from citizenship were either aliens or men of base and servile occupation, by definition incapable of civic life.[4] Apart from introducing us to one of the basic ambiguities in Aristotelian categorization, this dispute reveals a number of interesting things. One is the implication of such a term as *governo largo* as opposed to *governo stretto*: the former clearly does not mean a constitution which extends citizenship to all, or even to the *popolo* or "many" as a defined social group—the constitution of 1494 did not explicitly do that—but rather one which, by refusing to confine citizenship to an exactly defined (*stretto*) group among the inhabitants, acknowledges that civic participation is a good, something that men aim at, that develops men toward goodness, that it is desirable to extend to as many men as possible. *Governo*, the word most closely corresponding to our "constitution," is in the Florentine vocabulary almost interchangeable with *modo di vivere* or simply *vivere*; and it is observable that it is always *governo largo*, not *stretto*, which is indicated by the phrase *vivere civile*. To acknowledge civic participation as a good in itself was to acknowledge that it should be widely extended; but not all men thought it a supreme or an indispensable good that as many as possible should take part in public decisions, and this problem too was discussible in Aristotelian terms.

A further noteworthy point is the determination of those who defended the *governo largo* to retain the Venetian paradigm by denying that Venice was a closed aristocracy. A crucial moment in the history of Florentine ideas was the decision of 1494 to introduce widespread membership in the Consiglio Grande under the form of imitating the Venetian constitution.[5] We do not know exactly who made this decision or what was in their minds, but the consequence was that Venice continued to symbolize for most writers a constitution with an element of popular participation, one based on harmony between the participant non-elite and elite, the many, the few, and also possibly the one; and the theorists most intent on following the Venetian model are those who hold that the *ottimati*—that inner circle of influential Florentine families who considered themselves an elite and identified themselves with the few in the Aristotelian scheme—cannot exercise

[4] Gilbert, "Venetian Constitution," p. 488; for *governo largo* and *stretto*, see *Machiavelli and Guicciardini*, p. 60.
[5] *Machiavelli and Guicciardini*, pp. 9-11.

their natural function of leadership, or develop the virtues pertaining to it, unless there is a participant non-elite or many for them to lead. The *ottimati*, in this image or self-image of their role, are a civic aristocracy; their qualities exist and are displayed in their relations with other citizens.

It is therefore permissible to ask whether the "Venetian" formulation of the measures of 1494 was not the work of *ottimati* who considered that a *governo largo* would suit them better than a *stretto*. But the background to the debate over the real character of Venice, and the form of government best suited to Florence, was the increasing inability of the Consiglio Grande to govern in a way satisfactory to the *ottimati* as a class. At Venice the secret of government lay in the relations between the Consiglio Maggiore and the complex of magistracies and committees known collectively as the Senate,[6] and it was in the elaborate machinery of the latter's deliberations that political initiative was located. But the corresponding relationship at Florence— that between the Consiglio Grande and the group of executive committees with the Signoria as their center—worked less well, and a principal source of tension was the strong sense of a distinct identity possessed by those who ranked as *ottimati*. These distrusted the Consiglio as the unwieldy organ of an overweening *popolo* and did not find in the Signoria or the other executive bodies—whose members were appointed, usually for short terms of office, by a mixture of lottery and elective procedures in the Consiglio—an effective institutionalization of that principle of aristocracy which the *ottimati* considered they represented. The families to which they belonged had generally supported Medicean rule from 1434 to 1494, and they held that the Medici regime had rested on their cooperation and had fallen only when the last of Cosimo's line had forfeited their support by mismanagement and bad manners. Thereafter, they felt themselves to have been precipitated into a dangerous experiment in cooperation with the *popolo*, which had been sweetened for them only by the proclamation that it was to be conducted along Venetian lines. Now, as tensions between the elite and the non-elite grew worse, and the Consiglio Grande and Signoria proved increasingly incapable of conducting the republic's external affairs, it became more and more the complaint of the *ottimati* that the promise of a Venetian style of government was not being properly carried out.

Felix Gilbert has explored both the institutional and the ideological programs of the aristocratic movement against the constitution of

[6] For the Florentine use of this model, see Gilbert, "Venetian Constitution," p. 485.

1494. A leading figure of the ideological counteroffensive is Bernardo Rucellai,[7] a connection of the Medici by marriage who stood for all those who had supported the 1494 revolt less because they disliked Medicean rule as such than because they felt that Piero had become politically impossible. Their vision of the old regime depicted the Medici line as working with the inner ring of *ottimati* in the role of *primus inter pares*, and when bereft of the Medici they turned to the organization of direct rule by the inner circle. By 1500-1502 (it seems probable), Bernardo Rucellai was the center of a group of aristocratic intellectuals who met at the Orti Oricellari to criticize the regime by humanist means. These included the idealization of Lorenzo de' Medici (the "Magnificent") as the leader who had known best how to work with the aristocratic families in fellowship; the reevaluation of Venice as a closed aristocracy and the implication that such a *governo stretto* was best suited to Florentine needs; and systematic research into Roman history in order to ensure that the right lessons were drawn from the past for the government of affairs in the present. Gilbert sees in this program a decisive break with the style of earlier thinking and has even spoken of it as marking "the origin of modern political thought." Previously, he argues, all proposals for institutional reform at Florence had had to be cast in the form of a return to some pattern of things existing in the city's remote and mythical past, but since the Rucellai group were arguing for something unprecedented—a continuation of some features of an informal and dubiously legitimate regime of the preceding century—they had to adopt new techniques of argument and pioneered research into the past in search of the principles of government. The antithesis between old and new styles of argument may be a little strained, but the adoption of the Venetian paradigm in 1494 and its continuing importance are evidence that new methods of legitimation were felt to be needed. It seems clear that the Rucellai and aristocratic critique of the 1494 constitution intensified both the comparative study of Florentine, Venetian, and Roman institutions of government and the elaboration of Aristotelian categories of citizenship in the attempt to determine what the parts of a political society were and what virtues and functions were appropriate to each. The critique of the Consiglio Grande, as we shall see, rests almost wholly upon the Aristotelian concept of differentiation of function.

Bernardo Rucellai suffered a political disappointment in 1502. The agitation he had helped to promote had called, if not for the abolition

---

[7] Gilbert, *Machiavelli and Guicciardini*, pp. 80-81, 112-13, and "Bernardo Rucellai and the Orti Oricellari" (above, ch. IV, n. 27), for the character of Rucellai's political thought.

of the Consiglio, at least for the transfer of most of its powers to a senate of leading citizens chosen for life; but what came about, in circumstances that remain obscure, was the erection of the chief magistracy of the republic into a Gonfalonierate for life—a post immediately filled by Machiavelli's patron Piero Soderini. This measure, a clear imitation of the Venetian Dogeship, was presumably taken in the hope that relations between the few and the many would be stabilized by the addition of a properly functioning one, something which Savonarola had considered unsuited to Florentine conditions. Rucellai, who had worked for it initially, tells us[8] that he was unable to support it since it was not accompanied by the abolition of the Consiglio outright, but that most of his friends thought it worth trying to operate the tripartite system, even without an effective senate. A significant group of *ottimati*, we may conclude, were still interested in trying to find a role for aristocracy within a *vivere civile*, and the next phase in the development of Florentine political thought consists of an attempt to define the *politeia* in those terms.

The first writer of whom we require to take detailed notice is Francesco Guicciardini (1483-1540), a younger contemporary of Machiavelli (1469-1527)—whose great political writings were still to come—and, in the end, by general consent (including Machiavelli's) the only political intellect of a stature approaching his. The son of a "gray" or cautiously pro-Savonarolan optimate, this young and exceedingly ambitious man had, we know, begun about 1508 the composition of a history of Florence under Medicean rule,[9] which is distinguished from the line of thought emanating from the Orti Oricellari by its pronounced hostility to Lorenzo. Both Felix Gilbert and Vittorio De Caprariis,[10] the most valuable modern students of Guicciardini's thought, have observed that this attitude was to be progressively modified in his later discourses and histories;[11] but it is important that to condemn Lorenzo with the young Guicciardini and to idealize him with Rucellai and the older Guicciardini were two sides of the same medal. The *ottimati* admired the Medici for collaborating with them and hated the Medici for treating them as inferiors; on which side of the divide Lorenzo was placed might be little more than a matter of

[8] Gilbert, "Bernardo Rucellai," pp. 106-109, quoting Bernardo's *De urbe Roma*.

[9] Now available in translation by Mario Domandi, *The History of Florence* (New York, Evanston and London: Harper and Row, 1970). For a biography see Roberto Ridolfi, *Life of Francesco Guicciardini* (London: Routledge and Kegan Paul, 1967).

[10] V. De Caprariis, *Francesco Guicciardini: dalla politica alla storia* (Bari: Laterza, 1950).

[11] *Machiavelli and Guicciardini*, pp. 106-23.

family tradition or rhetorical convenience. The strength of Guicciardini's thought and that of one or two of his fellows lay in their endeavors to grapple with the ambivalences of the optimate position and bring out the implications. As we shall see, the ultimate problem was whether the *ottimati* were to continue to define themselves as citizens or to accept the role of servants of something neither a *vivere civile* nor a *governo stretto*.

Little of this, however, appears in Guicciardini's first formal treatise on politics, the so-called *Discorso di Logrogno*, published in the modern edition of his works under a title which means "On the right way of ordering our popular government."[12] Guicciardini wrote this in Spain, where he had gone as Florentine ambassador to Ferdinand of Aragon, and had perhaps not completed it[13] when he heard of the fall of the Soderini regime, which was swiftly followed by the return of the Medici in 1512. The work therefore coincides with the end of the *ottimati*'s efforts to adapt the restored republic to their purposes, and it is significant that the last practical measure they undertook before the Medici resumed power was the installation of a senate which took over from the Consiglio Grande nearly all functions except that of electing the Gonfaloniere, no longer for life but for a one-year term.[14] The problem at that stage was still one of reconciling aristocratic predominance with the principle of *vivere civile*; and it is of this that the *Discorso di Logrogno* is a theoretical treatment, which we may study as much for its conceptual vocabulary as for its concrete recommendations.

Guicciardini opens by declaring that the *vivere civile* has fallen into grave disorder; all men aspire indiscriminately to attain all honors and offices, and to meddle in all public affairs of whatever importance; there is no order.[15] In the terms of classical theory, which Guicciardini

---

[12] "Del modo di ordinare il governo popolare." Published in *Dialogo e discorsi del Reggimento di Firenze*, ed. Roberto Palmarocchi (Bari: Laterza, 1932)—hereafter referred to as *D. e D.*—pp. 218-59.

[13] A note at the end says so, but may perhaps be a literary embellishment.

[14] Gilbert, *Machiavelli and Guicciardini*, pp. 76-77.

[15] *D. e D.*, pp. 218-19: ". . . el vivere nostro civile è molto difforme da uno ordinato vivere di una buona republica, cosí nelle cose che concernono la forma del governo, come nelli altri costumi e modi nostri: una amministrazione che porta pericolo o di non diventare tirannide, o di non declinare in una dissoluzione populare; una licenzia universale di fare male con poco rispetto e timore delle legge e magistrati; non essere aperta via agli uomini virtuosi e valenti di mostrare ed esercitare la virtù loro, non proposti premi a quegli che facessino buone opere per la republica; una ambizione universale in ognuno a tutti li onori, ed una presunzione di volersi ingerire in tutte le cose publiche di qualunque importanzia; gli animi degli uomini effeminati ed enervati e volti a uno vivere delicato e,

does not use but which are never far from his mind, this is a chaos of the appetites and a general disorder of the means by which social men pursue value and virtue. If the disorder is as general as he says, and if the appetites are undergoing Platonic degeneration from the pursuit of honor to the pursuit of riches, what is needed is a correspondingly universal reform of human behavior, and we look for a definition of the intellectual means by which it is to be carried out. Here Guicciardini has recourse to analogy with other human arts, and in particular to the art of medicine, a device capable of being used in many ways and almost always worth scrutinizing carefully. If a man making *pasta*, he says, does not succeed with his mixture the first time, he makes a new heap of all his materials and stirs them together again; and if doctors find themselves dealing with a body afflicted by so many diseases that they cannot operate with a single goal, they attempt by medication to bring the whole body into a new disposition, which though very difficult is not impossible.[16] But the analogy is shifting ground; the human body is not the same as a mound of flour and water, and the intelligence which could deal in any total manner with all the value-oriented intelligent activities making up the life of men in society would be superhuman if not divine. At once we find Guicciardini admitting that procedures such as he describes are governed by circumstances beyond their control; doctors find the reordering of the whole body easier with a young patient than with an old one, and the city of Florence is already old.[17] He refuses to despair, but goes on to concede that a total reordering of the city's health would mean doing more things than the public could be brought to accept. The city is already *male abituata*:[18] we may gloss this as meaning that the "second nature" of use and acceptance has brought about that adjustment of human life to morally imperfect conditions which is the political equivalent of the "old Adam," but which there is no longer (since

---

respetto alle facultà nostre, suntuoso; poco amore della gloria ed onore vero, assai alle ricchezze e danari . . ."

[16] *D. e D.*, p. 219: "Non veggo già che una legge o dua particulare possino fare frutto, ma saria necessario fare uno cumulo di ogni cosa e ridurre tutta questa massa in una materia, e di poi riformarla e ridistinguerla tutta a uso di chi fa cose da mangiare di pasta: che se la prima bozza non viene bene, fa uno monte di tutto e riducela in una forma nuova; a esemplo ancora de' buoni medici, e' quali quando truovono uno corpo pieno di molte malattie ed in modo che non lo possono reggere con una intenzione particulare, attendono con medicine a resolvere tutte le male cause e fare una disposizione nuova di tutto el corpo, il che se bene è difficile ed ha bisogno di buono medico, pure non è impossibile." See above, ch. IV, n. 52, for Savonarola's depiction of Christ as just such a physician.

[17] *Ibid.*   [18] *D. e D.*, p. 220.

Savonarola) any rebirth of man to burn away. If we are right in uncovering this last implication, we have brought to light the Savonarolan streak which some scholars have detected in Guicciardini; overtly, however, he says merely that we must be content to do what we can, and that if we could establish a good beginning (*dare principio*) in the city's affairs, the process of time and the course of years might do more than we could ever hope for at that beginning itself.[19] But he leaves it unclear what is the nature of that knowledge by which men who have not the superhuman wisdom of the legislator are enabled to make a beginning at the legislator's task.

It is of interest that the first question which he turns to consider is that of the employment of citizen or mercenary troops. The writing of the *Discorso di Logrogno* coincided fairly closely with the tragic culmination of Soderini's and Machiavelli's attempts to defend the republic by organizing a militia, an experience which was to lead Machiavelli in later years to weave his theories of military organization more and more closely into his theories of citizenship and civic virtue; and we know that the relations of military and political structure at Rome, Venice, and elsewhere were much discussed in the Orti Oricellari both before and after 1512. Guicciardini in this *Discorso* shares both Machiavelli's general mistrust of mercenaries and his specific point that you must go on providing for them after the war is over, whereas citizens can be disbanded and sent home; citizens, furthermore, are easier to replace after a defeat. He makes the further point—to prove vital in Machiavellian theory—that since citizens will fight well only if the city is in good order, to commit yourself to a citizen army is to commit yourself to good laws and *una buona giustizia*, something easier to ordain than to maintain, as he will demonstrate in greater detail.[20] But though his work is based on this commitment, it is typical of Guicciardini that he clearly recognizes the function of an army as both internal and external; it exists to expand, as well as to defend, the dominions of the republic, and in the former sphere of action there is neither law nor justice. He makes here the striking but easily misunderstood remark that political power is nothing

[19] *Ibid.*: "E non sarebbe poco condurre la città di luogo tanto infirmo, almeno a una disposizione mediocre, anzi saria assai darli principio, perché lo essere una volta aperta la via ed el processo del tempo farebbono forse cogli anni maggiore successo che non paressi potersi sperare di uno principio tale."

[20] *D. e D.*, p. 221: "Né è el dare l'arme a' sua cittadini cosa aliena da uno vivere di republica e populare, perché quando vi si da una giustizia buona ed ordinata legge, quelle arme non si adoperano in pernizia ma in utilità della patria." P. 223: "È vero che, acciò che la città ed el paese non si empressi di fazione e discordie, sarebbe necessario tenerli con una buona giustizia, la quale nelle legge è facile a ordinare, ma è difficile nelle osservazione, come di sotto si dirà più largamente."

but an act of violence committed on those subject to it, sometimes palliated by some apparent justification but only to be maintained by armed force—which must be one's own and not another's.[21] It is clear that the words used here to denote political power (*lo stato e l'imperio*) refer to external power, the power of the city over those not of the city, such as the Florentines sought over the stubbornly resisting Pisans. The implication is not that the authority exercised by Florentines over Florentines is a species of violence, but rather that it is or may be the only sort of authority which is not;[22] and yet there is an intimate relationship between the internal zone, where justice may obtain, and the external zone where there can be nothing but violence. A citizen army, which necessitates *una buona giustizia* within the city, is the best means of keeping one's conquests, the only alternative to relying upon the power of another in the amoral world of external relationships. Through relying upon a *condottiere* the Venetians nearly lost their *libertà*.[23] The word here means, as it often does in Renaissance Italian, the city's independence from external control; yet so closely connected are the external and internal zones that Guicciardini turns immediately[24] to a consideration of liberty in a context of *governo di drento* or the relationships between citizens.

There is no need, he says, to consider whether government by one, few, or many is ideally the best. The facts are that liberty is natural and proper to the city of Florence, that Florentines are born under it, have inherited it from their forefathers and are consequently obliged to defend it with their lives.[25] His language recalls Savonarola's rejection of Thomist ideality in favor of the particular character of the

[21] *D. e D.*, p. 222: "Non è altro lo stato e lo imperio che una violenzia sopra e' sudditi palliata in alcuni con qualche titulo di onestà; volerlo conservare sanza arme e sanza forze proprie ma collo aiuto di altri, non è altro che volere fare uno esercizio sanza li instrumenti che a quello mestiere si appartengono. In somma male si può prevalere sopra altri, male si può difendere dalli inimici chi non vive armato."

[22] Cf. *Ricordi*, C, 48 (Francesco Guicciardini, *Ricordi: edizione critica a cura di Raffaele Spongano*, Florence: Sansoni, 1951, p. 57): "Non si può tenere stati secondo conscienza, perché—chi considera la origine loro—tutti sono violenti, da quelli delle republiche nella patria propria in fuora, e non altrove . . ."

[23] *D. e D.*, p. 222.

[24] Immediately following the words quoted in n. 20 above: ". . . più largamente. Ordinato questo capo, più importante di tutti, non merita poco considerazione el governo nostro di drento."

[25] *D. e D.*, p. 223: ". . . né accade disputare quale sia migliore amministrazione o di uno o di pochi o di molti, perché la libertà è propria e naturale della città nostra. In quella sono vivuti e' passati nostri, in quella siamo nutriti noi; né solo ci è suto dato dalli antichi nostri per ricordo che noi viviamo con quella volentieri, ma che bisognando la defendiamo e colle facultà e colla vita propria."

Florentines which makes them the fit instruments of regeneration. It could also—given what we know of Guicciardini's cast of mind—be read as having a conservative coloration, recalling the Burkean justification of the Revolution of 1688 on the grounds that liberty is an inherited trust which we are obliged to pass on intact, or even as an utterance of skeptical traditionalism on the lines of the famous *Spartam nactus es, hanc exorna*—"Sparta is your portion; make the most of this." But in the *Discorso di Logrogno*, Guicciardini defines liberty in terms which, while providing him with a flexible instrument of political analysis, at the same time carry the full universalism of the Aristotelian and civic humanist tradition. Liberty, he says, consists in the ascendancy of public laws and decisions over the appetites of particular men.[26] That is, it is that state in which my individual will is not subject to the will of any other identifiable individual or group; no other can bind me and carry me whither I would not. But the laws and decrees of the city can do this; in the Renaissance as in the Greek polis, public regulation of individual life could be meticulous and stringent. What matters in the unfree condition is not that I may be bound, but that I may be bound by another's particular will, acting in pursuit of his private interest (*appetito*). I then approach the condition which Aristotle defined as that of the slave, the instrument by which another's ends are achieved; ends which, incidentally, become baser as they are achieved through control of a slave, since such can only be private appetites and not the pursuit of a universal good. The latter can be pursued only through joining with one's equals in the exercise of public authority. Slave-masters can be free only in their relations with each other, since only there is public authority to be found.

The problem of liberty, then, to solving which Florentines stand committed by their civic inheritance (which is also their nature), is that of constituting a citizen body capable of exercising public authority; the antithesis of freedom is a state of affairs wherein authority which should be public is in fact exercised by particular men. As Guicciardini develops the first implications of a definition of liberty as non-dependence upon the particular, he reveals to us the concrete significance which this theory had in the conditions of post-1494 Florence. Laws, he says, do not enforce themselves; they must be executed by magistrates; and if we are to live under laws rather than men, the first necessity is that the magistrates should not owe their authority to particular men or find their wills swayed in exercising that authority by particular men's wishes.[27] There is here a very strong implicit reference

---

[26] *Ibid.*, following immediately: "Né è altro la libertà che uno prevalere le legge ed ordini publici allo appetito delli uomini particulari. . . ."

[27] *Ibid.*, following immediately: ". . . e perché le legge non hanno vita né si

to the conditions of Medicean rule before 1494, in which the heads of that family had governed the city by a technique of informally manipulating both the elections of magistrates and their subsequent exercise of their offices. It was this system about which the *ottimati* in 1512 still felt deeply ambivalent: on the one hand it had guaranteed them a monopoly of office, on the other hand it had made them feel that their offices were not truly theirs. They were experimenting with the republic in the hope that it would prove a better device for legitimating aristocratic ascendancy in office. This is certainly Guicciardini's position; his bias in favor of a political elite is always explicit; but it is important to note that here, as elsewhere in his writings, there is an equally strong rejection, whether implicit or explicit, of formally closed oligarchy. He says that the magistrates must not recognize one or a few as the source of their authority, or feel constrained to govern in accord with other men's wills, so that consequently the foundation of liberty is popular government. A small group of oligarchs—he seems to be thinking—sharing out magistracies among themselves in a smoke-filled room (as Cavalcanti had suspected was what went on), would not satisfy the essential condition of liberty, since they would always know to whom they owed their offices. If authority is to be free it must be public; if it is to be public it must be impersonal; if it is to be impersonal the group conferring it must be over a certain size. In his own words, if the foundation of liberty is popular government, at Florence the foundation of popular government is the distribution of magistracies and dignities by the Consiglio Grande.[28]

In another constitutional tradition, the distribution of magistracies was to be considered among the attributes of sovereignty. But here, in the Aristotelian and civic humanist mode, the distribution of magistracies by the many was intended not to endow them with a sovereign will, but to free the magistrates from dependence on anyone's will: to free the will that allocated authority from any taint of particularity by depersonalizing and universalizing it to the point where it ceased to be a will at all, or ceased at the moment of the magistrate's election. Yet the many in the Consiglio Grande consisted of individuals exercising their individual wills and intelligences, and the problem is to see

---

possono fare osservare da sé medesimo, ma hanno bisogno di ministri, cioè de' magistri che le faccino eseguire, è necessario a volere vivere sotto le legge, non sotto particulari, che e' magistrati non abbino a temere alcuno particulare, non a ricognoscere l'onore loro da uno o da pochi, acciò che non sieno constretti a governare la città secondo la volontà di altri."

[28] *Ibid.*, following immediately: "E però per fondamento della libertà bisogna el vivere populare, del quale è spirito e basa el consiglio grande, che ebbi a distribuire e' magistrati e degnità della città."

how Guicciardini intended to convert these into members of a public body. The clue lies in the differentiation of political function. Under the 1494 constitution, membership in the Consiglio was supposed to extend to all those capable of being elected to office themselves; and Guicciardini proposes as a reform that it should be extended further, to take in a sizable number of persons not so qualified. The trouble with the present system, he says, is that every man involved in electing officeholders thinks himself capable of office and aspires to hold it. Consequently his personal ambitions and preferences interfere with his choice, and more errors are committed at this point in the political process than at any other. If the function of choosing magistrates were entrusted to those not capable of exercising magistracy themselves, they would think only of the claims of those to be elected and not of their own ambitions, since it is the natural inclination of all men to follow the good if not distracted by their particular ends.[29]

At this point in the civic theory of Renaissance Aristotelianism, we are well placed to observe the origins of the doctrine of the separation of powers, and to note that the foundations of that doctrine are—as they were for John Adams—ethical rather than institutional. The elective and executive functions are to be separated in order to diminish the danger of the individual's being personally interested in the outcome of his choice for the public good, to prevent him from being judge in his own cause. The theory of the polity remains what we saw it to be earlier, a science of virtue. But Guicciardini's analysis further presupposes assumptions which have to do with epistemology and the theory of knowledge. Persons adjudged incapable of exercising magistracy are adjudged capable of choosing those best able to exercise it; by what process of cognition do they do this? He extends his account of the Consiglio Grande's functions from the election of magistrates to the establishment of laws, and remarks that though nobody supposes the Council capable of debating and formulating a law from the first proposal to the last, there is a question whether laws discussed and

[29] D. e D., pp. 224-25: "Fu adunche bene ordinato el consiglio grande in farlo generale a tutti quegli che participavano dello stato; ed io ho qualche volta considerato se e fussi bene che nella creazione de' magistrati intervenissino in consiglio non solo tutti quelli che oggi vi sono abili, ma ancora uno numero grande di quegli che non possono participare del governo, perché noi abbiamo veduto per esperienzia che la piú parte delli errori che fa el consiglio nello eleggere li ufici, nasche da uno appetito del distribuirli si larghi che ognuno di chi squittina, possi sperare di aggiugnervi. La quale ragione cesserebbe in quelli che non ne fussino capaci, perché non avendo speranza che alcuna larghezza ve li potessi tirare, non arebbono causa di conferirli se non in quelli che a iudicio loro li meritassino. . . . ed andrà drieto in questo alla inclinazione naturale di tutti li uomini, che è di seguitare el bene, se e' respetti propri non ritirano."

agreed upon in smaller deliberative bodies—presumably more highly qualified—should be submitted to the Council for its assent. This is an important matter, both because laws affect all men without exception and—we learn elsewhere—because they are capable of suddenly altering the form of government;[30] and the decision Guicciardini reaches is that though the Consiglio Grande should not debate the laws proposed to it—this has been done already—it should have the function of giving or withholding final assent. There seem to be two sets of reasons for this. In the first place, since laws bind all it must be impossible to say that they owe their being to a few, and this can be prevented by ensuring that they have the consent of all. In the second place, ratification by the Council will ensure that no law alters the form of government or has any other pernicious effect; and to this end, though there is to be no public debate, it would be well to publish the laws proposed a few days in advance, so that the members may know what they are to decide and may have talked about them among themselves.[31]

It seems fairly clear that Guicciardini's theory as regards both election and legislation rests upon an Aristotelian conception of decision-making by the many. Though not themselves capable of magistracy, they can recognize this capacity in others; though not themselves capable of framing or even debating a law, they are competent judges of the draft proposals of others. By excluding them from the functions they are to evaluate, the principle of impersonalization is secured; but it is still not clear what intellectual capacities they exercise in evaluation. Aristotle's doctrine—in essence a doctrine of experience—had been that each non-elite individual knew enough of how a particular man in office, or a particular law in operation, was likely to affect him to make the sum of many such judgments a more reliable prediction of the outcome than could be reached by individual wisdom. But as we have seen in chapter I of this study, the collective wisdom of the severally less wise was cumulative in character, and its efficacy decreased as the complexity of the particular decision to be faced increased the speed with which it must be understood, made, and put into effect. In a system of custom, the many were asked only to decide whether their former responses should be repeated in what appeared to be a recurring situation, and their decision emerged gradually, through action and memory rather than thought, as former usages were retained or abandoned; but in the popular assembly of a city-state decisions were more highly individualized and the pressure on their time was greater—Guicciardini's use of words like *occorrere* and *giornalmente* clearly reflects

[30] *D. e D.*, p. 244.   [31] *D. e D.*, pp. 230-31.

this.[32] Once it became a matter of deciding whether a particular individual was fit for office, a particular law fit to be made universally binding, the many must acquire and process their data at a speed far greater than that required for the formation of custom. It is significant that Guicciardini does not seem to have dealt with this problem by ascribing to the many a prudence, or ability to predict the outcome of actions, differing from that of the few, but rather through the ethically based strategy of arguing that since the many's decisions were undistracted by personal ambitions—and we have seen how he meant to secure that—it knew what was good more exactly than did any smaller deliberative body. At another time than that of composing the *Discorso di Logrogno*, but also in analysis of the constitution of 1494, he wrote two speeches[33] stating the cases for electing magistrates in the assembly either by majority vote or by casting lots, and caused the proponent of the vote—with whom his preferences lie—to say:

> A man's merits should not be judged by particular persons but by the people, which has better judgment than any of us, because it is prince and is without passion. . . . It knows each of us better than we know ourselves, and has no other end than to distribute things to those who are seen to deserve them.

> And further, I do not mean to deny that the people sometimes votes erroneously, since it cannot always know the quality of every citizen; but I affirm that these errors are incomparably less than those committed in any other way of proceeding, and that every day they will be corrected and grow fewer, because the longer we go on in our present way the better will it be known what each man is worth, since this man's actions can be observed today and that man's tomorrow; and now that the people has begun to get down to business in this Council and knows that the government is its own, it will pay more attention to each man's actions and character than ever it did before, so that every day it will become a better judge of men's merits and will not be prevented from giving them what they deserve.[34]

---

[32] *Ibid.*: "El modo che si usa nelle legge e provisione che occorrono di farsi giornalmente in una republica è molto stretto, sendo necessario che le sieno prima proposte da' signori, approvate da' fermatori, deliberate di nuovo da' signori, vinte di poi da loro e da' collegi, avendo a passare nelli ottanta ed ultimamente venire per tanti vagli e mezzi al consiglio grande."

[33] *D. e D.*, pp. 175-95: "Del modo di eleggere gli uffici nel consiglio grande."

[34] *D. e. D.*, pp. 178-79: ". . . se uno merita, non s'ha a stare a giudicio de' particulari ma del popolo, el quale ha migliore giudicio che nessuno altro, perché è el principe ed è sanza passione. . . . Lui cognosce meglio ognuno di noi che non

Here the perpetual assembly has taken the place of the customary community; day-to-day participation in political life has increased the speed at which relevant experience and knowledge are acquired; but still it is to be noted that popular decision is basically a matter of discerning the characters of individuals to compose a decision-making elite. The people choose men, and are praised for their ability to choose good men. The men chosen resolve on laws and policies, and the people have a final voice in accepting or rejecting their proposals. But we do not hear so much about their ability to discern good policies from bad—the most so far allowed them is the ability to know when a proposal will alter the form of government—and there is no hint whatever of their having any capacity to initiate policies, let alone reforms or innovations. They can perceive men's characters, but not the shape of events or the structure of society.

In the *Discorso di Logrogno*, Guicciardini's ideas about the moral character and powers of perception required, or likely to appear, in a decision-making elite first emerge in his consideration of the office of *gonfaloniere*, where the central question is whether the supreme magistrate should be appointed for a limited term or for life. The case for life appointment—which Guicciardini favors—is initially stated[35] in terms of the acquisition of information and the resultant making of decisions. Because the *gonfaloniere* is irremovable, he will not have to worry about keeping his office or about what may happen to him when his term is up, considerations which often produce lukewarmness (*freddezza*) in magistrates; nothing will distract him from learning how to deal with events as they occur and how to understand the nature of the people with whom he has to deal. It is evident how easily this argument can be transposed into ethical terms: the life appointee is undistracted by private considerations both from acquiring the information

---

facciamo noi stessi, nè ha altro fine se non di distribuire le cose in chi gli pare che meriti.

"Ma piú oltre, io non voglio negare che anche el popolo faccia qualche volta, con le piú fave, degli errori, perché non può sempre bene cognoscere la qualità di tutti e' suoi cittadini; ma dico che sono sanza comparazione minori che non saranno quegli che si faranno in qualunque altro modo, e che alla giornata sempre si limeranno e se ne farà manco, perche quanto si andrà piú in là, sarà ogni dì piú cognosciuto quello che pesa ognuno, perché si vedranno oggi le azione di questo, e domani di quello, ed el popolo che ha cominciato a porsi a bottega a questo consiglio, e cognoscere che el governo è suo, porrà piú mente agli andamenti e costumi di ognuno che non faceva prima, in modo che ogni dì sarà migliore giudice di quello che meritino gli uomini e non arà impedimento a dare a chi merita."

[35] *D. e D.*, p. 237.

and skills necessary to his office and from concerning himself exclusively with the public good. Having been appointed for life to the highest post the city has to offer, he has no motive for seeking to please particular interest groups, and very little for seeking to extend his authority beyond the limits set to it. But at this point the argument takes a new and interesting turn. The case for having an office of this kind, exalted above all private distractions and personal considerations—free even from the ancient check of having to answer for one's tenure of office at the expiry of its term—is that citizens may lawfully aspire to a reward elevated above all others, to the point where it becomes virtually impossible to exercise it to any end except the public good. This is the moment at which Guicciardini makes the observation—often quoted as proof of his optimate bias—that all republics, without recorded exception, are and have been governed (*retto*) by the very few who are rendered capable of glorious deeds by the spur of ambition, the appetite for greatness, and the desire to rise to the highest pinnacle;[36] and that the gonfalonierate for life seems on the whole the best means of giving this appetite lawful satisfaction.[37]

The remarkable thing about this passage is not its elitism. The Aristotelian tradition unequivocally differentiated citizens into the many, with neither the motive nor the knowledge to look far beyond their own affairs, and the few who sought, and had the capacity to exercise, a greater share in the control of affairs; it indicated that the few would always exercise power disproportionate to their numbers, and that the problem was to devise an institutional framework—the *politeia*—which would prevent this disproportion from running to excess and ensure that the preponderant minority governed with an eye to the good of others beside themselves. Guicciardini is plainly no exception here: on the one hand he insists that the highly participant few can function only in the context of a less participant (but still participant)

---

[36] *D. e D.*, pp. 238-39: "E se bene questo è pasto da infiammare pochi, non è però questo infiammarli inutile, perché in ogni republica bene ordinata ed in ogni tempo si è sempre veduto che la virtù di pochi cittadini e quella che ha retto e regge le republiche, e le opere gloriose ed effetti grande sono sempre nati da pochi e per mano di pochi, perché a volere guidare cose grande ed essere capi del governo in una città libera, bisogna moltissime parte e virtù che in pochissimi si coniungono. E' quali oltre a avere amore alla città, è bene, acciò che li operino piu ardentemente, che abbino uno sprone di ambizione, uno appetito di grandezza e di condursi in qualche summo grado; la quale quando e' cercano e desiderano di acquistare non col prevalere alle legge né per via di sette, ma collo essere reputati cittadini buoni e prudenti e col fare bene alla patria, chi può dubitare che questa ambizione è laudabile ed utilissima? La quale chi non sente è in una certa fredezza e li manca uno certo stimolo di gloria, che da lui non esce mai cose generose ed eccelse."
[37] *Ibid.*

many, and on the other he is constantly proposing devices to prevent decision-makers at all three levels from being distracted by the pursuit of their private ends. His thought is formally aristocratic, but never oligarchic. His originality lies in his insistence that as the many are differentiated from the few by their capacity to judge of others' fitness for offices they do not themselves seek, the few are differentiated from the many by their propensity to seek office; and that the *virtù*— a term he explicitly employs—which makes them seek it is not wisdom or goodness or any other moral quality which renders them fit for office, not even love for the city—though they must have that too— but, quite simply, ambition and the thirst for glory. Nor does he present this *virtù* as in any way nonmoral; on the contrary, he qualifies it with adjectives such as *generosa* and *onesta*.

Ambition was not among the Christian virtues; "by that sin fell the angels." Guicciardini's concern with the subject arises, so his biographers tell us, in part from a certain moral honesty; he was intensely aware of his own intense ambition and obsession with personal and family honor. But the role of ambition, honor, and the search for glory in his political theory must be further investigated. The feudal ethos of course centered upon honor, together with fidelity, and the literature of knightly ethics records many attempts to bring it into line with Christian morals; there is a lingering ambiguity in the words of Shakespeare's Henry V: "if it be a sin to covet honor, I am the most offending soul alive."[38] The problem of civilizing the warrior ethos was no new theme in European thought. We should be careful, however, about attributing a feudal code of values to the Florentine aristocracy; the *ottimati* with whom Guicciardini identified himself were merchants, bankers, and jurists—not to mention politicians—and it is not clear how great an impact knightly ethics made upon them. Perhaps the true point is that honor was preeminently the virtue of the political individual, the *particulare*—to use (and use as he spelled it) the central and most ambiguous term of Guicciardini's political thought. On the one hand the *particulare* was a deadly danger so long as he sought his private and particular good; ambition was what impelled him to do that, and the search for a position of preeminence in which one could satisfy one's appetites was something that individuals would pursue in defiance of all laws and public morality. On the other hand, glory was public; it consisted in the recognition accorded one by one's fellows; being pagan rather than Christian, it brought fame, rather than salvation, in and after life; and if the *particulare* could be made to conduct his search in a civic setting, where everyone was by definition engaged in making decisions aimed at a mutual and public good, his glory would

[38] *Henry V*, IV, 3, 28-29.

consist in the recognition by his fellows of his preeminence in this activity. His need for glory would drive him to attempt more than his fellows and to expose himself to public scrutiny; he would be under constant examination by the few and the many, who would know him better than he knew himself; and once his honor became a matter of recognized concern for the public good, his inward concern for the ideal of purely individual integrity which the notion expresses would make him disdainful of lesser satisfactions. In these circumstances, it would prove wise to have politicized his ambition with the offer of supreme and irremovable power, so long as that power functioned in a context of incessant public scrutiny and judgment; and the one and the few would be free to acquire the knowledge and experience needed for their tasks.

But having made ambition the distinguishing characteristic of the political elite, Guicciardini knew well enough what ambition must look like if the political structure failed to discipline it. In one passage of the *Discorso di Logrogno*,[39] he remarks that a set of arrangements which make constitutional change easy to propose, but hard to carry through, looks like an oligarchical device to keep existing groups in power; it would probably be better if such changes could be proposed only in committees difficult of access but rapidly submitted to the judgment of the many. And in the second of the two *discorsi* on methods of election in the Consiglio Grande, the critique of the *ottimati*'s oligarchic proclivities is carried further and in a new direction. Here the speaker in favor of election by lot—anciently considered a more democratic procedure than selection by voting—declares that the argument that the many necessarily choose the best man is vitiated by the presence of a hard core of *ottimati* who call themselves *uomini da bene*, consider that they have an inherited and inherent right to office, and invariably vote for one another in exclusion of those not of the inner ring; so that the only choice of strategies remaining to the non-elite is either to vote invariably against *ottimato* candidates—thus falsifying the whole rationale—or to abandon voting altogether in favor of sortition. He goes on to declare that the self-styled *uomini da bene* base their claim to elite status on the supposed superiority of their prudence, wisdom, and virtue; but in fact they occupy this status either because they have acquired or inherited wealth, or because their ancestors held high office—very often for reasons which will not bear much examination. Riches and ancestry, he adds, come one's way by fortune; and the case against the Florentine political aristocracy is that it owes its being to fortune rather than virtue,[40] which is why, in the last analy-

39 *D. e D.*, pp. 245-46.   40 *D. e D.*, pp. 189-92.

sis, it pursues private, not public ends. Guicciardini did not intend his readers to be convinced by this speech, to which he gives an unpleasant demagogic tone; we can be sure that he favored election by vote for more or less elitist reasons. But he knew the strength of the case that could be made against the Florentine elite. It was oligarchic because it was the child of fortune; and ambition, the virtue he had singled out as eminently capable of politicization, was what had made its members or their progenitors seek their fortunes. It was, at once and for the same reasons, potentially a civic aristocracy and potentially a self-seeking *intelligenza*—the Florentine word for clique or racket—of oligarchs. An extraordinary passage at the close of the *Discorso di Logrogno* bears witness to the importance which Guicciardini still attached to the systematic elimination of private satisfactions and appetites.

This is nothing less than a polemic against luxury, concluding with what is almost a Savonarolan proposal to "burn the vanities." Luxury corrupts men; it gives them an increasing appetite for wealth and display and everything antithetical to true glory and virtue. Corruption of this sort is not new in the world; ancient writers inveigh against it, and partial remedies will not serve against an evil "so universal, so old and so deeply rooted in the minds of men."[41] It is, in short, the "old Adam" which Savonarola had hoped to burn away in the fires of spiritual reformation; but Guicciardini's language is civic and classical where his predecessor's was apocalyptic. To cut out the evil, he says, one would need the scalpel (*coltello*) of Lycurgus, who eliminated all luxury from Sparta in a day, dividing up all property and prohibiting the use of money and personal adornment. A miraculous austerity and devotion to the public good at once overcame the Spartans, and it is the glory of Lycurgus's name that he had *grazia*—grace? good fortune?—to execute so durable a reform. Great philosophers were denied this, and it is no wonder that Lycurgus was thought to have had the aid of Apollo; for to reform a city is a work rather divine than human.[42]

[41] *D. e D.*, pp. 257-58: "Né incomincia questa corruttela oggi nel mondo, ma è durate già molti e molti secoli, di che fanno fede li scrittori antichi che tanto detestano ed esclamano contro a' vizi delle età loro.

"Rimedi ci sono forse qualcuni per potere un poco moderare questi mali, ma non già tanti che e' faccino effetto notabile in una malattia si universale, si vecchia e tanto radicata nelle menti delli uomini."

[42] *Ibid.*: ". . . felicissimo certo e glorioso che avessi grazia di ordinare si bene la sua republica, e molto piú felice di averla acconcia in modo che li ordine e le legge sue durassino molte centinaia di anni ed in tal maniera che, mentre visse sotto quelle, fu molte volte di potenzia e forze capo della Grecia, ma sempremai di gloria ed opinione di virtù apresso alle nazione forestiere la prima. Fulli piú facile a ridurle in atto che non fu facile a Platone, a Cicerone ed a molti uomini

Reformation, to Savonarola, had borne the precisely Aristotelian meaning of the imposition of form upon matter, the restoration of matter—the inhabitants of a city were the "material cause" of its being—to pursuit of its original end, which was why he had preferred to call it *rinnovazione*. But as a Christian, he had seen that end as the sanctified life; the *prima forma* was the gift of grace, and in consequence reformation could occur only in an apocalyptic context provided by the workings of grace in history. To burn away the "second nature" established in man by the pursuit of unsanctified goods, such as the "vanities," was a necessary part of restoration. It is of considerable significance to note Guicciardini's transmutation of these themes into a different and less specifically Christian rhetoric. He does not spell out the language of form and matter, or point out that it is the work of *virtù* to impose form upon *fortuna*; but his legislator achieves the superhuman success of reforming a city so that his laws and its virtues last for ages. The word *grazia* is used in connection with his doing this; it is a divine work that brings him the reputation if not the reality of divine assistance; and he carries it out by means of a systematic elimination of the pursuit of luxury, an evil anciently rooted in the minds of men. The parallels are as important as the divergences. On the one hand, where Savonarola had seen luxuries and vanities as distracting the soul from the pursuit of grace, Guicciardini sees them as distracting the citizen from the pursuit of the public good; Lycurgus accordingly takes the place of Jeremiah, and his reformation is an act of legislation rather than a summons to repentance. But it is an act performed directly upon the moral personalities of the citizens, and it has the effect of restoring them to their natural propensity, or "first nature," to seek the general good if not distracted by the pursuit of particular satisfactions. When we are told that men are by nature good, this is what is meant; the doctrine that men have a corrupted "second nature," which leads them to go whoring after private satisfactions whenever the opportunity offers, makes it possible, in the appropriate rhetorical context, to add without real contradiction that men are by nature bad.[45] What the legislator does is to eliminate the second nature (which is old) by a mixture of moral charisma and institutional provision, and leave the way free for the restoration of the first nature

---

dottissimi e prudentissimi metterle in scrittura; in modo che non sanza causa fu opinione ne' tempi sua che fussi aiutato del consiglio di Apolline Delfico, e ragionevolmente, perché riformare una città disordinata e riformarla in modi tanto laudabili è più tosto opera divina che umana."

[43] Perhaps it may be observed at this point that failure to grasp this has been the cause of much misunderstanding of both Guicciardini and Machiavelli.

(which is primal). This is divine work even if viewed in the light of the Christian concept of grace; but since it is performed wholly in and for a civic context of political decision and institution, the appropriate rhetoric in which to describe it is that of Greco-Roman politics, where the legislator regularly appears as receiving the aid of the Hellenic gods. What should be stressed here is less the secular divergence between the Christian and civic traditions than the extent to which they found common ground in an ideal of austerity and self-denial; there were civic humanist grounds for erecting this ideal after there were monastic and before there were Calvinist grounds.

But the task that the legislator performs is miraculous, and where Savonarola had believed that miracles were at hand, Guicciardini did not. For ourselves, he adds, it is illegitimate to hope or even desire to do the legislator's work; we must recognize ourselves for what we are, beings so far corrupted that only marginal adjustments of our moral character can be performed. If the city could be trained in the use of arms—the militia tradition emerging once more—and if magistrates could be elected for no other reason than public approbation of their good character, riches and luxuries would be less esteemed and it might even be possible to enact effective sumptuary laws to keep them permanently in check.[44] But we have in essence returned to the analogy of the doctor with which the *Discorso* began, and can now see clearly the difference between the doctor and the cook. It would be the legislator who stirred the whole *materia* of the city together, in the manner of the man making *pasta*, and imposed form on it anew. The doctor, faced with an organism of greater complexity, assumes it to be already diseased and hopes to control the course of the malady rather than eliminate it altogether. But this means that the *materia* on which he operates is already inherently unstable; he is exposed to the unpredictabilities of fortune. Guicciardini's ambivalence about designating the *ottimati* the class of those ambitious for honor can now be fully

---

[44] *D. e D.*, p. 258: "A noi è rimasto el poterci maravigliare ed esclamare di cosa tanto notabile, ma di ridurla in atto non ci è lecito non che sperarlo a pena desiderarlo; e però ritornando alle cose che sono in facultà nostra, io dico che questa malattia è tanto difficile che gli è impossibile estirparla; bisognerebbe come fece lui, levare li usi per e' quali le ricchezze si desiderano, e questo per la mollizie delli uomini non si può non che altro disegnare. Credo bene che dandosi la città alle arme ed essendo aperta la via di diventare glorioso con quelle, distribuendosi e' magistrati con riguardo della buona fama e portamenti delli uomini, sendo facile el punire e' delitti di chi errassi, che tutte queste cose insieme farieno e' ricchi essere in meno estimazione che non sono oggi. Aggiungereci una cosa tentata spessissime volte ma male osservata, di limitare e moderare quanto fussi possibile li ornamenti e suntuosità del vestire . . . ," a long indictment of which follows.

appreciated. On the one hand he was convinced that ambition was the quality which must be politicized and legitimized if the *politeia* were to have the elite it needed to take the initiative in particular decisions; on the other hand he was well aware that ambition might already have created an environment too unstable to permit of its own politicization, and might be already too corrupt to be capable of serving civic ends.

[III]

The role of ambition in determining the behavior of a civic elite remained of central concern to optimate thought in the years following the restoration of the Medici in 1512. Probably the principal fact in determining the character of the restored government was the election, in 1513, of Cardinal Giovanni de' Medici as Pope Leo X. This transformed the situation by absorbing Medicean rule at Florence into a wider political context. The family had been brought back by foreign arms, brutally underlining Florentine inability to control the external environment, but when Leo X reigned in the place of Julius II he assumed the role of a leading moderator of Italian politics, one who might possibly build a system which would lessen the domination of the non-Italian powers. In addition to this and to the reflected glory which the city derived from the enthronement of a Florentine pope, his election meant that the stability of Medicean rule depended neither on foreign arms nor on the ability of the ruling family to enter into political relationships satisfactory to the major political groups within Florence, but was underwritten by the legitimacy and durability still attaching to any system of papal politics. Leo's ascent thus gave a breathing space to the Medici and to those Florentines who had to decide whether to accept them and what terms would be exacted on either side as the price of acceptance. At the same time it removed from Florence the most able-seeming member of the family and left citizens with an unpleasant sensation of provinciality, of being no longer at the center where their fate was determined; and it made the whole Medicean system dependent, first on Leo's tenure of life (he reigned for eight years), and second on what the junior members of his house, who held power at Florence in his absence, might attempt to do in the context of a Medicean politics no longer confined to Florentine civic relationships. To optimate thinkers, already ambivalent in their feelings about the relationships between their circle and the Medici rulers before 1494, all this presented a new set of problems. Coinciding with each fresh crisis in affairs—with the election of Leo in 1513, with the death in 1516 of Giuliano de' Medici, who ran things for the family in Florence, with the death in 1519 of Lorenzo, his successor, who involved Florence in his attempt to capture the Duchy of Urbino—we find a recrudescence[45] of optimate writings, of which the point for our purposes is their endeavor to apply Aristotelian and humanist paradigms defining the civic aristocracy to a situation which the writers recognize as unprecedented. It follows that an equal degree of interest attaches to the terms in which they endeavor to state that the situation is unprecedented and what is unprecedented about it.

Guicciardini was one of these authors, but it is characteristic of him, his class, and the whole period that we should not think of him as involved in a sort of perpetual confrontation between the Florentine civic aristocracy and the Medici denying them the power which they sought. After his return from his Spanish embassy he practiced law at Florence and observed with optimate disapproval the increasing disinclination of Giuliano and Lorenzo to share power with anyone but their intimates; at the time of Giuliano's death in 1516, however, he accepted from the papacy the governorship of Modena and subsequently pursued under both Medici popes a career in the administration and defense of the papal territories in north-central Italy. Like the other optimate writers, and like Machiavelli, he was happy to serve the Medici if he could do so in ways consonant with his idea of himself; but at Florence that idea involved his membership in a civic aristocracy—a classic Few—whom the Medici must recognize as their peers and fellow citizens. If Giuliano and Lorenzo would not do that, he would not work with them and looked with foreboding on the future of a regime which could not adjust its relationships with the civic elite. At Modena and other papal cities, however, the issue of citizenship did not arise. As governor there, he was the lieutenant of an absent but lawful prince; in the terminology which James Harrington was to use in the next century, his empire was provincial, not domestic; and it would be legitimate to feel that he was exercising it over people so little politicized that citizenship was beyond them and subjection to monarchical authority—as Machiavelli was to observe— the only alternative. Guicciardini's life from 1516 to 1527, therefore, affords valuable insight into the relationships of theory to practice.[46] While living as the servant of a monarchy, he thought and wrote about the role (a limited one) of aristocracy in a polity; had he remained at Florence, he would have been directly involved—as he was to be after 1527—in the dilemma of his class, the choice between insisting on an elite role in a "proportionate equality" of citizenship, or accepting the

---

[45] For this see Rudolph von Albertini, *Das florentinische Staatsbewusstsein im übergang von der Republik zum Prinzipat* (Bern: Francke Verlag, 1955), who prints the texts of the *discorsi* in his appendix.

[46] Roberto Ridolfi, *Life of Francesco Guicciardini*, chs. VIII-XVI.

role of servants and courtiers of what was becoming increasingly a monarchy but could not be legitimized as such in Florentine terms. This is the choice with which, and with whose conceptual implications, optimate thought was increasingly concerned after 1512.

Soon after his return from Spain, and continuing the thought of the *Discorso di Logrogno* and the historical work he had written earlier, Guicciardini composed a short treatise "concerning the government of Florence after the restoration of the Medici in 1512."[47] This work breaks off abruptly and may well be incomplete, but contains language of much significance. If we look, to begin with, at the rhetorical exordium, we note that the familiar figures of the steersman and the doctor are present, but that of the cook-legislator is lacking. The implicit reason is stated in the second paragraph: a city is a body composed of an infinite diversity of individuals, and the accidents and difficulties that can arise in managing them are infinite likewise. Therefore the ruling virtue of steersman, doctor, and statesman alike is circumspection, prudence, diligence. This enables the steersman to hold his course and bring his ship to port; doctors employ it to apprehend the nature of the disease and all its accidents, and without it their prescriptions would be "disproportionate" to the disease and contrary to the "complexion" of the patient.[48] There is no question here of restoring the matter to its primary form; the word *materia* first appears in connection with the word *difficile*; the analogy with medicine presupposes that the body is sick and the ship in a storm. When speaking of a popular government, in which the many as well as the few were to be associated in political participation, it was appropriate to adopt a relatively sanguine note and speak in terms of the legislator and his divine

[47] *D. e D.*, pp. 260-66: "Del governo di Firenze dopo la restaurazione de' Medici nel 1512." This is the only one of this group of writings for which we are not dependent on Albertini.

[48] *D. e D.*, pp. 260-61: "Veggiano e' prudenti ed esperti medici in nessuna cosa usare piú esatta diligenzia che in conoscere quale sia la natura del male, e capitulare un tratto le qualità e tutti li accidenti sua per resolversi poi con questo fondamento quale abbi a essere el reggimento dello infermo, di che sorte ed in che tempo si abbino a dare le medicine; perché non fermando bene questo punto, ordinerebbono spesse volte una dieta, darebbono medicine non proporzionate alla malattia, contrarie alla complessione ed essere dello infermo; donde ne seguirebbe la totale ruina e morte del loro ammalato.

"Questa resoluzione se in cosa alcuna è laudabile e necessaria, bisogna sopra tutto in chi è principe e capo di governi di stati; poiche essendo una città uno capo [*sic*: corpo?] composto di infiniti uomini diversi di condizione, di appetiti e di ingegno, sono infiniti li accidenti, li umori, infinite le difficultà nel maneggiarli; e però è necessario in conoscerli a capitularli e pigliare lo ordine con che si abbino a governare, tanto piú cura e prudenzia quanto la materia è in sé piú difficile e quanto sono piú importanti li effetti che ne seguitano."

power to operate on all parts of the body politic at once; but in this *discorso* Guicciardini was restricting himself to the point of view of the *ottimati* and the problem of reordering their relations with the Medici, and since they were a part only—although the most prudent and experienced part—of the whole body, it would not have been proper for them to attempt to bring to bear on the whole body qualities over and above their prudence and experience. And where in his previous work he had been able to stress the legitimate ambition of the few and the contribution which their thirst for honor might make to the perfection of the whole, the note here is correspondingly more circumspect. Good medicine may keep a sick man alive, but bad will kill him; good government may conserve that civil association and accord than which nothing is more precious and unique (*singulare*) in the life of man, but from bad government we may predict *ruina, destruzione, esterminio*.[49] Even in the most Aristotelian context Guicciardini can here provide, the *summum bonum* is little more than the absence of the *summum malum*.

Further reasons for this disenchanted tone soon appear. He says—evidently on the grounds that a city is composed of an infinite diversity of humors and conditions—that it is useless to speak of government abstractly and in general; one must take into account the individual character (*natura*) of both the people and the area (*luogo, sito*) to be governed. Guicciardini is moving toward the standard characterization of the Florentines as a people unfitted by second nature and history for anything except liberty, but before doing so he lays down a set of categories which arrest the reader's eye and profoundly affect the remainder of his argument. There is, he says, one mode of government to be exercised by a king or *signore naturale*, another by one whose rule is founded in violence and usurpation; one to be exercised over a city used to subjection, another over one used to govern itself and dominate others. What catches the eye is that these are, as we shall see, important organizing categories of Machiavelli's *Il Principe* (there seems to be no trace of contact between the two men in 1512-1513, when this *discorso* and *Il Principe* were both being written), but that where Machiavelli employs them to isolate the "new prince"—the

---

[49] *D. e D.*, p. 261: "Perché del buono governo ne seguita la salute e conservazione di infiniti uomini, e del contrario ne resulta la ruina ed esterminio delle città, di che nella vita delli uomini nessuna cosa è piú preziosa e singulare che questa congregazione e consorzio civile. E come dallo essere uno infermo bene curato da' medici o no, si può pigliare potento argumento della salute o morte sua, così interviene nel governo di uno stato, perché essendo retto prudentemente e proporzionatamente, si può crederne e sperarne buoni effetti; essendo retto altrimenti e governato male, che si può crederne altro che la ruina e destruzione sua?"

usurper of power over a city—as an ideal type, and to define the class of political phenomena to which that type belongs, Guicciardini, declaring that an exhaustive analysis of the field would take too long, employs them to no other purpose than to define the character and problems of the government of the restored Medici.[50] He does this, of course, because he assumes himself to be closer to power and to practical questions than Machiavelli could; but at the same time, his analysis takes the form of a comparison between Medicean rule after 1434 and after 1512—it is a restatement of history—and has the effect of leaving it uncertain how far the restored Medici belong to the class of "new princes" and to what sources of stability and legitimation they may look.

The city of Florence, he proceeds, is anciently free and given to the exercise of dominion in Italy. This is due partly to its geographical location, but also to the character of its inhabitants, a restless and mobile people given to the acquisition of riches and power, and so— most important of all—addicted to concerning themselves with public business. The central fact of Florentine life is the existence of a large number of citizens accustomed to demand and exercise political participation (*participazione*), which has led to a built-in preference for the *vivere libero e populare* and to a hatred of deriving one's political status from powerful individuals (*particulari*).[51] Concerning this fact we know Guicciardini's feelings to be mixed; he acknowledged widespread participation to be a prerequisite of liberty, but distrusted the actual exercise of participatory initiative by the many. Consequently, it is not surprising to find that he asserted liberty, in these terms, to be ancient and ineradicable in the Florentine personality, but did not hold

[50] *Ibid.*: ". . . donde ne seguita che el parlare generalmente e con una medesima regola non basta, ma bisogna o parlare generalmente con tali distinzione che servino a tutti e' casi, il che sarebbe di troppa lunghezza, overo ristrignersi a uno particulare solo, come farò io, che solo insisterò in queste cose che io giudicherei doversi fare per questi Medici, volendo tenere lo stato e governo della città di Firenze. . . ."

[51] *D. e D.*, pp. 261-62: "La città di Firenze da lunghissimi tempi in qua è stata in libertà; essi governata popularmente ed ha avuto imperio e signoria in molti luoghi di Toscana; ha avuto ne' maneggi di Italia per el passato sempre piú reputazione e piú luogho tra li altri potentati, che non pareva convenirsi al dominio che ha; di che si può dare causa al sito dove la è posta, alla natura delli uomini che per essere inquieti hanno voluto travagliare, per essere industriosi lo hanno saputo fare, per essere suti danarosi hanno potuto fare. Queste condizioni hanno fatto che in Firenze e' cittadini communemente appetiscono el vivere libero e populare, non vorrebbono ricognoscere da alcuno particulare el grado loro ed hanno esosa ogni grandezze o potenzia eccessiva di alcuno cittadino, ed è la inclinazione loro attendere e pensare alle cose delli stati e governi." The word *participazione* first occurs on p. 263; see below, n. 53.

it to be sacred, especially legitimate, or even an unvarying norm. It could fail from time to time. However, since 1494, and again since 1502, it had been an institutionalized norm by reason of the Consiglio Grande,[52] and it was this which established an inescapable difference between the rule of the old and the restored Medici. In 1434 there was no *vivere populare*; the city was divided into factions and a struggle for power went on between their chiefs, so that when Cosimo de' Medici acquired control, it did not seem that he had taken it from the *popolo* or *universale*, but "from one Messer Rinaldo degli Albizzi, one Messer Palla Strozzi, and other such particular men." The *popolo*, to whom the factions had denied effective power, did not increase their political participation under Cosimo, but by the fall of the faction leaders experienced a lessening of relative deprivation. Furthermore, the Medici avoided seeming to control everything directly, but shared power with a circle of intimates, who were not their equals but nevertheless enjoyed a measure of *participazione*; so that even Lorenzo il Magnifico, who (Guicciardini is still implying) possessed too much power over the inner circle, acquired it piecemeal over the years.[53]

But in 1512 none of these conditions obtain. For eighteen years the Consiglio Grande has afforded a wide measure of political participation to a large number of citizens, whose appetite for it has not left them and cannot be expected to do so. The Medici acquired power direct from the *universale*, and did it suddenly and brutally, so that there has been no opportunity for the latter to forget the experience of citizenship; and having many enemies and few friends, the members of the restored family are constrained to exercise power directly and openly, thus exacerbating the differences between the present and the

---

[52] *D. e D.*, p. 262: "E questo interviene piú oggi che mai, per essersi e' cittadini nutriti ed avezzi del 1494 sino al 1512 a uno modo di governo popularissimo e liberissimo e nel quale parendo loro essere tutti equali, con piú difficultà si assettano a ricognoscere alcuno superiore, e massime vedendo uno solo tanto interamente assoluto arbitro e signore di ogni cosa."

[53] *D. e D.*, pp. 262-63: "Aggiugnevasi quello che importa assai, che la casa de' Medici non successe a uno governo meramente populare, ma essendo la città divisa ed in mano di piú capi di fazione e fluttuata in simili modi lungo tempo ... non parse che lo stato si togliessi allo universale, ma a' capi di una altra parte; il che non dispiaceva alli uomini mediocri e populari, che con queste mutazioni non pareva diminuissono el grado loro ma piú tosto, per essere battuti e' maggiori, miglioravano condizione. E cosí lo stato che nel 1434 venne in mano de' Medici non parse tolto al populo, ma a uno messer Rinaldo degli Albizzi, a uno messer Palla Strozzi ed a altri simili particulari; ed anche e' Medici non rimasono assolutamente padroni di ogni cosa ma con qualche compagno, li quali benché fussino inferiori a loro pure avevano qualche participazione [this is the first appearance of the word]; donde la grandezza che venne in Lorenzo non fu a un tratto in casa sua, ma venne a poco a poco col corso di molti anni."

recent remembered past.[54] The many and the few, the *popolo* and the *ottimati*, are alike alienated from the regime, and since power can hardly be shared with the many, the crucial problem confronting the Medici is that of their relations with the few.

In this analysis, Guicciardini is combining the doctrine that political participation is a thing desired by men for its own sake with the thought that innovation and mutation are dangerous, because swift and sudden changes do not leave men time in which to grow accustomed to their new circumstances. The Medici of the first line found power in nobody's hands, and acquired it by degrees; but in 1494 a sudden revolution brought about widespread political participation, which another in 1512 as suddenly took away. The restored Medici are, in two senses at least, "new princes": the innovation which brought them back has been so sudden that nobody is accustomed to their rule, and this alone is a reason why they cannot govern in an accustomed way; in addition, the circumstances of the city are radically altered from what they were before 1494, because eighteen years of *vivere populare* have given the *universale* an appetite for political participation—or rather, have given them back their normal appetite for it, which under Cosimo and his heirs was temporarily in abeyance. The natures of men, or at least their social and political dispositions, can be changed; but the only two forces recognized as capable of working such a change are custom and use on the one hand, which work slowly, and political participation on the other, which quickly works effects that it takes time to undo.

Innovation, then, has made the restored Medici insecure, by giving them many enemies who are unlikely to grow accustomed and resigned to their loss of *participazione*; but it is necessary to distinguish between the categories into which these enemies are divided. The enmity of the *universale* is irremediable, less because of its intensity than because it could not be appeased short of restoring the Consiglio Grande, by overthrowing which the Medici returned to power. That of the vari-

[54] *D. e D.*, p. 263: "Oggi ogni cosa è diversa: a uno stato afatto populare e larghissimo è succeduta in uno momento la potenzia de' Medici, e ridotta assolutamente la autorità e grandezza a uno; donde è nato che e lo stato si è tolto al populo ed a uno universale di una città, e questa mutazione si è fatta in una ora, e sanzo intervallo di tempo si è venuto da qual che era grato a' più, a quello che e' più avevono esoso. E però questa materia riesce per ogni conto più difficile [cf. the usage in n. 48 above] avendo per inimici uno numero grande di cittadini, e' quali oggi si può dire non abbino nulla ed in quello stato avevono qualche participazione; né solo sono inimici loro e' cittadini di questa sorte, ma ancora sono molti altri a chi dispiace questo governo, e' quale per conoscere meglio la natura di questo male e la complessione di questo corpo, è da distinguerli in più spezie."

ous elite groups is another matter, and it is with them that Guicciardini is principally concerned. In the relatively ideal world of the *Discorso di Logrogno*, we recall, the Few had been distinguished as the class of those ambitious for glory, the pursuit of which rendered them capable of exceptional service to the *res publica*; the treatment here is very different. He begins by discounting certain groups of irreconcilables: hereditary enemies of the Medici family, and those whose ambition and restlessness makes them incapable of serving under any superior.[55] There next appears a definition of the *ottimati* proper: those whose nobility of descent or whose reputation (*essere tenuti, avere fama*) for goodness or prudence brought them eminence in the 1494 regime and would probably ensure them elite status in any system of government. From these there ought in principle to be nothing to fear, for men whose prudence and wisdom brings them social distinction have something to gain from any government and something to lose by its fall. As Lodovico Alamanni was to put it more brutally a few years later, "there is nothing to fear from the wise, for wise men never innovate."[56] But since men are not all wise, and even the wise may be deceived where their own interests are concerned, Guicciardini says he would rather not predict the behavior of most of them.[57]

His tone concerning the *ottimati* has discernibly changed. Instead of stressing their ambition and love of honor, he is concerned here with their prudence or lack of it. Prudence is, after all, the second virtue of civic aristocracies; it is that ability to act in the present while looking ahead, that exceptional knowledge of affairs possessed by those who have had exceptional opportunities of acquiring it. But what has happened is less that Guicciardini now wishes to recommend a different virtue than that the situation determining the *ottimati*'s role has altered. Ambition was the virtue of those who enjoyed elite status in a *vivere populare* and acted conspicuously before an admiring yet critical audience of their fellow citizens. But now *ottimati* and *universale* have suffered loss in the extent of their civic participation, and the question

---

[55] *D. e D.*, pp. 263-64.

[56] Albertini, *op.cit.*, p. 370: "Questa fantasia da' vechi non si leverebbe mai, ma e' sono savii et de' savi non si de' temere, perché non fanno mai novità."

[57] *D. e D.*, pp. 263-64: ". . . uomini adoperati da loro, e nondimeno che o per essere nobili e di parentado, o per essere tenuti buoni, o per avere fama di prudenti, ebbono condizione nello stato populare, e darebbe loro forse el cuore trovare luogo in ogni modo di vivere. Di costoro, perché hanno secondo li altri condizione ragionevole con questo stato, non è da temere che si mettessino a pericolo per travagliare lo stato . . . se gli hanno prudenzia o bontà doverrebbono desiderare che questo governo durassi. . . . Ma perché li uomini non sono tutti savi ed e' piú si ingannano ne' casi loro particulari, io non darei iudicio fermo dello animo di una grande parte di costoro."

under discussion is essentially whether the former are going to be able to resume leading roles under Medici auspices. But since the Medici monopolize power, there is tension between them and the excluded *ottimati*; and since the *universale* are not going to resume power, they will be no friendly audience to the *ottimati*'s readmission to it. Because there has been innovation, there has been a general loss of security; men are become one another's enemies. Guicciardini's stress on the need for prudence rather than ambition—the prudence which teaches what course the ship should steer—occurs in, and is explained by, the same context as his characterization of the elite as distinguished by descent and reputation, which comes close to making them creatures of fortune.

He proceeds to consider a question which, significantly, he sees as one for the Medici rather than the *ottimati* to determine. Is the best strategy for the restored regime one of ingratiating itself with the *universale*, distributing honors and offices as nearly as possible as they would be distributed under a popular government, and making itself the protector of personal liberty against oppression by the great; or one of repressing all attempts at popular initiative and ruling by the aid of a small number of partisans to whom the distribution of honors is confined?[58] Behind the first alternative lies the question whether peace, order, and justice will reconcile the many to their loss of *participazione*; behind the second, the problem whether the *ottimati* can retain their elite status at a price less than that of becoming permanent dependents of the ruling family. In the rest of this *discorso*, Guicciardini rehearses the arguments in favor of the former strategy. For the *universale*, good government is no substitute for self-government; they will be content with no government, however just or liberal in its distribution of office, which does not give them back the *dolcezza* of participation in the Consiglio Grande, and if this cannot be given them their aspirations must be suppressed.[59] But the Medici cannot do this without enlisting a band of devoted adherents, and these must be

[58] *D. e D.*, p. 265.

[59] *D. e D.*, pp. 265-66: "Alleganne che el primo intento di chi regge e governi ha a essere di conservare sé e lo stato suo, ed avendo questo intento li bisogna tenere bassi e battuti quegli che li sono inimici e non si possono guadagnare per amici, e di questa sorte dicono essere non solo quelli che si sono scoperti particolarmente inimici de' Medici, ma in genere tutto lo universale della città, el quale non ha odio con loro per ingiurie e paure private, ne perché governino ingiustamente, ma solo perché avando gustata diciotto anni la dolcezza di quello vivere populare, vorrebbono ritornarvi ed ogni altra cosa dispiace loro. E però né co' portamenti buoni, né col favorire la giustizia, né col distribuire largamente li onori e li utili si satisfaranno; anzi sempre desidereranno mutazione per ritornare a quello consiglio grande e travagliarsi nel governo ed amministrazione publica."

recruited from the ranks of the ambitious, to whom shall be granted a monopoly of office in such a way as to make it clear that their monopoly depends on the Medici and would fall with them. Ambition will unite with self-interest to make these persons enthusiastic partisans instead of half-hearted friends. But at this point Guicciardini breaks off the treatise of 1513 with the remark that he is altogether opposed to these arguments.[60]

He may have thought it less than prudent for the *ottimati* to align themselves with the Medici in open hostility to the *popolo*, or less than honorable for them to acknowledge a condition so far short of freedom as open dependence on the Medici for their position. His immediate personal solution to the problem we know; but as a theoretical analyst he was employing a scheme which made it very hard to see how Medicean rule could lose the innovatory character that had made it enemies, or the aristocracy avoid a choice between the Medici and dependence, or citizenship and the Consiglio Grande. Guicciardini had contemporaries who were prepared to give advice even more ruthless than that he rejected. One of them, Paolo Vettori, had written in 1512 a memorandum for Cardinal de' Medici on his departure for Rome and the papal election. "Your ancestors," he told the head of the family, "held this city by management (*industria*) rather than force; you, however, must hold it by force. The reason is that since 1502 the city has been very well governed, and the memory of this will always make war on you; you have too many enemies to hold power through any combination you could possibly form within the walls. But the subject countryside—the *contado*—has been thoroughly badly governed, and if you arm it and place it under your direct patronage, in six months you will be safer than if you had an army of Spaniards to protect you."[61] Vettori was proposing a reversal of Machiavelli's policy of organizing the

---

[60] *D. e D.*, p. 266: ". . . le quali benché paino colorate, io nondimeno ne sono in diversa opinione." These are the *discorso*'s final words.

[61] Albertini, p. 345: "Li antecessori vostri, cominciandosi da Cosimo e venendo infino a Piero, usorno in tenere questo Stato piú industria che forza. A voi è necessario usare piú forza che industria, perché voi ci avete piú nimici e manco ordine a saddisfarli. . . . Tenere appresso intelligentia drento, tenere le gente d'arme a vostro proposito; ma tutte queste forze non bastano, perché questa città è troppo grossa e ci sono troppi malcontenti . . . perché voi avete a intendere che li dieci anni passati la citta è stata benissimo, in modo che sempre la memoria di qual tempo vi farà guerra. Da l'altra parte, il contado e distretto vostro è stato malissimo, talmente che la città voi non ve la potete riguadagnare, ma sibene il contado. E se voi lo armate, e li armati intrattenete con il difenderli da' rettori di fuori e da' magistrati di dentro che li assassinono, e che voi in fatto diventiate loro patroni, e non passano sei mesi da oggi, che vi parrà essere piú securi in Firenze che se voi avessi un esercito di Spagnuoli a Prato in favore vostro."

contadini as a civic militia, and his point was, of course, that since the
contadini lacked civic rights they had shown no wish to defend the city
against the Spaniards,[62] but would be glad to help the Medici hold
down a city that exploited them. But this would not make citizens of
them. Vettori was predicting what would in fact be a feature of Medicean rule under the ducal system which developed after 1530, when
the *contado* was favored if not actually armed; by that time, however,
all pretense that the Medici ruled as citizens among other citizens had
been given up.

But the nature of the optimate dilemma has now been plainly stated.
Their sense of being an exclusive elite was strong enough to make
them welcome the suppression of the Consiglio Grande and the prospect of exercising a *governo stretto* together with the Medici; but at
the same time it made them anxious to remain a civic aristocracy,
depending on no superior and exercising among themselves an equality
which left the Medici no acceptable role other than that of *primus
inter pares*. Both Guicciardini and Vettori, however, and there are
others, display a clear awareness that if this was possible under the
conditions of 1434-1494, it may not be so now: the fall of Piero, the
rise and fall of the Consiglio, have changed too much. The idealization
of Lorenzo il Magnifico had clearly something that was nostalgic about
it: the myth of a golden moment in which the ideal of *primus inter
pares*, of an Augustan principate, was for once realized. But the hard
cutting edge of Florentine political analysis is felt whenever it is
pointed out that the many as well as the few enjoyed *participazione*
under the Savonarolan constitution and feel its recent loss, so that
whenever the *ottimati* are thought of as bringing pressure to bear on
the Medici to take them into a partnership of equality, the jealous desire
of the *popolo* for rights which are not to be restored to them must be
thought of as exerting its own pressure: as making it desirable on the
one hand for the Medici to make concessions to the *ottimati*, but on
the other as rendering the *ottimati* so much the dependents of the
Medici as to cancel out much of the first effect. Guicciardini at this
stage may be thought of as representing those who doubted if the *ottimati* could survive as a civic aristocracy except in a context of civic
freedom, and so leaned (though increasingly as a theoretical exercise)
toward some restoration of *participazione* to the many, picturing the
Medici at the head of something like a Venetian constitution. Vettori
speaks for those who were prepared to safeguard optimate ascendancy
by becoming the associates of the Medici in a form of rule which was
not exercised through primacy among equals at all, even if this meant

[62] A point perhaps never recognized in Machiavelli's own writings.

148

winding up the whole experiment in classical citizenship at Florence. What is most striking is the employment by both men of the view that the Medici are innovators, that their rule is "new" both in the sense that people are unaccustomed to it and in the sense that it is the product of changed conditions. It is innovation—meaning less the many's acquisition of *participazione* in 1494 than their loss of it in 1512—that is making the exercise of citizenship by any significant number difficult if not impossible; and either former conditions must be restored, or the city must resign itself to new and non-civic political relationships.

This pattern of ideas is found restated in certain writings of the year 1516—by which date, it should be observed, there may have been time for the content of Machiavelli's *Il Principe* to become known in some Florentine circles, though it was only about then that he completed the dedication of that work to Lorenzo de' Medici, duke of Urbino. The occasion of that dedication was the growing illness of Giuliano and his death in March 1516, and the increasing military activity of Lorenzo and his acquisition of the duchy for which he was now named. Since, as we shall see, it is doubtful whether Machiavelli, insofar as he had the Medici in mind when he wrote his study of "new princes," was thinking of their role in Florentine politics, rather than their acquisition of new lordships and territories in central Italy, it is interesting that the parallels with his thought are especially plain in Guicciardini's *discorso* on "how to assure the government to the house of Medici,"[63] written to survey the situation after three years of the pontificate of Leo X. That pope's election, Guicciardini observes, brought about a marvelous access of confidence in the rule of the family at Florence, but its main effect has been to encourage his kinsmen to neglect consolidating their position there in pursuit of power elsewhere in Italy. The rashness of this course is obvious. In places such as Urbino their power is new and resentment of its acquisition still vivid, and it depends so largely on one man's tenure of life and papacy[64] that Guicciardini is led to draw what to any reader of *Il Principe* is the obvious parallel: that with Cesare Borgia, whose power was gam-

---

[63] *D. e D.*, pp. 267-81: "Del modo di assicurare lo stato alla casa de' Medici."

[64] *D. e D.*, p. 269: ". . . possono, vivente el pontefice, valersi assai della opportunità e potenzia di qui a acquistare stati e colorire e' loro disegni; morto el pontefice, chi non vede quanto importerà questo braccio a mantenersi quello che aranno acquistato? Gli altri stati da loro medesimi saranno difficili anzi difficillimi a conservarli, perché saranno nuovi, aranno tutti opposizione potentissime o di vicini potenti o di chi vi pretenderà su diritto, o di pessime disposizione di populi; in questo, adattandocisi bene drento, non sarà difficile el mantenercisi, perché el governare loro questo stato non offende né toglie a persona se non a' cittadini medesimi, a' quali satisfare, come di sotto si dirà, non è difficile."

bled on his father's papacy and perished with him. More remarkable
still, he goes on to analyze the case of Francesco Sforza, who acquired
power over a Milan already long used to the rule of the Visconti family and, by marrying the natural daughter of the last Visconti duke,
was able to appear as their legitimate inheritor.[65] But the Medici are
not hereditary rulers at Urbino, where their rule is analogous to that
of Borgia; while at Florence they are not *signori naturali* either, but
legitimized by their descent from citizens whose primacy was exercised
civilmente e privatamente.[66] As wise steersmen and navigators make
use of a calm to overhaul the ship's timbers and equipment, so they
must make use of Leo's lifetime to consolidate at Florence the only
basis on which their power can outlive him. This basis is, of course,
that of civic relationships within the city—and it is noteworthy how
the analogy of the steersman slides, almost in mid-sentence, into that of
the doctor dealing with a sick man whose malady can be remedied if
it cannot be wholly cured.[67]

The sickness in question is still that analysed in 1513: the Medici
propensity to believe that they must take all business openly into their

[65] *D. e D.*, pp. 270-71: ". . . abbiamo lo esemplo del Valentino e la ragione ci è
manifesta; perché privati acquistare stati grandi è cosa ardua ma molto piú ardua
conservarli, per infinite difficultà che si tira drieto uno principato nuovo, massime
in uno principe nuovo. Riuscí solo a Francesco Sforza el conservarsi nello stato
di Milano ma vi concorsono molti cagione. . . . Aggiunsesi che trovò uno stato
che, benché avessi goduto libertà, era solito a essere signoreggiato da altri, ed a
chi era tanto disforme la libertà quanto e disforme a' populi liberi la servitù; tutte
condizioni da fare facilità grandissima a conservare, e che rare volte si abattono
a chi acquista nuovi domini, e' quali el piú delle volte si tolgono a' populi liberi
o a' signori naturali. Lui piú tosto si può dire che occupassi una eredità vacante,
che togliessi nulla di quello di altri; anzi parve a qual populo avere beneficio
grande che li pigliassi, vedendosi per quello modo trarre di bocca a' viniziani, di
chi naturalmente erano inimicissimi." It would indeed be easy to believe that
Guicciardini was acquainted with *Il Principe* when he wrote this passage.

[66] *D. e D.*, p. 270: ". . . benché gli abbino uno papa, e' non sono però signori
naturali, anzi cittadini e discesi di padri che vissino benché fussino grandi, sempre
civilmente e privatamente."

[67] *D. e D.*, p. 268: "E se bene la grandezza del papato non lascia conoscere
questo danno, non è ragione sufficiente a sprezzarlo perché le qualità de' tempi e
felicità si mutono, ed è debole cosa essere tutto fondato in sulla vita di uno uomo
solo, quale quando morissi, se vedrebbono li effetti di questi disordini. . . . E però
come e' marinai prudenti quando sono in porto o in bonaccia rassettano el loro
legno e tutti li instrumenti di quello per potere resistere alla futura tempesta, cosí
chi ha in mano el timone di questo stato doverrebbe in tanto ocio e commodità
rassettare e disporre bene tutte le membre di questo corpo, per potere in ogni
accidente che venissi, valersi di tutto el nervo e virtù sua. Il che certo chi con-
siderassi bene le cause e le origine di questi mali, non doverrebbe diffidarsi di
potere sanza difficultà grande condurre questo ammalato se non in ottima, almeno
in buona disposizione."

own hands, trust nobody but regard all as potential rivals, and act swiftly to repress anyone whose rivalry looks like becoming actual.[68] This, Guicciardini sees plainly, is reducing their power to a base of support so narrow as to be increasingly insecure; and the pity of it is that this generalized mistrust is largely unnecessary. The aristocracy, he insists, have no longer any choice but to support the Medici. They connived at, and were identified with, the destruction of the Consiglio Grande in 1512 to such an extent that the populace now identifies them with the restoration of the Medici. There can be no repetition of the conditions of 1494, when the Medici were driven out but the *ottimati* left in a position of leadership in the regime that resulted; any popular revolt now would involve the destruction of their elite position (as Guicciardini was to see happen in 1529-1530).[69] Therefore the *ottimati* present no threat to the ruling family, which has everything to gain from seeking their friendship, allowing them liberty of action and strengthening its position by the aid, counsel, and affection which would then be given it.

In this *discorso* Guicciardini seems more than usually identified with the group for whom he is writing—the first person plural is constantly used—and there is an audible note of desperation. It may be wondered whether his arguments do not destroy the basis of the aristocracy's claim to be treated as equals, and leave their role one of deference and dependence. There is another *discorso*, dated later in 1516, on the consolidation of Medicean rule, in which the policy advocated is more drastic, because more subtle, even than that proposed by Paolo Vettori. The author of this, Lodovico Alamanni,[70] concurs with Guicciar-

---

[68] *D. e D.*, pp. 272-73.

[69] *D. e D.*, p. 275: ". . . e nondimeno era uno zucchero a petto a quello che diventerebbe se si facessi nuova mutazione, perché a iudicio mio, della larghezza che era allora a quella che si introdurrebbe sarebbe tanta differenzia quanta è dalla strettezza che è oggi a quella che era a tempo di Lorenzo.

"Cosi causerebbono e' sospetti, la rabbia e la ignoranzia degli uomini in chi verrebbe lo stato; ne sia alcuno che pensi che la fussi mutazione simile a quella del 94, dove li amici de' Medici, che erano el fiore della città, furono conservati e doppo pochi mesi messi insieme con li altri in participazione del governo. Oggi sarebbe pericoloso non si facessi crudelmente . . . porterebbe pericolo di esilio, di perdita di beni e simili ruine. . . ."

[70] Albertini, pp. 362-71: "Discorso di Lodovico Alamanni sopra il fermare lo stato di Firenze nella devozione de' Medici"—title given to the piece by Roberto Ridolfi. For Alamanni's career, and the need to distinguish him from his republican brother, Luigi, see Albertini, pp. 43-45. See also G. Guidi, "La teoria delle 'tre ambizioni' nel pensiero politico fiorentino del primo Cinquecento," in *Il Pensiero Politico*, vol. 5, pt. 2 (1972), pp. 241-59. An English translation of this *discorso* may be found on pp. 214-20 of *Social and Economic Foundations of the Italian Renaissance*, ed. Anthony Molho (New York: John Wiley and Sons, 1969).

dini in holding that the insecurity of Lorenzo's Italian position, as
dependent upon the life of Leo X, renders it all the more necessary to
consolidate a permanent tenure of power at Florence,[71] but differs from
him radically in his views on how this may be done. He agrees that the
widespread desire among citizens for a share in power constitutes a
permanent challenge to the retention of power in a few men's hands,
but claims to know of ways in which this desire may be converted into
something else. This is not to be achieved by terrorism, which if indis-
criminate must destroy friends as well as enemies and if discriminating
must wait for enemies to show their hands, by exiling citizens to form
groups of irreconcilable conspirators, or by killing men without trial,
which creates new tensions as well as disgracing oneself. The Roman
proscriptions were possible only because there was no center of power
left in the world outside Rome, while Agathocles of Syracuse and Oliverotto da Fermo were criminals of such desperation that they hardly
cared what were the consequences of their acts.[72] Alamanni was an
acquaintance of Machiavelli's and it does sound as if he had been reading *Il Principe*, where Agathocles and Oliverotto appear as types of
pure criminality. But the analysis develops in a direction where neither
Machiavelli nor Guicciardini could be said to follow. Alamanni knew,
with everyone else, that the Medici of 1434-1494 had ruled by creating
a group of citizens who owed office and status to them, and followed
their wishes in discharging their public duties. It was the essence of
both the optimate and the republican analyses that even if this had not
been a source of instability before 1494, it would be impossible to
resume it in the changed conditions after 1512. Alamanni denied this
contention at considerable length,[73] by arguments which culminated
in his denying the Savonarolan and Guicciardinian thesis that the addic-
tion of the Florentines to civic *participazione* was unalterable.

There were, he argued in a recension of familiar language,[74] three

---

[71] Albertini, p. 363. [72] Albertini, pp. 366-68.

[73] Albertini, p. 368: ". . . so che molti altri sono che contradicono col dire che
per essere e' tempi et le conditioni diverse, bisogna pensare ad diversi modi, perché
quegli medesimi non servirebbono. Ma io dico che d'alhora in qua le difficultà
son bene multiplicate, ma non già variate o cresciute. Et per quelle che son vechie
et consuete, sono optime e' vechi modi di Lorenzo vechio; et per queste che di
novo ce si conoscono, sono ancora de' remedii promptissimi et sicuri, in modo che
cosí sia facile il tenere hora questo stato come se fussi alhora il tener quello. Et
quando bene ad alcuni paressi il contrario, e' quali affirmassino quelli tempi havere
piú vantaggio che questi, alleghino quel che voglino, che a tucto responderà la
ragione."

[74] Albertini, pp. 368-69: "Diranno ancora che a tempo di Lorenzo non era stato
un Consiglio grande come è questo, che tanto aliena stato le menti de' cittadini:
et io dico che questa difficultà non è si grande che la non si medichi agevolmente,
perché infra e' cittadini fiorentini sono di tre sorte di animi. . . ."

levels of ambition discernible in a body of citizens. Some were ambitious to the point of desiring admission to the highest councils of government; others desired only to be the recipients of honors and offices; others again had little ambition beyond being left alone and unvexed in their private pursuits. These last, of course, were Aristotle's many, and it is easy to see how the limitations which an Aristotelian sociology of knowledge imposed on their political understanding could be used to reduce their *participazione* to near vanishing point. Alamanni had little difficulty in indicating how the Medici might manage both this and the second class. It was in dealing with the third—the elite of the honorably ambitious described by Guicciardini in the *Discorso di Logrogno*—that he achieved originality as a political thinker within the limits of the language of his time. Men were what they were, he agreed with a host of predecessors, because of the usages which had become second nature with them, and after a certain age or stage, this nature could not be altered by ordinary means. Among the highly ambitious of Florence, the older men were so deeply inured to seeking public honors through the pursuit of a citizen's career that they would never be reconciled to a regime which must deny them the chance of open competition and unlimited rewards. But the younger men were another matter, and there existed an alternative form of political culture which might be used to divert them from citizenship (*civilità*). This was the pursuit of honor *alli costumi cortesani*,[75] the courtier's life, in no way less honorable or—its devotees might assert—less free than the citizen's, of which Castiglione's classic study, completed in 1518, had as its setting that Urbino where Lorenzo's ambitions were fixed, and introduced Giuliano as a speaker in the dialogue. In serving his prince, the young aristocrat found a way of life; and Alamanni, drily and with none of Castiglione's devotion, outlined its features: the intimacy of the prince, command in the prince's guards, missions in the prince's diplomatic interests, the modes of dress specifically opposed to those of a civic patriciate—Guicciardini's interest

---

[75] Albertini, p. 370: "Ma e' sono avezzi in una certa loro asineria piú presto che libertà, che in Fiorenza non degnano di fare reverentia a qualunche, bene la meritassi, si non a' suoi magistrati, et a quegli per forza et con fatica. Et per questo sono tanto alieni da' modi delle corte, che io credo che pochi altri sieno tanto; non dimeno, quando sono di fuori, non fanno cosí. Credo proceda da questo che nel principio dovea parere loro cosa troppo disadacta il cavarsi quel loro cappuccio; et questa loro infingardagine si ridusse in consuetudine, et di consuetudine in natura; et per quel che io lo credo, è che quando e' sono fuor della loro terra et di quello habito, manco par loro fatica assai el conversare co' principi. Questa fantasia da' vechi non si leverebbe mai, ma e' sono savii et de' savi non si de' [sic] temere, perché non fanno mai novità. E' giovani facilmente si divezzarebbono da questa civilità et assuefarebbonsi alli costumi cortesani, se'l principe volessi."

in sumptuary legislation travestied and turned against him—by which an intelligent ruler might draw the young men to him, refute in advance the reproach that their way of life lacked liberty, and transform their usages, values, and personalities until the tension between authority and *participazione* lost all meaning.[76] The Grand Duchy of Tuscany, whose foundation by another Cosimo de' Medici lay two decades in the future as Alamanni wrote, was to be based on just such a political culture, whether or not he had correctly predicted the effects on the Florentine personality of replacing the citizen with the courtier ideal.

Alamanni, it may seem as we pursue the next stage of this study, had solved a problem which eluded Machiavelli if he did not evade it: that of showing how the "new prince" might reinforce his position by getting the stabilizing effects of custom on his side; and he had done so by utilizing the precept that "use is another nature" in the light of the existence of an alternative political culture to which Machiavelli and Guicciardini remained totally indifferent. But what concerns us immediately is the problem in whose context all these Florentines worked: that of innovation. Guicciardini, Vettori, and Alamanni all analyzed the position of the restored Medici in the light of what was unfamiliar and unprecedented about it, and examined the new to see what difficulties it had thrown in the path of the *ottimati*'s enjoyment of their chosen, and allegedly traditional, function of civic leadership. The more conservative and humanist among them (notably the circle of the Orti Oricellari, of whom more later) moved in a direction which led toward idealization of Venice on Aristotelian and Polybian grounds; the more radical and *deraciné* toward abandonment of the civic for the courtly ideal. But the central theme was innovation and the new prince. In this setting, Machiavelli's *Il Principe*, written for the most part in 1512-1513, takes on a new aspect, that of the greatest of all theoretical explorations of the politics of innovation. Machiavelli's lack of optimate status—he belonged to the second of Alamanni's three classes—

[76] Albertini, pp. 370-71: "Ultra questo, quel che piú è da stimare, gli divesserà da quella civilità che gli aliena sì da' suoi costumi; perciò che a quegli che per Sua Ex.tia piglieranno la cappa et lasciaranno el cappuccio, interverrà come se si facessino frati, perché renuntiaranno alla republica et faranno professione all'ordine suo et mai piú poi potranno pretendere al grado civile o alla benivolentia del populo: et per questo tucta la loro ambizione si volgerà ad guadagnarsi el favore de Sua Ex.tia. . . Et correndo li anni, di mano in mano, se si terrà il medesimo ordine di eleggere et di chiamare ad sé quegli giovani che verranno su, e quali hora sono fanciulli, rimettendo al governo della città quegli che hora son giovani et alhora saranno vechi, allevati nondimeno nella sua scuola, ne nascerà che nella città nostra non si saprà vivere senza un principe che gl'intractenga dove hora pare tucto il contrario."

set him free from optimate concerns; he could never be either a senator or a courtier, and his mind was liberated to explore the absorbing topic of the new prince's relations with his environment. It is this which gives *Il Principe* the standing of an act of intellectual revolution: a breakthrough into new fields of theoretic relevance.

CHAPTER VI

THE MEDICEAN RESTORATION

B) Machiavelli's *Il Principe*

MACHIAVELLI, beginning work on *Il Principe* in 1512, does not in this treatise consider innovation from the aspect of its impact on citizenship; that topic is reserved for his work on republics. That is to say, he identifies himself neither with the *ottimati*, struggling to retain their character as a citizen elite, nor with those—Alamanni in 1516 would group them with the Savonarolans—who demanded the restoration of the Council and widespread *participazione*. *Il Principe* is not a work of ideology, in the sense that it cannot be identified as expressing the outlook of a group. It is rather an analytic study of innovation and its consequences; but within that character, it proceeds straight to the analysis of the ultimate problem raised by both innovation and the decay of citizenship. This was the problem of *fortuna*, to which Guicciardini and the lesser *ottimati* had not yet addressed themselves, perhaps because the assumption that they belonged to an elite was still strong enough to carry the implication that they were relatively secure. Machiavelli led too vulnerable an existence to make any such assumptions concerning himself; but the theoretical exploration into which he was led was not inconsistent with the optimate intellectual position. If politics be thought of as the art of dealing with the contingent event, it is the art of dealing with *fortuna* as the force which directs such events and thus symbolizes pure, uncontrolled, and unlegitimated contingency. In proportion as the political system ceases to be a universal and is seen as a particular, it becomes difficult for it to do this. The republic can dominate *fortuna* only by integrating its citizens in a self-sufficient *universitas*, but this in turn depends on the freely participating and morally assenting citizen. The decay of citizenship leads to the decline of the republic and the ascendancy of *fortuna*; when this is brought about by innovation—the uncontrolled act having uncontrolled consequences in time—the point is underlined. Machiavelli's treatment of the "new prince"—the ruler as innovator—therefore isolates him from the desire of *ottimati* and others to continue acting as citizens, and considers him and those he rules as acting solely in their relations with *fortuna*. The confrontation of citizenship itself with *fortuna* is a topic reserved for the *Discorsi*.

A further point which can never be too often made is that the problem of *fortuna* is a problem in virtue. To every thinker in the Boethian tradition, *virtus* was that by which the good man imposed form on his *fortuna*. Civic humanism, identifying the good man with the citizen, politicized virtue and rendered it dependent on the virtue of others. If *virtus* could only exist where citizens associated in pursuit of a *res publica*, then the *politeia* or constitution—Aristotle's functionally differentiated structure of participation—became practically identical with virtue itself. If the good man could practice his virtue only within a frame of citizenship, the collapse of such a frame, whether through violent innovation or through the creeping dependence of some upon others, corrupted the virtue of the powerful as well as the powerless; the tyrant could not be a good man because he had no fellow citizens. But at this point the ability of the republic to sustain itself against internal and external shocks—*fortuna* as the symbol of contingency— became identical with *virtus* as the Roman antithesis to *fortuna*. The virtue of the citizens was the stability of the *politeia*, and *vice versa*; politically and morally, the *vivere civile* was the only defense against the ascendancy of *fortuna*, and the necessary prerequisite of virtue in the individual. What Machiavelli is doing, in the most notorious passages of *Il Principe*, is reverting to the formal implementation of the Roman definition and asking whether there is any *virtù* by which the innovator, self-isolated from moral society, can impose form upon his *fortuna* and whether there will be any moral quality in such a *virtù* or in the political consequences which can be imagined as flowing from its exercise. Since the problem only exists as the result of innovation, which is a political act, its exploration must be conducted in terms of further political action.

This study adopts a formal and analytical approach to *Il Principe*, which is not a formal or analytical treatise; it seeks to bring out certain of its implications by relating them to two schemes of ideas, the one rehearsing the modes of cognizing and acting upon the particular which appear to have been available in medieval and Renaissance political thought, the other detailing humanist and Florentine thought on the relation of citizenship, virtue, and *fortuna*. Any analytical approach must of necessity be limited to its own methodology, and there will be aspects of Machiavelli's thought in *Il Principe* not dealt with here. But so many works have attempted to interpret this classic either by plunging directly into such elusive problems as Machiavelli's moral outlook and his state of mind as he contemplated Florence and Italy in 1512, or by a purely textual exegesis not directed to previously specified problems, that there may be room for an exegesis conducted in terms of the heuristic models used in this book.[1]

Viewed in this way, then, *Il Principe* becomes a typology of innovators and their relations with *fortuna*. A classificatory approach is adopted at the outset and runs through key chapters of the book. All governments are either republics or monarchies; all monarchies (or principalities) are either hereditary or new. The latter are either totally new or a mixture of hereditary and newly acquired territories. Acquired territories have been accustomed either to liberty or to the rule of another prince; their new ruler has acquired them either by the armed force of others or by his own, either by *fortuna* or by *virtù*.

This typically Machiavellian rattle of antitheses, concluding with the word most crucial in the entire treatise, makes up the whole of chapter I.[2] The vital distinction, which the next chapter further explores, is that between the hereditary prince (*principe naturale*)[3] and the new. The former, Machiavelli explains, enjoys traditional legitimacy; the inhabitants are *assuefatti* to his *sangue*, used to being ruled by persons of his line and name, and the weight of use and custom on his side is such that as long as he observes ancestral conventions, he can only lose his *stato* if some extraordinary accident befalls him; and if his supplanter makes any slip or suffers any mischance, he will probably regain his position. In short, he is legitimized by custom and tradition, he is relatively invulnerable to *fortuna*, and he has little need of extraordinary *virtù*.[4] These propositions follow one from another, and

---

[1] For an earlier statement of this interpretation, see the author's "Custom and Grace, Form and Matter: An Approach to Machiavelli's Concept of Innovation," in Martin Fleisher (ed.), *Machiavelli and the Nature of Political Thought* (New York: Atheneum, 1972), pp. 153-74.

[2] Niccolò Machiavelli, *Opere* (a cura di Mario Bonfantini; Milan and Naples: Riccardo Ricciardi Editore; vol. 29 in series *La Letteratura Italiana: Storia e Testi*, undated but 1954), hereafter cited as *Opere*, p. 5: "Tutti gli stati, tutti e dominii che hanno avuto e hanno imperio sopra li uomini, sono stati e sono o republiche o principati. E' principati sono: o ereditarii, de' quali el sangue del loro signore ne sia suto lungo tempo principe, o e' sono nuovi. E' nuovi, o e' sono nuovi tutti, come fu Milano a Francesco Sforza, o e' sono come membri aggiunti allo stato ereditario del principe che li acquista, come è el regno di Napoli al re di Spagna. Sono questi dominii cosi acquistati, o consueti a vivere sotto uno principe o usi ad essere liberi; e acquistonsi o con le armi d'altri o con le proprie, o per fortuna o per virtù."

[3] Chapter II is entitled "Of Hereditary Principalities" in both the Latin and the Italian chapter headings, as in chapter I; but the alternative term first appears in the second paragraph: "Perché el principe naturale ha minori cagioni e minore necessità di offendere. . . ."

[4] *Opere*, p. 5: ". . . se tale principe è di ordinaria industria, sempre si manterrà nel suo stato se non è una estraordinaria ed eccessiva forza che ne lo privi . . ." Compare *Discorsi*, III, v, where it is made clear that a hereditary prince need fear

in each case the reverse is true of the new prince. Machiavelli, then, is employing ancient usage as the antithesis of *fortuna* and *virtù*; it is when the first is lacking that the relations between the second and third become crucial. We see at once that we are still in the conceptual world of medieval politics insofar as it is still impossible to conceive of legitimacy without tradition and ancient usage, but moving out of it fast insofar as Machiavelli is prepared to examine the nature of rule where legitimacy is lacking. It should further be emphasized that a fully developed transalpine monarchy of Machiavelli's day had more to legitimize it than ancient usage alone: it could claim to represent a universal order, moral, sacred, and rational; in addition to the people being anciently accustomed to its rule, it could derive legitimacy from the body of ancient customary law which it administered in its *juris-dictio*; and it could claim to exercise a perhaps providentially directed set of skills in its *gubernaculum*. Machiavelli does not paint a portrait in depth of such a trebly legitimized system of rule, though we know from his observations on French monarchy[5] that he was familiar with many of its features. The only instance of hereditary rule in this chapter of *Il Principe* is Italian, that of the Este of Ferrara,[6] and he indicates that such families are merely successful usurpers who have maintained themselves through enough generations for the original innovation to be forgotten.[7] It is a long stride from the Este to—let us say—the anointed Capetians; yet even the Este are posed antithetically to the "new prince." We now know that *Il Principe* is not a handbook for the use of kings—highly interesting though some of them found it—or a treatise on "absolute monarchy." An absolute monarch like Fortescue's king ruling *regaliter tantum* was defined by his relation to a body of law which was part of the complex scheme of his own legitimation; the "new prince" lacked legitimacy altogether and consequently was not what we mean by a king. A king was not new, and could deny that he was the child of fortune—except on the occasions when he

losing his throne only if he systematically disregards the ancient customs of his people.

[5] *Ritratto delle Cose di Francia*, in *Opere*, pp. 471-86. In "Niccolò Machiavelli politologo," published in Gilmore, ed., *Studies in Machiavelli*, Nicola Matteucci has juxtaposed his observations on the monarchy of France with his studies of the Roman republic, and has supposed that these represent Machiavelli's two most admired forms of government. This striking interpretation is characterized as "strutturale e non evolutivo" (Gilmore, p. 211).

[6] *Opere*, p. 6, and Bonfantini's note, in which he objects that the Este dukes were not lacking in *virtù*.

[7] *Ibid.*: "E nella antiquità e continuazione del dominio sono spente le memorie e le cagioni delle innovazioni: perché sempre una mutazione lascia lo addentellato per la edificazione dell'altra." It looks as if the *memorie* are themselves *cagioni*.

acquired a territory to which he had no previous title; Ferdinand of Aragon is Machiavelli's example here.

Il Principe is a study of the "new prince"—we know this from Machiavelli's correspondence as well as from internal evidence—or rather of that class of political innovators to which he belongs. The newness of his rule means that he has performed an innovation, overthrowing or replacing some form of government which preceded him. In doing this he must have injured many people, who are not reconciled to his rule, while those who welcomed his arrival now expect more from him than he is able to provide.[8] The situation is that analyzed by contemporary *ottimati* in the specifically Florentine context: because some are alienated and others unsatisfied, society is atomized into a chaos of unreconciled and conflicting wills, the ruler lacks legitimacy, and citizenship is not possible. Machiavelli, however, conducts his analysis neither in the specific context of Florence nor with regard to the specific problem of citizenship; his concern is solely with the relations between the innovator and fortune. For this reason it is never possible to say exactly how far *Il Principe* is intended to illuminate the problems faced by the restored Medici in their government of Florence. There is some evidence for the view that it was meant to advise Giuliano and Lorenzo on the acquisition of dominions elsewhere in Italy, but in doing this the Medici would differ little from other princely families. What was peculiar to them was the former nature and the history of their power in Florence, and it was partly in analyzing this that Guicciardini, Vettori, and Alamanni were led to ascribe to the restored Medici some of the characteristics of the *principe nuovo*. But where they specified, in varying degrees of detail, the exact historical changes that had constituted this innovation, Machiavelli in *Il Principe* starts from innovation as an abstract principle; and the specific case that most closely resembles that of the Medicean ruler—the case of a citizen who becomes a prince by the support of a party of his fellow citizens—is considered in chapter IX carefully, it is true, but without special emphasis, as one among a gallery of types of "new prince." *Il Principe*, formally anatomized, would seem to be a theoretical treatise, inspired by a specific situation but not directed at it. We must return to the themes of the innovator and his fortune.

Innovation, the overthrow of an established system, opens the door to fortune because it offends some and disturbs all, creating a situation in which they have not yet had time to grow accustomed to the new order. Usage is the only alternative to fortune; in republican theory

---

[8] *Ibid.*: ". . . in modo che tu hai inimici tutti quelli che hai offesi in occupare quello principato, e non ti puoi mantenere amici quelli che vi ti hanno messo, per non li potere satisfare in quel modo che si erano presupposto . . ."

we would investigate the prospects of a *vivere civile* being restored, but *Il Principe* is not concerned with republics or primarily with citizenship. The prince's new subjects are not accustomed to him, and consequently he does not have the assurance of their loyalty: ". . . one change always leaves the way open for the initiation of another."[9] He is contrasted with the hereditary prince, and so must be thought of as striving to attain the stability of the latter, whose family have maintained themselves for so long that the injuries and disappointments of the original innovation are forgotten and—as the term *principe naturale* implies—obedience to them has become part of the inherited "second nature" of the people. But how is the new prince to do this? How, we might ask though Machiavelli does not, did the hereditary prince's ancestors bring it off? Merely allowing time to elapse will not suffice, since the situation may change suddenly. Here as elsewhere in his writings, Machiavelli is intensely scornful of the advice, often given by contemporaries, to temporize and "enjoy the advantages of delay."[10] In a situation not prestabilized, so that nobody knew what time might bring, temporization was the least appropriate of strategies.

The new prince, therefore, required exceptional and extraordinary qualities, standing outside the norm defined by the case of the *principe naturale*. These qualities might be termed *virtù*, that by which form was imposed on the matter of *fortuna*, but since form and matter must be appropriate to one another it followed that the innovator's exposure to fortune, being extraordinary, must be met by extraordinary *virtù*. Machiavelli proceeded on the assumption that situations dominated by fortune were not uniformly chaotic; there were strategic variations in them, and various strategies which *virtù* might consequently adopt. He had prepared the ground for this assumption in two ways. First, by defining innovation as the destruction of a previously existing legitimatory system, he had established that previous systems might vary and the prince's new subjects react variously to their loss. Former citizens of a republic would be harder to accustom to his rule than former subjects of another prince, since in the one case established norms of behavior must be transformed and in the second they need only be transferred.[11] Secondly, he had distinguished between several modes

---

[9] See n. 7 above.

[10] The *principe naturale*, however, can afford "non preterire l'ordine de' sua [suoi] antenati, e dipoi temporeggiare con gli accidenti," *Opere*, p. 5. See Gilbert, *Machiavelli and Guicciardini*, p. 33, for this theme in the speech of the *pratiche*.

[11] Chapter III (*Opere*, p. 7): ". . . basta avere spenta la linea del principe che li dominava, perché nelle altre cose, mantenendosi loro le condizioni vecchie e non vi essendo disformità di costumi, gli uomini si vivono quietamente . . ." Chapter V (*Opere*, p. 18): "Ma quando le città o le provincie sono use a vivere sotto uno principe, e quel sangue sia spento, sendo da uno canto usi ad obedire,

of innovation. The prince might have acquired his position through his own arms or those of supporters; he might owe it to his own abilities or to sheer good luck. When Machiavelli uses *virtù* and *fortuna* to denote the second of these antitheses, he is not using them with absolute precision. Since it was almost unthinkable that a man should acquire power without displaying some *virtù* of his own, there was always a sense in which *virtù* was the instrument of the innovation which exposed him to *fortuna*; but on the other hand *virtù* continued to mean that by which fortune was controlled, and the essential distinction lay between an innovator having means of his own to stay where he was and one continuing in dependence on whatever had put him there. At this point the second antithesis opened to include the first, and *virtù* took on the double meaning of the instruments of power, such as arms, and the personal qualities needed to wield those instruments.

In two ways, therefore, the nature and circumstances of the innovation operated to vary the problem which the innovator confronted. The more he could transfer to himself the habitual legitimacy enjoyed by his predecessor, the less he was exposed to the naked confrontation of *virtù* and *fortuna*, and the less urgent his need of *virtù* (in either of its meanings) became. The more his innovation had rendered him dependent on circumstances and people outside his immediate control, the greater his exposure to *fortuna* and his need of *virtù* to emancipate him. His need of *virtù* might then vary along two scales, and since his position on either of these was determined by empirically determined circumstances, the actions strategically necessary and the qualities of mind required to take them—the two together constituting *virtù*—might similarly vary. It was therefore possible to construct a typology of innovations, of ways in which the innovator was vulnerable and of forms of *virtù* by which this vulnerability might be countered. The control case was that of the hereditary prince, in whom vulnerability and the need for *virtù* were at a minimum.

The analysis of innovation is carried out in the first third of *Il Principe* and supplies a key to the pattern of at least that part of the book. Chapters III to V deal with the relation between the new prince's power and the customary structure of the society over which he has acquired it; chapters VI to IX with the degrees to which innovation renders him dependent on fortune. To complete the conspectus which this approach to *Il Principe* suggests, we may observe that chapters XII to

dall'altro non avendo el principe vecchio, farne uno infra loro non si accordano, vivere liberi non sanno . . ." This chapter also deals with the problem of the former republic; see below, n. 15.

XIV deal with the prince's military strength and XV to XXI with his personal conduct in relation to his subjects; this is the section chiefly concerned with what came to be known as Machiavellian morality. In XXIV and XXV Machiavelli returns to his main theme and confronts the new prince once again with the hereditary prince and with *fortuna*, and the concluding chapter XXVI is the famous and problematic "exhortation to liberate Italy from the barbarians." *Il Principe* does not take the form of a systematic exhaustion of categories, but there are patterns discernible in it, of which this is one.

The insecurity of political innovation, as we have seen, springs from the fact that it injures some and unsettles all, while creating a situation to which they have not yet had time to grow accustomed. Perhaps the key to the thought of *Il Principe* is Machiavelli's perception that behavior in such situations is partly predictable, so that strategies for acting in them may be devised; his great originality is that of a student of delegitimized politics. But to the extent that structures of accustomed behavior survive the prince's acquisition of the territory, the discussion of human behavior outside such structures must be postponed and the question is how these will affect the prince's power and authority. In chapters III to V, Machiavelli examines aspects of this question, and the emphasis throughout is on the idea of the accustomed. If the prince's new territory is added to one in which he is already established—the word is *antico*, which suggests that here he is not a "new prince" at all—if the two territories are of the same nationality (*provincia*) and language, and above all if the new is already accustomed to princely rule, then his task is at its easiest; he has only to see that the previous ruling family is extinct and to make no alterations in the province's laws and taxes, and everything which operated to legitimize his predecessors will operate to legitimize him. Furthermore, the similarity in customary structure and language between his old dominions and his new will lead to their rapidly becoming *tutto un corpo*.[12] Machiavelli does not particularize how this union will be effected, and we should not expect him to; he is dealing with the new principality at the point where it most closely resembles the hereditary monarchy, and he is presenting the latter in its most simply traditional form, as a community united by a body of common customs, which include allegiance to a given lineage. If nothing but the lineage is changed, the structure of tradition will facilitate a new allegiance; and such a community will easily blend with one of similar customs. But if a prince acquires a territory differing from his old in language, laws, and customs he will need great good fortune and great industry to keep it, and one of the best techniques is to go and live there himself. Machia-

---

[12] Chapter III (*Opere*, p. 8).

velli does not tell us whether this implies the prince's acculturation to the usages of his new subjects, or what will be happening in his old lands meanwhile; he proceeds rather quickly to consider how the prince should deal with the situation rendered inherently unstable by his new acquisitions.[13] A further assumption which has been made hitherto is that the traditional society's former loyalty was to a single ruling family. In chapter IV Machiavelli points out this limitation by considering the case where traditional loyalty is shared between a monarch and a large number of feudal lords (*baroni*), constituting so many local foci of hereditary allegiance. Here the principle of inertia does not hold; since there will always be malcontents among the barons, it is easy enough to dethrone the monarch by fomenting rebellions, but after a new ruler has taken possession he will find, first, that the usual consequences of innovation apply—his supporters will be unreliable and his enemies inveterate; second, that each baronial family enjoys the continuing loyalty of its subjects; third, that the *baroni* are too numerous to be exterminated. The Romans were never secure in a province while its old nobility survived, since merely by existing these kept alive the memory of a former state of things; and they contrived to outlast the provincial nobilities—Machiavelli seems to indicate— only because they monopolized power in the known world.[14]

In all this it is noteworthy that Machiavelli seems to be presupposing an entirely traditional form of society, one based upon custom to the exclusion of the relations between citizens that formed the groundwork of the Aristotelian polis. In chapter V, however, he proceeds to say that just as a territory with customs of its own is harder to hold than one whose customs are easily assimilable, so a city accustomed to liberty and the use of its own laws is hardest to hold of all. It may be held by the establishment of an oligarchy dependent on external support, but the only certain method is to destroy it; and the reason is that the memory of its former liberties, which can never serve to legitimize the new prince, is extraordinarily tenacious. Once again Machiavelli's emphasis is on usage; nothing else seems capable of providing legitimacy, and the innovator's problem is always that his subjects are not used to him and are used to something of which he has deprived them. But in this case something more than use and custom is at work: ". . . in republics there is greater hatred and more desire for vengeance;

---

[13] *Ibid.*; the point is that the prince should be readily available to remedy the disorders caused by his officials.

[14] *Opere*, p. 16: "Di qui nacquono le spesse rebellioni di Spagna, di Francia e di Grecia da' Romani, per li spessi principati che erano in quelli stati; de' quali mentre duro la memoria, sempre ne furono e Romani incerti di quella possessione; ma spenta la memoria di quelli, con la potenzia e diuturnità dello imperio ne diventorono securi possessori."

the memory of their ancient liberty does not and cannot leave them in peace."[15] Time is here inoperative. We are reminded here of Guicciardini's doctrine that civic freedom had become part of the second nature of the Florentines, and this chapter is one in which Machiavelli may be adverting to the character of restored Medici government, though formally at least the case is one of a former republic being added to the territories of an external ruler. But the real question is why the usage of liberty is so hard to shake off, so impossible to forget. The answer seems to be that when men are used to obeying a ruler, they do not have to alter their natures in order to obey someone else; but the experience of citizenship, especially if prolonged over several generations, sets an indelible mark upon their natures, so that they must indeed become new men if they are to learn willing obedience to a prince. Unlike Lodovico Alamanni, Machiavelli does not seem to think this transformation can be effected; indeed, it is essential to his whole theory of fortune that men cannot change their natures, except perhaps at the infinitely slow rate indicated by the concept of custom. And at the back of our minds must lurk the possibility that even for Machiavelli, men who have been citizens have known the realization of their true natures or *prima forma*.

By now the new prince has entered the domain of contingency; the time he is living in is shaped by human behavior as it is when men are no longer guided by structures of habitual legitimacy. He is therefore vulnerable to fortune, but it is perhaps the central assertion of *Il Principe* that the time-realm he now inhabits is not wholly unpredictable or unmanageable. It is a Hobbesian world in which men pursue their own ends without regard to any structure of law; that they do so is partly the innovator's own doing, that he inhabits this world is almost wholly so; and that by which they pursue their ends is power, so defined that each man's power constitutes a threat to every other's. The second half of chapter III is the first essay in that strategic analysis of the delegitimized world of the power-seekers which, as has always been recognized, brings Machiavelli's thought into sharpest focus; and

[15] *Opere*, p. 17: "E chi diviene patrone di una città consueta a vivere libera e non la disfaccia, aspetti di essere disfatto da quella: perché sempre ha per refugio nella rebellione el nome della libertà e gli ordini antiqui suoi; li quali né per la lunghezza de' tempi né per benefizii mai si dimenticano. E per cosa che si faccia o si provegga, se non si disuniscono o dissipano gli abitatori, e' non sdimenticano quel nome né quelli ordini, e subito in ogni accidente vi ricorrono: come fe' Pisa dopo cento anni che l'era suta posta in servitù da' Fiorentini."

P. 18: "Ma nelle republiche e maggiore vita, maggiore odio, più desiderio di vendetta; né li lascia né può lasciare riposare la memoria della antiqua libertà: tale che la più secura via e spegnerle o abitarvi." There seems no discussion of how living there will help.

it is here that we hear for the first time the assertion that the prime necessity of strategic behavior is action. The alternative to action is delay and temporization, and once time has become the domain of pure contingency it is impossible to temporize because there can be no secure assumptions about what time will bring; or rather, the only assumption must be that, unless acted upon, it will bring change to one's disadvantage. One has power, and others have not; the only change that can come is that others will gain power, to the loss of one's own. The Romans knew that war is not to be avoided, and always chose to fight their enemies now rather than later.[16] What Machiavelli would have said of modern deterrent strategies of "buying time" we can only guess; perhaps that they make sense only as a collusive strategy between powers aiming to stabilize and legitimize their relations. In the simpler but sufficiently terrible world of the Renaissance he could afford to see the prince as launched on a career of the indefinite maximization of his power, with no more final question to be asked than what would become of him if he should achieve universal empire—and *Il Principe* does not ask that question.

Strategy is the science of the behavior of actors defined by the power they possess; and the strategic world inhabited by the prince as acquisitor of power is best understood in terms of his relations with his fellow princes. But these relations are external to the subsystems, command of which gives each prince his power; and the relations between individuals seen as composing (or decomposing) separate political societies are the subject of an analysis for which "strategic" is not a sufficiently comprehensive word. It is here that we enter fully into the question of the relations between an individual's *virtù* and his *fortuna*, which is always a moral and a psychological, as well as a simply strategic problem. Chapter VI and its successors are dedicated to the role of *virtù* in acquiring and holding new dominions,[17] and Machiavelli enters the realm of moral ambiguity by the single step of defining *virtù* as an innovative force. It is not merely that by which men control their fortunes in a delegitimized world; it may also be that by which men innovate and so delegitimize their worlds, and we shall see in a moment

[16] *Opere*, p. 10: "Però e' Romani vedendo discosto gli inconvenienti vi rimediorno sempre, e non li lasciorno mai seguire per fuggire una guerra, perché sapevono che la guerra non si leva ma si differisce a vantaggio di altri. . . . Né piacque mai loro quello che tutto dì è in bocca de' savii de' nostri tempi, di godere el benefizio del tempo, ma si bene quello della virtù e prudenzia loro: perché el tempo si caccia innanzi ogni cosa, e può condurre seco bene come male e male come bene."

[17] *Opere*, p. 18: "De principatibus novis qui armis propriis et virtute acquiruntur."

that it may even be that which imposes legitimacy on a world which has never known it. The only constant semantic association is now that between *virtù* and innovation, the latter being considered rather as an act than as a previously accomplished fact, and *virtù* is preeminently that by which the individual is rendered outstanding in the context of innovation and in the role of innovator. Since innovation continues to raise ethical problems, this use of the word *virtù* does not deny its association with ethics, but it employs the word to define the situations within which the ethical problems arise.

In chapter VI the prince is internal rather than external to the society over which he acquires power; we are not now concerned with a prince adding to his dominions, but with a private individual who becomes a prince. This, says Machiavelli, presupposes either *virtù* or *fortuna*;[18] but it is clear that the relation between the two is more than simply antithetical. On the one hand *virtù* is that by which we innovate, and so let loose sequences of contingency beyond our prediction or control so that we become prey to *fortuna*; on the other hand, *virtù* is that internal to ourselves by which we resist *fortuna* and impose upon her patterns of order, which may even become patterns of moral order. This seems to be the heart of the Machiavellian ambiguities. It explains why innovation is supremely difficult, being formally self-destructive; and it explains why there is incompatibility between action—and so between politics defined in terms of action rather than tradition—and moral order. The politicization of virtue had arrived at the discovery of a politicized version of original sin.

Within the central ambiguity, it was possible to isolate the antithetical relation between *virtù* and *fortuna*; and Machiavelli's thought was now concentrated upon it. The more the individual relies upon his *virtù* the less he need rely upon his *fortuna* and—since *fortuna* is by definition unreliable—the safer he is. But if *virtù* is that by which we acquire power, the ideal type we are now seeking is the individual who acquires it wholly by the exercise of his personal qualities and not at all as the result of contingencies and circumstances outside himself. This explains why we must examine the acquisition of power by one who is a private individual and not a power-wielder at the moment of acquiring it; but to do so does not exhaust the difficulties. The career of any individual in a given society is conditioned by the particular circumstances of that society, which, not being of his making, are part of his *fortuna*. But to find an individual unconditioned by social membership is next to impossible; he must be Aristotle's "beast or god." The

[18] *Ibid.*: ". . . questo evento, di diventare di privato principe, presuppone o virtù o fortuna . . ."

quasi-solution is given by Machiavelli's declaration that the ideal type (*li più eccellenti*) of those who have become princes through their own *virtù* and not by *fortuna* is to be found in "Moses, Cyrus, Romulus, Theseus and their like."[19] These are the classical legislators in the strictest possible sense of state-founders (Lycurgus and Solon, who might be termed reformers rather than creators, are not named); the divine or divinely aided beings who could create societies because their *virtù* was such that it did not need the social frame which was the precondition of virtue in ordinary men; gods with (at least in such figures as Theseus and Romulus) a little of the beast about them. But Machiavelli has introduced the legislators for a reason peculiarly his own. If we examine their lives and actions, he says,

> it will not appear that they owed anything to fortune except opportunity (*l'occasione*), which gave them matter into which to introduce whatever form they thought good; without the opportunity their *virtù* would have been wasted, and without *virtù* the opportunity would have been in vain. It was then necessary that Moses should find the people of Israel slaves in Egypt and oppressed by the Egyptians, so that they were disposed to follow him in order to escape from servitude. It was necessary that Romulus should take no root in Alba and should be exposed at his birth, in order that he become king of Rome and founder of that nation. It was necessary that Cyrus find the Persians ill content with the rule of the Medes, and the Medes soft and effeminate through long peace. Theseus could not have displayed his *virtù* if he had not found the Athenians dispersed.[20]

A comparison of Machiavelli's poems on *Fortuna* and *Occasione* will show how far he had blended these two symbolic figures with one another. His insistence that *Fortuna* is a woman who can be temporar-

[19] *Opere*, pp. 18-19.

[20] *Opere*, p. 19. "Ed esaminando le azioni e vita loro, non si vede che quelli avessino altro dalla fortuna che l'occasione; la quale dette loro materia a potere introdurvi drento quella forma parse loro: e sanza quella occasione la virtù dello animo loro si sarebbe spenta, e sanza quella virtù la occasione sarebbe venuta invano.

"Era dunque necessario a Moise trovare el populo d'Isdrael, in Egitto, stiavo e oppresso dalli Egizii, acciò che quelli per uscire di servitù si disponessino a seguirlo. Conveniva che Romulo non capissi in Alba, fussi stato esposto al nascere, a volere che diventassi re di Roma e fondatore di quella patria. Bisognava che Ciro trovassi e' Persi malcontenti dello imperio de' Medi, e li Medi molli ed effeminati per la lunga pace. Non posseva Teseo dimostrare la sua virtù se non trovava li Ateniesi dispersi. Queste occasioni pertanto feciono questi uomini felici, e la eccellente virtù loro fece quella occasione essere conosciuta: donde la lora patria ne fu nobilitata e divento felicissima."

ily mastered if you do not hesitate with her[21] is reinforced by his presentation of the classical figure of *Occasione* as a woman with a forelock by which she can be seized from before but tonsured so that she cannot be taken by the short hairs behind;[22] and the language addressed to either daemon could be appropriately used to the other. But the antithesis of form and matter tells us even more about the meaning of this passage. It is the function of the legislator to impose the form of *politeia*—the constitution—upon the matter of *politeuma*, the citizen body; and it is the function of *virtù* to impose form upon *fortuna*. But when the subject is innovation, there is a pressing danger that *virtù* may deliver itself into *fortuna*'s power, and therefore the ideal type of innovator is he who depends as little as possible on circumstances beyond his control. The more the innovator is thought of as subverting and replacing a previously existing structure of custom and legitimacy, the more he will have to cope with the contingencies of suddenly disoriented behavior and the greater will be his exposure to *fortuna*. To attain the ideal type, therefore, we must suppose a situation in which the matter has no form, and above all no previously existing form, but what the innovator gives it; and the innovator must be a legislator. It was therefore a logical necessity that each hero should find his people in a condition of total anomie; since if the matter had had any vestige of form, that would have detracted from his *virtù*'s total independence of *fortuna*.

It is difficult to imagine so ideal a situation in concrete terms. Apart from the problem of envisaging a specific society in a totally anomic condition, the more we insist that there is nothing for the legislator to

---

[21] *Capitolo della Fortuna*, lines 10-15:

> Perché questa volubil creatura
> Spesso si suole oppor con maggior forza
> Dove più forza vede aver natura.

> Sua natural potenza ognuno sforza;
> E il regno suo è sempre violento
> Se virtù eccessiva non lo ammorza.

Lines 124-26:

> Però si vuol lei prender per sua stella;
> E quanto a noi è possibile, ognora
> Accomodarsi al variar di quella.

[22] *Capitolo dell'Occasione*, lines 10-15:

> Li sparsi mia capei dinanti io tengo:
> con essi mi ricuopro il petto e'l volto
> perch'un non mi conosca quando io vengo.

> Drieto dal capo ogni capel m'è tolto,
> onde invan s'affatica un, se gli avviene
> ch'i' l'abbi trapassato o s'i' mi volto.

replace the less can there be anything for him to build upon; and we face the problem of finding any terms in which to describe what he does or how he does it. The legislator has such *virtù* that his command of *occasione* is absolute and he has unconditioned ability to dictate form to matter; but he has now become a species of demiurge, able to actualize all potentialities by a single creative command, and very much above the level of ordinary humanity. One of the classical legislators of course stands apart from the others.

> Of Moses one ought not to speak, since he was no more than an executor of commands given him by God; still, he should be admired if only for that grace (*grazia*) which made him worthy to speak with God. But if we consider Cyrus and others who have acquired or founded kingdoms, we shall find them all admirable; and if we consider their particular actions and laws, they will not appear different from those of Moses, although he had so great an instructor.[23]

Machiavelli's language is irritatingly orthodox. It was only by God that a chaos of particulars (matter) could be commanded into a whole (form), and it was only by divine grace and instruction that an individual could be authorized to do this. The impious thoughts probably[24] hinted at above arose only because it was difficult to explain how pagan legislators could have done their work without furnishing an explanation which would account just as well for Moses; but the impulse to assimilate the prophet to the categories of "legislator" and "innovator" was not irreligious in its origin. The problem of innovation was such that the divine authorization and inspiration enjoyed by the prophet furnished one—but only one—of the acceptable answers. We have seen that Guicciardini employed the word *grazia* in connection with Lycurgus, and that his allusion to the Spartan legislator was such as to assimilate him to Savonarola. Our analysis of chapter VI of *Il Principe* is approaching Machiavelli's allusion to Savonarola as typifying the "unarmed prophet" who invariably fails where the "armed prophets" succeed;[25] but this observation has to be studied in the light of Machia-

[23] *Opere*, p. 19: "E benchè di Moise non si debba ragionare, sendo suto uno mero esecutore delle cose che li erano ordinate di Dio, *tamen* debbe essere ammirato *solum* per quella grazia che lo faceva degno di parlare con Dio. Ma consideriamo Ciro e li altri che hanno acquistato o fondato regni: li troverrete tutti mirabili. E se si considerarranno le azioni e ordini loro particulari, parranno non discrepanti da quelli di Moise, che ebbe si gran precettore. Ed esaminando le azioni e vita loro . . . ," etc., as quoted in n. 20 above.

[24] But not certainly; it could always be argued—and James Harrington was to do so—that the works of grace and wisdom might prove identical. See below, ch. XI.

[25] *Opere*, p. 20: "È necessario pertanto, volendo discorrere bene questa parte, esaminare se questi innovatori stanno per loro medesimi o se dependano da altri;

velli's identification of the prophet and the legislator. Both are attempting a task beyond normal human powers, and both require more than normal *virtù*; we must not say that divine inspiration is being lowered to the level of *realpolitik* without adding that *realpolitik* is being raised to the level of divine inspiration, and that Machiavelli may have been a pagan but was not a *philosophe*. Moses was an armed prophet, but need have been no less a prophet for his use of the sword. The prophet requires arms because, as an innovator, he must not be dependent on the contingent goodwill of others, and must therefore possess the means of compelling men when they cease to believe in him. It would be perfectly orthodox to contend that God provided Moses with a divinely authorized message, but did not provide that the Israelites would invariably obey him, and that the prophet's dealings with the stiff-necked by means of the secular sword[26] were authorized as part of his inspiration.

Prophets, whether true or false, require the sword because they are innovators. It is essential to realize that chapter VI is an analysis of innovation, and that Moses and Savonarola have both come into it because the legislator is part of the definition of the ideal type of innovator and the prophet part of the definition of the ideal type of legislator. The most that Machiavelli is saying is that the prophet's inspiration and mission do not deliver him from the political context created by innovation and that he must continue to use the secular arm for

---

cioè, se per condurre l'opera loro bisogna che preghino o vero possono forzare. Nel primo caso capitano sempre male e non conducano cosa alcuna; ma quando dependano da loro proprii e possono forzare, allora è che rare volte periclitano. Di qui nacque che tutti e' profeti armati vinsono, e gli disarmati ruinorno. Perché oltra alle cose dette, la natura de' populi è varia; ed è facile a persuadere loro una cosa, ma è difficile fermarli in quella persuasione. E però conviene essere ordinato in modo che quando e' non credano più, si possa fare credere loro per forza.

"Moise, Ciro, Teseo e Romulo non arebbono possuto fare osservare loro lungamente le loro costituzioni se fussino stati disarmati; come ne' nostri tempi intervenne a fra' Ieronimo Savonarola, il quale ruinò ne' suoi ordini nuovi come la moltitudine cominciò a non credergli, e lui non aveva modo a tenere fermi quelli che avevano creduto, né a far credere e' discredenti."

[26] *Exodus* 32:26-28: "Then Moses stood in the gate of the camp and said, Who is on the Lord's side? let him come unto me. And all the sons of Levi gathered themselves together unto him. And he said unto them, Thus saith the Lord God of Israel, Put every man his sword by his side, and go in and out from gate to gate throughout the camp, and slay every man his brother, and every man his companion, and every man his neighbour. And the children of Levi did according to the word of Moses; and there fell of the people that day about three thousand men." See Michael Walzer, "Exodus 32 and the Theory of Holy War: The History of a Citation," *Harvard Theological Review* 61, no. 1 (January 1968), 1-14, for a history of the exegesis of this text.

reasons inherent in that context, which make it the appropriate weapon for use there. (He may also be hinting that the same constraints apply to the Lord God of Israel if he chooses—as he does choose—to act upon a particular nation in its history.) Innovation is the theme. It is the most difficult and dangerous of human enterprises for reasons which we already know. It makes enemies who are fervent because they know what they have lost, and friends who are lukewarm because they do not yet know what they have gained, not having yet had enough experience of it: precisely the problem of the fleshpots of Egypt. For this reason the innovator is delivered, on disadvantageous terms, to the contingencies of human behavior: to *fortuna*. That by which he confronts *fortuna* is to be found within him, except in the one case where he receives direct divine inspiration, and is to be termed his *virtù*—except where it must be described as *grazia*. Since it was also his *virtù* (where it was not his inspiration) which made him an innovator and exposed him to *fortuna*, we must seek for that *virtù* which involves the minimum of dependence on *fortuna*. The ideal and extreme case of the innovator whose initial *virtù* was unconditioned by external circumstance is found in the category of legislators and prophets; yet the greatest genius or most inspired prophet operates only by inducing men to follow him and is exposed to *fortuna* unless he has means to ensure that they continue to do so—means which Machiavelli can only characterize in terms of the sword, so that *virtù*, which could not have manifested itself without *occasione*, cannot maintain itself without an external instrument for coercing men's wills. Subject to these limitations, we have succeeded in defining the *virtù* which involves the minimum dependence on *fortuna*.

At this stage in the analysis, it must be evident that the category "innovator" has substituted itself for the category "new prince," in the sense that it is more comprehensive and capable of greater theoretical precision. *Il Principe* continues to be about new princes, but the new prince belongs to the class of innovators, to which legislators and prophets also belong; and they have characteristics which the new prince does not possess, while those characteristics which they share with him are those which all members of the class of innovators have in common. Each innovator is specifically located, within the class of innovators, by the degree and quality of his *virtù*'s dependence or independence with respect to *fortuna*. The legislator and prophet constitute the extreme limiting case of minimum dependence, and the greatest precision which we can now give to the term "new prince" is to make it inclusive of all those innovators who fall short of minimum dependence.

Chapters VII to IX, it may be said, constitute an exploration of the category "innovator," still in terms of the *virtù-fortuna* polarity, with attention to those new princes who lack the superhuman *virtù* of legislators and prophets. Since the last-named are considered independent of *fortuna*, chapter VII opens by positing the case of the new prince who owes his position wholly to it.[27] But while it is possible to imagine a man becoming a prince by sheer luck while having absolutely no *virtù* of his own, the exercise is of little theoretical interest. Something would happen to him so quickly that it hardly matters what it would be. Moreover, since *virtù* and *fortuna* are not mutually exclusive terms, the amount of luck a man has bears no necessary relation to his personal abilities. It is therefore possible to consider the case of a man unusually indebted to *fortuna* while possessing unusual ability with which to counteract his dependence: one

> of so great *virtù* that he can promptly take steps to preserve what *fortuna* has thrown into his lap, and lay after becoming a prince those foundations which others lay in anticipation of it.[28]

This is the context in which we are introduced to Cesare Borgia. Machiavelli was notoriously fascinated by this figure; and so much has been written on the assumption that he is the hero of *Il Principe*, and that its main themes are all to be understood by reference to his role, that it is desirable to define the exact status which he occupies in the book. If we apply the *virtù-fortuna* criterion, it defines his position as that of one among a number of ideal types, all located along a spectrum of degrees to which *virtù* is independent of *fortuna*. The legislator's *virtù* endows him with almost complete independence, but in Cesare we see combined the maximum *virtù* with the maximum dependence on fortune. He is presented as a man of extraordinary ability who got his chance only because his father happened to become pope, and whose *virtù* was displayed in the efforts he made to establish his power in the Romagna on an independent basis before his father should happen to die.[29] Alexander VI's election, clearly, was the *occasione* for Cesare's *virtù* to manifest itself, but the case is quite different from that

[27] *Opere*, p. 21: "Coloro e' quali solamente per fortuna diventano di privati principi. . . ."

[28] *Opere*, p. 22: ". . . di tanta virtù che quello la fortuna ha messo loro in grembo e' sappino subito prepararsi a conservarlo, e quali fondamenti che gli altri hanno fatti avanti che diventino principi, gli faccino poi."

[29] *Ibid.*: ". . . acquistò lo stato con la fortuna del padre, e con quella lo perde; nonostante che per lui si usassi ogni opera e facessi tutte quelle cose che per uno prudente e virtuoso uomo si dovea fare per mettere le barbe sua in quelli stati che l'arme e fortuna d'altri gli aveva concessi."

of the seizure of *occasione* by the legislator. When that happens, we are told, the legislator owes nothing to *fortuna* except the *occasione*; his *virtù* is all within himself, and we are left with the image of extraordinary personal creativity imprinting itself on circumstance as on a *tabula rasa*, so that the contingent world becomes the inert matter on which *virtù* imposes form. But Cesare's seizure of *occasione* merely made of him a rider on the wheel; he entered a situation in which he owed much to *fortuna* that might at any moment be taken away, and this dependence on *fortuna* endured while he endeavored by his *virtù* to establish a power independent of the wheel's next turn.

Cesare's position differs formally from that of the legislator in that his *virtù* and his *fortuna* are not in a simple inverse relation. Because the legislator's *virtù* is superhuman, *fortuna* has no power over him; Cesare's *virtù* is only human—he is related to the legislator somewhat as the Aristotelian "man of practical wisdom" is to the Platonic philosopher-king—and is seen in his struggle to escape the power which *fortuna* exercises. Not only this, but in addition Cesare occupies a somewhat specialized position in the gallery of innovators. When we were told in chapter VI that innovation was the most difficult and dangerous of all things to accomplish,[30] the innovator's exposure to *fortuna* was derived from the fact that his innovation disturbed all human relationships and alienated some individuals more violently than it attracted others. But that is not the point with Cesare. The measure of his dependence on *fortuna* is not the uncertainty of the Romagna's reactions to his rule, but the uncertainty of Alexander VI's tenure of life. It is true that the measure of his *virtù* is the excellence which Machiavelli ascribes to his military and other techniques of assuring that his power in the Romagna will survive Alexander's death, but in fact it remains wholly dependent on papal and curial politics and Machiavelli was unable to assert convincingly that it does not.[31] *Fortuna* has become externalized; what happens in the Romagna is dependent on what happens elsewhere, and is not the simple consequence of the impact of Cesare's innovation on the Romagna's accustomed life. Nor do we hear very much about the character of Romagnuol society before Cesare went there, and this is not because we are to see Cesare as potentially the Theseus of the Romagna and the Romagnuoli as the inert matter to which he might have given form; his relation to *fortuna* is not that of the legislator.

[30] *Opere*, pp. 19-20.

[31] *Opere*, p. 26: "E che e' fondamenti sua fussino buoni, si vidde: che la Romagna lo aspettò piú di uno mese . . ." His success is measured by his mastery of the short term.

If Cesare is not a legislator, it may be that—as Machiavelli indeed avers—he is the ideal type which every new prince in his (carefully defined) category should follow.[32] But from this we should have to deduce, contrary to some interpreters of Machiavelli, that the new prince is not a potential legislator, and that the legislator is an ideal type situated at one extreme of the category of innovators, of which genus the new prince is a species. Not only is the legislator's *virtù* related to *fortuna* in a way utterly different from that of the new prince; he is performing an innovation of a different order. He finds his *materia*—the people he is to mold—in a condition so anomic that his *virtù* needs only a sword to impose form upon it; very little is said of the previous structure of accustomed behavior which other innovators displace. Moreover, in imposing form upon matter he is the founder of a political order: Cyrus, Theseus and Romulus founded kingdoms, Lycurgus a polity and Moses a nation in covenant with God. The word *stato*—normally employed by Machiavelli and Guicciardini to mean "rule by some over others"—does not appear to denote what the legislator brings into being, a highly viable political community, stabilized by his *virtù* and (at least if it is a republic) by the *virtù* of its citizens; a kingdom is stabilized by use and inheritance. By contrast, the new prince does not find matter lacking all form; he takes possession of a society already stabilized by customs of its own, and his task—relatively hard or easy according as it is used to liberty or obedience—is to replace this "second nature" with another. The function of his *virtù* is not to impose *prima forma* (in the phrase used by Savonarola and Guicciardini) but to disturb old forms and change them into new. The old form being rooted in custom and "second nature," his innovation disorients men's behavior patterns and this exposes him to *fortuna*. What he is seen to establish is *stato*, a limited form of government only partly legitimized, only partly rooted in customs and "second nature" new to the people; and to get past this stage would require *virtù* of a kind the more extraordinary because it would not be identical with the *virtù* of the legislator.

   J. H. Hexter has pointed out[33] that the phrase most frequently used by Machiavelli to describe the purposes of the new prince is *mantenere lo stato*, and that this carries short-term implications; it seems to mean little more than to maintain himself in the position of power and

[32] *Opere*, p. 27: ". . . anzi mi pare, come ho fatto, di preporlo imitabile a tutti coloro che per fortuna e con l'armi d'altri sono ascesi allo imperio."

[33] "*Il Principe* and *lo stato*," *Studies in the Renaissance* 4 (1957), 113-38; now included in *The Vision of Politics on the Eve of the Reformation* (New York: Basic Books, 1972). Cf. Gilbert, *Machiavelli and Guicciardini*, pp. 326-30.

insecurity which innovation has brought him. On this view, the prince is not to look so far ahead as to hope to achieve for his *stato* either the near-immortality achieved by the creation of the legislator or the legitimacy achieved by use and inheritance in the hereditary principality. *Stato* means that one's eye is always upon immediate dangers; *virtù* is that by which one resists them, not that by which one is emancipated from the need to fear them. The new prince does not hope to transform the conditions of his political existence, or look to a time when he will be anything but a parvenu. If *virtù* and *fortuna* should happily go together, his line may last long enough to achieve the habitual stability of the Este of Ferrara, who are legitimized to the point where they have little need of *virtù*. Meanwhile, in the short view, there is *virtù*: the *virtù* of Philopoemon the Achaean, who never took a walk without planning a campaign.[34] *Virtù* is in the present, and for the future it begets glory. The *virtù* of the legislator is quite different; it builds nations to last.

This interpretation seems to be borne out if we consider the preceptive as opposed to the analytical chapters of *Il Principe*: after those which explore the category of innovators, those which isolate the new prince and tell him what to do. The transition from one to the other comes about two chapters after the profile of Cesare Borgia. The dominant themes do indeed appear concerned with the prince's techniques for rendering himself safe against immediate threats. He inhabits a world of competitors, and so we return to the theme of inter-princely relationships in which his chief need is an army and the skill to use it. There is perhaps the question, given Machiavelli's intense concern with the Florentine militia tradition and his belief that only a civic militia could render a citizen body capable of maintaining its liberty, whether he did not have in mind that the prince's command of the army was a means of transforming his relations with those he governed. We recall Vettori's advice that the Medici should arm the *contado* against the city, Alamanni's that young aristocrats should become captains in the prince's guard. But if this was in Machiavelli's mind, he did not follow it out in detail. The military chapters of *Il Principe* (XII-XIV) passionately assert the inferiority of mercenary and auxiliary troops to those who are "one's own" (*proprie*), but the social relationship between the prince and "his" soldiers is not explored, except for one sentence in which it is observed that they consist either of subjects (*sudditi*), citizens (*cittadini*), or one's own dependents (*creati*, creatures, those raised up by one).[35] This is suggestive, but it is not enough to substan-

[34] *Opere*, pp. 48-49.

[35] *Opere*, p. 47: "E l'arme proprie son quelle che sono composte o di sudditi o di cittadini o di creati tua: tutte l'altre sono o mercenarie o ausiliarie. E il modo

tiate a theory. Machiavelli's great explorations of the politics of military organization, in the *Discorsi* and the *Arte della Guerra*, presuppose the republic as the political norm.

If the military chapters on the whole depict arms as a weapon against short-term dangers, the famous chapters (xv-xix) on the morality of princely behavior adopt a similar perspective. Here it is simply assumed that by the fact of his own innovation, the prince inhabits a context in which human behavior is only partly legitimized and only partly subjected to the rules of morality. Consequently, the intelligence of the prince—his *virtù*—includes the skill necessary to know when it is possible to act as if the rules of morality (whose validity in itself is nowhere denied) were in force and to be relied on as governing the behavior of others, and when it is not. Formally, this has reference to a specific political context, that which is the result of innovation; if it is possible to detect moments at which Machiavelli speaks as if it had reference to all political contexts whatsoever, the reason may be that he had adopted a short-term perspective in which the consequences of innovation were not expected to be lived down, and that this had enabled him to see that all political situations were in part the products of innovation and contest for power, and that the short-term perspective never ceased altogether to be valid. But further consequences follow. The prince's moral and social, like his military and diplomatic behavior, was carried on in a context dominated by *fortuna*, in which time brought with it good things and bad indifferently, and the greater part by far of his *virtù* was his ability to discern what time was bringing and what strategies were required to cope with it. Discussion of whether the prince should obey moral law therefore becomes discussion of when he should obey it,[36] and this in turn blends into discussion of whether it is better to be loved or feared, to be audacious or prudent. The answer is always the same. The essence of *virtù* is to know which of these paired courses is appropriate to the moment; but other things being equal, the better course is always the more aggressive and dramatic—to be audacious, to act so as to be feared. To be loved takes time.

We know that it is in the long-term context—the eternity of reason, the antiquity of custom—that legitimation resides. Since by his own act the innovator inhabits a delegitimized context, where *fortuna* rules

---

a ordinare l'arme proprie sarà facile a trovare se si discorrerà gli ordini de' quattro sopra nominati da me [i.e., Cesare Borgia, Hiero of Syracuse, David of Israel, and Charles VII of France], e se si vedrà come Filippo, padre di Alessandro Magno, e come molte republiche e principi si sono armati e ordinati: a' quali ordini io al tutto mi rimetto."

[36] The fox knows this better than the lion does (ch. xviii).

and human behavior is not to be relied on, he is obliged to take the short view and continue to act—and in that sense, to innovate. In a very precise sense, then, action is *virtù*; when the world is unstabilized and the unexpected a constant threat, to act—to do things not contained within the structures of legitimacy—was to impose form upon *fortuna*. Aggression was the better part of value. It is this, and not the erotic fantasies to which Machiavelli was admittedly given, that lies behind his repeated descriptions of *fortuna* as a woman who could be taken by force but would destroy you if you did not—the words should be weighed carefully—act in time.

But the *virtù* of action did not legitimate its environment. The forms it imposed existed only for a short time, whereas those of the legislator aimed at secular immortality. In the concluding group of chapters (XXIV-XXVI), it is true, Machiavelli opens by declaring that the *virtù* of the new prince will

> make him appear ancient, and render him swiftly more secure and established than if he were established from of old. For a new prince is always more observed in his actions than a hereditary one, and when these are seen to be virtuous he wins men over far more and they become more bound to him than to the ancient blood. For men are more taken by things present than by things past, and when they find themselves well off in the present, they enjoy it and ask no more; they will even undertake to defend him, so long as he does not fail of himself in other respects. And so he will have the double glory of having founded a new principate and adorned and strengthened it with good laws, good arms, and good examples; as he will have double shame who was born a prince and has lost it through lack of prudence.[37]

But this is not a declaration that the new prince can found a system more durably institutionalized and legitimized than by use and tradition, so much as a declaration that men in the world of innovation live in the present. Given a world which they see and experience as action

[37] *Opere*, p. 78: "Le cose suprascritte, osservate prudentemente, fanno parere uno nuovo antico, e lo rendono subito piú securo e piú fermo nello stato che se vi fussi antiquato drento. Perché uno principe nuovo è molto piú osservato nelle sua azioni che uno ereditario; e quando le sono conosciute virtuose, pigliano molto piú li uomini e molto piú gli obligano che il sangue antico. Perché li uomini sono molto piú presi dalle cose presenti che dalle passate, e quando nelle presenti truovono il bene, vi si godono e non cercono altro; anzi piglieranno ogni difesa per lui, quando non manchi nelle altre cose a se medesimo. E cosi arà duplicata gloria di avere dato principio a uno principato nuovo, e ornatolo e corroboratolo di buone leggi, di buone arme e di buoni esempli: come quello ha duplicata vergogna che, nato principe, lo ha per sua poca prudenzia perduto."

and fluctuation rather than as tradition and legitimacy, their feelings about the present are bound to be the stronger; action is more exciting than custom, it holds the attention and stirs up the emotions. In the present, the new prince can outshine the hereditary and evoke more loyalty; his *virtù*—functioning where rational and traditional authority are both absent—is a kind of charisma. But if we ask whether the charisma has been institutionalized, we must move from the short view to the long, and Machiavelli will not be moving with us; just as *Il Principe* does not inform us what is meant by "good laws, good arms and good examples," for which we must wait till the *Discorsi*. The examples he gives of hereditary rulers who have lost their states do not conform to the pattern laid down in chapter ii, because the individuals he names were clearly not fortified by the habitual loyalty of their subjects.[38] As for the spectacular *virtuosi* of the new principates, if there is one thing certain about them it is that they continue to exist in fortune's world. In chapter xxv Machiavelli returns to the themes of how far men may hope to resist *fortuna*, and whether audacity or caution is the best means of dealing with her. In a crucial passage he lays down that sometimes one and sometimes the other is appropriate strategy; but men are audacious or cautious by nature, and so succeed or fail according to the times they have the fortune to live in. A man may have succeeded by either strategy,

but if time and circumstances change he will be ruined, because he does not change his mode of procedure. No man is found so prudent as to be able to adapt himself to this, either because he cannot deviate from that to which his nature disposes him, or else because having always prospered by walking in one path, he cannot persuade himself that it is well to leave it; and therefore the cautious man, when it is time to act suddenly, does not know how to do so and is consequently ruined; for if one could change one's nature with time and circumstances, fortune would never change.[39]

[38] *Ibid.*: ". . . come il re di Napoli, duca di Milano e altri, si troverrà in loro: prima uno commune defetto quanto alle arme per le cagioni che di sopra a lungo si sono discorse; dipoi si vedrà alcuno di loro, o che arà avuto inimici e' populi o, se arà avuto el populo amico, non si sarà sapputo assicurare de' grandi. . . ."

[39] *Opere*, p. 81: "Da questo ancora depende la variazione del bene, perché, se uno che si governa con respetti e pazienzia, e' tempi e le cose girono in modo che il governo suo sia buono, e viene felicitando; ma se li tempi e le cose si mutano, e' rovina, perché non muta modo di procedere. Ne si truova uomo si prudente che si sappi accomodare a questo; sì perché non si può deviare da quello a che la natura lo inclina, sì *etiam* perché, avendo sempre uno prosperato camminando per una via, non si può persuadere partirsi da quella. E però l'uomo respettivo, quando egli è tempo di venire allo impeto, non lo sa fare; donde e'

Machiavelli is saying that our second nature, the product of use and wont—he does not revert to the concept of *fantasia* employed in his letter to Soderini[40]—is acquired as we become habituated to acting audaciously or cautiously. No *virtù* can so completely dominate *fortuna* as to ensure that the same strategy remains always appropriate; and what is more important still, no *virtù* of this order gives men power to change their own natures, or consequently to act "in time." If the prince cannot change his own acquired second nature, it does not seem that he can change those of his subjects. The legislator and prophet impose something of the kind on the anomic personalities they come to rule; but the new prince finds men habituated to a certain *vivere* and must, if he is to legitimize his power, habituate them to another. This his *virtù* does not seem capable of doing, least of all when they have been habituated to the usages of civic liberty which Machiavelli describes as ineradicable. Lodovico Alamanni, writing a few years after 1513, and possibly after reading *Il Principe* and reflecting on its limitations, thought he knew a way of doing even this. But the new prince as a type of innovator can only be said to transform the conditions of political existence if we mean that he transposes them into a context of innovation and fortune, where only the short view has validity. The only two agencies so far known to be capable of creating a context of stability were custom, which established second nature, and grace (or the superhuman *virtù* of the legislator), which established *prima forma*. Since legislators established highly stable republics, we must turn to Machiavelli's republican theory to know what he thought about the stabilization of political life; and, it should seem, we are forced in the same direction by the effort to solve the riddle of chapter xxvi. *Il Principe* concludes with a passionate "exhortation to liberate Italy from the barbarians." This is addressed to a "new prince," and the question has consequently been how far the preceding chapters are to be seen as leading up to and progressively delineating the portrait of this liberating hero. But on the assumption used here—that *Il Principe* does not present a single rounded portrait, but a gallery of specimen types of innovator—the question must rather be to which subcategory, or combination of them, the liberator belongs. Rhetorically, it seems that he is a legislator: Moses, Cyrus, and Theseus are invoked once more, and we are told that the Italians are as prostrate as the Hebrews, Persians, and Athenians were in their generations, so that the *virtù d'uno spirito italiano* can be displayed in the imposition

---

rovina: che se si mutassi di natura con li tempi e con le cose, non si muterebbe fortuna."

[40] Above, ch. IV, n. 23.

of form upon matter, as fully as were those of the ancient liberators.[41]
But are we to understand that the anomie of Italians has reached the
point where the *virtù* of a legislator will owe nothing to *fortuna* except
occasione? Machiavelli was a Florentine, and knew perfectly well that
there were republics and *principi naturali* to be met with, the acquired
or natural characteristics of whose subjects would complicate the liberator's task. Italy was not inert matter to be organized into form,
though he says it is; he had himself worked against Cesare Borgia's
intended *regno* in the Romagna. The other thing we are told about the
hero of chapter XXVI is that he is to be a military organizer, whose
tactical principles will revive *virtù militare* and (in Petrarch's phrase)
antico valore.[42] It has been hinted that there are ways in which military
virtù can be associated with—can perhaps be the foundation of—civic
virtù, but we have not yet learned what they are; and the language of
this chapter seems to preclude the possibility that the liberator can stop
short of restoring both kinds of virtue to Italy. If he does less he will
be a "new prince" at a low level, a victim of *fortuna* obliged to live
in the present; if he is to be a figure of the magnitude of Moses, Romulus, and Theseus, the army he trains must evolve into a people. Machiavelli admired military leaders—Borgia early in his career, Giovanni

[41] *Opere*, p. 83: "Considerato adunque tutte le cose di sopra discorse, e pensando meco medesimo se al presente in Italia correvono tempi da onorare uno
nuovo principe, e se ci era materia che dessi occasione a uno prudente e virtuoso
di introdurvi forma che facessi onore a lui e bene alla università delli uomini di
quella, mi pare concorrino tante cose in benefizio di uno principe nuovo che io
non so qual mai tempo fussi piú atto a questo. E se, come io dissi, era necessario
volendo vedere la virtù di Moise che il populo d'Isdrael fussi stiavo in Egitto, e
a conoscere la grandezza dello animo di Ciro ch'e' Persi fussino oppressi da' Medi,
e la eccellenzia di Teseo che li Ateniesi fussino dispersi; cosí al presente, volendo
conoscere la virtù di uno spirito italiano, era necessario che la Italia si riducessi
nel termine che ella è di presente, e che la fussi piú stiava che gli Ebrei, piú serva
ch'e Persi, piú dispersa che gli Ateniesi, sanza capo, sanza ordine, battuta, spo-
gliata, lacera, corsa, e avesse sopportato d'ogni sorte ruina."

[42] *Opere*, pp. 84-85: "E non è maraviglia se alcuno de' prenominati Italiani non
ha possuto fare quello che si può sperare facci la illustre Casa Vostra, e se in tante
revoluzioni d'Italia e in tanti maneggi di guerra e' pare sempre che in quella la
virtù militare sia spenta. Questa nasce che gli ordini antichi di essa non erano
buoni e non ci è suto alcuno che abbi saputo trovare de' nuovi: e veruna cosa fa
tanto onore a uno uomo che di nuovo surga, quanto fa le nuove legge e li nuovi
ordini trovati da lui. Queste cose, quando sono bene fondate e abbino in loro
grandezza, lo fanno reverendo e mirabile: e in Italia non manca materia da
introdurvi ogni forma. . . . Volendo dunque la illustre Casa Vostra seguitare
quelli eccellenti uomini che redimerno le provincie loro, è necessario innanzi a
tutte le altre cose, come vero fondamento d'ogni impresa, provedersi d'arme
proprie: perche non si può avere nè piú fidi nè piú veri né migliori soldati. . . .
E necessario pertanto prepararsi a queste arme, per potere con la virtù italica
defendersi dalli esterni."

delle Bande Nere in his later years—and in the idealized Fabrizio Colonna of the *Arte della Guerra* he hinted that a *condottiere* might in theory become a legislator. But a mere hegemon does not reach men's civic personalities. In the *Discorsi sopra . . . Tito Livio* we meet both the military leader who founds a republic, and the republic itself as hegemon.

CHAPTER VII

ROME AND VENICE

A) Machiavelli's *Discorsi* and *Arte della Guerra*

[1]

J. H. WHITFIELD has rightly warned students of Machiavelli against commencing their interpretation of his thought with *Il Principe* and confining it to the *Principe* and the *Discorsi*.[1] The present study, which is indeed confined as regards Machiavelli to the two works named, may seem to ignore Whitfield's warning as it ignores much more in recent Machiavelli scholarship; but there is a reason for this. We are engaged in an attempt to isolate "the Machiavellian moment": that is, to isolate the continuous process in the history of ideas which seems the most promising context in which to treat his contribution to that history; and the enterprise is selective, in the sense that it does not commit us to interpreting the totality of his thought or the totality of its development. "The Machiavellian moment" entails less a history of Machiavelli than a historical presentation of Machiavelli, and within the context that has so far been established, the *Principe* and *Discorsi* are selected—as Guicciardini's *discorsi* and *Dialogo* have been selected—because they may be used to present those aspects of his thought which tell us most about the context and about his role in it. The test of this method is its ability to narrate a process actually taking place in the history of ideas, and to show that Machiavelli and Guicciardini were, and are to be understood as, major actors in it; the aim is not to provide a complete intellectual biography—if such a thing can be written—of either man.

This inquiry, then, which has long been principally concerned with the politics of time, has assumed the further shape of an investigation of the concept of virtue. We have distinguished two meanings of the term, each of which has something to do with time and something to do with the Aristotelian concept of form. By the institutionalization of civic virtue, the republic or polis maintains its own stability in time and develops the human raw material composing it toward that politi-

---

[1] J. H. Whitfield, *Discourses on Machiavelli* (above, ch. IV, n. 63), pp. 17, 43, 57-58, 111, 141-42.

cal life which is the end of man. By the exercise of a partly nonmoral *virtù*, the innovator imposes form upon *fortuna*: that is to say, upon the sequence of happenings in time disordered by his own act. In Machiavelli's *Discorsi* (*Discourses on the First Ten Books of Livy*) and his *Arte della Guerra* (*The Art of War*), both these concepts are brought together, and an analysis of these works may start from the conceptual framework used to interpret *Il Principe*. In the earlier work, the innovator has need of *virtù* because he has disturbed the fabric of custom by which a previously existing government was legitimized; it is this that has exposed him to *fortuna* and the unpredictable wills of men. The test which *virtù* exists to meet, but never quite surmounts, is that of modifying men's natures from what custom has made them after custom itself has ceased to be operative. All through *Il Principe*, however, the customary community is exemplified in the hereditary monarchy or principality, whose subjects are simply habituated to obeying a particular man or family. The republic is certainly included in the category of those political structures by disturbing which the innovator renders himself vulnerable to *fortuna*, but we found cause to suspect that something more than customary allegiance gave it solidarity: when men have been accustomed to liberty, we were told, the memory of it does not leave them and they cannot be reconciled to princely rule. We found it not altogether impossible to interpret this as meaning that the experience of citizenship—of what Guicciardini called *participazione*—had changed their natures in a way that mere custom could not. Custom at most could affect men's second or acquired natures, but if it was the end of man to be a citizen or political animal, it was his original nature or *prima forma* that was developed, and developed irreversibly, by the experience of a *vivere civile*.

Machiavelli's thought can now be related to a Savonarolan tradition, and at this point the notion of civic virtue takes on added depths of meaning. It was the virtue, as it was the end, of man to be a political animal; the polity was the form in which human matter developed its proper virtue, and it was the function of virtue to impose form on the matter of *fortuna*. The republic or polity was in yet another sense a structure of virtue: it was a structure in which every citizen's ability to place the common good before his own was the precondition of every other's, so that every man's virtue saved every other's from that corruption part of whose time-dimension was *fortuna*. The republic was therefore a structure whose organizing principle was something far more complex and positive than custom.

But not only was it a fact of experience and history that such structures of virtue could become corrupt and disintegrate; it was, by a terrible paradox, inherent in the very nature of republics that this should be so. The republic attempted to realize a totality of virtue in the relations of its citizens with one another, but did so on a footing that was temporally and spatially limited. Because it had a beginning in time, it must both offer an account of how that beginning had been possible and acknowledge that, since it must in theory have an end, its maintenance was no less problematic than its foundation. Because it had a site or location in space, it was surrounded by neighbors with whom its relations were not governed by the virtue existing only as between citizens. Temporally if not spatially, it faced problems arising from the fact that it was in its own way an innovator; spatially if not temporally, it was involved in a world of unlegitimated power-relationships. The structure of virtue inhabited the domain of *fortuna*, in part at least for the reason that its virtue was itself an innovation, and in consequence it must possess its share of that *virtù* which imposed form on fortune. Study of the "new prince" had already shown that this was largely a question of manipulating human behavior which was unlegitimized and power-centered. The Machiavellian ambiguities did not simply disappear once a republic was founded; they survived in its internal as well as its external relations, and the republic might suffer corruption in the former no less than defeat in the latter. But whereas the prince whose *virtù* failed lost his *stato*, the citizens whose republic failed lost their virtue, in the sense of their citizenship.

For Florentine theorists concerned with republican values, therefore, it was both a practical and a theoretical problem of the first order to show how republics came into being and how they might be maintained. The stakes were very high, being nothing less than the establishment of virtue as a principle of active life; the risks were equally high, because of the difficulty of grounding the enterprise on any but an insecure and transitory foundation. In Guicciardini we have located a tradition of optimate thought, looking in many ways back to Savonarola, which accepted that there was a Florentine impulse toward liberty, an acquired characteristic rooted in the deep but shifting sands of inherited tradition and "second nature," and sought means of transforming this into a fulfilled *prima forma*. Pessimistically but persistently, Guicciardini since 1512 had been exploring the theoretical realm of Aristotelian polity and mixed government, and the less remote exemplary realm of the 1494 constitution and the Venetian model. This train of thought, seeking to combine aristocratic leadership with *governo largo*, seems to have been carried on by the circle who met in the Orti Oricellari after Bernardo Rucellai's death in 1514.[2] This group,

[2] For discussion of this group, and the problems of dating raised by Machiavelli's association with them, see Gilbert, "Bernardo Rucellai and the Orti Oricellari" (above, ch. IV, n. 27), pp. 101-31, and "The Composition and Structure of

aristocratic in membership yet popular in their sympathies, seem to have included men who admired Venice as attaining the structure of virtue through the principle of blending the simple forms of power. Guicciardini's absence in the grim world of the papal territories prevents our regarding him as a member of the Oricellari circle. Machiavelli, who did belong to it, was prevented by birth and belief from sharing its aristocratic idealism, and his *Discorsi*, as we shall see, are best interpreted as a systematic dissent from the Venetian paradigm and a diffuse pursuit of the consequences of that dissent. Guicciardini's *Dialogo del Reggimento di Firenze*, which at times reads like a series of replies to leading ideas of the *Discorsi*, carries on the optimate and philo-Venetian tradition. We may treat the two works as expounding different approaches to the problem of the republic, while studying in later chapters the strange way in which these ideas came together to form the classical republican tradition of northwest Europe and the Atlantic world.

[ii]

Whereas Guicciardini began with the inherited disposition of the Florentines toward liberty, and remained throughout the *Dialogo* anchored within the context of Florentine institutions, Machiavelli, true to form, operated at a higher level of theoretical generality. Like *Il Principe*, the *Discorsi* open with a typology, a classification of republics in terms of their modes of origin. All cities are founded either by natives of the territory or by immigrants;[3] their founders, at the moment of institution, are either independent or remain dependent on some external power, and cities in the latter category, lacking liberty in the first place, rarely come to much. In what reads like a direct challenge to the Salutatian tradition, Machiavelli adds that Florence, a foundation of either Sulla or Augustus, is such a city,[4] a point he will take up again in the *Florentine Histories* and use to develop his argument that Florence has never succeeded in achieving stability of either

Machiavelli's *Discorsi*," *Journal of the History of Ideas* 14, no. 1 (1953), 136-56; Whitfield, *Discourses*, pp. 181-206; and Baron, "Machiavelli: the Republican Citizen and the Author of *The Prince*," *English Historical Review* 76 (1961), 217-53.

[3] *Discorsi*, I, 1; *Opere*, p. 91.

[4] *Opere*, p. 92. "E per non avere queste cittadi la loro origine libera, rade volte occurre che le facciano progressi grandi, e possinsi intra i capi dei regni numerare. Simile a queste fu l'edificazione di Firenze, perché (o edificata da' soldati di Silla o a caso dagli abitatori dei monti di Fiesole, i quali confidatisi in quella lunga pace che sotto Ottaviano nacque nel mondo si ridussero ad abitare nel piano sopra Arno) si edificò sotto l'imperio romano, ne pote ne' principii suoi fare altri augumenti che quelli che per cortesia del principe gli erano concessi."

dominion or liberty.[5] In the present work, he declares (after an interlude on whether cities should be founded in barren or in fertile lands),[6]
it is not his intention to deal with cities in this category, but only with
those which have been wholly autonomous from the moment of
origin;[7] a fairly clear indication that Florence is not a principal object
of reference in the treatises which are to follow.

Reverting to a schematic treatment, Machiavelli next distinguishes
between those cities which have been founded by a legislator[8] such as
Lycurgus, whose work was so near perfection that nothing needed to
be added to it;[9] those whose initial foundation was imperfect and which
consequently are so unfortunate as to be obliged to reform themselves;
those which have degenerated from their foundations; and those whose
initial institution was radically unsound.[10] This classification, crucial to
all that follows in the three books of the *Discorsi*, turns out on inspection to have a number of implications. In the first place, the distinction
is not simply that between all-wise and less-wise *ordinatori*, but also
that between foundation by a single lawgiver and foundation in circumstances that do not permit of attribution to *uno solo* at all. Solon was
less effective than Lycurgus;[11] Romulus, as we shall see, comes somewhere between the two; but Machiavelli is concerned with modern
republics as well as ancient, and cities such as Venice, whose foundations occurred within the Christian era, do not look back to single
legislators, but at best to patron saints who were not truly founders.
The possibly paradigmatic history of Venice begins with a leaderless
swarm of refugees, whose subsequent ascent in the scale of civic virtue

[5] *Istorie Fiorentine*, II, 2; *Opere*, pp. 620-22. See also *Discorsi*, I, 49, where the
statement that Florence has failed to overcome her unfree origins is even more
specific. Cf. Nicolai Rubinstein, "Machiavelli and Florentine Politics," in Gilmore,
ed., *Studies on Machiavelli*, pp. 21-22.

[6] *Discorsi*, I, 1; *Opere*, pp. 93-94.

[7] II, 2, the opening sentences; *Opere*, p. 95.

[8] The word for this is sometimes *ordinatore*, but Machiavelli prefers periphrases
such as *uno solo, il quale ordino*, etc. *Latore delle leggi* is found in II, 1; *Opere*,
p. 205.

[9] *Opere*, pp. 95, 98, 99, 107.

[10] *Opere*, p. 95: "Talché felice si può chiamare quella republica la quale sortisce
uno uomo si prudente che gli dia leggi ordinate in modo che, sanza avere bisogno
di ricorreggerle, possa vivere sicuramente sotto quelle; e si vede che Sparta le
osservò più che ottocento anni sanza corromperle o sanza alcuno tumulto pericoloso. E pel contrario tiene qualche grado d'infelicità quella città che non si sendo
abbattuta a uno ordinatore prudente, è necessitata da se medesima riordinarsi: e
di queste ancora è più infelice quella che è più discosto dall'ordine; e quella ne
è più discosto che co' suoi ordini e al tutto fuori del diritto cammino che la
possa condurre al perfetto e vero fine, perché quelle che sono in questo grado è
quasi impossibile che per qualunque accidente si rassettino."

[11] *Opere*, pp. 98-99.

presents a problem in explanation.[12] Since Machiavelli does not in fact regard Venice as the model to be followed, this particular problem does not trouble him unduly; but the *Discorsi* are throughout to focus on those situations in which, because the legislator was imperfect or non-existent, the citizens have been called upon to reform their own *ordini* and themselves—those in which the matter has had to shape itself into form.

It is also apparent that the distinction being drawn is one between relative freedom from, and relative subjection to, the accidents of time. Lycurgus gave the Spartans "by a single act, all the laws they needed"; thereafter they had only to conserve them, and though—as we shall learn later on—this may be difficult, it is nothing compared to the problems facing those cities which have received their laws "by chance (*caso*), at several times (*più volte*) and through accidental happenings (*accidenti*), as Rome did."[13] To have had a perfect legislator is to enjoy that stability which is freedom from time; to be in any other position is to have to rely on one's own *virtù* in the context of *fortuna*. But once again, as we did in *Il Principe*, we descend from the legislator as ideal type through varying degrees of the insecurity of *virtù*. To have started with vicious institutions is to be in a hopeless condition; to be obliged to reform the laws by efforts originating within an imperfectly formed body is to be unhappy in comparison with Sparta. Nevertheless, republics which started with good but imperfect institutions may become perfect *per la occorrenzia degli accidenti*; we know that *fortuna* responds favorably only to *virtù*, and the implication is reinforced by Machiavelli's observation that self-improvement is difficult for the familiar reasons that make innovation dangerous.[14] The way is now

---

[12] I, 1; *Opere*, pp. 91-92: ". . . cominciarono infra loro, sanza altro principe particulare che gli ordinasse, a vivere sotto quelle leggi che parevono loro più atte a mantenerli. Il che successe loro felicemente per il lungo ozio che il sito dette loro, non avendo quel mare uscita, e non avendo quelli popoli che affliggevano Italia navigli da poterli infestare, talché ogni piccolo principio li pote fare venire a quella grandezza nella quale sono."

[13] *Opere*, p. 95: ". . . alcune le hanno avute a caso ed in più volte e secondo li accidenti, come ebbe Roma." In II, 1, Machiavelli reverts to this theme and explains that *fortuna* is not the cause or agency of Roman greatness; we might render his meaning by saying that it is the context.

[14] *Ibid.*: "Quelle altre che, se le non hanno l'ordine perfetto, hanno preso il principio buono e atto a diventare migliore, possono per la occorrenzia degli accidenti diventare perfette. Ma sia bene vero questo: che mai non si ordineranno sanza periculo, perché gli assai uomini non si accordano mai ad una legge nuova che riguardi uno nuovo ordine nella città, se non è mostro loro da una necessità che bisogni farlo; e non potendo venire questa necessità sanza periculo, è facil cosa che quella republica rovini avanti che la si sia condotta a una perfezione d'ordine."

open to consideration of the case of Rome, where Romulus failed to render the kingship perpetual but did his work well enough to permit its transformation into an exceptionally successful republic. But the typology is significantly incomplete. The case of a republic where the citizens had from the beginning to manage without a legislator to guide them is envisaged but not specified; and in particular we are left wondering what Machiavelli thought of Venice, where there had never been a legislator but exceptional stability had from the beginning supposedly obtained. It is not certain that we are ever to hear in full.

When citizens perfect their own relationships in a context of time, they practice *virtù*, in the sense that they seek superiority over *fortuna*; as practiced by the new prince, this is an art of which little theoretical study has been made before *Il Principe*. But they also practice virtue, in the sense that they establish, maintain and actually improve structures of ethical and political relationships, and here the theoretical literature is very much larger. At this stage, without mentioning the author by name, Machiavelli embarks on a long exposition of Polybius's theory of the constitutional cycle.[15] Since the *Discorsi* cannot possibly be reduced, as we shall see, to a treatise on how to establish the perfectly balanced constitution that escapes from the cycle into timelessness, it is natural to wonder what he meant to achieve by drawing on Polybius. An answer is to be found toward the end of chapter II, where he repeats his earlier distinction between cities with and without perfect legislators. Lycurgus, on a single *occasione*—Machiavelli does not use this word here, but it helps if we insert it—established a distribution of power between kings, nobles, and people which maintained itself for more than eight hundred years. Solon failed to do this, and Athens never achieved stability in consequence. But the case of Rome—from which Polybius had developed the whole theory—exhibits the most extraordinary phenomena of all. Here no legislator attempted to integrate the one, few, and many; the kingship established by Romulus fell with Tarquin; under the republic there ensued generations of strife between patricians and plebeians; and yet from all this disunion emerged the constitution admired by Polybius and stable enough to conquer the world.[16]

---

[15] II, 2; *Opere*, pp. 96-99.

[16] *Opere*, pp. 99-100: ". . . Roma, la quale non ostante che non avesse uno Licurgo che la ordinasse in modo nel principio che la potesse vivere lungo tempo libera, nondimeno furo tanti gli accidenti che in quella nacquero, per la disunione che era intra la Plebe ed il Senato, che quello che non aveva fatto uno ordinatore lo fece il caso. Perché se Roma non sortí la prima fortuna, sortí la seconda: perché i primi ordini suoi se furono difettivi, nondimeno non deviarono dalla diritta via che li potesse condurre alla perfezione . . . alla quale perfezione

Machiavelli has carried out a drastic experiment in secularization. He has established that civic virtue and the *vivere civile* may—though not that it is necessary that they should—develop entirely in the dimension of contingency, without the intervention of timeless agencies. The goal defined by Polybius and achieved by Lycurgus may still be to escape from time and change, but there are circumstances in which citizens move toward this goal through the efforts of their own time-bound selves. The interesting case is not that of Sparta, where a formula for timelessness was written in a single moment by a legislator virtually independent of time; it is that of Rome, where the goal was achieved— as nearly as men can achieve it—by the disorderly and chance-governed actions of particular men in the dimension of contingency and fortune. Men who do this escape from *fortuna* by the exertion of a *virtù* which is their own and not that of a superhuman legislator, and if they erect a conquering republic—even though that takes generations to achieve— what they set up is more durable, and more virtuous, than any attainment open to the *principe nuovo* unless he too is a legislator, which we have found to be improbable. But in detaching himself from the type-figure of Lycurgus, Machiavelli has accepted payment of a price which will have momentous consequences. We learned from the conjunction of legislator and prophet in *Il Principe* that Machiavelli was not free from the need to visualize the republic, or any other body politic, as originating in the realm of the sacred. Being the precondition of virtue in man, it must be created by a virtue more than human. But certain historical ironies arose from the association of the canonical prophet, inspired by the scriptural God, in the class of state-founders along with the pagan hero-legislators acting out of no more than a superhuman grasp of *occasione*. Moses seemed little more archetypal than Lycurgus, and Christian grace, while remaining part of the concept of the legislator, scarcely appeared as an independent variable in its own right. Irony deepened when one contemplated the temporal principality supposed to have been founded by Peter, the only other figure of the Judeo-Christian pantheon (except perhaps Constantine) to whom the role of legislator by grace could possibly be attributed. In chapter XI of *Il Principe* there is a withering, but not wholly dismissive, analysis of ecclesiastical principalities such as the states of the church.

> These rulers alone have states and do not defend them, subjects and do not keep them in order; and these states, through being undefended, never are snatched away; and their subjects, through not

venne per la disunione della Plebe e del Senato, come nei dua prossimi seguenti capitoli largamente si dimosterrà."

being kept in order, never feel any concern, and do not imagine being alienated from them nor can be. These states alone, then, are secure and happy.[17]

The author of the *Tao Te Ching*, from which these sentences might almost come, would have said there was nothing here that needed explaining, but to Machiavelli there is. Since neither virtue nor fortune (as he specifically says)[18] can account for the fact that such principalities exist and survive, we are reminded of the joke that they must be of divine institution since no merely human foundation conducted with such knavish imbecility could last a fortnight. Machiavelli echoes this jest with the perhaps not wholly ironical comment that since they are ordained and maintained by God, it would be impious and imprudent for the human mind to attempt analysis of such matters.[19] But he further says that they are maintained by *ordini antiquati nella religione*—laws grown ancient in religion and hence possessing some of the quality of custom—"which are so powerful and of such kind that they keep their princes in power, in whatever manner they act and live."[20] If the dispositions of providence are beyond finding out, they cannot be used to explain the behavior of mankind. The ecclesiastical principality can be thought of as a species of customary community, more stable than the hereditary monarchy in that it matters even less what the prince is and does. When, especially in the *Discorsi*, we resume a perspective in which the figures of classical antiquity are as visible as those of the Judeo-Christian canon, we are reminded that there have been other religions than this, which can only have been founded by human action. A new category of innovators emerges, and we are told:

> Of all men who have been praised, those have been praised the most who have been the authors and founders of religions. Next come those who have founded republics or kingdoms. After these are celebrated those who have commanded armies and enlarged their

[17] *Opere*, p. 37: "Costoro soli hanno stati, e non li defendano; sudditi, e non li governano; e li stati, per essere indifesi, non sono loro tolti; e li sudditi, per non essere governati, non se ne curano, ne pensano ne possono alienarsi da loro. Solo adunque questi principati sono sicuri e felici."

[18] *Opere*, p. 36: ". . . si acquistano o per virtù o per fortuna, e sanza l'una e l'altra si mantengano . . ."

[19] P. 37: "Ma sendo quelli retti da cagione superiori alle quali mente umana non aggiugne, lascerò il parlarne; perché sendo esaltati e mantenuti da Dio, sarebbe offizio di uomo prosuntuoso e temerario discorrerne."

[20] Pp. 36-37: ". . . sono sustentati dalli ordini antiquati nella religione, quali sono suti tanto potenti e di qualità che tengono e' loro principi in stato, in qualunque modo si procedino e vivino."

kingdom or that of their fatherland. To these may be added men of letters. . . .[21]

A complex distribution of emphasis is going on here. Insofar as the prophet is thought of as doing something explicable in human terms, he is the founder of a structure which possesses some property that makes it even more durable than a structure of inherited allegiance. For this reason he ranks above the legislator; yet we know that the legislator, at least if he is to found a republic, aims at creating a structure of virtue, which is once again something more than a structure of custom. Machiavelli is working toward his contention that a substructure of religion is a prerequisite of civic virtue, and that Rome could not have endured without the contribution of Numa Pompilius, her second king, who devoted his life to developing a religion and implanting it in the natures of the Romans.[22] But if religion is a prerequisite of civic virtue because it can change men's natures, it is not virtue itself if that can exist only in a civic frame. This thought will become part of Machiavelli's subordination of religion to politics, his critique of Christianity on the grounds that it gives men other than civic values.[23] The prophet may rank above the legislator, on the grounds that in any event his work is the most durable; but the prophet should aim at being a legislator and providing a religion which will serve as a substructure for citizenship. It also follows that religious usages are only a part of whatever constitutes civic virtue, and here we should note that after the prophet and legislator the warrior is next to be praised. Romulus was a lawgiver and a warrior, who could "establish civil and military institutions without the aid of divine authority"; Numa was a lawgiver in the sense that he was the author of Roman religion; and there are apparently contradictory passages in Book I of the *Discorsi*, devoted to the problem of which figure is more to be praised and studied.[24] On

---

[21] *Discorsi*, I, 10; *Opere*, p. 118: "Intra tutti gli uomini laudati, sono i laudatissimi quelli che sono stati capi e ordinatori delle religioni. Appresso dipoi quelli che hanno fondato o republiche o regni. Dopo a costoro sono celebri quelli che, preposti agli eserciti, hanno ampliato o il regno loro o quello della patria. A questi si aggiungono gli uomini litterati . . ."

[22] I, 11, generally.   [23] See below, n. 76.

[24] I, 11; *Opere*, p. 123: "E vedesi, chi considera bene le istorie romane, quanto serviva la religione a comandare gli eserciti, ad animire la Plebe, a mantenere gli uomini buoni, a fare vergognare i rei. Talché se si avesse a disputare a quale principe Roma fusse piú obligata, o a Romolo o a Numa, credo piú tosto Numa otterrebbe il primo grado: perché dove è religione facilmente si possono introdurre l'armi, e dove sono l'armi e non religione, con difficultà si può introdurre quella."

I, 19; *Opere*, p. 144: ". . . pensò che a volere mantenere Roma bisognava volgersi alla guerra, e somigliare Romolo, e non Numa. Da questo piglino esemplo

the one hand, Numa's work was more difficult than his predecessor's, since it is easier to teach men military skill and valor than to change their natures by religion; on the other, Numa's successors wisely chose to follow the ways of Romulus, since the hostility of their neighbors rendered a peaceful policy too dependent on "time and fortune." We look back to the antitheses of *Il Principe*: the unarmed and the armed prophet, the cautious man and the daring; and we have returned to the world of *fortuna* and *virtù*. It is clear that custom, religion, and the military spirit all enter into some as yet undefined concept of civic virtue; that virtue in this sense is not separable from the *virtù* that seeks to master *fortuna*; and that there are many types of legislator in addition to the ideal figure we met in *Il Principe*. All these are key ideas in the conceptual structure of the *Discorsi*.

It looks, then, as if Machiavelli was in search of social means whereby men's natures might be transformed to the point where they became capable of citizenship. The combination of Romulus and Numa suggested ways in which the legislator might be freed from the necessity of acting merely as the "armed prophet" of *Il Principe*, who must coerce men the instant they ceased to believe in him; but this freed him at the same time from the need to be the superhuman demiurge we met in the same chapter, who needed only *occasione* to speak the word that transformed the unshaped matter. The legislator-prophet is an even rarer figure in the *Discorsi* than in the *Principe*, because the legislator's *virtù* is becoming less significant than the social and educational processes he sets in motion, and he can thus afford to live in time and be a lesser figure than Lycurgus or Moses. But in diminishing the role of the legislator, Machiavelli has diminished his need of the Savonarolan doctrine that the establishment of the republic—the *prima forma*—must be the work of grace. If men do not need the superhuman in order to become citizens, but achieve citizenship in the world of time and fortune, the earthly and heavenly cities have ceased once again to be identical; and this again may be an ethical as well as a historical distinction. We are moving back to the point at which it is seen that "states are not governed by paternosters," and civic ends—including the virtue of citizenship—are divorced from the ends of

---

tutti i principi che tengono stato: che che somiglierà Numa lo terrà o non terrà secondo che i tempi o la fortuna gli girerà sotto; ma chi somiglierà Romolo, e sia come esso armato di prudenza e d'armi, lo terrà in ogni modo, se da una ostinata ed eccessiva forza non gli è tolto." It should be noted how the language used of the prince *armato di prudenza e d'armi* echoes that used in *Il Principe*, ch. II, of the *principe naturale* who is safe against anything but *una estraordinaria ed eccessiva forza*. See above, ch. 6, n. 4.

redemption. This is to be the most subversive suggestion contained in the *Discorsi*—more so, it may well be argued, than any to be found in *Il Principe*.

[III]

The stage is now set for Machiavelli to offer the daring and arresting hypotheses which are the foundation of the *Discorsi*, and both of which Guicciardini was to find unacceptable.[25] The first is that the disunion and strife among nobles and people was the cause of Rome's attaining liberty, stability, and power[26]—a statement shocking and incredible to minds which identified union with stability and virtue, conflict with innovation and decay, but increasingly intelligible once we have reminded ourselves of the ambiguities of *virtù*. The Romans were innovating in a context not yet sufficiently stable to permit of legitimized behavior, when they established by their own efforts a structure of legitimacy; we must consequently look for actions not themselves legitimate, which nevertheless contributed to such a result. But if union arises from disunion, it comes about through irrational rather than rational action. Of this the inscrutable workings of fortune might seem the only possible explanation, and indeed Machiavelli says once that chance (*caso*) and once that *fortuna* brought about what a legislator (*ordinatore*) had failed to do.[27] But *fortuna* is not a term exclusive of *virtù*; it is a response to it; and we are therefore to look for a special *virtù* which the Romans displayed at this stage in their history. With *Il Principe* in mind, we are aware that *virtù* in these circumstances is more likely to take an active than a passive, a daring than a prudent form, and will exhibit qualities of both the lion and the fox. Here, however, it must appear in the behavior of individuals and groups of citizens toward each other, rather than in the solitary mastery of a prince over his environment, and its social and ethical content must of necessity be greater. *Virtù* must be constitutive of virtue.

There follows a summary of early Roman constitutional history.[28] Though Romulus and his successors did their work less than perfectly, the laws they established were not unsuited to a *vivere libero*.[29] When

[25] See below, ch. 8; and generally his *Considerazioni intorno ai Discorsi del Machiavelli*.

[26] I, 2-6.

[27] See above, n. 16, and the reference there cited.

[28] *Opere*, pp. 99-100.

[29] *Ibid.*: "Perché Romolo e tutti gli altri Re fecero molte e buone leggi, conformi ancora al vivere libero; ma perché il fine loro fu fondare un regno e non una republica, quando quella città rimase libera vi mancavano molte cose che era

the kings turned to tyranny—a reader with the Polybian cycle in mind would note this as a normal instance of corruption following imperfectly stabilized power—much remained to be done for the establishment of freedom. Consequently, the kingly power was not abolished at the expulsion of Tarquin, but was retained in the form of the consulate and now shared authority with the nobility in the senate. When the nobles in their turn became corrupt and arrogant, it was not necessary to destroy the whole frame of government in order to check their power, since that was already limited to some degree by the consuls. The tribunes of the people were established to give weight to the popular voice, and Rome was now a mixed and "perfect" society in which each of the three elements was able to hold back the others from excess.[30]

In this less than absolutely clear narrative, it is evident that the decisive step was taken early and accounts for the establishment of the consulate at the expulsion of the kings. Machiavelli does not specify the causes of this measure, though he may have linked it with a fear lest the Tarquins should return; this fear, he says, caused the nobles to behave moderately toward the people for as long as it lasted.[31] But the emphasis laid on the statement that Rome had laws suited to liberty even before becoming a free city indicates that Romulus and his successors made a legislative contribution of some kind. Machiavelli takes issue with those—Guicciardini was to be one of them—who hold that Rome was an inherently disorderly republic, saved from destruction only by good fortune and extraordinary military prowess. The error here, he says, is to forget that where there is good military organization, there must also be good laws; and where there are *buoni ordini* and *buona milizia*, there will almost certainly be *buona fortuna* also.[32] Good laws produce in addition *buona educazione*, which is exhibited at Rome by the relative bloodlessness of the struggles between the orders—down at least to the time of the Gracchi—and the comparative ease with which concessions were made.[33] The means by which

---

necessario ordinare in favore della libertà, le quali non erano state da quelli re ordinate."

[30] *Ibid.*: "perfezione" used twice and "perfetta" once.

[31] I, 3; *Opere*, pp. 100-101.

[32] I, 4; *Opere*, p. 101: ". . . contro la opinione di molti che dicono Roma essere stata una republica tumultuaria, e piena di tanta confusione che se la buona fortuna e la virtù militare non avesse sopperito a' loro difetti, sarebbe stata inferiore a ogni altra republica. Io non posso negare che la fortuna e la milizia non fussero cagione dell'imperio romano; ma è mi pare bene che costoro non si avegghino che dove è buona milizia conviene che sia buono ordine, e rade volte anco occorre che non vi sia buona fortuna."

[33] *Ibid.*, p. 102: "Né si può chiamare in alcun modo con ragione una republica

the plebeians asserted their demands were to demonstrate, to close their shops, to refuse military service, and to march out of the city, none of which was really as destructive of order as it may appear. A republic which desires to make use of its people—the phrase is pregnant with meaning for the next stage of the analysis—ought to allow them means of expressing their aspirations,[34] which in free peoples are seldom harmful to liberty; such a people fears only oppression and has the capacity to understand when its fears are mistaken.[35]

We have still no definition of the "freedom" first established in the people by the kings, but links are emerging which connect it in some way with military service. *Buoni ordini* produce both *buona milizia* and *buona educazione*; the liberty of the Roman *plebs* consisted at least partly in its ability to refuse military service, and from its *buona educazione* Machiavelli seems to deduce the relative bloodlessness of civil conflict and the progressive improvements of the constitution by which conflicts were resolved. Freedom, civic virtue, and military discipline seem then to exist in a close relation to one another.

The second major hypothesis of the *Discorsi* is put forward in I, 5 and 6. The question initially raised is whether something called "the guardianship (*guardia*) of liberty" is better entrusted to the nobles or to the people,[36] and as Guicciardini was early to point out, it never becomes very clear whether "guardianship" means a preponderance of power or some specialized form of authority.[37] But it emerges before

---

inordinata, dove sieno tanti esempli di virtù, perché li buoni esempli nascano dalla buona educazione, la buona educazione dalle buone leggi, e le buone leggi da quelli tumulti che molti inconsideratemente dannano; perché che esaminerà bene il fine d'essi, non troverrà ch'egli abbiano partorito alcuno esilio o violenza in disfavore del commune bene, ma leggi e ordini in beneficio della publica libertà."

[34] *Ibid.*: ". . . dico come ogni città debbe avere i suoi modi con i quali il popolo possa sfogare l'ambizione sua, e massime quelle città che nelle cose importanti si vogliono valere del popolo . . ."

[35] *Ibid.*, pp. 102-103: "E i desiderii de' popoli liberi rade volte sono perniziosi alla libertà, perché e' nascono o da essere oppressi, o da suspizione di avere ad essere oppressi. E quando queste opinioni fossero false e vi è il rimedio delle concioni, che surga qualche uomo da bene che orando dimostri loro come ei s'ingannano: e li popoli, come dice Tullio, benché siano ignoranti sono capaci della verità, e facilmente cedano quando da uomo degno di fede è detto loro il vero."

[36] I, 5, title: "Fove piú sicuramente si ponga la guardia della libertà, o nel popolo o ne' grandi . . ."

[37] "I do not understand the title of the question, that is, what it means by placing the guardianship of freedom with the people or the nobles, because it is one thing to say who is to have power, the nobles or the plebs—and of this Venice is an example, for there it is so far in the hands of the nobles that all the plebs are excluded—and it is quite another thing, where all take a share in government,

long that Machiavelli is not talking about the distribution of power or the construction of a constitution, so much as exploring the relationship of military and political *virtù*. He assumes from the start that Sparta and Venice entrusted "guardianship" to the nobles, Rome to the people. All three have been presented as successful examples of the balanced constitution, but where Sparta enjoyed this condition from the time of Lycurgus and Venice attained it through the deliberations of her citizens and the aid of fortune, Rome arrived at it through internal strife and a process of development. An equation of some kind is being established between peaceful stability and the aristocratic principle. Early in chapter v, Machiavelli says unequivocally that liberty lasted longer in Sparta and Venice than at Rome, where the plebeian desire to engross all offices led to the ascendancy of Marius and the ruin of the republic; so that if we were to attach the normal value to the attainment of the greatest possible stability and duration, we would clearly opt for the aristocratic version of liberty.[38] But Machiavelli does not leave it there, or make the choice indicated by his argument. Embarking on a discussion of which is the more dangerous to a republic, the desire of the nobles to keep what they have (a monopoly of office) or the desire of the people to acquire what they have not (unrestricted entry into office), he says, parenthetically as it were, that the crucial question is whether the republic is to grow and establish an empire, as was always the aim of Rome, or simply to maintain its independence, as was originally the sole purpose of Sparta and Venice.[39]

The ideal type of perfectly stable government has already been equated with aristocratic predominance; now we learn that the ideal of stability itself is not the only value to be pursued, since a republic may pursue empire at the sacrifice of its own longevity—a choice which involves a preference for a more popular form of government. The point here is in part Machiavelli's concern, typical of his generation, with the republic's ability to control its external environment.[40]

---

to say who should have special responsibility or care for the defence of liberty, placed either in plebeian magistrates or in noble ones." Cecil and Margaret Grayson, eds. and trans., *Francesco Guicciardini: Selected Writings* (London: Oxford University Press, 1965), p. 70.

[38] *Discorsi*, I, 5; *Opere*, p. 103: "E se si andasse dietro alle ragioni, ci è che dire da ogni parte; ma se si esaminasse il fine loro, si piglierebbe la parte de' Nobili, per avere la libertà di Sparta e di Vinegia più lunga vita che quella di Roma."

[39] *Ibid.*, p. 104: "Ed in fine chi sottilmente esaminerà tutto, ne farà questa conclusione: o tu ragioni d'una republica che voglia fare uno imperio, come Roma, o d'una che le basti mantenersi. Nel primo caso gli è necessario fare ogni case come Roma; nel secondo può imitare Vinegia e Sparta, per quelle cagioni, e come nel seguente capitolo si dirà."

[40] The whole of I, 6, requires to be read in this connection.

All cities have enemies and live in the domain of fortune, and it must be considered whether a defensive posture does not expose one more to unexpected change than a bold attempt to control it; the antithesis between prudence and audacity is at work again. But the crucial association is that between external policy and the distribution of internal power. Sparta and Venice, for as long as they were able to avoid the pursuit of empire and to adopt the posture of the prudent man who waits upon events,[41] did not need to arm the people or to concede them political authority; consequently they were able to enjoy stability and internal peace. Rome resolved upon empire, upon a daring attempt to dominate the environment, and consequently upon innovation and upon a *virtù* which would enable her to control the disorder which her own actions had helped to cause. She had therefore to arm the people, to suffer the strife caused by their demands for more power, and to make concessions to those demands.[42] The arming of the plebeians contributed to Rome's military greatness; the struggle between the orders to the consolidation of a mixed government; but some continuing disequilibrium, yet to be analysed, to shortening the life of Roman liberty. Rome is, as it were, the "new prince" among republics, and Machiavelli would rather study Rome than Venice as he would rather study the new prince than the hereditary ruler: the short view is more interesting than the long, and life in it more glorious. But unlike the hereditary ruler, Sparta and Venice did not escape the domain of fortune; from defending their independence, they were led to dominate their neighbors and this task proved too much for the Spartan military elite as for the mercenaries employed by Venice; indeed, it destroyed the internal constitution of Sparta, and Machiavelli plainly would not have cared if the same thing had happened to Venice. A republic which could avoid all contact with her neighbors might limit her arms and live in aristocratic stability for ever; but since this cannot be done,[43]

---

[41] *Opere*, p. 109: ". . . se la è difficile a espugnarsi, como io la presuppongono, sendo bene ordinata alla difesa, rade volte accaderà o non mai che uno possa fare disegno di acquistarla. Se la si starà intra i termini suoi, e veggasi per esperienza che in lei non sia ambizione, non occorrerà mai che uno per paura di sé le faccia guerra; e tanto più sarebbe questo, se e' fussi in lei constituzione o legge che le proibisse l'ampliare. E sanza dubbio credo che potendosi tenere la cosa bilanciata in questo modo, che e' sarebbe il vero vivere politico e la vera quiete d'una città."

[42] *Opere*, p. 108: ". . . dare luogo a' tumulti e alle dissensioni universali il meglio che si può, perché sanza gran numero di uomini e bene armati non mai una republica potrà crescere, o se la crescerà mantenersi."

[43] *Opere*, p. 109: "Ma sendo tutte le cose degli uomini in moto, e non potendo stare salde, conviene che le salghino o che le scendino, e a molte che la ragione non t'induce, t'induce la necessità; talmente che avendo ordinata una republica atta a mantenersi non ampliando, e la necessità la conducesse ad ampliare, si verrebbe a tor via i fondamenti suoi ed a farla rovinare più tosto. Così dall'altra parte,

to reject expansion is to expose oneself to fortune without seeking to dominate her—the thought of chapter xxv of *Il Principe* is being repeated. The Roman path does not guarantee against ultimate degeneration, but in the present and foreseeable future—in the world of accidental time, in short—it is both wiser and more glorious.[44]

But there is more to Roman *virtù* than the will of an aggressive republic to dominate in a disordered world. It has already been made clear that the military discipline established by the first kings had something to do with the development of liberty and stability in the republic; and now we have learned that there is an intrinsic connection between military expansion, the arming of the plebeians and the *vivere popolare*. What we need next is to understand the relations existing in Machiavelli's mind between the military and civic capacities of the individual—in shorter language, between the soldier and the citizen. Evidence on this question is scattered through the pages both of the *Discorsi* and of the *Arte della Guerra*, written, it seems, in 1519-1520, not long after the completion of the *Discorsi*; the two works can without overinterpretation be brought together.

"The Art of War," while almost inevitable as an English translation of the title of the later book, misses something of the richness of the original. *L'arte della guerra* has a double meaning: it signifies both the "art" of war in the sense of the creative skill of generalship, and the "profession" of war, in the sense in which the principal skilled occupations of Florence were organized into greater and lesser *arti* or guilds. But the *arte della guerra* is not like any other; it is true that Machiavelli is writing in part to show how the business of war can become as honorable and useful to the republic as, say, the *arte della lana*—the woolen-manufacturers' guild on which so much in Florentine economics and politics depended—but his central point is that it must on no account become a separately organized profession to which men look for the whole of their living. A soldier who is nothing but a soldier is a menace to all other social activities and very little good at his

---

quando il Cielo le fusse si benigno che la non avesse a fare guerra, ne nascerebbe che l'ozio la farebbe o effeminata o divisa; le quali due cose insieme, o ciascuna per sé, sarebbono cagione della sua rovina."

[44] *Ibid.*: "Pertanto non si potendo, come io credo, bilanciare questa cosa, né mantenere questa via del mezzo a punto, bisogna nello ordinare la republica pensare piú onorevole, ed ordinarla in modo che quando pure la necessità la inducesse ad ampliare, ella potesse quello ch'ella avesse occupato conservare. E per tornare al primo ragionamento, credo ch'e' sia necessario seguire l'ordine romano e non quello dell'altre republiche, perche trovare un modo mezzo infra l'uno e l'altro non credo si possa; e quelle inimicizie che intra il popolo e il senato nascessino, tollerarle, pigliandole per uno inconveniente necessario a pervenire alla romana grandezza."

own. We have returned, of course, to the well-worn theme of Machiavelli's hatred of mercenaries and his exaltation of the civic militia, but the relation of this theme to Aristotelian theory of citizenship is the vital point if we wish to understand his political thought. A man who should devote the whole of his energies to the *arte della lana* and none to participation in public affairs would appear in classical theory as less than a citizen and a source of weakness to his fellows; but a man who should devote the whole of his energies to the *arte della guerra*— Machiavelli sometimes uses phrases like "make war his *arte*"[45]—is an infinitely greater danger. The banausic tradesman is pursuing a limited good to the neglect of the common good, and that is bad; he may set that good in the place of the good of the city, and that is worse, as it would be if the *arte della lana* were to become the exclusive government of Florence; but the banausic soldier is far more likely to do this, and to do it in a far more antisocial way, because his *arte* is to exercise the means of coercion and destruction. For a whole string of reasons, therefore—from the unreliability of *condottieri* to the danger of Caesarian tyranny—it is important "to restrict the practice of this art to the commonwealth" (*al pubblico lasciarla usare per arte*).[46] This *arte*, more than any other, must be a public monopoly; only citizens may practise it, only magistrates may lead in it, and only under public authority and at the public command may it be exercised at all.

The paradox developed in Machiavelli's argument is that only a part-time soldier can be trusted to possess a full-time commitment to the war and its purposes. A citizen called to arms, with a home and an occupation (*arte*) of his own, will wish to end the war and go home, where a mercenary, glad rather than sorry if the war drags on indefinitely, will make no attempt to win it.[47] Because the citizen has his

---

[45] E.g., *Opere*, p. 503: ". . . (la) guerra, che è l'arte mia . . . essendo questa una arte mediante la quale gli uomini d'ogni tempo non possono vivere onestamente, non la può usare per arte se non una republica o uno regno; e l'uno e l'altro di questi, quando sia bene ordinato, mai non consentí ad alcuno suo cittadino o suddito usarla per arte; né mai alcuno uomo buono l'esercitò per sua particulare arte."

[46] *Opere*, p. 505: "E dico che Pompeo e Cesare, e quasi tutti quegli capitani che furono a Roma dopo l'ultima guerra cartaginese, acquistarono fama come valenti uomini, non come buoni; e quegli che erano vivuti avanti a loro, acquistarono gloria come valenti e buoni. Il che nacque perché questi non preserò lo esercizio della guerra per loro arte, e quegli che io nominai prima, come loro arte la usarono." P. 507: "Debbe adunque una città bene ordinata volere che questo studio di guerra si usi ne' tempi di pace per esercizio e ne' tempi de guerra per necessità e per gloria, e al publico solo lasciarla usare per arte, come fece Roma. E qualunque cittadino che ha in tale esercizio altro fine, non è buono; e qualunque città si governa altrimenti, non è bene ordinata."

[47] *Ibid.*: ". . . se uno re non si ordina in modo che i suoi fanti a tempo di

own place in the body politic, he will understand that the war
fought to preserve it; a mercenary with no home but the ca
become the instrument of tyranny over the city he was
defend—a tyranny which may well be exercised by a Po
Caesar, once a citizen but now so far perverted as to use the sword as
an instrument of political power. Machiavelli presses these arguments
with a vigor that was to earn them three centuries of close attention,
but they are limited to the extent that they explain why only the citizen can be a good soldier. The contention that only the soldier can
be a good citizen is also being made, but much less explicitly. The
thought implementing it is complex, but rests in part on some assertions
made in the preface:

> And if, in every ordering of a city or kingdom, the greatest care
> is taken to keep men faithful, peaceable and full of the fear of God,
> in military government this care should be doubled. For of whom
> should the commonwealth require greater faith than of him who
> must promise to die for her? In whom should there be more love
> of peace than in him who may be attacked only in war? In whom
> should there be more fear of God than in him who, having to sub-
> mit himself to infinite dangers, has greatest need of Him?[48]

Military *virtù* necessitates political virtue because both can be presented in terms of the same end. The republic is the common good;
the citizen, directing all his actions toward that good, may be said to
dedicate his life to the republic; the patriot warrior dedicates his death,
and the two are alike in perfecting human nature by sacrificing particular goods to a universal end. If this be virtue, then the warrior displays it as fully as the citizen, and it may be through military discipline
that one learns to be a citizen and to display civic virtue. In the anatomy of early Roman virtue given in the *Discorsi*, Machiavelli seems

---

pace stieno contenti tornarsi a casa e vivere delle loro arti, conviene di necessità
che rovini: perché non si truova la più pericolosa fanteria che quella che è composta di coloro che fanno la guerra come per loro arte; perché tu sei forzato o a
fare sempre mai guerra, o a pagargli sempre, o a portare pericolo che non ti
tolgano il regno."

[48] *Opere*, p. 496: "E se in qualunque altro ordine delle cittadi e de' regni si usava
ogni diligenza per mantenere gli uomini fedeli, pacifichi e pieni del timore d'Iddio,
nella milizia si raddoppiava. Perché in quale uomo debbe ricercare la patria maggiore fede, che in colui che le ha a promettere di morire per lei? In quale debbe
essere più amore di pace, che in quello che solo dalla guerra puote essere offeso?
In quale debbe essere più timore d'Iddio, che in colui che ogni dì sottomettendosi
a infiniti pericoli ha più bisogno degli aiuti suoi?"

(The Ricciardi edition of the *Opere*, which is being cited here, does not contain the full text of the *Arte della Guerra* and this must be sought elsewhere.)

to depict it as built on military discipline and civic religion, as if these were the two socializing processes through which men learned to be political animals. He distrusted Christianity—or at least he divorced it from the political good—because it taught men to give themselves to ends other than the city's and to love their own souls more than the fatherland.[49] But if it followed that no end was to transcend the social, the social good must cease to be transcendent. Of early Roman religion Machiavelli said that it was founded principally on augury, men regarding as divine that which offered means of foretelling the future.[50] Pagan religion, which he preferred to Christianity as a social instrument, served a purpose identical with that of the republic: the control of fortune. But the republic, being a structure of action, did this better than augury; the lies and fallacies of the latter were justified if they gave men confidence in themselves, helped them display military *virtù*—most of Machiavelli's anecdotes of Roman religion have to do with augury and auspices before battle[51]—and so to develop that dedication of oneself to a common good which was the moral content of pagan religion and is the essence of civic virtue. It was their civic religion which made the Roman plebeians good soldiers; their military discipline and their civic religion which made them attentive to the public good in the midst of civil conflict, and thus able to control their future in the teeth of augury where necessary.[52]

It is evident by now that Machiavelli is employing the concept of armed *virtù* to transform the question of the participation of the many in citizenship. The usual way of defending a *governo largo* was to assert that the many were peaceable, desired little more than the enjoyment of a private liberty, had common sense enough to reject what was not for their own good and moral sagacity enough to elect and defer to their natural superiors in the civic elite. Machiavelli used this line of argument in the *Discorsi*, and again in a work contemporary with the *Arte della Guerra*, the "Discourse on Reforming Florentine

[49] *Discorsi*, II, 2; see below, n. 77.

[50] I, 12; *Opere*, p. 126: "La vita della religione Gentile era fondata sopra i responsi degli oracoli e sopra la setta degli indovini e degli aruspici; tutte le altre loro cerimonie, sacrifici e riti, dependevano da queste. Perché loro facilmente credevono che quello Iddio che ti poteva predire il tuo futuro bene o il tuo futuro male, to lo potessi ancora concedere."

[51] I, 13-15.

[52] *Opere*, p. 132: Papirius defied the auguries and won a battle; Appius Claudius defied them and lost; "di che egli fu a Roma condannato, e Papirio onorato: non tanto per avere l'uno vinto e l'altro perduto, quanto per avere l'uno fatto contro gli auspicii prudentemente, e l'altro temerariamente. Né ad altro fine tendeva questo modo dello aruspicare, che di fare i soldati confidentemente ire alla zuffa, dalla quale confidenza quasi sempre nasce la vittoria."

Government Written at the Request of Pope Leo X";[53] but he does not, as Guicciardini repeatedly does, elaborate it into a theory of the distribution of functions between the many and the few. His emphasis is as always on innovation, *fortuna*, and *virtù*; we shall see that the *Discorsi* is in part a treatise on the different forms which may be assumed by the fixed quantity of *virtù* there is in the world at any one time, and on how this quantity may be conserved and canalized. In Roman virtue he has discovered a new form of active *virtù* which is peculiar to the many, and exists only in dynamic warrior states which arm the people and give them civic rights; and his debt to the militia tradition in Florentine theory, plus his experience under Soderini in actually organizing a militia, leads him to ground citizenship upon military virtue to the point where the former becomes the outgrowth of the latter. The plebeian as Roman citizen is less a man performing a certain role in a decision-making system than a man trained by civic religion and military discipline to devote himself to the *patria* and carry this spirit over into civic affairs, so that he conforms to the dual model of the Machiavellian innovator displaying *virtù* and the Aristotelian citizen attentive to the common good. The Roman *plebs* displayed *virtù* in demanding their rights, virtue in being satisfied when their demands were granted.

The analysis of the *Arte* defines both the moral and the economic characteristics of the citizen warrior. In order to have a proper regard for the public good, he must have a home and an occupation of his own, other than the camp. The criterion is identical with that applied to the Aristotelian citizen, who must have a household of his own to govern so that he may not be another man's servant, so that he may be capable of attaining good in his own person and so that he may apprehend the relation between his own good and that of the polis. The mercenary soldier is a mere instrument in another man's hand; but the citizen-warrior is more than an instrument in the public hand, since his *virtù* is his own and he fights out of knowledge of what it is he fights for. We have seen that for Bruni and Guicciardini, loss of liberty and the corruption of the body politic occurred when men, by compulsion or out of effeminacy, expected from others what they

---

[53] *Discorso sopra il riformare lo stato di Firenze a instanza di Papa Leone*, in *Tutte le Opere di Niccolo Machiavelli*, ed. Francesco Flora and Carlo Cordié (Rome: Arnaldo Mondadori Editore, 1949), II, 526-40. He insists that the *universalità dei cittadini* must be given back the *autorità* which rests on membership in the Consiglio Grande (p. 534), but adds that "li pochi cittadini non hanno ardire di punire gli uomini grandi" (p. 537) and that if arrangements are made to restore popular access to office by degrees, "non veggiamo ancora come la universalità dei cittadini non si avessi a contentare, veggendosi rendute parte delle distribuzioni, e l'altre vedendo a poco a poco cadersi in mano" (p. 538).

should have expected from themselves as members of the public. It is clear that this would apply, in a double sense, when a city ceased to use its own citizens in its armies and employed mercenaries instead. The citizens would be corrupted because they permitted inferiors to do for them what should be done for the public good; the mercenaries would be agents of that corruption because they performed a public function without regard for the public good; and any ambitious individual could set himself above the republic and destroy it, by bringing the unthinking mercenaries to do for him what should only be done for the public, but had been allowed by unthinking citizens to pass out of public control. If we now examine the theory and the instances of corruption set out by Machiavelli in the *Discorsi*, we shall observe how far it is founded on the concept of the individual citizen's autonomy and how far the test of that autonomy is his willingness and ability to bear arms.

Corruption appears, initially, as a generalized process of moral decay whose beginnings are hard to foresee and its progress almost impossible to resist. The constitutional order is rooted in the moral order, and it is the latter which corruption affects; on the one hand there cannot be *buoni ordini* without *buoni costumi*, but on the other, once *buoni costumi* have been lost there is a very slender chance that *buoni ordini* alone will succeed in restoring them. Institutions are dependent on the moral climate and laws which work well when the people are not corrupt produce effects the reverse of those desired when they are.[54] For this reason we should study the failure of the Gracchi, who with the best of intentions precipitated the ruin of Rome by attempting to reactivate the institutions of her former virtue.[55] When Machiavelli lays down that political and religious bodies must be preserved by being brought back to their initial principles,[56] he does not mean that

[54] *Discorsi*, I, 18; *Opere*, p. 140: "E presupporrò una città corrottissima, donde verrò ad accrescere piú tale difficultà; perché non si truovano né leggi né ordini che bastino a frenare una universale corruzione. Perché cosí come gli buoni costumi per mantenersi hanno bisogno delle leggi, cosí le leggi per osservarsi hanno bisogno de' buoni costumi. Oltre a di questo, gli ordini e le leggi fatte in una republica nel nascimento suo, quando erano gli uomini buoni, non sono dipoi piú a proposito, divenuti che ei sono rei. E se le leggi secondo gli accidenti in una città variano, non variano mai, o rade volte, gli ordini suoi: il che fa che le nuove leggi non bastano, perché gli ordini che stanno saldi le corrompono."

[55] I, 37: *Opere*, p. 173: "Del quale disordine furono motori i Gracchi, de' quali si debbe laudare piú la intenzione che la prudenzia. Perché a volere levar via uno disordine cresciuto in una republica, e per questo fare una legge che riguardi assai indietro, è partito male considerato: e come di sopra largamente si discorse, non si fa altro che accelerere quel male a che quel disordine ti conduce; ma temporeggiandolo, o il male viene piú tardo, o per sé medesimo, col tempo, avanti che venga al fine suo, si spegne."

[56] III, I; *Opere*, p. 309: "E perché io parlo de' corpi misti, come sono le repub-

a corrupt state can make a fresh beginning[57] and start again, or that the Polybian cycle is reversible, but that the onset of corruption must be prevented by exemplary and probably punitive enforcement of the *principii* at intervals of ten years or thereabouts;[58] we must refrain from entering the time-process as far as it is possible to do so. Institutional devices may reinforce and renew themselves, and may even prevent the onset of corruption, so long as corruption has not actually begun; once it has, however, they are probably powerless. The advantage of institutional machinery for reinforcing the *principii* every now and again is that otherwise the beginnings of corruption can only be detected by the prescience of a wise man, who (assuming that he exists at all) will find it hard to convince his neighbors, and increasingly hard the more they are actually corrupted. The tragic perplexity of the situation is that corruption is easily visible only after it has taken general hold, and by this time the *costumi* of the people will have changed, so that old laws and remedies no longer apply. Under these conditions, Machiavelli suspends his normal preference for bold action over tem-

---

liche e le sette, dico che quelle alterazioni sono a salute che le riducano inverso i principii loro. E però quelle sono meglio ordinate, ed hanno piú lunga vita, che mediante gli ordini suoi si possono spesso rinnovare, ovvero che per qualche accidente, fuori di detto ordine, vengono a detta rinnovazione. Ed è cosa piú chiara che la luce che non si rinnovando questi corpi non durano.

"Il modo del rinnovargli è, come è detto, ridurgli verso e' principii suoi; perché tutti e principii delle sette e delle republiche e de' regni conviene che abbiano in sé qualche bontà, mediante la quale ripiglino la prima riputazione ed il primo augumento loro. E perché nel processo del tempo quella bontà si corrompe, se non interviene cosa che la riduca al segno, ammazza di necessità quel corpo." For the application of this to religions, see below, n. 81.

[57] Though the sack of Rome by the Gauls comes close to a beginning again from matter reduced to chaos; *ibid.*, pp. 309-10.

[58] *Opere*, pp. 310-11: "Le quali cose [Machiavelli has been listing exemplary punishments recounted by Livy and discussed more than once in the *Discorsi*] perché erano eccessive e notabili, qualunque volta ne nasceva una, facevano gli uomini ritirare verso il segno [more than Cesare Borgia can be said to have achieved by the execution of Ramirro de Orca]; e quando le cominciarono a essere piú rare cominciarono anche a dare piú spazio agli uomini di corrompersi e farsi con maggiore pericolo e piú tumulto. Perché dall'una all'altra di simili esecuzioni non vorrebbe passare il piú diece anni, perché passato questo tempo, gli uomini cominciano a variare con i costumi e trapassare le leggi: e se non nasce cosa per la quale si riduca loro a memoria la pena, e rinnuovisi negli animi loro la paura, concorrono tosto tanti delinquenti che non si possono punire sanza pericolo." This is true irrespective of the justice of the original *principio*; Machiavelli goes on to say that the Medici rulers of Florence between 1434 and 1494 used *ripigliare lo stato*, i.e., to dissolve their own system so as to renew it in its original severity—a procedure recalling the "great purges" and "cultural revolutions" of modern times.

porization; it is wrong to legislate, as the Gracchi did, contrary to established customs even when these are corrupt, and Cleomenes of Sparta did better by conducting a blood-purge of the corrupted elements before attempting to restore the laws of Lycurgus.[59] If you cannot do this you should temporize;[60] but there is clearly not much more to be hoped for from a time-process governed by increasing corruption than from one governed by *fortuna*. The only real hope lies in the absolute power of one man of transcendent virtue, who will end corruption by restoring virtue in the people. But he faces an even harder task than the charismatic legislators of *Il Principe*; for whereas they found their peoples completely anomic and plastic, so that they owed nothing to fortune but the *occasione*, he finds a people corrupt and an environment delivered over to fortune by the perversity of their behavior. In these circumstances, even the armed prophet may fail; the methods by which he seizes power may corrupt even him,[61] and should this not happen, his charisma will not restore the people to virtue in one lifetime,[62] so that they will return to their vomit at his death (as de Gaulle is supposed to have prophesied of the French). The chances that one superhuman legislator will be succeeded by another are clearly remote, though in view of Machiavelli's insistence on military and

[59] I, 9 (Cleomenes), 17, 18 (Cleomenes again), 33, 38, 46.

[60] I, 33: *Opere*, pp. 164-65: "Dico adunque che, poi che gli è difficile conoscere questi mali quando ei surgano, causata questa difficultà da uno inganno che ti fanno le cose in principio, e piú savio partito il temporeggierle, poi che le si conoscono, che l'oppugnarle: perche temporeggiandole, o per loro medesime si spengono o almeno il male si differisce in piú lungo tempo. E in tutte le cose debbono aprire gli occhi i principi, che disegnano cancellarle o alle forze ed impeto loro opporsi, di non dare loro in cambio di detrimento augumento, e credendo sospingere una cosa tirarsela dietro, ovvero suffocare una pianta a annaffiarla; ma si debbano considerare bene le forze del malore, e quando ti vedi sufficiente a sanare quello, mettervi sanza rispetto, altrimenti lasciarlo stare né in alcun modo tentarlo."

[61] I, 18; *Opere*, p. 142: ". . . a fare questo non basta usare termini ordinari essendo i modi ordinari cattivi, ma è necessario venire allo straordinario, come è alla violenza ed all'armi, e diventare innanzi a ogni cosa principe di quella città e poterne disporre a suo modo. E perché il riordinare una città al vivere politico presuppone uno uomo buono, e il diventare per violenza principe di una republica presuppone uno uomo cattivo, per questo si troverrà che radissime volte accaggia che uno buono, per vie cattive, ancora che il fine suo fusse buono, voglia diventare principe; e che uno reo, divenuto principe, voglia operare bene, e che gli caggia mai nello animo usare quella autorità bene che gli ha male acquistata."

[62] I, 17; *Opere*, p. 139: ". . . ma morto quello, la si ritorna ne' primi disordini suoi. La cagione è, che non può essere uno uomo di tanta vita che'l tempo basti ad avvezzare bene una città lungo tempo male avvezza. E se uno d'una lunghissima vita o due successioni virtuose continue non la dispongano, come la manca di loro, come di sopra è detto, rovina; se già con di molti pericoli e di molto sangue e' non la facesse rinascere."

religious *virtù* (as exemplified in Romulus and Numa) as the two tools of creative state-founding, it is interesting that he did not use the instances of the warrior Joshua succeeding to the prophet Moses, or of the judges succeeding him as inspired war leaders. The attempt to discover legislators in the prophets of Jewish and sacred history is not significantly resumed in the *Discorsi*.

Down to this point it might seem as if corruption were little more than an extension of *fortuna*—an irrational succession of divergencies from a norm, uncontrollable because unpredictable and inherently subversive of order. But in reality the phenomenon is subjected to a more detailed analysis than this suggests. It is noteworthy how often in his treatment of corruption Machiavelli employs teleological language: laws and constitutions, even structures of virtue, are *forma*, and the legislator and law-enforcer (not to mention the reformer) seek to impose form on the *materia* of the republic, which is of course its human constituent matter. In certain chapters of the *Discorsi* we note a habit of using *materia* as a quasi-colloquial term for the population of a city; but in the theory of corruption its employment is technical.[63] What happens as corruption develops, we are told, is that the *materia* itself undergoes change, and the reason why old laws lose their efficacy when this happens is that the same form cannot be imposed upon, or educed from, different matter. It is at times almost suggested that the Romans ought to have devised new laws to suit their changed state, though as long as this change is summarized as corruption it must seem virtually impossible that they could have done so.

There seems a certain ambiguity as to whether the *materia* is changing into something else or merely decomposing. But we recall that to

[63] I, 17; *Opere*, p. 139: ". . . dove la materia non è corrotta, i tumulti ed altri scandali non nuocono: dove la è corrotta, le leggi bene ordinate non giovano, se già le non son mosse da uno che con una estrema forza le faccia osservare tanto che la materia diventi buona . . . una città venuta in declinazione per corruzione di materia, se mai occorre che la si rilievi, occorre per la virtù d'uno uomo che è vivo allora, non per la virtù dello universale che sostenga gli ordini buoni . . ." I, 18; *Opere*, p. 141: ". . . altri ordini e modi di vivere si debbe ordinare in uno suggetto cattivo che in uno buono, nè può essere la forma simile in una materia al tutto contraria." III, 8; *Opere*, p. 342: Manlius Capitolinus "venne in tanta cecità di mente, che non pensando al modo di vivere della città, non esaminando il suggetto, quale esso aveva, non atto a ricevere ancora trista forma, si misse a fare tumulti in Roma contro al Senato e contro alle leggi patrie. Dove si conosce la perfezione di quella città e la bontà della materia sua. . . ." P. 343: "se Manlio fusse nato ne' tempi di Mario e di Silla, dove già la materia era corrotta, e dove esso arebbe potuto imprimere la forma dell'ambizione sua arebbe avuti quegli medesimi seguiti e successi che Mario e Silla. . . . Però è bisogno, a volere pigliare autorità in una republica e mettervi trista forma, trovare la materia disordinata dal tempo, e che a poco a poco e di generazione in generazione si sia condotta al disordine . . ."

Savonarola reformation had been a question of restoring the *prima forma*, and as this meant to him no less than the end of man, which was to know God through living virtuously, he had looked on reformation as a total restoration of man's moral nature, to be carried out only through grace. As other Florentine intellects had increasingly equated virtue with the *vivere civile*, its necessary conditions had appeared increasingly temporal; and time was governed by such forces as use and custom, the creators of "second nature." If the *materia*'s aptitude to assume the *forma* of republican virtue was governed by its second nature, a condition determined by time, then change within the *materia* might be qualitative change from one temporal condition to another. Accordingly, the question could arise of how far the prince or the legislator could modify the second nature, or structure of custom, which was the product of time and circumstance. Since the republic was a structure of virtue, it was more than a structure of custom; yet virtue was rooted in *buoni costumi*, and these could become corrupted in time, so that the *materia* itself was changed and less capable of virtue. On the one hand, virtue appeared an ideally realized state, from which there could be no change but degeneration; on the other, it was seen to rest in temporally determined conditions, so that the loss of virtue could be described in terms of historical and qualitative change—even though such a description must be circumscribed by ideas of what was conducive or nonconducive to virtue.

There is consequently a sociological as well as a merely moral analysis of corruption to be found in the *Discorsi*. At the end of the first chapter (I, 17) in which corruption is considered, Machiavelli says unequivocally that corruption has a cause, other than the generalized wickedness of men.

> Such corruption and lack of aptitude for liberty arise from inequality in a city; and in order to restore equality it is necessary to use the most extraordinary of means, for which few have the knowledge or the will.[64]

What this "inequality" is we are not told in any formal expository way; it is necessary to collect evidence about Machiavelli's thoughts on the subject. In the next chapter, devoted to explaining how the old laws of Rome became inoperative under corruption, he says that after the Romans had conquered all their enemies and had ceased to fear them, they began electing to office, not those best fitted for it, but those most skilled at gaining the favor (*grazia!*) of others. They next

[64] *Opere*, p. 139: "Perché tale corruzione e poca attitudine alla vita libera nasce da una inequalità che è in quella città, e volendola ridurre equale è necessario usare grandissimi straordinari, i quali pochi sanno o vogliono usare . . ."

descended to giving office to those who had most power, so that fear of the powerful dissuaded good men from seeking office themselves and even from speaking freely in public.[65] These are the conditions under which reform becomes almost impossible. A republic having got so far will not reform itself; since the laws have become inoperative, reform must be carried by violent means; and since some men are now more powerful than the law they must be controlled by the almost kingly power of one man, who will find it difficult to restore either law or liberty by the means he must adopt.[66] It looks as if some quasi-cyclical return to monarchy has become nearly inevitable.

But if the above constitutes an account of the rise of "inequality," that term connotes neither inequality of wealth nor inequality of political authority—there is no reason to suppose that Machiavelli objected to either—but a state of affairs in which some individuals look to others (Guicciardini's *particulari*) when they should be looking to the public good and public authority; and "equality" must be a state of affairs in which all look to the public good alike. Corruption is the rise of factions, of overmighty citizens, a moral condition affecting the powerful and their dependents with equal corrosiveness; and its origins in this instance are purely moral, a change of Roman *costumi* for the worse. We are not told at this stage of any social conditions which would necessarily carry corruption with them, but it is easy to imagine, given the equation of citizen with self-maintained warrior that runs through Machiavelli's theories of the militia and the popular state, that they would have something to do with the many's nonpossession or surrender of the means of war.

In I, 55, the concepts of corruption and inequality recur in a way that constitutes a social analysis of the conditions propitious and unpropitious to republican government. The latter, Machiavelli says, becomes altogether impossible where there are many persons of the kind he calls *gentiluomini*. These are either such as live in luxury off the returns from their landed estates, or—more dangerous still—such as have in addition castles and subjects (*sudditi*). Naples, Rome, the Romagna, and Lombardy "are full of these two sorts of men"; unfortunately, it is not quite clear from the context whether Machiavelli has in mind the two "sorts" of *gentiluomini*, military and nonmilitary, or the two

---

[65] I, 18; *Opere*, pp. 140-42.

[66] *Ibid.*, pp. 142-43: "Da tutte le soprascritte cose nasce la difficultà o impossibilità, che è nelle città corrotte, a mantenervi una republica o a crearvela di nuovo. E quando pure la vi si avesse a creare o a mantenere, sarebbe necessario ridurla più verso lo stato regio che verso lo stato popolare, acciochè quegli uomini i quali dalle leggi per la loro insolenzia non possono essere corretti, fussero da una podestà quasi regia in qualche modo frenati. E a volergli fare per altre vie diventare buoni, sarebbe o crudelissima impresa o al tutto impossibile . . ."

classes of castle-dwelling lords and their *sudditi*. The latter is at least a possible interpretation, since it is the power of the *gentiluomini* that makes them incompatible with free government, and it is hard to see what power the idle absentees of the first category exert. It is the absence of *signori di castella* from Tuscany, as well as the extreme rarity of *gentiluomini*, that makes republican life there at least possible; and just as a republic cannot be established unless the *gentiluomini* are first wiped out, since otherwise the *materia* is so corrupt that laws cannot govern it and kingly power must be set up, so a kingdom or principality cannot be established where there is equality unless an ambitious few are given castles and men, and made dependent for them on the monarch.[67] Here Machiavelli's thought has nearly caught up with that of Lodovico Alamanni, except that he stresses the baron where Alamanni stressed the courtier.

If it is the castles and retainers of the *gentiluomini* that make them a cause of inequality and corruption, the uncorrupt republic must be a state lacking military dependencies and one characteristic of "equality" must be that all are warriors alike. There must be the political conditions which permit the arming of all citizens, the moral conditions in which all are willing to fight for the republic and the economic conditions (lacking in the case of a lord's retainers) which give the warrior a home and occupation outside the camp and prevent his becoming a *suddito*, *creato*, or mercenary whose sword is at the command of some powerful individual. The economic independence of the warrior and the citizen are prerequisites against corruption. If these conditions are lacking, a city which eschews expansion and cuts itself off from the world may still limit its armies and its citizen body and escape corruption; in spite of the contempt with which Machiavelli describes Venetian policies, he never quite says that Venice has been corrupted by the employment of mercenaries. But a city which had

---

[67] *Opere*, p. 205: "Ed a volere in provincie fatte in simil modo introdurre una republica non sarebbe possibile. Ma a volerle riordinare, se alcuno ne fusse arbitro, non arebbe altra via che farvi uno regno: la cagione è questa, che dove è tanto la materia corrotta che le leggi non bastano a frenarla, vi bisogna ordinare insieme con quelle maggior forza, la quale è una mano regia che con la potenza assoluta ed eccessiva ponga freno alla eccessiva ambizione e corruttela de' potenti."

P. 206: "Trassi adunque di questo discorso questa conclusione: che colui che vuole fare dove sono assai gentiluomini una republica, non la può fare se prima non gli spegne tutti; e che colui che dove è assai equalità vuole uno regno o uno principato, non lo potrà mai fare se non trae di quella equalità molti d'animo ambizioso ed inquieto, e quelli fa gentiluomini in fatto e non in nome, donando loro castella e possessioni e dando loro favore di sustanze e di uomini, acciochè, posto in mezzo di loro, mediante quegli mantenga la sua potenza ed essi mediante quello la loro ambizione, e gli altri siano costretti a sopportare quel giogo che la forza, e non altro mai, può fare sopportare loro."

chosen popular government, aggressive *virtù*, and an armed people, and then allowed the citizen-soldiers to become the clients and retainers of a powerful few, would be miserably corrupt indeed. This had been the ultimate fate of Rome. Machiavelli gives two principal causes for the collapse of the Roman republic.[68] The first[69] is the revival by the Gracchi of the law limiting landownerships and dividing conquered lands among the people, which caused such hatreds between nobles and people that each faction appealed to its own military leaders and their armies; the second[70] is the prolongation of military commands, which tempted the armies to forget public authority and become the partisans of the politicians who commanded them. It is noteworthy that neither statement quite explains the corruption of the Roman citizen-soldier, and curious (as James Harrington observed) that Machiavelli never quite arrived at the point of uniting the two explanations by saying that the distribution of lands fell under the control of soldier-politicians, so that armies became the clients and factions of their generals, who alone could reward them, until the most successful *imperator* emerged to rule Rome with his now mercenary army. But this thesis became a commonplace with civic humanists of the seventeenth and eighteenth centuries, whose thought in this and other regards was based on premises entirely Machiavellian: with Harrington, Montesquieu, Jefferson, and Gibbon.

[IV]

A sociology of liberty, then, is emerging, founded very largely upon a concept of the role of arms in society and in a *vivere civile*; and at its negative pole, the concept of corruption is tending to replace that of the mere randomness of *fortuna*. This of course is a consequence of the politicization of virtue, which has made the latter's decline explicable in political terms. On the one hand, corruption is still an irreversible, one-way process, part of the mutability and entropy of sublunary things; personality and polity may be kept in equilibrium or may decay, and there is no third possibility; but on the other hand, the concepts of autonomy and dependence, which the notion of arms serves to organize, are beginning to offer an objective and almost materialist, as opposed to a subjectively ethical, explanation of how corrup-

---

[68] In I, 5, he says that the people became disposed to adore all politicians who attacked the nobility, "donde nacque la potenza di Mario e la rovina di Roma." In I, 37, the agrarian law appears as the cause of this.

[69] I, 37.

[70] III, 24. The theme of the professionalization of the armies by the emperors is further developed in Book I of the *Arte della Guerra*.

tion may occur. Men lose their *virtù* because they have lost their autonomy, and their autonomy does not consist solely in their *virtù*; the Roman republic was not destroyed by the mysterious power of the *volubil creatura*, but through describable causes whose consequences were not arrested while there was yet time.

But although secondary causes are rapidly encroaching upon the figure of *fortuna*, there is a deeper sense in which the *virtù-fortuna* polarity is still operative; and this is integral to the *Discorsi*'s democratic theory. By basing the popular republic on the *virtù* of the armed citizen, Machiavelli had transformed the problem of popular participation from one of knowledge to one of will. In the mainstream of Aristotelian theory, the many possessed a knowledge based on experience, which made them capable of electing their superiors and exercising a judgment of policies that differed little from the judgment of use, custom, and tradition. To Machiavelli, however much he might praise it,[71] this was too slow-moving and entrusted too much to the aristocracy to suit a world of sudden dangers and challenges to the very existence of states. Accordingly, he had substituted the armed popular state, the *senatus populusque*, which could both confront its enemies and display a disciplined and dynamic will to alter and improve its internal relationships. The strength of Rome was that it could mobilize the maximum of *virtù* for purposes both military and civic, and continue doing so for centuries. But in the last analysis all depended on *virtù* as a quality of the individual personality, a devotion to the *respublica* which rested on political, moral, and economic autonomy. If the citizen in arms had all these things, and *buona educazione* besides, he would display Roman *virtù*, though higher than that he could not rise. Republics mobilized more *virtù* than monarchies, and the multiplicity of their leadership made them more flexible and adaptable to the shifts of *fortuna* than could be expected of the single personality of the ruling individual;[72] it was only when changed circumstances (probably cor-

---

[71] I, 58; *Opere*, p. 212: "E non sanza cagione si assomiglia la voce d'un popolo a quella di Dio: perché si vede una opinione universale fare effetti maravigliosi ne' pronostichi suoi, talché pare che per occulta virtù ei prevegga il suo male ed il suo bene."

[72] III, 9; *Opere*, pp. 344-45: "E se Fabio fusse stato re di Roma poteva facilmente perdere quella guerra; perché non arebbe saputo variare col procedere suo secondo che variavono i tempi [cf. *Il Principe*, ch. xxv; above, ch. vi, n. 39]. Ma essendo nato in una republica dove erano diversi cittadini e diversi umori, come la ebbe Fabio, che fu ottimo ne' tempi debiti a sostenere la guerra, cosí ebbe poi Scipione ne' tempi atti a vincerla.

"Quinci nasce che una republica ha maggiore vita ed ha piú lungamente buona fortuna che uno principato, perché la può meglio accomodarsi alla diversità de' temporali, per la diversità de' cittadini che sono in quella, che non può uno

ruption) necessitated alterations in their structure that the need to obtain consensus made them slow to act.[73] For all this, however, success was a function of *virtù* and *virtù* was a matter of the autonomy of personalities mobilized for the public good. Only in republics could it be mobilized, and every republic was a finite particular in which only a finite number of individuals could be trained and assembled to display *virtù*. However defined, the *virtù* of every individual depended on the *virtù* of every other; its decline was impossible to arrest once it was well started; and it must be manifested in arms as well as in citizenship, in the external world of war as well as in the civic world of justice. Once it was established that the *governo largo*, which aimed at maximizing *participazione*, required an armed many and a republic organized for expansion, then civic virtue became dependent upon the republic's ability to conquer others, a *virtù* displayed in a world where *fortuna* ruled and *giustizia* did not. Florence could not be a republic if she could not conquer Pisa; but the Pisans could not be virtuous if they could not stop her.

The militarization of citizenship makes the *Discorsi* in an important sense more morally subversive than *Il Principe*. The prince existed in a *vivere* so disordered that only if he aimed as high as Moses or Lycurgus did he undertake any commitment to maintaining civic virtue in others; but the republic can be morally and civilly virtuous in itself only if it is lion and fox, man and beast, in its relation with other peoples; the image of the centaur found in *Il Principe*[74] may be repeated at a higher level of complexity. Recognition of this duality, relatively easy for Polybius who had a less developed concept of a God who might be directing the universe on principles of justice, was for Machiavelli directly linked with his implicit refusal to treat the republic as a creature of grace. Its justice was spatially and temporally finite; toward other republics it could display only a *virtù militare*, and its ability to do this was determinative of its ability to maintain civic virtue internally. Virtuous republics were at war with one another. For this reason the Christian virtues and the civic could never coincide;

---

principe. Perché un uomo che sia consueto a procedere in uno modo, non si muta mai, come è detto e conviene di necessità che quando e' si mutano i tempi disformi a quel suo modo che rovini."

[73] *Ibid.*: ". . . in uno uomo la fortuna varia, perché ella varia i tempi ed egli non varia i modi. Nascene ancora le rovine delle cittadi, per non si variare gli ordini delle republiche co' tempi, come lungamente di sopra discorremo. Ma sono più tarde, perche le penono più a variare; perché bisogna che venghino tempi che commuovino tutta la republica, a che uno solo col variare il modo del procedere non basta."

[74] Ch. xviii; *Opere*, p. 56; "mezzo bestia e mezzo uomo."

humility and the forgiveness of injuries could have no place in the relations between republics, where a prime imperative was to defend one's city and beat down her enemies. Machiavelli does indeed insist that "if religion had been maintained in the beginnings of the Christian republic according to the precepts of its founder, Christian states and republics would be more united and happier than they are,"[75] and that Christianity does not prohibit us from loving and defending our country;[76] but he also makes it plain, both that a pursuit of other-worldly felicity makes us endure injuries to our republic as well as to ourselves,[77] and that the civic virtues flourished best when there was no mercy to enemies and the defeat of a city meant death or slavery to its inhabitants.[78] The implications of the *vivere civile* are becoming pagan, secular, and time-bound; it is most itself in a world where there is no religion but augury and no values that transcend those of this life.

If the republic does not exist in a dimension of grace, religion may be seen as existing in a dimension identical with that inhabited by the republic. At the beginning of Book III, we are told that all the things of this world have a time-limit set to their existence, but that only those run the course appointed for them by heaven which keep their bodies unaltered as at first organized (*ordinato*) or change in such a way as to bring them back to their first principles. This is especially true of mixed bodies, such as republics or religions (*sette*).[79] In just what sense a religion is a *corpo misto* Machiavelli does not specify—the conventional answer, once given of the church by Savonarola, was that it was a compound of heavenly and earthly things[80]—but, in order to leave no doubt that *la nostra religione* can be considered among the

---

[75] I, 12; *Opere*, p. 127: "La quale religione se ne' principi della republica cristiana si fusse mantenuta secondo che dal datore d'essa ne fu ordinato, sarebbero gli stati e le republiche cristiane piú unite, piú felici assai che le non sono."

[76] II, 2; *Opere*, pp. 227-28: "Perché se considerassono come la ci permette la esaltazione e la difesa della patria, vedrebbono come la vuole che noi l'amiamo ed onoriamo, e prepariamoci a essere tali che noi la possiamo difendere."

[77] *Ibid.*, p. 227: "La religione antica . . . non beatificava se non uomini pieni di mondana gloria, come erano capitani di eserciti e principi di republiche. La nostra religione ha glorificato piú gli uomini umili e contemplativi che gli attivi. Ha dipoi posto il sommo bene nella umiltà, abiezione, e nel dispregio delle cose umane: quell'altra lo poneva nella grandezza dello animo, nella fortezza del corpo ed in tutte le altre cose atte a fare gli uomini fortissimi. E se la religione nostra richiede che tu abbi in te fortezza, vuole che tu sia atto a patire piú che a fare una cosa forte. Questo modo di vivere adunque pare che abbi renduto il mondo debole, e datolo in preda agli uomini scelerati, i quali sicuramente lo possono maneggiare, veggendo come l'università degli uomini per andare in Paradiso pensa piú a sopportare le sue battiture che a vendicarle." Cf. Guicciardini, *Ricordi*, B 27.

[78] II, 2, *passim*.   [79] Above, n. 56.   [80] Above, ch. 4, n. 38.

cose del mondo, he examines the work of Francis and Dominic in imitating the poverty of Christ and thus restoring religion *verso il suo principio*. The orders founded by these saints then preached that wicked rulers should not be disobeyed but their punishment left to God, with the result that the wicked do as they please, not fearing a punishment in which they do not believe. The wicked in question are corrupt princes of the church rather than secular tyrants; but this, says Machiavelli, is how religion has been maintained by a *rinnovazione* which the saints carried out.[81] The irony at the expense of the reforming orders and their attempt to restore clerical poverty could not be much plainer; and it does not seem that the faithful who attend to the teachings of Francis and Dominic will pay much attention to the liberty or civic virtue of their republics.

The dimension of grace being thus lost, the republic and its virtue ceased to be universal and became once more spatially and temporally—it will enhance the contrast if we say "historically"—finite. In time and space there were many republics and the virtue of each abutted upon the virtue of others. To admit this was to confront the problem of showing how a republic, any more than a prince, could reconstitute an Italy which was already partly organized into republics. Savonarola had been able to envisage Florence as reforming the world only in a context of apocalypse and only in terms which seemed to promise that city earthly riches and power. To Machiavelli that route was not open, and the relations of a republic with other republics presented a problem of real difficulty. Confederation, hegemony, and naked dominion seemed to be the available possibilities, and if the last was ruled out as radically unstable, the first was open to the same criticism as the aristocratic republic: voluntarily to limit expansion was too dangerous. Rome, the expanding democracy, had taken the middle path, and Machiavelli devotes much space[82] to examining and recom-

---

[81] III, 1; *Opere*, pp. 312-13: "Ma quanto alle sette, si vede ancora queste rinnovazioni essere necessarie per lo esempio della nostra religione, la quale se non fossi stata ritirata verso il suo principio da Santo Francesco e da Santo Domenico sarebbe al tutto spenta: perché questi con la povertà e con lo esempio della vita di Cristo, la ridussono nella mente degli uomini, che già vi era spenta; e furono si potenti gli ordini loro nuovi che ei sono cagione che la disonestà de' prelati e de' capi della religione non la rovinino, vivendo ancora poveramente, ed avendo tanto credito nelle confessioni con i popoli e nelle predicazioni, che ei danno loro a intendere come egli è male dir male del male, e che sia bene vivere sotto la obedienza loro, e se fanno errori lasciargli gastigare a Dio. E cosí quegli fanno il peggio che possono, perché non temono quella punizione che non veggono e non credono. Ha adunque questa rinnovazione mantenuto, e mantiene, questa religione."

[82] II, 2, 3, 4, 19, 23.

mending the various devices by which the Romans associated their allies and former enemies with themselves in relations which were those of subordination without involving the conscious loss of all freedom. It is partly in this context that we should view the famous, if slightly opaque, dictum that to be ruled by a free people is worse than to be ruled by a prince, apparently because the prince desires your love and allegiance and so may respect your customs, whereas the free people, being morally self-sufficient, have no interest in anything other than your total subjection.[83] The Romans sought to avoid exerting this tyranny, but Machiavelli has no illusions about their long-term success. They could manage their relations with the formerly free republics of Italy, but once their rule was extended to peoples who had always been less than free and whom they governed accordingly, the Italians found themselves assimilated to the status of the barbarian provincials.[84] In this way, "the Roman empire destroyed by force of arms all the republics and free cities," so that their virtue could never afterwards recover; and this, together with the spread of other-worldly values, explains the weakened love of liberty displayed by moderns as compared with ancients. It was the Roman conquest of Tuscany which ultimately caused Florence's inability to develop as a free and stable republic.[85]

[83] II, 2; *Opere*, p. 229: "E di tutte le servitù dure quella è durissima che ti sottomette a una republica: l'una perché la è piú durabile e manco si può sperare d'uscirne, l'altra perché il fine della republica è enervare ed indebolire, per accrescere il corpo suo, tutti gli altri corpi: il che non fa uno principe che ti sottometta . . . s' egli ha in sé ordini umani ed ordinari, il piú delle volte ama le città sue suggette equalmente, ed a loro lascia . . . quasi tutti gli ordini antichi . . ." Compare Guicciardini, *Ricordi*, C 107.

[84] II, 4; *Opere*, pp. 232-33: ". . . avendosi lei fatti di molti compagni per tutta Italia, i quali in di molti cose con equali leggi vivevano seco, e dall'altro canto, come di sopra è detto, sendosi riserbata sempre la sedia dello imperio ed il titolo del comandare, questi suoi compagni venivano, che non se ne avvedevano, con le fatiche e con il sangue loro a soggiogar se stessi. Perché come ei cominciorono a uscire con gli eserciti di Italia, e ridurre i regni in provincie, e farsi suggetti coloro che per essere consueti a vivere sotto i re non si curavano di essere suggetti, ed avendo governatori romani ed essendo stati vinti da eserciti con il titolo romano, non riconoscevano per superiore altro che Roma. Di modo che quegli compagni di Roma che erano in Italia, si trovarono in un tratto cinti da' sudditi romani ed oppressi da una grossissima città come era Roma; e quando ei s'avviddono dello inganno sotto il quale erano vissuti, non furono a tempo a rimediarvi. . . ."

[85] II, 2; *Opere*, p. 228: "Fanno adunque queste educazioni e si false interpretazioni, che nel mondo non si vede tante republiche quante si vedeva anticamente, né per consequente si vede ne' popoli tanto amore alla libertà quanto allora. Ancora che io creda piú tosto essere cagione di questo, che lo imperio romano con le sue arme e sua grandezza spense tutte le republiche e tutti e viveri civili. E benché poi tale imperio si sia risoluto, non si sono potute le città ancora rimet-

Since military (and consequently civic) virtue is both emulative and competitive, the loss of virtue in the other peoples helped cause the decline of virtue in the Romans themselves; and this is in part[86] the context in which Machiavelli propounds the view that the amount of *virtù* in the world at any one time is finite,[87] and that when it is all used up through corruption there will be some kind of cataclysm, after which a few uncorrupted barbarian survivors will emerge from the mountains and begin again.[88] The theory is cyclical and presupposes a closed, because not transcended, system in the human and moral world; the neo-stoic overtones recall the *aeternitas mundi* of the heterodox Aristotelians. Machiavelli arrives at it both through his abandonment of the dimension of grace and through his decision to regard virtue as existing only in republics—that is, in finite quantities themselves finite in number, space, and time; we should remind ourselves that the only alternative to a cyclical *aeternitas mundi* was a Christian eschatology. But it follows that virtue itself, not merely a *virtù* limited to new princes, has now become cannibal—Shakespeare's "universal wolf" that

---

tere insieme né riordinare alla vita civile, se non in pochissimi luoghi di quello imperio." For references to the Roman overthrow of Tuscan virtue, see pp. 228, 235, 237.

[86] The context is also that of the question how it is that the memory of former times is now and again completely destroyed, obscuring the problem of whether or not it has existed from eternity. This Machiavelli says is brought about by changes of religion and of language: a concept which in some respects anticipates Gibbon's "triumph of barbarism and religion."

[87] II, *proemio*, *Opere*, pp. 218-19: ". . . giudico il mondo sempre essere stato ad uno medesimo modo, ed in quello essere stato tanto di buono quanto di cattivo; ma variare questo cattivo e questo buono di provincia in provincia, come si vede per quello si ha notizia di quegli regni antichi, che variavano dall'uno all'altro per la variazione de' costumi, ma il mondo restava quel medesimo: solo vi era questa differenza, che dove quello aveva prima allogata la sua virtù in Assiria, la collocò in Media, dipoi in Persia, tanto che la ne venne in Italia e a Roma. E se dopo lo Imperio romano non è seguito Imperio che sia durato nè dove il mondo abbia ritenuta la sua virtù insieme, si vede nondimeno essere sparsa in di molte nazioni dove si viveva virtuosamente . . ."

[88] II, 5; *Opere*, p. 236: "Quanto alle cause che vengono dal cielo, sono quelle che spengono la umana generazione e riducano a pochi gli abitatori del mondo. E questo viene o per peste o per fame, o per una inondazione d'acque, e la più importante è questa ultima: si perché la è più universale, si perché quegli che si salvono sono uomini tutti montanari e rozzi, i quali non avendo notizia di alcuna antichità, non la possono lasciare a' posteri. . . . la natura, come ne' corpi semplici quando e' vi è ragunato assai materia superflua, muove per sè medesima molte volte e fa una purgazione la quale è salute di quel corpo, cosí interviene in questo corpo misto della umana generazione, che quando . . . la astuzia e la malignità umana e venuta dove la può venire, conviene di necessità che il mondo si purchi . . ."

"last eats up himself." If the republic quarreled with grace, the consequences were universal. The truly subversive Machiavelli was not a counselor of tyrants, but a good citizen and patriot.

A republican scheme of history therefore continued to be *fortuna*-dominated and cyclical, a matter of finite quantities of energy, rarely mobilized, inclined to be self-destructive and moving toward total entropy until some unpredictable force should mobilize them again. Machiavelli's contributions to republican theory were extraordinarily original, but were based on and limited to his decision that military dynamism was to be preferred before the search for stability. It was this decision that led him to investigate the military and social bases of political action and personality; but meanwhile, other minds were making the more traditional decision in favor of stability and, without abandoning the problems of arms and war, were turning back toward the Venetian example, which they used as a paradigm for exploring the constitutional distribution of power. The combination of their thought with Machiavelli's helped to form the classical republican tradition of early modern England and America.

CHAPTER VIII

ROME AND VENICE

B) Guicciardini's *Dialogo* and the Problem of Aristocratic Prudence

UNLIKE THE WRITINGS of Machiavelli, those of Guicciardini are always specifically related to the context of Florentine politics and lack the older man's theoretical and speculative freedom. This is an index not merely to Guicciardini's greater concern with the actual and the practicable, but also to his aristocratic conservatism. The specific and particular world, almost by definition, could be known and controlled only with a considerable admixture of experience, and at the heart of Guicciardini's thinking we shall always find the image of the *ottimati* as a politically experienced inner ring who could govern because they knew by experience the city they had to deal with, and because they knew by experience that they could not do too much with it. Yet there could be no greater mistake than to treat Guicciardini as the mere mouthpiece of his class; if he regarded the *ottimati* as the keystone of the governing structure, he had no illusions whatever about the way they would behave if allowed to monopolize power and office. The minimum which he allows to the other political classes—even if he generally allows them no more than that minimum—is the role of providing the structure within which the virtues of the aristocracy, namely practical experience and the pursuit of honor, may remain uncorrupt and efficacious.

It follows also from his determination to anchor his thought within the context of an actual historical Florence that the highly abstract universal concepts, easy to discern in *Il Principe* and the *Discorsi*, do not meet the eye in the *Dialogo del Reggimento di Firenze*.[1] Fortune and innovation, matter and form, are not the objects of regular allusion and it is not easy to uncover their implicit presence; the degree of abstraction is less than that dictated by Machiavelli's decision to deal with republics and principalities, innovation and corruption, as general topics and does not call for the same degree of categorization. Guic-

---

[1] The text used here is that of Palmarocchi's *Dialogo e Discorsi* (*D. e D.*), pp. 3-174; see above, ch. v, n. 12.

ciardini indeed liked to profess a certain contempt for speculative reasoning. The principal speaker of the *Dialogo* is one who has learned his politics by experience, without studying either philosophy or history, though he does not deny the role of history in making the experience of the dead available to those who lack it among the living; and he does not mean that the lessons of experience are incapable of organized exposition. We must avoid at all costs the pitfall of supposing that thought centered on the concept of experience lacks a conceptual structure, to understand which is to understand the thought. Experience itself is a concept as well as an irreducible reality, and this book is largely concerned with a conceptual structure in which the notions of experience and prudence played a prominent and revealing part. Guicciardini's treatment of these and related ideas tells us much about his conceptions of political knowledge and action, and so about his version of what is usually called political theory. We examine his thought by examining its theoretical structure, first in the *Dialogo*, where it is still possible to imagine Florence possessing an institutional organization in which experience could do its proper work, and later in the *Ricordi*, where the historical structure of Florence has collapsed and experience is left to function in a world not unlike that of Machiavelli's *Prince*.

The *Dialogo* is the last of Guicciardini's *discorsi* on Florentine government: the last, that is, of a series of works, commencing with the *Discorso di Logrogno* in 1512, in which he thought it possible to make normative recommendations for a stable political structure to be established at Florence.[2] Felix Gilbert and Vittorio De Caprariis have studied the evolution of his thought *dalla politica alla storia*, to use the latter's title:[3] from an attempt to establish the conditions necessary for a stable political life to a conviction that human existence could only be depicted in the streams of *fortuna*-directed change; and it is significant that the *Dialogo* is set at a point in the past history of Florentine politics, one moreover to which Guicciardini had already averred there could be no returning. It takes place in 1494, shortly after the overthrow of the Medici; there is significant mention of Savonarola, but the focus lies on the problems of the *ottimati* as participants in the revolution. The speakers are three younger *ottimati*—Piero Capponi, Paolantonio Soderini, and Guicciardini's father Piero—who to varying degrees support the expulsion of the Medici as conducive to *libertà*,

---

[2] *D. e D.*, p. 6: "Come se la volontà ed el desiderio degli uomini non potessi essere diverso dalla considerazione o discorso delle cose, o come se da questo ragionamento apparissi quale di dua governi male ordinati e corrotti mi dispiacessi manco; se già la necessità non mi costrignessi a biasimare manco quello di che s'ha piú speranza potersi riordinare."

[3] See above, ch. v, n. 10.

and an older man, Bernardo del Nero, Guicciardini's mouthpiece, who tends to regret the overthrow of the ruling family but is prepared to consider what can be made of a regime founded on the Consiglio Grande. We know that Guicciardini held the establishment of the Council to have worked such changes in Florentine politics that there could be no return to Medicean rule as it had been before 1494; and he also held that the role of the *ottimati* in restoring the Medici and overthrowing the Council in 1512 meant that the former were now bound irrevocably to that family and would never again have the chance to help set up a republic based on their exclusion. The whole dialogue therefore takes place at a moment of opportunity which is gone forever; and as if to rub this point in further, Guicciardini chose in Bernardo del Nero a principal interlocutor who had been illegally put to death by the Savonarolan regime—one, moreover, whose personality he had analyzed with detachment in his earlier historical writings.[4] Time and a worsening world separate Guicciardini from the scene of his dialogue, at once emphasizing and diminishing its ideal character; he does not write its recommendations in the expectation that they will be carried out.

In Guicciardini's version of the year 1494, then, three friends call on Bernardo del Nero and begin to discuss with him whether the recent *mutazione dello stato* will prove beneficial or not. Bernardo bleakly observes that he has found by experience that all *mutazioni* are for the worse, but Soderini asks whether there may not be such a thing as change from a bad form of government to a good, or from a good to a better.[5] In reply, Bernardo begins, half ironically, by going back to a point at which Savonarola had once found himself: is it not the teaching of philosophers, in particular Marsilio Ficino, that among the three species of government that of the one is better than that of the few or the many? Guicciardini causes his father Piero to reply, on the grounds that he was once Ficino's pupil and that Capponi has no learning except a little astrology; there is some sort of joke against political philosophers going on here, which we must be careful not to interpret

---

[4] Domandi ed. (above, ch. v, n. 9), pp. 134-35.

[5] *D. e D.*, p. 8: "[Bernardo:] . . . in tanto tempo che io ho, ho veduto per esperienzia che le mutazioni fanno piú danno alla città che utile, di che vi potrei molti esempli allegare . . .

"[Soderini:] Si forse, quando le sono di quella sorte che sono state l'altre de' tempi vostri, le quali si debbono mutazioni da uomo a uomo, o come meglio avete detto voi, alterazione che mutazioni di stati . . . questo ultimo, nel quale solo a' dì vostro si è fatta mutazione di una specie di governo a un' altro. E quando questo accade, e si muti di una specie cattiva in una buona, o d'una buona in una migliore, io non so perché la mutazione non sia utile . . ."

too coarsely.[6] Piero says apologetically that, as everybody knows, it is a commonplace of political theory that there is a good and a bad form of each of the three species, and that the rule of one man is best only when all three are good. The question is whether it has come about "by the choice or the free will of the governed," "according to their will and natural propensities (*naturale*)," or by force, faction or usurpation," according to the appetite of the ruling element (*secondo lo appetito di che prevale*)." Piero seems to be leaving room for elective and hereditary succession, and to be running together the unjust acquisition of power and its unjust exercise. He remarks that the rule of one is the best when good, but the worst when bad—a Savonarolan dictum—and further that since it is easiest for one man to impose his will on the public, it is the likeliest to become bad. If one were creating a new government and considering the possibility of monarchy, one would have to ask whether the prospect of good outweighed the risks of evil.[7]

All this is indeed commonplace; but Guicciardini has begun to exploit the ambiguities of the word *naturale*. Applied to a form of government, it might mean "elective," "hereditary," or simply "suited to the character and propensities of the governed," and Guicciardini is about to steer a course through its ambiguities of such a kind as to involve rejection both of the idea that one form is inherently better than any other, and of the Savonarolan doctrine that the historically conditioned "nature" of the Florentines requires a regime of wide popular participation. In reply to Piero, he makes Bernardo agree that a ruler whose position is *naturale* or based on *elezione e voluntà* has no

[6] *D. e D.*, pp. 11-12: note also Bernardo's remark (p. 11): ". . . esperienzia della quale nessuno di voi manca, avendo già piú e piú anni sono, atteso alle cose dello stato; ed oltre a questo ed el naturale buono, avete davantaggio le lettere con le quali avete potuto imparare da' morti gli accidenti di molte età; dove io non ho potuto conversare se non co'vivi, né vedere altre cose che de' miei tempi." For a relationship of some sort between Ficino and the elder Guicciardini, see Carlo Dionisotti, "Machiavelli letterato," in Gilmore, ed., *Studies on Machiavelli*, p. 110.

[7] *D. e D.*, pp. 12-13: "[Piero:] È vera cosa che di questi tre reggimenti, quando sono buoni, el migliore è quello di uno, ma difficilmente può essere buono se è fatta piú per la forza o per fazione o per qualche usurpazione, che per elezione o volontà libera de' sudditi; e di questa sorte non si può negare che non fussi quello de' Medici, come quasi sono tutti oggidi e' domini di uno, che el piú delle volte non sono secondo la volontà o el naturale de' sudditi, ma secondo lo appetito di chi prevale; e però siamo fuora del caso de' filosofi, che mai approvorono reggimento di specie simigliante. Potrei ancora dire, secondo e' medesimi filosofi, che el governo di uno, quando è buono, è il migliore de' tutti, ma quando è cattivo è el peggio. . . . e quale fussi migliore sorte di una città che nascessi ora e che si avessi a ordinare el governo suo, o che fussi ordinate in uno governo di uno, o in governo di molti [?]"

need to commit evil deeds unless ignorance or his own *mala natura* move him thereto, whereas one whose rule is originally violent or grounded in usurpation is often obliged to do things to preserve it that offend his own moral nature, as was repeatedly seen in the cases of Cosimo and Lorenzo de' Medici.[8] But now we have distinguished between the location of power, the legitimacy of its acquisition, the moral personality of the ruler, and—by implication—the inherited characteristics of the governed; and since all these are denoted by different applications of words like *natura* and *naturale*, it is evident that no form of government is by nature good or bad, and that we must look for other criteria. If we imagine a legitimate prince ruling unjustly and a usurper ruling justly, or—since Capponi objects that the latter is impossible to imagine—that they both rule unjustly, it becomes plain that it is the effects (*effetti*) of a particular government and not its origins or defining circumstances (the output, so to speak, and not the input) that we use to evaluate it.[9]

Bernardo goes on to argue that if we are discussing forms of government in the abstract, we must certainly say that a voluntary origin is preferable to a violent one, since its *natura* does not carry the *necessità* of further violence in the future. But when we come to particular cases and to governments actually in being, we must proceed empirically: we must observe how they are working and evaluate their effects by obvious standards of morality and utility, before presuming to rank one of them before the others.[10] But this raises an evident difficulty

[8] *D. e D.*, p. 14: "E quella distinzione che ha fatta Piero, tra el governo di uno quando è naturale e per elezione e voluntà de' sudditi, ed uno governo usurpato e che ha del violento, ha anche in sé ragione capace agli idioti, perché che domina amorevolmente e con contentezza de' sudditi, se non lo muove la ignoranzia o la mala natura sua, non ha causa alcuna che lo sforzi a fare altro che bene. E questo non interviene a chi tiene lo stato con violenzia, perché per conservarlo e per assicurarsi da' sospetti, gli bisogna molte volte fare delle cose che egli medesimo non vorrebbe e che gli dispiacciono, come io so che spesso fece Cosimo, e . . . Lorenzo qualche volta lagrimando e a dispetto suo fece deliberazione . . . contrarie alla natura sua . . ."

[9] *D. e D.*, pp. 14-15: "Questa diversità adunche tra l'uno governo e l'altro non procede perché la spezie del governo in sè faccia buono o cattivo quello che fussi d'altra condizione, ma perché secondo la diversità de' governi, bisogna tenerli con mezzi diversi. . . . dico che a volere fare giudicio tra governo e governo, non debbiamo considerare tanto di che spezie siano, quanto gli effetti loro, e dire quello essere migliore governo o manco cattivo, che fa migliori e manco cattivi effetti. Verbigrazia, se uno che ha lo stato violento governassi meglio e con più utilità de' sudditi, che non facessi un altro che lo avessi naturale e voluntario, non diremo noi che quella città stessi meglio e fussi meglio governata?"

[10] *D. e D.*, pp. 15-16: "Però ogni volta che sanza venire a particulari, si ragiona quale governo è migliore, o uno violento o uno volontario, risponderei subito

when we are discussing *mutazione*, the replacement of an old government by a new. The effects of the former may be observed, those of the latter may only be predicted;[11] and we may add, in criticism of Guicciardini's argument, that the origins of the former may be discounted, whereas those of the latter must be taken into account in the act of prediction itself. Bernardo has now to explain the nature and methods of prediction in politics. He explains to his interlocutors that as he has lived a very long time in Florence, been immersed in the city's affairs both as actor and observer, and talked often with men of great experience, he thinks he has enough knowledge of the nature (*natura*; several times repeated) of the people, the citizens, and the city as a whole (*universalmente*) to be able to predict well enough the effects of every constitution (*modo di vivere*). He may go wrong in matters of detail (*particulari*), but in general statements (*universali*) and in all matters of substance he hopes to make few mistakes.[12] Where he does err, he can be corrected by the younger men, who may lack his age and experience but have read diligently, as he has not, in the histories of many nations and have been able to converse with the dead where he has spoken only with the living. The lessons of history will reinforce those of experience, because everything that is has been and everything that has been will be again. The only difficulty is to recognize it and to avoid the error of taking it for something new; in this pursuit Bernardo and his interlocutors must go hand in hand, and he

---

essere migliore el volontario, perché cosí ci promette la sua natura e cosí abbiamo in dubio a presummere, avendo l'uno quasi sempre seco necessità di fare qualche volta male, l'altro non avendo mai cagione di fare altro che bene. Ma quando si viene a' particulari ed a' governi che sono in essere . . . io non guarderei tanto di che spezie siano questi governi, quanto io arei rispetto a porre mente dove si fa migliori effetti e dove meglio siano governati gli uomini, dove piú si osservino le leggi, dove si faccia migliore giustizia e dove si abbia piú dispetto al bene di tutti, distinguendo a ciascheduno secondo el grado suo."

[11] *Ibid.*: ". . . considerata la natura sua e la natura della città e di questo popolo, possiamo immaginarci che effetti producerà . . ." and the objection of Piero Guicciardini.

[12] *D. e D.*, pp. 16-17: ". . . la lunga età che io ho, e lo avere molte volte veduto travagliare questa città nelle cose di drento, e quello che spesso ho udito ragionare de' tempi passati da uomini antichi e savi, massime da Cosimo, da Neri di Gino e dalli altri vecchi dello stato, mi hanno dato oramai tanta notizia della natura di questo popolo e de' cittadini ed universalmente di tutto la città, che io credo potermi immaginare assai di presso che effetti potrà portare seco ciascuno modo di vivere. Né voglio mi sia imputato a arroganzia, se essendo io vecchissimo, ed avendo sempre atteso alle cose di drento e quasi non mai a quelle di fuora, fo qualche professione d'intenderle; la quale è di questa sorte, che io credo che facilmente molti particulari potrebbono variare dalla opinione mia, ma negli universali ed in tutte le cose di sustanzia spero ingannarmi poco."

leaves it unclear whether the qualities of mind needed to recognize the recurrent and predict its effects can be acquired by education or only through experience.[13]

The argument is clearly pragmatic and loaded in favor of conservatism. Forms of government can be studied and evaluated only in action and in actuality, and the question has arisen how even this can be done—and whether such a procedure does not necessarily favor the existing, or even the recent, constitution. By admitting historical knowledge to an apparent equality with the knowledge based on experience, Guicciardini has avoided giving the existing an inherent superiority over the nonexisting, but he is already well on the way toward his later position that the lessons of history are, though not inapplicable, extremely difficult to apply. But there is another way in which the pragmatic argument contains conservative implications. If we are to evaluate constitutions solely by their results, we shall presumably use the same set of values as criteria in all cases; but it is perfectly well known that different forms of government give priority to different values, so that we cannot proceed pragmatically unless we standardize our values in advance. At this stage in the *Dialogo*, Soderini puts forward what we have seen to be a cardinal assumption of Florentine thought after 1494-1512: that a *vivere libero* is natural to Florence, because a desire for liberty is in that city an *appetito universale*, engraven in men's hearts as it is on their walls and banners. Since philosophers will agree that, of the three forms of government, that is best which is most natural to the people whom it is to govern, the case for the inherent superiority of popular rule at Florence seems to be made in advance.[14]

[13] *D. e D.*, p. 17: "E dove mi ingannassi io, potrete facilmente supplire voi, perche avendo voi letto moltissimo istorie di varie nazioni antiche e moderne, sono certo le avete anche considerate e fattovene uno abito, che con esso non vi sarà difficile el fare giudizio del futuro; perché el mondo è condizionato in modo che tutto quello che è al presente è stato sotto diversi nomi in diversi tempi e diversi luoghi altre volte. E cosí tutto quello che è stato per el passato, parte è al presente, parte sarà in altri tempi ed ogni dì ritorna in essere, ma sotto varie coperte e vari colori, in modo che chi non ha l'occhio molto buono, lo piglia per nuovo e non lo ricognosce; ma chi ha la vista acuta e che sa applicare e distinguere caso de caso, e considerare quali siano le diversità sustanziali e quali quelle che importano manco, facilmente lo ricognoscer[à], e co' calculi e misura delle cose passate sa calculare e misurare assai del futuro. In modo che senza dubio procedendo noi tutti insieme cosí, erreremo poco in questi discorsi e potremo pronosticare molto di quello che abbia a succedere in questo nuovo modo di vivere."

[14] *D. e D.*, p. 18: ". . . uno vivere libero, quale se negli altri luoghi è buono, è ottimo nella nostra città dove è naturale e secondo lo appetito universale; perché in Firenze non è manco scolpita ne' cuori degli uomini la libertà, che sia scritta nelle nostre mure e bandiere. E però credo che e' politici, ancora che ordinaria-

This contention, given the assumption on which it rests, seems as fully anchored in the concrete and the *particulare* as Guicciardini could desire. But he makes Bernardo give a double reply: that even a form of government rooted in the nature of the people, though clearly preferable in theory, may in specific cases produce harmful effects; and that the purpose of *libertà* is not to ensure the participation of everyone at all levels of government, but to ensure the conservation of the rule of law and the common good (the verb *conservare* is used twice in the same sentence), an aim which may be better achieved under the rule of one man than in other ways.[15] The latter argument is secondary to the former, which incidentally suggests the question how we can predict harmful effects from a government visibly rooted in the nature of the people; but by introducing it, Guicciardini has redefined *libertà* to suit his own values. What Soderini means, and Guicciardini has himself argued as recently as 1516,[16] is that the experience of the Consiglio Grande has given (or is giving) the Florentine *popolo* a taste of direct personal participation in government which has changed them, so that things in the city cannot be the same again. Now this argument is rejected,[17] and there is being conveyed a value judgment as to the proper meaning of the term *libertà*. It is seen to have two meanings: it denotes a state of affairs in which every citizen participates as fully as possible in decision-making, and it denotes one

---

mente ponghino tre gradi di governi, di uno, di pochi e di molti, non neghino però che el migliore che possi avere una città sia quello che è el suo naturale. Però io non so come in termini tanto sproporzionati si potrà procedere colla regola vostra, e come potremo mai dire che el governo della libertà, che a Firenze come ognuno sa è naturalissimo, non sia migliore che qualunche altro che ci si possa introdurre."

[15] *Ibid.*: ". . . parlando in genere, tu mi confesserai che uno governo di libertà non è di necessità migliore che gli altri. E' vostri filosofi, o come tu dicesti ora politici, ne sono abondante testimoni, che ordinariamente appruovano più la autorità di uno quando è buono, che la libertà di una città; e ragionevolmente, perché chi introdusse la libertà non ebbe per suo fine che ognuno si intromettersi nel governore, ma lo intento suo fu perché si conservassino le leggi ed el bene commune, el quale, quando uno governa bene, si conserva meglio sotto lui che in altro governo."

[16] Above, ch. 5, n. 69.

[17] *D. e D.*, pp. 18-19: "E quella ragione in che tu hai fatto fondamento grande, di essere la libertà naturale in Firenze, non contradice alle cose dette prima, perché el filosofo ed ognuno che abbia giudicio, dimandato in genere, risponderà che el migliore governo che si possa mettere in una città sia el suo naturale. . . . Ma se venendo agli individui, si vedessi che uno vivere libero, ancora che naturale di una città, per qualche cagione particulare non facessi buoni effetti, allora né e' filosofi vostri né alcuno che fussi savio, lo proporrebbono a un altro vivere, anzi loderebbono più ogni altro governo che portassi seco maggiori beni."

in which laws, not men, are supreme and the individual receives his social benefits from impersonal public authority and not at the hands of individuals. Machiavelli had used *equalità* in a somewhat similar sense. These two definitions are not logically identical, and Guicciardini is implicitly denying that they have anything to do with one another; but it was commonly argued that the former state of affairs was the best (radicals held the only) guarantee of the latter, and if Bernardo was to contend that the many could enjoy *libertà* in the sense of legality and impersonality where they were excluded from *libertà* in the sense of *participazione*, he had (irrespective of the question whether they could be denied *participazione* having once known it) to show how such a state of things could be rendered permanent. This, needless to say, became the problem of preventing corruption in the limited group which enjoyed power while excluding others from it.

Bernardo's interlocutors next explain that at the time of Piero de' Medici's expulsion from the city, they had no intention of setting up a government so broadly based as that of the Consiglio Grande, but that their hand was forced by Savonarola. He replies that in that case they should be deeply obliged to the Friar, because experience has shown (*ha insegnato la esperienzia de' tempi passati*) and will always show (*cosí sempre mostrerrà la esperienzia*) that there can be nothing less stable at Florence than a government monopolized by a few; it invariably falls after a while and power passes to the one or the many[18]—more probably to the latter, since one man to make himself supreme needs prudence, wealth, reputation, much time, and an indefinite succession of favorable circumstances, a combination so unlikely to be enjoyed by a single person that there has only been one Cosimo de' Medici in Florentine history (words which may well have taunted their author in later life).[19] The rule of a few is rendered unstable by the nature of the Florentines, which is to love equality and resent the

---

[18] *D. e D.*, p. 20: ". . . voi abbiate uno obligo grande a questo frate . . . Ma io sono di ferma opinione, e cosí sempre mostrerrà la esperienzia, che a Firenze sia necessario o che el governo sia in mano di uno solo, o che venga totalmente in mano del popolo; ed ogni modo di mezzo sarà pieno di confusione ed ogni dì tumultuerà. Questo me lo ha insegnato la esperienzia de' tempi passati, ne' quali tutti, quando lo stato è venuto in mano di pochi cittadini . . . finalmente in breve spazio di tempo lo stato uscito di mano di quelli pochi, o si è ristretto in uno solo o è ritornato alla larghezza . . ."

[19] *D. e D.*, pp. 21-22: "Bisogna che a fare questo effetto concorrino in uno medesimo, il che è cosa rarissima, prudenzia, tesoro e riputazione; e quando bene tante qualità concorressino tutte in uno, è necessario siano aiutate da lunghezza di tempo e da infinite occasioni, in modo che è quasi impossibile che tante cose a tante opportunità si accumulino tutte in uno medesimo; e però poi in fine non è mai stato in Firenze piú che uno Cosimo."

superiority of others. Consequently, the few are divided by their ambition, and since those who are not of the inner ring (*ognuno che non è nel cerchio*) hate them for their power, they are destroyed by their refusal to support one another.[20]

In this argument Guicciardini is adopting the criterion of the *natura dello universale* which he has rejected a little earlier, and is using it in unexpected ways. The idea that the "second nature" of the Florentines made them restless, egalitarian, and desirous of sharing in the public authority had appeared in his and others' writings before the composition of the *Dialogo*; but it had usually been ascribed to the many and made part of the case for a *vivere popolare*, since the qualities that made the individual anxious for a share in power were also those that made him refuse to accept dependence on others, the characteristic which remained central to Guicciardini's definition of *libertà*. In this passage, however, the "nature of the Florentines" is indeed ascribed to the many (those who are "not of the circle"), but it is much more prominently a characteristic of the few. The "circle" of ambitious men compete for leadership, and their "natural love of equality" becomes the refusal of the losers to accept the predominance of the winners. It can be calculated by reason (*ragione*) and shown by *esperienzia* that the odds against a regime of this kind proving stable are of the order of twenty to one.[21] Not only are *equalità* and *libertà* being depicted as tending to self-destruction; the same harsh light is being thrown on that *ambizione* and pursuit of *onore* which Guicciardini in earlier writings had thought the characteristic of the *ottimati* which made them anxious to serve liberty by playing on the public stage the role of great servants of the public good. Everything in the "nature of the Florentines" which tends to intensify political individuality is being depicted as a characteristic of the few rather than the many; and the rhetoric at this stage depicts all such characteristics as politically disruptive.

But the ambivalences of Guicciardini's attitude toward the *ottimati*

[20] *D. e D.*, p. 21: "A Firenze li uomini amano naturalmente la equalità e però si accordano mal volentieri a avere e ricognoscere altri per superiore; ed inoltre e' cervelli nostri hanno per sua proprietà lo essere appetitosi ed inquieti, e questa secondo ragione fa che quelli pochi che hanno lo stato in mano sono discordi e disuniti. . . . Ed el non amare gli altri la superiorità di alcuno, fa che a ogni occasione che venga, vanno in terra; perché dispiacendo naturalmente a Firenze a ognuno che non è nel cerchio la grandezza d'altri, è impossibile che la durí se la non ha uno fondamento ed una spalla che la sostenga. E come vi può essere questa spalla e questo fondamento, se coloro che reggono non sono d'accordo?" Cf. *Ricordi*, C 212.

[21] *D. e D.*, p. 24: ". . . se e' si ha a arguire dalla ragione, si doverà credere a venti per uno el contrario; se dalla esperienzia, el medesimo."

ensure that the dialogue form is used to present a number of points of view. In what follows, Capponi and Soderini present the case against Medicean rule, of the sort overthrown in 1494, in terms of an ideal of liberty which becomes more and more visibly aristocratic. Capponi denounces as tyranny the essentially manipulative nature of this government, in which actions nominally performed within a code of public laws and approved values were actually evaluated according to the interests of an informal ruling group, and the same conduct might be approved in one whom they considered a friend and condemned in one whom they considered an enemy;[22] one had to find out what one was really meant to do, adds Soderini, by observing the unspoken hints which Lorenzo excelled at giving.[23] Soderini further attacks Bernardo's distinction between governments good by nature and governments which produce good effects by pointing out that to deny the natural and laudable propensities of mankind is to produce bad effects by definition, and *vice versa*.[24] When he says that men by nature desire liberty and hate slavery (*servitù*), however, Soderini proves to mean something which appears to the full only in men of unusually high spirit and talent: namely, the desire to perform actions which are, and are seen to be, excellent because they are to the public good. Liberty is the freedom to perform these actions; slavery is the state of having them evaluated, permitted or prevented by particular men according to the latter's idea of what suits their interests—of knowing that one's actions, "which ought in reason to be free and to depend on nothing

[22] *D. e D.*, pp. 27-28: "E che sdegno, anzi disperazione crediamo noi che si generassi nelli animi degli altri, quando vedevano che quello che in loro era peccato mortale si trattava in una sorte di uomini come veniale; che l'uno era trattato come figliuolo della patria, l'altro come figliastro? E quanto era inumana e tirannica quella parola con la quale pareva loro scaricare, anzi per dire meglio ingannare la conscienza, a che già era venuta come in proverbio: che negli stati si avevano a giudicare gli inimici con rigore e li amici con favore; come se la giustizia ammetta queste distinzioni e come se la si dipinga con le bilancie di dua sorte, l'una da posare le cose delli inimici, l'altra quelle degli amici!"

[23] *D. e D.*, p. 35: "E che misera . . . avere a interpretare la volontà di chi vuole essere inteso a' cenni! In che, come ognuno sa, Lorenzo preme sopra tutti gli uomini."

[24] *D. e D.*, p. 34: "Però non so come Bernardo potrà aguagliare il vivere di simili stati al governo populare, nel quale quando bene gli effetti non fussino migliori che quegli della tirannide, l'uno è secondo lo appetito naturale di tutti gli uomini che hanno per natura lo appetire la libertà, l'altro è direttamente contrario, avendo ognuno in orrore la servitù; donde eziandio con disavantaggio si debbe preporre quello che satisfa piú alla naturalità, che el contrario. E questa ragione è generale in tutti gli uomini, perché ordinariamente gli istinti naturali sono in ognuno."

but oneself and the good of the country, must be regulated by the wills of others whether just or capricious."[25]

Soderini proceeds to define what makes us behave in this way as *virtù*.

> And if the principal object of those who have rightfully governed cities, the principal care of philosophers and others who have written of civic life, has been to give them such a foundation as will encourage the virtues, excellence of character and honourable deeds, how much should we condemn and detest a government in which the greatest pains are taken to root out all generosity and all virtue! I speak of those virtues by which men prepare themselves to perform actions excellent because beneficial to the republic. . . .

> And so I say again that whenever the government is not legitimate on the grounds that it honours virtue, but tends to tyranny whether fierce or tolerant, one ought at whatever sacrifice of property or prosperity to seek after any other form of rule; for no government can be more abominable and pernicious than one which seeks to destroy virtue and prevent its subjects from attaining, I will not say greatness, but any degree of glory attained through nobility of character and generosity of mind.[26]

What distinguishes the arguments of Soderini from those of modern theorists of "participatory democracy" and "repressive tolerance" is that whereas the biases of the latter are populist, those of the former are explicitly aristocratic. Those who take as their aim the ideal of *virtù*—stated here less as the imposition of form upon *fortuna*, which is not a key idea of the *Dialogo*, than as life, liberty, and the pursuit of excellence in moral autonomy—are, practically by definition, the few,

[25] *Ibid.*: ". . . le azioni loro, che arebbono ragionevolmente a essere libere nè avere dependenzia da altri che da sé medesimo e dal bene della patria, bisogna che si regolino secondo la arbitrio di altri, o sia giusto o sia a beneplacito . . ."

[26] *D. e D.*, p. 35: "Adunche se el primo obietto di coloro che hanno retto legitimamente le città, se la principale fatica de' filosofi e di tutti quegli che hanno scritto del vivere civile, è stata di mettervi quella instituzione che produca le virtù ed eccellenzia di ingegno e di opere generose, quanto sarà da biasimare e detestare uno governo, dove per contrario si fa estrema diligenzia di spegnere ogni generosità ed ogni virtù! Parlo di quelle virtù con le quali gli uomini si fanno atti alle azioni eccellenti, che sono quelle che fanno beneficio alla republica . . .

"Però io replico di nuovo che ogni volta che el governo non sia legitimo, perché allora la virtù è onorate, ma abbia del tirannico o fiero o mansueto, che con ogni disavantaggio ed incommodità di roba o di altra prosperità, si debbe cercare ogni altro vivere; perché nessuno governo può essere piú vituperoso e piú pernizioso che quello che cerca di spegnere la virtù ed impedisce a chi vi vive drento, venire, io non dico a grandezza, ma a grado alcuno di gloria, mediante la nobilità dello ingegno e la generosità dello animo."

and in earlier writings Guicciardini has clearly indicated just how small a number they may be. Nevertheless, tyrants hate and fear them, since it is the aim of the tyrant to bring everything into dependence on himself; Soderini says he need not tell his hearers who he has in mind.[27] He concluded this part of his discourse by observing that, as is usual with *stati stretti*, the Medici have been at pains to disarm the citizens, thus depriving them of their *virilità* and of the *vigore de animo* which belonged to their ancestors. One has only to consider the difference between those who make war with their own arms and those who do it by means of mercenaries; the Swiss, fierce and warlike when they appear in Italy, live in liberty, under law, and at peace when in their own homes.[28] Here the rhetoric of the civic militia tradition appears in a context which suggests, as was certainly not the case in Machiavelli's *Discorsi*, that liberty, civic virtue, and political individuality are essentially the ideals of an elite.

Bernardo's reply to this statement of the civic humanist position is long and diffuse; the conversation in which it is worked out forms the remainder of Book I of the *Dialogo*. It is not only lengthy but complex, and many of its shafts are indirectly aimed. As we have already seen him doing, Bernardo attempts to identify liberty in Soderini's sense with the display of ambition, and the desire to perform noble actions with the lust to dominate others; and he makes the interesting suggestion that the performance of public services does not necessitate a regime of *libertà*, since what is to be served is the *patria*, "which embraces so much that is good, so much that is sweet, that even those who are subject to princes are lovers of country and have many times been known to put themselves in danger for its sake."[29]

[27] *D. e D.*, pp. 34-35: ". . . gli bisogna andare nascondendo la sua virtù, perché al tiranno dispiaciono tutti gli spiriti eccelsi, ogni potenzia eminente, massime quando procede da virtù, perché la può manco battere; e questo fa qualche per invidia, perché vuole essere lui singulare, spesso per timore, del quale per l'ordinario è sempre pieno. Non voglio applicare queste parole a particulare alcuno, ma voi sapete tutti che io non le dico senza proposito."

[28] *D. e D.*, pp. 35-36: ". . . la casa de' Medici, come fanno tutti gli stati stretti, attese sempre a cavare l'arme di mano a' cittadini e spegnere tutta la virilità che avevano; donde siamo diventati molto effeminati, né abbiamo quello vigore di animo che avevano gli avoli nostri; e questo quanto sia di danno a una republica lo può giudicare chi ha considerato che differenzia sia a fare le guerre con le arme proprie, a farle con le arme mercennarie . . . E che questo sia facile lo dimostrano le antiche republiche e se ne vede oggi qualche vestigio in questi svizzeri, che ora cominciano a farsi conoscere in Italia; e' quali ancor che siano feroci ed armigeri quanto si vede, intendo che in casa loro vivono in libertà, sotto le leggi ed in somma pace."

[29] *D. e D.*, p. 39: "Si può dire piú tosto che questi simili abbino fatto per amore della patria che della libertà; la patria abbraccia in se tanti beni, tanti effetti dolci,

Where Soderini has defined liberty in terms of *virtù* and *partici-pazione*, Bernardo reverts to one of Guicciardini's earlier definitions of the term: liberty is that state of things in which we are beholden to the law for what is our own, and not to the power or personality of particular men. In its implied stress on the moral and political auton-omy of the individual, this is of course a civic humanist ideal; but, in comparison with the *Discorso di Logrogno*, there is the all-important difference that the ideal of participatory *virtù* is now being, as it were, subtracted from the definition of liberty and set in opposition to it. Liberty defined as the rule of law might very well be endangered by the compulsive and competitive magnanimity which Soderini has praised so highly,[30] and a man might enjoy his own under the law with minimal or even with no participation in decision-making on his own part or anybody else's. It could be said that Guicciardini is here developing a negative as opposed to a positive concept of liberty, mak-ing it the freedom from other men's ascendancy rather than the free-dom to develop positive human capacities and qualities; and with this change in definition goes a change in the values which he is setting before the eyes of the *ottimati*. Two codes of value are now visible, both representing poles of Guicciardini's own personality: on the one hand, the ideal of excellence displayed in public action; on the other, that *esperienzia* and *prudenzia* which only an elite has time to acquire. Throughout his life Guicciardini felt the tension between ambition and caution, and it is fascinating to observe how he moves in the oppo-site direction to Machiavelli when faced with the choice between audacity and prudence. Where the *Discorsi* had opted for the armed popular state and depicted *virtù* as the dynamic spirit of the armed many, Bernardo in the *Dialogo* is allowed to dismiss—as we shall see—Soderini's revival of the civic militia tradition and to reject as far as possible his idealization of *virtù*. But the *virtù* in question is a property of the few, not the many. In its place—or rather in the place of that ambition and thirst for *onore* which he had once praised—Guicciardini makes Bernardo, in a concluding passage of Book I, exhort his optimate hearers to recognize that the city of Florence is old and hard to reform, and that the natural course of senescence in states has more power than human *ragione* or *prudenzia*.[31]

---

che eziandio quegli che vivono sotto e' principi amano la patria, e se ne sono trovati molti che per lei si sono messi a pericolo."

[30] *D. e D.*, pp. 45-46: ". . . faccendo differenzia da uno che è savio e non ani-moso, a uno che è savio, animoso a non inquieto, e da questo a chi ha ingegno ed animo ed inquietudine."

[31] *D. e D.*, pp. 81-82: "Quando le città sono vecchie, si riformano difficilmente, e riformate, perdono presto la sua buona instituzione e sempre sanno de' suoi

All that he says is addressed to the *ottimati*, but Guicciardini's aristocratic bias is expressed rather in his having regarded the *ottimati* as the only people worth talking to or about, than in his having crudely ascribed to them—as he never did—every political virtue or legitimate claim to power. Bernardo's refutation of Soderini takes the form of a defense of the Medici against Soderini's more embittered charges, and this in turn becomes a critique of the Consiglio Grande and the participation of the many in certain types of decision-making.[32] But the target is rather the few, considered as the authors of the popular constitution of 1494, than the many. It is as if the *ottimati*, dissatisfied by their alliance with the Medici, had set up an alliance with the *popolo* instead, and as if Bernardo were asking them how much they had really gained by the change. But this challenge implicitly raises the question of optimate values. The justification of the 1494 regime, set forth by Soderini and by Guicciardini in his own person when he wrote the *Discorso di Logrogno*, was stated in terms of *virtù*, of that conspicuous excellence which the *ottimati* displayed before an appreciative *popolo*. To attack that regime involved both recommending the ideal of caution in place of that of *virtù* and casting doubt on the many's ability to recognize *virtù* when they saw it; the attack on the many, however, was not an exaltation of the few but a criticism of their values. Once we realize that in Guicciardini's mind the ideal of *virtù* was coming to stand less for the pursuit of excellence than for an unhealthy competition for preeminence, we can understand better his unswerving insistence that a *governo stretto*, in which the *ottimati* monopolized power, would be a disaster for Florence. If the elite were really to conduct a competition in excellence, they needed the *popolo* (or the Medici) as audience and judges; but if what they were competing for was really power and ascendancy, they needed the *popolo* (or the Medici) to limit the competition by limiting the power. At the same time, Guicciardini recommended to his order a less competitive code of values. He may have thought the *ottimati* the only people worth criticizing, but he criticized them no less pertinaciously for all that.

---

primi abiti cattivi; di che, oltre alle ragioni che si potrebbono assegnare, potete pigliare lo esemplo di molte republiche antiche, le quali se nel suo nascere, o almanco nella sua giovanezza, non hanno avuto sorte di pigliare buona forma di governo, ha durato fatica invano chi ve la ha voluta mettere tardi; anzi quelle che sono use a essere bene governate, se una volta smarriscono la strada e vengono in qualche calamità e confusione, non tornano mai perfettamente al suo antico buono essere. È così el naturale corso delle cose umane, e come solete dire voi altri, del fato, che ha bene spesso più forza che la ragione o prudenzia degli uomini."

[32] See in general *D. e D.*, pp. 42-47.

Bernardo's defense of the Medicean regime and his critique of popular unwisdom are therefore, on this interpretation, to be read as stating the case for the Medici and against the *popolo*, or Consiglio Grande, as allies of the *ottimati*. His criticisms are directed against the belief, which Guicciardini had himself expressed in earlier writings, that the many are good judges of their superiors, able to recognize qualities which they themselves lack, and so fit to be trusted with the selection of the few to hold office. Once the distinguishing quality of the leader ceases to be *virtù* and becomes *esperienzia*, this belief becomes less plausible, since *esperienzia* is an acquired characteristic which can be evaluated only by those who have acquired some of it themselves; and since a republic is not a customary but a policy-making community, there is little opportunity for the many to acquire experience of what only governors do—a form of experience whose expression is not custom but prudence. This is the point of Bernardo's assertion that they are incapacitated for this sort of judgment by an outlook limited to "their businesses and their shops";[33] lack of leisure would not prevent their recognizing *virtù* as a quality of the personality, nearly so certainly as it would prevent their acquiring knowledge of affairs or the ability to understand what those who possessed such knowledge were doing. However, Bernardo is prepared to agree with Soderini that the Florentine *popolo* under the constitution of 1494, like that of Venice, may choose its officeholders tolerably well so long as it retains the technique of election by majority vote—on the vexed question of which Guicciardini had written two *discorsi*; but, Bernardo darkly adds, one cannot tell how long this sensible procedure will last. Soderini is left to maintain that no form of government can be made perfect at the beginning, but may learn by experience to confirm and improve its good qualities.[34] He is in short hoping that the *popolo* will learn by experience to retain a method of election assumed to favor the political elite, and Guicciardini is presumably appealing to the optimate belief that there had been too much selection of officeholders by lot.

But Bernardo is mainly concerned to defend the pre-1494 Medici against Soderini's charge that they had repressed *virtù* by advancing to office only those whom they considered safely dependent. He does this by conceding most of the accusation and proceeding to argue that a government of this kind is nevertheless superior to a popular regime—a debating strategy very likely to mask a shift in values and assump-

[33] *D. e D.*, p. 43: ". . . fondato . . . in sugli esercizi ed in sulle botteghe . . ."
[34] *D. e D.*, p. 47: ". . . non solo ne' governi, ma nelle arti, nelle scienzie ed in ogni altra cosa, non furono mai perfetti ne' principi, ma si va aggiungendo alla giornata secondo che insegna la esperienzia."

tions. Certainly, he says, the Medici advanced those they considered safe and kept down those they considered dangerous, but it does not follow, as Soderini suggested, that they regarded all *virtù* as potentially dangerous to them. The qualities of the political elite are wisdom and enterprise; it is possible to be wise (*savio*) without being enterprising (*animoso*), and it is possible to be both without becoming a threat to the established order (*inquieto*).[35] The Medici were able to draw these distinctions the better because they already possessed preeminent power; this gave them the experience with which to judge men and the security in which to exercise their judgment.[36] There are two causes of error in judgment of this kind: ignorance and jealousy (*malignità*). Ignorance, which is preeminently the fault of popular assemblies, is the more dangerous of the two in its effects because by its nature it is without limits, whereas jealousy ceases with the removal of the individual who is its object.[37]

Guicciardini is allowing Bernardo to beg the question. Soderini had defined Medicean rule as a tyranny, and had very clearly stated the classic view that the jealousy of the tyrant is without limits, since he regards everything not subject to his power as a threat to it, and fears especially the *virtù*—the innate moral quality—of every other individual. In defense of *malignità*, Bernardo says that men are by nature inclined to the good and that anyone who preferred evil to good would be rather a beast than a man.[38] It was of course the classic contention that the tyrant was precisely such a beast, but Bernardo is here exploiting the assumption—to which Soderini has been made to assent—that Medicean rule was a tyranny of a peculiar kind, *mansueto* rather than *fiero*, operating by manipulating men's good qualities rather than by seeking to destroy them. But a "moderate tyranny" is almost a contradiction in terms, and Bernardo's rhetoric is tending to empty the term "tyranny" of much of its meaning. The Medici subjected the good in men to their wills by using it; but in order to use it they must have known it and been able to evaluate it, and to go on using it they must have been able to refrain from destroying it. Reason in them cannot have been overthrown by fear and appetite to the extent to which it was in the typical tyrant; and the weakness of human nature, by which its natural love of the good is so easily overthrown, cannot have been inherently more pronounced in them than in any other class of rulers.

[35] Above, n. 30.   [36] *D. e D.*, pp. 44-46.   [37] *D. e D.*, pp. 46, 55.

[38] *D. e D.*, p. 55: "Quanto alla malignità, io vi dico che per natura tutti gli uomini sono inclinati al bene, né è nessuno a chi risulti interesse pari dal male come dal bene, che per natura non gli piaccia più el bene; e se pure si ne truova qualcuno, che sono rarissimi, meritano essere chiamati più presto bestie che uomini, poi che mancano di quella inclinazione che è naturale quasi a tutti gli uomini."

This leads Bernardo, at the end of his argument in Book I, to deny that Medicean rule was doomed by its nature to degeneration and corruption. It operated by utilizing the qualities of the *ottimati* and had therefore to leave them intact; and this necessity acted as a *freno*, a bridle or limitation, on any tendency of the ruling will to run to excess. Furthermore, the *ottimati* could not be of service to the Medici unless they acted as autonomous beings, that is to say freely; and Medicean rule, though it was a tyranny in the sense that everything was done in accordance with their will, was never conducted like *uno stato di uno principe assoluto*, in which the sovereignty of the ruling will is institutionalized and visible. The appearances and the image (*le dimostrazioni e la immagine*) were always those of free government.[39] To take away the image would have been to take away the life and the soul of the city; because this was not done (and only a madman would have done it) the Medici ruled a city stronger for the circumstance that it was governed by a mixture of love and force, rather than by naked violence.[40] Love, after all, is a self-moved activity; the weight of the words used by Guicciardini tells against the view that he wished to represent Florentines as governed by illusion. There must have been something real about a liberty, the need to respect which was a real limitation on Medicean power. But in defending the Medici against the charge of tyranny, Guicciardini has in fact represented their government as something to be distinguished from a *principato assoluto*—

[39] *D. e D.*, p. 77: "Lo stato de' Medici, ancora che, come io ho detto, fussi una tirannide e che loro fussino interamente padroni, perché ogni cosa si faceva secondo la loro voluntà, nondimanco non era venuto su come uno stato di uno principe assoluto, ma accompagnato co' modi della libertà e della civiltà, perché ogni cosa si governava sotto nome di republica e col mezzo de' magistrati, e' quali se bene disponevano quanto gli era ordinato, pure le dimostrazioni e la immagine era che el governo fussi libero; e come si cercava di satisfare alla moltitudine de' cittadini con la distribuzione degli uffici, cosí bisognava satisfacessino a' principali dello stato non solo con le dignità principali, ma ancora col fare maneggiare a loro le cose importanti, e però di tutto si facevano consulte publiche e private."

[40] *D. e D.*, pp. 77-78: "E però nessuno de' Medici, se non fussi publico pazzo, arebbe mai fatto questo, perché potevano conservare la autorità sua, sanza fare uno passo che gli avessi a inimicare ognuno, e bisognava che, facendolo, pensassino o uscire di Firenze a ogni piccola occasione che venissi, o aversi a ridurre tutti in su le arme ed in su la forza; cosa che e' tiranni non debbono mai fare, se non per necessità, di volere fondarsi tutti in su la violenzia, quando hanno modo di mantenersi col mescolare lo amore e la forza. Aggiugnesi che chi togliessi alla nostra la sua civiltà ed immagine di libertà, e riducessila a forma di principato, gli torebbe la anima sua, la vita sua e la indebolirebbe e conquasserebbe al possibile; e quanto è piú debole e manco vale la città, tanto viene a essere piú debole e manco valere che né è padrone; e cosí se e' Medici avessino preso el principato assoluto, arebbono diminuito e non cresciuto la sua potenzia e riputazione."

that is to say, though he does not use the term, a mixed monarchy. We are approaching the doctrine of French and English kingship when we learn that Medicean power was limited by the obligation to consult and respect the chief men and magistrates of the city—not to share power with them in any formal sense. This obligation is not very unlike that to respect the forms of republican government, which kept Medicean rule a monarchy in disguise.

Bernardo's argument, however, is still directed toward recommending the Medicean system to the *ottimati*, and is consequently as much aristocratic as monarchic in character. It departs furthest from the Aristotelian or Polybian doctrine of the coordination of distinct powers in its thrust toward the view that a man or group of men in supreme authority are fitted and enabled by that supremacy to perform all the functions of power, and do not need the support of any coordinate intelligence; but it falls short of a theory of sovereignty in its refusal to locate supreme power in either one or a few. It is noteworthy that Bernardo's discussion of the role of the *ottimati* under Medicean rule is perfectly compatible with the assumption that their supreme value is *virtù*, whereas there is another aspect of his argument which rests entirely on the concept of prudence and in which the distinction between monarchy and aristocracy is far less pronounced. This is the section in which he assails the participation of the Consiglio Grande in decisions on external policy (*cose di fuora*).[41]

Here the train of thought carries us directly back to concepts of the particular event, of intelligence, number, and time, such as we have repeatedly seen to be basic to this aspect of Renaissance thinking. Affairs of external policy, we are told, have no regularity or certain course, but vary every day with the happenings of the world, so that our thinking about them must be largely a matter of conjecture. The smallest cause can have the greatest effect, and identical causes have effects of the greatest diversity. "So it is necessary that the governors of states should be men of prudence, vigilantly attentive to the smallest accident, and weighing every possible consequence in order to obviate at the beginning, and eliminate as far as possible, the power of chance and fortune."[42]

---

[41] *D. e D.*, pp. 60-65.

[42] *D. e D.*, pp. 60-61: "Perché le cose di questa sorte non hanno regola certa ne corso determinato, anzi hanno ogni dì variazione secondo gli andamenti del mondo, e le deliberazioni che se ne hanno a fare, si hanno quasi sempre a fondare in su le conietture, e da uno piccolo moto dependono el piú delle volte importanze di grandissime cose, e da' principi che a pena paiano considerabili nascono spesso effetti ponderosissimi. Però è necessario che chi governa gli stati sia bene prudente, vigili attentissimamente ogni minimo accidente, e pesato bene tutto quello che ne

There could be no clearer statement of Guicciardini's refusal to enter into that world of *virtù* that so fascinated Machiavelli. *Virtù* as audacity, the dynamic and perhaps creative power of a prince or a people in arms, sought to dominate fortune rather than eliminate it; Machiavelli found this characteristic in the innovator of genius and in the equation of citizen and warrior. But Guicciardini is identifying (if not replacing) *virtù* with prudence, the steersman's or doctor's power to observe events and accommodate oneself to them, rather than seeking to shape or determine them; his is a politics of maneuver rather than of action. It calls for the maximum degree of information and deliberation compatible with the unrelenting and unpredictable speed of events, and the case against popular control of external policy is that the many cannot achieve this. One man or a few, Bernardo says, have the time and the application to acquire this intuitive sense for affairs and to translate it into action. An assembly of many men has not;[43] but it is not quite clear whether the reasons for this are quantitative or qualitative. On the one hand it is indicated that a problem, knowledge of which has to be diffused among many men, is unlikely to be studied and inwardly digested, and that decisions which require the concurrence of many minds will be too slow in the making or the alteration. On the other hand there is language which suggests that an assembly of many will be an assembly of individuals each intent on his private affairs, and consequently lacking the leisure in which experience, prudence, and an understanding of power politics can alone be acquired; Bernardo even suggests that the many are especially corruptible because, as private individuals, they do not regard the common good as their own, whereas a single ruler thinks of the common good as his own property.[44] At all events, an assembly cannot develop the delib-

---

possi succedere, si ingegni sopra tutto di ovviare a' principi ed escludere quanto si può la potestà del caso e della fortuna."

[43] *D. e D.*, p. 61: "Questo è proprio di uno governo dove la autorità è in uno solo o in pochi, perché hanno el tempo, hanno la diligenzia, hanno la mente volta tutta a questi pensiere, e quando cognoscono el bisogno, hanno facultà di provedere secondo la natura delle cose; che tutto è alieno da uno governo di moltitudine, perché e' molti non pensono, non attendono, non veggono e non cognoscono se non quando le cose sono ridotte in luogo che sono manifeste a ognuno, ed allora quello che da principio si sarebbe proveduto sicuramente e con poco fatica e spesa, non si può poi ricorreggere se non con grandissime difficultà e pericoli, e con spese intollerabili."

[44] *D. e D.*, p. 65: "Dove hanno a deliberare molti è el pericolo della corruttela, perché essendo uomini private e che non hanno el caso commune per suo proprio, possono essere corrotti dalle promesse e doni de' principi . . . questi non si ha a temere da uno, perché essendo padrone di quello stato, non si lascerà mai comperare per dare via o per disordinare quello che reputa suo."

erative and intuitive knowledge which an understanding of power politics requires, and so can never attain continuity of policy; but the powers with whom they must conduct their relations will for the most part be governed by princes, who do have durable conceptions of their own interests and so can understand and work with one another, but who will consequently refuse to enter upon relations with democracies that do not know their own minds.[45]

For the same reason, princes can usually deal with mercenary captains and soldiers, but these are the natural enemies of popular governments. A prince regards war as a normal activity and his relations with mercenaries are durable; but a democracy makes war only when it must, employs mercenaries only as an emergency measure and tries to get rid of them, if possible unpaid, as soon as the emergency is over.[46] It is useless, adds Bernardo, to allege the success of the Romans in conducting war and foreign policy under a popular government, since it is possible to deny that their military success was related to their governmental structure. Since the latter was full of discord and confusion, it cannot have contributed to their *virtù* in war, which was in any case as great under the kings as under *libertà*. The Roman military system was not the consequence of popular government, but contributed two things to its success. In the first place, it enabled the Romans to rely wholly on their own power and so to do without that *vigilanzia e diligenzia sottile* necessary to those who must rely on diplomacy amid the power of others. In the second, it placed control of war and policy in the hands of the consuls, experienced military men who looked on war as the source of their civic greatness and even as a profession (*bottega*). We cannot imitate the Romans unless we can duplicate the conditions of their civic life.[47]

[45] *D. e D.*, pp. 63-64: ". . . Queste coniunzione continuate si fanno difficilmente con uno popolo, perché non essendo sempre e' medesimi uomini che governono, e però potendosi variare e' pareri ed e' fini secondo la diversità delle persone, uno principe che non vede potere fare fondamento fermo con questi modi di governo, né sa con chi si avere a intendere o stabilire, non vi pone speranza né si ristrigne teco, disegnando che ne' bisogni o nelle occasioni tue tu ti vaglia sì poco di lui come lui spera potersi valere di te."

[46] *D. e D.*, p. 65: "Sanza che, molto manco si possono confidare de' capitani e de' soldati, che possa fare uno solo, perché tra' soldati mercenari ed e' populi è una inimicizia quasi naturale: questi se ne servono nella guerra, perché non possono fare altro; fatta la pace non gli remuneranno, anzi gli scacciano e gli perseguitano, pure che possino farlo; quegli altri, cognoscendo non servire a nessuno, o pensano tenere la guerra lunga per cavare più lungamente profitto dalla sua necessità, o voltono lo animo a gratificarsi col principe suo inimico; o almeno gli servono freddamente . . ."

[47] *D. e D.*, p. 68: "Né mi allegate in contrario lo esemplo de' romani, che benché avessino el governo libero e largo, acquistano tanto imperio; perché . . . a me non

Whether or not Guicciardini was aware of the content of Machiavelli's *Discorsi* or of the debates in the Orti Oricellari, his argument can only be read as forming an antithesis to what Machiavelli had to say. It is to be observed that he takes for granted the impossibility of duplicating Roman conditions, that is, of making military training and discipline part of the civic personality of every Florentine citizen. In Book II Bernardo is made to deplore the decline of the civic militia, but to argue that it is now too late to bring it back;[48] he does not, however, argue that it would be bad to restore it on the grounds that this would mean conceding too much power to the people. Guicciardini merely assumes that Florence cannot exert dominant military strength, but must exist by diplomatic subtlety in a world of princes and *condottieri*; and he remarks at a later point that if the Romans had employed mercenaries and so had had to live "as unarmed cities do," by means of wit rather than arms, their form of government would have ruined them in a very few years.[49] Intelligence of this order is possible only to one or a few, and the form of government in a *città disarmata* must conform to that. But once again, Guicciardini is not singing the praises of the *ottimati* so much as telling them to change their values. In setting up a constitution in which the Consiglio Grande has such power, they were relying on *virtù* in Soderini's sense; that the military and diplomatic condition of the city forbids their relying on *virtù* in Machiavelli's philo-Roman sense is one more reason why the quality required of them should be seen as prudence. Bernardo remarks that the architects of the 1494 constitution meant well, but could not know how their experiments would turn out:

---

pare che el modo del governo di Roma fussi di qualità da fondare tanta grandezza; perché era composto in modo da partorire molte discordi e tumulti, tanto che se non avessi supplito la virtù delle arme, che fu tra loro vivissima ed ordinatissima, credo certo che non arebbono fatto progresso grande. . . . e dove si fa el fondamento in sulle arme proprie, massime eccellenti ed efficaci come erano le loro, si può intermettere quella vigilanzia e diligenzia sottile che è necessaria a chi si regge in su le pratiche ed aggiramenti. Né avevano allora e' capi della città a durare fatica a persuadere al popolo . . . perché erano uomini militari, e che non sapevano vivere sanza guerra, che era la bottega donde cavavano ricchezze, onori e riputazione. Però non si può regolare secondo questi esempli chi non ha le cose con le condizione e qualità che avevano loro."

[48] *D. e D.*, pp. 90-93.

[49] *D. e D.*, p. 155: "Se avessino guerreggiato con le arme mercenarie ed in consequenzia avuto a valersi come fanno le città disarmate, della sollecitudine, della diligenzia, del vegghiare minutamente le cose, della industria e delle girandole, non dubbitate che vivendo drento come facevano, pochi anni la arebbono rovinata."

nor is this any wonder, since none of them had seen the city free or managed the humours of free men; and those who have studied liberty in books have not observed and digested its peculiarities as have those who know it by experience, which teaches us many things that learning and innate intelligence never impart.[50]

They should also have considered that the city of Florence is already old, and that such cities are very hard to reform or to prevent from reverting to their former harmful usages.[51] Guicciardini does not mention here the reforming legislator whom Machiavelli had depicted as having so inhumanly hard a task in the like circumstances; there was little point in doing so where his main concern was to enjoin prudence and caution upon the *ottimati*, and this is a moment at which Bernardo adjures his hearers to fling away ambition and be content with what is possible. They might have done better not to overthrow the Medici, but having done so they must learn to live with the consequences.

But if we read Book I simply as recommending the abandonment of *virtù* in favor of prudence or of the civic ideal in favor of the quasi-monarchical authority of a ruling group, we shall be little prepared for what is to follow in Book II. Here Bernardo is invited to state his conception of the best form of government attainable for Florence in post-1494 circumstances; and he does so in terms of a complex distribution of authority between a *gonfaloniere*, a senate, and a Consiglio Grande, in which Venice is consciously copied as the best example ever to have existed of a constitution uniting the three forms of government. The tone is classical and humanist throughout. Bernardo displays an erudition in ancient and modern history hard to reconcile with his earlier disclaimers of learning; he mentions with respect—though, significantly, he does not feel able to adopt—the ideal of a civic militia; and, most perplexing of all, he accepts as a postulate that one of the criteria for judging any form of government is its success at encouraging *virtù* in a sense fundamentally indistinguishable from Soderini's. A drastic shift in perspective would seem to have occurred.

To Vittorio De Caprariis, one of the most penetrating of Guicciardini's modern analysts, it seemed inescapable that Book II was pointless, an unprofitable excursion into the realms of the ideal and (like

[50] *D. e D.*, p. 81: "Chi ha ordinato queste cose ha avuto buoni fini, ma non ha avertito particularmente a tutto quello che bisognava; né me ne maraviglio, perché non vive nessuno che abbi mai veduto la città libera, né che abbi maneggiato gli umori della libertà, e chi gli ha imparati in su' libri non ha osservato tutti e' particulari e gustatigli, come che gli cognosce per esperienzia, la quale in fatto aggiugne a molte cose dove la scienza ed el giudicio naturale solo non arriva."

[51] Above, ch. v, n. 10.

the *Ricordi*) of no use or value to the student of his thought's real development.[52] But De Caprariis was a brilliant expositor of the tradition of Crocean historicism; he was exclusively concerned to study Guicciardini's transition *dalla politica alla storia*, from devising stable constitutional schemes for Florence to the realization, expressed in the great history of his later years, that the civic lives of Florentines and all other Italians now existed in a current of profound historical change which was hardly any longer of their own making. De Caprariis was Crocean enough to feel that human self-knowledge was essentially historical knowledge, and awaited only the rise of intellects strong enough to realize that man's life was led in history and nowhere else; and he experienced an evident impatience when Guicciardini seemed to turn aside after advancing so rapidly on the road to that discovery. It was also—and rightly—an essential part of his argument that Guicciardini's realization that the *ottimati* now existed solely in their history was based upon the realization that their fortunes had become irretrievably bound to those of the Medici; and therefore he had stressed those passages of Book I which depict the Medici and the *ottimati* as jointly exercising a supreme and self-moderating power, interpreting them as constituting a wholesale abandonment of the Aristotelian-Polybian tradition. This left him unable to accept the revival of that tradition and of the *ottimati*'s position within it, which forms the theme of Book II. He accordingly accused the second half of the *Dialogo del Reggimento di Firenze* of the deadly sin of unhistoric "abstractness" (*astrattezza*) and denied it any significance whatever.

But such thinking is itself unhistorical. Men like Guicciardini are not so naive as to engage at length in merely conventional writing unless the convention itself has some high degree of significance for them; and the problem is to find out what it was. At about the time when Guicciardini was writing the *Dialogo*, Machiavelli composed the *Discorso delle cose fiorentine dopo la morte di Lorenzo*, in which he genuinely seemed to believe that the ecclesiastics now heading the Medici family—Pope Leo X and the future Pope Clement VII—not being themselves permitted to found hereditary princedoms, might be content with a constitutional settlement at Florence in which the family was secured by a kind of hereditary lien on the role of the One in a government very much of the Venetian pattern. It is conventional to ascribe to Machiavelli a streak of idealism which Guicciardini lacked, and we may agree with De Caprariis[53] that though Guicciardini would have happily enough seen the Medici exercise the effective power in his imaginary constitution, he did not expect to see them

[52] De Caprariis, pp. 78-82.   [53] *Ibid.*, p. 71.

institute it. Since 1512 it had been his belief that though the Medici needed the *ottimati* to legitimate and stabilize their rule, the objective necessities of power did not render them dependent on optimate support, but rather the reverse. There was a moral necessity, but political necessity did not support it. Consequently we may see Guicciardini, writing the *Dialogo* in 1520 and 1521, as facing the dilemma which Joseph Levenson has described as that between "value" and "history";[54] what ought to be is not what is going to happen, but nonetheless it requires to be affirmed. In these circumstances, to affirm one's values is not an act of unreal abstraction, but precisely a moral necessity. If the *ottimati* and the city were not going to get what their natures required them to enjoy, the only way to evaluate what they were going to get was to study in depth what they ought to have had. There is room within this dichotomy for that duality of values which Guicciardini always sensed when he thought about his own order. In the world as it was after 1512—or after 1494—the pursuit of *ambizione*, *onore*, and *virtù* might be most dangerous and inappropriate behavior for the *ottimati* to display; but in the world as their own values and nature required that it should be, *virtù* in this sense must be given freedom to develop. It was therefore permissible to describe a *vivere* in many ways founded on aristocratic *virtù*, as a means to evaluating— and therefore to understanding—a world in which the aristocratic strategy must be prudence. We shall see that the last-named concept is never out of reach all through Book II, and that a return to the historical world is made toward its conclusion.

The way to interpret the remainder of the *Dialogo*, then, is to observe how the dialogue between *virtù* and prudence gives rise to what were to become key ideas in the tradition of republican constitutionalism: a generalization which will support the thesis that many of the roots of that tradition were in Aristotelian politics considered as a "science of virtue." As with Machiavelli's *Discorsi*, we are in a conceptual world related to, but not dependent on, such formalized theories of mixed government as the Polybian cyclical scheme, and one of the main differences which distinguish the two Florentines from their ancient masters is the special emphasis which the former give to the related themes of arms and civic virtue. Book II of Guicciardini's work opens with a reexamination of the concept of *virtù*, and an early point raised by the interlocutors is the possibility of reviving at Florence the tradition of a citizen militia. Capponi contends that a popular government will do better than Bernardo has suggested at maintaining the

[54] Joseph R. Levenson, *Liang Ch'i-ch'ao and the Mind of Modern China* (Berkeley and Los Angeles: University of California Press, 1953 and 1959), introduction.

city's power over surrounding territories, because it will attract to this end the active enthusiasm of more citizens than will a *governo stretto*, especially should the citizenry be rearmed.[55] Bernardo—somewhat surprisingly if we are to hear in his voice the immediate tones of Francesco Guicciardini—agrees without much sign of skepticism, though it is characteristic of him that he does not use the argument that personal military service heightens the individual's personal *virtù*, and that his two reasons for thinking a citizen army beneficial to popular government are first, that it enables such a city to defeat its enemies despite the internal disorders to which it will be prone, and second, that the *potenzia e virtù* resulting will do much to nullify the weaknesses of popular government, because an armed state has less need of the *vigilanzia* and *industria* which only the few can provide.[56] The association between an armed people and *virtù* can never quite be eliminated and Bernardo thinks that the abandonment of the civic militia, if it did not originate in popular persecution of the nobility—a class of military leaders—was the work of faction leaders who felt their power safer when the people were disarmed and too much engrossed in business to care for risking their persons.[57] Harmful as the results have been, he does not see much hope of restoring the militia; to alter the habits and values of the people would take many years of good government, during which (a glance at 1512) the risks of relying on an imperfectly restored militia would be too great.[58]

In the world as it is, the city is disarmed and requires the rule of prudent men; in a world dominated by theoretical values, a civic *milizia* might be the basis of civic *virtù*. But though Guicciardini will allow that a citizen army may make popular government strong and success-

---

[55] *D. e D.*, pp. 89-90.

[56] *D. e D.*, p. 90: "Che lo essere armati di arme vostre fussi non solo utile ed el modo di conservarvi, ma ancora el cammino di pervenire a grandezza eccessiva, è cosa tanto manifesta che non accade provarla, e ve lo mostrano gli esempli delle antiche republiche e della vostra ancora, che mentre che fu armata, benché piena di parte e di mille disordini, dette sempre delle busse a' nostri vicini e gettò e' fondamenti del dominio che noi abbiamo, mantenendosi secondo e' tempi e condizione di allora, in sicurtà e riputazione grandissima. E la potenzia e virtù che vi darebbono le arme vostre quando fussino bene ordinate, non solo sarebbe contrapeso pari a' disordini che io temo che abbi a recare questa larghezza, ma di gran lunga gli avanzerebbe, perché chi ha le arme in mano non è necessitato reggersi tanto in su la vigilanzia ed in su la industria delle pratiche."

[57] *D. e D.*, pp. 90-91: "La cagione di questa mutazione bisogna che nascessi o dalla oppressione che fece el popolo a' nobili, e' quali avevano grado e riputazione assai nella milizia, o pure ordinariamente dagli altri che tennono per e' tempi lo stato, parendo loro poterlo meglio tenere se la città era disarmata, o da comminciare el popolo a darsi troppo alle mercatantie ed alle arte e piacere più e' guadagni per e' quali non si mittava in pericolo la persona."

[58] *D. e D.*, p. 92.

ful, he will not accept the thesis that the strongest and most successful
form of government is a popular one because it generates a citizen
army. Bernardo repeats at this stage his earlier contention that Roman
military discipline owed nothing to the popular form of government;
it was established by the kings and merely continued by the republic,
and in those days every city in Italy armed its people.[59] It is hard to
think of the argument he is seeking to repudiate without expressing it
in the terms of Machiavelli's *Discorsi*, and this impression is heightened
when the problem of Rome is reexamined at the end of Book II. In a
lengthy discussion,[60] which seems to take place after the main business
of the dialogue is concluded, Piero Guicciardini is made to take up the
question of the connections between disorder in the early republic and
the arming of the people. Since the Romans had *buona milizia*, he says,
they must have had *buoni ordini*; since they had *grandissima virtù*,
they must have had *buona educazione* and hence *buone leggi*. The
struggles between the orders looked more alarming than they were and
brought no fundamental disorder.[61] The senate, being greatly outnum-
bered by the people, could either leave them unarmed at the price of
military weakness or make enough concessions to their *umori* to ensure
their military and political support.[62] No doubt it would have been

[59] *Ibid.*   [60] *D. e D.*, pp. 148-58.

[61] *D. e D.*, p. 148: ". . . ponendo quello fondamento che nessuno nega né può
negare, che la milizia sua fussi buona, bisogna confessare che la città avessi buoni
ordini, altrimenti non sarebbe stato possibile che avessi buona disciplina militare.
Dimostrasi ancora perché non solo nella milizia ma in tutte le altre cose laudabili
ebbe quella città infiniti esempli di grandissima virtù, e' quali non sarebbono stati
se la educazione non vi fussi stata buona, né la educazione può essere buona dove
le leggi non sono buone e bene osservate, e dove sia questo, non si può dire che
l'ordine del governo sia cattivo. Dunche ne seguita che quegli tumulti tra e' padri
e la plebe, tra e' consuli ed e' tribuni, erano piú spaventosi in dimostrazione che
in effetti, e quella confusione che nasceva non disordinava le cose sustanziali della
republica."
Compare Machiavelli, *Discorsi*, I, 4 (*Opere*, p. 102): "Né si può chiamare in
alcun modo con ragione una republica inordinata, dove sieno tanti esempli di
virtù, perché li buoni esempli nascano dalla buona educazione, la buona educazione dalle buone leggi, e le buone leggi da quelli tumulti che molti inconsidera-
mente dannano; perche chi esaminerà bene il fine d'essi, non troverrà ch'egli
abbiano partorito alcuno esilio o violenza in disfavore del commune bene, ma
leggi e ordini in beneficio della publica libertà."

[62] *D. e D.*, pp. 148-49: "Di poi essendo el numero del senato piccolo, quello del
popolo grandissimo, bisogna che e' romani si disponessino o a non servire del
popolo nelle guerre, il che arebbe tolto loro la occasione di fare quello grande
imperio, o volendo potere maneggiarlo, gli comportassino qualche cosa e lascias-
singli sfogare gli umori suoi, che non tendevono a altro che a difendersi dalla
oppressione de' piú potenti ed a guardare la libertà commune."
Cf. Machiavelli, *loc. cit.*: ". . . le quali cose tutte spaventano non che altro chi
legge; dico come ogni città debbe avere i suoi modi con i quali il popolo possa

better to have the people armed but not tumultuous, but nothing in the social world is so perfect that it lacks some accompanying evil.[63] Disorder at Rome therefore arose more from the nature of things than from any specific defect in the constitution, and the tribunate, a series of devices intended to protect the people against the senate, contained this disorder so effectively that Bernardo might well have included something of the kind in his ideal constitution.[64]

It is very difficult to believe that Guicciardini was unacquainted with Machiavelli's *Discorsi* when he completed the *Dialogo*; but the arguments which he puts in the mouth of his father, and has Bernardo refute, are essentially those of Machiavelli whether he knew this or not. It is important to grasp clearly just what he aimed to refute: first, that the struggle between the orders was the necessary consequence of arming the people; second, that the tribunate was the means of containing this struggle; third, that Roman military prowess forms an argument in favor of the popular element in government. Bernardo's first contention is that the turbulence of the plebeians was not the simple consequence of the assertiveness of men in arms, but arose from specific defects in the social order. The patricians formed a distinctive hereditary class who monopolized all honors and offices and formally excluded plebeians from these; and they treated the latter with arrogance and oppressiveness, especially in matters of debt. Under the kings all these conditions obtained, and the people were enrolled in the army; yet there were no overt conflicts. The reason is that the kings used their supreme magistracy to protect the plebeians against the aristocracy, and promoted significant numbers of plebeians into the senatorial

sfogare l'ambizione sua, e massime quelle città che nelle cose importanti si vogliono valere del popolo. . . . E i desiderii d' popoli liberi rade volte sono perniziosi alla libertà, perché e' nascono o da essere oppressi, o da suspizione di avere ad essere oppressi."

[63] *D. e D.*, pp. 148-49: "Né negano che se si fussi potuto trovare uno mezzo che sanza avere el popolo tumultuoso si fussino potuti valere di lui alla guerra, sarebbe stato meglio; ma perché nelle cose umane è impossibile che una cosa sia el tutto buona sanza portare seco qualche mali, è da chiamare buono tutto quello che sanza comparazione ha in se piú bene che male."

Cf. Machiavelli, *Discorsi*, I, 6 (*Opere*, pp. 107-8): "Ed in tutte le cose umane si vede questo, chi le esaminerà bene, che non si può mai cancellare uno inconveniente, che non ne surga un altro. Pertanto se tu vuoi fare uno popolo numeroso ed armato, per poter fare un grande imperio, la fai di qualità che tu non lo puoi maneggiare a tuo modo; se tu lo mantieni o piccolo o disarmato per poter maneggiarlo, se tu acquisti dominio, non lo puoi tenere, o ei diventa si vile che tu sei preda di qualunque ti assalta, e però in ogni nostra deliberazione si debbe considerare dove sono meno inconvenienti, e pigliare quello per migliore partito, perché tutto netto, tutto sanza sospetto non si truova mai."

[64] *D. e D.*, pp. 148-49.

order; but when they were overthrown the leading plebeians saw all magistracies closed to them by their class enemies and the *plebe bassa* saw their only protector taken away. Conflict occurred as the latter supported the former in their struggle to force themselves into office. The city was still young, however, and fortune favorable inasmuch as the evils in this state of affairs were observed in time for their cure to become apparent; the patricians steadily if reluctantly gave way—it was again fortunate that they were so few—and opened more and more magistracies to plebeian leaders, and in proportion as this happened the *plebe bassa* showed themselves content that others should enjoy magistracy so long as they were protected in their lives and goods. In proportion also, the tribunate ceased to be a significant office; and the conclusion to be drawn is that the whole struggle, including the necessity for tribunes, could have been avoided from the beginning if magistracies had been awarded without distinction between patricians and plebeians. There was no causal relation between the arming of the people and the existence of enmities between the orders.[65]

As for Roman military *virtù*, this is not to be taken as proving that the *ordini* and *leggi* under which it flourished were good because the cause of it. The causes of Roman military success, says Bernardo, were *costumi*—love of glory, love of the *patria*; and he explains these by reference to historical rather than institutional causes. The city was poor and surrounded by enemies; when these were defeated and incorporated in an empire which brought wealth and luxury with it, corruption ensued and inordinate vices flourished under the best of laws.[66]

[65] *D. e D.*, pp. 150-53. That Guicciardini, while contravening the interpretations of the *Discorsi*, is operating within a very similar conceptual scheme, is shown by the following passage (p. 153): "E certo se voi leggete le antiche istorie, io non credo che voi troviate mai o rarissime volte che una città in una ordinazione medesima sia stata ordinata perfettamente; ma ha avuto qualche principio non perfetto, e nel processo del tempo si è scoperto quando uno disordine quando un altro, che si è avuto a correggere. Però si può dire con verità che a ordinare una bella republica non basta mai la prudenzia degli uomini, ma bisogna sia accompagnata dalla buona fortuna di quella città, la quale consiste che e' disordini che scuopre la giornata ed esperienzia si scuoprino in tempo ed in modo e con tale occasione che si corregghino."

[66] *D. e D.*, p. 157: "Né io ho biasimato el governo romano in tutti gli ordini suoi anzi oltre al laudare la disciplina militare, laudo e' costumi loro che furono ammirabili e santi, lo appetito che ebbono della vera gloria, e lo amore ardentissimo della patria, e molte virtù che furono in quella città piú che mai in alcuna altra. Le quali cose non si disordinorono per la mala disposizione del governo nelle parti dette di sopra, perché le sedizioni non vennono a quegli estremi che disordinano tutti e' beni delle città, ed el vivere di quella età non era corrotto come sono stati e' tempi sequenti massime sendo la città povera e circundata di inimici che non gli lasciava scorrere alle delizie ed a' piaceri; in modo che io credo che non tanto le legge buone, quanto la natura degli uomini e la severità

It is clear that Guicciardini felt that military *virtù* and a civic militia might exist without a popular government and brought more to the latter than they derived from it. But he does not go to the length of arguing that a civic militia should be avoided because it necessitates the follies of popular government; indeed, his argument is formally incompatible with this position. He is against popular government at Florence because the city cannot be armed; he argues, not that it should not be armed on normative grounds, but that it cannot be armed on historical grounds. This must sooner or later carry us back into the realm of prudence. But the debate about *virtù* is far from being at its end. Guicciardini's critique of the patrician order indicates that his aristocratic preferences were compatible with a firm rejection of any legally or institutionally *stretto* class monopolizing office. He was not (in his writings at least) an oligarch and had no interest whatever in an order of nobility; his elitist model of government is at every point in the analysis a competitive meritocracy, in which those possessing *virtù*—whatever role social position may play in affording the opportunity to develop it—acquire and maintain political ascendancy by publicly displaying that quality, which can only be acquired and displayed in civic and political action.[67] The only other role for the Florentine *ottimati* was that of collaborators with the Medici, and even this state of affairs was one in which the Medici replaced the *popolo* as judges of the display of *virtù*, more than it was one in which the nature of *virtù* was fundamentally modified. If *virtù* was not ascriptive, but had to be acquired, displayed and recognized, there must be a certain openness about the political system founded upon it.

As we probe the nature of *virtù*, moreover, it becomes clear that such a political system places magnificence among its central values. Following the discussion of the militia early in Book II, Soderini is

---

di quegli antichi tempi . . . producessino quelle virtù e quelli costumi tanto notabili e la conservassino lungamente sincera da ogni corruzione di vizi. Vedete che ne' tempi sequenti la città fu sempre meglio ordinata di legge ed era unita e concorde, e pure gli uomini andorono imbastardendo, e quelle virtù eccellente si convertirono in vizi enormi, e' quali non nascono dalle discordie della città, ma dalle ricchezze, dalle grandezze degli imperi e dalle sicurtà."

[67] *D. e D.*, p. 93: "[Soderini:] E quegli ingegni piú elevati che sentono piú che gli altri el gusto della vera gloria ed onore, aranno occasione e libertà di dimostrare ed esercitare piú le sue virtù. Di che io tengo conto non per satisfare o fomentare la ambizione loro, ma per beneficio della città, la quale . . . si troverà che sempre si regge in su la virtù di pochi, perché pochi sono capaci di impresa si alta, che sono quegli che la natura ha dotati di piú ingegno e giudicio che gli altri. . . . la gloria ed onore vero . . . consiste totalmente in fare opere generose e laudabili in beneficio ed esaltazione della sua patria ed utilità degli altri cittadini, non perdonando né a fatica né a pericolo."

allowed to restate the case for *virtù* as he sees it. In reply to Bernardo's earlier arguments, he maintains that it is not a sufficient definition of *libertà* that each man is able to enjoy his own under law, without owing it to any powerful protector or fearing any powerful oppressor. This is essentially a private ideal, he says, and is not conducive enough to a sense of the *res publica*. Soderini is arguing for a government of *libertà* and *virtù*, that is to say one in which the unusually talented few are allowed to satisfy their thirst for *onore*, which can be attained only by the performance in public of outstanding deeds beneficial to the *patria* and the public good; his liberty is that of the elite to develop their *virtù* to the full; and it is in this statement of his case that we realize how far *virtù* and *onore* have become identified. It is necessary, he goes on, to consider honor, magnificence and majesty and to rate *generosità* and *amplitudine* above *utilità* alone. It may be that cities were founded to conserve the security and convenience (*commodità*) of individuals, but for the very reason that these are private ends, cities cannot endure unless their citizens and rulers aim to make them magnificent and illustrious and to acquire for themselves the reputation among other peoples of being *generosi, ingegnosi, virtuosi e prudenti* (the last two epithets especially catch the reader's eye). In private men we admire humility, frugality and modesty, but in public affairs the desirable qualities are generosity, magnificence and splendor.[68] Not only is *onore* the end of *libertà*; it is shame and dishonor that are particularly to be dreaded in losing it, especially in the case of a city which is publicly committed to liberty *ed ha fatta questa professione*.

This is plainly an extreme case of that honor-centered scheme of values which many would consider characteristic of "Renaissance man." It should not be forgotten, however, that even here *onore* is a form of civic *virtù*; it is attained in serving the common good, and in pursuing it and its concomitant values above all others, we are pro-

---

[68] *D. e D.,* pp. 94-95: ". . . al bene essere di una città si abbi a considerare non solo che la sia governata giustamente e sanza oppressione di persona ed in modo che gli uomini godino el suo con sicurtà, ma ancora che la abbia uno governo tale che gli dia dignità e splendore: perché el pensare solo allo utile ed a godersi sicuramente el suo, è più presto cosa privata che conveniente a uno publico, nel quale si debbe . . . considerare più quella generosità ed amplitudine che la utilità. Perché se bene le città furono instituite principalmente per sicurtà . . . la commodità che ricerca la vita umana, nondimeno si appartiene pensare . . . in modo che gli abitatori acquistino . . . riputazione e fama di essere generosi, ingegnosi, virtuosi e prudenti; perché el fine solo della sicurtà e delle commodità è conveniente a' privati considerandogli a uno per uno, ma più basso e più abietto assai di quello che debbe essere alla nobilità di una congregazione. . . . Però dicono gli scrittori che ne' privati si lauda la umilità, la parsimonia, la modestia, ma nella cose publiche si considera la generosità, la magnificenzia e lo splendore."

claiming the supremacy of the common good. What is noteworthy is that republican and patriotic values are being expressed in the form of ego-serving ideals like honor, reputation, and generosity, rather than in the distributive, social, and far more traditional ideal of justice. It is also observable that Soderini thinks of the supremacy of *libertà*, *onore*, and *virtù* rather as historically conditioned and determined by human choice than as natural to political man from the beginning. Referring to Bernardo's contention that in evaluating any form of government one should examine the effects it produces and not whether *libertà* is one of its formal components, he observes that this may be true when a city is being established for the first time, but that when a city is committed to liberty to the point where it can be said that freedom has become part of its nature (*naturale* is the noun used, not *natura*), to lose liberty by force is utterly intolerable;[69] as Bernardo himself has observed in another context, it is to lose the city's soul. Here we are back at the key contention of Florentine libertarianism, that whatever is the best form of government in theory, a high level of participation in government is natural to Florence; but as always, it is "second" or "acquired" nature that is meant.

Soderini's admission that liberty is a product of Florentine history links his thinking with Bernardo's. When he asks the latter to expound his conception of the best form of government for Florence, Bernardo is enabled not only to accept the invitation—which in Book I he would have turned aside—but to go far toward including Soderini's ideal of liberty, by stressing that what is under discussion is not the best form of government in the abstract—presumably monarchy—which could only be considered in the context of a city being founded for the first time, but the best form for Florence as she is: that is, for a city which has "made profession" of liberty to the point where the exclusive rule of one or a few could only be imposed by force. To escape the ensuing evils, which would be at their worst in the case of oligarchy, the best hope is offered by popular government; in theory the worst of the tolerable forms, it is *proprio* and *naturale* to Florence and involves least imposition by violence. Further, if we were devising a popular government for a new city, we could rely on the teachings of philosophy and the lessons of recorded history, but since we are concerned

[69] *Ibid.*: "Dunche quando voi dite che chi ha trattato de' buoni governi non ha avuto questo obietto che le città siano libere, ma pensato a quello che fa migliori effetti . . . io crederrei che questo fussi vero, quando da principio si edifica o instituisce una città. . . . Ma quando una città e già stato in libertà ed ha fatta questa professione, in modo che si può dire che el naturale suo sia di essere libera, allora ogni volta che la si riduce sotto el governo di uno, non per sua voluntà o elezione, ma violentata . . . questo non può accadere sanza scurare assai el nome suo ed infamarla appresso agli altri."

with a city actually existing, we must take into account "the nature, the quality, the circumstances (*considerazione*), the inclinations and, to express all these terms in a single word, the humours (*umori*—Montesquieu might have said *esprit*) of the city and the citizens." Knowledge of these *umori* is not gained through the study of history in the bookish sense. Guicciardini here employs his favorite analogy of the physician who, though freer than the statesman since he can give the patient whatever medicines he chooses, nevertheless administers only those which are both good for the disease and such as the patient's body can tolerate, "given its complexion and other attributes."[70] It is not stated how the physician acquires his knowledge of *complessione* and *accidenti*, but one suspects that this is through practical experience.

The doctrine of accidents enables Bernardo to accept Soderini's scheme of values as part of the world with which he has to deal. The Florence of actuality is characterized by an acquired second nature, a tissue of accidents built up through experience, use, and tradition, which can only empirically be known. This accidental fabric has come to embody the values to which Soderini makes appeal—*equalità*, *libertà*, *onore*, and *virtù*; and Bernardo, who in Book I had tended to dismiss them in favor of a rigorous inspection of the predictable consequences of specific governmental arrangements, is now prepared to admit them as facts, that is as values which Florentines cannot afford (being what they are) not to acknowledge, and even to acknowledge them himself as values, with the proviso that it is only the need to study Florentine actuality which compels him to do so. His attitude to values, then, is empirical; he is consenting to erect a scheme of government based on civic *virtù* because it is prudent to acknowledge the facts of Florentine nature, of which a commitment to *virtù* is one.

Guicciardini is not now locating the *ottimati* and their values in the highly specific context created by the events of 1494 and 1512, but in that created by usage and tradition, in which accidents accumulate and second nature is acquired. This much may be conceded to De Caprariis's opinion that at this point he fell short of a rigorous historicism; but it can be argued in reply that the context he employed was

---

[70] *D. e D.*, pp. 97-99; especially p. 99: ". . . non abbiamo a cercare di uno governo immaginato . . . ma considerato la natura, la qualità, le considerazioni, la inclinazione, e per strignere tutte queste cose in una parola, gli umori, della città e de' cittadini, cercare di uno governo che non siamo sanza speranza che pure si potessi persuadere ed introducere, e che introdotto, si potessi secondo el gusto nostro comportare e conservare, seguitando in questo lo esemplo de' medici che, se bene sono più liberi che non siamo noi, perché agli infermi possono dare tutte le medicine che pare loro, non gli danno però tutte quelle che in se sono buone e lodate, ma quelle che lo infermo secondo la complessione sua ed altri accidenti è atto a sopportare."

the appropriate one for presenting optimate values in a historical setting, and that once this had been done the constitution depicted in
Book II of the *Dialogo* became somewhat less abstract and unreal than
De Caprariis seems to have believed—though we shall find that Guicciardini did not, indeed, think it likely to be historically realized. In
Book I the *ottimati* were offered the choice between *onore* considered
as a species of civic *virtù*, and a prudence which might well involve
recognition that in the actual world the civic framework and its values
had been destroyed by Medicean rule. In Book II existing optimate
values are to be paramount; it is recognized that they are *libertà*, *onore*,
and *virtù*; and an attempt is to be made to discover the constitutional
structure which these values necessitate. But Bernardo has begun by
establishing that they are less intrinsic than given, part of the actual
world which prudence must acknowledge, and he has committed the
ottimati as well as himself to this recognition. They must acknowledge
that *ambizione* and the thirst for *onore* are part of their temporal
natures, that they require to be satisfied but at the same time to be
kept in check; the exercise of prudence may be the highest form of
the display of *virtù*, and it may entail acceptance of a scheme of government in which the pursuit of *onore* is limited by the power of others. As against this, however, such a scheme may ensure that the exercise of prudence is identical with that free pursuit of excellence which
is the essence of *libertà* and *virtù*.

Meanwhile, that part of the argument in which Florence is contrasted, as a *città disarmata*, with Machiavellian Rome serves to establish that the conduct of external relations in a world not determined
by Florentine power is the most important single activity of government, and that this requires the constant exercise of *vigilanzia e diligenzia sottile*. Only an experienced few can develop and display this
quality, and the problem of constitution-making is largely a matter of
reconciling their control of affairs with the maintenance of liberty.

> It is difficult to find the right medicine, because it must be of such
> a kind that in curing the stomach one does not injure the head; that
> is, one must be careful not to alter the substance of popular govern-
> ment, which is liberty, or, in taking important decisions away from
> those incompetent to make them, to give so much authority to par-
> ticular persons as to risk setting up some kind of tyranny.[71]

[71] *D. e D.*, p. 101: ". . . è difficile trovare el medicina appropriata, perché
bisogna sia in modo che medicando lo stomaco non si offenda el capo, cioè provedervi di sorte che non si alteri la sustanzialità del governo populare che è la libertà,
e che per levare le deliberazioni di momento di mano di chi non le intende, non
si dia tanta autorità a alcuno particulare, che si caggia o si avii in una spezie di
tirannide."

Since the external world is nonmoral, this problem may appear as one of reconciling facts with values, the brute necessities of survival with the need for moral relations within the city. Guicciardini is known for his skepticism and realism, and we may quite properly see it in this light. But Book II of the *Dialogo* is essentially value-oriented, and the reconciliation of leadership with liberty is a value problem on both sides of the equation. In exercising leadership and control the elite are displaying a virtue, which is prudence, and they are also pursuing values characteristically theirs, which are *onore* and *virtù*. At this level prudence and *virtù* have become identical, so that the choice between them has disappeared. But we have repeatedly seen that *onore* and *virtù* are civic qualities which require a civic and public setting for their development. The point of Soderini's emulative conception of *virtù*, which Bernardo is now able to adopt, is that it brings about the identification of aristocratic with popular government; since *virtù* is *onore*, a public and popular audience is required to acclaim it and give it meaning. The few exist only in the many's sight. This must be so, since their special excellence, like any other secular and republican virtue, is liable to self-corruption if suffered to exist in isolation. If the recognition of *virtù* was left to the few who possess and seek to display it, the result could only be disastrous competition (*ambizione*) or corrupt connivance and wheeler-dealing (*intelligenza*). For *virtù* to be recognized purely for what it is—for the recognition to be unflawed by extraneous or private considerations—for the elite to be truly free to develop it—recognition must be a public act performed by a public authority. Leaving aside the possibility, not further considered in Book II, that this authority might be a quasi-monarchical Medicean government, the remaining alternative is the Consiglio Grande. Meritocracy necessitates a measure of democracy. The *libertà* of the few is to have their *virtù* acknowledged by the *res publica*; the *libertà* of the many is to ensure that this acknowledgment is truly public and the rule of *virtù* and *onore* a true one.

A complex polity, or "mixed government," is required both by the need to balance *libertà* against prudence (the stomach against the head), and by the nature of *libertà* itself. In both formulations it is essential that the popular assembly be prevented from trying to exercise itself those virtues and functions whose exercise it oversees and guarantees in the few; and it is no less essential that the few be prevented from setting up an oligarchy, that is from monopolizing those virtues and functions within a rigidly closed *governo stretto*. In his theoretical constitution, therefore, Bernardo has two overriding, and interlocking, purposes: to confine the Consiglio Grande to those functions which are essential to the maintenance of liberty, and to ensure that participation in the governing elite, which discharges all other functions, is determined solely by the public display of *virtù*. These aims necessitate a great deal of careful differentiation and distribution of powers, and it is striking to observe how nearly Guicciardini agreed that they had been attained in the Venetian model.

The Consiglio has three essential functions.[72] By its existence alone it provides every person capable of holding office, that is to say every member of the city—Guicciardini does not revive the proposal, made in the *Discorso di Logrogno*, to enlarge the Consiglio by adding persons not capable of office—with access to decision and opportunity of office; this is to ensure that equality which is the prime foundation of liberty. In theory, the governing elite was to be an open meritocracy; no prior qualifications of wealth or birth were to be laid down, and promotion to office was to rest solely on one's fellows' opinion of one's merits. As a corollary, then, the Consiglio must fill all or nearly all the offices and magistracies of the city; the aim here is to ensure that no magistrate is indebted to any individual (*privato*) or clique (*setta*) for his office. The point is less that the people or many as a distinct group should have power to choose the government they want, than that the process of recognizing fitness for office should be conducted as publicly and as impersonally as possible. The people do not exercise sovereignty so much as ensure that the *res publica* (here a remote forerunner of the general will) is the choosing agency, and we enter upon no discussion of the qualities of mind that enable them to recognize *virtù* in others. These qualities, however, do not disappear, for Guicciardini continues to prefer election of magistrates by vote (*le più fave*) to the wholly impersonal machinery of sortition. Men are unequal in merit, and only the reasoning mind is capable of choosing its superior.

The third function which, in order to ensure the protection of liberty, is to be left in the Consiglio's hands is that of "making new laws and altering old." It is a temptation to refer to this as "the legislative power" and to see its inclusion here as a rudimentary attempt at a definition of sovereignty. But we must be quite clear as to just what this legislative function is. The *leggi* or *provisioni* of which Guicciardini speaks are essentially what Machiavelli calls *ordini*: those fundamental ordinances which give the polity its form by determining the distribution of the several political functions or powers. They must be kept in the hands of the Consiglio, first, to ensure that the determination of the city's form is untouched by particular interests or pressures; secondly, because a free government can be altered only by laws or by arms,

[72] For this and the following paragraph, see *D. e D.*, pp. 102-103.

and if we render impossible any *mutazione* by means of law, other devices will prevent *mutazione* by armed force. In other words, the Consiglio's function is less to legislate than to prevent legislation, which is still thought of largely as the determination of political form—a task which should be done once and then left unaltered. Nonetheless, there is implicit here the notion of some continuous activity of "making new laws and altering old," which may bring about *mutazione* if improperly exercised, but can presumably be properly exercised so that it does not. Guicciardini does not define this permissible legislation for us, but since he did not believe that the form of a city could be perfectly established once and for all,[73] it is likeliest that he thought of it as the correction of earlier deficiencies and the rounding out of first principles in the light of further experience. But he does tell us how it is to be carried on. The Consiglio is assumed incapable of initiating legislation—only in *consigli più stretti* is there the prudence which can cognize specific defects and remedies—and is excluded from all *deliberazione*, all framing and discussing of proposed legislation. It retains only the bare power of *approvazione*, of accepting or vetoing the proposals laid before it by smaller deliberative bodies. Significantly, Guicciardini does not examine here, as he had in the *Discorso di Logrogno*, the nature of the cognitive intellect which makes the many capable of evaluating what they cannot initiate or verbalize. If he had, he would no doubt have reproduced the Aristotelian doctrine of the cumulative judgment of the many, but it is more noteworthy that he did not and that, in place of their knowing what was best for themselves, he stressed once more their function of universalizing decision, of ensuring that it was free from corrupting particular interests. The role of the many was less to assert the will of the non-elite than to maximize the impersonality of government; and, with many more extreme exponents of the *mito di Venezia*, we wonder whether a machine might not be devised to do this more efficiently.

Guicciardini, however, shows no desire to see this done. He remains (in this respect) a civic humanist: the essence of his governmental ideal is that the elite shall display *virtù* before the eyes of the non-elite. It is for this reason that the *deliberazioni* of the few require the *approvazione* of the many, and he is strongly opposed to any attempt by the former to trespass on the province of the latter. He repeats from the *Discorso di Logrogno*[74] his condemnation of existing Florentine procedure, whereby new laws are proposed in the Consiglio, but must pass through a tangle of committees on their way to approval; this

[73] See above, ch. v, nn. 17, 18, 44, 48.
[74] See above, ch. v, nn. 30, 31.

practice, he says, is plainly oligarchical, a device of existing power-holders to expose all possible reforms to destructive intervention by their confederates (*sette*). The correct procedure is to have new legislation initiated and discussed only in open senate, accepted or rejected only in open Council.[75] Guicciardini's assumptions are in a sense rationalist; he affirms that reason and virtue are most likely to prevail where there is unrestricted access to decision, and though the functional differentiation between elite and non-elite must be maintained, there comes a point where limiting the size of councils serves only to give undue weight to particular and sinister interests. The idea that the self-determination of the elite must be a public and open process is even more pronounced when he deals with election than when he deals with legislation.

Since Florentine politics were not conceived of as those of a jurisdictional society, legislation—the alteration of substantive law by sovereign will—did not seem as important to theorists as in the politics of a northern monarchy, and we already know that Machiavelli and Guicciardini regarded the management of external affairs as the most momentous single function of government. Since affairs of this kind were in constant daily change, they made the greatest demand on the *prudenzia* of the decision-makers, and it was therefore important both that their direction should be in the hands of a few and that these few should combine the greatest experience of such affairs with the maximum opportunity of enlarging that experience. The selection of magistrates to compose the political elite was very largely a matter of appointing men to deal with external affairs, and at this point there arose a clash of desiderata. On the one hand, the principles of *equalità* and *libertà* required that all citizens should have the maximum opportunity of office, which suggested—as it had to the framers of the constitution of 1494—that all magistracies should rotate as rapidly as possible; on the other, those of *esperienzia* and *prudenzia* required that magistrates should remain in office long enough to acquire experience and put it to use. Yet there was the danger that they would come to regard their offices as their own and behave corruptly and tyrannically. Guicciardini now argues that the Venetians have hit upon the best solution of this dilemma, in electing their *doge* for life, thus ensuring the benefits of his experience, but seeing to it that his authority is kept from becoming dangerous by requiring the constant concurrence of others to make it effective.[76] He proposes to adopt the Dogeship to

[75] D. e D., pp. 124-25.

[76] D. e D., pp. 103-104: "Però a me pare che a questo punto abbino proviso meglio e' viniziani che facessi mai forse alcuna republica, con lo eleggere uno doge perpetuo, el quale è legato dagli ordini loro in modo che non è pericoloso alla

Florentine conditions in the form of a gonfalonierate for life, instead of for very short terms as in the 1494 constitution; but this will necessitate changes in the *signoria*, the executive board with whom the *gonfaloniere* is required to work. At present membership of the *signoria* rotates very rapidly; every citizen wants his turn and the board is filled with men who understand what is happening so little that even a short-term *gonfaloniere* can do much as he likes with them. To develop a long-term *signoria* to balance a *gonfaloniere* for life would probably prove too difficult, and the best course may be to downgrade the *signoria* altogether, leaving the *gonfaloniere* to share power with a senate and its daily presidium, the "ten of war." He is to be permanent chairman of the latter, possessing no formal powers but relying on his personality and experience to bring him authority.[77]

The senate is to be the central organ and the embodiment of the elite of *virtù*. Guicciardini observes that it is a problem in constitutional theory whether membership in a senate should be for life or for a limited term. The ancients opted for life; the Venetians rotate membership so rapidly that the *pregati*, as they call the equivalent body, are always largely made up of the same individuals. It makes relatively little difference which model we adopt.[78] The technical problem is that of combining the maximum continuity and therefore concentration of experience with the maximum expectation of eventual membership in the part of the aspiring, and if we have a large enough senate vacancies through death will occur often enough to give everyone the hope of election some day if he deserves it. Guicciardini prefers a senate elected for life for the same reasons as make him favor life tenure for the gonfalonierate: it ensures maximum concentration of experience, and it enables men to hope that their *virtù* will carry them to an office so secure that they need never fear, or feel indebted to, any other individual. In the case of the senate, as well, he seems to prefer election for life to rapid rotation because the individual will be the more certain that he owes his membership to public recognition, and not to the random operations of constitutional machinery. It is also suggested that Florentines, being more restless and ambitious than Venetians, are less willing to wait for their turns;[79] better therefore to

---

libertà, e nondimanco, per stare quivi fermo né avere altra cura che questa, ha pensiero alle cose, è informato delle cose, e se bene non ha autorità di deliberarle, perché questo sarebbe pericoloso alla libertà, vi è pure uno capo a che riferirle e che sempre a' tempi suoi le propone e le indirizza."

[77] *D. e D.*, pp. 104, 113-14.   [78] *D. e D.*, p. 115.

[79] *D. e D.*, p. 116: "Ma questa misura ed ordine che ha partorito in loro la lunga continuazione del governo è forse la natura de' loro cervelli più quieta, non si potrebbe sperare in noi di qui a molti anni; e se noi facessimo questo consiglio

create as large a senate as possible—150 instead of the 80 of 1494—and bring in the maximum number of aspirants on a permanent basis.

As the letter and spirit of this scheme emerge, more attention seems to be paid to the mobilization of *virtù* and the prevention of corruption than to ensuring the ascendancy of prudence; and the first two aims seem to require, in ways that the third does not, that the competition to have one's *virtù* recognized be an open one. When Piero Guicciardini asks whether a *doge* or *gonfaloniere* for life is not better suited to Venice than to Florence, since the former is an aristocratic and the latter a popular republic, Bernardo replies that there is no essential difference between the two. In each city there is a grand council made up of the whole citizen body, that is of all who have the right to hold office; if it is harder for incomers to secure that right at Venice, the difference is one of *ordini* only and does not amount to one in the *spezie del governo*. What is important is that within each citizen body—the *popolo* of Florence, the *gentiluomini* of Venice—there is formal equality of access to office; "they make no distinctions of wealth or lineage, as is done where optimates rule," and the Venetian system is as popular as the Florentine, the Florentine as optimate as the Venetian.[80] In each system, we are to understand, the ruling elite emerge solely through the display of the necessary qualities and the recognition and choice of their fellows.

If there is a difference of substance between Venice and Florence, it lies not in the formal commitment of either city to the principle of equality, but in that greater restlessness and ambition which marks the Florentine personality in the pursuit of *onore*. Bernardo treats this characteristic with highly Aristotelian ambivalence. On the one hand it is desirable that men should be ambitious for that *onore* which can

---

per sei mesi o per uno anno, se ne troverrebbono bene spesso esclusi tutti quelli che sarebbe necessario che vi fussino."

[80] *D. e D.*, p. 106: "E se bene ha nome diverso da quello che vogliamo fare noi, perché si chiama governo di gentiluomini ed el nostro si chiamerà di popolo, non per questo è di spezie diversa, perché non è altro che uno governo nel quale intervengono universalmente tutti quegli che sono abili agli uffici, né vi si fa distinzione o per ricchezza o per stiatte, come si fa quando governano gli ottimati, ma sono ammessi equalmente tutti a ogni cosa, e di numero sono molti e forse più che siano e' nostri; e se la plebe non vi participa, la non participe anche a noi, perche infiniti artefici, abitatori nuovi ed altri simili, non entrano nel nostro consiglio. Ed ancora che a Vinezia gli inabili sono abilitati con più difficultà agli uffici che non si fa a noi, questo non nasce perché la spezie del governo sia diversa, ma perché in una spezie medesimi hanno ordini diversi . . . e però se noi chiamassimo gentiluomini e' nostri, e questo nome appresso a noi non si dessi se non a chi è abile agli uffici, troveresti che el governo di Vinegia è popolare come el nostro e che el nostro non è manco governo di ottimati che sia el loro."

be won only by serving the *res publica* and to exclude ambition, so that they are content with mere security, is no longer the pragmatic realism of Book I, but an unattainable Platonic ideal. On the other, it is dangerous that *ambizione* should reach a point where honor is desired for its own sake, since the private good will now be set above the public good and men will soon become capable of doing anything whatever to get and retain it. However, men have this appetite, whether it is to be praised or condemned, and the political theorist must take account of it.[81] Nor should a free government need to fear the ambition of its citizens; if properly directed it should lead to the emergence not merely of a governing elite, but of those three or four highly exceptional men on whose *virtù*, at any one time, nearly everything depends.[82]

The proper direction of this *laudabile o dannabile* ambition takes several forms. In the first place, one must ensure that no office carries so much power that it is not limited by the power of some other; this is why the *gonfaloniere* is to share executive authority with the "ten" and the senate, and the senate to share legislative power with the Consiglio. This will not only keep the corrupt magistrate harmless, but actually prevent his corruption by reminding him constantly that what he has and is he shares with the public. In the second place, there must be offices of honor sufficiently numerous and graded, and changing hands often enough, to ensure that nobody is without hope of promotion according to the merit he displays. In Bernardo's ideal system, these *gradi* begin with election to the senate for life, rise through the

---

[81] *D. e D.*, pp. 118-19: "E se bene io dissi ieri che e' cittadini buoni non hanno volontà di governare, e che al bene essere delle città basta che vi sia la sicurtà, nondimeno questo è uno fondamento che fu piú facile a Platone a dirlo, che a chi si è maneggiato nelle republiche a vederlo, e piú rigoroso che non è oggi el gusto degli uomini, e' quali hanno tutto per natura desiderio di essere stimati ed onorati. Anzi, come io dissi poco fa, è forse piú utile alle città, che e' suoi cittadini abbino qualche instinto di ambizione moderata, perché gli desta a pensieri ed azione onorevoli, che se la fussi al tutto morta.

"Ma non disputando ora questo, dico che poiché negli uomini è questo appetito, o laudabile o dannabile che sia, ed appicato in modo che non si può sperare di spegnerlo, a noi che ragioniamo di fare uno governo, non quale doverebbe essere, ma quale abbiamo a sperare che possi essere, bisogna affaticarsi che tutti e' gradi de' cittadini abbino la satisfazione sua, pur che si facci con modo che non offenda la libertà."

[82] *D. e D.*, p. 112: ". . . le città benché siano libere, se sono bene ordinate, sono sostentate dal consiglio e dalla virtù di pochi; e se pigliate dieci o quindici anni per volta insieme, troverete che in tale tempo non sono piú che tre o quattro cittadini da chi depende la virtù ed el nervo delle consulte ed azioni piú importanti." Note that this is the first time we have found *virtù* used as a quality pertaining to actions, rather than to persons.

various magistracies which senators may assume and culminate with the supreme office of the gonfalonierate.[83] But in the third place, it must be made plain at every point that office is the reward of public recognition of *virtù* and can never be owed to the private favor of individuals or cliques.[84]

Bernardo's determination to ensure the last of these drives him to several proposals designed to open up the system, at some points going well beyond the confines of the Venetian paradigm. When the senate elects persons to those offices which are not in the gift of the Consiglio Grande, it is to be afforced either by a variety of lesser magistrates not otherwise of its body, or else by one hundred commissioners elected by the Consiglio and sitting with the senate for this purpose only. The aim here is to prevent the senate from becoming a closed corporation, by reminding its members that they must still take account of those whose good opinion put them in the senate originally, and to break up the *sette* and *intelligenzie* which will otherwise form within its body.[85] Deliberation, as opposed to election, is to be rigorously confined to the life membership of the senate, but all debate is to take place in open and plenary sessions and the *gonfaloniere*, in his capacity as president, is to ensure that as many speak as possible, notably the reluctant, the inexperienced, and the relatively unknown.[86] Guicciar-

[83] *D. e D.*, pp. 119-20: "E questo che noi abbiamo detto è sanza dubio grado che non gli nuoce, perché se bene sono senatori a vita, pure sono molti, hanno la autorità limitata in modo che non diventano signori, e nondimeno el grado è tale che debbe bastare a uno cittadino che non ha la stomaco corrotto di ambizione; perché se ha virtù mediocre, si debbe contentare di essere senatore; se è più eccellente, verrà di grado in grado agli onori più alti: essere de' dieci, essere della pratica, essere uno de' disegnati per gonfaloniere quando vacassi."

[84] *D. e D.*, p. 112: "A questi (i.e., those of the highest *virtù*) sia proposta la speranza di uno grado estraordinario dove pensino di arrivare, non con sette, non con corruttele, non con violenzia, ma col fare opere egregie, col consumare tutta la sua virtù e vita per beneficio della patria, la quale, poiché ha a ricevere più utile da questi tali che dagli altri, debbe anche allettargli più che gli altri."

[85] *D. e D.*, p. 121: "Le ragione che mi muovono a fare questa aggiunta sono due: l'una, che io non vorrei che a alcuno per essere diventato senatore paressi avere acconciò in modo le cose sua che giudicassi non avere più bisogno degli altri che non sono del senato e tenessi manco conto della estimazione publica, come se mai più non avessi a capitare a' giudici degli uomini . . . L'altra, che io non vorrei che per essere e' senatori sempre quegli medesimi, una parte di essi facessi qualche intelligenzia che facessi girare e' partiti in loro, esclusi gli altri, . . . Questa aggiunta rimedia benissimo a tutt'a dua gli inconvenienti, perché romperà le sette, intervenendovi tanto più numero e di persone che si variano; e da altro canto non potendo questi aggiunti essere eletti loro, non aranno causa di favorire per ambizione sua la larghezza, ma si volteranno ragionevolmente con le fave a chi sarà giudicato che meriti più; e quando parte del senato malignassi, questi daranno sempre el tracollo alla bilancia."

[86] *D. e D.*, p. 122.

dini is balancing the hierarchical principle that the most experienced should take the lead against the egalitarian principle that the elite must be reinforced by giving the greatest number opportunity to acquire experience and develop *virtù*; he is also not unaware that cliques and corruption could arise if the same individuals took the lead all the time. But a reputation as an intelligent commentator in debate, he says, will bring a man more esteem than a two-months tenure of the gonfalonierate, even if he never holds office at all; and if this is the accepted road to office and advancement, crooked means will not be used.[87]

Guicciardini's antipathy to private alliances and relationships in politics, and his belief in countering these by wide public participation, are most clearly stated in his discussion of the mode of electing the *gonfaloniere*. Here he holds the Venetians to have made a mistake: anxious to avoid the extremes of popular ignorance and optimate ambitions and rivalries, they have set up an elaborate machinery of indirect election and drawn ballots, designed to produce at the end of the process forty-one men to choose the *doge*, whose names could not possibly have been predicted at the beginning, so that no intrigues or canvassing can occur. But all this is beside the point. Either the forty-one will be nobodies, in which case they will be ignorant and inexperienced; or they will be men of substance, with interests, alliances, and ambitions of their own, in which case their choice will be predetermined by private considerations. In practice the latter is what happens; a knowledgeable observer of Venetian politics can usually predict who will be *doge* once he knows the names of the forty-one, because he will know their *dependenzie*. It is true that even so they will elect one of the five or six best qualified citizens, but corruption has not been sufficiently eliminated.[88]

Here we return to basic principles. Every city consists of a many and a few, a *popolo* and a *senato*, and the normal road to power and influence lies through alliance with one or the other. Guicciardini now develops a somewhat Polybian argument;[89] it may be legitimate enough to defend people against senate or senate against people, but the nature of man is insatiable and we pass imperceptibly from defending our own to claiming what is another's.[90] Either strategy in the end produces harmful results, but it is easy in principle so to arrange matters that the aspirant to office must be acceptable to both parties. Let the senate

---

[87] *D. e D.*, p. 123.   [88] *D. e D.*, pp. 130-32.   [89] *D. e D.*, pp. 132-35.

[90] *D. e D.*, p. 133: "E queste contenzione, se bene qualche volta nascono da onesti principi, pure vanno poi piú oltre, perché la natura degli uomini è insaziabile, e chi si muove alle imprese per ritenere el grado suo e non essere oppresso, quando poi si è condotto a questo, non si ferma quivi ma cerca di amplificarlo piú che lo onesto e per consequente di opprimere ed usurpare quello di altri."

meet and choose persons by lot to draw up a panel of forty or fifty candidates. The three of these who receive the most votes—irrespective of whether one has an absolute majority or not—must be voted on by the Consiglio Grande on another day, and if one has an absolute majority, let him be *gonfaloniere*; if not, let three other finalists be selected and the process repeated until a victor emerges. The participation of the senate ensures that the final candidates are men of standing; that of the people ensures that the final outcome is not determined by intra-elite rivalries. Each contributes to ensure that the merit of the individual is recognized as publicly and impersonally as possible.[91]

Guicciardini, it is clear, is not an uncritical follower of the *mito di Venezia*, but he has Bernardo conclude his constitutional exposition with a conventional panegyric on the best form of government known to all time; he has already praised it—with the qualification *per una città disarmata*—on the grounds of its centuries-old stability,[92] and here he even more conventionally adds that it combines the merits, while avoiding the disadvantages, of rule by the one, the few, and the many.[93] But this is not the real scaffolding of his thought on the subject of Venice. A fully Polybian theory would assert that monarchy, aristocracy, and democracy had each its peculiar merit, or *virtù*, but that each tended to self-corruption in isolation; a true mixed government would employ each *virtù* to check the degeneration of the others, and in fully developed versions of the *mito*, as we shall see, it was usually added that the Venetians had achieved this by mechanical and self-perpetuating devices. Guicciardini set little store by these last, in comparison with the open recruitment of an elite of *virtù*; and it is his use of that key term that distinguishes his thought from schematic Polybianism. He does not attribute a separate *virtù* to each of the three forms, because he uses the word in such a way as to define it as a quality of the elite or few. We have repeatedly seen that the many are essential to his scheme, and they do not function in it without exercising some form of intelligence and judgment which is their own and not that of the elite. But Guicciardini nowhere tells us what it is or defines it as a *virtù*; the function of his many is to be a context for the few, and when in the passage under scrutiny he states that the chief good of popular government is "the conservation of liberty," he instantly adds "the authority of the laws and the security of every

[91] *D. e D.*, p. 135.

[92] *D. e D.*, p. 106: "A me pare che el governo viniziano per una città disarmata sia così bello come forse mai avessi alcuna republica libera; ed oltre che lo mostra la esperienzia, perché essendo durato già centinaia di anni florido ed unito come ognuno sa, non si può attribuire alla fortuna o al caso, lo mostrano ancora molte ragioni che appariranno meglio nel ragionare di tutta questa materia."

[93] *D. e D.*, pp. 138-39.

man"[94]—moving down the scale toward that private and nonpartici-
patory definition of liberty set out in Book i. Nor has the one—the
gonfaloniere or *doge*—any *virtù* of his own distinguishable from the
esperienzia, prudenzia, and honorable ambition of the few; he is simply
the culmination of the elitist edifice.

Guicciardini does not idealize Venice as a synthesis of different
forms of *virtù* because, at bottom, he recognizes only one, and since
this is an attribute of the few, the roles of the one and the many must
remain ancillary. Machiavelli had departed even further from the
Polybian-Venetian paradigm because he saw *virtù* as the attribute of
the armed many; Guicciardini's skepticism about this reading of Roman
history is of less importance than his regretful conviction that the
Florentine militia was beyond revival. But in terms both of historical
reality and of preferred values, his conception of *virtù* was aristocratic. The problem then was to prevent the corruption and decay of
the few, specifically of the Florentine *ottimati.* The one and the many
provided the structure in which the *virtù* of the few—more prudent
and less dynamic than Machiavellian *virtù*—might continue to be
autonomously directed toward the common good; but since they did
not exercise *virtù* specifically their own, we are not being shown a
Polybian structure in which the polity is a combination of different
forms of *virtù* and its stability is ensured by their checking each other
from degeneration. The *Dialogo* is not a treatise on how the mixed
government may remain stable in a world where degeneration is the
norm, or on how *virtù* may act to prevent the ascendance of *fortuna.*
Guicciardini was too directly concerned with the historic dilemma of
the Florentine *ottimati* to engage in so theoretical an inquiry; he knew
that the alternative to a successful *vivere civile* was not some generalized form of cyclical decay, but the reestablishment of Medicean rule
in a new and less advantageous relationship to the optimate class. It
can however be shown that the supremacy of fortune is, in some ultimate sense, one of the poles within which his highly individual thought
developed.

Bernardo concludes by remarking that as far back as can be read in
Florentine history, the city has never enjoyed good government; there
has been either the tyranny of one (as under the Medici), the insolent
and self-destructive domination of the few, the license of the multitude,
or the supreme irrationality of oligarchy and mob rule in conjunction.
"Unless chance (*sorte*) or the mercy of God give us grace (*grazia*) to
arrive at some such form of government as this, we must fear the same

---

[94] *D. e D.,* p. 139: "El consiglio grande ha seco quello bene che è principale nel
governo del popolo, cioè la conservazione della libertà, la autorità delle leggi e la
sicurtà di ognuno . . ."

evils as have come about in the past."[95] Soderini asks what hope there is that this will ever happen, and Bernardo's reply is a disquisition on the ways in which good governments are founded.[96] They come about either by force or by persuasion. A prince possessing absolute power may decide to lay it down and institute a republic. In theory this will be very easy, as none can resist him and a people passing suddenly from tyranny to liberty will think themselves in paradise and repose infinite faith in him; they will see, says Guicciardini in language which recalls Machiavelli's treatment of the ideal legislator, that fortune has played no part in his decision, but that all depends upon his *virtù* to a degree which makes the latter more than human.[97] In the real world, however, the exercise of absolute power will either have created such hatreds that he dare not lay it down or (more probably) will have so far corrupted his character that he will not really want to (Augustus is the example here).[98] A private citizen may seek supreme power in order to reform the city, as did Lycurgus, but the same considerations apply; force and power tend to be self-perpetuating.[99] There remains persua-

[95] D. e D., pp. 139-40: "Sarebbe adunche el governo vostro simile al governo loro; ed essendo el suo ottimo, el vostro almanco sarebbe buono e sarebbe sanza dubio quale non ha mai veduto la città nostra. Perché o noi siamo stati sotto uno, come a tempo de' Medici, che è stato governo tirannico, o pochi cittadini hanno potuto nella città . . . che in fatto hanno oppressi e tenuti in servitù gli altri con mille ingiurie ed insolenzie, e tra loro medesimi sono stati pieni di sedizioni . . . o la è stata in arbitrio licenzioso della moltitudine . . . o è stato qualche vivere pazzo, dove in uno tempo medesimo ha avuto licenzia la plebe e potestà e' pochi. . . . Però se la sorte o la benignità di Dio non ci dà grazia di riscontrare in una forma di governo come questa o simile, abbiano a temere de' medesimi mali che sono stati per el passato."

[96] D. e D., pp. 141-45.

[97] D. e D., pp. 141-42: "E' governi buoni si introducono o con la forza o con la persuasione: la forza sarebbe quando uno che si trovassi principe volessi deponere el principato e constituire una forma di republica, perché a lui starebbe el commandare e ordinare; e questo sarebbe modo facilissimo, si perché el popolo che stava sotto la tirannide e non pensava alla libertà, vedendosi in uno tratto menare al vivere libero con amore e sanza arme, benché si introducessi ordinato e con moderato larghezza, gli parebbe entrare in paradiso e piglierebbe tutto per guadagno . . . gli sarebbe prestata fede smisurata . . . Non si potrebbe di questa opera attribuire parte alcuna alla fortuna, ma tutto dependerebbe dalla sua virtù, ed el frutto che ne nascessi non sarebbe beneficio a pochi né per breve tempo, ma in quanto a lui, a infiniti e per molte età."

[98] D. e D., p. 142.

[99] D. e D., pp. 142-43: "Si introducerebbe anche el governo per forza quando uno cittadino amatore della patria vedessi le cose essere disordinate, né gli bastando el cuore poterle riformare voluntariamente e dacordo, si ingegnassi con la forza pigliare tanta autorità che potessi constituire uno buono governo *etiam* a dispetto degli altri, come fece Licurgo quando fece a Sparta quelle sante leggi. . . . Però bisogna che la forza duri tanto che abbia preso piede; e quanto più durassi,

sion, by which is evidently meant a collective decision by the citizens to set up good government; but for this to come about they must have had sufficient experience to know both the evils of bad government and the remedies for it, and must have suffered misfortunes great enough to teach them without either destroying them or driving them into violent conflicts and extreme causes. If the 1494 constitution should miscarry, there will be a move for a *stato stretto* but—Guicciardini is exercising hindsight here—a likelier outcome is a *gonfaloniere* with increased powers.[100] All will then depend on his character and position; Guicciardini's readers know that what is to come is the ineffective rule of Piero Soderini, but Bernardo says there is a slim chance that a strong and wise *gonfaloniere*, especially if appointed for life, will institute a constitution truly of the Venetian pattern.[101]

The explicit conclusion is that Florence in 1494 is still too much at the mercy of fortune to allow much hope of a stabilized republic.[102] It seems also to be implied, at least to some extent, that such a republic is the only alternative to the rule of fortune; Guicciardini, we know, believes that its power over its own citizens is the only form of power not radically violent or unjust. But the realm of fortune is not—in theory it could but need not be—one of totally random and unpredictable happenings. Since 1513 Guicciardini had been anatomizing what was in fact emerging out of the failure of republican government—a restored Medicean system in which the intense hostility of the *popolo*, deprived of their Consiglio Grande, rendered the Medici more suspicious and the *ottimati* less able to act as an independent counterweight to them. He now has Bernardo conclude the main theme of the

---

tanto piú sarebbe pericoloso che non gli venissi voglia di continuarvi drento. Sapete come dice el proverbio: che lo indugio piglia vizio."

[100] *D. e D.*, p. 143: "Ci è adunche necessario fare fondamento in su la persuasione, e questa ora non sarebbe udita; ma io non dubio che le cose andranno in modo che innanzi che passi troppo tempo, si cognoscerà per molti la maggiore parte de' disordini, e combatterà in loro da uno canto la voglia di provedervi, da l'altro la paura di non ristringere troppo el governo. Ed in questo bisognerà, a mio giudicio, che giuochi la fortuna della città . . . Potrebbe ancora essere che questi disordini fussino grandi, ma tali che piú presto travagliassino la città che la ruinassino, ed allora el punto sarà che chi arà a fare questa riforma la pigli bene, perché sempre farà difficultà grande el dubio ch'e' cittadini principali non voglino ridurre le cose a uno stato stretto; però potra essere che gli uomini si voltino piú presto a uno gonfaloniere a vita o per lungo tempo che a altro, perché darà loro manco ombra che uno senato perpetuo, e perché per questo solo la città non resta bene ordinata."

[101] *Ibid.*

[102] *D. e D.*, p. 144: "Però concludendo vi dico che ho per molto dubio e mi pare che dependa molto dalla potestà della fortuna, se questo governo disordinato si riordinerà o no . . ."

Dialogo—Roman history and some other topics are still to be discussed—by expatiating on this possibility, after which he reminds Soderini, Capponi, and Piero Guicciardini that though they will doubtless endeavor to reform the republic, they may not succeed. Success in any political enterprise is a matter of *tempo* and *occasione*, and the times cannot be said to be propitious. If the times are against one, circumstances may arise in which the only strategy is to temporize and conform, since the attempt to innovate may bring about worse evils yet.[103]

With this we return from the realm of value into that of history, or, to use the terminology we have found most effective in interpreting Guicciardini, from that of *virtù* into that of prudence. In the ideal republic prudence appeared as a form of *virtù*, that is, of morally free and unforced civic behavior. But it could always bear the meaning of doing the best one could with what one could not help getting; and in this sense it might be the appropriate conduct for a world in which the republican experiment had collapsed and the *ottimati* found themselves allied not with the *popolo*, among whom they could display *virtù* if they were ever accepted as natural leaders, but with the Medici on terms which could never again be those that had obtained before 1494. Guicciardini never failed to emphasize that the revolution of that year had been a *mutazione*, an *innovazione*, after which everything was changed and the future was hard to predict or to control. The rhetoric for depicting such consequences was the rhetoric of fortune; and the quality we have been calling prudence might therefore appear preeminently the quality of intellect and personality with which the intelligent aristocrat sought to govern himself and others, in the world of *fortuna*.

When Guicciardini wrote the *Dialogo*, it still seemed worthwhile to devise a civic setting in which *virtù* and prudence could function together and develop to the full. The world of *fortuna* and prudence in naked confrontation does not appear in his writings until the *Ricordi* of 1528 and 1530, because only then did he face the full reality of optimate isolation between Medici and *popolo*. These were the years of the last republic and the Great Siege, in which an increasingly revolutionary popular government drove out the *ottimati*—including Guic-

---

[103] *D. e D.*, p. 146: "Perché le medesime imprese che fatte fuora di tempo sono difficillime o impossibile diventono facillime quando sono accompagnate dal tempo o dal occasione, ed a chi le tenta fuora del tempo suo non solo non gli riescono ma è pericolo che lo averle tentate non le guasti per quello tempo che facilmente sarebbono riuscite, e questa è una delle ragione che e' pazienti sono tenuti savi . . . e del resto più presto andate comportando e temporeggiatevi el meglio che potete, che desiderate novità, perché non vi potrà venire cosa che non sia peggio." The language of Lodovico Alamanni: the wise never innovate.

ciardini himself—and defied the Medici in ways which ensured that the latter could return only as absolute princes. At the end of the Siege, Guicciardini was to react by helping the Medici reimpose themselves and by engaging personally in their savage purge of the defeated popular leaders;[104] but during its course he employed his enforced leisure by completing a critique of Machiavelli's *Discorsi* and a collection of aphorisms in which we clearly see the world as it then appeared to him. A dominant—perhaps the overmastering—theme of these *Ricordi* is the extraordinary difficulty of applying intelligence to the world of events in the form of personal or political action. When all the books have been read, the lessons learned, and the conclusions digested— Guicciardini never for a moment suggests that these preliminaries do not have to be gone through—there remains the problem of converting thought into action;[105] and even when experience has brought an accidental knowledge of particulars that natural intelligence cannot provide,[106] that problem remains, lying beyond any conceivable systematization of knowledge, as the problem of judging time, of determining the moment to act, and the considerations relevant to both the moment and the action.[107] It is easy to see that the fool may fail to understand what is happening; Guicciardini sees that the very intelligent man may overreact to what he sees happening,[108] so that he

---

[104] For this phase of Guicciardini's career see Ridolfi, *Life*, chs. XVIII-XX.

[105] *Ricordi*, C 22 (Spongano, p. 27, cited above, ch. v, n. 22): "Quante volte si dice: se si fussi fatto o non fatto cosi, saria succeduta o non succeduta la tale cosa! che se fussi possibile vederne el paragone, si conoscerebbe simile openione essere false."

[106] *Ricordi*, C 9, 10 (Spongano, pp. 13-14): "Leggete spesso e considerate bene questi ricordi, perché è piú facile a conoscergli e intendergli che osservargli: e questo si facilita col farsene tale abito che s'abbino freschi nella memoria.

"Non si confidi alcuno tanto nella prudenza naturale che si persuada quella bastare senza l'accidentale della esperienzia, perché ognuno che ha maneggiato faccende, benché prudentissimo, ha potuto conoscere che con la esperienzia si aggiugne a molte cose, alle quali è impossibile che el naturale solo possa aggiugnere." Cf. B 71, 100, 121.

[107] *Ricordi*, C 78-85; especially 79 (Spongano, p. 90): "Sarebbe pericoloso proverbio, se non fussi bene inteso, quello che si dice: el savio debbe godere el beneficio del tempo; perché, quando ti viene quello che tu desideri, chi perde la occasione non la ritruova a sua posta; e anche in molte cose è necessaria la celerità del risolversi e del fare; ma quando sei in partiti difficili o in cose che ti sono moleste, allunga e aspetta tempo quanto puoi, perché quello spesso ti illumina o ti libera. Usando cosí questo proverbio, è sempre salutifero; ma inteso altrimenti, sarebbe spesso pernizioso."

[108] *Ricordi*, B 96 (Spongano, p. 28): "Le cose del mondo sono si varie e dependono da tanti accidenti, che difficilmente si può fare giudicio del futuro; e si vede per esperienzia che quasi sempre le conietture de' savi sono fallace: però non laudo el consiglio di coloro che lasciano la commodità di uno bene presente,

imagines it to be happening faster and more completely than it is.[109] Where Machiavelli had thought it better to act than to temporize, since time was likely to worsen one's position, Guicciardini can see the strength of the case for temporization, since nothing can worsen one's position more than one's own ill-considered actions. But both men are clear that the domain of imperfectly predictable happenings—Guicciardini salutes Aristotle for laying it down that there can be no determined truth about future contingencies[110]—is the domain of *fortuna*. All the *ricordi* which are relevant to this problem should be read as the counterpart to chapter xxv of *Il Principe* and to those chapters of the *Discorsi* which deal with the problems of action in a society which has begun to be corrupt.

On several occasions in the *Ricordi*—echoing passages in the *Dialogo* and in the *Considerations on Machiavelli's Discourses* which Guicciardini wrote about this period—there appear criticisms of Machiavelli's treatment of Roman history, a recurrent theme of which is the naiveté of supposing that one can imitate Roman examples under very different conditions.[111] Around this there has sprung up a literature which contrasts Machiavelli's supposedly idealistic belief in historical parallels and recurrences with Guicciardini's supposedly more realistic understanding that no two situations are exactly alike and that one must play them by ear rather than by the book.[112] But it is possible that this con-

---

benché minore, per paura di uno male futuro, benché maggiore, se non è molto propinquo o molto certo; perché, non succedendo poi spesso quello di che temevi, ti truovi per una paura vana avere lasciato quello che ti piaceva. E però è savio proverbio: di cosa nasce cosa."

[109] *Ricordi*, C 71 (Spongano, p. 82): "Se vedete andare a cammino la declinazione di una città, la mutazione di uno governo, lo augumento di uno imperio nuovo e altre cose simili—che qualche volta si veggono innanzi quasi certe—avvertite a non vi ingannare ne' tempi: perché e moti delle cose sono per sua natura e per diversi impedimenti molto piú tardi che gli uomini non si immaginano, e lo ingannarti in questo ti può fare grandissimo danno: avvertiteci bene, che è uno passo dove spesso si inciampa. Interviene anche el medesimo nelle cose private e particulari, ma molto piú in queste publiche e universali, perché hanno, per essere maggiore mole, el moto suo piú lento, e anche sono sottoposte a piú accidenti." Cf. C 34, 115, 116, 162, 191; B 76, 103.

[110] *Ricordi*, C 58 (Spongano, p. 67): "Quanto disse bene el filosofo: *De futuris contingentibus non est determinata veritas!* Aggirati quanto tu vuoi, che quanto piú ti aggiri, tanto piú truovi questo detto verissimo."

[111] *Ricordi*, C 110 (Spongano, p. 121): "Quanto si ingannono coloro che a ogni parola allegano e Romani! Bisognerebbe avere una città condizionata come era loro, e poi governarsi secondo quello esemplo: el quale a chi ha le qualità disproporzionate è tanto disproporzionate, quanto sarebbe volere che uno asino facessi el corso di uno cavallo."

[112] E.g., Sir Herbert Butterfield, *The Statecraft of Machiavelli* (London: G. Bell and Sons, 1940, 1955).

trast has been overstated. Both men lived in a conceptual world where *fortuna* was held to be both unpredictable and recurrent; Guicciardini declares in both final drafts of the *Ricordi* that everything recurs, though it does not look the same and is very hard to recognize;[113] and Machiavelli knew well enough that the lessons of history were difficult to apply and that this was part of the whole problem of action in time. There is little separating them here but emphasis and temperament. The important difference between the two men is not a question of historical sophistication, but lies in the fact that Machiavelli used the term *virtù* to denote the creative power of action to shape events, whereas Guicciardini had little faith in this power and did not use the term *virtù* to describe it. Both men found *virtù* used to denote behavior constitutive of a system of morality in action; but Machiavelli's most daring intellectual step was to retain the term to denote aspects of the individual's behavior in the domain of war outside the city and after the civic universe had collapsed, and Guicciardini employed it only with reference to the civic setting. *Il Principe* and the *Ricordi* both depict the individual in the post-civic world; but Machiavelli's individual is a ruler seeking to shape events through *virtù* in the sense of audacity, Guicciardini's a patrician seeking to adapt himself to events through prudence. Both men hold that audacity and prudence are appropriate in different circumstances, that these circumstances are brought to us by *fortuna*, and that it is exceedingly difficult for the individual to tell what they require.

If we compare the two writers' thoughts on the civic and republican framework, we find that their conceptions of *virtù* can be further differentiated in relation to their thought about arms and war. From *Il Principe*, where *virtù* appears as limited but real creative power, Machiavelli went on to complete the *Discorsi* and the *Arte della Guerra*, concerned with the armed popular state where the foundation of civic was military *virtù* and the republic could tame its environment by arms. Before he wrote the *Ricordi*, Guicciardini had completed the *Dialogo*, in which he considered and rejected the Roman paradigm and

---

[113] *Ricordi*, C 76 (Spongano, p. 87): "Tutto quello che è stato per el passato e è al presente, sarà ancora in futuro; ma si mutano e nomi e le superficie delle cose in modo, che chi non ha buono occhio non le riconosce, nè sa pigliare regola o fare giudicio per mezzo di quella osservazione." Cf. B 114 (*ibid.*): ". . . le cose medesime ritornano, ma sotto diversi nomi e colori." B 140 (Spongano, p. 82): "Le cose del mondo non stanno ferme, anzi hanno sempre progresso al cammino a che ragionevolmente per sua natura hanno a andare e finire; ma tardano piú che non è la opinione nostra, perché noi le misuriamo secondo la vita nostra che è breve e non secondo el tempo loro che è lungo; e però sono e passi suoi piú tardi che non sono e nostri, e si tardi per sua natura che, ancora che si muovino, non ci accorgiamo spesso de' suoi moti: e per questo sono spesso falsi e' giudici che noi facciamo."

settled for the *città disarmata*, where the essential skill was that of adaptation to the environment through prudence. Consequently, *virtù* had no meaning for him outside the civic setting, where it was identical with prudence; and when the republic and its *virtù* had vanished together, prudence remained the instrument of the post-civic individual.[114] The only alternative remaining—our basic model informs us—was faith, reposed in providence or prophecy, as operations of grace: that faith which Savonarolans were still placing in the messianic destiny of Florence. Guicciardini inserts in the *Ricordi* an analysis of the faith which moves mountains, considered as a purely unreasonable persistence in the teeth of circumstances; capable, if raised to a sufficient height of exaltation, of doing the work of *virtù*, triumphing over contingencies and shaping them in ways which no reasonable observer could have predicted. It is faith of this order which has nerved the Florentines to defy the armies of pope and emperor together for more than seven months, and the faith in question is reposed in the prophecies of Savonarola.[115] It is also indicated that this faith is a madness, which consists in trusting oneself wholly to *fortuna*.[116]

[114] *Ricordi*, C 51 (Spongano, p. 60): "Chi si travaglia in Firenze di mutare stati, se non lo fa per necessità, o che a lui tocchi diventare capo del nuovo governo, è poco prudente, perché mette a pericolo sè e tutto el suo, se la cosa non succede; succedendo, non ha a pena una piccola parte di quello che aveva disegnato. E quanta pazzia è giuocare a uno giuoco che si possa perdere piú sanza comparazione che guadagnare! E quello che non importa forse manco, mutato che sia lo stato, ti oblighi a uno perpetuo tormento: d'avere sempre a temere di nuova mutazione."

[115] *Ricordi*, C 1 (Spongano, p. 3): "Quello che dicono le persone spirituali, che chi ha fede conduce cose grandi, e, come dice lo evangelio, chi ha fede puo comandare a' monti ecc., procede perché la fede fa ostinazione. Fede non è altro che credere con openione ferma e quasi certezza le cose che non sono ragionevole, o se sono ragionevole, crederle con piú resoluzione che non persuadono le ragione. Chi adunche ha fede diventa ostinato in quello che crede, e procede al cammino suo intrepido e resoluto, sprezzando le difficultà e pericoli, e mettendosi a soportare ogni estremità: donde nasce che, essendo le cose del mondo sottoposte a mille casi e accidenti, può nascere per molti versi nella lunghezza del tempo aiuto insperato a chi ha perseverato nella ostinazione, la quale essendo causata dalla fede, si dice meritamente: chi ha fede ecc. Esemplo a' dì nostri ne è grandissimo questa ostinazione de' Fiorentini che, essendosi contro a ogni ragione del mondo messi a aspettare la guerra del papa e imperadore sanza speranza di alcuno soccorso di altri, disuniti e con mille difficultà, hanno sostenuto in sulle mura già sette mesi gli eserciti, e quali non si sarebbe creduto che avessino sostenuti sette dì, e condotto le cose in luogo che, se vincessino, nessuno piú se ne maraviglierebbe, dove prima da tutti erano giudicato perduti: e questa ostinazione ha causata in gran parte la fede di non potere perire, secondo le predizione di fra Ieronimo da Ferrara."

[116] *Ricordi*, C 136 (Spongano, p. 148): "Accade che qualche volta e' pazzi fanno maggiore cose che e' savi. Procede perché el savio, dove non è necessitato, si

But the thought of Guicciardini diverges from that of Machiavelli at the point where each man assesses the role of armed *virtù* and of arms themselves as a cause of *virtù*: a problem closer to the ultimate concerns of Western political thought than has always been understood. Guicciardini was as well aware of the nonmoral element in politics as Machiavelli, but he employed *virtù* only as a compendium for the values of civic humanism. Machiavelli was as well aware of those values as Guicciardini, but he held them to be contingent on a people's ability to control its environment by arms, which he called its *virtù*. Guicciardini—the greater realist, perhaps, in his assessment of Florentine military capacity—was able, in choosing Venice as typical of the *città disarmata*, to develop the image of a society in which those values were realized in purity; Book II of the *Dialogo* is a statement of the civic ideal such as Machiavelli never attempted. The role of Venice was to be paradigmatic for civic humanism, and below the level at which the Venetian image was a myth of Polybian stability, it furnished paradigms for the conversion of classical political values into actual or nearly actual political arrangements. The writings of Donato Giannotti, like those of Guicciardini himself, show us the paradigms in action as conceptual tools; those of Gasparo Contarini show us the symbolic development of the myth.

---

rimette assai alla ragione e poco alla fortuna, el pazzo assai alla fortuna e poco alla ragione: e le cose portate dalla fortuna hanno talvolta fini incredibili. E' savi di Firenze arebbono ceduto alla tempesta presente; e' pazzi, avendo contro a ogni ragione voluto opporsi, hanno fatto insino a ora quello che non si sarebbe creduto che la città nostra potessi in modo alcuno fare: e questo è che dice el proverbio *Audaces fortuna iuvat*."

CHAPTER IX

GIANNOTTI AND CONTARINI

Venice as Concept and as Myth

[1]

DONATO GIANNOTTI (1492-1573) is known, if at all, to readers of English as "the most excellent describer of the commonwealth of Venice" (the phrase is Harrington's 1656)[1] and by less specific statements to the effect that he was the intellectual heir of Machiavelli and the last major thinker in the Florentine republican tradition. No detailed study of his thought has yet been written in English,[2] but we have gone far enough in the present analysis to have uncovered an anomaly in his received reputation: it is odd, on the face of it, that the same man should have been at once an admirer of Venice and an admirer of Machiavelli. And the oddity grows as we look deeper, for Giannotti proves to have employed his detailed knowledge of Venetian procedures to construct a model of Florentine government which was both markedly popular and founded upon a citizen militia; both concepts very far removed from the aristocratic *città disarmata* discerned by Machiavelli and Guicciardini. The fact is, as already indicated, that his conception of Venice is rather instrumental than ideal; he does not set up the *serenissima republica* as a model to be imitated, but treats it as a source of conceptual and constitutional machinery which can be adapted for use in the very difficult circumstances of Florentine *popolare* politics. He is aided to do this by the fact that the Aristotelian-Polybian model of mixed government, which Venice

---

[1] At the beginning of the Preliminaries to *Oceana*; see Toland, ed., p. 35 (above, ch. I, n. 28).

[2] For his life and career, see Roberto Ridolfi, *Opuscoli di Storia Letteraria e di Erudizione* (Florence: Libr. Bibliopolis, 1942); Randolph Starns, *Donato Giannotti and his Epistolae* (Geneva: Libr. Droz, 1968); and the publication by Felix Gilbert described in the next note. R. von Albertini (*op.cit.*) devotes pp. 14-66 to a study of his thought, as does Starns in "*Ante Machiavel*: Machiavelli and Giannotti" (Gilmore, ed., *Studies on Machiavelli*) and there is a short account, which seeks to relate him to English thought of the Shakespearean age, in C. C. Huffman, *Coriolanus in Context* (Lewisburg: Bucknell University Press, 1972), pp. 17-20.

exemplifies, can be given either an aristocratic or a democratic bias without losing its essential shape. Giannotti, who specifically acknowledges his indebtedness to Aristotle and Polybius, as well as to Machiavelli, may be thought of, from our point of view, as a contributor of originality, if not of direct influence, to the theory of mixed government; he is the first author we shall meet of certain general assertions which were to recur in the history of this branch of republican thought. At the same time we may see him as continuing a tendency whereby Machiavelli's thought was reabsorbed into the tradition of Aristotelian republicanism and the edges of its drastic originality softened and blurred. On neither *innovazione, virtù,* nor even *milizia* is Giannotti's thinking as abrasive or as creative as that of his older friend. But the more we discount the legend of the "wicked Machiavel," the harder it becomes to see just how Machiavelli's true intentions were imparted to European tradition. As later Western republicanism grew, at all events, his image became progressively more orthodox and moral.

As already indicated by his habit of citing his authorities, Giannotti is a more formally academic thinker than either Machiavelli or Guicciardini; his political commitment is real, but his thought does not grow out of the tormenting experience of citizenship in the same way that theirs did. As a young man he frequented the Orti Oricellari and was friendly with Machiavelli while the latter was writing his history of Florence. From 1520 to 1525 he taught (and it is highly probable from the tone of his later writings that at some time he taught political theory) at the university of Pisa. In 1525-1527 he spent much of his time in Padua and Venice, and it was during this time that he wrote most of his *Libro della Repubblica de' Vineziani,* the work by which he is best known to posterity.[3] He returned to Florence after the fall of the Medici—he seems to have regarded his absence hitherto as an exile—and during the Great Siege of 1528-1530 held Machiavelli's old post as secretary to the Ten of War and like him was involved in the organization of a civic militia. Expelled from the city in 1530, he suffered the longevity of the exile; and his second major work, the *Della Repubblica Fiorentina,* is an expatriate's vision of a Florentine popular republic which was never to come into being. The work was not even printed until 1721, and though the study of Venice was published in 1540 and had an extensive reputation, we do not study Giannotti as one whose thought greatly affected the mind of his age. He was not a genius, as Machiavelli and Guicciardini both were; but his writings are those of a very intelligent man, in which we see what could be done

[3] Felix Gilbert, "The Date of the Composition of Contarini's and Giannotti's Books on Venice," in *Studies in the Renaissance,* xiv (New York: The Renaissance Society of America, 1967), pp. 172-84.

with Aristotelian, humanist, Venetian, and Machiavellian concepts under significant and revealing circumstances. They further contain some new departures in thought concerning the politics of time.

Although Felix Gilbert has assembled evidence connecting Giannotti's composition of his work on Venice with the fall of the Medici in May 1527—which he and his friends eagerly anticipated while he was writing his first draft[4]—it would probably not be inappropriate to consider the *Repubblica de' Vineziani* as a fact-finding service which Giannotti intended to perform for his contemporaries. The Venetian model had been endlessly talked about since 1494; there existed a great deal of disseminated information about its workings; but the only written work of reference on the structure of Venetian government, that of Marcantonio Sabellico, was in Giannotti's view so unmethodical as to be uncritical. If the Medici regime were to fall, the *popolare* optimates among whom he moved must resume their struggle to erect a government in which their leadership would be combined with liberty, and Venice was paradigmatic for such a program. Giannotti therefore set out to inform them of the facts. He envisaged a tripartite study,[5] in which one book would outline the general governmental structure (*l'amministrazione universale*), a second would deal with the various magistracies in detail (*particolarmente*), and a third with *la forma e composizione di essa Repubblica*—a phrase suggesting theoretical analysis. But he had completed only the first section when revolution did break out at Florence and he returned, to serve under both the moderate regime of Niccolò Capponi and the much more radical government of the Siege, to experience (it may be) a greater degree of commitment to popular government than he anticipated in 1526-1527, and to suffer exile. Long afterwards, in 1538, he began preparing (but not revising) his incomplete work for the printer.[6] He may by then have completed the manuscript of his blueprint for a popular government at Florence; if so, it would be interesting to know why he did not publish the latter, but we should know why he did not complete the former. His theoretical work was done, and had been devoted to a different subject.

This being so, we are not to expect too much theoretical structure

[4] *Ibid.*, pp. 178-79.

[5] Donato Giannotti, *Opere* (3 vols., ed. G. Rosini, Pisa, 1819), I, 9: "E perché nel primo ragionamento fu disputato dell'amministrazione universale della repubblica; nel secondo particolarmente di tutti i magistrati; nel terzo della forma e composizione di essa repubblica, noi dal primo penderemo il principio nostro, non solamente perché naturalmente le cose universali sono di più facile intelligenza, ma perché ancora del primo ragionamento il secondo, il terzo dall'uno e dall'altro depende."

[6] Gilbert, "Date and Composition," pp. 180-82.

from the essentially incomplete *Repubblica de' Vineziani*. The first section is all that we have, and it suffers from almost the same inadequacies as those ascribed to Sabellico; for what his work lacked, we are told, was any account of *la forma, la composizione, il temperamento di questa Repubblica*[7]—precisely the themes which Giannotti himself was reserving for the third section which he never wrote. Even when it is laid down that the first section will deal with universal topics, leaving particulars to be treated later on, for the reason that universals are easier to understand, this does not mean that the essential principles of the republic's structure are to be expounded first and their specific applications followed up later; for the defense offered of this procedure is that painters begin by sketching in their outlines and sculptors by roughing out their marble, so that one can see what part of the block is going to be the head before the actual shape emerges. The *cose universali* are the general characteristics of the natural object which make it fit for the shape or form which it afterward assumes, and this is why the geographical site of Venice—itself, of course, an extraordinary phenomenon—is to be described before even the governmental structure.[8] In going from *universale* to *particolare*, then, we are not traveling from the principle to its application, so much as examining the matter before we study its form; and even then the scholastic image may be less appropriate than the artistic, for we are told that

> each republic is like a natural body, or rather it would be better to say that it is a body produced by nature in the first place and afterwards polished by art. When nature makes a man, she intends to make a universal whole, a communion. Since each republic is like a natural body, it must have its members; and since there is a proportion and relationship between the members of each body, who knows not this proportion and relationship knows not how the body is made. This is where Sabellico falls short.[9]

[7] *Opere*, I, 20.

[8] *Opere*, I, 34-35: "I dipintori, e scultori, se drittamente riguardiamo, seguitano nello loro arti i precetti dei filosofi; perciocché ancora essi le loro opere dalle cose universali cominciano. I dipintori, prima che particolarmente alcuna imagine dipingano, tirano certe linee, per le quali essa figura universalmente si dimostra; dopo questo le danno la sua particolare perfezione. Gli scultori ancora osservano nelle loro statue il medesimo; tanto che chi vedesse alcuno dei loro marmi dirozzato, direbbe piú tosto questa parte debbe servire per la testa, questa per lo braccio, questa la gamba: tanto la natura ci costringe, non solamente nel conoscere ed intendere, ma eziandio nell'operare, a pigliar il principio dalle cose universali! Per questa cagione io incominciai dalla descrizione del sito di Venezia, come cosa piú che l'altre universale."

[9] *Opere*, I, 21: "Perciocché ciascuna repubblica è simile ad un corpo naturale, anzi per meglio dire, è un corpo dalla natura principalmente prodotto, dopo

But if—to simplify the argument a little—nature supplies the matter of a republic and art the form, it follows that the principles of political harmony are not the work of nature and cannot be intuitively known; they can only be discovered once we see how the political artist has shaped his material. Sabellico merely described the various magistracies of Venice and did not consider the relationships between them which compose the form of the state. But this is all that Giannotti found time to do; Sabellico's deficiencies were to be made good only in the third section. We have not his theoretical analysis of Venetian government, and can only draw conclusions from the language of what we have, and its intimations, as to what that might have been. It is certainly significant, for instance, in the light of various doctrines which he was to develop in the book on Florentine government, that Sabellico should be blamed for failure to show how each magistracy is linked with and dependent upon every other, so that the *composizione* of the republic could be seen in its perfection.[10]

The *Repubblica de' Vineziani* would not have been a humanist work if it had not contained some consideration of the place of the individual in political time. The book is in dialogue form, and the principal speaker—the Venetian scholar Trifone Gabriello or Gabriele—is compared, in his leisurely retirement at Padua, with the Roman Pomponius Atticus. He acknowledges the compliment, but proceeds to draw a distinction. Pomponius Atticus lived when his republic was far gone in corruption, and withdrew into philosophic privacy because he could not save it and was unwilling to perish with it. But Venice is not corrupt, rather more perfect than ever before, and his retirement is that of a man free to choose between action and contemplation.[11] The tran-

---

questo dall'arte limato. Perciocché quando la natura fece l'uomo, ella intese fare una università, una comunione. Essendo adunque ciascuna repubblica come un'altro corpo naturale, dove ancora i suoi membri avere. E perché tra loro è sempre certa proporzione e convenienza, siccome tra i membri di ciascuno altro corpo, chi non conosce questa proporzione e convenienza, che è tra l'un membro e l'altro, non può come fatto sia quel corpo comprendere. Ora questo è quello dove manca il Sabellico."

[10] *Ibid.*: ". . . non dichiara come l'uno sia collegato con l'altro, che dependenza abbia questo da quello, tal che perfettamente la composizione della repubblica raccoglier se ne possa."

[11] *Opere*, I, 16-17: ". . . Pomponio considerando che la repubblica sua era corrottissima, e non conoscendo in sé facoltà di poterle la sanità restituire, si ritrasse da lei per non essere costretto con essa a rovinare. Perciocché la repubblica, quando è corrotta, è simile al mare agitato dalla tempesta, nel quale chi allora si mette, non si può a sua porta ritrarre. Io già non mi son ritratto dalle cure civili per questa cagione, perciocché la mia repubblica non è corrotta, anzi (se io non m'inganno) è piú perfetta ch'ella mai in alcun tempo fosse . . ."

quillity of Venice, favorably compared with the military glory of Rome,[12] is further contrasted with the present miserable state of Italy. Trifone says he does not know whether the present should be compared with the times when the Caesars were destroying Roman liberty, or with those when the barbarians were overrunning Italy; nor does it much matter, since the Caesars were the cause of the barbarian invasions and they in their turn the cause of the present calamities.[13] Giannotti's sense of history is notably causal and linear. Nevertheless it is the happiness of Venice to have escaped history, and this she has clearly done through her success in retaining inner stability and civic *virtù*. We look at this point for an account, Aristotelian or Polybian, of how stability may be retained through time by some harmony or mixture of the different elements composing a political society. The language is in many ways suggestive of such doctrine, and yet, as Gilbert has pointed out, the term "mixed government" and the apparatus of Polybian thought nowhere appear in the *Repubblica de' Vineziani*. They do appear in the *Repubblica Fiorentina*, and yet we cannot say for certain what principles of *composizione* and *proporzione* Giannotti would have educed from the functioning of Venetian magistracies if he had written his third section.

So far as our evidence goes, there is no indication that he would have presented Venice as a Polybian balance of monarchy, aristocracy, and democracy. Certainly we are told that the republic consists of a Consiglio Grande, a Consiglio de' Pregati, a Collegio, and a Doge; and of these the first, second, and fourth obviously correspond to the classical many, few, and one, while the Collegio is an executive presidium of serving magistrates which renders more efficient the aristocratic element of the *pregati*. But there is far less indication than there was in

---

[12] *Opere*, I, 17: "E quantunque i Romani possedessero tanto maggiore imperio quanto è noto a ciascuno, non però giudico la repubblica nostra meno beata e felice. Perciocché la felicità d'una repubblica non consiste nella grandezza dell'imperio, ma si ben nel vivere con tranquillità e pace universale. Nella qual cosa se io dicessi che la nostra repubblica fosse alla romana superiore, credo certo che niuno mi potrebbe giustamente riprendere."

[13] *Opere*, I, 15: ". . . due tempi mi pare che tra gli altri siano da ricordare: Uno, nel quale fu il principio della ruina sua [i.e., Italy's] e dello imperio Romano, e questo fu quando Roma dalle armi Cesariane fu oppressa: l'altro, nel quale fu il colmo del male italiano; e questo fu quando l'Italia dagli Unni, Goti, Vandali, Longobardi fu discorsa e saccheggiata. E se bene si considerano gli accidenti che da poco tempo in qua, cosi in Oriente come in Occidente, sono avvenuti, agevolmente si può vedere che a quelli che oggi vivono in Italia soprasta uno di quelli due tempi. Ma quel di loro più si debba avere in orrore non so io già discernere: perciocché dal primo si può dire nascesse il secondo, e dal secondo tutta quella variazione, che ha fatto pigliare al mondo quella faccia, che ancora gli veggiamo a' tempi nostri, e lasciar del tutto quella che al tempo de' Romani aveva . . ."

Guicciardini that the four members balance or check one another. We may suspect that Giannotti would in the end have put forward some such theory, but the fact remains that his study of the Venetian constitutional structure is developed in a double context, that of a historical account of how Venice came to be a closed aristocracy and that of a detailed investigation of Venetian voting procedures, neither of which has any obvious connection with the principles of Polybian balance.

When he wrote about Florentine politics, Giannotti as we shall see advocated a *vivere popolare*; he wished to extend membership in the Consiglio Grande to all who paid taxes, not merely to those whose ancestry qualified them to hold magistracies. How far these sympathies were developed when he was writing about Venice in 1525-1527 is not quite clear,[14] but there is evidence that he was aware of the problem raised by the law of 1297, which had limited membership in the Venetian Consiglio to the descendants of those who sat in it at that date. In Florence the constitution of 1494, consciously modeled on that of Venice, was almost archetypically *the* popular constitution because it was based on a Consiglio Grande open to all qualified citizens; so long as there was no such provision as the Venetian law of 1297, there was bound to be tension within this image. Giannotti does not adopt Guicciardini's view that Florence is as aristocratic as Venice and Venice as democratic as Florence, since in either case there is a finite citizen body and the terms "aristocratic" and "democratic" have meaning only in relation to the distribution of power within that body. He points out, as he is to do again in the case of Florence, that in Venice there are poor, middling, and elite persons, *popolari*, *cittadini*, and *gentiluomini*. The first are those whose callings are too ignoble and whose poverty too great to qualify them for any kind of civic membership; the second are those whose descent and occupations give them standing and wealth enough to rank as sons of the *patria*; and the third are those who are truly of the city and the state.[15] When Giannotti writes as a

---

[14] But see I, 42: ". . . non è dubbio alcuno che gli uomini, dove eglino non si trovano a trattar cose pubbliche, non solamente non accrescono la nobiltà loro, ma perdono ancora quella che hanno e divengono peggio che animali, essendo costretti viver senza alcun pensiero avere che in alto sia levato."

[15] *Opere*, I, 35-36: ". . . per popolari io intendo quelli che altramente possiamo chiamare plebei. E son quelli, i quali esercitano arti vilissime per sostentare la vita loro, e nella città non hanno grado alcuno. Per cittadini, tutti quelli i quali per essere nati eglino, i padri e gli avoli loro nella città nostra, e per avere esercitate arti più onorate, hanno acquistato qualche splendore, e sono saliti in grado tal che ancora essi si possono in un certo modo figliuoli di questa patria chiamare. I gentiluomini sono quelli che sono della città, e di tutto lo stato, di mare o di terra, padroni e signori."

Florentine advocating popular rule, he wishes to admit the second category to membership of the Consiglio, if not to magistracy itself;[16] but it is the characteristic of Venice that there is a Consiglio Grande, but that the law of 1297 limits it forever to persons in the last and highest grade. Once again, if we had Giannotti's final reflections upon the government of Venice, we might know how he thought this closed council contributed to Venetian stability; but it is noteworthy that in what we have, a first sketch in which the shape of the republic is roughed out (*dirozzato*),[17] the dialogue takes the form of a discussion of the history of the Venetian Consiglio and of the cause (*cagione*) and occasion (*occasione*)[18] of each form which it has assumed. It is noteworthy also that, though to a humanist writing history the cause of political innovation would normally be the perception by reforming legislators of some principle on which government should be modeled, Giannotti is unwilling to go too far in ascribing such perceptions to the ancestral Venetians; a caution which reveals a number of things about the problems which Venice presented to the political intellect.

In Venetian constitutional history he sees two critical moments: one occurring about 1170, when a Consiglio Grande was established, the other in 1297, when its membership was closed.[19] Both are moments in the institutionalization of a citizen body on a footing of proportionate equality among its increasingly finite membership. The Venetians constitute a civic aristocracy, and it is the characteristic of such an aristocracy—we know by now that it was hard to define the civic ethos in other than aristocratic terms—that its members pursue glory (Giannotti's term is *chiarezza*) in the public service. In this way individuals become renowned and their families preserve the memory of their deeds. This, Trifone explains, is why we know relatively little of Venetian history before 1170. Since there was no Consiglio, there was no institutionalized pursuit of *chiarezza*; there were no families constituted by the *chiarezza* of their ancestors and impelled to preserve records of past deeds and lineal continuities. The condition of Venice was not unlike that of Rome under the kings; in both cases only the advent of a civic aristocracy led to the institution of historic memory, and in the case of Venice it may be added that the term *gentiluomo*, before 1170, probably meant only what it means in other cities—an individual outstanding for his birth or for some other reason—and had not the precise civic and political significance it acquired with the development of the Consiglio.[20]

[16] See below, nn. 93-95; cf. Guicciardini in 1512, above, ch. v, n. 29.

[17] E.g., p. 50.   [18] E.g., p. 77.   [19] *Opere*, I, 42-43.

[20] *Opere*, I, 61-62, 63-64: "Ma poscia che il consiglio fu ordinato, e che l'autorità de' dogi fu co' magistrati e coi consigli temperata, allora i cittadini, adoperandosi

Giannotti is grappling with several problems in Venetian studies. One is the general paucity of historical information, and the circumstance that more is preserved in private archives than in public chronicles. Another is a problem of considerable importance in constitutional theory, already familiar to us from Machiavelli's *Discorsi*: since Venice claimed no hero-legislator and retained the memory of no great political crisis, it was difficult to explain how a citizen body could have perfected itself, especially since Giannotti does not spend much time on the possibility that the whole apparatus of perfection had existed since the beginning. When his interlocutors discuss the innovation of 1170, they face the question of how the Venetians could have thought of organizing themselves into a Consiglio Grande, seeing that no such institution existed anywhere in the world at that time. Very few men, they agree, are capable of political invention, and citizen bodies never approve proposals which have not been tested by experience, either their own or that of others. Innovation is almost always imitation; even Romulus is said to have borrowed from the Greeks, and Florence, after imitating the Venetian Consiglio in 1494 and the perpetual Dogeship in 1502, might have been saved from disaster if she had imitated what goes with them. It would therefore have been a miracle (*cosa miracolosa*) if the Venetians of 1170 had been able to excogitate the form of a Consiglio Grande without imitating it from somebody else, since it is this which has not only kept them free but raised them to unparalleled heights of grandeur. But we need not suppose that any such miracle occurred. Apart from a few hints in the scanty historical materials, it is reasonable to believe that some sort of Council was maintained by the Doges before 1170, so that those are right who maintain that the Council is of highest antiquity, so long as they do not mean the Consiglio Grande as established in that year.[21] In a passage faintly recalling

---

nelle faccende, acquistarono gloria e riputazione. Ed è accaduto alla nostra città quel medesimo che avenne a Roma. . . . E da questo, credo, che nasca che noi non abbiamo molta notizia dell'antichità delle famiglie de' gentiluomini innanzi a Sebastiano Ziani . . . e . . . che in tutte le nostre memorie non trovo menzione alcuna di questo nome *gentiluomo*, eccetto che nella vita di Pietro Ziani doge XLII, figliuolo del sopradetto Sebastiano.

". . . e non credo che questo nome *gentiluomo* significasse quello che oggi significa . . . ma che . . . s'intendesse quello che oggi nell'altre città significa, cioè chiunque o per antichità, o per ricchezze o per autorità piú che gli altri risplende."

21 *Opere*, I, 66-68: "Ma quello che piú mi stringe è che gran cosa saria stata, che i nostri maggiori senza esempio alcuno avessero trovato si bell'ordine, si bel modo di distribuire i carichi e le onoranze della città, cioè il gran consiglio. Perciocché egli non è dubbio alcuno che quando questo consiglio fu trovato, non era simile forma di vivere in luogo alcuno di mondo, di che s'abbia notizia. E le cose, le quali senza esempio alcuno s'hanno ad introdurre, hanno sempre tante difficoltà,

Machiavelli's views on early Roman history, Giannotti suggests that reformers in 1170, wishing to strip the Doge of certain powers, resolved to transfer them to the Council, but realizing that there would be dangers and tensions if they were conferred upon a few, decided to transfer them to the citizens as a whole (while retaining a special degree of authority for themselves) and devised an annually elected Consiglio Grande to be truly representative of the whole.[22] No miraculous legislator is thus called for; Venetian history proceeds through pragmatic reflection on past experience and, far from hitting upon some miraculous recombination of elements, merely displays in 1170 a political sagacity exceeding that of the Roman patricians after the expulsion of the kings.

In the civic humanist perspective, a Consiglio Grande—whether Venetian or Florentine—was the foundation of all *libertà* in a *vivere civile*, because it brought together all citizens, on a footing of equality, in a competition for office and in *virtù*. Its appearance at Venice, then, could not as we have seen be left unexplained. But the closing of the Venetian Consiglio in 1297, so that membership became hereditary and new *gentiluomini* were next to never created, was a phenomenon of a different order. Giannotti writes that nothing can be learned of it from publicly commissioned histories, so that if one did not read the private records of noble houses one would remain almost wholly ignorant; and even in these sources nothing whatever is known about the *cagione* or the *occasione* of that law. From experience and history one recognizes that changes on this scale do not occur unless there has been some major emergency; but he has been unable to find out what this was, and he specifically says that he can see no imperfection in the Consiglio

---

che come impossibile sono le piú volte abbandonate. Il che nasce perché gli uomini nel azioni umane non approvano quegli ordini, l'utilità de' quali non hanno né per la propria, né per l'altrui esperienza, conosciuta; e pochissimi sono sempre stati e sono quelli che sappiamo cose nuove trovare e persuaderle. E perciò nelle innovazioni degli ordini si vanno imitando i vecchi cosí proprii come gli altrui. . . . Saria stata adunque cosa miracolosa, che i nostri maggiori senza averne esempio alcuno, avessero, nel riordinare la nostra repubblica, saputo trovare ed introdurre sì bella, sì civile, sì utile ordinazione come è questa del gran consiglio, la quale senza dubbio è quella che non ha solamente mantenuto libera la nostra patria, ma eziandio, procedendo di bene in meglio, l'ha fatta salire in quella grandezza d'imperio e riputazione, alla quale voi essere pervenuta la vedete. È adunque credibile per le due dette ragioni, oltre a quelle poche memorie che ce ne sono, che innanzi a Sebastiano Ziani fosse qualche forma di consiglio. . . . Quegli adunque i quali dicono che il consiglio è antichissimo, se non intendo quel consiglio che s'ordino per distribuire i magistrati, forse non s'ingannano; ma se intendono questo altro, senza dubbio sono in errore."

[22] *Opere*, I, 72-74.

as established in 1170 which could have necessitated the *variazione* of 1297. It is possible, as he has earlier suggested, that all natives of good family were by now included in the Consiglio and that the closure was applied in order to keep out foreign merchants and preserve purity of lineage. But all this is mere conjecture, and nothing is known for certain.[23] It seems clear that Giannotti had encountered a double difficulty. He had really been unable to find any traditional or historical account of the closing of the Council; and, no less significantly, he could not deal with it by supposing that civic experience had led to the discovery of some political principle, because he could not imagine any principle which it exemplified. His attitude toward the closure is not free from ambiguity. When he first discusses it he asserts that Venetian *chiarezza* mounted higher than ever after 1297, and that few families of note already resident in Venice were excluded from power by the change; but in his subsequent treatment, while insisting that it was a change for the better, he concedes that some were excluded and embittered and allows the suggestion to be made that these declined in nobility and vanished from the historic record in consequence of their exclusion. Possibly the last word may be found in something that he writes in another context—admittedly with reference to a *particolarità* of much less importance than the great measure of 1297:

> You are to understand that in every republic there are many institutions (*costituzioni*) for which one can give no probable reason, let alone the true one. And this is to be found not only in those cities where the form of government has changed, but in those which have long been ruled and governed by the same laws. For although the usages have been kept up, their causes are none the less lost in antiquity.[24]

[23] *Opere*, I, 77: ". . . dico che io nell'antiche nostre memorie non ho trovato mai che si fossa cagione di far serrare il consiglio; come voi dite, non par da credere che un ordine tanto nuovo potesse nascere senza qualche grande occasione. Di che noi potremmo addurre infiniti esempii, non solamente di quelle repubbliche che hanno variato in meglio, tra le quali è la nostra, siccome io stimo, ma di quelle che sono in peggio trascorse. Ma le variazioni della nostra repubblica medesima, se bene le considerate, vi possono dare di quello che diciamo certissima testimonianza. Nondimeno io non ho letto mai, né inteso, che cagione e che occasione facesse il consiglio serrare. Né da me stesso posso pensare che da quella forma del consiglio potesse nascere disordine alcuno, che avesse ad essere cagione della sua variazione; tanto che io credo che coloro che furono autori di tal mutazione . . . vedendo nella città nostra concorrere quantità grandissima di forestieri per conto di faccende mercantili. . . . Ma questa è tutta congettura; perciocché, come ho detto, non ne ho certezza alcuna."

[24] *Opere*, I, 116: "Ed avete ad intendere che in ogni repubblica sono assai costituzioni, delle quali non si può assegnare alcuna probabile non che vera ragione. E questo non solamente avviene in quelle città che hanno il loro governo variato,

There are political phenomena which usage may justify, but cannot explain. If we know neither the occasion, the cause nor the principle on which the Council was closed in 1297, that measure is dangerously close to being one of them.

Giannotti's Venice, then, does not seem to have effected her escape from history through the divine intelligence of the legislator, or through achieving some Polybian or even Aristotelian combination of principles. If we now ask what are the salient features of Venetian government as he roughs them out in this initial sketch, the answer seems to emerge in two ways. In the first place there is what Giannotti's introductory remarks have prepared us to encounter: a description of the various councils and officers making up the Venetian pyramid, which ought at least to prepare the way for the never-written account of how they are linked together to compose *la forma di essa Repubblica*. It is a safe assumption that this account would have dealt both with the distribution of functions among the various magistracies and with the ways in which the Doge, the Collegio, and the Pregati came to be elected; for it was a characteristic of Aristotelian political science that the functions performed by public officials were not differentiated from the function of electing those officials, and that membership in the *ekklesia* or *consiglio* where magistrates were chosen was considered in itself a species of magistracy. This point is borne out when Giannotti, like Guicciardini a few years earlier, enumerates in more or less classic terms the principal powers of government. "It is said that there are four things which constitute the directive force (*il nervo*) of every republic: the creation of magistrates, the determination of peace and war, the making of laws and the hearing of appeals."[25]

Magistracies, or forms of power, are rendered interdependent by the ways in which they share these four modes of authority; but in that case the election of magistrates must itself be a kind of magistracy and enter into the complex distributions of authority. What rendered both Florence and Venice, in the eyes of both Giannotti and Guicciardini, governments of the *popolo* and of *libertà*, was the fact that in both (at least during Florence's republican interludes) there existed a Consiglio Grande in which all magistracies were distributed. The further problem, at least to minds trained on Aristotelian and humanist presumptions, was whether the Consiglio, as the assembly of all citizens,

---

ma in quelle ancora le quali con le medesime leggi si sono lungo tempo rette e governate. Perciocché quantunque l'usanze si siano mantenute, nondimeno le cagioni di quelle sono dall'antichità oscurate."

[25] *Opere*, I, 51: "Dicono adunque che quattro sono le cose nelle quali consiste il nervo d'ogni repubblica. La creazione de' magistrati; le deliberazioni della pace e della guerra; le introduzione delle leggi; e le provocazioni." Cf. p. 86.

should have any other function than that of election. On the one hand it was possible, though as we know not very easy, to attribute to undifferentiated citizens species of intelligence which rendered them capable of other forms of decision. On the other it was possible to deny them any independent intelligence, to suppose that any specific type of decision needed a corresponding elite group or "few" to take it, and to reduce the role of the Consiglio Grande to that of ensuring that the election of these elite groups, which may now be termed "magistracies," took place under conditions of equality and impersonality. The latter we have seen to be the thrust of Guicciardini's argument; Giannotti, when writing some years later about Florentine government as one committed to some kind of popular supremacy, had to decide whether control of elections was a sufficient guarantee of this, or whether the Consiglio Grande must intervene also, to some degree, in the exercise of the other three powers making up the *nervo della repubblica*.

But when he wrote his description of Venice such problems did not demand his attention. The limited size of the Venetian citizen body precluded any division into *ottimati* and *popolo*, and he was able to ignore what would in a Florentine context have been the strongly elitist implications of the circumstance that the Consiglio discharged no functions other than the electoral, none at least that need detain his readers. In observing that new legislative proposals are dealt with by the Pregati, he remarks quite casually that some laws are also laid before the Consiglio Grande for its approval, if the initiating magistrate thinks they need the *maggior riputazione* which this brings.[26] Focussing his attention exclusively on the electoral organization of the Venetian Consiglio, he is able to deal at length[27] with a major constituent of the "myth of Venice" of which we have so far said little: the complex and fascinating routinization of nominating, voting and ballotting which visitors to the republic delighted to observe and describe. By a series of physical devices—the benches on which men took their seats at random, but rose up in a fixed order to cast their votes; the containers from which names and numbers were drawn at random, but in which positive or negative votes might be placed in secrecy—the Venetians were held, so to speak, to have mechanized *virtù*. That is, they had blended the elements of chance and choice in such a way as

[26] *Opere*, I, 125-26: "Usano ancora i nostri fare confermare alcune leggi non solamente nel consiglio dei pregati, ma ancora nel grande; la qual cosa, credo che sia in potestà di quel magistrato che principalmente le introduce. E credo che questo s'usi fare, accioché a questo modo s'acquisti a quella legge maggior riputazione . . ."
[27] *Opere*, I, 91-117.

to present each voter with a clear set of alternatives, and to liberate him from every pressure and every temptation which might cause him to vote to please somebody else instead of stating his rational choice of the better candidate. If one thought of *virtù*, as one might, as the taking of decisions directed at the public good, and if one thought of the *sala del consiglio grande* as an enormous physical device for eliminating extraneous pressures and ensuring—almost enforcing—rationality in choosing for the public good, then one thought of Venetian government in a way for which such a phrase as "the mechanization of *virtù*," though anachronistic, is not inappropriate. No less than the image of a Polybian perfection of equilibrium, the belief that the Venetians had achieved this was a potent element of the *mito di Venezia*.

Giannotti's account of Venetian voting procedures was the first written and printed by a Florentine for Florentines, but their general nature had of course been known at Florence for a long time.[28] Guicciardini, we recall, did not believe in their efficacy; private interests and relationships could not be eliminated from what electors did in secret, and it would be better to have them declare their choices in public where their fellow-citizens could observe and respond to what they were doing. Mechanized secrecy of choice, in his view, was at once too oligarchic and not elitist enough. Guicciardini's criticism carries the very important implication that decision and *virtù*, in the last analysis, exist in the web of interactions between men; that what matters is less the rationality with which I choose what is for the public good than the concern for that good which I communicate to others in the act of choosing; and James Harrington, who admired the Venetian system, was to admit the force of the criticism that in these routinized and ritualized procedures, men did not learn to know each other.[29] In a secret ballot, each man chooses between alternatives that have been found for him and, even if his choice can be made perfectly rational, he does not have opportunity to declare his reasons to his fellows. If the Venetian Consiglio did nothing but choose magistrates and officers in this way, it would represent an extreme development of the principle that the many had no function but to ensure equality and impersonality in the choice of the governing elites. Giannotti does not comment on these problems, but it is possible to see from his subsequent

---

[28] Gilbert, "Venetian Constitution," pp. 463-500 (above, ch. IV, n. 26).
[29] See the speech of Epimonus de Garrula in *Oceana* (*Works*, ed. Toland, 1771; p. 110): "The truth is, they have nothing to say to their acquaintance; or men that are in council sure would have tongues; for a council, and not a word spoken in it, is a contradiction. . . . But in the parliament of Oceana, you had no balls or dancing, but sober conversation; a man might know and be known, shows his parts and improve 'em."

writings that Venetian procedures reinforced in his mind the idea of a political activity which consisted purely in a silent and rational choice between alternatives found and presented by others. To understand the full range of his political thought, one must turn to those works in which he applied Venetian and other ideas to the problem of devising a popular government for Florence.

[II]

We have two short treatises which he wrote during the period of the last Florentine republic and the Great Siege (1527-1530). The first of these is a *discorso* on reordering the government, of familiar type, which, according to an appended letter of later date, Giannotti wrote at the request of the Gonfaloniere Niccolò Capponi, shortly before he fell from power and was replaced by a more radical ruling group. Assuming that this *Letter to Capponi*[30] retains the original text and was not revised in the light of later experience, Giannotti's thinking at this time (say late 1528) was so markedly aristocratic in character that it is hard to distinguish from that of Guicciardini's *Dialogo*, and Felix Gilbert has defined it as typical of the liberal *ottimati* who wanted to maintain elite rule within a popular system. Giannotti begins by laying down that the citizens of any republic are of diverse natures, and that the aspirations of all must be satisfied if the republic is to survive (an Aristotelian maxim). There are those who desire only liberty, and these are the many; there are those who seek that honor (*onore*) which is the reward of greater prudence (*prudenza*), and these are fewer; and there are those who seek the highest position of all, which can be enjoyed by only one man at a time. This variant of the traditional one-few-many differentiation was something of a Florentine cliché; Guicciardini, Machiavelli, and Lodovico Alamanni had used it already; but it was not a formula which had been found necessary by the student of Venetian affairs. There the citizen body was so homogeneous that it could be treated as consisting of equals; but in the sharply divided city of Florence, where an elite and a non-elite confronted each other (so it was thought) within the citizen body, it was far more necessary to categorize the different types of citizen and plan a mixed government as a combination of the one, few and many which the categories employed inevitably suggested. Though Giannotti does not use the language of *governo misto* when writing directly about Venice, the city begins to appear in that light as soon as its principles and methods are applied to the ordering of Florence.

---

[30] *Discorso al . . . Gonfaloniere . . . Niccolò Capponi sopra i modi di ordinare la Repubblica Fiorentina; Opere,* III, 27-48.

The Consiglio Grande had been restored as soon as the Medici collapsed in 1527, and Gilbert presents Giannotti's *discorso* as one of a number of proposals to lessen its power in favor of the optimate *cerchio*.[31] So no doubt it is, but we should observe that Giannotti's criticisms of the existing system are directed at its over-narrow and over-restrictive character. The Gonfaloniere has too much influence over the Signoria; the Ten of War (to whom he was secretary) have too much power in matters of peace and war, and their procedure is so disorderly that decisions are often made by one or two men. All this is *strettissimo* and *violento*. Like the Guicciardini of the *Dialogo*, Giannotti argued that aristocratic leadership could function only on a footing of equality among aristocrats, and that this could be secured only by a regime of *libertà*, guaranteed by a Consiglio Grande. His threefold classification of citizens necessitated a four-step pyramid of government, exactly following that he had observed in Venice. The many who desired liberty were to be represented (the term is in the original Italian) by a Consiglio Grande; the few who pursued *onore* by a senate elected for life. The role of the One was obviously to be played by a Gonfaloniere *a vita*, but since there would always be more than one seeking the supreme glory which could formally be vested in only one man at a time, he was to be assisted by a council of *procuratori*, like the *collegio* at Venice, consisting of the most experienced magistrates of all, sharing his preeminence and aspiring legitimately to his office should it fall vacant. Though election to the senate, the *procuratori* and the gonfalonierate was to be for life, the essence of *libertà* was to be retained by keeping all elections in the hands of the Consiglio. In this way, competition for elite membership was to be open, and men would owe their preeminence to public and not private favor. Giannotti no doubt assumed that there would be a sufficient turnover through death to satisfy the aspirations of the young to office.

It appears at this stage that the Consiglio Grande has been confined to the single function of preserving liberty through rendering public and political the emergence of elites. But Giannotti introduces the further principle that every public action is divisible into three phases, which he calls *consultazione*, *deliberazione*, and *esecuzione*.[32] If we place the first two beside Guicciardini's *deliberazione* and *approvazione*, some apparent confusion may arise; but the distinction being drawn in either case is that between the activity of proposing alternative courses of action and the activity of choosing between such alternatives. We know that it had already been used by Guicciardini, and it might have been suggested by many, though it corresponds exactly

[31] Gilbert, "Venetian Constitution," p. 498 and n.
[32] *Opere*, III, 32-33.

287

with none, of the distinctions between different modes of political activity drawn in Aristotle's *Politics*. In a Renaissance setting, it must necessarily have to do with the distinctions which the age observed between different modes of political understanding; and Giannotti proceeds to say that *consultazione* must be left to the few, since only a few possess the faculty of invention (*invenzione*) and these do not need the counsel of others[33] (though presumably they take counsel among themselves). To Florentines interested in Venetian procedures, the idea of a silent, routinized, rational choice implicit in the mechanisms of the ballot might well have heightened the sense of a distinction between invention and selection; but when Giannotti proceeds to lodge *deliberazione* in the many, it is characteristic of the way Florentine thought seems to have been developing that he says nothing about the intellectual or moral faculties which render the many capable of choosing where they cannot initiate. The reason why they should have this function is that if the few choose, or if *consultazione* and *deliberazione* are in the same hands, the temptations of power will pervert their reason; their choice will be determined by private ambitions, and in consequence *consultazione* will be exercised not by the few qualified, but by the even fewer ambitious. Here, once again, we are looking at the origins of the doctrine of the separation of powers, and it should be observed both how far these origins lay in the fear of corruption, and how little a role was played by any clear theory of a democratic mode of understanding.

If *consultazione* is left to the few, rationality is assured; if *deliberazione* is left to the many, "liberty will be secured, and those who have authority will have it by virtue (*virtù*) of the republic and not through their own presumption and importunity."[34] Execution may be left to the few, and it is not unfitting that those who proposed a policy should have responsibility for carrying it out. But as we examine what Giannotti is saying on these matters, we make two further discoveries. The first is that the composition of a public action by *consultazione*, *deliberazione* and *esecuzione* is depicted as occurring primarily within the senate, which is the organ of the few and *rappresenta lo stato degli ottimati*. When we read that *deliberazione* is carried out "by the many, that is, by the senate,"[35] we realize that the few in this case are

[33] III, 32: "Tutti quelli che consigliano è necessario che sieno valenti, e di quel primo ordine, che scrive Esiodo, nel quale sono connumerati quelli che hanno invenzione per loro medesimi, e non hanno bisogno di consiglio d'altri."

[34] III, 41: "Il consiglio saria in pochi, cioè nei valenti; la deliberazione in molti; e perciò la libertà saria sicura, e quelli che avrebbero la autorità, l'avrebbero per virtù della repubblica, e non per loro presunzione e importunità."

[35] *Ibid.*: ". . . essendo le cose determinate da molti, cioè dal senato . . ."

the *procuratori* or the Ten of War, and that the numerical few-many distinction does not after all coincide with the qualitative distinction between the many who seek liberty through the Consiglio and the few who seek honor through the senate; it is internal to the latter. But we next discover a further reason for this. The analysis of action has so far been conducted solely with reference to the determination of questions of peace and war, which Giannotti like Guicciardini regarded as the most important single function of government once internal liberty was secured (if it was not more important even than that). These questions were to go no further than the senate. When he deals with the *procuratori* as initiators of new legislation,[36] however, Giannotti makes it clear that the final *deliberazione* must take place in the Consiglio Grande. He makes more specific provision for this than he had described as existing in Venice, and the reason may well have been the acute awareness possessed by Florentines that a new law could easily affect the distribution of political power—a thing assumed not to occur at Venice. But the legislative power ranks in importance after the power of peace and war, and the feeling that the latter was a matter of *prudenza*, and *prudenza* the characteristic of the few,[37] was to drag Giannotti's thought in an aristocratic direction even after he was much more openly committed to popular government than he was when he wrote the *Letter to Capponi*.

It was probably the siege of 1528-1530 that brought about an undeniable change in Giannotti's thinking. After the fall of Capponi he remained in Florence to the end and seems, not unlike Guicciardini, to have had ambivalent feelings toward the radical leaders, at once condemning their recklessness and admiring their courage. He had no good opinion of their Savonarolan religiosity or of the way they conducted the government of the city, but even before Capponi's removal from the scene, the defense of Florence was raising a political issue which may have formed the bridge between Giannotti's earlier philo-Venetian and his later *popolare* writings. This was the question of the militia. Machiavelli and Guicciardini had agreed in contrasting Venice, as an aristocratic *città disarmata*, with Rome as an armed, popular, turbulent, and expanding state; and in the *Repubblica de' Veneziani* Giannotti had allowed Trifone to contrast Roman military glory with Venetian peace and stability, to the latter's apparent advantage. Nevertheless, there was the militia tradition at Florence; there were Machia-

---

[36] *Opere*, III, 30: "Vorrei dare a costori una cura speciale di considerar sempre le cose della città, e i primi pensieri d'introdurre nuove leggi e correggere le vecchie, secondo che ricerca la varietà de' tempi."

[37] *Opere*, III, 28: the *ottimati* are "quelli che il piú delle volte hanno prudenza, il premio della quale pare che sia l'onore come testimonio d'essa."

velli's writings, with which Giannotti was acquainted; and before as well as after Capponi's overthrow, the republic set about organizing a militia which was held to have performed great deeds during the siege and became part of the legend cherished by Giannotti and other exiles in subsequent years. As secretary to the Ten, he was involved in organizing this force, and we have a *discorso* on the subject which is accepted as his work and seems to belong to the latter part of 1528.[38] It forms part of a substantial contemporary literature of the revived militia, with which it should be read; but in the context of Giannotti's own thinking, it can be seen working a change.

Giannotti opens by refuting various arguments against the establishment of a militia, the chief of which is that arms are contrary to the nature of the Florentines, since this has been so long formed by mercantile pursuits that it will be too difficult to accustom them to military exercises.[39] His reply is an appeal from second to first nature: there is an absolute necessity for the city to be armed, since it is the nature of every creature to defend itself and a city must not lack the *virtù* which is given it in order to do so.[40] The fact that some men never develop their intellect does not alter the fact that men are endowed with intellect by nature; and as for the argument that the Florentines have grown used to other pursuits, this can be dealt with by saying that since use (*assuefazione*) is so mighty a power that it can operate even against nature, it can do even more when operating with nature on its side.[41] The revival of the militia, then, will restore the Florentines to what they are by the universal nature of all men, and this is a sufficient refutation of those who see it as somehow incompatible with civic life. If it is natural to men to bear arms, Giannotti means, and if it is natural to them to follow citizenship, there can be no incongruency between the two, and this is much more than a for-

[38] *Archivio Storico Italiano* (hereafter *A.S.I.*), ser. 5, vol. 8 (1891), G. R. Sanesi (ed.), "Un discorso sconosciuto di Donato Giannotti intorno alla milizia," pp. 2-27.

[39] *Ibid.*, p. 14: ". . . non tanto perché da natura non hanno questa inclinazione, quanto perché, essendo la città lungo tempo vivuta tra gli esercizii mercantili, difficilmente si potria assuefare a uno esercizio tanto diverso e contrario."

[40] *Ibid.*: ". . . dico che assolutamente la città si debbe armare: perché lo essere disarmato repugnia alla natura, ed alla autorità di tutti quelli che hanno trattato delli governi delle città. Repugnia alla natura, perché noi vediamo in ogni uomo particulare, essere d'appetito naturale di potersi difendere; ed a qualunche non sopliscano le forze di poterlo fare, pare che sia imperfetto, per mancare di quella virtù: la quale è ordinata dalla natura per conservazione di sé stesso."

[41] *Ibid.*, p. 16: "E chi dicie che lo essersi assuefatto ad altri esercizii impediscie tale ordinazione, si inganna interamente: perché, essendo di tanta forza la assuefazione, che ella puote operare contro alla natura, tanto più facilmente potrà in una cosa che è secondo la natura, cioè l'esercizio delle armi."

mal reconciliation: Giannotti goes on to argue that the militia is a powerful, indeed an indispensable, socializing, and politicizing agency. Military service makes men equal, in the sense that all who serve are equally subject to the public authority, and the private loyalties and affiliations which may disfigure and corrupt civic life have no place there and are eliminated.[42] Because men in arms defend the same things without distinction, they come to have the same values; because they are all disciplined to accept the same authority, they are all obedient to the *res publica*; because the public authority monopolizes force, there can be no subjection of one private citizen to another, so that liberty and authority are strengthened and guaranteed simultaneously.

But there is a dynamic involved in the view that the militia makes men citizens, as the military discipline imposed by Romulus made Romans out of a random collection of bandits;[43] it is that the more men we arm, the more citizens we must make. The inhabitants of Florence, Giannotti proceeds, are of three kinds: those capable of membership in the Consiglio, those capable only of paying taxes and those capable of neither. He now states the case for enrolling the second category in the militia as well as the first. The *beneficiati*—as in his later writings he calls the first class—are too few in numbers; the second class have the same material and emotional interests (fatherland, property, and families) as the first, and must be given the same opportunity to defend them. Once you give some men the right to defend their property with their own persons, to deny it to others who have the same property is to render them worse than slaves; the city would become a collection of masters and servants, and the latter would be lower than the dwellers in the subject cities and the countryside.[44] To leave them unarmed would divide the city, to arm

[42] *Ibid.*, p. 17: "Ma vuol dire regolare gli uomini, e rendergli atti al potere difendere la patria da gli assalti esterni e dalle alterazioni intrinseche, e porre freno a' licenziosi: li quali è necessario che ancora essi si regolino, vedendo per virtù della ordinanza ridotti gli uomini alla equalità, né essere autorità in persona, fuori che in quelli a chi è dato dalle leggi. . . . Non è adunque da omettere di introdurre tale ordinanza: la quale, oltre alle predette cose, toglie ogni autorità a chi per ambizione estraordinariamente cercassi riputazione; perché, sapiendo ciascuno chi egli abbia a ubbidire, non si può destinare alla ubbidientia di persona."

[43] *Ibid.*, p. 20: ". . . Romulo, il quale messe l'ordinanza in quella sua turba sciellerata ed assuefatta a ogni male: il che poi che ebbe fatto, tutti quelli uomini diventorno buoni; e quello furore che usavano nel male operare, lo convertirono in far bene." Note how arms serve to convert habit, and how *virtù* is a reversed *furore*.

[44] *Ibid.*, p. 18: "Sono alcuni che dicono che le armi non si dovriano dare se non a quelli che sono abili al consiglio, dubitando se elle si dessino a quelli altri che sono a graveza, essendo maggior numero, non rovinassino lo stato. Chi seguitassi

them would unite it. Giannotti goes on from this point to state the case against excluding from the militia those suspected of collaboration with the Medici, and argues that to give them arms will be to reunite them with the city of which they are members. He does not put it into words at this stage, but it is clear that arms and a full equipment of civic rights are inseparable: on the one hand, to deny men arms which are allowed to others is an intolerable denial of freedom; on the other, those who bear arms in the militia become morally capable of a citizenship which it would be equally impossible to deny them. In the *Repubblica Fiorentina*, written a few years later, he followed a similar logic and contended that membership in the Consiglio Grande should be conceded to all who paid taxes, whether their ancestors had held magistracies or not.

We have returned to the point where it is seen that the armed state must be the popular state. Machiavelli had opted for Rome and against Venice on these grounds, and there is one moment in Giannotti's Venetian dialogue where the Florentine interlocutor asks how many men in Venice there are capable of bearing arms and how many *gentiluomini* enjoying the rights of citizenship.[45] The answer reveals a disproportion of 40,000 to 3,000, but no comment is made either on the meaning of this for Venetian political stability or on Venice's reliance on mercenary soldiers. In general, the case for the restricted size of the Venetian citizen body must rest on the assumption that those who are not *gentiluomini* are either resident aliens or plebeians of too base a calling to rank as political animals at all; neither claim could be made in the case of Florence. Even more than Machiavelli, Giannotti was driven by Florentine realities toward the ideal of the armed popular state, and he specifically applies the idea to Florentine conditions in a way that Machiavelli's *Discorsi* do not. We know from the *Repubblica Fiorentina* that he recognized Machiavelli as an authority on the military and civic role of the militia, but it should be observed that the theory set forth in the militia discourse of 1528 is much more overtly Aristotelian than is Machiavelli's. It is natural to man to defend his own, and it is natural to him to pursue common goods in citizenship.

---

tale oppinione, primamente armerebbe poco numero di uomini, e lasciando gli altri, che sono a graveza, disarmati, saria necessario che restassino mal contenti, e conseguentemente nimici della repubblica; talché quelli pochi che sarebbono armati, a poco altro servirebbono che a guardia dello stato contro a quelli, che rimanessino disarmati. . . . A' quali se si togliessi anche il potere difendere le cose sue con la persona propria, sarebbano peggio che stiavi; di modo che la città sarebbe uno agregato di padroni e servi; e sarebbano in peggiore grado, che i sudditi e contadini."

[45] *Opere*, I, 45-46.

To restore him his power to do the former contributes to the restoration of his power to do the latter; both restorations constitute *riformazione* in the Aristotelian sense, the return of man to his prime nature. This is why militia service is an agency transforming men into citizens.

There was another dimension which thought on this subject could easily assume. In Giannotti's proposals for organizing the militia there is provision for a solemn ceremony on the feast-day of San Giovanni, at which the citizens in arms, mustered by their officers, shall hear mass, take an oath of obedience at the altar, and listen to an oration making clear the religious as well as civic meaning of their duties.[46] Such ceremonies were actually held, and we have the texts of several orations delivered to the militia by figures of the post-Capponi regime.[47] All of them strike a note essentially Savonarolan, in the sense that the Aristotelian idea of a *riformazione* of man as citizen is extended into the sphere of personal holiness and proclaimed with religious exaltation as a *rinnovazione*. Florence has been chosen by God to restore *libertà*,[48] and to exhibit men living socially according to the values of Christianity; "*vivere a popolo*," says one of them, "*non è altro che vivere da cristiano*."[49] Since militia service teaches men to be citizens,[50] it is part of this process of eschatological restoration; it is itself holy and miraculous, and arms are more than once spoken of as a "garment"—*sacratissima veste, incorruttibile veste dell' arme*.[51] The idea that the citizen-in-arms dedicates himself to the public good is of course dominant, and he is many times told why he should not fear death in doing so; but

[46] *A.S.I.* (1891), pp. 26-27.

[47] *A.S.I.*, vol. 15 (1851), "Documenti per servire alla storia della Milizia Italiana . . . raccolti . . . e preceduti da un discorso di Giuseppe Canestrini," pp. 342-76 (orations of Luigi Alamanni and Pier Filippo Pandolfini); R. von Albertini, *op.cit.*, pp. 404-11 (oration of Piero Vettori).

[48] *A.S.I.* (1851), p. 355 (Pandolfini): ". . . questa libertà non è opera umana, tanti anno sono che la fu predetta, et vedesi nata et data a questo popolo miracolosamente . . ."

[49] *Ibid.*, p. 356.

[50] *Ibid.*, p. 354: "Chi exaerita il corpo, lo dispone ad ubbidire al consiglio, e fa l'appetito obbediente alla ragione; et così l'uomo diventa facile a sopportare il dolore, et disporsi a disprezzare la morte. L'obbedienza è necessaria in ogni cosa, et maxime in una republica. A buon cittadino niente più si conviene, che sapere comandare et ubbidire."

[51] *Ibid.*, p. 345 (Alamanni): ". . . et allor tutti insieme parimente si vestiron l'arme, et dieron forma a questa militar disciplina; alla quale oggi noi, dalla divina grazia illuminati, darem principio . . ." P. 347: "Nessuno sia, non volendo offendere Dio, le leggi, la libertà et se medesimo, che si cinga questa sacratissima veste dell'arme con altra privata speranza che con quella di salvare la sua patria et i suoi cittadini." Albertini, p. 409: ". . . per salvatione et libertà di voi medesimi vi siate cinta questa incorruttibil veste dell'arme . . ."

there is one significant passage in which the austerity and discipline of the soldier's life is equated with the Christian ideal of poverty, and we are told that poverty is the origin of every art, profession and study known to man, and that only the lovers of poverty have pursued liberty, founded republics and overthrown tyrants.[52] Poverty—we are looking here at the heritage of the radical Franciscans—is the ideal which impels the citizen to sacrifice his private satisfactions to the common good, and the warrior, the citizen, and the Christian have here become one; but as is usually the case in Christian thought, it is the will to sacrifice goods, not the nonpossession of goods, which is being praised. There is no contradiction between utterances such as these and those in which we are introduced once again to the Aristotelian doctrine that a city is supported by its *mediocri*—those who are neither too poor to be citizens nor so rich that they are tempted to self-regard.[53] Poverty is the virtue of the *mediocri* rather than the *poveri*.

Giannotti's thought nowhere follows this path, or extends Aristotelian citizenship into a realm of radical saintliness and eschatological vision, unless it be in the remark, made more than once in the *Repubblica Fiorentina* that the republic and the militia were restored and succeeded "contrary to the opinion of the wise"[54]—and Guicciardini, making the same point, had come close to equating faith with madness. But if he did not think with Savonarola that the citizen must be one in whom Christian ideals were realized, he did not think with Machiavelli that Christian and civic values were ultimately incompatible. His doctrine that military and civic life alike realized and "reformed" man's

[52] *Ibid.*, p. 344 (Alamanni): "Oh! se fusse, o popolo mio Fiorentino, ben conosciuta da te quello che ella vale, et quanto sia da essere onorata la povertà, come ti faresti lieto di ritrovarti al presente in questo stato! Quanti pensieri, quante fatiche, quanti affanni si prendon gli uomini indarno, che si lascerieno indietro! Guarda pure quale arte, quale esercizio, quale studio lodevole oggi o mai furono in terra, et gli vedrai fabbricati tutti et messi avanti dalla povertà, unica inventrice di tutti i beni."

[53] *Ibid.*, pp. 358-59 (Pandolfini): ". . . la mediocrità et il mezzo sendo ottimi in ogni cosa, manifesta cosa è che la mediocre possessione della fortuna è ottima [note that fortune here can be possessed]; imperocché questi tali felicissimamente obbediscono alla ragione: ma se eccedono il modo in una o altra parte . . . è difficile obbedischino alla ragione. . . . Cosí si fa una città di servi et padroni, non di uomini liberi. . . . Adunque la città vuol essere di pari et simili quanto piú si può, et da questi la città è ben governata, et questi si conservano nella città; perché non desiderano le cose d'altri, né i loro beni son desiderati da altri. . . . Per la qual cosa è manifesta che la società e ottima, che si mantiene per uomini mediocri; et quelle città son ben governate, nelle quali son molti mediocri et possono assai." Pandolfini's *discorso* throughout is an interesting document of revolutionary Aristotelianism.

[54] Giannotti, *Opere*, II, 37, 46, 98, 141.

true nature precludes anything so radical as the latter; and in a sense it was his continued use of the Venetian model which indicated his separation from the former. If we think of the fall of Niccolò Capponi as the moment at which the radical Savonarolans broke finally with the liberal *ottimati* like Guicciardini, it would also be the moment at which the eschatological and "Venetian" projections of the republican image, introduced jointly by Savonarola and Paolantonio Soderini in 1494, split apart. Giannotti, a liberal optimate who remained with the republic to the end, had nothing of the Savonarolan about him, and was left by default to express the ideals of 1494 in Venetian terms.

It was not impossible to reconcile Venetian paradigms with the idea of the supreme importance of a Consiglio Grande; the significant tensions in Giannotti's thought lay elsewhere. The revival of the militia had convinced him of the need for *popolare* government; but the theory which asserted that such a form of rule must rest on a warrior citizenry, though it could be stated in Aristotelian and even Savonarolan terms, could not escape a strongly Machiavellian coloring in the mind of one who, like Giannotti, had read the *Arte della Guerra* and known its author. The whole tradition of debate in the Orti Oricellari, to which Machiavelli and Giannotti both belonged—and to which Guicciardini must in some way be related—posed an antithesis between Venice and armed popular government as typified in Rome. Machiavelli's treatment of *innovazione* and *virtù* contains a latent dynamism hard to reconcile with Aristotelian theory of the civic life as fulfilling a static human nature; yet the *Repubblica Fiorentina*, Machiavellian though it is at many points, explicitly declares its debt to Aristotle, "from whom, as from a superabundant spring that has spread through all the world overflowing streams of doctrine, I have taken all the fundamentals of my brief discourse,"[55] and this is in no way an empty compliment. When we add the variations that were beginning to appear within the Venetian model, between the idea of Polybian balance, the idea of a mechanized virtue, the idea of fundamental powers of government and the idea of differentiation between the component parts of a political act, and reflect that these concepts must now be applied to the theory of a government *popolare* in a sense in which that of Venice could never be defined, it becomes plain that the *Repubblica Fiorentina*, the wishful fantasy of an exile forever divorced from political action, is nevertheless a remarkable case study in the history of political conceptualization.

The aim of the work, we are told in language by now familiar, is to

[55] *Opere*, II, 12: "Aristotile, dal quale io come da uno abbondantissimo fonte, che ha sparso per tutto'l mondo abbondantissimi fiumi di dottrina, ho preso tutti i fondamenti di questo mio breve discorso . . ."

devise a durable if not a perpetual form of government for Florence.[56] No general theory of cities and their characteristics need be constructed, since the basic characteristics (*qualità*) of Florence have already been determined by those who live there. But the form of government is to the character of a city as the soul to the body, and if a human soul were to be placed in a bestial body, or *vice versa*, the two would corrupt and destroy one another—a use of the term *corruzione* differing somewhat from its technical employment. We must therefore consider what is the best form of government, but ask whether Florence has those characteristics which render a city capable of such a form, and how this can be imposed without altering Florentine manners and customs too greatly. Where the choice of a concrete and specific context drove Guicciardini to employ the analogy of the physician treating a sick man, Giannotti employs that of an architect rebuilding a house upon foundations already laid; the difference indicates the comparative radicalism and compulsive optimism of the refugee hoping to return.[57]

He proceeds to a theoretical disquisition purely Aristotelian and Polybian, in which the latter's Book VI is cited by name[58] for the first time among the writers we have studied. There are in principle three types of government, and which should obtain ought to be determined by the location of *virtù* in the one, the few, or the many. He does not specify what is meant by *virtù*, but the context shows it to have the standard ethical meanings, with the interesting modification that the concentration of *virtù* in the many "is found in those cities which have military virtue, which is the property belonging to the multitude."[59]

[56] *Opere*, II, 2: ". . . ho deliberato ragionare in che modo si possa in Firenze temperare un'amministrazione che non si possa alterare senza extrema forza estrinseca."

[57] *Opere*, II, 9-10: "È adunque il subietto nostro la città di Firenze tale quale ella è, nella quale vogliamo introdurre una forma di repubblica conveniente alla sue qualità, perché non ogni forma conviene a ciascheduna città, ma solamente quella la quale puote in tal città lungo tempo durare. Perciocché siccome il corpo prende vita dall'anima, così la città dalla forma della repubblica, tal che se non è conveniente tra loro, è ragionevole che l'una e l'altra si corrompa e guasti, siccome avverrebbe se un'anima umana fusse con un corpo di bestia congiunta, o un'animo di bestia con un corpo umano; perche l'uno darebbe impedimento all'altro, di che seguirebbe la corruzione . . . siccome anco fanno i prudenti architettori, i quali chiamati a disegnare un palazzo per edificare sopra i fondamenti gettati per l'addietro, non alterano in cosa alcuna i trovati fondamenti; ma secondo le qualità loro disegnano un edificio conveniente a quegli; e se hanno a racconciare una casa, non la rovinano tutta, ma solo quelle parti che hanno difetto; ed all'altre lassate intere si vanno accomodando."

[58] *Opere*, II, 17.

[59] *Opere*, II, 13-14: "Queste tre specie di reggimento nascono da questo, perché

If *virtù* in the one or the few means the ability to govern with regard to the good of all, it would be valuable to know if Giannotti shared Machiavelli's reasons for holding that this ability can only exist among the many if it takes a military form. However, he does not clarify his remark, but goes on to explain that each of the three types can exist only in ideality. There is no difference between the good and the bad form of each except the virtue or corruption of the ruling group; and it follows, first, that nothing prevents the degeneration of each type except the rulers' ability to escape the moral corruption which is rooted in their natures,[60] and second, that it would be morally impossible to establish any of the three pure types in the actual world, where we must presuppose that men are corrupt already.[61] Nothing is said about *fortuna*, and, despite his acknowledged debt to Polybius, Giannotti employs neither the idea of the cycle as a determinate order of succession of the forms nor the concept that each pure type is corrupted by the excessive power of its own special virtue; but we are clearly in that Christian world in which history is the dimension of the Fall of man, to which all these concepts could be rhetorically appropriate.

A theory of mixed government (*governo misto* or *stato misto*) now makes its appearance, in a form markedly more Aristotelian than Polyb-

---

in ciascuna città o egli si trova uno che è virtuosissimo, o pochi o molti virtuosi. . . . Ma dove i molti sono di virtù ornati, quivi nasce quella terza specie di governo chiamata repubblica, la quale amministrazione si è trovato in quelle città, che hanno virtù militare, la quale è propria della moltitudine."

[60] *Opere*, II, 16: ". . . bene è vero, che nelle tre rette, quelli che ubbidiscono stanno subietti volontariamente; nelle tre corrotte, stanno paziente per forza; e perciò si può dire che le buone siano dalle corrotte in quello differenti. . . . Nondimeno a me pare . . . che questa differenza non sia propria, ma piuttosta accidentale, perché può essere che i subietti nella tirannide volontariamente ubbidiscano, essendo corrotti dal tiranno con largizioni ed altre cose, che si fanno per tenere gli uomini tranquilli e riposati. Non essendo adunque altra differenza tra i buoni e tra i corrotti governi che quella che è generata dal fine da loro inteso e seguitato, seguita che i buoni senza alcuna difficoltà, cioè senza intrinseca o estrinseca alterazione, si possono corrompere e divenir malvagii."

[61] *Opere*, II, 18: ". . . tale introduzione è impossibile, perché essendo gli uomini più malvagii che buoni, e curandosi molto più de' privati comodi che del pubblico, credo fermamente che nei tempi nostri non si trovi subietto che le possa ricevere, perché in ciascuna di quelle tre sorte si presuppongono gli uomini buoni: tal che avendo i subietti a ubbidire volontariamente a quello, se è uno, o a quelli, se son pochi o molti virtuosi, non saria mai possibile indurre a ciò gli uomini non buoni, i quali per natura loro sono invidiosi, rapaci e ambiziosi, e vogliono sempre più che alle sua natura non conviene . . . Per la qual cosa non si potendo le buone repubbliche, e le malvagie non essendo convenevole introdurre, è necessario trovare un modo e una forma di governo, che si possa o sia onesto introdurre: questo modo e questa forma per questa via, si potrà agevolmente trovare."

ian, and Christian rather than Hellenic in the sense that it is intended for fallen and imperfectly rational men. In every city there are different types of citizens with different desires. There are the rich and great who desire to command; these are necessarily few in number, and the differentiation of the "one" from the "few" appears only because there are degrees of authority and preeminence which only one man can enjoy at a time. There are the many poor, who do not wish to command, or to be commanded by any authority less universal than that of the laws; and there are the *mediocri*, who as well as desiring *libertà* in the sense just defined have sufficient fortune to desire *onore*— plainly meaning a share in command—in addition.[62] It is the latter who fulfill Aristotle's definition of the citizen as one who rules and is ruled, and if only for this reason it would be erroneous to assign them the role of the "few." The *grandi* clearly possess many "oligarchical" characteristics, and it emerges a little later, in the true Aristotelian tradition, that it is possible for the *mediocri* to be so numerous that they absorb the category of the "many poor" altogether; Giannotti's numerical and his qualitative categories do not, as they need not, perfectly coincide. What is important at this stage is that we are studying men's desires, not their virtues. These *desideri* are also called *umori*, a term which carries nonrational connotations; they are irrational because they are incompatible, there being no way of combining, without modifying, the desire of some to command with the desire of others to be commanded by none. Formally, it might seem, this could be done by establishing a rule of laws, or by incorporating all citizens within the category of *mediocri* who both command and are commanded; but whether as a Christian, an Aristotelian, or a Machiavellian, it is important that Giannotti was convinced that the *umori* could never wholly be abolished and consequently that no mixed government could ever be a perfect blend.[63]

[62] *Opere*, II, 18-19: ". . . i grandi, perché eccedono gli altri in nobiltà e ricchezze, vogliono cómandare non ciascuno da per sé, ma tutti insieme, perciò vorriano una forma di governo nella quale essi solo tenessero l'imperio; e tra loro ancora sempre alcuno si trova che aspira al principato e vorrebbe comandar solo. I poveri non si curano di comandare, ma temendo l'insolenza de' grandi, non vorriano ubbidire se non a chi senza distinzione a tutti comanda, cioè alle leggi, e però basta loro esser liberi, essendo quegli libero che solamente alle leggi ubbidisce. I mediocri hanno il medesimo desiderio de' poveri, perché ancora essi appetiscono la libertà; ma perché la fortuna loro è alquanto piú rilevata, perciò oltre alla libertà, desiderano ancora onore. Possiamo adunque dire che in ogni città sia chi desidera libertà, e chi oltre alla libertà onore, e chi grandezza, o solo o accompagnato."

[63] *Opere*, II, 19-20: "A volere adunque istituire un governo in una città, dove siano tali umori, bisogna pensare di ordinarlo in modo che ciascuna di quelle parti ottenga il desiderio suo; e quelle repubbliche che sono cosí ordinate si può dire

Governo misto is, initially at least, a beneficent deception practiced on irrational men. It is possible to introduce a *modo di vivere*—in fact, if we look closely, this is the only way in which a *modo di vivere* can be introduced—in which men are given part of what they want, or are given it conditionally, in such a shape that they believe they have been given the whole of it, or have been given it absolutely.[64] The incompatibility of their desires is an incompatibility arising from the nature of power; some men cannot command all while others are free from command by any; and therefore the beneficent deception consists in the fact that the former receive authority and the latter liberty, in such a way that each party's enjoyment of its desire is conditional upon the will of the other.

In the form of government we are seeking it is necessary that one man be prince, but that his principate is not dependent on himself alone; that the great command, but that their authority does not originate with themselves; that the multitude be free, but that their liberty involves some dependence; and finally that the *mediocri*, as well as being free, can attain to honours (*onori*—the word in the plural has the secondary meaning of "offices"), but in such a way as is not placed entirely at their will . . . .[65]

But the deception may lead men beyond the point of illusion. Assuming that it is the property of man as a rational political animal to rule with an eye to the common good, and assuming that this state of mutual political dependence will compel men so to rule whether they intend to or not, such a distribution of functions (Giannotti calls it *amministrazione*) will make men rational; *umori* will become *virtù*. But the agency precipitating them from unreason into reason is a structure of

---

che sono perfette, perché, possedendo in esse gli uomini le cose desiderate, non hanno cagione di far tumulto, e perciò simili stati si possono quasi eterni reputare. A' desiderii di queste parti similmente non si può soddisfare, perché bisogneria introdurre in una città un regno, uno stato di pochi ed un governo di molti, il che non si può immaginare, non che mettere in atto, salvo che in Genova, dove innanzi che Messer Andrea Doria le avesse con grandissima sua gloria renduta la libertà, si vedeva una repubblica ed una tirannide."

[64] *Opere*, II, 20: "Possonsi bene detti desiderii ingannare, cioè si può introdurre un modo di vivere nel quale a ciascuna di quelle parti paja ottenere il desiderio suo, quantunque pienamente non l'ottenga."

[65] *Ibid.*: "Onde in questo governo che cerchiamo bisogna che uno sia principe, ma che il suo principato non dependa da lui; bisogna che i grandi comandino, ma che tale autorità non abbia origine da loro; bisogna che la moltitudine sia libera, ma che tal libertà abbia dependenza; e finalmente che i mediocri, oltre all'esser liberi, possano ottenere onori, ma che tal facoltà non sia nel loro arbitrio collocata . . ."

powers, arranged so that they depend upon and condition one another. Once these powers are exercised rationally, they become faculties in the individual whereby he acts rationally and politically and governs the actions of others (as they govern his) so that they act in the same way. That is, powers too have become *virtù*; and it is characteristic of the active connotations which this word always bore that Giannotti is able on occasion to use it interchangeably with terms like *forze* and *potestà*. The polity, once again, is a contrivance of human intelligence for the institutionalization of *virtù*: for assigning men functions which will require them to act in such a way that their natures are reformed and are once again what they *are*, instead of what they *have become*.

Such a contrivance depends on the existence of *mediocri*, the only people capable of governing and being governed, and therefore of substituting rational behavior for the irrationalism of those who can only command or only obey. If there were a city consisting wholly of *mediocri*, it could be a democracy of the pure type—we know that the *virtù* of the *mediocri* would be military—but there is none.[66] Where the *mediocri* are stronger than, or equal to, the *grandi* and *poveri* in combination, or where they hold the balance of strength between the two, a *governo misto* is possible and indeed necessary, if the city is not to suffer that corruption which comes when the soul is disproportionate to the body. It remains to be shown that Florence satisfies these conditions and Giannotti proceeds to do so, in the form of a history of the city which indicates how his Aristotelian grounding had given him a more subtle and sanguine grasp of historical causation, and delivered him further from the grip of *fortuna*, than a merely Polybian theory of cycles could have done. His thought will also be found strikingly anticipatory of that of James Harrington in the next century.

Giannotti contends that Florence used to be a city of *grandi* and *poveri*, and has in the last century become increasingly one of *mediocri*. To understand this, he claims, is to understand Florentine history both before and after the Medicean regime of 1434-1494. Had he employed the scheme of Polybius's sixth book to this end, it would have suggested that rule by the few (*grandi*) had given place to rule by the many (*poveri*) and then to rule by a tyrant (Cosimo) and so round the clock again; each form would have existed in its purity, decayed through spontaneous inner degeneration and collapsed through some combination of circumstances precipitated by unpredictable *fortuna*. But such a scheme was unlikely to satisfy Florentines of the 1530s, whether historically or philosophically; they knew too much about the past by way of data, and demanded too much by way of explanation.

[66] *Opere*, II, 24.

Giannotti lays it down that in considering every event (*azione*), one must examine the general cause (*cagione*), the precipitating cause (*occasione*), and the immediate cause (*principio*). In the case of the fall of the Florentine republic in 1512, the *cagione* was the discontent of certain ambitious oligarchs with the form of government, the *occasione* was the war between Pope Julius and the king of France, and the *principio* was the attack of the Spanish army on Prato and Florence. *Cagione* is a disposition of things, which makes itself felt when *occasione* offers, and very frequently it is also the cause why *occasione* appears.[67]

In the case of Florentine politics in the thirteenth and fourteenth centuries, we are concerned with an unstable alternation between the *stati* of *grandi* and *popolo*—Giannotti is clearly not thinking of it as a cycle—and the *cagione* or *disposizione* was the rough equality between the forces (*forze*) of the two. The monopoly of *qualità* by the one was answered by the ascendancy of quantity in the other, so that neither could prevail or destroy its adversary—Giannotti would have agreed with Machiavelli's further contention that neither could devise a system of government acceptable to the other—and the victory of either party was the result of *occasione*, which might at some future date, and generally did, prove propitious to the other.[68] In this case *cagione* was all, and it is clearly of no importance what the various *occasioni* may have been. It is useful to contrast Machiavelli's use of *occasione* in *Il Principe*, where it signified the extreme irrationality and

[67] *Opere*, II, 37-38: "Ed è da notare che in tutte le azioni sono da considerare tre cose, la cagione, l'occasione e il principio. Sono molti che pigliano l'occasione per la cagione, e della cagione non fanno conto, come saria se alcuno (poniamo) dicesse che la cagione della rovina dello stato di Firenze nel MDXII fosse la differenza che nacque tra Papa Giulio ed il re di Francia, e l'aver perduto il re di Francia Milano; la qual cosa non fu la cagione, ma l'occasione, e la cagione fu la mala contentezza d'alcuni cittadini malvagii ed ambiziosi; il principio poi fu la venuta ed assalto degli Spagnuoli per rimettere i Medici. Non è adunque la cagione altro che una disposizione, la quale si risente qualche volta l'occasione si scopre, e molto spesso è tanto potente la cagione, che non aspetta, anzi fa nascere l'occasione."

[68] *Opere*, II, 39: ". . . era necessario che le parti tumultuassero, e quando reggesse l'uno, e quando l'altro; e se alcuno domandasse qual sia stata l'occasione, perché i grandi non prevalessero mai tanto al popolo, né il popolo ai grandi, che l'una parte e l'altra potesse lo stato suo fermare, dico che la cagione di tal cosa era perché le forze del popolo e de' grandi erano uguali, e però l'una non poteva abbassare mai l'altra intieramente; e quando l'una prevaleva all'altra nasceva dall'occasioni, che erano ora a questa parte, ora a quell'altra conformi, e non era possibile, quando l'una prevaleva all'altra, che interamente si assicurasse . . ." Cf. pp. 42-43 for the contrast between quantity in the *popolo* and *qualità*—"nobilità, ricchezze e favori, dignità, disciplina e simili cose . . . reputazione, ricchezze, clientele, favori, cosí esterni come domestici"—in the *nobili*.

unpredictability of the particular event in a world of *fortuna*. Machiavelli knew far more about historical causation than that, but the contrast is still worth drawing. Giannotti's *occasione* is still the random unpredictable which turns the wheel and overthrows power systems, but the instability of politics is now caused rather than inherent. *Grandi* and *poveri*, quality and quantity, authority and liberty, constitute an unstable equilibrium from which most men cannot escape, being what they are; but one can see why their natures constitute instability, and consequently one can see how stability might replace it. *Fortuna* consequently plays little role in his system, and the word is hardly used. He relies instead on an Aristotelian theory of causation, and an Aristotelian theory of social forces.

Harrington, constructing in the next century an account of English history along comparable lines, ascribed to the king and barons of medieval England a role very like that of Giannotti's *grandi* and *poveri*; they were locked in an unstable equilibrium until the Tudors undermined baronial power by raising up a landowning people, whose advent proved no less ruinous to a monarchy that could no longer govern them.[69] A similar role is allotted by Giannotti to the Medici of the fifteenth century, who, by advancing poor men to office and depriving the aristocrats of any chance to display *generosità* and *grandezza* except at the nod of the ruling family, depressed some and exalted others to form a new and growing class of *mediocri*, who now hold the balance of power and make a stable *governo misto* possible in Florence.[70] Since 1530 the Medici have ruled with the support of a few *grandi* who owe them their advancement and a few more whom the excesses of the siege have *alienat[i] dal vivere universale e politico*, but their tyranny is self-abolishing; it deprives all men of what they desire and increases the number of *mediocri* whose presence alone can ensure that they achieve their various ends.[71] Like Harrington, Giannotti was a poor prophet but a successful enricher of the conceptual vocabulary; both

---

[69] See below, pp. 388-89. [70] See, at length, *Opere*, II, 45-48.

[71] *Opere*, II, 47-48: "È succeduto poi il secondo ritorno de' Medici nel MDXXX con quella violenza che è nota a tutto'l mondo, e perché nella resistenza grande che s'è fatta loro, sono stati offesi molti cittadini di gran qualità, è necessario che abbiano l'animo alienato dal vivere universale e politico, parendo loro essere stati da quello maltrattati; la qual cosa pare che generi quella stessa difficultà all'introduzione d'un vivere civile che saria se la città, cosí come già era, fusse piena di grandi, e mancasse di mediocri, come di sopra discorremmo. Ma questa difficultà a poco a poco manca, per il violento modo di vivere che al presente si osserva, nel quale tutti i cittadini, di qualunque grado, appariscono conculcati ed abbietti, senza onore, e senza reputazione, e senza autorità. Talché è necessario che ciascuno, deposti gli odii particolari ed unite le volontà, viva con desiderio grande di pacifico e quiete vivere, ed aspetti l'occasione di ricuperarlo."

men developed schemes of causation which wrongly predicted political stabilization and an end to historical turbulence, but increased the extent to which sequences of political change could be talked about in terms, concrete and social, which were not those of the irrational particularities of *fortuna*. One is tempted to say that both offered ways out of the Polybian cycle and into the rotating spheres of ordered government; but in fact their causal vocabularies were so rich that they never had recourse to the Polybian model at all. The vocabulary of Aristotle was less stilted, and it is this that Giannotti is using.

The apparatus of political analysis which it is possible to bring to bear on the city's problems continues to be a crucial question in Book II of the *Repubblica Fiorentina*, which is devoted to a criticism of the republican constitutions of 1494-1502-1512 and 1527-1530. Reforming legislators, Giannotti begins, like Numa and Lycurgus, have a harder task than those who found cities where none have existed before (we should remember that Machiavelli in the *Discorsi*, though not in *Il Principe*, had on the whole treated Lycurgus as belonging to this class). The latter have only to know what is good and may be fairly sure of the support of the unformed matter whom they lead and mold; but the former have to know what has been wrongly managed in previous constitutions, and there are familiar difficulties about this. In the first place there are always those who are used (*assuefatti*) to the previous order and will change only with difficulty; this is why Numa had to feign divine assistance and Lycurgus to use violence[72] (we recall the armed prophet of *Il Principe*). In the second place constitutional defects belong in the category of *cose particolari*, which are hard to understand by any means over and above mere experience; and in the third place no man is so free from human affections that he can always see clearly defects in which he has himself been involved.[73] Savonarola, both as a foreigner and as a friar, could hardly be expected to know much about the workings of Florentine institutions; nevertheless, the Consiglio Grande which he helped introduce would have reformed itself by degrees, if given time and if the treachery of certain *grandi* had not brought back the Medici.[74]

[72] *Opere*, II, 52-53.

[73] *Opere*, II, 53: "A che si aggiugne che la considerazione de' difetti, nei quali hanno di bisogno di reformazione, è molto malagevole, non solamente perché in cose particolari consistono, le quali con difficoltà si possono altrimenti che per esperienza conoscere, ma perché ancora niuno mai si trovò che tanto fosse libero dalle umane affezioni che in ogni cosa il difetto e mancamento suo potesse vedere . . ."

[74] *Opere*, II, 54-55: "Non conobbe adunque Fra Girolamo questi particolari mancamenti, né è da maravigliarsene molto; perché essendo forestiero e religioso, non poteva trovarsi nelle pubbliche amministrazioni; talché veduti egli i modo del

It is therefore of great importance to know if we can develop a political science by which the deficiencies of previous constitutions can be exposed and corrected. Giannotti proceeds to a critique of both republican constitutions, in which he argues that although the Consiglio Grande was nominally the foundation of the system, in practice the various magistracies—including the Ten and in some respects the Gonfaloniere—exercised so much irresponsible power that effective authority was in the hands of a few.[75] This disguised oligarchy should not be confused with a disguised aristocracy; Giannotti's links with the liberal *ottimati* are still strong enough to make him stress that this state of things alienated them from the government so much that their hostility grew worse under the gonfalonierate for life of 1502-1512, of which he otherwise approves, and that one's detestation of their treachery should not blind one to its causes (*cagioni*, not *occasioni*).[76] In these chapters he is essentially resuming and reworking the themes of the *Letter to Capponi*, and two lines of constitutional analysis are reappearing. In the first place it is evident that the irresponsibility of the various magistracies arose from a failure to separate powers: they could do as they liked because they had *deliberazione* as well as *consultazione*. When Giannotti reverts, as he does some chapters later, to the recommendation of Venetian voting procedures, it is because these decisively separate the function of resolving from the function of proposing. But in the second place—and this is less unambiguously Venetian—there is the thought that the irresponsibility of the magistrates meant that their power was not, as it should have been, dependent on the power of some authority outside themselves. The structure of mutual interdependence which was the essence of *governo misto* must at some stage be worked out in full. But at this moment Giannotti strikes a new note, indicative of the movement of his ideas toward popular supremacy, by saying that the familiar four powers—election of magistrates,

---

procedere in esse, avesse potuto far giudizio di quello che era bene o male ordinato . . ."

[75] *Opere*, II, 59: "In Firenze adunque nei due passati governi, la creazione de' magistrati senza dubbio era in potere degli assai, perché tutta la città dependeva dal gran consiglio, e però in questa parte la città era libera; la deliberazione della pace e guerra era in potere del magistrato dei dieci, i quali di quelle due cose, e conseguentemente di tutto lo stato della città potevano disporre; di che seguitava che i pochi e non gli assai fossero signori dello stato della città: e dove tal cosa avviene, quivi non può esser vera e sincera libertà."

[76] *Opere*, II, 81-82: ". . . talché costretti da questa mala contentezza, consentirono alla rovina di quello stato, ed a rimettere i Medici; benché questi tali non meritino laude alcuna, anzi biasimo e vituperio, non è però che quel modo di procedere sia da biasimere e da correggere, per tor via le cagioni di quelle male contentezze. . . ."

peace and war, hearing of appeals, and legislation—which constitute the *vigore* (formerly the *nervo*) of government, must be in the control of whoever is to be *signore* of the city. If the many are to rule they must possess the four powers, or such a city will not be truly free.[77] Clearly the problem is where the four powers are to be located in a *governo misto*, but all Giannotti has to say at the moment is that it was insufficient to vest the election of magistrates in the Consiglio Grande— even though in that respect the city might be termed free—if peace and war were to remain in the irresponsible control of the Ten.[78] This rendered the right of appeal against magistrates' decisions virtually meaningless; while as for legislation, though it was nominally determined by the Consiglio, it was for all practical purposes in the hands of a few men. That election of magistrates alone is insufficient is shown by the practice of the Medici, who always controlled the appointment of those who managed the three remaining powers and left the election of others entirely free. The master of the three, not the four, powers is master of all.[79]

Giannotti is on the point of breaking new ground, which will lead his thought away from a simple mixture of three elements or a simple institutionalization of *virtù*. But for the present he has finished his analysis of the remedial knowledge which a reforming legislator of Florence must possess, and has now to blend it with the universal principles on which such a figure must proceed. The aim of the legislator, we read at the beginning of Book III, is to erect a state which will last; states fall either through internal dissension or through external assault; a *buon governo* provides against the former danger, a *buona milizia* against the latter—though it may also be considered part of *buon governo* and functioning to the former end. We now enter upon the

[77] The first occurrence of this thought is at *Opere*, II, 58-59: "Ma è da notare che quattro sono le cose nelle le quali consiste il vigore di tutta la repubblica; l'elezione de' magistrati; la deliberazione della pace e guerra; e provocazioni; e l'introduzione delle leggi; le quali quattro cose sempre devono essere in potere di chi è signore della città. Per la qual cosa in quei governi, dove gli assai reggono, è necessario che sieno in potestà degli assai, altrimenti in quella città, dove sieno tali amministrazioni, non sarebbe libertà."

[78] Cf. the *Letter to Capponi*, above, and nn. 32, 75.

[79] *Opere*, II, 59-60: "Veniva adunque la città quanto alla creazione de' magistrati ad esser libera, ma quanto all'altre tre cose, che non sono di minore importanza, non era libera ma all'arbitrio e podestà di pochi soggetta. Che le tre ultime cose non fossero di minor momento che la creazione de' magistrati è manifesto, se non per altra, perché chi è stato padrone delle tirannidi passato non si è curato dell'elezione de' magistrati, eccetto quelli ne' quali era posto l'autorità delle tre dette cose, parendo loro che chi è signore di quelle sia signore di tutto; e senza dubbio, chi può deliberare della pace e guerra, introdurre leggi ed ha il ricorso de' magistrati, è padrone d'ogni cosa."

Machiavellian problem of deciding whether civil or military organization should come first, and the figure of Romulus makes his appearance. But whereas it was Lycurgus who attended to *governo* and *milizia* simultaneously, before Romulus gave a thought to either he devoted himself to acts of violence against his neighbors and to the aggrandizement of his people's empire. It might seem that this choice was conducive to, if not identical with, military organization; but it appears to have been the Rape of the Sabines that Giannotti had principally in mind, and he comments that behavior of this kind can only have originated in the lust for domination, since Romulus had enough men to make a city and there were, after all, other ways of procuring women for them.[80] A little later Romulus is stated to have attended to civil before military organization; so that the effect of Giannotti's analysis is to separate him sharply from Machiavelli's view that because Rome was from the beginning organized for expansion, she was developed along military and therefore along popular lines. This initial repudiation of the Roman model, to be carried further in later chapters, assists in the reintroduction of Venetian concepts; and it rests in part on the implication that the function of the militia is preservative rather than aggressive. Venice, preferring stability to empire, went so far as to have no civic militia at all; but Giannotti, with the experience of the Siege behind him, is clear that the function of the militia is defensive. Rome was held by Bruni and Machiavelli to have destroyed republican *virtù* in the rest of the world and to have lost her own in consequence; but a nonaggressive militia may remain a means of inculcating *virtù* in the citizens. Men defended the republic of 1527-1530 where that of 1512 fell without a struggle, and the main reason was that a citizen militia existed at the later date but not at the earlier (Machiavelli's had been a militia of *contadini* and Giannotti was aware of the theoretical difference). The ideal Florence is to be armed and popular like Rome, but stable and peaceable like Venice; and Giannotti has moved decisively away from the restless dynamism of Machiavelli. The militia in its politicizing aspects is only a part of the apparatus of *buon governo*, and he now gives the latter so great a priority that for the

[80] *Opere*, II, 96-97: "Pensò adunque Romulo a fare violenza, e d'avere a vincere, e per conseguente al propagare l'imperio, e far grande la sua repubblica. La cagione ancora, che l'indusse a far tal violenza, non fu altro che la cupidità dell'imperio, perché se non voleva quello accrescere, non gli era necessario usare tal violenza; perciocché aveva tanti uomini, che facevano conveniente corpo d'una città non ambiziosa, la quale si voglia solamente mantenere, e non desideri accrescimento; e delle donne per gli uomini suoi avrebbe trovato in spazio di tempo, senza che quelle d'Alba non gli sariano mai mancate."

rest of the book he lays, on the whole, less stress on the militia's power to make men virtuous than he had in 1528.[81]

Since what he is designing for Florence is a *governo misto* and not a pure democracy, we have to understand the role in a *governo misto* both of a militia—we have been told that military virtue is a democratic characteristic—and of the four powers of government, since their location determines who shall be *signore* of a city and we do not yet know the place of such a *signore* in a mixed government. Giannotti proceeds to develop a critical analysis of the idea of mixed government. This can mean, he says, either that the three parts (one, few, and many; *grandi, mediocri, popolari*) exercise powers equal to one another, or that some one of them exercises power (*forze, potenza*) greater than either of the other two; the aim in each case is to produce an equilibrium. If we think carefully, we shall see that the former is bound to be defective. The reason is that a mixture of political elements is not like a mixture of natural elements, in which each component (*semplice*) loses its distinctive *virtù* and the compound acquires a *virtù* of its own. A political mixture is made up of men, of *grandi, mediocri* and *popolari*, each of whom remains after mixture what he was before (unless, presumably, all have become *mediocri*, in which case we are not constructing a mixed government at all). Each retains his distinctive characteristic, which Giannotti is now calling *virtù*, not *umore* or (as he might have done) *fantasia*; and these *virtù* consist of desires and the power to pursue them, which we merely institutionalize in the construction of a polity. It is therefore impossible to "temper a state so perfectly that the *virtù*—let us call it power—of each part is not apparent," and if these are equal, then the oppositions and resistances between them will be equal, and the republic will be full of dissensions which will bring about its ruin.[82] Giannotti has analyzed the

---

[81] *Opere*, II, 98-99: "Ma se noi consideriamo bene, è di maggiore importanza introdurre una buona forma di repubblica, perché dietro a questa agevolmente s'introdurrà buona milizia: ma dove fosse la milizia introdotta, non saria forse cosí agevolmente introdurre buona ordinazione; perché naturalmente gli uomini militari sono meno che gli altri trattabile. E perciò Romulo primieramente introdusse gli ordini civili, e poi gli ordini militari; e potette costui in brevissimo tempo ogni cosa condurre, perché essendo principe assoluto non aveva che contradicesse. . . . In Firenze adunque, essendo di maggiore importanza introdurre un buon governo che una buona milizia (perché invero la città ne' tempi passati ha piuttosto patito per mancamento di governo che di milizia, forse per le qualità dell'armi e de' tempi) tratteremo prima di quella parte . . ."

[82] *Opere*, II, 99-100: ". . . il primo modo, secondo il quale le forze di ciascuna parte sono eguali a quelle dell'altra, senza dubbio è difettivo e non si debbe seguitare, perché non è possibile temperare uno stato tanto perfettamente che la virtù (vogliamo dire potestà di ciascuna parte) non apparisca; perciocché in tal mistione

term *virtù* in such a way as to bring about the substitution of a mechanistic for a pseudo-organic model in political analogy; Guicciardini's cook, stirring a mound of *pasta*, has disappeared.

It further follows that Polybius was wrong in seeing the Roman republic as the model of mixed government. He declares that ambassadors to Rome, when dealing with the consuls, thought they were in a kingdom; when with the senate, in an aristocracy; when with the *populus*, in a democracy. But this indicates that the power of each was equal to and uncontrolled by that of each other, and if this was so it is small wonder that the republic was prey to civil dissensions. Had it been well-ordered, ambassadors would have sensed in dealing with the consuls their dependence on the senate and the people, with the senate their dependence on the consuls and the people, and with the people their dependence on the consuls and the senate; and the *virtù* of each would have been *temperata* by the others. This should have been attended to by Brutus and his colleagues at the expulsion of the kings, and it can be argued that they tried to vest superiority in the senate; but assuming that Polybius is right in his facts, the equality of power between the three organs of government exposed Rome to that instability and strife which destroyed her in the end.[83]

The repudiation of Polybius carries to a further stage Giannotti's repudiation of Machiavelli on the subject of Rome. He has already implicitly rejected Machiavelli's contention that the armed popular state must be one organized for expansion; he now rejects his contention that Roman civil strife was a sign of health because it led to the institution of the tribunate (of which Giannotti has very little to say). The more Rome is eliminated from paradigmatic stature, the more fascinating becomes his evident intention of employing Venetian forms and concepts for the organization of an armed popular state. The crucial point, however, is Giannotti's drastic remodeling of the concept of *governo misto*, not least because this anticipates so much in English and American constitutional thought during the seventeenth and eighteenth centuries. His contention at the moment is that you cannot construct a balance of equal and independent forces because the pressures

---

avviene il contrario che nella mistione delle cose naturali, nella quale le virtù particolari delle cose di che si fa mistione non rimangono nel misto apparenti, ma di tutte se ne fa una sole; la qual cosa non può nel temperare una repubblica avvenire; perché bisogneria pestare e tritare in modo gli uomini, che dei grandi, popolari e mediocri se ne facesse una sol cosa diversa in tutto da quelle tre fazioni; la qual cosa senza dubbio è impossibile. Rimanendo adunque le virtù di ciascuna parte apparenti nella mistione, è necessario che essendo l'opposizioni e resistenze eguali, non manchino le repubbliche in tal modo temperate di civili dissensioni, le quali aprano la via alla rovina loro."

[83] *Opere*, II, 101-103.

and counterpressures between them will be equal and there will be no resolution of the contest. But we know that political authority is of so many kinds and can be distributed in so many combinations that it is possible to render three agents mutually dependent, and it may seem theoretically possible to erect a system of three equal yet interdependent parts. Giannotti does not examine this possibility; he assumes that interdependence requires inequality, to the extent that one part must enjoy a preponderance over the other two (*la repubblica deve inclinare in una parte*). A principal reason seems to be that one must institutionalize conflict; there will always be competition among the powers, and if all are theoretically equal a loser may blame a victor for his loss and pursue internecine strife instead of the common good, whereas if the loser's inferiority is built into the structure of the republic it will be accepted as legitimate. Giannotti stresses that he does not mean the preponderant part to enjoy an *imperio* from which the others are excluded, but merely that it shall be less dependent on them than they on it. He has yet to make clear what is the relevance to all this of his doctrine that the four powers of government must belong to the *signore* or *padrone*, and whether indeed such terms are applicable to that part to which *la repubblica inclina*.[84]

The next step is to consider whether the preponderant part should be the *grandi* or the *popolo* (that it might be the one on whom the few and the many depend he does not consider a contemporary possibility, though he holds that this provided a stable government in prerepublican Rome). Giannotti argues the case for the people at considerable length, much as Machiavelli had, and not all his arguments need detain us. The indictment of Roman institutions is resumed, but in a way revealing some significant tensions. We are told that if the people feel themselves oppressed by a particular individual, they rush to his house and revenge themselves by burning it down—such at least is the way of Florence—whereas if they feel that their wrongs are the result of the maldistribution of public authority they agitate for legal and institutional reforms which will assure them of greater justice and a greater

---

[84] *Opere*, II, 103: ". . . quella parte dove la repubblica inclina, viene ad esser più potente che l'altra; e però facilmente può opprimere gli insulti che le fossero fatti; e perché quella potenza che le nasce dalla forma della repubblica, però se la parte contraria si reputa ingiuriata, non l'imputa alla fazione avversa ma alla forma della repubblica. E perché la repubblica è temperata in modo che non vi è adito a rovinarla, però è necessato che viva quieta; onde in tale repubblica non può nascere alterazione alcuna. È ben da notare che quando io dico che la repubblica deve inclinare in una parte, non dico che quella parte abbia sola l'imperio, e l'altra sia esclusa dall'amministrazione, ma che l'una abbia poca dependenza e l'altra assai. . . . Concludendo adunque dico che è necessario che una repubblica inclina ad una parte, a volere che sia diuturna e viva sempre senza alterazioni civili."

share of power; and this explains why the struggle between the orders at Rome was relatively bloodless until the time of the Gracchi and brought the plebeians increasing participation in authority.[85] This point clearly owes much to Machiavelli's argument concerning the beneficent effects of strife at Rome, which Giannotti otherwise wished to reject. Elsewhere we read that if at the expulsion of the Tarquins the senate had been made dependent on the people instead of the reverse, the people would have been free from injuries and the senate weaker than the people, and Rome would as a result have been more tranquil and escaped the dissensions which ultimately destroyed her; the republic would have been eternal and her empire *stabilissimo*.[86] Rome, a popular state to Machiavelli, is to Giannotti as to Guicciardini a rather unstable optimacy. There are some, he adds—though Machiavelli is plainly meant here—who argue that Rome could not have expanded (*crescesse*) without these civil dissensions, but that is true only of Rome as she was organized and it can be held that she would have expanded much more efficiently without them if organized on a popular basis.[87] But Giannotti has already indicated that imperial expansion is not a necessary mark of the armed popular state. One is left feeling that he had considerable difficulty in getting out of Machiavelli's shadow, if only because he aimed at establishing positions so like and yet unlike his—the armed popular state without Rome, Venice without her aristocracy or mercenaries.

He is happier developing Aristotelian and Machiavellian arguments for the superiority of the *popolo*. These are, in general,[88] that the few desire to command, an impulse easily destructive of the common good, where that *libertà* which the many desire to preserve—that condition in which each enjoys his own under law—is close to being the common good itself. Furthermore, the few command and the many obey—i.e., they obey the laws, rather than the few—and it is easier for one who

---

[85] *Opere*, II, 107-108: ". . . se possono apporre la cagione delle ingiurie ricevute a qualche particolare, subito li corrono a casa, e coll' armi e col fuoco si vendicano, siccome in Firenze molte volte si trova essere avvenuto. Ma se tali cagioni nascono dall'ordinazione della repubblica, talché a nessuno particolare si possano applicare, allora i popolari, non avendo contro a chi voltare l'ira sua, si separano da' grandi, e chieggono o legge o magistrato per lo quale si possano difendere ed ottenere la loro ragione; e questo fu grandissima cagione che ne' tumulti del popolo Romano contro al senato, non si venne mai al sangue de' cittadini, insino ai Gracchi; perché le ingiurie che pativano i popolari non da' privati cittadini, ma dalla forma della repubblica nascevano, e perciò l'ingiuriati non de' cittadini ma dell'ordine della repubblica si potevano lamentare; onde avveniva che nelle sovversioni non chiedeva altro che qualche legge o qualche magistrato, per virtù della quale si difendesse, e la potenza de' pochi si venisse ad abbassare, ed essi più della repubblica partecipassero."

[86] *Opere*, II, 114-15.   [87] *Opere*, pp. 115-16.   [88] *Opere*, II, 104-16.

knows how to obey the laws to learn how to give commands than for one whose aim is always to command to subject his will to law. The habit of obeying a wide variety of laws gives the many a certain prudence, which the few often lack since their passions know fewer restraints; practical experience and book-learning, the sources of prudence considered as information, are as accessible to *popolari* as to *grandi*;[89] and since the former outnumber the latter, "it can be said with probability that they make up a greater aggregate of prudence."[90]

Giannotti puts forward a democratic theory of *prudenza*. Instead of being the reward of the elite who thrust themselves into public service in pursuit of *onore*, it is the reward of those who obey the laws, pool their experience, suffer injuries rather than inflict them and react by the collective pursuit of public remedies rather than by the aristocratic pursuit of revenge on particular enemies. The many's interest in *libertà* means that they are better politicized, more apt to accept public authority as legitimate, than the ambitious few. Last and strongest argument of all, in a city where there are many *popolari* or *mediocri*, it would be *violenza* to subject them to the authority of the *grandi*.[91]

The rest of Book III is taken up with the anatomy of an ideal constitution. We know that this is to be a *governo misto*, owing much of its detail to Venice, and satisfying the aspirations, by combining the powers, of those who desire *grandezza*, *onore*, and *libertà*. The powers of each group are to be interdependent, but there is to be one—the power of those whose aim is *libertà*, namely the people—which preponderates, at least in the sense of being less dependent on the other two than they are on it; but there has also been mention of four powers or functions which constitute the *vigore* or *nervo* of government and belong to whatever individual or group is to be *signore*. To modern readers, this *signore* sounds very like a sovereign, and a sovereign does not seem to fit into the balanced distribution of powers which constitutes a *governo misto*, even of the weighted kind which Giannotti has in view. We have a problem, therefore, and perhaps Giannotti had too, in relating these concepts to one another.

Giannotti begins by declaring that the republic is to be composed of three principal members, but that, just as in Venice, there is to be a fourth, called the Collegio, to go between the senate and the *gonfaloniere* (or prince) and satisfy the aspirations of those who seek *grandezza* by associating them as closely as possible with the supreme

---

[89] *Opere*, II, 110: "Quanto al leggerle, cosí le può leggere un popolare come un grande; e la pratica non veggio maggiore nell'una parte che nell'altra . . ."

[90] *Opere*, II, 111: ". . . perché i popolari fanno molto maggiore numero che i grandi, si può probabilmente dire che facciano maggiore aggregato di prudenza . . ."

[91] *Opere*, II, 116.

authority which only one man can exercise.[92] The members of this Collegio are to be magistrates rather than counselors, in the sense that specialized functions in regard of war (the Ten), justice (the *procuratori*), and so on, are to be assigned to each of them; and it is assumed that they excel in respect not only of ambition, but also of intellectual qualities, perhaps including experience, but certainly extending to originality, initiative, and the ability to propose policies. If at this end of the scale there is to be overlap between the one and the few, between *grandezza* and *onore*, at the other end the Consiglio Grande, though its function is to preserve *libertà* and therefore to represent the *popolari* who look no higher, is to be open to all citizens, whether *grandi*, *mediocri*, or *popolari*, whether (we may add) they seek *grandezza*, *onore*, or *libertà*. It is in fact to be composed of citizens reckoned as equals and by number. Giannotti goes on to explain why there will be a category of *plebei* who find no place in the Consiglio because they are not members of the city; their trades are vile and they are foreigners with homes to go to (he may have in mind peasants from the surrounding villages). But he insists at some length that those who pay taxes, but are not eligible for magistracies, must be members of the Consiglio Grande.[93] Since it seems to have been the experience of the militia of 1528-1530 which convinced him of the need to treat these *non-beneficiati* as citizens, it is interesting, and possibly significant of the way his thought was turning, that the arguments he now deploys are stressed as being operative when the city is not armed, no less than when it is. If the *non-beneficiati*—he is now calling them *popolari*— are not admitted to *onori* (membership of the Consiglio is plainly an *onore*), they will not love the republic or voluntarily contribute to or defend it; they will be liable to follow particular leaders; and these dangers will be exacerbated in time of arms. Aristotle would certainly

[92] *Opere*, II, 117: "Per il consiglio adunque si soddisfa al desiderio della libertà; per il senato all'appetito dell'onore; per il principe al desiderio del principato. Resta di trovar modo di soddisfare a chi appetisce grandezza, non potendo più che uno ottenere il principato. Bisogna adunque collocare un membro tra il senato ed il principe, e questo sarà un aggregato d'alcuni magistrati, i quali col principe consiglieranno, ed eseguiranno le faccende grandi dello stato e della città . . . e questo membro si può chiamare, se vogliamo imitare i Veneziani, il collegio."

[93] *Opere*, II, 118: "Il consiglio grande essere un aggregato composto di quei tre membri, i quali noi di sopra descriveremmo, cioè grandi, mediocri e popolari; de' plebei non occorre far menzione, come ancora di sopra dicemmo, essendo gente forestiera che vengono alla città per valersi delle fatiche corporali, e ne vanno a casa loro, qualunque volta torna loro a proposito. Quelli che io chiamai popolari (cioè quelli che sono a gravezza, ma non sono abili a' magistrati) è necessario connumerare in detto consiglio, perché sono poco meno che principal membro della città per fare grandissimo numero, e per non potere la città senza quelli stare, e per mantenere la sua grandezza."

condemn both Venice and Florence for failure to mobilize this class in citizenship;[94] and Giannotti is plainly aware that not membership in the Consiglio alone, but all forms of magistracy and *onore*, should be open to them, though he concedes that this may not be practicable as things are. There is no one who is not ambitious of exaltation and glory, he says, unless repressed and debased as the French have been; and the arming of a city serves to bring this truth to the surface.[95] At this stage the class of those, once called *popolari*, who desire *libertà* alone would seem to have disappeared, but perhaps it would be truer to say that it has become open-ended: it is a category to which all men may, and to some extent do, belong, but this is in no way incompatible with the existence of a constant competition in *virtù*, from which governing elites emerge and in which all citizens may take part. Giannotti is as hostile as Guicciardini to the imposition of qualifications of wealth or birth for membership in the higher magistracies.

He now explicitly declares that the Consiglio Grande is to be *signore* of the city and consequently must exercise those "functions which are sovereign in the republic and embrace all the power of the state."[96] We ask ourselves how such a monopoly can be reconciled with a mere lessening of dependence in a structure of interdependence. The functions or powers in question, we recall, are the election of magistrates, the determination of peace and war, the hearing of appeals and the approval and promulgation of new laws. Giannotti is able to explain a modified version of Venetian procedure whereby the Consiglio elects all magistrates, from the senate up through the Collegio to the Gonfaloniere. The last is to be elected for life, but the senate, he decides after consideration—and contrary to his opinion in the *Letter to Cap-*

[94] *Opere*, II, 119-20: ". . . di qui nasce che i popolari amano piú molte volte un privato che la repubblica, e per lui prendere l'armi contro alla patria, sperando avere ad esse da quello arricchiti ed onorati. . . . Appresso, se Aristotile, il quale ha trattato con tanta dottrina e sapienza de' governi di tutte le repubbliche, entrasse in Venezia o in Firenze, dove vedesse d'una gran moltitudine d'uomini non esser tenuto conto alcuno, salvo che ne' bisogni della città, senza dubbio si riderebbe di tali ordinazioni, avendo nel settimo libro della sua Politica distribuiti gli ufficii della città convenienti a tutte le qualità degli abitanti della medesima."

[95] *Opere*, II, 120-21: "E se alcuno dicesse che questi popolari non sono ambiziosi . . . questo curarsi (poco?) de' magistrati non è naturale, ma accidente, perche non è uomo si misero che non desideri essere esaltato. Ma perché questi popolari sono stati tenuti bassi dalla superbia dei grandi, perciò son divenuti non ambiziosi, siccome ancora ne' tempi nostri sono i Franzesi, i quali per essere stati sbattuti dalla nobiltà loro, sono divenuti vilissimi. Non essendo adunque naturale tal viltà di animo in questi popolari, non è da privarli de' magistrati, e massimamente perché armandosi la città, diverriano subito desiderosi di gloria come gli altri . . ."

[96] *Opere*, II, 122: ". . . azioni le quali sono principali nella repubblica ed abbracciano tutta la forza dello stato."

poni—is to be reelected every year, with no bar to the serving of successive terms; this will ensure a stable elite, in which it will however be possible to lose one's place.[97] But

> the determination of peace and war must terminate in the senate . . . and though it cannot pass to the Consiglio, it will nevertheless depend upon the latter since this is where the senate in which it terminates is elected. It might perhaps be well, when a new war is proposed for the first time, to refer the decision to the Consiglio Grande, as did the Romans, who used to ask the people if it was their will and command that war be made on this or that prince or republic; but all consequent decisions (*accidenti*) must terminate in the senate.[98]

Similarly the power of hearing appeals must terminate in a specialized body of magistrates, imitated from the Venetians, called the Quarantie. Giannotti subsequently remarks that the *signore* of a state or city, whose *proprietà* this power rightfully is, often finds that it takes up too much of his time to exercise it in person (one suspects that it was also the problem of time which made Giannotti withhold the *accidenti* of war from the Consiglio), and for this reason the Consiglio Grande which is *signore* of Venice has set up the Quarantie, and the king of France has deputed his judicial power to four *parlements*.[99] It is arguable, then, that the power of election safeguards the *dependenza* of the judicial as of the military power upon the Consiglio. The difficulty is the vigor with which Giannotti earlier contended that a city might be free—i.e., that its Consiglio might be supreme—in respect of the election of magistrates but unfree in respect of the way those

[97] *Opere*, II, 129-30.

[98] *Opere*, II, 123: "Le deliberazioni della pace e guerra abbiano a terminare nel senato . . . e quantunque elle non passino nel consiglio, avranno pure da lui la dependenza, essendo da quello il senato, dove l'hanno a terminare, eletto . . . Saria forse bene, quando si ha a muovere una guerra di nuovo, vincere questa prima deliberazione nel consiglio grande (siccome facevano i Romani, i quali domandavano il popolo, se volevano e comandavano che si movesse guerra a questo ed a quello altro principe o repubblica); dipoi tutti gli accidenti di essa avessero a terminare nel senato."

[99] *Opere*, II, 157: ". . . è da notare che questo atto dell'ascoltare le provocazioni pare che sia proprietà di quello che è signore dello stato e della città: ma perché chi è signore, o egli non vuole, o egli non può se non con difficoltà tal cosa eseguire, perciò vediamo tale uffizio essere attribuito ad un altro giudizio dagli altri separato. Laonde perché in Francia il re non vuole, ed anco con difficoltà potrià occuparsi in tal faccenda, sono ordinati quattro parlamenti, i quali odono e giudicano le provocazioni di tutto il regno. In Venezia, perché il consiglio grande, che è signore di tutta la repubblica, non può fare tale effetto, perché bisogneria che stesse tutto l'anno occupato in tal materia (il che saria impossibile rispetto alle faccende private) sono ordinate tre quarantie . . ."

magistrates exercised their power, and that it was precisely this, in relation to military and judicial matters, which had made the republics of 1494 and 1527 violent and unfree governments. It was insufficient to keep—as Giannotti's plan continues to keep—the final approval of legislation in the power of the Consiglio, since legislation was not thought of as regulating the military and judicial functions.

It is possible to modify what seems a theoretical failure on Giannotti's part by pointing out that the former magistrates' irresponsibility had consisted in his view not only in their independence of control by the Consiglio Grande, but also in the fact that the same men proposed, resolved upon, and executed policies.[100] This alone had sufficed to make them closed cliques of the self-seeking, and he now takes up again his earlier proposals to separate *consultazione* and *deliberazione* and in this way to make men functionally responsible to each other. He effected this by detailing the relations between the senate and the various boards composing the Collegio, and he is able (as in the *Letter to Capponi*) to use the terms "few" to denote the body, e.g., the Ten, which exercises *consultazione*, and "many" to denote the senate which resolves on their proposals.[101] Yet as long as military and judicial matters do not reach the Consiglio, the term "many" cannot carry its usual meaning, and as long as the election of magistrates is thought of as one among four powers, and not as a prior and separate determinant of the other three, such a Consiglio cannot qualify as a *signore* exercising all four; but that is the only definition of *signore* which we have. It can of course be argued—and this is much more plausible—that if the Consiglio elects the senate, the Collegio, and the Gonfaloniere, it exercises indirect control over those two of the four powers which do not remain under its immediate authority, and is therefore very much less dependent on the one and the few than they are on it. But the problem throughout has been the relation between the concept of lesser *dependenza* and that of *signore*, and the two cannot be said to have been reconciled, much less identified. If we take Giannotti's theory of the *signore* and its four powers as a primitive attempt at a theory of sovereignty, we may add that the linguistic confusions which arose when one spoke of sovereignty in a context of mixed government, and vice versa, were to bedevil political discourse to the American Revolution and beyond.

Giannotti's mind was independent, forceful, and original, but lacked the unpredictable creativity of genius which we find in Machiavelli; and for this reason it may be taken as displaying in some detail the bent

---

[100] See his criticisms of the arrangements made in 1502, 1512, and 1527 at pp. 140-41.

[101] See generally pp. 139-47, and particularly 144-45.

and the limitations of humanist political thought. His chief originality consists in his perception that *virtù* in a mixed government was a kind of power, and in his consequent attempt to define the four functions of government whose location determined the *signore*. But he failed to concentrate these functions and was obliged to distribute them instead; and the ultimate reason was that humanist political thought was overmasteringly concerned with the ideal of civic virtue as an attribute of the personality, and in the last resort always turned from the establishment of institutionalized authority to the establishment of conditions, termed *libertà*, in which virtue might have free play and escape corruption. Our analysis of the *Repubblica Fiorentina*, like that of the *Discorsi*, should close with its distinctive contribution to the theory of corruption: Giannotti condemns the way in which, under the Savonarolan regime of 1529-1530, the brethren of San Marco became involved in politics and ambitious politicians sought conspicuous association with them as a means to enhanced authority with the citizens. This, he says, was no less corruption than was the open bribery of voters at Rome—it was, so to speak, an attempt to buy authority with coin other than that existing for the purpose—and to make things worse, bribery was at least acknowledged to be an evil, whereas if you attacked hypocrisy you were taken for an enemy of Jesus Christ.[102] Humanist political thought excelled at this sort of analysis, and subordinated the consideration of power to it; liberty, virtue, and corruption, rather than the location of authority, were its prime concerns.

It is not even certain that Machiavelli was an exception. As we complete this study of the last phase of Florentine political theory, the most vivid impression remaining should be that of the continuity of a basically Aristotelian republicanism from which Machiavelli did not seem to his friends (who were each other's enemies) to have greatly departed. Certainly we can discover areas of his thought where he seems to have radically departed from the medieval concept of a teleologically determined human nature, though equally there are moments at which he seems to be using, if he does not formally reason from, the idea that men are formed to be citizens and that the reformation of their natures in that direction may be corrupted but cannot be

[102] *Opere*, II, 194-99; especially p. 196: "Questo modo di vivere che tengono questi che fanno professione di religione, conversando coi frati di San Marco e continuando simulatamente l'orazione e la comunione, senza dubbio è pessimo nella nostra città; perché egli fa il medesimo effetto che facevano in Roma le largizioni. Ma questi è ancora molto peggiore, perché dove le largizioni si potevano in qualche modo correggere, a questa così fatta vita con difficoltà si trova rimedio; perché chi ragionasse di proibire questi modi di vivere, parrebbe che volesse vietare agli uomini il bene operare, e sarebbe ributtato non altrimenti che un pessimo nemico nella fede di Cristo."

reversed; the prince cannot make them anything else. But it is of some significance that the revolutionary aspects of his thinking—those in which man appears most dynamic and least natural—did not arrest the attention of his friends. Guicciardini's concept of citizenship remains a concept of *virtù*, loaded in the midst of its realism with Aristotelian language and assumptions, and in Giannotti the principle that man's nature is that of a citizen is explicitly stated, explicitly Aristotelian, and stops short only of becoming Savonarolan. It was in the Aristotelian and civic humanist channel that the stream of republican tradition was to flow, and Machiavelli as a historical figure, to whom theorists like Harrington and Adams referred, was to swim quite successfully in that channel. And the tradition to which the Florentines belonged was to be supported rather than impeded by their tough-mindedness in retaining a basically moralist concern with liberty and corruption; it continued to present politics as the erection of conditions under which men might freely exercise active virtue.

Giannotti also reveals to us the high capacity of Aristotelian political science, as an analytical and explicatory system, to absorb theories put forward as variations on its basic ideas. The Polybian theory of cycles, Machiavelli's doctrine of the militia, the model (rather than the myth) of Venice—all these are alluded to, explored, but finally used rather than followed; and they are used in the service of a basically Aristotelian method of categorizing the elements composing a city and showing how their interactions lead to stability, instability, or change in the polity. The classical republicanism to which John Adams still adhered was basically a Renaissance rephrasing of the political science set forth in Aristotle's *Politics*, and it possessed a high degree of capacity for dealing with the social phenomena of the seventeenth and eighteenth centuries. For Giannotti, however, perhaps its main importance was its ability to provide causal explanations of particular happenings and particular characteristics of cities; the *Repubblica Fiorentina*, is after all, a partially successful attempt to show how Venetian procedures and their underlying principles can be used in devising a different style of government for the very different conditions obtaining at Florence; and we have seen how, using Aristotelian categories both of causation and political composition, he was able to construct historical explanations and predictions concerning Florentine conditions which may have been misleading, but nevertheless dispelled much of the sense of mystery surrounding the particular. He is less dependent on concepts of usage, providence, or *fortuna*, when it comes to explaining how Florence has come to be as she is or what she may expect in the future, than either Savonarola or Machiavelli; he does not expect a miracle, like the former or his epigoni in 1529-1530—he has seen what

their faith could and could not do—and he has less than the latter's
sense of the desperate difficulty of creative action in the face of *fortuna*, or the almost miraculous qualities required for its success. This
no doubt has much to do with his choice of a rational Venice, rather
than a dynamic Rome, as the source of his principles of organization.[103]
His theory is highly articulated and he is relatively confident of its
applicability in practice.

Guicciardini, had he ever read the *Repubblica Fiorentina*, would
have acidly remarked that its author had never had to put his theories
into effect; and certainly it is sad, as one reads Giannotti's demonstrations that the regime of the early 1530s cannot possibly last, to reflect
that this intelligent man had forty more years of life in which to see
himself proved wrong (Guicciardini was just as wrong about the same
regime in his own way). But in the present study we are concerned
less with the predictive capacity of ideas than with their capacity to
enlarge the paradigmatic vocabulary of a civilization; in this sense, an
unsuccessful prophecy can be reused. Giannotti found Aristotelian
political analysis complex and plausible enough to give him confidence
that he understood something of the way things happened in time, and
for this reason his thought is not focused on apocalyptic expectation,
like Savonarola's, or on *innovazione* and *occasione* like Machiavelli's.
Time is not in the foreground. The work concludes—as do *Il Principe*
and the *Dialogo del Reggimento di Firenze*—with what we can now
see as an almost conventional section[104] on the problems of actualiza-
tion. Like Machiavelli and Guicciardini, Giannotti reviews the occasions on which, and the personalities by whom, republics may be
securely founded; but his thought is directed toward Florentine actuality, and the fact that he writes as an exile in time of tyranny leaves
him, as he recognizes, very little to say. Only a liberator (like Andrea
Doria at Genoa) can be legislator for Florence, and concerning a liberator we can say only that either he will come or he will not. Others—
presumably including Machiavelli—have written so well on the theory
of conjurations and conspiracies as to teach him all he can learn about
the *occasione* of the overthrow of governments; our part is to study

---

[103] But cf. *Opere*, II, 255-56: "Conchiudendo adunque dico che tal forma di
repubblica della nostra città non potrebbe patire alcuna intrinseca alterazione: e
per virtù della milizia nel sopradetto modo ordinata, si difenderebbe dagli assalti
esterni, e se la fortuna concedesse a questa repubblica colle sue armi armata una
sola vittoria, acquisterebbe la nostra città sola tanta gloria e reputazione che toc-
cherebbe il cielo; e non saria maraviglia alcuna se Firenze diventasse un'altra
Roma, essendo il subbietto per la frequenza e natura degli abitatori, e fortezza
del sito, d'un imperio grandissimo capace." At this point Giannotti is drawing
nearer to both the Savonarolan and the Machiavellian modes of thinking.

[104] Book III, ch. 8 (the last); pp. 258-69.

the theory of establishing them, since it is better that we should complain of Fortune that she never sent us a liberator, than she of us that we did not know what to do when he came.[105] In these concluding words of his treatise, Giannotti accepts the role of the theorist in exile, and indicates once more that his attitude to time and *fortuna* is realistic. He is not naive about the difficulties of action, neither does he think them capable only of a miraculous solution (Machiavelli, who has been accused of the former, is nearer to the latter position). When he acknowledges the primacy of *fortuna*, he means only that there are always things beyond our control.

If this is largely the reason why Giannotti prefers Venice to Rome, and does not adopt Machiavelli's concept of a dynamic *virtù*, it is also a reason why he does not present Venice as a miracle or a myth. The problem of time was not, to his mind, such that only a Venetian miracle could solve it. He accepted the view that the purpose of legislation—and of his own planning for Florence—was to found constitutions that would endure, and he profoundly admired Venice's success in achieving near-perpetual stability. But the components of the *mito di Venezia* were the belief that only miraculous wisdom could bring such stability, and the belief that Venice had achieved a miracle by the art and contrivance of many; and since Giannotti did not adopt the former position, he presented neither a Polybian balance nor the mysteries of Venetian electoral machinery as constituting a miraculous solution to the problem of duration. He was obliged to see Venice's success as the product of many causes, simply by the circumstance that he was applying Venetian paradigms to the problem of achieving the same success in the very different conditions of Florence, and his mainly Aristotelian vocabulary gave him so many ways of differentiating conditions and causes that he could not see the problem as apocalyptic or its solution as miraculous or simple. The problem of legislation for durability was capable of complex solutions, and these could be built up over time. In both Giannotti's major works, his account of Venetian history, while serving as a kind of antithesis to

---

[105] *Opere*, II, 269: "Saria ben necessario esser accorto nel prender l'occasione; perché questa è quella che ha le bilance delle faccende umane e tutte quelli che in tal cosa non usano prudenza grandissima sono costretti a rovinare. Ma di questa materia non è da parlare, perché appartiene delle congiure, la quale è stata da altri prudentissimamente trattata.

"Conchiudendo adunque dico che questi sono i modi per i quali alcun cittadino potrià recare si gran benefizio alla nostra città; e benché la malignità della fortuna abbia oppressati quelli che hanno questi modi seguitati, non è però da disperare . . . acciocché la città nostra s'abbia piú tosto a lamentare della fortuna per non avere mostrato mai alcuna intera occasione, che ella della città, per non v'essere stato chi l'abbia saputa conoscere e pigliare."

Machiavelli's history of Rome, is equally an account of a complex historical process.

But we have seen that republican theory is in essence Aristotelian political science, selectively simplified by a drastic emphasis on the problem of time. It was possible to move away from such an emphasis, into a conceptual world so rich in its vocabulary that the potentialities of action increased and the problem of time grew less. But it was equally possible to move in the reverse direction, toward a position where only divine grace, the heroic action of a Lycurgus, or the attainment of a miraculous equilibrium seemed to offer solutions to the problem. The Renaissance obsession with time and fortune ensured that, since Venice was the paradigm of the solution last mentioned, the *mito di Venezia* would endure; and if Giannotti's nonmythical account became one of the standard books in the literature of the *mito*, it is valuable to study the contemporary and no less widely read treatise of Gasparo Contarini, in which the mythical element is far more pronounced.

[III]

Contarini, a Venetian aristocrat and churchman, wrote his *De Magistratibus et Republica Venetorum* at an uncertain time[106] during the twenties and thirties of the sixteenth century, and it was printed only in 1543, after which it became a book of European reputation and was many times reprinted. Though its renown exceeded that of Giannotti's *Repubblica de' Veneziani*, it is a work of rather less intensive and technical character as far as its treatment of the Venetian magistracies and their history is concerned; but it is completed where Giannotti's treatise is incomplete, and Contarini has found space to state his philosophy of government as relevant to the Venetian theme. Since his book had a traceable impact in many countries, it is of some value to quote it in the English of its Elizabethan translation, the work of Lewes Lewkenor, which appeared in 1599.

Contarini's language is panegyrical from the start: he states that Venice appears, both physically and politically, "rather framed by the hands of the immortal Gods, than any way by the arte, industry or inuention of men."[107] But it is a crucial point with him that Venice

---

[106] Perhaps 1522-25. See Gilbert, "Date of the Composition," *loc. cit.* (above, n. 3).

[107] Lewkenor, *The Commonwealth and Government of Venice. Written by the Cardinall Gasper Contareno and translated out of Italian into English by Lewes Lewkenor* (London, 1599), p. 2. The Latin text runs (Contarini, *De Magistratibus et Republica Venetorum*, Paris, 1543, p. 1): ". . . deorum immortalium potius quam hominum opus atque inuentū fuisse . . ."

is the work of human art and above all of human virtue. Following a line of thought opened up by the Florentines, but becoming usual with Venetian writers, he states that virtue may appear in either a civil or a military form, but that although the latter is glorious and necessary it must exist only for the sake of the former. He is in the mainstream of Aristotelian and Christian thought in insisting that the end of war must be peace, but as an Italian writing in the civic humanist tradition he has also to explain how it is that Venetian *virtù* involves the employment of mercenaries while the citizens remain unarmed themselves. To Lewkenor, who furnished his own commentary by way of introduction, this paradox—and it seemed one to him no less than to a Florentine—was part of the generally miraculous way in which Venetian political procedures controlled, both rationally and morally, all departments of civic life.

> Besides, what is there that can carrie a greater disproportion with common rules of experience, thē that unweaponed men in gownes should with such happinesse of successe give direction & law to many mightie and warlike armies . . . and long robed citizens to bee serued, yea and sued unto for entertainment by the greatest princes and peers of *Italy*; amidst which infinit affluence of glorie, and unmeasurable mightinesse of power, of which there are in soueraignty partakers aboue 3000 gentlemen, yet is there not one among them to bee found that doth aspire to any greater appellation of honour. . . .[108]

Contarini does not go quite as far as his translator, though he does explain later that, because the civil constitution of Venice grew up under conditions of separation from the *terra firma* and therefore from military life—like most writers on these questions, he does not regard maritime power as posing any problems for civil organization—when the city finally became a land power, it was thought better not to let citizens exercise military commands for fear that

> this their continual frequentation of the continent, and diuorcement as it were from the ciuile life, would without doubt haue brought forth a kinde of faction different and disioyned from the other peaceable Citizens, which parcialitie and dominion would in time have bred ciuile warres and dissentions within the City. . . . To exclude therefore out of our estate the danger or occasion of any such ambitious enterprises, our auncestors held it a better course to defend their dominions vppon the continent, with forreign mercenarie souldiers, than with their homeborn citizens, & to assigne them

---

[108] Lewkenor, sig. A3.

their pay & stipende out of the tributes and receipts of the Prouince, wherein they remayned. . . .[109]

But he does not mean that military and civic virtue are necessarily incompatible, or that it is the mechanized routine of decision at Venice which keeps the former subordinate to the latter. This is the work of virtue, and of a virtue which Contarini depicts as inherent in the Venetian aristocracy as a whole. In a passage which a knowledge of Florentine thought greatly illuminates, he bases this assertion on the familiar themes that Venice has never had a legislator, that a legislator has a difficult task with those less virtuous than himself, and that there is little historical evidence preserved concerning the city's early history. Giannotti had been puzzled to account for the creation of stable orders by the early Venetians' unaided intelligence, but to Contarini the mystery is to be proudly affirmed rather than explained.

There were in *Athens, Lacedaemon* and *Rome*, in sundry seasons sundry rare and vertuous men of excellent desert and singular pietie towards their country, but so fewe, that being ouerruled by the multitude they were not able much to profit the same. But our auncestors, from whome wee have receyued so flourishing a commonwealth, all in one did vnite themselues in a consenting desire to establish, honour and amplifie their country, without hauing in a manner any the least regarde of their owne priuate glorie or commodity. And this any man may easily coniecture . . . in regarde that there are in *Venice* to bee found none, or very few monuments of our auncestors, though both at home and abroad many things were by them gloriously atchieued, and they of passing and singular desert towards their countrie. There are no stately tombes erected, no military statues remaining, no stemmes of ships, no ensignes, no standards taken from their enemies, after the victory of many and mighty battailes. . . .[110]

[109] Lewkenor, p. 130. Contarini, pp. 100-101: "Haec vero frequens consuetudo cõtinentis, ac intermissio urbanae, factionẽ quandam ciuium paritura facile fuerat ab aliis ciuibus disiuncta: quapropter proculdubio res Veneta breui ad factiones et ad bella ciuilia deducta fuisset. . . . Ne ergo huiusmodi quispiam morbus in Venetam ciuitatem obreperet, satius esse maiores statuerunt, ut continentis imperium externo ac conducto milite quam Veneto defenderetur. Stipendiũ uero illi statuit ex uectigalibus totius prouinciae. Aequũ enim erat eius regionis impensis militem uiuere, qui ad eam tuendam accersitus fuerat . . ."

[110] Lewkenor, p. 6. Contarini, pp. 5-6: "Fuere Athenis, Lacedaemone, ac Romae nonulli ciues uitae probitate, atq: in Rempub. pietate insignes uiri, sed adeo pauci, ut multitudine obruti, non multum patriae rei profuerint. At maiores nostri, a quibus tam praeclaram Rempub. accepimus, omnes ad unum consensere in studio patriae rei firmandae et amplificandae, nulla prope priuati commodi et honoris

With this then exceeding vertue of mind did our auncestors plant and settle this such a commonwealth, that since the memory of man, whosoeuer shal go about to make compare between the same & the noblest of the ancients, shal scarcely find any such: but rather I dare affirme, that in the discourses of those great Philosophers, which fashioned and forged commonwealths according to the desires of the mind, there is not any to be founde so well fayned and framed. . . .[111]

To Florentine theorists it was evident that ambition and the pursuit of *onore* and *chiarezza* motivated any civic aristocracy, and that a problem in government was to prevent this thirst from corrupting itself. Giannotti considered the need to give it the appearance of satisfaction, while rendering that satisfaction dependent on the concurrence of others, one of the necessities that kept *governo misto* a second best, appropriate to an imperfect world. But if Contarini is prepared to endow the Venetians with virtue in the full sense of a disregard of all except the public good, then the *governo misto* of Venice must be much less a contrivance against corruption, much more an expression of its absence. When he proceeds to state his philosophy of government, it involves the usual case against the simple rule of the one, the few or the many, but on grounds less close to Polybius than to the main lines of Christian Aristotelian politics. As beasts are governed by men, so should men be governed by that which is higher than man. God does not govern commonwealths directly, but there is in man an element of the divine, which is "the mind, pure and devoid of perturbation"; a long way from Giannotti's conception of *virtù.* Since there are also in man "inferior and brutish powers," we cannot ensure the rule of the mind by entrusting government to any man, group or combination of groups of men, but "by a certaine diuine counsell when by other meanes it might not, mankinde through the inuention of lawes seemeth to have attained this point, that the office of gouerning assemblings of men should be giuen to the mind and reason onely. . . ."[112]

---

habita ratione. Huiusce rei coniecturam facere quiuis facile poterit . . . q: nulla, aut admodū pauca antiquorū monumēta Venetiis extent: alioquin domi forisq: praeclarissimorum hominū, et qui de Rep. bene meriti fuerint, non sepulchra, nō equestres aut pedestres statua, nō rostra nauiū, aut uexilla ab hostibus direpta, ingentibus praeliis superatis."

[111] Lewkenor, p. 7. Contarini, p. 6: "Hac ergo incredibili uirtute animi maiores nostri hanc Remp. instituere, qualē post hominū memoriam nullam extitisse, si quis hāc nostram cum celeberrimis antiquorum cōferar, meridiana luce clarius intuebitur. Quin adfirmare ausim, neq: monumentis insignium philosophorum, qui pro animi uoto Reip. formas effinxere, tam recte formatam atq: effictam ullam contineri."

[112] Lewkenor, p. 11. Contarini, pp. 8-9: ". . . menti purae, ac motionum animi

If laws can attain the status of pure reason—the apocryphal authority of Aristotle is given for the view "that God was the same in the vniuersity of things, as an ancient lawe in a civill company"[113]—then laws must rule and not men; the participation of individuals and groups in government is subordinate to this. But the argument is in danger of becoming circular: laws ensure that reason rules and not particular passions, but they are invented and maintained by men and can prevail only when men are guided by reason to the public good and not by passion to private ends. The laws must maintain themselves, then, by regulating the behavior of the men who maintain them; and in "assemblings of men," in cities, that is to say, where men regularly meet face to face to enforce and make laws and to transact public business, the term "laws" must have the principal meaning of a set of orders and regulations for the conduct of assemblies and the framing of decisions. Such laws must have the effect of directing men's energies solely toward the public good, which is to say solely in the paths of pure reason. The *mito di Venezia* consists in the assertion that Venice possesses a set of regulations for decision-making which ensure the complete rationality of every decision and the complete virtue of every decision-maker. Venetians are not inherently more virtuous than other men, but they possess institutions which make them so.

An individual in whom pure mind always reigned, without the need for external controls or assistance, would as we know be an angel rather than a man. As Hobbes's Leviathan was an "artificial man" and a "mortal god," so Contarini's Venice, it may be suggested, was an artificial angel: men who were not wholly rational functioned as members of an institutional framework which was. Lewkenor seems to have sensed this:

> beholde their great Councell, consisting at the least of 3000 Gentlemen, whereupon the highest strength and mightinesse of the estate absolutely relyeth, notwithstanding which number all thinges are ordered with so diuine a peaceablenesse, and so without all tumult and confusion, that it rather seemeth to bee an assembly of Angels, then of men.

---

immuni id munus conferendum est. Quamobrem diuino quodam consilio, cum alia ratione id fieri non posset, inuentibus legibus hoc assecutum humanum genus uidetur, ut menti tantum ac rationi nullis perturbantibus obnoxiae, hoc regendi hominum coetus officium demandatum sit . . ."

[113] Lewkenor, p. 12. Contarini, pp. 9-10: "Aristoteles philosophorum facile princeps, in eo libello quē de mundo ad Alexandrum regem Macedonum scripsit, nihil aliud reperit cui similem deum optimum faceret, praeter antiquam legem in ciuitate recte instituta: ut id propemodum tam magni philosophi sententia sit deus in hac rerum universitate, quod antiqua lex in ciuili societate."

. . . their penall Lawes most unpardonably executed; their encouragements to vertue infinite; especially by their distribution of offices and dignities, which is ordered in such a secrete, straunge, and intricate sort, that it utterly ouerreacheth the subtiltie of all ambitious practises, neuer falling upon any but upon such as are by the whole assembly allowed for greatest wisedome, vertue and integritie of life.

. . . there are sundry other so maruellous and miraculous considerations, and in their owne exceeding singularitie, beyond all resemblance or comparison with any other Commonwealth so unspeakeablie straunge, that their wonderfull rarenesse being verified, maketh the straungest impossibilities not seeme altogether incredible. . . .[114]

To an Elizabethan mind, Venice could appear a phenomenon of political science fiction: a series of marvelous devices for keeping men virtuous, where in other states this was left to individual reason or divine grace. Contarini, who was after all a churchman, does not press the language of mystery and miracle so far, but he has endowed his Venetians with exceptional virtue by whose means they have evolved political procedures which maintain it. Inevitably, the theoretical language he adopts obliges him to present virtue as the maintenance of a balance between the one, the few, and the many; these are the categories into which persons fall and which must consequently be transcended if an impersonal government is to be maintained. But in his ideal constitution it is the laws which rule, and the distribution of authority between one, few, and many is a means of keeping all three subject to law and reason:

yet is the multitude of itselfe unapt to governe, unlesse the same be in some sort combined together; for there cannot bee a multitude without the same bee in some vnitie contayned; so that the ciuill society (which consisteth in a certain vnity) will bee dissoluted, if the multitude become not one by some meane of reason. . . .[115]

The language reveals that older philosophical traditions are directing and binding the simpler formulae of mixed government. We do indeed read, shortly after this, that Venice has combined the princely, noble, and popular forms of authority "so that the formes of them all seeme

[114] Lewkenor, sig. A 2v.-3.
[115] Lewkenor, p. 13. Contarini, p. 11: "Ac equidem multitudo omnis est per se inepta gubernationi, nisi in unum quodammodo coalescat: quandoquidem neque esse ulla multitudo queat, nisi unitate aliqua contineatur. Qua de re ciuilis quoque societas dissipabitur, quae unitate quadam cōstat, nisi quapiam ratione multitudo unum efficiatur."

to be equally balanced, as it were with a paire of weights . . . ,"[116] but it is not a question of distinguishing political functions as distinct modes of power, and ascribing them to the one, few, and many so as to form a balance. This raised, as we have seen, the problem of explaining just how one mode of power could be said to "balance" another; Giannotti had decided that the question could not be resolved in those terms and would have to be rephrased (a task in which he had not been very successful), but Contarini, writing apparently without knowledge of the Florentine's work,[117] may be found at one point repudiating the very language in which Giannotti had restated it.

> there cannot happen to a commonwealth a more daungerous or pestilent contagion, then the ouerweighing of one parte or faction aboue the other: for where the ballance of iustice standeth not euen, it is vnpossible that there should bee a friendly societie and firme agreement among the citizens: which alwaies happeneth where many offices of the commonwealth meete together in one. For as every mixture dissolueth, if any one of the elementes (of which the mixed body consisteth) ouercome the other: and as in musicke the tune is marred where one string keepeth a greater noyse than hee should doe: so by the like reason, if you will haue your commonwealth perfect and enduring, let not one part bee mightier than the other, but let them all (in as much as may bee) have equall share in the publique authoritie.[118]

Read in conjunction with Giannotti, this may seem a simple recession to the theory of Polybian balance; but there is rather more to it than that. The context in which it occurs is that of a provision which forbids more than three members of a family holding office in the senate at any one time, so that the "partes or factions" which must not overbalance one another are not merely the traditional Polybian three, but might include any grouping whatever into which the citizens might fall. Polybian theory, we remember yet again, was a paradig-

---

[116] Lewkenor, p. 15. Contarini, p. 13: ". . . adeo ut omnium formas pari quadam librameto commiscuisse uideatur . . ."

[117] Gilbert, "Date of the Composition," pp. 172-74, 182.

[118] Lewkenor, p. 67. Contarini, p. 53: "Nam nulla perniciosior pestis in Rempublicam obrepserit, q[uam] si quaepiā eius pars caeteris praeualuerit. Sic nanque (?) quoniam ius non seruatur, impossibile est societatem inter ciues consistere. Quod usu euenire solet ubicunque plura in unum conueniunt. Sic soluitur mixtum, si quodpiā elementorū ex quibus constat, alia superauerit. Sic omnis consonantia dissonans sit, si fidem seu uocem unā plus intenderis quam par sit. Non dispari ratione si ciuitatem aut Rempublicam constare uolueris, necesse est id in primis seruari, ne qua pars aliis efficiatur potentior, sed omnes, quoad fieri possit, participes fiat publicae potestatis."

matic simplification of Aristotelian political science, and Aristotle had known well enough that the one, few, and many were categories which it was convenient and necessary to employ. A durable constitution must satisfy all social groups; a one-few-many analysis was merely an operationally satisfactory means of ascertaining whether it was doing so.

But Contarini, far more than Giannotti, is self-consciously a philosopher in politics; and where the Florentine developed the concept of *virtù* in the direction of power, the Venetian retained it primarily with the connotation of rationality. Government was an act of wisdom directed at the common good, so that "equall share in the publique authoritie" meant, among other things, "equal share in the exercise of public intelligence." But a body politic in which every conceivable part or category exercised the mode of intelligence appropriate to it would be one whose rationality was perfect, and participation in its public intelligence would also be perfect. It is not insignificant that from the beginnings of the *mito*, Venetian mixed government had been idealized by equation less with Polybius's Book vi than with Plato's *Laws*.[119] The "artificial angel" was miraculously, because rationally, stable, perfect, and timeless, relatively free from the shadows of ambiguity and ultimate doom that overhung Polybius's Rome or Machiavelli's Florence. Where Giannotti, knowing that his own city's history was one of instability, had first asked questions about Venetian history which he left unanswered,[120] and had later felt obliged to devise means of analyzing instability and providing for stability that carried him away from all three of his masters—Aristotle, Polybius, and Machiavelli—Contarini needed to take neither of these steps. Nor did he follow Savonarola in presenting his republic as playing a messianic role at an apocalyptic moment.

Yet we must avoid dismissing Venetian republican thought as the mere projection into myth of a Platonic self-image. In a most magisterial treatment of the subject, William J. Bouwsma has shown that Venetian thought did not stand still with Contarini but developed during the next eighty years, first with Paruta and afterwards with Sarpi, a sense of the particularity and moral autonomy of history which was founded on a series of assertions of Venice's unique individuality against the universalist claims of the Counter-Reformation papacy.[121] And just as for Florence, the republican vision of history carried with

119 Gilbert, "Venetian Constitution," pp. 468-70.
120 Above, nn. 23, 24.
121 William J. Bouwsma, *Venice and the Defense of Republican Liberty: Renaissance Values in the Age of the Counter Reformation* (Berkeley and Los Angeles: University of California Press, 1968).

it shadows as well as lights; Sarpi's *History of the Council of Trent* is as disenchanted a record of human failure and frailty as anything in Guicciardini.[122] The timeless myth and the history that lacked finality were, we must recollect, two responses to the same problem: the republic's struggle to attain self-sufficient virtue and stability in a context of particularity, time, and change. It might escape from history by a self-constituent act of timeless rationality; it might seek to tame history by combining in a grand synthesis all the elements of instability, identified and interwoven; or it might confess that the problem could not be solved and that the pitfalls of history remained forever open. Contarini is nearer to the first position than to the second; Machiavelli, Guicciardini, and Sarpi nearer to the third than to the second. Giannotti's significance lies in the originality of his contributions to the second, to the science that pursued stability.

He has appeared in these pages, it is true, as a thinker who to some extent sought to draw Machiavelli's fangs, reconciling Rome with Venice, transcending both models, and presenting the armed popular republic as devoted to its own virtue rather than to conquest and expansion—thus seeming to free it from the Ragnarok of the "universal wolf." Partly because he was less interested in war than was Machiavelli, and more interested in the theory of constitutional equilibrium, he was able to carry the science of mixed government to points not reached by other Florentine analysts; but while on the one hand this means that fortune's role in his thought is restricted by the wealth of his explanatory devices, his failure to develop a theory of sovereignty resting on the legislative power meant that he had not escaped from the world in which Contarinian myth and Machiavellian or Guicciardinian realism were the confining alternatives, since a republic which could not legislate itself must be restricted to the struggle to maintain *prima forma*. It reverted to being the political form in which was attained the universal good, which meant that there was no political activity other than the maintenance of form. If Machiavelli and Guicciardini did not, with all their brilliance, succeed in seeing political activity as creative, but only in showing just how difficult, or impossible, the maintenance of republican order really was, we are obliged to think of *cinquecento* civic realism, even at its height, as a kind of negative capability of the Aristotelian mind. Its awareness of the qualitative character and even the irreversibility of historical change was arrived at by recombining the categories of Aristotelian thought, and its concern with *fortuna* varied inversely as these categories could suggest new conceptual means of controlling her. It can be suggested also

---

[122] Bouwsma, ch. x.

that these limitations were in part imposed upon Machiavellian thought by its obstinately durable moralism.

Aristotelian republicanism was exclusively concerned with the citizen, and there was no need for Florentine and Venetian theorists to abandon it so long as they too were concerned only with him and his chances of escaping corruption; indeed, within its traditions they found it possible greatly to enlarge their vocabulary for discussing his problems. But for all the tough-mindedness of Machiavelli and Guicciardini, the fact remains that the weakness of the Aristotelian and humanist tradition was the insufficiency of its means for discussing the positive, as opposed to the preservative, exercise of power. We earlier considered the possibility that some political agency might acquire so developed a capacity for dealing with particular and changing problems as they arose that society's institutional means of dealing with such problems were in constant change and capable of changing themselves. It is evident that such an agency would be government in the modern sense, that it would be legislating in the modern sense, and that such a political society would be a modern administrative state possessed of a dimension of historical change and adaptation. But a body of political theory exclusively concerned with how the citizen is to develop his human capacities by participating in decisions aimed at the subjection of private to public goods is unlikely to develop a concern for, or a vocabulary for dealing with, government as a positive or creative activity. Under sixteenth-century conditions, it tended to reduce politics to the structure within which the individual asserted his moral autonomy, and legislation to the purely formal activity of establishing and restoring such a structure, so that any but a destructive innovation in time became virtually impossible. We have also seen that a view of politics which confined it to the assertion of values, or virtues, by individuals in public acts discouraged, every time that it encouraged, any attempt to treat it as the concurrent exercise of different kinds of power. Giannotti took a first step in that direction, but was unable to take a second; and the Polybian concept of a balance between different agencies exercising power seems so far to have been acutely self-limiting. We may say that all this reveals the deficiencies of Aristotelian theory, but it is possible also—though debatable—that power in a face-to-face polis must be so far dispersed and personal as to render difficult the growth of theory about the several specialized ways of exercising it. The next step will be to study the development of humanist and Machiavellian thought in a society made up of several institutionalized agencies exercising different kinds of power: post-Tudor England, with its king, its law, its parliament, and its church. But we shall find that each of these agencies secreted and disseminated its own ideology, its own modes of defining political society and the political individual; with the consequence that it was only with difficulty, and in a variety of very special senses, that the English realm could be defined as a civic community or republic, in which politicized individuals pursued a *vivere civile*. We shall have to study how it happened that Englishmen could begin to project an image of themselves and their society in Machiavellian terms; but we shall find that this process involved a restatement of civil history in terms both positive and negative, which defined government as modern in the act of rebelling against its modernity. Exported to the Atlantic's western shores, this contributed powerfully to the complexity of American values.

PART THREE

VALUE AND HISTORY IN THE PREREVOLUTIONARY ATLANTIC

CHAPTER X

THE PROBLEM OF ENGLISH MACHIAVELLISM

Modes of Civic Consciousness before the Civil War

[I]

IN THE PRECEDING CHAPTERS we have been engaged upon an exploration of a mode of thought which may be termed "Machiavellism," and consisted in the articulation of civic humanist concepts and values under the stresses of the Florentine predicament in the years 1494 to 1530. A conceptual world dominated by the paradigms of use, faith, and fortune was subjected to strain by the republican decision to pursue universal values in a transitory form, and this strain was intensified by happenings in the world of experience after 1494, when the Florentine republic failed to maintain itself against Medicean reaction and the Italian republics failed to maintain their system of relationships against French and Spanish intruders. From these complex tensions we have noted two major outputs: Machiavelli's revision of the concept of *virtù*, finding its most controversial expression in the advice given to the *principe nuovo* and its most durable lessons in the theory of arms as essential to liberty; and a renewed and intensified study of the Aristotelian-Polybian theory of mixed government, in which Venice figured as both paradigm and myth and, in her capacity as antithesis to Rome, helped deflect attention from Machiavelli's military populism. The concepts of custom, apocalypse, and *anakuklōsis*, based on the triad of use, faith, and fortune, have remained operable throughout, and we have noted only an observable tendency—of great importance to republican theory—to replace the concept of fortune with that of corruption: a means, it may be suggested, of introducing secondary causes into what was otherwise an image of pure randomness. In this respect there has been an intensification of historical self-understanding; but the medieval triad remains intact.

We have next to embark upon a study of how patterns of "Machiavellian" thought became operative in England, and at a later period in colonial and revolutionary America; and, as regards England at least, the greatest single difficulty we face is that there occurred in that culture nothing like the relatively simple options for *vita activa, vivere civile* and the republican remodeling of the historical self-image, which were all we found necessary to posit in order to account for the highly complex conceptual rearrangements which ensued. Republican and Machiavellian ideas had to become domiciled in an environment dominated by monarchical, legal, and theological concepts apparently in no way disposed to require the definition of England as a polis or the Englishman as a citizen. Our first problem will be to ascertain how it was that they became domiciled at all, and we cannot do this without initially reviewing the modes of consciousness with which they had to compete; we shall have to see whether these earlier political languages encountered problems which made a partial recourse to the republican vocabulary convenient or necessary.

There is a *prima facie* case for holding that an ideology of civic activism was incompatible with either the institutions or the beliefs of territorial monarchy. To use the terminology of Walter Ullmann,[1] the "descending thesis" of authority left the individual under a king with little function but to obey those above him in a hierarchical order and to pass on the duty of obedience to those below him; while the "ascending thesis" of corporate rationality served mainly as a theoretical means of constituting a people as a body intelligent enough to recognize that it had a head, a stalagmite of intelligence capable of rising toward the descending stalactite of authority. The *corpus mysticum* which Fortescue recognized as needing to be governed *politice*[2] was far from being an Aristotelian polis, it was a fellowship of reason, capable of cognizing rational laws, a fellowship of experience, capable of generating a body of remembered customs which became its second nature, but not a fellowship of action or a partnership of directing virtues in which men were intelligently participant according to the diversity of their individualities. Fortescue could never have recognized predicaments like those diagnosed by Machiavelli and Guicciardini as part of the very stuff of political life, or devised machinery like that of Guicciardini and Giannotti as the means by which such predicaments could be resolved; Venice to him was a legal entity distinguished by the antiquity and rationality of its municipal laws,[3] just as England was. The *corpus misticum* was, indeed, exposed to the solvents of methodological individualism: a body whose head was the prince, it was

---

[1] *Principles of Government and Politics in the Middle Ages* (above, ch. I, n. 32); *History of Political Thought in the Middle Ages* (Harmondsworth: Penguin Books, 1965); *The Individual and Society in the Middle Ages* (Baltimore: The Johns Hopkins University Press, 1966). For a vigorous critique, see Francis Oakley, "Celestial Hierarchies Revisited: Walter Ullmann's Vision of Medieval Politics," *Past and Present* 60 (1973), 3-48.

[2] *De Laudibus Legum Anglie*, ch. XIII. [3] Above, pp. 14-16.

nevertheless made up of individuals who had heads of their own—as in the frontispiece to *Leviathan*—and the problem of relating the intelligence of the subject to the intelligence of the prince could be productive of tensions. But reason and experience alone could never provide grounds for characterizing the individual as a citizen; that could only happen if there were revival of the ancient notions of political *virtus*, of the *zōon politikon* whose nature was to rule, to act, to make decisions; and so far, only the ideology of the *vita activa*, operating in a communal climate where men were indeed called to assemble and make decisions, has emerged as showing how such a revival could take place. In the territorial and jurisdictional monarchy, the individual took on positive being primarily as the possessor of rights—rights to land, and to justice affecting his tenure of land—and a structure of "ascending authority" existed mainly as a structure of customs, jurisdictions, and liberties, in which such rights were embodied and preserved and which rose to meet the descending structure of authority that existed to command its continuance and enforcement. In the world of *jurisdictio* and *gubernaculum* the individual possessed rights and property—*proprietas*, that which rightfully pertained to him—and was subject to authority which, since it descended from God, was never the mere reflection of his rights; and the central debate was, and has remained, how far the two conceptual schemes—ascending and descending powers, *jurisdictio* and *gubernaculum*, rights and duties—were integrated with one another. It can be strongly affirmed, however, that to define the individual in terms of his rights and his duties, his property and his obligations, is still not enough to make him an active citizen or a political animal.

It is not surprising, then, that for some time scholars have sought to raise not only the question of how the values and concepts of civic humanism could become established in a territorial-jurisdictional monarchy such as England,[4] but the larger question of how and when, in what terms and under what conditions, the Englishman could develop a civic consciousness, an awareness of himself as a political actor in a public realm. One of these books, Donald Hanson's *From Kingdom to Commonwealth*,[5] is noteworthy for the stringency of its assertion that *jurisdictio* and *gubernaculum* were never integrated and hardly related; that medieval and Tudor Englishmen lived under a conceptual scheme of intractable duality which the author terms "double majesty"; and that the collapse of this duality, which Hanson considers did not take place until the Civil War of 1642-1646, was the necessary and (it

---

[4] E.g., Denys Hay in A. Molho and J. Tedeschi (eds.), *Renaissance: Studies in Honour of Hans Baron* (De Kalb: Northern Illinois University Press, 1971).

[5] For full title see above, ch. I, n. 30.

would almost seem) the sufficient condition of "the growth of civic consciousness." If this is a correct summary, the argument would appear somewhat too drastic, but it has the merit of posing a challenge which historians have been tardy in recognizing. The growth in England of civic consciousness as he defines it does indeed present a problem; it is a difficult subject of which less than enough has been written; but there is evidence to suggest that it grew along a number of lines, and that we should proceed cautiously as we approach the further problem of how the Englishman acquired the means of seeing himself, in Aristotelian, Machiavellian, or Venetian terms, as a classical citizen acting in a republic.

One powerful and persuasive argument presents the saint as preceding the citizen. Walzer's *The Revolution of the Saints*[6] presents the Calvinist or classical Puritan individual as the type of the first revolutionary, the first radically alienated man in modern Europe, filled with a sense of his loneliness—a loneliness before God—associating with others on the basis of their common responsibility to values which are not those of society, and possessing a program of action whereby these values are to become the foundation of a reformation of the world. Walzer salutes—though he does not share—the older Marxism of Christopher Hill,[7] in which the alienation and activism of the Puritan creed appear as the ideology of middling and industrious persons emerging from the broken forms of feudal society. Walzer's saints are clerics, gentlemen, and lesser nobility, and the social origins of their alienation are not located in a feudal-to-bourgeois transition. But if the abortive revolutions of seventeenth-century England were not made by middling and industrious persons, they were not made by the classical Puritan ministers depicted by Walzer—indeed, his analysis specifically stops short of the sectarians who made them.[8] The abortive revolutions were the work of an army—a unique phenomenon in itself—inspired by millennial hopes which were only half accepted, and led by legally educated lesser gentry profoundly split in their ideologies, almost to the point where this amounted to a split in personalities. With half their minds they were radical saints; with the other half they were conservative reformers, deeply committed to a traditional order in which they saw the source of all secular values, even those which should reform it. Their revolution failed less because there were not enough of them— revolutions are the work of minorities—than because they constantly

[6] Walzer, *Revolution of the Saints* (see above, ch. II, n. 22).

[7] Christopher Hill, *Puritanism and Revolution* (London: Secker and Warburg, 1958); *Society and Puritanism in Pre-Revolutionary England* (New York: Schocken Books, 1964).

[8] Walzer, pp. viii, 115, n. 3.

and fatally insisted that their radical and chiliastic reformation must be endorsed and legitimized by the ancient liberties of England. It can even be argued that their chiliasm was part of their failure to detach themselves wholly from the secular world. The pure Calvinism isolated by Walzer was too austere, too rigid in its alienation, to need the visionary hopes of apocalyptic promise; but chiliasm was a more prominent feature of the Puritan mind than he has recognized.

There are dimensions which need to be added to Walzer's portrait, and it will appear that these are dimensions of time. In the first place, there is need to study the eschatological dimension of the saint's activism—the sacred present in which he acted, the sacred future which he expected to determine it—and this would take us all the way from Calvin's rigorous (and perhaps Augustinian) refusal of all speculation upon this question, through the steadily increasing chiliasm of the sects and the steadily increasing antinomianism which accompanied it. But it would not be sufficient to study this dimension in isolation, since we shall find that in England—apparently to a greater degree than in any other Protestant society—apocalyptic was national, a mode of envisaging the nation as existing and acting in sacred time, with the consequence that the English saint might see his election and his nationality as co-inherent: he was a saint as he was one of "God's Englishmen." But "England" remained an obstinately national and secular concept— there was no Puritan Logres, the mystical and esoteric Britain of the Arthurian romantics—and the English apocalypse, the doctrine of the Elect Nation, has therefore to be considered as, in part, a means of conceptualizing, in a complex and particular time-frame, a public realm, at once secular and godly, in which the individual, at once saint and Englishman, is to act. In these terms it becomes a mode of civic consciousness, one of those modes for whose emergence in English history we have begun to seek; and since there could be tensions—the whole history of the Cromwellian years is testimony to them—between the individual's veneration for the institutions of his Elect Nation and the radical acts which his election might call him to perform upon them, chiliasm's evident concessions to the *saeculum* become important. Since it was in part a mode of national consciousness, it could take a conservative or a radical form; and since it might pose the dilemma between conservative and radical action, it might raise the problem of innovation in a form greatly but not overwhelmingly remote from that in which Machiavelli had considered it under the heading of *virtù*. The apocalyptic mode can therefore be studied as one of those modes of secular consciousness which blurred the purity of the "revolution of the saints," and as one of those modes of civic consciousness which antedated the arrival of the classical concept of citizenship.

The problem now becomes that of exploring what further modes there were, available to Englishmen of the post-Reformation era, of conceptualizing a public realm in which they might act and modes of action appropriate to the realm thus defined. Since there is already reason to suspect that the dilemma of Cromwellian Puritanism was a dilemma between several modes of action, one of which was that of the radical saint, we may further suspect that the alternative modes, whatever they may have been, had grown up together with the last-named and were in some measure co-inherent with it. If we can trace such a growth, it will deliver us from the oversimplification apparently to be found in Hanson—in which there is nevertheless some truth— that Englishmen, denied civic consciousness by the prevalence of "double majesty," were pitchforked into it by the trauma of "double majesty's" collapse; as from the oversimplification, possessing a long and more or less Marxist pedigree, that an intensely religious consciousness of individuality was secularized into bourgeois rationalism overnight, since it had never been more than the ideology of an emergent class—though there is much evidence to suggest that rapid secularization of consciousness did occur and requires explanation. There is an interesting passage in *The Revolution of the Saints* in which Walzer, following H. G. Koenigsberger, presents revolutionary consciousness as developing in response to the "modern state's" impact upon consciousness in general;[9] but he appears to visualize this "state," very much in the romantic tradition, as a leveling, centralizing and rationalizing force, to which an appropriate response is the hardness of individual alienation. Both Walzer and Hanson, in their very different ways, seem much under the influence of the concept of "traditional society" as the inert and prepolitical antithesis of "modernization";[10] and this concept, however carefully refined, is liable to dichotomize our thinking. We have seen at considerable length that Old Western men had access to more modes of consciousness and articulation than the merely traditional; and the paradigm of "humanism," within which this book so largely operates, should suggest a similar diversity of modes of intensifying the individual's consciousness of himself in relation to the *saeculum* and the secular culture.

An impressive literature of recent historiography indicates that English humanism developed its civic awareness by projecting the image of the humanist as counselor to his prince. To the extent to which the humanist thus envisaged possessed, like Fortescue's lawyer,

[9] Walzer, pp. 1-2, 16. He refers to Koenigsberger, "The Organisation of Revolutionary Parties in France and the Netherlands during the Sixteenth Century," *Journal of Modern History* 27 (1955), 335-51.

[10] Walzer, pp. 1-4, 13-16, 19; Hanson, pp. viii-ix, 2, 7, 9, 11, 18, 336-44, 349-54.

awareness and skills which the prince did not, he was contributing to an association a virtue of his own, an individual capacity for participation in rule, and had thus taken a step in the direction of the Aristotelian image of the citizen. In *The Articulate Citizen and the English Renaissance*,[11] Arthur B. Ferguson has traced through Thomas More, Thomas Starkey, and Thomas Smith the growth of the self-image of the counselor: of his understanding of the role he played, the intellectual and political capacities he must possess in order to play it, and the public realm in which he played it, seen as an association of ruler and subjects whose relationships might be defined in terms of their reciprocal obligations to seek counsel and to give it. As Ferguson's narrative develops, there is in some respects a growing stress on association at the expense of hierarchy; the counselor is increasingly known by his capacities, on which the prince relies, and is becoming something more than a "good" subject appealing to the conscience of a "good" ruler; and words like "civic" and "citizen" become usable by Ferguson and by some of his central figures. But the community of counsel does not become a republic in the acephalous sense; "common weal" or *res publica*, it remains a *corpus* of which the prince is head, a hierarchy of degree in which counsel is given by every man sitting in his place. (Walzer points out that the image of a diversity of particular virtues was actually better preserved in the medieval hierarchy of degree than in the inscrutable individualism of the predestinarian Calvinists.)[12] In the same way, Ferguson traces how the increasing humanist ability to control secular concepts gave rise in England, as it so often did elsewhere, to an enhanced capacity to see the realm as an entity undergoing change over time;[13] but it is highly significant to note what forces he sees as setting limits to this increase. The social idealists of the mid-sixteenth century saw government—the wisdom of the prince counseled by the wisdom of the realm in parliament—as capable of legislation, and legislation as capable of bringing about a more just and a more prosperous distribution of the common weal than actually existed; the humanists who "discoursed of the common weal" dedicated themselves to an understanding of the economic forces at work in society. This thrust, however, together with what ideologies of dynamism it carried with it, was turned back in favor of the static and medieval ideal of maintaining the realm as a hierarchy of degree, a

---

[11] Arthur B. Ferguson, *The Articulate Citizen and the English Renaissance* (Durham, N.C.: Duke University Press, 1965).

[12] Walzer, ch. v, "The Attack upon the Traditional Political World," pp. 148-98.

[13] Ferguson, ch. xiii, "The Commonweal and the Sense of Change: Some Implications," pp. 363-400.

frame of order which must not be shaken; there was only one order and chaos lay outside it.

What is significant here is that Ferguson's exploration of "civic" aspects of English humanism has led us to the concepts of parliament and legislation. As we broaden our view of the different versions of civic humanism, we look for local variants of the figure of the "citizen," the *zōon politikon* who rules and is ruled. In French legal humanism and the political thought of the Wars of Religion, he seems to appear chiefly in the guise of the subordinate magistrate (whether *seigneur* or *officier*) who rules and is ruled; and we ask the question, to which Bodin returned on the whole a negative answer, whether a society of such magistrates could constitute a *polis* or community of participation. But England possessed, in court, common law and parliament, a more intensive organization of national consultation, and instead of the magistrate exercising his subordinate or derived *imperium* we meet with the more many-sided, and in that respect more civic, figure of the counselor, who may appear as the country gentleman, representing a shire or borough to counsel his prince in parliament, under a writ which enjoins him to treat of all matters affecting the realm and to serve as representative of the whole body politic, in a *commune consilium regni*. As the sixteenth-century gentry moved massively into the representation of boroughs, they moved massively into the schools, universities, and inns of court, seeking in all these an education which equipped them to serve the prince, to counsel the prince, and to compete for local office and influence in a structure of government and jurisdiction which was at once the prince's and theirs. The education they received may in a highly general sense be termed humanist, and in search for an English variant of politically active humanism, and for a humanist-derived mode of civic consciousness available to Englishmen, we may turn from the idealists of the mid-century toward the emergent ideologies of the parliamentary gentry.

Mid-century humanism had, perhaps, entertained the vision of parliament legislating for the commonweal; but by the end of the century, the gentlemen of the House of Commons more and more saw parliament's function as the preservation of liberty, and liberty as rooted in a fabric of immemorial custom with which it was possible to identify every major juridical and governmental institution, up to and including parliament itself. The ideology of the Ancient Constitution can be accounted for by means of a purely structural explanation: all English law was common law, common law was custom, custom rested on the presumption of immemoriality; property, social structure, and government existed as defined by the law and were therefore presumed to be immemorial.[14] But if we think of it as ideology, as coming into being as social creatures sought new ways of conceptualizing themselves, we can characterize it as a mode of civic consciousness particularly appropriate to a gentry asserting itself in parliament, in litigation, and in the local administration of the common law. And the word "civic" is not used inadvertently. Nothing could be more misleading than to picture the vehement assertion of the antiquity of English laws and liberties as an inert acceptance of "traditional society." It was rather traditionalist than traditional—to adopt a distinction of Levenson's[15]—an assertion of conservatism; and conservation is a mode of action. The Englishman who saw his realm as a fabric of custom, and himself as a custom-generating animal, saw proprietor, litigant, judge, counselor, and prince as engaged in a constant activity, one of preserving, refining and transmitting the usages and customs that made him and England what they were. The cult of customary antiquity was a peculiarly English brand of legal humanism, and the great Jacobean antiquaries, who asserted it as they began undermining it, were humanists of a very special sort; and, however remote from civic humanism in the republican and Florentine sense, it was, unmistakably and post-medievally, a species of civic consciousness. It defined, in traditionalist terms, a public realm and a mode of action therein.

We have seen that custom, as the origin of second nature, served as the best means of explaining what made a people and its laws uniquely and autonomously themselves; and wherever we read that a people must be governed by laws suited to its nature, it is second nature and customary law that are primarily intended. A claim to uniqueness was a claim to autonomy, and when it was asserted that there was nothing in English law and government that was not customary and autochthonous, the claim was being made that the English possessed a historical and immemorial sovereignty over themselves; they were not, and they had never been, anything which was not of their own making. More effectively even than the Henrician assertion that England was "an empire

[14] Pocock, *The Ancient Constitution and the Feudal Law*, chs. II and III.

[15] This antithesis recurs throughout Levenson's writings (above, ch. VIII, n. 54), denoting a difference to be drawn between the mere transmission of a tradition and the defensive conceptualization of either tradition or transmission. (For another elaboration of this theme, cf. Pocock, *Politics, Language and Time*, pp. 233-72.) The theme of *Confucian China and its Modern Fate* led Levenson to stress how a tradition might die when it needed to be conceptualized in traditionalistic terms; but for his comparison between China and late 18th-century England—where this did not follow—see his *Liang Ch'i-ch'ao and the Mind of Modern China* (2d ed., 1967), pp. 151-52.

and hath so been acknowledged in the world,"[16] this articulated a claim to national secular independence of the universal church. In French thought of the later sixteenth century, an affinity has been traced between Gallicanism, which asserted the jurisdictional autonomy of the church in France, and the labors of great scholars and antiquaries who used the sheer complexity of French legal and institutional history to argue that it was *sui generis* and of its own making.[17] Conceptually of less sophistication, the cult of the Ancient Constitution did the same service for the Church of England as by law established.

But the historical autonomy of England in religious affairs was asserted—as that of France was not, and as does not seem to have been the case on a comparable scale in any other Protestant nation—by means of the construction of a national apocalyptic, primarily a product of the Marian exile and classically expressed in John Foxe's *Acts and Monuments*. It seems not impossible that the conceptual origin of this English restatement of sacred history lay in the Henrician claim that England was an "empire." If Henry VIII's servants intended no more than an assertion of juridical status, nevertheless an empire must have a historical affiliation with Rome; and the figure of Constantine, born at York and playing a role in the Trojan and Arthurian legends of "Britain," was ready to hand.[18] But Constantine in his role as first Christian emperor, maker and unmaker of popes and councils, author or non-author of the supposed Donation, could also figure at the highest level of argument concerning the derivations of church and empire. He might appear as the "equal of the apostles" who had established the church as an extension of imperial authority, or he might appear as the grand apostate who had established a false church by an unwarranted abdication of that authority; and variations on both these themes were numerous and bewildering. Any or all of them, however—and sooner or later the same must be true of any interpretation of the church in terms of rival legal systems—must present the Body of Christ, or church militant, as appearing in history, and consequently must present a scheme of sacralized history for it to appear in. We are back at the point where the secular prince and the anti-Augustinian heretic might join hands; both desired to deny that the church on earth pos-

[16] Preamble to the *Act in Restraint of Appeals* (1533). R. Koebner, *Empire* (Cambridge University Press, 1961), pp. 53-55, and below, n. 18.

[17] Donald R. Kelley, *Foundations of Modern Historical Scholarship*, especially chs. VI, IX, and X.

[18] F. J. Levy, *Tudor Historical Thought* (San Marino: The Huntington Library, 1967), p. 83; he cites R. Koebner, " 'The Imperial Crown of this Realm': Henry VIII, Constantine the Great and Polydore Vergil," *Bulletin of the Institute of Historical Research* 26 (1953), 29-52.

sessed an authority derived from the unmoving celestial hierarchies and willed by God from the extra-temporal perspective of the *nunc-stans*, and both had an interest in reidentifying human salvation with human history, in order to deny that the pope possessed such an authority and to explain how he had asserted a false claim to it. But if human history and human salvation were coterminous processes, a sustained historical injustice—such as one which denied this identification—must be the work of forces hostile to salvation; and it was to become near-dogma that the pope was identical with Antichrist, the false image of Christ's return who figured in so many versions of the eschatological drama.[19] The pope's falsehood consisted not in any claim to be the returning Messiah, but in his assertion that Christ was present throughout time, in the substances of the sacrament and in the institutions of the church. Against him godly princes, upholding their purely secular authority, upheld the purity of that time in which Christ had not yet returned and it was known that he had not but would. The *saeculum* was more truly Christian than the false pretense of eternity maintained by Rome. If the new radical saints, each conscious of his own utter isolation before God and the utter uniqueness of each believer's relation with God, did not see the secular prince as exercising a Christ-like authority—some probably did—they nevertheless saw him as a witness and protector of witnesses to the truth concerning Christ's return: a judge, and at least a protector of prophets, in the new Israel.

But the growth of an English apocalyptic also stems from the circumstance that it was *England* which now claimed to stand responsible for its own acts in the drama of sacred history. In a sense, the imperial and apocalyptic mythologies were only means of projecting this new mode of consciousness. In the seminal modern study of Foxe, Haller points out—from a standpoint far removed from Walzer's—that the leaders of the Marian exiles were not alienated rebels, "but high-ranking members of a displaced hierarchy and intellectual class cherishing a real prospect of returning by legitimate means to legitimate power."[20] The sign from heaven which convinced them that their nation was elect—the death of Mary and the advent of Elizabeth—ensured their legitimate return and delivered them from resort to tyrannicide and rebellion; how far they could have been pushed toward truly revolutionary alienation, had this event been long delayed, we cannot know. The point is that it was not delayed, and that the "empire" which they saw as adversary of Antichrist and witness to the truth remained "Eng-

---

[19] William M. Lamont, *Godly Rule*; Christopher Hill, *Antichrist in Seventeenth-Century England* (London: Oxford University Press, 1971).

[20] Haller, *Foxe's Book of Martyrs* (above, ch. II, n. 22), p. 85.

land"—a complex of secular laws, secular legitimacy, and secular history. This complex occupied an apocalyptic moment and discharged an apocalyptic role; we have another illustration of the thesis that it was the secular which necessitated the apocalyptic; but there is an important difference between this and the last time we saw such a thing happen. To Savonarola the affirmation of Florence's apocalyptic role involved both an affirmation and a repudiation of the city's secular past; it was the "second nature" of the Florentines which fitted them to inaugurate the renovation of the church, but in that renovation "second nature" was to be burned away. To the legal and legitimist minds of Tudor Englishmen, renovation—if they thought of the word—was primarily a matter of recovering a rightful jurisdiction over themselves (even the saint was radically legal-minded). But a jurisdiction—especially to men disposed to think of law in terms of precedent and custom—must be rooted in a past, and that past must constantly be affirmed. Consequently, the vision of England as occupying a moment of apocalyptic election entailed the vision of England discharging a special role—largely identical with the maintenance of an autonomous jurisdiction—throughout church history. Archbishop Parker, as well as John Foxe, labored to recover the details of this history, in which Joseph of Arimathea, Constantine, King John, Wyclif, and Elizabeth all played important parts;[21] and the idea of England's uniqueness in sacred history culminates in Milton's much-quoted but quite un-John-Bullish remark that God revealed himself "as his manner is, first to his Englishmen."[22]

The English apocalyptic was therefore past-facing and, initially at least, tended toward the postmillennialist assertion that the thousand years of the devil's binding are over and the climactic struggle with Antichrist at hand, rather than to the premillennialist proclamation of a thousand-year reign of Christ and the saints, in which the renovation of all things is imminent. The former is more likely to affirm the validity of existing institutions, the latter to proclaim their imminent transcendence; two attitudes which Savonarola had brought very close together, but which here appear widely separated. The difference between them is one of choice and emphasis; the postmillennialist may still look to a reign of Christ on earth yet to come, but is frequently dramatizing his decision not to do so; but we have now returned to the point of studying apocalyptic as a mode of civic consciousness. The Elect Nation—England seen as occupying a moment and possessing a dimension in sacred history—was a theater of action, and the individual

[21] Haller, pp. 63-70, 108-109, 137-38, 149-72; Levy, pp. 87-97, 101-105, 114-23.
[22] Milton, *Areopagitica*; *Works*, IV (New York: Columbia University Press, 1931), p. 340.

was by its structure defined—as "God's Englishman" rather than simple "saint"—as acting a role therein. The modes of his action, however, could be and were defined in more than one way. As a subject of the "godly prince," successor perhaps of Constantine, who ruled the Elect Nation and preserved it against encroaching Antichrist, his action was defined as his obedience; it has been convincingly shown how, to Foxean Puritans, the sin of the Laudian episcopate was that they derogated from the prince's authority, not that they made it absolute.[23] But the uniqueness of England, and so the purity of its immunity from Antichrist, could also be defined in terms of its antiquity as a community of custom; and here the activity of God's Englishman was that of an inheritor at common law, receiving property, liberties, and customs from his ancestors and passing them on in a perpetual condition of refinement. To the men of 1628 the reaffirmation of Magna Carta and the struggle against Antichrist at home and abroad were to be much the same.[24] But finally, the activity of God's Englishman must sooner or later be defined as that of the Puritan saint; and here, a disjunction could become visible between the Elect Nation and the community of the elect. If the emphasis fell on the former, the individual's business was to obey the prince, to continue the customs, to maintain the realm; if it fell on the latter, then the elect might do what they were called to do, and the theater of political action might consist exclusively of their relations, with God and with each other, as they did it. We can easily see that God's Englishman might have to choose between acting as Englishman, as traditional political being, and as saint; but it is not certain that to see this is to see to the bottom of the problem.

It is suggested that the English apocalyptic—to which no close parallel seems to exist among the phenomena of Protestantism—developed because of the intensity of the English Protestant's involvement with the secular institutions of his realm; simultaneously Erastian and chiliastic, he saw his election as identical with his membership in a historic nation, and rewrote sacred history to accommodate his election on the only terms possible. Recent work on the fairly close connection between John Foxe and John Knox suggests that the latter had relatively little sense of historic Scottish nationality, and the apocalyptic thinking of Scots Calvinism before 1637 contains no coherent account of Scottish history as that of an Elect Nation.[25] If then it was a secular

---

[23] William M. Lamont, *Marginal Prynne, 1600-1669* (London: Routledge and Kegan Paul, 1963), pp. 15-21.

[24] See the speech of Rouse against Manwaring in Cobbett, *Parliamentary History of England*, II (1807), 377-79.

[25] Arthur H. Williamson, "Antichrist's Career in Scotland: The Imagery of Evil and the Search for a National Past," unpublished doctoral dissertation, Washington University, 1973.

commitment which impelled the Puritan saint in the direction of apocalyptic, we must see him as markedly less alienated from the social order
and its governance than Walzer at times suggests; and we must
reexamine the role in Puritan thinking of that antinomianism which
Walzer abstained from studying. Antinomianism classically arises when
the believer comes to feel that the authority of God or Spirit, exercised
directly over and within him, takes precedence over, and annuls, the
authority of some law which he formerly acknowledged as uttering
commands necessary to his salvation; in extreme cases he may symboli-
cally break the old law to signify that he has passed beyond or above it.
Christians were antinomian in respect of the Mosaic law; Joachite
Spirituals in respect of the Age of the Son and the authority of the
successors of St. Peter; and a premillennial chiliasm is almost invariably
antinomian in respect of existing forms of authority. But we think of
antinomianism, considered as a phenomenon in the sociology of religion, as a characteristic of independent sects radically alienated from
both ecclesiastical and magistratical authority; and in Anabaptists, Men-
nonites, and other sects of the Radical Reformation, there is plenty of
evidence for this phenomenon. Radical and antinomian sects of many
kinds were of course abundant in the Cromwellian phase of Puritanism,
but in general they were characterized by a greater degree of politicization, a greater willingness to advance programs of drastic secular
reform in fields such as government, law, and the distribution of property, than characterized their Swiss, German, and Dutch equivalents;
and the problem for historians has been to determine whether this
simply indicates the impact, on the relatively self-conscious and highly
governed society of England, of the difference between Calvinism and
chiliasm, between the magisterial and radical Reformations.

It has seemed possible that this was simply a difference of degree;
that the same alienation, conviction of depravity, and experience of
conversion, that led to the triumph of discipline in personalities of the
Calvinist kind, produced the triumph of the antinomian Spirit in personalities of the sectarian kind; but Walzer, in deliberately cutting off
his analysis short of the sectarians, may be hinting that a simple further
stage of extrapolation is not enough to explain the phenomena of
antinomianism. If it can be accepted, as we have been suggesting, that
the English saint was not radically alienated from the secular order,
but on the contrary radically involved in it, and that his apocalypticism
was the measure and product of this involvement, the difference
between Calvinism and chiliasm will cease to appear a simple matter of
two stages in the same sequence of alienation. The crucial moment
will be that at which God's Englishman, having initially believed that
his *nation* was elect because of the intensity of his involvement in its

institutions, comes to believe that some or all of these institutions are unworthy of the work to which the nation is *elect*. This moment has been identified by Lamont as one, frequently to be found about 1641 or 1643, at which the believer abandons the apocalyptic of Foxe in favor of that of Thomas Brightman, who declared that the Church of England was no more than the Laodicea of the third chapter of Revelations, and that the Philadelphia lay elsewhere or was yet to come.[26] This is plainly a moment of antinomianism; but the laws which the elect are now rejecting are—since the church rejected is one "by law established"—of a secular character and possess a well-known secular history which must now be reevaluated and condemned. One by one, church, monarchy, and parliament itself passed into this highly specialized limbo, and each time a new sector of English history was denied and rewritten; and while the political capacities of God's more antinomian Englishmen were bent upon the devising of new institutions to replace them, those of Englishmen of an older stamp fell back on a sullen preference for what was ancient even if it was not elect. William Prynne—again in Lamont's analysis—emerges as one who opted for the Ancient Constitution at the end of a lifelong commitment to the Elect Nation; he closed his career heroically studying Tower records in search of the origins of Parliament, while rather pathetically comparing himself to Hilkiah the high priest who "found the book of the law in the house of the Lord."[27] There was no covenant to be found in the Tower; only usage and precedent.

Radical or conservative, God's Englishmen might inadvertently secularize their thought either in asserting or in resisting a revolutionary impulse which we may now see as antinomian, the paradoxical outcome of a commitment to English institutions so complete that chiliasts would feel called to transform them even if the process made rational utilitarians of its adepts; while conservatives would abandon, in order to defend them, the apocalyptic they had taken up in order to affirm their significance. The dialectic of Ancient Constitution and Elect Nation was complex and made up of many more than two theses. But—at the cost of looking far ahead into the Civil War and Cromwellian years—we have now constructed a survey of modes of civic consciousness which we may hold in mind while exploring the origins of Machiavellian humanism in England. If there was ever a moment—some locate it under Protector Somerset midway in the Tudor century[28]—when

---

[26] Lamont, *Marginal Prynne*, pp. 59-64; *Godly Rule*, pp. 49-52.

[27] Pocock, *Ancient Constitution*, p. 159, and generally, pp. 155-62; Lamont, *Marginal Prynne*, pp. 175-92.

[28] W. K. Jordan, *Edward VI: the Young King* (Cambridge, Mass.: Belknap Press, 1968), pp. 416-26, 432-38; Ferguson, *The Articulate Citizen*, pp. 271-73.

"commonwealth" humanists might hope to use the legislative power of parliament to bring about a regime of social justice, many forces conspired to strangle it. Sheer fear of disorder compelled an obstinate adherence to the vision of England as a hierarchy of degree; the determination of the gentry to retain their established hold on land and local office ensured that, as they flocked into parliament, schools and a new expansion of consciousness, their ideology would be one which presented parliament as a court and political activity as the maintenance of a heritage of customs. The hard core of Protestants returned from exile armed with an ideology intended as much for institutionally committed Englishmen as for radically alienated saints, and sought to implement their program of radical church reform through action in parliament, inaugurating its career of claiming a political initiative even against the crown. From the use of parliament to press Puritan demands it was never possible finally to drive them, and their efforts did much both to destroy the cohesion of crown and parliament and to institute that strange partnership of antiquity-upholding gentleman and lawyer with activist and organizing saint, which was to split the Puritan mind and give it its dynamism, ensuring both revolution and the failure of revolution in the next century.

God's Englishman was a complicated animal. If there was a revolution of the saints there was also a revolution of the counselors; but what the parliamentary gentry learned from classis, congregation and common law was a technique for organizing the House into committees which could defy the Court while inventing new precedents and new claims to antiquity. This was a far cry from citizenship in the classical sense. New modes of civic consciousness and action there were in some profusion, but as yet there was no way of envisaging the political community as the sum of these interacting modes, which we have seen to be the essence of the theory of the polis. In an important sense it is true after all that post-Elizabethan England lacked a fully developed civic consciousness, and was under the thralldom of a doctrine of double majesty. The literature of debate down to 1614 and even 1649 shows that there was a highly wrought theory of kingship and authority, a highly wrought theory of privilege and custom, a religious veneration for both, and no known means of bringing them together. Yet to say that this reveals a lack of civic consciousness is less true than to say that there was an excess of it, more than the available institutional and conceptual schemes could contain. In the unheralded collapse of the forties and fifties, attempts both radical and conservative were made to restate the terms on which Englishmen as civic beings lived with one another; and in this endeavor theories of classical republicanism played their part.

[II]

Custom and grace, then—two of the three components of the model on which this book is based—served as means of explaining a highly autonomous, late Tudor England to itself and affording it images of its own particular yet continuous existence in time. We are in search of the circumstances in which it became important to make use of the model's third language of particularity: that based on the concepts of fortune and virtue, which in Florence appears to have become crucial only when republican consciousness reached a certain degree of intensity. Elizabethan Englishmen were well acquainted with these concepts, and not a few of them were diligent students of humanist political theory in its republican form—Shakespeare's *Coriolanus* could only have been played to an audience sensitive to the idea that a balanced republic was necessary to prevent the corruption of civic virtue[29]— but they were not in themselves republicans. Consequently, the enormous literature of Fortune in their historical and dramatic writings is preponderantly subservient to the theme of order; the image of the Wheel is used to warn the individual against vaulting ambition which may tempt him out of his degree.[30] This is not wholly incompatible with a classical vision of citizenship; it is possible within limits to say that the Few and the Many are estates which must stay in their due places and practice their proper virtues, and to that extent the republic and the hierarchy are one. Yet there is a radical difference between elements ranked in a descending chain and elements balanced against one another. The latter order is kinetic; the balance is maintained by the counterpressures, the countervailing activities, of the elements, and these must practice a relationship among themselves as well as each remaining fixed in its prescribed nature (or virtue). We have seen Donato Giannotti pursuing the implications of a balance of activities to the point where contradictions began to emerge. In the final, Boethian, analysis, the price to be paid for a life of civic activity was vulnerability to fortune; and the republic, being that community in which each individual was defined by his activity, was the community committed by its political form to contend against that vulnerability. States and nations, like individuals, might rise and fall as ambition condemned them to mount upon the Wheel, but only the republic obliged

---

[29] See Huffman, cited above (ch. x, n. 2).

[30] Levy, *Tudor Historical Thought*, pp. 212-25. For a concept of *fortuna* prevalent among noble houses and their dependents, very far from the Court, but not basically different from the more traditional images there prevailing, see M. E. James, *Past and Present* 48 (1970), 71-78, and 60 (1973), 52.

the individual to pit his virtue against fortune as a condition of his political being. Virtue was the principle of republics.

A corollary is that, once a political society was envisaged as a community of active beings, we should expect to find signs of the virtue-fortune polarity and—given the Europe-wide dissemination of Florentine literature—of a true understanding and sharing of Machiavelli's main concerns. But we have premised that in post-Reformation England, such a consciousness would have to contend with others—the hierarchy of degree, the community of custom, the national structure of election—which defined the individual as public actor, while fixing his activity at levels lower than that which made Machiavellian man existentially dependent on his own virtue. As long as these modes of consciousness held, it would be difficult if not unnecessary to envisage the Englishman as Machiavellian citizen or England as a Machiavellian Rome; and as long as it was presumed that the individual acted in a stable scheme of moral authority, consciousness of Machiavelli would be confined to—and would distort—the disturbing and morally subversive aspects of his thought. The distortion may be further explained by the hypothesis that his moral subversion can only be fully understood when his republicanism has been fully understood and digested. The subjects of Christian princes who raged against the wicked author of *Il Principe* were unlikely to get things in the right perspective.[31]

If we premise that a true Machiavellism is to be looked for where a political society becomes highly conscious that its *vita* is *activa* to the point of creating its own morality, it is significant that the first English Machiavellians were courtiers. Post-Reformation England was still a princely society, and the social microcosm around the prince was the milieu in which men became most conscious of themselves as actively governing beings. Ideally, a court's vision of itself was Platonic, a matter of degree and of planets revolving in their appointed orbits around a central sun; and even when it became evident that Greenwich and Whitehall were not beautiful and harmless Urbinos but restless, ruthless, and sadomasochist vortices of power, the older perspective ensured that the Wheel of Fortune remained the image of the courtier's life in a sense enduringly medieval. He fell only because he had sought to rise. But the literature also betrays a perception—which Augustine and Boethius would have understood even while repudiating—that the courtier was what he could scarcely help being. He had his *virtus*, his *ingenium*, which impelled him to act, to seek both service and power, and which exposed him to *fortuna*. The more this was realized, the

---

[31] The best account of English anti-Machiavellism is Felix Raab, *The English Face of Machiavelli* (London: Routledge and Kegan Paul, 1968).

more the court became a world with its own moral laws, and the courtier must by his nature expose himself not only to the insecurities but to the moral dilemmas of life there. A late, Caroline, expression of this awareness is to be found in the great letter written by Sir Edward Stanhope to Wentworth as the latter was resolving to take up the Lord Deputyship for Ireland.[32] But though the Elizabethan and Jacobean Court produced much memorable language articulating the loathing and fascination felt toward it, no guide or manual to the courtier's life attained to the level of political vision found in Machiavelli or Han Fei. As a political community, the court was not fully natural to man; it engaged too few aspects of too few personalities. Only the republic posed the full moral challenge.

It may be arguable that something of the politicized consciousness of the Court was transferred to the Country; that as discontented noblemen and gentlemen intensified their sense of community in parliament and the shires, England itself came to be envisaged as a commonwealth in which the relationships between the estates and the sovereign were kinetic, liable to disturbance by fortune and capable of being described in terms bordering upon the Machiavellian. But our language here must still be tentative. Older modes of expression, centered upon the medieval image of authority descending from God and defining each degree in its place, were still so strong that elements of a republican vision must be thought of as making head, slowly and piecemeal, against a prevailing stream; and when we encounter—as we do—fragments of thought which are recognizably Machiavellian, there is the further difficulty that these may have been filtered through an intervening mode of expression known as Tacitism, whose relationship to Machiavellism is ambiguous.[33] The Tacitean vision accepted the prince's authority as natural, or at least established, rather than innovative, and was thus enabled to share in the general denunciation of Machiavelli as skeptical toward authority to the point of atheism; but it focused upon the relations of courtiers, senators, and other aristocrats with a jealous and suspicious prince and was thus able to draw upon Machiavellian modes of depicting a restless and dangerous political world which, however, was part of the universal structure of authority. The Tacitean prince did well to be suspicious, since he reigned naturally and legitimately over men who were no better than the real (or fallen) world allowed them to be; yet he might not be

[32] Perez Zagorin, "Sir Edward Stanhope's Advice to Thomas Wentworth . . . ," *The Historical Journal* 7, no. 2 (1964), 298-320.

[33] Levy, pp. 237-51; Peter Burke, "Tacitism," in T. A. Dorey (ed.), *Tacitus* (New York: Basic Books, 1969).

able to resist the tendency of his suspicion to run to excess and distort the natural and legitimate functioning of his power—it was a trope that jealousy was a characteristic of tyrants. Bacon's Henry VII is a portrait of a prince who was, on the whole, successful in keeping his suspicion in check; but we are more than once told that though this king's nobles were not in terror of him, yet they did not cooperate with him more than they must.[34]

To the extent to which such language, Tacitean, Machiavellian, or other in its origins, came to be applied to the relation between the king and the estates or orders of his realm of England, the problem of stability within the realm would come to be described in terms other than those, predominantly medieval, which Tudor writers had used for dealing with the wars of Lancaster and York. In the writings of some of the most powerful—and unhappy—theoretical intellects among the post-Elizabethan courtiers, we can—subject to the above warnings—detect signs that such a thing was beginning to happen. Fulke Greville's long versified *Treatise of Monarchy* is, on the face of it, couched entirely in terms of a descending thesis of power: the king's authority is absolute, not to be resisted by men, and compared with aristocracy and democracy only to the entire disadvantage of the latter as alternative modes of sovereignty. But it exists only in response to an imperfection in the world, and that imperfection is the result of a mutation, innovation, or fall. There was a golden age "before the tymes of story," in which order maintained itself without rule by sword or scepter, but

> some disproportioned tyde
> Of times self humours hath that commerce drown'd
> To which this image showes those tymes were bound.[35]

"The tymes of story" began when men required to be ruled by a sovereign whose dread must keep them in order; and he is presented not simply as a judge, enforcing those eternal laws which men no longer obey of themselves, but a ruler practicing a manipulative statecraft, which works upon his subjects' now perplexed, fearful, and power-seeking natures in ways they do not fully understand. As an art it is arcane, because the beings on whom it is practiced are no longer wholly

[34] Bacon, "History of the Reign of King Henry VII," *Works* (eds. Spedding, Ellis, and Heath, London, 1890), VI, 242; "Of Empire," VI, 422. Levy, pp. 252-68, examines Tacitean historiography as exemplified in Bacon and Sir John Hayward. See also his introduction to his edition of *The Reign of King Henry VII* (Indianapolis: Bobbs-Merrill, 1972).

[35] G. A. Wilkes (ed.), *Fulke Greville, Lord Brooke: The Remains, Being Poems of Monarchy and Religion* (London: Oxford University Press, 1965), pp. 34 (stanza 1, line 1), 39 (stanza 18, lines 3-5).

rational, and to the extent to which the king is a man, sharing in the general depravity, it may be arcane even to him. In a fallen world, even divinely commanded authority has the character of praxis rather than of pure norm. What makes the king's power absolute is the fact of moral imperfection, and the conclusion seems inescapable that it may share in moral imperfection itself. Through the king, God commands it so; but even the king may not know why. The distance between the king as God's deputy executing his judgments and the conqueror as God's scourge executing his punishments is great but not unbridgeable; and in this context many writers and preachers were to rehearse the ambiguities of God's warnings to the Israelites when they would have a king. Greville, taking up a classical theme, explains how the "strong tyrant" will, if he is wise, rule in a manner almost indistinguishable from that of a good king[36]—a subject treated by Aristotle and disturbingly exploited by Machiavelli. But since what makes the tyrant rule virtuously is not moral wisdom and rationality, but mere worldly prudence, he does not fully understand the reason for his own virtue. We are back in the world of Machiavelli's centaur, and there is a disturbing suggestion that all kings were centaurs in the beginning— "strong tyrants" in at least half of their natures.

There is a disjunction between the king's authority and his intellect: the former is absolute because the latter is imperfect, and since the imperfection of intellect is shared by the king with all men, the authority which God commands over all fallen men is located in the individual as king only providentially and must be exercised absolutely, but at the same time only prudentially and not rationally. The way is now open to say that because the king shares imperfection of intellect with his subjects, he should take counsel of their laws and customs and of themselves in occasional and regular assemblies; but that because authority is, under God, his alone, he can never be obliged to take counsel of law or parliament and does so only because prudence enjoins it. But this is to say merely that his descending authority meets, in imperfection of intellect, with the imperfect intellects of his subjects, to pool experience and take counsel of one another; to the extent to which experience is cognate with reason, one can say that here the head and members are forming a fairly rational *corpus misticum* (if rationality can be a matter of degree at all). There is, however, a shift of emphasis, perceptible and important in the Jacobean mind, away from counsel and toward statecraft. If, at the point where king and people meet in imperfection of intellect, the people are thought of as desirous, fearful, and perplexed, the king is not only exercising a

---

[36] Wilkes, pp. 78-82 (stanzas 171-91).

thunderous authority over them, not merely pooling their experience with his prudence, but also practicing upon them arcane arts of manipulation.[37] To do this he must possess arts unknown to them; he must perhaps know things about their natures which they do not know themselves; but since it is possible to conceive that his authority is the effect of an imperfection of intellect from which he is not himself exempt, and the arts of his statecraft arcane even to him, it is also conceivable that he might, when meeting with his estates, be manipulated as well as manipulator, and the head and members engaged in a competitive exercise of statecraft upon one another. But here the Tudor passion for descending authority interposed a most effective obstacle; such a thing could be thought of only to be denounced; but we can see that if the point were ever reached where it must be admitted that the estates were practicing an active and effective statecraft of their own, and that the *arcana imperii* had become available to the few and the many, the only means of remoralising the *corpus misticum* would be to reconstitute it as a republic, in the proper sense of a partnership between different modes of virtue and intelligence. Such a republic might be seen as a response, even more effective than monarchically descending authority, to the imperfection of intellect and the disorder of time; or it might be seen as the restoration of the golden age "before the tymes of story." To the subjects of James I, however, such a conceptual—let alone actual—reconstitution of the realm was as good as inconceivable.

It was, then, possible to incorporate elements of civic and even Machiavellian thought with the dominant paradigm of monarchy. As the descending authority of the prince met with the civic capacity of the estates, these could be thought of as contributing either their experience or their activity—and as the two houses of parliament learned increasingly to take the initiative, the latter became increasingly apparent. There was an upper house embodying the nobility, a lower house representing the commonalty, and no shortage of classically based language in which these might appropriately be termed the few and the many; and there is consequently no great need to establish the first occasions on which it was said that English government associated the monarchy with the aristocracy and the democracy in ways approved by the best philosophers of antiquity.[38] So long as

[37] Hence perhaps the contemporary fascination with the moral problem of how far a king might dissimulate with an unmoral subject, short of actually lying to him. See George L. Mosse, *The Holy Pretence: A Study in Christianity and Reason of State from William Perkins to John Winthrop* (Oxford: Basil Blackwell, 1957) where Puritan and Machiavellian lines of thought are shown converging.

[38] Corinne Comstock Weston, *English Constitutional Theory and the House of Lords* (London: Routledge and Kegan Paul, 1965), pp. 9-23.

authority remained essentially with the king, however, his need to consult or even treat with the nobility and the commons remained merely prudential, and language savoring of the mixed government of Aristotle and Polybius was technically inappropriate. It was nevertheless far from unknown, and we shall see that when the monarchical paradigm collapsed and the king was forced to admit that, whether of force or of right, he shared his authority with others, terminology was already available for characterizing the government of England as a balanced relationship of king, lords, and commons.

The important point here, however, is that a normative theory of balanced or mixed government was incompatible with Tudor notions of descending authority, and that the elements of republican theory were therefore best adapted to dealing with imperfectly legitimized situations. A king was likely to appear most Machiavellian where there were fewest laws, or even *arcana*, to guide him, and where the independent wills of the upper or lower estates were most active and least guided by legitimate authority. It was consequently in the study of statecraft that Jacobean intellects were most likely to lay hold upon those elements of the republican tradition which ascribed distinctive characteristics—interests, humors, *particulari*—to kings, nobilities and peoples, and considered how these might conflict or be reconciled. The concern with secondary causes, often presented as a distinguishing mark of Jacobean historiography, might arise in this way and, to the extent that it did, would appear Machiavellian and skeptical rather than sanguine and scientific.

The most recent authority on the writings of Sir Walter Ralegh desires to exclude *The Maxims of State*—as *The Cabinet Council* was excluded earlier—from the canon of works composed by Ralegh, while conceding the possibility that it was found among his papers "et faisai[t] partie de sa documentation."[39] There is no reason to suppose the same of *The Cabinet Council*, though the latter seems to be by a contemporary and perhaps by a minor courtier;[40] but if Ralegh knew *The Maxims of State*, he knew a work in which the classical types of government, both good and bad, simple and mixed, are set out and enlarged by the distinction of monarchies into hereditary and elective, absolute and mixed, inherited and acquired by conquest, and in which means are considered for the preservation of every type and divided into "rules," which are ethically centered, and "sophisms," which are not. *The Maxims of State* alludes to Machiavelli with disapproval, but any contemporary reader would see that it was "Machiavellian" in the

---

[39] Pierre Lefranc, *Sir Walter Ralegh Ecrivain* (Paris: Armand Colin, 1968), pp. 67-70.

[40] Lefranc, p. 64.

sense that it was a work of *ragione di stato*, in which intelligence was applied to the preservation of unsanctioned as well as sanctioned forms of rule. What is striking is the amount of attention paid to the distribution of arms in ways appropriate to monarchies, aristocracies and popular states;[41] for we have learned to consider this a characteristic of works written in the Florentine tradition, where the distribution of arms was among the most important "secondary causes" of the prevalence of aristocracy or democracy, liberty or corruption; and evidence of prior theoretical study by Ralegh on this theme would be of value in explaining its prominence in *The Prerogative of Parliaments*, the most challenging and original of the political works accepted as by his hand. This dialogue between a councilor of state and a justice of the peace, both of whom have served in the House of Commons, is the first among several analyses of the disordered relations between Stuart kings and their parliaments, with which we shall be concerned because of the "Machiavellian" character of their social analysis.[42] An ironical and enigmatic quality pervades the whole work, with the councillor becoming increasingly overbearing and corrupt; and it is assumed throughout that prudence, rather than justice in the obligatory sense, enjoins the king to consult the wishes of his parliaments, aiming at keeping them attached to him while himself retaining complete freedom of action. Yet there is no need to suppose anything ironical about Ralegh's acceptance of royal authority as legitimate; he merely accepts that its nature is such that it cannot be exercised except by means that must be ironically regarded, that is to say by statecraft. The king governs by art; that is, he governs in a world which is not to be perfectly known, which is therefore mutable and a prey to secondary causes. It is in this context that we learn from Ralegh that part of the king's problems in dealing with his parliaments lies in the decay of the private military power formerly possessed by great nobles. The maintenance of arms and soldiers is now a matter for the public authority, and the public purse.[43]

Here we are without doubt looking, from one angle, at a direct awareness possessed by Englishmen of changes going on in their social and political life. Everyone knew about the wars of York and Lancaster, fought by armies which followed great magnates and overmighty subjects; and in the absence of any dominant literary paradigm to account for knowledge of retainers and "bastard feudalism," we must accept the documentary evidence which suggests that there was a true oral tradition conveying the memory of these fairly recent phenomena.

---

[41] Oldys and Birch (eds.), *The Works of Sir Walter Ralegh, Kt.* (Oxford: at the University Press, 1829), VIII, 1-36.

[42] *Ibid.*, 157-221.   [43] *Ibid.*, pp. 163, 183-85.

Down until the late seventeenth century, cases can be found of speeches and pamphlets alluding to "blue coats" and "coats and badges" in ways which indicate that the audience knew of these marks of livery which gentlemen had once worn to show their dependence upon great lords, and that it took little pleasure in being reminded.[44] But Ralegh, like others, is clearly employing the statement that magnates have lost their former military power in order to develop the general hypothesis that a change has taken place in the social and political relations between king, nobility, and people; and while this passage in *The Prerogative of Parliaments* forms part of an increasing historical awareness that England possessed a feudal past, the Florentine tradition of regarding the distribution of arms as an index to the distribution of political capacity furnishes the appropriate paradigmatic context for the growth of ideas about the significance of this past in explaining English political change. Ralegh knew his Machiavelli; and Francis Bacon, who also knew him to a degree which might have been discussed at much greater length, not only alludes—both in his *History of Henry VII* and in his *Essays*—to the emancipation of the yeomanry from military dependence on their lords, but discusses, in contexts emphasizing empire, expansion, and the greatness of states, the idea that infantry form the nerve of an army.[45] He was tapping the tradition—most authoritatively stated by Fortescue—of contrasting the sturdiness of English yeomen with the misery of French peasants, and suggesting that what made the former tough fighters also made them difficult to tax and govern without their consent;[46] but once this tradition was stated in a Machiavellian context, it must seem as if made for it.

There were, then, elements of Machiavellism in Jacobean thought: elements, that is, of a "machiavellian" account of the English polity, depicting it as a one, few and many held together by arms, statecraft, and moral ambiguity. From such an account it might not be too long a step to recommending its reconstitution on the higher (if still not unambiguous) moral level of the republic. But only the breakdown of monarchy and civil war permitted such a step to be actually taken. So long as descending authority met with ascending custom, the king's

---

[44] E.g., Andrew Marvell, *An Account of the Growth of Popery and Arbitrary Government in England* . . . (London, 1677), pp. 74-81: "It is as well known among them"—i.e., factious members of the House of Commons—"to what Lord each of them retaine, as when formerly they wore Coats and Badges." See also Henry Neville, below, p. 418.

[45] Bacon, "History of the Reign of King Henry VII," *Works*, VI, 93-95; "Of the True Greatness of Kingdoms and Estates," VI, 446-47. N. Orsini, *Bacone e Machiavelli* (Genoa, 1936), remains an important study of this relationship.

[46] Fortescue, ed. Plummer, *The Governance of England* (London: Oxford University Press, 1926), pp. 137-42.

obligation to respect the privileges of his subjects remained prudential; it was not the consequence of a division and sharing of authority between him and them. John Pym, the future leader of revolution, impeaching Manwaring in 1628 for stating the descending thesis so strongly as to suggest that the sovereign had right to every man's goods, used language which revealed this in an interesting way. He said:

> The form of government is that which doth actuate and dispose every part and member of a state to the common good; and as those parts give strength and ornament to the whole, so they receive from it again strength and protection in their several stations and degrees. If this mutual relation and intercourse be broken, the whole frame will quickly be dissolved, and fall in pieces, and instead of this concord and interchange of support, whilst one part seeks to uphold the old form of government, and the other part to introduce a new, they will miserably consume and devour one another. Histories are full of the calamities of whole states and nations in such cases. It is true that time must needs bring some alterations, and every alteration is a step and degree towards a dissolution; those things only are eternal which are constant and uniform. Therefore it is observed by the best writers upon this subject that those commonwealths have been most durable and perpetual which have often reformed and recomposed themselves according to their first institution and ordinance, for by this means they repair the breaches and counterwork the ordinary and natural effects of time.[47]

Pym's language blends hierarchy with republic. On the one hand, there is a "great chain of being" which can be thrown into disorder by the defection of any one link from its due place or degree; on the other, the chain is a "whole," its members parts and their participation far enough from the observance of a static order to be termed "mutual relation and intercourse . . . concord and interchange of support"; and the resistance of order to the naturally debilitating effects of time is to consist of a Machiavellian *ridurre ai principii*. But it is still unclear whether this is to be more than the reconstitution of the hierarchy. The language is close to suggesting that the king is one of the parts of the whole, in which case it would become necessary to specify what he, and what each other part, contributes toward the "mutual . . . intercourse" which would in turn become a partnership in shared government. But Pym does not seem to be taking this crucial step from mixed monarchy to mixed government. The language of degree guards him

---

[47] Quoted in J. P. Kenyon (ed.), *The Stuart Constitution, 1603-1688* (Cambridge University Press, 1966), p. 17.

from taking it, and the *ridurre ai principii* could consist of the maintenance of ancient custom as well as of "priority and place." He goes on:

There are plain footsteps of those laws in the government of the Saxons; they were of that vigour and force as to overlive the Conquest, nay, to give bounds and limits to the Conqueror, whose victory gave him first hope. But the assurance and possession of the Crown he obtained by composition, in which he bound himself to observe these and the other ancient laws and liberties of the kingdom, which afterwards he likewise confirmed by oath at his coronation. From him the said obligation descended to his successors. It is true they have been often broken, they have been often confirmed by charters of kings, by acts of parliaments, but the petitions of the subjects upon which those charters and acts were founded were ever petitions of right, demanding their ancient and due liberties, not suing for any new.[48]

Here is the mythology of the Ancient Constitution, in 1628 at a high tide with the great debate over the Petition of Right to which Pym alludes. But if the liberties of the subject were rooted in custom and birthright, property and inheritance—the mechanisms of antiquity—they could not arise from, or entail, any sharing of positive authority between king and people. Pym was successful enough in arguing that the king had not made, and implying that he had not granted or conceded, the liberties; but that is all which separates him from the argument to be used by Wentworth six months later, in which descending authority and ascending liberty have only degree and custom to unite them.

Princes are to be indulgent, nursing fathers to their people; their modest liberties, their sober rights, ought to be precious in their eyes; the branches of their government be for shadow, for habitation, the comfort of life, repose, safe and still under the protection of their sceptres. Subjects on the other side ought with solicitous eyes of jealousy to watch over the prerogatives of a crown; the authority of a king is the keystone which closeth up the arch of order and government, which contains each part in due relation to the whole, and which once shaken . . . all the frame falls together. . . . Verily, these are those mutual intelligences of love and protection descending, and loyalty ascending, which should pass . . . between a king and his people. Their faithful servants must look equally on both: weave, twist these two together in all their counsels; study, labour to preserve each without diminishing or enlarging either, and by run-

[48] *Ibid.*

ning in the worn, wonted channels, treading the ancient bounds, cut off early all disputes from between them. For whatever he be that ravels forth into questions the right of a king and of a people, shall never be able to wrap them up again into the comeliness and order he found. . . .[49]

The disputes were not cut off, and the questions were not wrapped up again; but only when debates of this order had become utterly unmanageable did reformulations of the English political order in either republican or Machiavellian terms become more than the expression of a private alienation like that of Ralegh. Once it was admitted that the partnership of authority and liberty had broken down, it could be admitted that government was a sharing of power in a Polybian mixed constitution, and the way was open for further conceptual explorations. But the admission was made reluctantly, by minds clinging to the vocabularies of monarchy and common law; and even after the breach was made, the minds that moved out on to the fortune-tossed waters of republican theory did so under the guidance of theologically based concepts, of casuistry and apocalyptic, which did much to prevent and divert the development of Machiavellian categories of thought. We shall see that English Machiavellism appeared—as Machiavelli's own thinking had done—in the defeat of a chiliastic revolution; but we shall also find that there was an unexpected sequel.

[49] Kenyon, pp. 18-19.

CHAPTER XI

THE ANGLICIZATION OF THE REPUBLIC

A) Mixed Constitution, Saint and Citizen

[I]

ON 21 JUNE 1642, WITH ABOUT TWO MONTHS to go before the formal beginnings of civil war, two of Charles I's advisers—Viscount Falkland and Sir John Colepeper—drafted, and persuaded him to issue, a document in which the king, not parliament, took the step of declaring England a mixed government rather than a condescending monarchy. *His Majesty's Answer to the Nineteen Propositions of Both Houses of Parliament*, as has been emphatically and correctly asserted by Corinne C. Weston,[1] is a crucial document in English political thought, and among other things one of a series of keys which opened the door to Machiavellian analysis. In essence, it asserts that the government of England is vested in three estates, the king, the lords, and the commons, and that the health and the very survival of the system depend upon maintenance of the balance between them. This drastic departure from the thesis of descending authority was both constitutionally incorrect and a disastrous tactical error in royalist polemic; but it was, in a very short time, so widely accepted and so diversely employed as to present us with a clear case of paradigmatic innovation—here, we must believe, was a new formulation of a kind for which many men had been searching for many reasons.

The crucial fact is that the crisis making civil war imminent in June 1642 could no longer be seen as arising from the collision of authority with custom, or prerogative with privilege, but from a far more disruptive series of rifts in what all could now perceive as the nerve center of English government—the conjoined authority of king and parliament. The House of Commons, having forced through much legislation against the king's wishes, were now close to claiming the right to issue ordinances without his consent; they were demanding that con-

---

[1] See above, ch. x, n. 38. The question of authorship is discussed on pp. 26-27, following Clarendon, who stressed Colepeper's role rather than Falkland's. It may be remarked, however, that Falkland was an intellectual—and a friend of Clarendon's, who disapproved of the document—and that Colepeper was not.

trol of the county militia should be placed in their hands, and that they should possess at least a veto over the king's choice of counselors. Faced with these demands, the framers of the *Answer to the Nineteen Propositions* differed from monarchical tradition, from their colleagues, and in the long run from the king himself, in their willingness to concede that the problem was not one of adjusting descending to ascending authority, but one of sharing specifiable powers, and to represent the government of England as a sharing of power. In this willingness they wrote:

> There being three kinds of government among men, absolute monarchy, aristocracy and democracy, and all these having their particular conveniences and inconveniences, the experience and wisdom of your ancestors hath so moulded this out of a mixture of these acts as to give to this kingdom (as far as humane prudence can contrive) the conveniences of all three, without the inconveniences of any one, as long as the balance hangs even between the three estates, and they run jointly on in their proper channel (begetting verdure and fertility in the meadows on both sides) and the overflowing of either on either side raise no deluge or inundation. The ill of absolute monarchy is tyranny, the ill of aristocracy is faction and division, the ills of democracy are tumults, violence and licentiousness. The good of monarchy is the uniting a nation under one head to resist invasion from abroad and insurrection at home; the good of aristocracy is the conjunction of counsel in the ablest persons of a state for the public benefit; the good of democracy is liberty, and the courage and industry which liberty begets.[2]

The king—as his adversaries remarked with glee and his friends with dismay[3]—was here made to describe himself as a part of his own realm, one of three "estates" between which there must be balance and (it followed) proportionate equality. But the implications of the language above reach farther still. Government in England is no longer a direct emanation of divinely or rationally enjoined authority; it is a contrivance of human prudence, blending together three modes of government—the only three that can exist—each of which possesses its characteristic virtues and vices (we have to remember that the words "conveniences" and "inconveniences" were far less low-keyed in seventeenth-century speech than they are now). This blend is a balance, an association in which each partner contributes its particular virtue, while

---

[2] A modernized text is in Kenyon, *The Stuart Constitution*, pp. 21-23. Cf. Weston, Appendix 1, pp. 263-65.

[3] The earlier reactions to the *Answer* are studied by Weston, pp. 27-50.

inviting the others to check its particular vice. The government of England, in short, without ceasing to manifest the element of monarchy, is being presented as a classical republic; and we catch a glimpse of Machiavelli's imagery of fortune. The three elements constitute a river, that ancient symbol of time: while it runs in its proper channel, bringing richness and fertility, the themes of order and descending grace are still being invoked; but once we hear that the balance is necessary to prevent "deluge and inundation," the river has become that of fortune, against which princes and republics erect dykes by the aid of virtue.

The framers of the *Answer* were, we shall shortly see, placing themselves in a position to appeal to the Lords against the Commons; but, with a far more lasting resonance, they were intimating that English government was a balance of the only three elements out of which government could be constructed, and that outside that balance lay only disorder. We have seen enough of republican theory by this time to know that such a balance must be one of virtues and of powers. The virtues, and the corresponding vices, of the three components have already been stated; what of the powers? From the words last quoted, the *Answer to the Nineteen Propositions* goes on:

> In this kingdom the laws are jointly made by a king, by a house of peers, and by a house of commons chosen by the people, all having free votes and particular privileges. The government according to these laws is trusted to the king; power of treaties of war and peace, of making peers, of choosing officers and counsellors for state . . . and some more of the like kind are placed in the king. And this kind of regulated monarchy, having this power to preserve that authority without which it would be disabled to preserve the laws in their force and the subjects in their liberties and properties, is intended to draw to him such a respect and relation from the great ones as may hinder the ills of division and faction, and such a fear and reverence from the people as may hinder tumults, violence and licentiousness. Again, that the prince may not make use of this high and perpetual power to the hurt of those for whose good he hath it . . . the House of Commons (an excellent conserver of liberty, but never intended for any share in government, or the choosing of them that should govern) is solely entrusted with the first propositions concerning the levies of monies (which is the sinews as well of peace as war). . . . And the Lords, being trusted with a judicatory power, are an excellent screen and bank between the prince and people, to assist each against any encroachments of the other[s], and by just

judgements to preserve that law which ought to be the rule of every one of the three. . . .[4]

It was, as we already know, a recurrent problem in Aristotelian theory to relate specific political functions to elements defined by their virtues; and in the case of English government, the problem was to prove peculiarly recalcitrant. The legislative power, being lodged in the trinity-in-unity of king-in-parliament, could not be further employed in distinguishing between the powers supposedly allotted to the three elements; and we notice how, in the passage just quoted, it is easier to state how each may check the excesses of the others than to specify just what powers the lords and commons wield. In stating that the House of Lords is "entrusted with a judicatory power," however, the framers of the *Answer*, while perhaps intending little more than an allusion to their role in impeachments, have given voice to a durable belief that the lords are peculiarly fitted to arbitrate, to trim the balance, to act as a supreme court of constitutional law or as Machiavelli's *guardia della libertà* (a Giannottian *signore* they cannot be). This in turn appears in retrospect a step toward the later theory which equated "mixed government" with "separation of powers," assigning to the lords a judicial function while seeking to separate executive, judiciary, and legislative in a way which clearly revealed how Aristotelian analysis was bedeviled by English parliamentary monarchy.

The doctrine that king, lords, and commons together constituted a marvelously equilibrated and gloriously successful distribution of powers was to be endlessly celebrated throughout the eighteenth century; but the purpose of the *Answer to the Nineteen Propositions* was minatory, not congratulatory; it was intended less to offer a new and generally acceptable theory of the constitution than to warn Englishmen that nothing but the balance of the three estates stood between them and anarchy. In language diminishingly coherent, the document goes on to warn that any surrender to the demand for parliamentary control of the king's choice of counselors will

> beget eternal factions and dissensions (as destructive to public happiness as war), both in the chosen, and in the Houses that chose them, and the people who chose the choosers, since so new a power will undoubtedly intoxicate persons who were not born to it, and beget not only divisions among them as equals, but in them contempt of us, as become an equal to them, and insolence and injustice towards our people, as now so much their inferiors, which will be the more grievous unto them, as suffering from those who were so lately of a nearer degree to themselves, and being to have redress only from

[4] Kenyon, pp. 21-22.

those that placed them, and fearing they may be inclined to preserve what they have made, both out of kindness and policy, since all great changes are extremely inconvenient, and almost infallibly beget yet greater changes, which beget yet greater inconveniences.[5]

The Machiavellian overtones are audible enough to warn us that there is more here than the familiar rhetoric of anarchy following the destruction of subordination and degree. Similarly in what follows, when we hear that

> at last the common people . . . set up for themselves, call parity and independence liberty, devour that estate which had devoured the rest, destroy all rights and proprieties, all distinctions of families and merit, and by this means this splendid and excellently distinguished form of government end[s] in a dark, equal chaos of confusion, and the long line of our many noble ancestors in a Jack Cade or a Wat Tyler,[6]

it is obvious enough who is to be frightened of whom; but this is not simply the appeal of Shakespeare's Ulysses. The king's subjects are being warned, not merely that they must observe due subordination, but that nothing stands between them and these horrors but the maintenance of a balance which men have made. To offend against degree is to offend against a divinely ordered universe, and "the powers above" may "put on their instruments" for some terrible judgment and restoration;[7] but to offend against balance may be to go out into a mindless chaos where nothing reigns except fortune and the treading of the wheel. The theory of the mixed constitution was imported into English political rhetoric in order to naturalize there the Polybian and Machiavellian doctrine of the republic, in which the virtues of all may neutralize the vices from which none is free, but which is historically fragile and may be overthrown at the slightest departure from balance. The alternative and opposite to balance is fortune and may be corruption; but there is an important difference between the Florentine and the English functions of this antithesis. The Florentines opted for the republic because it was in their nature to do so, and found fortune their enemy, virtue and balance their only defenses; but the English, monarchical and customary animals by nature, took up the rhetoric of balance and republic only because their traditional constitution was threatened by disorder in such a form—a dispute over the sharing of power— as to make this an appropriate response. In consequence older levels of rhetoric remained apparent; the language of order and degree was still outwardly dominant, and the suggestion that disorder had taken the

---

[5] Kenyon, p. 22.   [6] Kenyon, p. 23.   [7] Macbeth, IV, 3, 278-79.

form of fortune was operative but partially concealed within it. All this, as we shall next see, further concealed the naked opposition of *fortuna* and *virtù* to which the logic of republican rhetoric might otherwise have led.

If the citizen's republic collapsed about him, he might be left with his personal integrity so far bereft of social reinforcement in a world of changing particulars that only an act of divine grace might suffice to fortify him; and if this was not forthcoming, his only recourse might be to Machiavellian *virtù* or Guicciardinian prudence in their least comfortable forms. As the Englishman's Ancient Constitution collapsed about him, its fragility was indeed dramatized by presentation in a quasi-republican shape. But not only was it far from occurring to Calvinists and Arminians alike that grace might fail them; their responses were still fortified by the imageries of custom, of degree, and of a universe still both God-centered and monarchical. A simply Machiavellian response was hardly to be expected. Civil War thought is to a large degree casuist; it asks where the individual's duty lies when the legitimate authorities under which he has lived are locked in conflict; and classical republicanism, one way of projecting this problem, was not the only way of seeking to solve it.

In *A Treatise of Monarchy* (1643), the sensitive moderate Philip Hunton, taking his cue in part from the *Answer to the Nineteen Propositions*, accepted the premise that England's was a mixed government and indicated how far this was seen as a republic by alluding to the problem—raised for Florentines by the case of Venice—that there was no legislator involved in its foundation. It was marvelous to him, he remarked, that the wits of men in rude and unpolished times could have contrived so delicate a balance.[8] But when he turned to the problems of duty and allegiance raised by the breakdown of balance in civil war, he discovered that there was no ready-made answer. If constitutional law was the fruit of collaboration between three powers, among whom legitimate authority was distributed, there could be no constitutional law which directed allegiance to any one of the three in the event of conflict between them; if any one did possess such an authority, then (Hunton pushes the point far past Giannotti) it lay outside

8 Hunton, *A Treatise of Monarchy* (London, 1643), p. 44: "what ever more then humane wisedom had the contriving of it, whether done at once, or by degrees found out and perfected, I conceive it unparalleld for exactnesse of true policy in the whole world; such a care for the Soveraignty of the Monarch, such a provision for the liberty of the People, and that one may bee justly allayed, and yet consist without impeachment of the other, that I wonder how our Forefathers in those rude unpolisht times could attain such an accurate composure."

the balance and the latter could never have existed.[9] From this premise, many discussants were to draw the conclusion reached by Sir Robert Filmer (and earlier by Bodin): a mixed government was an anarchy, indeed an absurdity.[10] Hunton, writing as a casuist rather than a polemical theorist, takes another and an equally significant path. Mixed government is legitimate in England, but it has broken down. The individual is consequently without any legitimate authority in the form of positive law, to tell him how to act or what side to choose; but he is under an imperative, moral as well as practical, obliging him to act and choose. He must now employ his judgment as to the facts and his conscience as to the issues, and act as these direct him.[11] It is clear that, as to the outcome, he is in the hand of God and might almost be said to be appealing to that judge.

Hunton's argument has therefore reminded scholars[12] of the "appeal to heaven" which appears in Locke's *Treatises of Government*, some forty years later; but there are differences. In the first place, Hunton presupposes a conscience inhabiting a world of disordered legitimacy, whose fragments may be partly reassembled by a scrupulous casuistry.

---

[9] Hunton, p. 69: "To demand which Estate may challenge this power of finall determination of Fundamentall controversies arising betwixt them is to demand which of them shall be absolute: For I conceive that in the first part hereof, I have made it good, that this finall utmost controversie arising betwixt the three Legislative Estates, can have no legall, constituted Judge in a mixed government: for in such difference he who affirmes that the people are bound to follow the Judgement of the King against that of the Parliament, destroyes the mixture into absolutenesse: And he who affirms that they are bound to cleave to the Judgement of the two Houses against that of the King, resolves the Monarchie into an Aristocracie or Democracie, according as he places this finall Judgement. Whereas I take it to be an evident truth, that in a mixed government no power is to be attributed to either Estate, which directly, or by necessary consequence, destroyes the liberty of the other." See also pp. 28-29.

[10] Sir Robert Filmer, *The Anarchy of a Limited or Mixed Monarchy* (1648), in Laslett (ed.), *Patriarcha and Other Political Writings of Sir Robert Filmer* (Oxford: Basil Blackwell, 1949).

[11] Hunton, p. 73: "If it be demanded then, how this cause can be decided? and which way must the People turne in such a contention? I answere, If the non-decision be tolerable; it must remaine undecided, whiles the Principle of legall decision is thus divided, and by that division each suspends the others power. If it be such as is destructive, and necessitates a determination, this must be made evident; and then every Person must aide that Part, which in his best Reason and Judgement stands for publike good, against the destructive. And the Lawes and Government which he stands for, and is sworne to justifies and beares him out in it, yea; bindes him to it."

[12] A. H. Maclean, "George Lawson and John Locke," *Cambridge Historical Journal* 9, no. 1 (1947), 69-77, and "The Origins of the Political Opinions of John Locke," unpublished Ph.D. dissertation, Cambridge University, 1947.

If the conscience seeks to assess the political situation and its immediate past history, it must employ the methods of political and moral prudence to determine what has happened, what might have happened, and what should be done now; and since this presupposes objective standards of morality and law, the conscience is as far from Machiavellian *virtù* in one direction as it is from Locke in another. But in the second place, heaven has not made its will known by prior endorsement of any specific form of authority,[13] so that the individual, taking his stand on conscience in the midst of civil war, may well be appealing—whether or not he draws the sword himself (Hunton goes on to propose means of reconciliation)[14]—to *jus gladii* or *jus conquestus*, to the judgment of heaven as expressed in the outcome of a trial by battle. There was an extensive contemporary literature of this appeal procedure, which Hunton does not use, but to which we may refer at this point. Should the verdict go against him, he may conclude that he has been proved wrong; but if his conscience still assures him that he made a justified choice, he may reflect that the judgments of providence are too deep to be found out. The conquering sword, for its part, may go so far as to claim not only a providential, but a prophetic and apocalyptic authority for what it does with its victory.[15]

Locke's appeal to heaven is an appeal to the sword, but it is lodged by a people, not by a congeries of individual consciences. Hunton clearly does not think of the people as in any way incorporated except by the orders of the republic, or mixed government, which have now broken down and left each man on his own.[16] The republic, we observe, is no covenant, uniting a people by making them one with God, nor is it a social compact incorporating them by rational and non-Sinaitic processes; it is a human construct, blending imperfect elements into an equilibrium, and for Hunton it is a conservative and legitimating device as well. After it comes conscience; but if the people had in any prior sense been incorporated, the appeal to heaven would have been predetermined. Henry Parker, the most formidable parliamentary apologist of the First Civil War,[17] exploits every opportunity offered him by the *Answer to the Nineteen Propositions* to show that royal authority, being coordinate, is not preeminent; but when he comes to the question of where the individual's allegiance is to lie in

---

[13] Hunton, p. 4. [14] Hunton, pp. 77-79.

[15] For this see John M. Wallace, *Destiny His Choice: The Loyalism of Andrew Marvell* (Cambridge University Press, 1968), pp. 22-28.

[16] Hunton, p. 73 and above, n. 11.

[17] On him see W. K. Jordan, *Men of Substance: A Study of the Thought of Two English Revolutionaries, Henry Parker and Henry Robinson* (Chicago University Press, 1942).

civil war, he argues that the people are indissolubly incorporated in parliament. There is, says Parker, a "reason of state" which must be kept entirely distinct from anything in Machiavelli (he seems to have thought that Machiavelli had propounded a doctrine under that name). This is nothing other than the natural and rational impulse of any body of persons to become a body politic, or state; it is "reason" of state because for men to act rationally is to act politically; and on the premise that parliament represents the people, their will to be a people can be expressed nowhere but in that body.[18] The individual in time of civil war, then, need not consult his conscience and appeal to the arbitrament of providence. He need only consult his reason, which will direct him to incorporate himself in parliament.

An Aristotelian populism of this kind could plainly have the effect of disrupting mixed government altogether and substituting a democratic sovereignty; but, as with other Civil War writers,[19] the question arises whether Parker had a normal or an emergency sovereignty in mind. He might, that is, have thought of mixed government as sufficiently descriptive of the normal state of affairs, and have regarded "reason of state" simply as that which came into play when the norms had collapsed and the state was obliged to reconstitute itself, reasserting as it did so its claim to the allegiance of individuals. "Reason of state" in that sense would be a far cry from the intelligence of Lycurgus or any Machiavellian *ordinatore*; Parker is no kind of classical republican; but it would accord interestingly with the possibility that, like Hunton, he accepts the mixed constitution in order to say that when it collapses, the individual is alone and must move to reorder his life by the discovery of something in himself. In Hunton's scheme this is conscience; in Parker's a predetermined political rationality; but from "reason of state" it is a short step to *salus populi suprema lex*,[20] a formula whose implications might easily appear premoral. Before moral norms could exist, it might be said, *res publica, populus* or *status* must exist; consequently the first command of reason was that something by one of these names should be, and its institution could not be carried out by acts subject to the norms which it alone could commend. This thought of course lay behind all that Machiavelli had had to say about

---

[18] Parker, *Observations upon Some of His Majesties Late Answers and Expresses* (1642), pp. 15-16, 22-24, 34. For his denunciations of Machiavelli, see pp. 2, 10, 19, 20.

[19] E.g., Prynne; see Lamont, *Marginal Prynne*, 85-118.

[20] Parker, *Observations*, pp. 3-4: ". . . the transcendent of all Politiques . . . the Paramount Law that shall give Law to all humane Lawes whatsoever, and that is *Salus Populi. . . .* The Charter of nature intitles all Subjects of all Countries whatsoever to safetie by its supreme Law. . . ."

the nonmoral imperatives laid upon the legislator; but we are upon a rather different path here. The individual, assailed by civil war and seeking to reconstitute his allegiance, is no legislator, since his aim is to subject himself to authority rather than to found and rule a city; but he may visualize himself as forced back into a prepolitical and premoral situation, seeking that in himself which will reestablish order. The entity whose *salus* is *suprema lex* is now not *populus* but ego; he may make a Cartesian discovery that his first movement as an active being must be to assert and perpetuate himself, or a Christian and Calvinist discovery that, having been created to an end unfixed by him, by a being of whom he knows nothing, his first duty is to preserve himself to that end. He may now locate himself in a state of "nature," antedating society, covenant or revelation, and seek means of constituting an intelligible authority-structure, starting with nothing more than a primal impulse and duty to preserve himself. If he follows this path, he is less likely to emerge as Lycurgus establishing a republic than as the natural man erecting and obeying an artificial Leviathan.

Hobbes, not an English Machiavelli, is the radical master of Civil War political thought; the English individual, when stripped of all protection and legitimation and reduced to the extreme of prepolitical dereliction, was liable to establish himself in the state of nature, not under the dominion of fortune. This is in a sense an index to his resourcefulness, and to the difficulty of stripping him of all means of self-legitimation; but the important difference between Hobbesian and Machiavellian man is that the state of nature is ahistorical and logically timeless, whereas every moment on the rotating wheel forms one of a sequence in time. The *anakuklōsis* is wholly secular and time-bound, and nowhere intersects the state of nature; this indeed was a principal reason for deeming it atheistic; but the recourse to the state of nature—capable though it was of being described in terms which struck contemporaries as close to atheism—was a movement out of time, followed by a return to politics and history. Only by invoking a prophetic God could Hobbes make it clear that every moment, even the moment of nature, was in history.[21] But the complex armory of ideas that takes shape along the line leading from Parker to *Leviathan* provides yet another set of reasons why the individual isolated by the collapse of the mixed constitution need not define himself in terms of a Machiavellian polarity.

Mixed government—the term which rendered it possible for the king's subjects to accept the republican tradition—was supposed to

[21] *Leviathan*, Books III and IV. See Pocock, "Time, History and Eschatology in the Thought of Thomas Hobbes," in *Politics, Language and Time*, pp. 148-201.

ensure stability by setting up an equilibrium of virtues and powers. The enemy of balance was fortune, and the enemy of fortune was virtue; in this case, one would expect, the virtue of respecting the virtue of other parties to the equilibrium. But the paradigm of mixed government, though it defined the moment of breakdown as one of individual isolation and dereliction, did not oblige the individual to define that moment in terms of fortune and virtue. In the first place, there were too many alternative vocabularies. Hunton's moment, of conscience and the appeal to heaven, was capable of being developed in the direction explored by John M. Wallace,[22] in which a prudential submission to the will of providence rose to heights of sophisticated and latitudinarian piety; Parker's moment, of reason of state and *salus populi*, in the direction explored by Quentin Skinner, where prudence and providence gave way to the radical naturalism of Hobbes.[23] Others, like William Prynne, dealt with the problem by pitting Ancient Constitution against Elect Nation, and did not employ a quasi-republican rhetoric at all. In the second place, it may well seem that the individual who saw the Civil War as posing a problem in casuistry and allegiance would not affirm his virtue in terms strong enough to expose it immediately to fortune; virtue, when all is said and done, is an ideal of action, not merely of legitimation. To understand how the classical ideal of the citizen came to play its role in Interregnum thinking, we have still some way to go and must travel a route of utterances less apologetic and more activist; but the irreducible conservatism of the period will continue to have something to say to us.

[II]

Robert, Lord Brooke, encouraging his officers in 1643 to appear in arms against the King in the name of king and parliament, referred to "that great commonwealthman of the Romans, Cicero,"[24] and such words as "commonwealthman" and "patriot" were indeed used now and again to denote those who could think of king, parliament, and

[22] Above, n. 15.

[23] Skinner, "Hobbes's *Leviathan*," *Historical Journal* 7, no. 2 (1964), 321-32; "History and Ideology in the English Revolution," *ibid.* 8, no. 2 (1965), 151-78; "The Ideological Context of Hobbes's Political Thought," *ibid.* 9, no. 3 (1966), 286-317, and revised version in Cranston and Peters (eds.), *Hobbes and Rousseau* (New York: Doubleday Anchor Book, 1972), pp. 102-42; "Conquest and Consent: Thomas Hobbes and the Engagement Controversy," in G. E. Aylmer (ed.), *The Interregnum: the Quest for Settlement, 1646-1660* (London: Macmillan, 1973), pp. 79-98.

[24] Robert E. L. Striver II, *Robert Greville, Lord Brooke* (Cambridge, Mass.: Harvard University Press, 1958), p. 68.

people as forming a polity in which any part might be resisted and restrained in the name of the whole. But such language, though observably classical in its connotations, was hindered in its development by those other styles of thought we have been studying; there are clearly many grains of salt to be taken with Hobbes's opinion that republican principles, imbibed at the universities and from Greek and Latin histories, helped dispose men's minds to civil war.[25] We have next to look at the languages prevalent in the great radical movements of the late 1640s; and here the crucial utterances are of course those to be found in the manifestos of the officers and soldiers of the army. In these a body of men of diverse social origins, having in common that they had been mobilized into a military society which had just won a civil war of an unprecedented kind, declared themselves to be self-motivated and self-reliant in matters both civil and religious. They were, they said, "not a mere mercenary army, hired to serve any arbitrary power of a state," but were "called forth . . . to the defence of our own and the people's just rights and liberties."

> And so we took up arms in judgment and conscience to those ends, and have so continued them, and are resolved according to . . . such principles as we have received from your [parliament's] frequent informations, and our own common sense, concerning these our fundamental rights and liberties, to assert and vindicate . . . those common ends premised, against . . . all particular parties and interests whatsoever.[26]

These men, declaring a common sense that the arms they had taken up had engaged them to a common end, were declaring a political self-consciousness of a kind unheard of in England before. To do so was a revolutionary act, and it is not surprising that the documents employ and transcend every political language available to Englishmen in the attempt to make their statement. There is, for example, the appeal to ancient liberties, radicalized by the imputation that these have not been inherited, as the doctrine of the Ancient Constitution maintained, but have on the contrary been lost, since early but not forgotten times, and must now be restored.[27] There is the appeal to *salus populi suprema lex*, but we shall penetrate deeper into the character of radical thought

[25] Hobbes, *Behemoth* (ed. Tonnies, London, 1889; repr. London, Frank Cass, 1969), pp. 3, 23, 43.

[26] *A Representation of the Army* (14 June 1647); Woodhouse, *Puritanism and Liberty* (London: E. J. Dent, 1950), pp. 403-404.

[27] To neglect this distinction, as is still sometimes done, is to confuse the Ancient Constitution with the Norman Yoke; for the latter, see Christopher Hill, *Puritanism and Revolution*, pp. 50-122. Cf. *The Ancient Constitution and the Feudal Law*, pp. 125-27.

by citing a document in which this is made in a very different spirit from Parker's; the purpose being now not to make some ultimately conservative appeal to an irreducible principle of legitimation, but to assert that a people is itself and acts as itself before God.

> For God hath given no man a talent to be wrapped up in a napkin and not improved, but the meanest vassal (in the eye of the world) is equally obliged and acceptable to God with the greatest prince or commander under the sun, in and for the use of that talent betrusted to him. . . . For, Sir, should you [Fairfax]—yea, should the whole parliament or kingdom—exempt us from this service, or . . . command our silence or forbearance, yet could not they nor you discharge us of our duties to God or to our own natures. . . . And if by any one your Excellency should be suborned that we are transgressors of all order and form, and in that sense to look upon us, we desire to mind your Excellency that the law of nature and of nations, attested in our public declarations and papers, may be an answer to such for the justification of our present expedient. For all forms are but as shadows, and subject to the end. And the safety of the people is above all forms, customs, etc.; and the equity of popular safety is the thing which justifieth all forms, or the change of forms, for the accomplishment thereof; and no forms are lawful longer than they preserve or accomplish the same.[28]

Here "the safety of the people" is no premoral principle of socialization (as in "it is expedient that one man die for the people"). With the words "all forms are but as shadows," an appeal to "the law of nature and of nations" moves out into the language of apocalyptic *rinnovazione*. One is not merely obliged to preserve one's self, as created to an end; the emphasis is transferred to the end itself and to the "talent" which must be employed in pursuing it. And many readers of these words would interpret "the safety of the people" as indicating not merely the material preservation of the community of end-pursuing creatures, but the continued pursuit of that historic end to which a peculiar nation was elect. "All forms are but as shadows" is the language of apocalypse; it suggests that all earthly things shall pass away before the end; it is potentially antinomian, since it may very well indicate that the types are exhausted; and yet it is still Aristotelian in a way that would have made it intelligible to the Thomist Savonarola. The context in which men attain their final end—or recover their *prima forma*, though this concept might not have been antinomian

---

[28] From the letter to Fairfax, signed by eleven Agitators, accompanying *The Case of the Army Truly Stated* (Oxford, 1647); see Woodhouse, p. 437n.

enough for the radical saints of the New Model[29]—is that of apocalypse; the "end" of Aristotelian teleology is still united with the eschatological "end" of prophetic time.

Applying the mode of analysis adopted in the preceding section of this chapter, one might argue that the radical saint was reacting to the same situation as Hunton and Parker. Bereft of all traditional structures of legitimation, Hunton had appealed to conscience and to heaven; Parker had moved in the direction of a pre-Hobbesian naturalism; and it would have been theoretically possible for a Machiavellian to appeal to the confrontation of *virtù* with *fortuna*. Our model suggests, however, that alongside the moments of fortune, of nature and of providential judgment, we may detect—almost as an extension of the last-named—the moment of apocalyptic grace; army radicalism, then, would be responding to a moment of acute particularity by adopting one of a limited range of languages by which such a moment might be met. But it is fairly clear that such an explanation would not be adequate. Apocalyptic conviction in the men of the army had helped (like the *virtù* of Machiavelli's new prince) to create the situation which intensified the need for it, and was operating as an independent variable. It presents us with a case, not simply of minds seeking to regularize a delegitimized and chaotic situation, but of a new level of civic consciousness finding means of becoming articulate. The sense of a calling peculiar to the Puritan saint had operated to give these soldiers a sense of the irreducible personality—the "talent" or "nature"—inherent in each one of them. This could be expressed in terms of each man's unique relation, accountability, or duty to God, and also in terms of the radical equality of rights and powers which had been given to each to enable him to perform that duty. So far the Walzerian analysis holds good; and it continues to hold when we add that the calling, as an act of grace, must be thought of as operating upon the individual in time, and that time conceived in such terms must be conceived prophetically or apocalyptically. But if we add, along the lines suggested in the previous chapter, that the English saint was—at the opposite extreme from being alienated from his inherited laws and liberties—involved in them to the point where his calling did not liberate him from them, but liberated him to transform them, a great many points in the analysis will become clear. We can now understand why he felt himself called to restore those liberties to their original form, while insisting that what that original form had contained was the freedom of a people to be both naturally and apocalyptically them-

[29] A thorough antinomian might hold that the state of redeemed man would be higher than that of the unfallen Adam, not a mere recovery of it; see the article by Rosenmeier cited above, ch. i, n. 5.

selves. We can see how the individual's conviction of a radically free natural capacity within himself intensified his ability to engage in radical action based upon radical criticism of his laws and liberties in their inherited form; the Agreement of the People was the antinomianism of the Ancient Constitution. Lastly, we can see that, while we are not yet at a Machiavellian moment in English thought, we are at something comparable to the Savonarolan moment, at which civic consciousness, apocalyptic conviction, and inherited second nature were in a complex relationship. The prophets, furthermore, were armed; they had only to continue to believe in themselves.

The radicals of 1647 may therefore be thought of as standing at a moment—whether one at which a true millennium seemed imminent or, more spiritually, one at which some liberation amounting almost to divinization of human capacities seemed to be taking place—of freedom triumphing over necessity. Where the casuists of allegiance had come in some cases to a timeless moment from which authority could and must be reconstituted, the illuminists of liberty had come to an apocalyptic moment, at which their swords and spirits appeared at the point of remodeling the laws and reinstituting freedom. But at Putney[30] there came to a head their debate with their own commanders, who desired to tell them that they still stood within a structure of continuing necessity from which they were not altogether free to move, and that to be so located was inseparable from the condition even of the saint (as it had necessitated Machiavelli's prophet to bear arms). Ireton, backed by Cromwell, insisted that there must be engagements which no inner conviction entitled men to break, and that there must be structures of positive law, against which the "law of nature" was not a sufficient plea. His chief reason for saying this, he declared, was that the law of nature might decree that each man should have his own, but could not determine what was to be each man's.[31] Property, an affair of particulars—Harrington was to call it "the goods of fortune"—must be distributed by human decisions, not by universal principles.

> The Law of God doth not give me property, nor the Law of Nature, but property is of human constitution. I have a property and this I shall enjoy. Constitution founds property.[32]

The individual—Ireton was declaring—must be defined by human society if the latter was to exist; law and property must give him his social rights and personality if law and property were to have any security at all—and without them, what would he be? Yet the social institutions which made men what they were must themselves be of

---

[30] The full text of these debates is to be found in Woodhouse.
[31] Woodhouse, pp. 54, 58, 60, 63.   [32] Woodhouse, p. 69.

human creation; and consequently the individual must be born into, and obliged to, a structure of human law which was not of his making. Since this was England, property and custom supplied the answer to the problem of how this might be achieved. The fabric of common law, within which each man lived and moved and had his being, was a structure defining modes of holding, inheriting, and transmitting land in terms of immemorial custom; and the only individual Ireton would admit to civic participation was one who had inherited—or had acquired the means of bequeathing—a minimum of land in freehold tenure. If it be true, as is contended,[33] that the Levellers meant to exclude from the franchise those who were so far propertyless as to live as servants in other men's houses, that does not bridge the gap between Ireton and Rainborough. For Ireton the land must be freehold, or at least assimilable to the legal concept of freehold tenure;[34] it must be capable of being conceived of as an inheritance at common law, which was itself an inheritance of customs from time immemorial, since there was no other way of anchoring the individual, from birth and at the moments of majority and inheritance, within a structure of law and property he could be obliged and committed to defend.[35] Sir Robert Filmer, inconspicuous in Kent, was working out a way of achieving the same denial of natural liberty by means of a theory of patriarchalism;[36] but Ireton's argument was by far the more widely intelligible.

It should be stressed that the necessity being imposed upon the individual is in an important sense more formal than specific: an obligation to respect *some* system of law and property, rather than *the* specific system now obtaining. Ireton was capable of conceiving and designing far-reaching and extremely intelligent plans of reform,[37] and the social structures which defined men were, as we have seen, themselves to be man-made. But his insistence on an inheritable freehold, a "permanent interest," qualifying the individual for citizenship by committing him to an inherited structure of obligations, is strong evidence that in the last analysis he desired to anchor the individual in custom, in a law made by men indeed, but by men who could not be identified. His arguments at Putney suggest the ideological explanation of why, a year and a half later, he rejected one of the few opportunities for revolutionary action ever afforded an English statesman. To purge parlia-

---

[33] E.g., by C. B. Macpherson, *The Political Theory of Possessive Individualism* (Oxford: The Clarendon Press, 1962), pp. 107-59.

[34] Woodhouse, pp. 57-58.   [35] Woodhouse, pp. 66-67.

[36] See Laslett's introduction to his edition; above, n. 10.

[37] E.g., the *Heads of the Proposals*; Kenyon, pp. 302-308, but the full text in John Rushworth, *Historical Collections of Private Passages of State* (London, 1659-1701), VIII, 731-36.

ment, instead of dissolving it and calling for elections on a new franchise, was to admit that the army—as led into political action by the senior officers—would always demand legitimation by elements of the traditional constitution, and was purging the House of Commons with no other end than to get a House of Commons which would legitimate its actions.[38] Such an attitude issued logically enough from Ireton's mode of arguing that social structures, laws, and institutions were prerequisite to the political wills of men.

Because the revolution of 1648-1649 had this unfulfilled character, its apologetics took the form of a justification of departure from existing ways—something for which revolutions seldom find it necessary to apologize. A main theme, for instance, of the declaration which the Rump Parliament published following the King's execution, was that the monarchy had failed—not just in the recent crisis, but throughout its history—to provide England with political stability;[39] and since it was necessary in addition to justify the abolition of the House of Lords, this could easily become an argument that the mixed constitution of the *Answer to the Nineteen Propositions* had failed in the purpose for which balanced governments were designed and must be replaced by a better one. A vehemence of feeling against a hereditary or entrenched aristocracy, moreover, remained part of the content of army radicalism and outlived the Leveller decline. But the defensive tone of the Rump's declaration points toward that of the main theoretical debate of 1649 and the years following: the so-called Engagement controversy,[40] which reveals to us the diversity of directions in which Independent thought must go, once deprived of radical conviction. For the Engagement was little more than an undertaking to be obedient to the government as at present constituted, and the complex and important controversy that ensued was concerned with the problem of granting obedience to a government *de facto* but not *de jure*—one possessed of effective power rather than legitimate authority. In short, the casuist search for authority was now resumed, and it is testimony to the enduring strength of English conservatism under catastrophic conditions that so colorless a theme produced so much thought of major importance.

[38] Kenyon, p. 294; David Underdown, *Pride's Purge* (Oxford University Press, 1971).

[39] *A Declaration of the Parliament of England, Expressing the Grounds of their Late Proceedings, and of Setling the Present Government in the way of a Free State* (London, 22 March 1648/9), pp. 6, 14, 17; for the Lords, p. 20. See also *The True Portraiture of the Kings of England . . .* (London, 1650).

[40] For this see Wallace (above, n. 15) and Skinner (above, n. 23), and Wallace, "The Engagement Controversy, 1649-52: an annotated list of pamphlets," *Bulletin of the New York Public Library*, 68 (1964), 384-405.

An analysis of the tangled strategy of this debate will carry us in the direction of Hobbes, but it will also furnish us with some of the conditions for a revival of Machiavellian and republican solutions.

Both in theory and in the actual conditions of 1649, rule *de facto* was rule by the sword. To all participants in this debate, the problem to be confronted was that of establishing the exact conditions under which government by human law had broken down and given place to government by human power, and in so doing to determine the modes in which power might be seen as supplying its own justification. The simplest and most obvious strategy was the appeal direct to providence: God's inscrutable will had brought these things to pass, and it was not for his creatures to resist his instruments. But not only was this argument vulnerable to a number of counterattacks; to the highly and diversely articulate minds of the time there were too many tempting directions in which it might be further developed. It was, for instance, no more than a single step from the providential to the prophetic; Cromwell, who repeatedly averred that he could not have put his hand to the work if he had not felt himself called to it, was surrounded by men anxious to interpret his and their roles in the context of prophecies about to be fulfilled and an apocalypse or millennium about to occur. But it is noteworthy—and typical of that divided mind in the saints which was discussed earlier—that, as his power mounted after 1653, Cromwell declined to see himself as any specific actor in the eschatological scenario and repeatedly insisted that his power was but that of a constable; thus marking, in Lamont's opinion, the definitive transition from godly (in the Foxean sense) to "godless rule."[41] The Protector himself was willing to acknowledge by implication that his authority was *de facto* rather than *de jure prophetico*; the rhetoric of Davidic kingship, with its shadowings of types to be renewed, might cling to him nevertheless;[42] but his attitude does much to explain why the doctrine that the saints, expecting Christ, now ruled in England remained the asseveration of a minority.

De facto argument, strictly speaking, could never adopt the full apocalyptic perspective and remain itself. Apocalyptic had grown antinomian in its willingness to proclaim that all human authority was, or soon might be, overturned and a true *regnum Christi* at hand; and it was only on the assumption that this was not the case, that the downfall of the old and the erection of the new government had occurred

---

[41] Lamont, *Godly Rule*, ch. 6, pp. 136-62.

[42] J. A. Mazzeo, "Cromwell as Davidic King," in *Renaissance and Seventeenth-Century Studies* (New York: Columbia University Press, 1964), pp. 183-208, and Wallace, *Destiny His Choice*, ch. 3, pp. 106-44. The discussion turns on the interpretation of Marvell's Cromwellian poems.

within continuing human time, that the problem of the Engagement was worth debating at all. The appeal to providence was the first move in a strategy for dealing with time; but if the event were not apocalyptic, it would not be unique and would form one of a class of revolutions occurring from time to time—Ascham's *Confusions and Revolutions of Government* is a key title, as well as an important text, of this controversy.[43] If governments fell from time to time, how was authority restored; or, in different yet familiar language, what was the nature of the individual's obligation in this predicament? In a brilliant and patient exploration of the richly textured thought of Andrew Marvell, John M. Wallace has demonstrated that the providential perspective was far from being exhausted at this point; it was possible to develop, with the wealth and complexity of poetic genius, a sense of the individual's implication in events to whose very ambiguity he owed a certain *pietas*; but, in accepting this interpretation of Marvell, it remains important to notice what languages spin off, as it were, at lower levels of his thought and other men's, to express the idea of a radical fracture of legitimacy. If such fractures occurred with any regularity in human affairs, it would follow that every government might be traced to a time when it had been founded not in right but in the sword; and the assertion that all are indeed radically unjust at the outset is found expressed—by Anthony Ascham and Marchamont Nedham among others—in terms which seem at last unmistakably Machiavellian. "This is that circle we so painfully move in," wrote Ascham,[44] alluding plainly enough to the Polybian *anakuklōsis*, though he did not go on to propose either a legislator or a republic as the way out of the pain of which his writings are full; a combination of providence and nature continued to dominate his thinking. Similarly, Marvell—though Wallace's analysis indicates that this is only one dimension of his vision—introduces into his *Horatian Ode* a number of no less unmistakable images of Cromwell as a Machiavellian prince-legislator akin to Romulus in the necessary illegality and ruthlessness of his proceedings, and into his *Ode on the First Anniversary of the Government under . . . Cromwell* a portrait of Oliver as both a Davidic restorer of prophetic authority and a classical legislator capable of bridging the instabilities of time in a single creative act.[45] David, it is worth recalling, is not

[43] For Ascham, see Wallace, *Destiny His Choice*, pp. 30-38, 45-48, 54-58.

[44] *Confusions and Revolutions* (2d ed., 1649), pp. 73-74. Cf. Nedham, *The Case of the Commonwealth of England Stated* (1650), ed. Knachel (Charlottesville: University of Virginia Press, 1969).

[45] Mazzeo, "Cromwell as Machiavellian Prince in Marvell's *Horatian Ode*" and "Cromwell as Davidic King," *op.cit.*; Wallace, *Destiny His Choice*, chs. 2-3; Felix Raab, *The English Face of Machiavelli*, pp. 144-46; Pocock, "The Onely Politician" (above, ch. x, n. 1), pp. 284-85.

unlike Romulus in the ambiguities of his relationships with Saul before his anointing and with the sons of Zeruiah after it; there were points at which the Machiavellian and the prophetic perspectives lay not far apart.

But the moment of the sword, while it could be occupied by prince, legislator or prophet—all types appearing in Machiavelli's gallery—could also be occupied by figures normative in quite another way; we have already seen something of this while treating of Henry Parker. In *jus gentium* it was possible for a conqueror to intervene at this moment, bearing his sword as proof of the judgment of heaven in his favor, so that it was forbidden to oppose him however violent and extralegal his behavior. The type of this conqueror was not William the Norman so much as Nimrod of the Bible, the primeval despot whose power was not unwilled by God;[46] but to Nedham and other writers the *jus conquestus* could be seen as in the possession of the army collectively, those Englishmen in arms whose conquest proved both their natural and their providential right to rule in circumstances such as these. From this point a single step would of course equate the conquerors with the saints; but another, in a different direction, would lead to *salus populi*, reason of state and the state of nature, in the way which we have already studied and which Skinner, in a series of essays, has shown to be the crucial breakaway from the providential strategy of the *de facto* controversy at its outset[47]—crucial because it supplies the context in which Hobbes completed, published and at one level of perception must have intended *Leviathan* (1651). This work was the most radical portrayal, among all those which appeared during the revolutionary years in England, of the human individual existing at a moment of near-total delegitimation and artificially recreating authority from a state of dereliction; it differed altogether in structure from the Machiavellian vision and may seem to have reduced the latter's role in English thinking to one of secondary importance.

It can be seen, however, that *de facto* argument heightened the importance of some elements of Machiavellism; the prince, the legislator, and the cycle can be observed emanating, so to speak, from the moment of the sword; but the republic was not to reassert itself—as in theory it might have done—simply as a *de facto* device of stabilization. It is one of the more interesting discoveries in all this long story that the classical republic made its appearance in English thought as an activist ideal, at a point where the *de facto* "moment of the sword"

---

[46] For these different types of conqueror, see Wallace, *Destiny His Choice*, pp. 22-28, 98-102, 132-34.

[47] Above, n. 23.

came into contact with the radicalism of the army, whose half-realized revolution had precipitated the conceptual and political problem in this form.

A speaker at Putney opposed to the Levellers—Colonel Nathaniel Rich, afterwards a somewhat conservative fifth-monarchist and yet a foe to the Protectorate—had attacked the proposal to give votes to the poor, not only on the ordinary grounds that they would use their power to abolish all property, but also with the rather more realistic argument that to do this would be to give undue weight to a few great men on whom the poor would assuredly be dependent. This had happened at the end of the Roman republic, he indicated, and it would be no use pulling down the king to set up an emperor in his place.[48] The importance of Rich's speech is that it reveals the presence, in the mind of at least one officer, of that classically derived association between republican liberty and a popular army which we have found as a standard theme in Florentine thought, although his attitude toward the prospect is indeed more negative than positive. We now know, however, that it was not beyond the resources of the army's vocabulary to justify their intervention in political affairs by presenting themselves as "no mere mercenary army," but a body of free citizen-soldiers, a claim which, if made in sufficiently Machiavellian terms, would entail the transformation of England into a popular republic. Such was not the language of Sexby and Rainborough, but it is possible to find a time and place, after the suppression of the Levellers, when such an ideology w˙ energetically disseminated by a writer well placed to reach a wide audience.

The writer in question was none other than Marchamont Nedham,[49] the journalist who shuffled the dominant concepts of the Civil War and Rump years with a brilliance if anything enhanced by what seems to have been a signal lack of sincerity or consistency. He won release

[48] Woodhouse, p. 64: "I remember there were many workings and revolutions, as we have heard, in the Roman Senate; and there was never a confusion that did appear (and that indeed was come to) till the state came to know this kind of distribution of election. That is how the people's voices were bought and sold, and that by the poor; and thence it came that he that was the richest man, and [a man] of some considerable power among the soldiers, and one they resolved on, made himself a perpetual dictator. And if we strain too far to avoid monarchy in kings [let us take heed] that we do not call for emperors to deliver us from more than one tyrant."

[49] For this reassessment of Nedham's activities, see Pocock, "James Harrington and the Good Old Cause: A Study of the Ideological Context of His Writings," *Journal of British Studies* 10, no. 1 (1970), 36-39. Also, J. Frank, *The Beginnings of the English Newspaper* (Cambridge, Mass.: Harvard University Press, 1961) and Knachel (ed.), *The Case of the Commonwealth*, introduction.

from prison for a Royalist phase in his activities by engaging to write, and in 1650 publishing, *The Case of the Commonwealth of England Stated*, an appeal for *de facto* obedience which contains certain Machiavellian elements but recommends submission to a conquering sword with arguments involving extensive reliance on the pre-*Leviathan* works of Hobbes. The Rump regime rewarded him with editorship of a new government weekly entitled *Mercurius Politicus*, which he retained for many years; and in the summer of 1650 he began furnishing it with leading articles at first excerpted from *The Case of the Commonwealth* and later, when this material was used up, with other editorials which did not then appear in book form. These carried him through to mid-1652, and thus cover the period of the Dunbar and Worcester campaigns, when the radical zeal of the regiments—the suppression of the Levellers notwithstanding—seems still to have been at a high level. The note struck by the articles is consistently radical and democratic. The claims of a Presbyterian ministry to *jure divino* authority is denounced as the work of Antichrist;[50] the commons of Scotland are to be liberated from the power of their chieftains;[51] and above all, the editorials add up to the first sustained English exposition of republican democracy in classical and Machiavellian terms. What can only be called a democratic government is to be based on the popular possession of arms[52] and the rapid succession—Nedham calls it "revolution," as Harrington was to call it "rotation"—of the representatives and magistrates the people elect.[53] There is repeatedly expressed a bitter mistrust of hereditary aristocracies and of senates which, not being regularly dissolved, come to almost the same thing.[54] The politics of the Roman republic are presented from a point of view militantly plebeian; Athens—a rare thing at this period—is preferred over Sparta;[55] and Venice, usually the paragon of mixed governments, becomes the archetype of "standing aristocracies."[56] Any mode of power in a republic which is not contained within a balance and within

[50] *Mercurius Politicus* 99 (22-29 April 1652), 1553-56; 114 (5-12 Aug. 1652), 1785-89.

[51] *Ibid.*, 65 (28 Aug.-4 Sept. 1651), 1033-34; 73 (23-30 Oct. 1651), 1161.

[52] *Ibid.*, 103 (20-27 May 1652), 1609-13.

[53] *Ibid.*, 74 (30 Oct.-6 Nov. 1651), 1173-75; 78 (27 Nov.-4 Dec. 1651), 1237; 79 (4-11 Dec. 1651), 1255-56; 91 (26 Feb.-4 March 1652), 1442 ("revolution").

[54] *Ibid.*, 70 (2-9 Oct. 1651), 1100-1101; 72 (16-23 Oct. 1651), 1142-43; 73 (23-30 Oct. 1651), 1158; 84 (8-15 Jan. 1652), 1334, 1337; 86 (22-29 Jan. 1652), 1365-68; 89 (12-19 Feb. 1652), 1409-13.

[55] *Ibid.*, 71 (9-16 Oct. 1651), 1126; 73 (23-30 Oct. 1651), 1158; 84 (8-15 Jan. 1652), 1335; 88 (5-12 Feb. 1652), 1394; 91 (26 Feb.-4 March 1652), 1445.

[56] *Ibid.*, 70 (2-9 Oct. 1651), 1100; 73 (23-30 Oct. 1651), 1158; 84 (8-15 Jan. 1652), 1338.

a rapid rotation of office is, we are told, "monarchical," whether exercised by one man or a number.[57]

Nedham, writing after the Levellers and deriding them, had hit upon a new mode of expressing democratic ideas in English; one with a long and complex history before it. For our purposes, what matters is that he was describing a *vivere civile e popolare*, based on the classical ideal of the armed citizen and the Machiavellian ideal of the armed and militant people. He was doing this because the appropriate paradigms were available in this form for articulating the claims which the army was still capable of making for itself as a revolutionary movement. With the other side of his none too admirable journalistic personality, he was articulating—still in a fairly democratic form—the doctrine of *de facto* authority made necessary by the army's inability to press its revolutionary claims to the full. In those editorials drawn from *The Case of the Commonwealth*, army and people appear as exercising the *jus conquestus* to be found in *jus gentium*;[58] but the trend of Nedham's *de facto* arguments would carry him to advocating submission to any power exercising effective authority. When that power was the Cromwellian Protectorate, and elements of the army for which he had written in *Mercurius Politicus* were in opposition, Nedham was to find himself in an awkward position and the history of English Machiavellism was to make a fresh start.

[III]

From what we know of the circumstances in which James Harrington's *Oceana* was published during the late summer or fall of 1656, the immediate background seems to have been the increasing discontent of some army circles with the way in which the Protectorate had been developing since 1654.[59] There are shadowy links associating Harring-

---

[57] *Ibid.*, 72 (16-23 Oct. 1651), 1143; 87 (29 Jan.-5 Feb. 1652), 1385; 92 (4-11 March 1652), 1457-62; 100 (29 April-6 May 1652), 1569-73. The last especially.

[58] *Ibid.*, 17 (26 Sept.-3 Oct. 1650), 277-78; 18 (3-10 Oct. 1650), 293-96; 19 (10-17 Oct. 1650), 309-12; 20 (17-24 Oct. 1650), 325-26; 21 (24-31 Oct. 1650), 341-43; 22 (31 Oct.-7 Nov. 1650), 357-59; 23 (7-14 Nov. 1650), 373-74; 24 (14-21 Nov. 1650), 389-90 (the kings of England); 25 (21-28 Nov. 1650), 407-408; 26 (28 Nov.-5 Dec. 1650), 423-25 (Nimrod and the kings of Israel); 27 (5-12 Dec. 1650), 439-40; 28-30 (12 Dec.-2 Jan. 1651), at large, for the necessity of obedience to the sword; 31 (2-9 Jan. 1651), 503-504, for the body politic originating in subjection; 35 (30 Jan.-6 Feb. 1651), 567-68, for the danger of a conquering people's losing their liberty; 75 (6-13 Nov. 1651), 1189-91; 93 (11-18 March 1652), 1457-60; 98 (15-22 April 1652), 1540.

[59] For further detail, see Pocock, "James Harrington and the Good Old Cause," *loc. cit.*

ton with former officers and others who disliked the assumption of power by a military leadership, unrepresentative of regimental feeling, which showed no sign of establishing the frequently elected parliaments called for since 1647 and had placed the army under the control of the Protector as chief of the executive power. Rumors may well have been circulating during 1656 concerning the intentions of some Protectoral grandees which took shape, in the spring of 1657, as the *Humble Petition and Advice*,[60] the crucially antirevolutionary step of the Cromwellian decline, with its proposals to convert the office of Protector into a hereditary monarchy and establish a nominated "Other House," to maintain a balance between the "single person" and unicameral "parliament" of which the constitution was otherwise held to consist. This was plainly a return to the form of government described in the *Answer to the Nineteen Propositions* fourteen or fifteen years previously, and indeed the words "the three estates" are to be found in the *Petition and Advice*.[61] A bitter opposition, both to the erection of an entrenched aristocracy and to any return to the historic constitution, now became a motif of that surviving republicanism which promulgated the slogan of "the good old cause," and it may be suspected that an anticipation of what the *Petition and Advice* would contain accounts for the opposition literature of the preceding summer. At all events, it can have been no accident, and must have been a miscalculation, when Nedham, in June 1656, published his *Mercurius Politicus* editorials of 1650-1652 in book form as *The Excellency of a Free State*, with little abatement of their fury against monarchical and aristocratical intrusions—there is evidence that he subsequently regretted this step and the association with *Oceana* it had brought him[62]—or when Sir Henry Vane, about the same time, brought out his *Healing Question*, the only one of these works to be prosecuted by the authorities, in which the army appears as the justly conquering "people of God," now unhappily divided against itself, and proposals are made for restoring it to its proper function of exercising the rule of the saints in England.[63]

But *Oceana* is one of those works that transcend their immediate context. The book's historical significance is that it marks a moment of paradigmatic breakthrough, a major revision of English political theory and history in the light of concepts drawn from civic humanism and Machiavellian republicanism. The immediate reason for undertak-

[60] Text in Kenyon, *The Stuart Constitution*, pp. 350-57.

[61] Kenyon, p. 353 (clause 7).

[62] Pocock, "James Harrington and the Good Old Cause," pp. 38-39.

[63] Margaret Judson, *The Political Thought of Sir Henry Vane the Younger* (Philadelphia: University of Pennsylvania Press, 1969).

ing such a revision was the impulse to justify the military republic in England as the rule of a *popolo armato*. The lengthy survey we have been conducting of the modes of articulating political consciousness available to Englishmen is enough to show us, however, that the language of *vivere civile* had a hard struggle to establish itself in the teeth of competing alternatives; and we will not expect to find Harrington, in the role of an English Machiavelli, staging a dramatic conflict between virtue and fortune, or playing the part of an accuser of the brethren, thrusting a sword into the side of English moral consciousness and making it cry out against the wound. That distinction was reserved for Hobbes. Harrington's purposes seem to have been,[64] first, to argue against any return to the traditional "ancient" or "balanced" constitution by showing that it had rested on foundations which had always been insecure and were now swept away; second, as the occupant of what we may term a post-Savonarolan moment, to show that this transcendence of ancient use and custom was rather a secular than an apocalyptic process (we should not forget that it was possible to be both), which did not, however, necessitate a rule of the saints. For the first purpose, he constructed a civil history of the sword,[65] based on a Machiavellian theory which depicted the possession of arms as crucial to both the distribution of power and the exercise of civic virtue; for the second, he developed a theory of citizenship which, in conjunction with the first group of arguments, showed the Englishman as citizen and the English republic as standing nearer to God than any oligarchy of self-selected saints. In the former respect, he threw a bridge of theory over the gap between Ireton's conviction of the necessity of property and Rainborough's assurance of the opportunity of freedom, and found means of depicting the English freeholder as the classical citizen returned to earth from Parnassus;[66] in the latter, he stood back-to-back with Hobbes at a strange and significant moment in the evolution of the Puritan millennial consciousness. In his long-term historical significance, however, he appears in a somewhat different light, and this will be explained in further chapters.

Harrington's work has been described as "a Machiavellian meditation on feudalism."[67] Among the pre-1642 generation of English scholars,

---

[64] The author is preparing an edition of Harrington's political writings, for the Cambridge University Press, to which the reader is referred. See also *The Ancient Constitution*, ch. VI, 124-47.

[65] *Oceana*, "Second Part of the Preliminaries." References are to Toland (ed.), *The Oceana and Other Works of James Harrington* (1771); see pp. 57-72.

[66] Traiano Boccalini's *Ragguagli da Parnasso* (Venice, 1612-13) was one of Harrington's favorite sources.

[67] Pocock, *Ancient Constitution*, p. 147.

there has been traced a growing understanding of the nature of baronage, knight's service, and dependent military tenures in general, which
were seen as periodizing English history, having entered the realm with
either the Saxons or the Normans and having faded from dominance
over law and society at a subsequent date hard to fix with precision.
Historical perception of the knight and vassal of true feudalism tended
to merge with the memory—which we have already found expressed
in a Machiavellian context by Bacon and Ralegh—of the military
power which more recent magnates had based upon their retainers;
and this telescoping of images permitted Harrington to think of a distribution of power based on the *feudum* as entering England with the
Saxons and leaving it only as the result of legislation devised by Henry
VII.[68] It was not new to suggest that the decline of military power in
the hands of the nobility had led to important changes in political
power, or that it had left the king face to face with his commons. Harrington's crucial innovation—which makes him the true pioneer of
civic humanist thought in England—was to erect these perceptions into
a general history of political power in both Europe and England,
founded on the Machiavellian theory of the possession of arms as necessary to political personality. The Florentines had stressed that if a
man bore arms not for himself but for another, he was incapable of
citizenship, since the use of arms—the crucial act in asserting both
power and virtue—must be at his command if he was to be at the
republic's; and they had perceived the transition from Roman republic
to empire in terms of the rise and fall of armed individuality. Harrington's acquaintance with English legal antiquarianism permitted him at
this point to add a further dimension—one which, as he put it, Machiavelli had very narrowly missed:[69] the bearing of arms, once it was seen
as a function of feudal tenure, proved to be based upon the possession
of property. The crucial distinction was that between vassalage and
freehold; it determined whether a man's sword was his lord's or his
own and the commonwealth's; and the function of free proprietorship
became the liberation of arms, and consequently of the personality, for
free public action and civic virtue. The politicization of the human
person had now attained full expression in the language of English
political thought; God's Englishman was now *zōon politikon* in virtue
of his sword and his freehold.

If the basis of political personality was now to be property, in the
real or (less probably) in the movable sense, it was anchored in something more concretely material than the Aristotelian *oikos*, and Harrington showed himself inclined to discount Machiavelli's emphasis on

[68] Toland, pp. 60-65. [69] Toland, p. 39.

a strictly moral corruption, an actual disintegration of the civic personality, as a main cause of the decay of governments. When a government became "corrupt," he thought, it was less because the citizens had ceased to display the virtues appropriate to it than because the distribution of political authority was no longer properly related to the distribution of property that should determine it.[70] When this happened, it would be found that equals were attempting to behave as lords and vassals, or lords and vassals to behave as equals; and in each case political power, exercised in ways no longer justified by the distribution of objective freedom, must be either forcibly and despotically imposed or (what came to the same thing) weak and failing, destined to be replaced by a distribution of authority geared to the actually existing distribution of land. The classical sixfold typology of constitutions—monarchy, aristocracy, and democracy, each exercised either justly, with an eye to the common good, or unjustly, with an eye to the good of the ruling part only—could now be modified and become a scheme in which each either was or was not related to the actual distribution of land. Harrington, however, introduced a further distinction between monarchy of the Turkish type, in which one man owned all the land and others held it from him at pleasure, and monarchy of the "Gothic" or feudal type, in which a few held of the king and the many held of the few. This last, he suggested, was not a true monarchy so much as an ill-designed and unstable balance. Feudal rebellions in the Gothic case, and rebellions of the palace guard—janissaries or praetorians—in the Turkish type (to which the later Roman empire had belonged), ensured that monarchy, even in its pure form, never became a truly stable mode of government.[71]

Harrington described property as "the goods of fortune,"[72] and had no particular conception of social laws regulating its distribution. But he did think that it could be redistributed, or that its redistribution might be prevented, by human legislation;[73] and the English conceptual context ensured that he was not so far committed to the notion of *fortuna* that he need present each mode of government as necessarily degenerating into its dysfunctional form, or his sixfold classification as moving inescapably in a Polybian *anakuklōsis*. He did, however, hold that only a democracy of landholders—that is, only a society where a *demos*, or many, of landed freemen held land in relative equality—pos-

---

[70] Toland, p. 68.
[71] Toland, pp. 37, 50, 65-67, 129-30, 248-52.
[72] Toland, pp. 36-37.
[73] This point is dwelt upon—I think a little too emphatically—by J. R. Pole in *Political Representation in England and the Origins of the American Republic* (London: Macmillan, 1966).

sessed the human resources (Machiavelli might have said the *materia*) necessary to distribute political authority in the diversified and balanced ways that created a self-stabilizing *politeia*; and such a commonwealth, he contended, might prove theoretically immortal.[74] He also presented a history of political authority in the Western world which did indeed follow a cyclical pattern: Moses and Lycurgus, Solon and Romulus, appeared as agrarian legislators who had established commonwealths of freeholding warriors, but their work had been undone by Roman conquest and the growth of *latifundia*; after the Gracchi failed to prevent this, the Caesars and their client armies had established an unstable monarchy in which land and military powers were shared between the emperor and the senate; the Goths, called in as mercenaries in the oscillations of this system, had taken over the entire empire and established feudal imbalances of monarchy and aristocracy. The "Gothic balance," or "modern prudence," Harrington said, though traditionally praised as a political masterpiece—an allusion to the kind of thinking represented by the *Answer to the Nineteen Propositions*—had nowhere been anything more than a "wrestling match" between king and nobility, an instability rendered persistent by the circumstance that each party could neither adjust to the other's power nor become independent of it.[75] In "Oceana"—his lightly idealized England—"modern prudence" had lasted from the Anglo-Saxon invasions to the advent of the Tudors. Henry VII, however—the portrait owes much to Bacon—had played a role very like that which Giannotti had assigned to the Medici; he had emancipated the military tenants (whom Harrington confounds with retainers) from the authority of their lords and, in rendering the latter impotent to harm him in future, had begun the elevation of the former into a landowning people (Giannotti's *mediocri*) over whom monarchy had no hold.[76] It had been reserved for Charles I to discover his own obsolescence; challenged by the power of the commons, he had found the nobility without authority to uphold his and had been forced to attempt rule by an army; but, there being no reservoir of soldiers other than landholding freemen in no way committed to fight for him, he had failed and his monarchy

---

[74] Toland, pp. 178-80. See Z. S. Fink, *The Classical Republicans: An Essay in the Recovery of a Pattern of Thought in Seventeenth-Century England* (Evanston: Northwestern University, 1945), and Charles Blitzer, *An Immortal Commonwealth: The Political Thought of James Harrington* (New Haven: Yale University Press, 1960).

[75] Toland, pp. 63, 129.

[76] Toland, pp. 64-65, 364-66. For references to Bacon (both the *History of Henry VII* and the *Essays*), see pp. 32, 64. For Giannotti, see above, ch. IX, n. 5.

had fallen.[77] The armed "people" of proprietors now held the field and might repeat the work of Moses and Lycurgus. A cycle was completed, and there was an opportunity for the construction of an immortal commonwealth. Harrington had outdistanced Ireton; he had anchored politics in a history of property, but one consisting of a cyclical series of transformations rather than a mere tradition of inheritance.

In addition, he had completed his theoretical demolition of the claims of the ancient constitution to be regarded either as a structure of use and custom adapted to the genius of the people, or as an exemplary balance of the one, the few, and the many. If he had not shown, like the Levellers, that it was rooted in Norman usurpation, he had depicted it as a phase in a cycle of unstable forms, a system which never had or could have brought peace or order to England. To the extent to which his thought can be seen as growing out of the casuist and *de facto* controversies of preceding years, he was prepared to argue that the incoherence of the old regime had left the choice between king and parliament to the conscience of the individual, and that no man could be justly punished for exercising such a choice;[78] and to readers who might fear, in the tradition of Ascham or Nedham, that all government was rooted in the sword, he had offered a civil theory and a civil history of the sword which led to conclusions far more sanguine and positive than those of *Leviathan*. His *popolo armato* is not the collective Nimrod exercising *jus conquestus* that had been imagined by Nedham, nor is it the mystically selected band of saints envisaged by Vane; the sword here is neither Leviathan's nor Gideon's, but the foundation on which a republican people erects the structure of its civic virtue.

The political individual depicted in Harrington's scheme is still the exponent of civic virtue presupposed—however skeptically—in all Florentine schemes of civic humanism, but we have already seen that Harrington emphasizes less the moral than the material bases of his personality. There is less in *Oceana* about the moral degradation

[77] Toland, p. 65: ". . . for the house of peers, which alone had stood in this gap, now sinking down between the king and the commons, shew'd that Crassus was dead, and the isthmus broken. But a monarchy devested of its nobility, has no refuge under heaven but an army. Wherfore the dissolution of this government caus'd the war, not the war the dissolution of this government.

"Of the king's success with his arms it is not necessary to give any further account, than that they prov'd as ineffectual as his nobility; but without a nobility or an army (as has bin shew'd) there can be no monarchy. Wherfore what is there in nature that can arise out of these ashes, but a popular government, or a new monarchy to be erected by the victorious army?"

[78] Toland, p. 69.

involved in corruption than there had been in the sixteenth century or was to be again in the eighteenth; and the worst thing Harrington's "people" ever has to fear is loss of government,[79] by which he means less a coercive sovereign than the "orders" or *ordini* which guide men into the opportunities of virtue. As in Machiavelli, the bearing of arms is the essential medium through which the individual asserts both his social power and his participation in politics as a responsible moral being; but the possession of land in nondependent tenure is now the material basis for the bearing of arms. That tenure might entail modes of social dependence other than vassalage Harrington does not seem to have considered; his stress on the importance of arms may have led him to lump together all tenures which did not impose the duty of military service; but if, like Ireton and Rainborough at Putney, he did not explore the vast area intermediate between true freehold and servitude, he combined elements from both their arguments in his. Like Ireton, he insisted on a transmissible and hereditary property in land as the prerequisite of any interest or participation in the commonwealth. Servants, he declared, were no part of the latter and any danger they presented came from without,[80] as did the danger from foreign enemies. But like Rainborough, he seems to have regarded the economic autonomy of citizenship as including men who worked for wages, so long as they inhabited cottages of their own and were not servants living in other men's houses and families.[81] Harrington's attitude to the economy has been much debated, and an attempt has been made to show that he thought of land as basically a market commodity, to be bought and sold at a profit, which would make his citizenry a fluctuating and mobile class of entrepreneurs.[82] But a good argument can be adduced to suggest that his economics were Greek and based on the relations of *oikos* to *polis*. When land was acquired, it was in order to bequeath it:[83] to found families or *oikoi* based on a security of inheritance, which set the sons free to bear arms and cast ballots in the muster of the commonwealth. As with Aristotle, the end of land is not profit, but leisure: the opportunity to act in the public realm or assembly, to display virtue. We return toward an ethos of civic excellence, in which politics are peculiarly suited to "the genius of a gentleman,"[84]

[79] Toland, p. 469 (*A System of Politics*, IV, 18, 19, 22).

[80] Toland, pp. 77, 138: "The causes of commotion in a commonwealth are either external or internal. External are from enemies, from subjects, or from servants."

[81] Toland, p. 247, where it is argued that such a man would have no interest in using his voting power to level property.

[82] C. B. Macpherson, *The Political Theory of Possessive Individualism*, ch. 6, especially pp. 82-88.

[83] Toland, p. 480 (*System of Politics*, X, 4-5).

[84] Toland, p. 53.

but the poor freeholders are not dismissed from the role of the crit. cally applauding Many.

Harrington knew that property might exist in real or in mobile forms, and specifically declared that his general laws concerning the relations of property to power would operate as well in the latter case as in the former.[85] But, though he was acquainted with Holland and is said to have served in an English regiment there, he nowhere draws the lineaments of a society whose military and political structure are based upon property in goods and money; the Dutch, rather far from being a classical people in arms, would have given him difficulty if he had. Holland and Genoa—not Venice, be it noted—appear as his types of the wholly mercantile society only in the context of a discussion as to whether "the balance in trade eats out the balance in land." This proves to be an examination of the impact of usury upon landed property. Holland and Genoa, profit-making societies, clearly have no need of regulations against usury; ancient Israel and Sparta, basing their constitutions upon the distribution of land where the agrarian territory was of limited extent, had to limit the operations of usury rigorously in order to prevent the distribution of real property becoming entangled in a web of debt.[86] For the same reason, the modern Jews should be reestablished in a territory where they could revert to the condition of agriculturists.[87] Oceana, however, is of sufficient extent to permit its merchants the practice of lending upon interest (though not, apparently, to readmit the Jews); the landed system cannot be disturbed by usury and may therefore be stimulated and enriched by it.[88] The pleasure of bourgeois-spotting scholars at finding Harrington engaged in justifying speculative profit in seventeenth-century England should not obscure the fact that he saw speculation in money as related to the inheritance of land more negatively than positively. The end of property was stability and leisure: it anchored the individual in the structure of power and virtue, and liberated him to practice these as activities. The objection to market profit as the basis of civic personality was its mobility; "lightly come," said Harrington, "lightly go."[89] What a man had he might lose; what he was, he might lose at the same instant. The superior man, observed Confucius, was not a utensil; and civic personality was not a commodity.

Should Oceana's volume of trade expand, of course, it might well be necessary for the republic to increase its territorial extent. This may have been one reason why Harrington echoes Machiavelli's insistence that an armed popular republic must be "a commonwealth for

[85] Toland, pp. 38, 228.
[86] Toland, pp. 228-29.
[87] Toland, pp. 33-34.
[88] Toland, p. 229; also 100-101.
[89] Toland, p. 227.

expansion";[90] but there are some important differences. Both men have in common the idea that a popular republic must place arms in the people's hands, and that these will be for use rather than ornament or ritual. But Machiavelli—affected, like Bruni before him, by thoughts of the Roman conquest of the free cities of Etruria—envisaged the republic in Polybian style as contiguous with other republics and kingdoms, and as necessarily involved in wars with its equals; and the destiny of Rome appeared to him cannibalistic, destructive of other peoples' virtue and ultimately of her own. Of England, however, Harrington wrote: "the sea gives law to the growth of Venice, but the growth of Oceana gives law to the sea."[91] Both were islands, insulated by water from the constant threat of enemies at their gates; but whereas Venice had room only for merchants, craftsmen, and mariners, and abstained from empire and democracy through lack of an independent citizenry, England was both island and agrarian territory, capable of breeding an armed people who should be democrats at home and conquerors abroad. The lack of *terra-firma* contacts, moreover, meant that there were no neighbor republics whose liberty and virtue might be subverted and that Oceana might expand without fear of self-corruption; but Harrington is unclear as to just what this means in the real world. True to the mood in which Marvell had declared that Cromwell, as bearer of the public sword, "to all states not free, shall climacteric be," he imagines the English republic as hegemon, liberating adjacent Europe from the Gothic (and probably papal) yoke;[92] but there is an alternative vision, oceanic rather than continental, in which the conquering and land-hungry freemen are seen colonizing an Ireland depopulated of its ancient inhabitants, "where every citizen will in time have his villa."[93] (The Puritan army in Ireland was a refuge for anti-Protectoral opinions, and several of Harrington's associates and admirers were connected with it.) "There be other plantations," the passage observes, "and the commonwealth will have more."[94] In view of the importance which his thought was later to enjoy in the Thirteen Colonies, it is tempting to say that Harrington visualized the settlement of an empty Ireland carried across the Atlantic; but there is a reference to "the colonies in the Indies,"[95] which may very well be the American settlements, as certain to become independent in no distant time. If it is obscure, however, just where the uncorrupting expansion of Oceana is to take place, it is certain that Harrington, like Giannotti before him, is determined to have the best of both alternatives posed

[90] Toland, pp. 178-85.   [91] Toland, p. 34.
[92] Toland, pp. 185-88.   [93] Toland, p. 103.
[94] Toland, p. 100.   [95] Toland, p. 41.

by Machiavelli at the beginning of the *Discorsi*. Oceana was to be a Rome in respect of unlimited expansion, a Venice in respect of perpetual stability, liberty, and virtue. To this end he made his legislator, in a speech of even more than usual length,[96] rehearse the whole passage from *Discorsi* i, 6, in which the antithesis of Rome and Venice had first been stated, and conclude that Machiavelli had been wrong in contending that the price paid for arming the people had been constant strife between the nobility and plebeians (whose effects had been fatal to the republic when the wealth of empire was the prize contended for). Like Machiavelli's philo-Venetian critics, he argued that civil strife at Rome was the result, not of plebeian turbulency, but of the patricians' hereditary monopoly of office, which was causally unrelated to the arming of the people. Venice had solved this problem by making her aristocracy a body elected by and rotating among the many, and Machiavelli had been wrong in supposing that the disarmament of the people was the cause of her internal peace.[97] Oceana, rising out of the wreck of the Gothic balance and the disappearance of its hereditary baronage, had an insular situation and a landowning and arms-bearing people; she had only to adopt the rotatory aristocracy of the Most Serene Republic, and she could be Venice and Rome in one. There need be no fear of an English Caesar.

The "orders" of Oceana are rehearsed at wearisome length and in utopian detail. They have as their objective the construction of a scheme of participation for all citizens, based on the frequent assemblies of local communities or "tribes"—a term equally of Greco-Roman or of Hebrew resonance—which in many ways resemble the county assemblies of the traditional English system: not least in their combining the functions of mustering and drilling the county militia and electing representatives to a national assembly. It is actually as they advance and retire in companies of horse and foot that the citizenry cast the "golden volleys" of Venetian ballots which elect members of the assembly and senate of Oceana; Harrington is consciously dramatizing the identity of *milizia* and *polizia*.[98] But the persons elected are less representatives in the proper sense than citizens taking their turn at participation and service, and lot as well as choice enters into the complex, and deliberately Venetian, structures by which the various assemblies and councils are chosen and function. Harrington is not unaware of that aspect of the *mito di Venezia* in which virtue appeared to have been mechanized and men fed into processes which made their behavior intelligent and disinterested whether they so intended it or not—

---

[96] Toland, pp. 132-44.   [97] Toland, pp. 139-40.
[98] See the speech of Hermes de Caduceo; Toland, pp. 92-94.

the Platonic overtones noted in Contarini appear in the last and most systematic of his political writings[99]—but his dominant purpose is the release of personal virtue through civic participation. There is to be frequent rotation—Nedham had called it "revolution"—in office, including the office of representation, not to ensure the supremacy of popular choice so much as to ensure the reality of the individual's participation; he is to take frequent turns at office, and is not to depute or alienate civic function to others. Rotation is Harrington's equivalent—as he thought it was Venice's—for Machiavelli's *ridurre ai principii*; it is the constant renewal of virtue in and through action, and the astronomical language—"galaxy," *"primum mobile,"* "orb"—he liked to employ in the technical jargon of his utopia carries the suggestion of the self-perpetuation of light, warmth, and life. So too did his invocation of Harvey's discovery of the circulation of the blood.

Rotation is also his solution for the problem of aristocracy. The members of the senate who discharge in his system the functions of the few—it should be noted that, the work of the legislator once done, there is not much role for a one—are regularly elected and regularly retire by thirds. They are defined, that is, less by their quality as a social group than by the political function they perform, which, according to the classical and Renaissance tradition, is rigorously confined to proposing laws and policies among which the people or assembly are to choose. The absolute separation of "debate" from "result," in his terminology,[100] was Harrington's method of mechanizing virtue, of distinguishing and distributing the elements of the decision process so that men were obliged to act disinterestedly. But to have the few regularly emerging from and returning to the body of the many was his way of demonstrating that there was no need to have an aristocratic class in order to have a functioning few. Some social differentiation, nevertheless, there had to be; the whole Aristotelian technique is built upon the relation of political functions to social characteristics. The senate is to be chosen by the people from members of an equestrian order, for which there is a property qualification of £100 per annum;[101] but greater importance seems to be attached to his firm belief that the many can be trusted to know the talented few when they see them. Out of twenty men, he says, six will be of superior ability and the remaining fourteen will follow their lead; there is no need to establish elaborate mechanisms to ensure their selection, and the most important precaution is to ensure that the differentiation of "debate" and

[99] *A System of Politics,* IV (Toland, pp. 468-70), IX (pp. 478-79).

[100] Toland, pp. 43-45, 48, 50-51, 71, 214-15, 416, 418-19. See above, pp. 255-6, 260, for Guicciardini's, and pp. 287-9, 304, for Giannotti's use of the same distinction.

[101] Toland, p. 78.

"result" provides for the performance of their proper functions by the six and the fourteen.[102] It is clear that the difference of talent between these two groups corresponds, in Harrington's mind, to a difference of wealth, birth, and standing; the six will be gentlemen, they will have more property, leisure, experience, and tradition than the fourteen.[103] But what matters is that the fourteen are left free to recognize these qualities for themselves, and that no hereditary and not much of a property qualification is imposed to regulate their choice. The concept of deference—to employ a term favored by modern scholars—which we are here meeting for the first time in English republican theory, though assuredly not for the first time in English social thought, is familiar to us from Aristotle, Machiavelli, and Guicciardini, and the last-named had employed it to distinguish carefully between aristocracy in a *governo largo* and in a *governo stretto*.[104] From Harrington to John Adams, its role in Atlantic thought[105] was to argue that the relations of aristocracy to democracy, crucial in any theory of mixed government, took shape best in a society of relative freedom, mobility, and outspokenness: that aristocracy, although a function of property as well as personality, was a natural rather than an institutional phenomenon, which worked best when it was not entrenched but left to the recognition of the many. An entrenched aristocracy, in Nedham's or Harrington's view, was hard to establish in any way that did not ensure either conflict or corruption; and there was no need to make the attempt.

The coincidence in time between Harrington's writings and those of Vane or Milton or the Fifth Monarchists meant, however, that he had to consider the possibility of another kind of aristocracy, more formidable even than a hereditary order: that of a rule of the saints, an elite of spiritual experience whose qualifications could not, by their nature, be judged by the many. To understand the full depth of this problem we must consider that he had successfully relocated England in a context not of traditional, but of classical time; English history now appeared, more positively than Florentine history had ever appeared to anyone after the early Bruni, part of the rise, fall, and rebirth of republican virtue, and the present moment was one at which England had the opportunity to recreate the commonwealth of armed freemen in such a form as had not existed since the days of Livian Rome. It has been a recurrent theme of this book that the moment of recreating the republic, that society in which men were what they

---

[102] Toland, pp. 44-45, 236-38.   [103] Toland, pp. 53, 125, 127.

[104] See above, pp. 130-35, 227, 248, 253.

[105] See especially Gordon S. Wood, *The Creation of the American Republic* (Chapel Hill: University of North Carolina Press, 1969), and below, ch. xv.

ought to be, was hard to conceive without adding the concept of the apocalyptic moment, or moment at which grace acted in history; and Harrington is not an exception. Oceana, we are told at one point, is "as the rose of Sharon and the lily of the valley"; the legislator chants over her beginnings the full rhapsody of the *Song of Solomon*,[106] which any orthodox Christian would associate with the imagery of the church as Bride of Christ; and we hear elsewhere that the republic is the reign of the Son as the Mosaic commonwealth was the reign of the Father.[107] But this is the moment at which the rule of the saints makes its appearance, to challenge in its own fashion the equality of the citizens before God.

The Elect Nation, that peculiarly English assertion of the priesthood of all believers, had since its first appearances been affirming the primacy of secular authority in a curious and characteristic blend of the languages of laicism and apocalyptic. If the pope's claim to represent the presence of God, acting from the *nunc-stans*, in time was dismissed as false, then the secular community could assume the role of the community of faithful expecting Christ's return in time. The supremacy of secular authority over any spiritually based challenge to its primacy thus became the test of the repudiation of Antichrist, and one by one Romish priests, Arminian bishops, and Scottish presbyters had appeared in the Antichristian role. To the Independents of the sixteen-fifties Rome remained the paradigmatic enemy, but *jure divino* presbyterianism ranked next; when Harrington's legislator—who is in part a portrayal of Cromwell—approaches the end of his labors, it is largely for his victories over a foreign invader, obviously the Scot, that he is commemorated.[108] But a rule of the saints, claiming a spiritual authority, election, or illumination, not accessible to other men, presented a threat to the secular community in its spiritual role that was basically of the same order—hence William Prynne's announcement that Quakers were Jesuits or Franciscans in disguise.[109] In Books III and IV of *Leviathan*, Hobbes had set out to erect a fortification against all these threats together. In his own highly individual way, he had employed the arguments of radical Protestantism to demonstrate the impossibility of any earthly agency's exercising an authority peculiarly derived from Christ between his ascension and his return, or one immediately derived

---

106 Toland, p. 188.

107 Toland, p. 187: "as the kingdom of God the father was a commonwealth, so shall the kingdom of God the son: *the people shall be willing in the day of his power*." Cf. p. 195: "I cannot conclude a circle (and such is this commonwealth) without turning the end into the beginning."

108 Toland, p. 199. Antichrist, however, is not mentioned by name.

109 Lamont, *Marginal Prynne*, p. 141 and note.

from God between the Mosaic theocracy that had ended with the election of Saul and the theocracy that would be exercised by Christ following his return and the resurrection of the dead. The natural and artificial civil authority of Leviathan, which held the stage meanwhile, had indeed undivided sway over the preaching and interpretation of the prophetic word concerning God's return; but this could be exercised only at the cost of incessant repetition of that word, which swept away all Leviathan's pseudo-spiritual rivals, but located him within a scheme of apocalyptic time and spoke of a day when his authority should be no more because theocracy had returned with the risen Christ.[110]

Hobbes and Harrington—the theorist of absolute sovereignty and the theorist of the commonwealth of participatory virtue—might seem as certain to quarrel as any two ideologues could be; and indeed Harrington is fertile in attacks upon Hobbes's theory of power, his hatred of the Greco-Roman heritage, and his substitution of private and voluntary subjection for public and active virtue.[111] But there is a further, and to them a deeper, sense in which they were at one, having the same enemies. Harrington, like Hobbes, was anxious to prove that the first presbyters and deacons ordained by the Apostles were not consecrated in a priestly succession, but elected in assemblies;[112] and, like most Independents, whether Erastian or congregationalist in their leanings, he desired to prove this against papists, episcopalians, and presbyterians all together. There was a wealth of literature on the subject from which he might have drawn arguments; what held him close to Hobbes must have been the desire of both men to show that the agency electing the presbyters and deacons had been a civil agency, and that—to Harrington at least—the primitive *ecclesiae* had been assemblies of citizens in the Athenian sense of the noun *ekklesia*.[113] The impulse was to prove that the choice of a clergy is a civil choice, carried out by the civil sovereign; and, profoundly as Harrington and Hobbes differed in their theories of sovereignty, a self-sufficient polis or commonwealth is, as Hobbes emphasized, as sovereign over its own affairs as any kingdom subject to Leviathan can possibly be. And the enemies were the same. Harrington's longest polemic on the question of primitive ordination, directed against the Anglican Henry Hammond, is aimed at a

---

[110] *Politics, Language and Time*, pp. 148-201.

[111] Toland, pp. 35-37, 38-39, 42-43, 45-46, 49-50, 53, 54, 65, 71, 241.

[112] *Prerogative of Popular Government*, Book II (Toland, pp. 304-54); *Art of Lawgiving*, ch. VI (Toland, pp. 398-400); *Leviathan*, Book III, ch. 42 (ed. Oakeshott, Oxford: Basil Blackwell, n.d.), pp. 322-83.

[113] Toland, pp. 48 ("the church or assembly of the people"), 316-17, and *Prerogative of Popular Government*, II, *passim*.

passage of the latter's writings, page by page and point by point, where Hammond had been attacking Hobbes.[114]

Hobbes had presented Leviathan's kingdom as occupying the present interval between the direct rule of God exercised in the Mosaic theocracy and the direct rule of God that would be exercised by the risen Christ. He had consequently emphasized the identity of both theocracies and their monarchical character; the authority that God would exercise through the human nature of Christ, he had exercised through his vice-gerents from Moses to Samuel. Harrington, however, insisted that the Mosaic commonwealth had been a true classical republic, and that the authority electing the officers of religion had been that of the people in their orders, as when they elected the officers of state.[115] He did not feel obliged to part company with Hobbes when he said this. The overriding aim was the destruction of any claim on the part of a clergy to independently derived spiritual authority, and a republic could assert civil sovereignty as effectively as could a monarchy. The appeal to theocracy—another mode of denying the independence of a priesthood—would be maintained by repeating, and Harrington does repeat, that a republic, that regime in which all citizens are equal, is that in which they are all equally free under God. Consequently, a republic is a theocracy; it is that realm of which Christ is King.[116] Savonarola had said this long ago, and Vane and the Fifth Monarchists were saying it still. To Harrington, however, their claim was false, since they were claiming for themselves an authority, as an elite or elect, which they denied to other citizens.[117] They were denying the republic, and denying Christ's kingdom by claiming it for themselves. Their role was not far from becoming that of Antichrist.

Even at Sinai, however, the republic had not been a simple matter of revelation. Harrington insisted that the orders of civil society, which it developed and embodied, were accessible to human reason, and that

---

[114] Toland, pp. 335-54. Henry Hammond, *A Letter of Resolution to Six Quaeres, of Present Use in the Church of England* (1653), in *Works of Henry Hammond* (London, 4 vols., dated between 1671 and 1684; here vol. 1, dated MDCLXXIV). The fifth "quaere" concerns ordination and is answered by an attack on ch. 42 of *Leviathan* (vol. 1, pp. 512-29). Harrington concludes that Hammond's attack has failed, and mentions Hobbes by name.

[115] Toland, pp. 46-48, 75, 99, 147, 166-67 (*Oceana*); 234-41, 272-74, 283-84, 320-33, 357 (*Prerogative of Popular Government*); 363, 372-98 (*Art of Lawgiving*).

[116] Toland, pp. 187 above, and 194: ". . . but a commonwealth is a monarchy; to her God is king, in as much as reason, his dictat, is her soverain power." Thus Toland; the original (as corrected by Harrington) reads "where God is king."

[117] Toland, pp. 469 (*A System of Politics*, IV, 23), 574 (*A Discourse upon this Saying* . . .), 580-84 (*A Parallel of the Spirit of the People with the Spirit of Mr. Rogers*).

God did not act contrary to the intelligible natural order.[118] Where Machiavelli had juxtaposed Moses with the heathen legislators in a way which cannot be stripped of irony, Harrington many times cited a text in which Moses accepted advice on the foundation of civil institutions from his Midianite father-in-law Jethro, a gentile and a heathen.[119] Here, he liked to say, were prophet and legislator, divine word and natural reason, working in harmony. But there is a further sense in which the republic displays a millennial aspect beyond anything to be found in Hobbes. If theocracy was exercised through a direct representation of God in the person of Moses, and is to be exercised through another in the person of the risen Christ, then Leviathan, who is only God's representative naturally and artificially, cannot exercise theocracy and can only expect its return. But if Israel's being a republic made it also a theocracy, then Oceana, the restored republic which is both Israel and Rome *redivivus*, may be in an intelligible sense Christ's kingdom returned. Hence the imagery of the Bride of Christ, and the other apocalyptic significances with which Oceana is invested. Leviathan can only expect Christ's kingdom at the end of time; Oceana may be that kingdom already come, and merging the millennium with the after-world. There is a difference between a mortal god and an immortal commonwealth.

But only a few of the types and shadows attending the serene edifice of Oceana are millennial. We are more likely to feel that Harrington and Hobbes, like Prynne and Marvell, ended by subordinating spiritual experience to political, and paradoxically employed to this purpose the prophetic dimension which their thought could not escape. Hobbes deliberately undermined the possibility of direct religious experience in all but the rarest of cases, and reduced the religious life to obeying Leviathan and acknowledging the power of God and the soterial mission of Jesus. Harrington, following the humanist path, obliterated the saint—while retaining a soterial function for "gathered congregations"[120]—and came close to leaving the practice of civic virtue by citizens as the sole prerequisite for the *regnum Christi*.[121] His

[118] Toland, pp. 214-15, 248, 272-73, 300, 342 ("Neither God nor Christ ever instituted any policy whatsoever upon any other principles than those of human prudence"), 347, 371-72, 401.

[119] E.g., Toland, pp. 48, 74 (". . . my Lord Archon, taking council of the commonwealth of Israel, as of Moses; and of the rest of the commonwealths, as of Jethro"); and *passim*.

[120] Toland, p. 55.

[121] Toland, p. 489: "As the natural body of a *Christian* or Saint can be no other for the frame, than such as has bin the natural body of an *Israelit* or of a Heathen; so the political bodys, or civil governments of *Christians* or Saints can be no other for the frame, than such as have bin the political bodys or civil

clergy are to be mere men of learning, interpreting the word of God because they know the ancient tongues in which it was delivered;[122] Pentecost has almost disappeared. But because of the availability of an eschatological rhetoric which implied the imminence of a millennium or return, Harrington—whatever may be true of Hobbes—avoided speaking of his republic as existing in a rigorously secular time. He did not use the terms *virtù* and corruption, as Machiavelli had used them, in such a way as to depict civic man in a world which neither custom nor grace was stabilizing. That perspective was to return when Harrington's ideas were used in a society no longer millennially oriented.

governments of the *Israelits*, or of the Heathens." P. 490: "The highest earthly felicity that a people can ask, or God can give, is an equal and well-order'd commonwealth. Such a one among the *Israelits*, was the reign of God; and such a one (for the same reason) may be among *Christians* the reign of Christ, tho not every one in the *Christian* commonwealth should be any more a *Christian* indeed, than every one in the *Israelitish* commonwealth was an *Israelit* indeed."

[122] Toland, pp. 82, 166-69, 421, 476.

CHAPTER XII

THE ANGLICIZATION OF THE REPUBLIC

B) Court, Country and Standing Army

[1]

IN THE TWO PRECEDING CHAPTERS we have examined the emergence and establishment of civic and Machiavellian modes of understanding politics in the language and thought of Stuart and Puritan England. The conceptual universe which obtained there was very different from that of Florence, and we had to go a long way about to understand why it became necessary to envisage England as a classical republic at all; but it may still be described as the same universe, dominated by the same paradigms, as those employed in constructing the model which has guided this book. The world of particular events was ill understood and regarded as a consequence of human irrationality, a zone of secular instability which it was the business of politics to control (if it was not the sin of politics to have created it); and the paradigms of custom, grace, and fortune provided the vocabularies available for guiding the intellect through the dangerous paths of historical existence. When civil war afflicted a monarchy which had been considered a representation of eternal order, we encountered one group of thinkers (to which Hobbes in a sense belonged) prepared to isolate a timeless "moment of nature," and out of it to reconstitute authority as a rigorously natural phenomenon; but the heterogeneous arguments of Nedham, and the paradoxical relationship discovered between Hobbes and Harrington, showed us the appeal to nature and authority coexisting closely with an appeal to fortune, *anakuklōsis*, and the republic, and this latter with a further appeal to grace, illumination, and apocalypse. It can be contended, therefore, that down to the exhaustion of the Puritan radical impulses, English political thought continued to face the challenge of the epistemology of the *saeculum*, and that the vision of England as a classical republic was constructed as a means of meeting that challenge, in the terms in which the languages familiar to us both posed it and recommended its solution.

During the late seventeenth and the eighteenth centuries, however, Western political and social thought passed from its post-medieval to its early modern stage. A massive increase in the capacity for historical self-understanding was one feature of this transition, and it could not have occurred without considerable modification of that rigorously limited epistemology of the secular with which we have been concerned. The causes of epistemological change in this era were numerous and complex, but we are going to find that the language of republican humanism played an important part in the process, and consequently entered upon a paradoxical relationship with the epistemology that had helped to give it birth. The civic humanists of the Renaissance had faced the almost insoluble problem of constituting the republic as both a universal community of value and a phenomenon in the world of particularity; their theory had consequently presented it as a device for mobilizing all rationality and all value, and remaining stable as a totality of virtue. This set of problems remained fundamental for post-Renaissance and Enlightenment minds; but in the intellectual lineage running through Bruni, Machiavelli, and Harrington, theories of mixed government, of arms, and finally of property had provided—at least for those able to overlook Machiavelli's underlying pessimism—a set of norms for the attainment of stability which reduced the totality of virtue to concrete and manageable terms. What we shall see happening is that these became parameters for the measurement of historical change. To the extent that they did so they greatly increased the capacity for historical understanding, simply by enriching its technical vocabulary. But at the same time they obliged thinkers to evaluate change negatively, as a movement away from the norms which defined it, as they defined stability, rationality, and virtue. The ancient equation of change with degeneration and entropy thus held fast; what was new in the situation was that it could now be defined not as sheer disorder, but in terms of intelligible social and material processes. The antithesis of virtue ceased to be *fortuna*, but became corruption instead. An increase in the capacity of Western men to understand history presented itself in the form of an acute and growing awareness of the potential quarrel between value and history, virtue and history, personality and history; and the growth of theories of progress during the eighteenth century is not to be understood without understanding of this counterpoint. Such was to be the final contribution of the classical image of man as finding his fulfillment in citizenship. A romantic theory of personality was the necessary response.

These movements of thought will be considered as occurring mainly in an English and American context, and as a preliminary step it is desirable to ask what general changes seem to have taken place in the languages of custom, grace, and fortune, following the revolutionary upheavals of the middle seventeenth century. First it should be noted that the habit of presenting English politics in terms of grace and apocalyptic underwent after 1660 a rather sharp decline. The vocabulary of Godly Rule and the Elect Nation, already perhaps eroded by disillusionment, now seemed part of that spirit of "enthusiasm" which resurgent Anglicanism sought to expunge for the next century and more. The apocalyptic dimension was, indeed, too integrally a part of the age's thinking to be merely canceled and annulled; it survived in preaching, in literature, and in several areas of the public mind;[1] but as a recognized political language with radical possibilities it was long eclipsed and never fully recovered. Foxe's *Acts and Monuments* survived as a martyrology and a source of atrocity stories, but ceased to form part of the essential scaffolding of the English mind. Ernest Tuveson[2] has, however, shown that there were ways in which apocalyptic continued to perform its characteristic if paradoxical function as a means of secularization. The revolutionary chiliasts had increasingly envisaged the millennium as a period in which the rational powers of the human mind should be sanctified, illumined, and set free to rule; and as rational religion steadily prevailed over prophetic "enthusiasm," the apocalyptic mode remained viable, and appealed to Anglicans of the latitudinarian tradition as a means of depicting a future utopia in which men should have learned from God all that he had to teach them. There are signs of a paradox in the English intellectual scene: republicans like Toland, in so many ways the heirs of the Puritans, emerge as Deists and foes of the prophetic tradition, while the apocalyptic mode of thought is carried on by latitudinarians who are professed enemies of "enthusiasm." But the republic as millennium has been important enough to our theme to warn us to watch for apocalyptic overtones in post-Puritan republicanism, and it is significant also that in the American colonies, where the revulsion against "enthusiasm" was never so great, Tuveson finds it possible to speak of an "apocalyptic Whiggism" and audible notes of messianism may be heard to this day. But it was one thing for millennial expectation to serve as a framework in which to present schemes of rational optimism and rational explanation; quite another for it to serve as a surrogate in the absence of any ability to supply them. Its day was not done, but it was for the present removed from the center of attention.

[1] See William M. Lamont, "Richard Baxter, the Apocalypse and the Mad Major," *Past and Present* 55 (1972), 68-90; M. C. Jacob and W. A. Lockwood, "Political Millenarianism and Burnet's *Sacred Theory*," *Science Studies* 2 (1972), 265-79.

[2] *Millennium and Utopia: A Study in the Background of the Idea of Progress* (Berkeley and Los Angeles: University of California Press, 1949); *The Redeemer Nation: the Idea of America's Millennial Role* (University of Chicago Press, 1968).

The language of custom, on the other hand, seems to have both survived and revived during and after the restoration of the monarchy. The ideological context of Harrington's writings was that of an unsuccessful attempt to prevent the revival of a house of lords and the return of government by three estates—the formula of the *Answer to the Nineteen Propositions* which had equated the classical balance of one, few, and many with the traditional structure of king, lords, and commons. Every step in the process of restoration which began in 1658— the return to the traditional franchise, to the hereditary peerage, and finally to the historic monarchy itself—was a return, under an increasingly thin veil of "mixed government," to that Ancient Constitution whose legitimacy and authority were held to derive from the immemorial continuities of custom. The writings of Sir Matthew Hale (d. 1675), the Chief Justice who had upheld the common law throughout the Protectorate, form one of the most brilliant articulations[3] of the philosophy of custom—of usage, presumption,[4] and prescription—that links Fortescue, Coke, and Edmund Burke. It is true that, a few years after Hale's death, the doctrine of the Ancient Constitution underwent unforgettably damaging attacks from a group of Tory scholars led by Robert Brady, who employed the feudal interpretation of English history to demonstrate that the constitution was neither immemorial nor customary, but owed its being to royal action and social change.[5] But it would be an oversimplification to suppose that the historic constitution was now prepared to abandon its foundation in antiquity. It is argued by Corinne Weston[6] that the assertion by Exclusionists of the antiquity of the commons, which called down the rebuttals of Brady and his friends, was intended to claim for the two houses that coordinate authority in legislation which the *King's Answer* had seemed to concede them in 1642, and that the intention of the Tory writers was to refute this claim and leave the king in possession of the initiative. If this interpretation can be accepted, it would follow that it was not their main purpose to set the authority of the Crown above that of custom, but to deny that the constitution was reducible to any formal distribution of powers. Its true character, they argued, must be found in complex processes and the actions of past kings and parliaments, dictated

[3] *The Ancient Constitution*, pp. 170-81; *Politics, Language and Time*, pp. 216-22, 262-64.

[4] But it has been pointed out by Paul Lucas that Burke was modifying the normal legal usage of this term; see "On Edmund Burke's Doctrine of Prescription: or, an Appeal from the New to the Old Lawyers," *The Historical Journal* 11, no. 1 (1968), 35-63.

[5] *The Ancient Constitution*, pp. 182-228.

[6] See her "Legal Sovereignty in the Brady Controversy," in *The Historical Journal* 15, no. 3 (1972), 409-32.

by the needs of the moments in which they were taken. Such a perspective is not altogether unlike that of Hale's philosophy of custom, in which every moment is unique and part of a continuous flow of emergencies; the only, if crucial, difference is that the historian proposes to know and resurrect each past moment in its particularity, the lawyer merely to presume its existence in its continuity with others. But wherever there were common lawyers, the language of use, tradition, and immemorial antiquity was sure to flourish; it did so throughout the eighteenth century, alongside many different modes of thought, and its reassertion by Burke himself was neither archaism nor antiquarianism.[7]

The third language of our model is that with whose further history we are concerned, but we should remind ourselves that it was no longer founded upon the primacy of ideas about fortune. Calvinist predestinarianism, the growth from many sources of a vocabulary of secondary causation, perhaps the decay of the Aristotelian stress upon form and *telos*, had heavily eroded the conception of external circumstance as a random, irrational, deforming force. It may also be arguable (it usually is) that changing social conditions were exercising an influence as well; an interesting study in historical semantics might be written to show how a man's or woman's "fortune" came to bear the predominantly monetary meanings of inheritance, acquisition, or dowry.[8] At all events, we are about to enter upon a period in which the terms virtue, *virtus*, and *virtù* are of great significance in their Roman and Renaissance connotations, but their antithesis is no longer circumstantial *fortuna* so much as historical corruption. A general reason for this we already know. The material and moral conditions necessary to the commonwealth in which virtue was possible had been established in a series of increasingly acceptable paradigms; the problem now seemed to be legislative and political—could these conditions be established, and if so could they be maintained?—and to admit of answers in material and moral, rather than voluntarist or charismatic, terms. The *virtù* of the prince seemed of less immediate concern than the virtue of the legislator, senator, or citizen. But to understand the exact shapes in which these problems presented themselves, we have to begin by understanding how it was that the formulations of Machiavellian and Harringtonian republicanism came to appear appropriate in the parliamentary monarchy of Restoration England.

---

[7] *Politics, Language and Time*, pp. 227-31.

[8] The older terminology survives in usages such as "soldier of fortune," meaning a mercenary, or "gentleman of fortune" (if anyone ever really said this), meaning a pirate. The notion of a woman's "virtue," it is interesting to note, acquired as specifically sexist a meaning as that of her "fortune."

[II]

The moment at which this began to happen can be conveniently located at—and in fact has not yet been traced much earlier than—the year 1675, in which also Hale died and the controversy over the feudal origins of parliament began again to get under way. The first known authors of what has been called the neo-Harringtonian interpretation[9] of English politics were the writer of a pamphlet entitled *A Letter from a Person of Quality to his Friend in the Country*,[10] who may just possibly have been John Locke and was certainly someone as close as he was to the Earl of Shaftesbury,[11] and Shaftesbury himself in a speech to the House of Lords.[12] Other more or less Shaftesburean pamphlets may be associated with these, and in 1677 Andrew Marvell, a more independent figure, published his *Account of the Growth of Popery and Arbitrary Government*, which belongs to the same intellectual stream. Finally, in 1680, at the height of the controversy over the Bill of Exclusion, Henry Neville, an old associate of Harrington himself and not, strictly speaking, an Exclusionist at all,[13] published *Plato Redivivus*, a political dialogue which may be taken as the culmination of the first attempt to restate Harringtonian doctrine in a form appropriate to the realities of the Restoration.

There are three circumstances which are crucial to the understanding of this first manifestation of neo-Harringtonianism. The first is that Shaftesbury was contending against the endeavors of the king's minister, Danby, to build up a "Court party" in the House of Commons by means involving patronage, places, and pensions. The second is that he chose to link this allegedly sinister influence with the growth of a professional or "standing" army. The third is that his argument was not only delivered in the House of Lords—in which he sat—but was, like Neville's after him, intimately bound up with the fact of the House's continued existence. To take these in order, the policies of Danby are usually taken as marking the revival of the Crown's efforts to master the arts of parliamentary management, at which the first two Stuarts, as well as Oliver Protector, had been notably unsuccessful; its impor-

[9] *Politics, Language and Time*, p. 115. This essay was first published in 1966. For the beginnings in 1675 of the "Brady controversy" see *The Ancient Constitution*, ch. 7.

[10] Printed in *State Tracts . . . in the Reign of Charles II . . .* (London, 1693), pp. 41-56, and in *Parliamentary History of England*, IV, xxxviii-lxvii.

[11] For a discussion of this question, see K.H.D. Haley, *The First Earl of Shaftesbury* (Oxford: The Clarendon Press, 1968), pp. 390-93.

[12] Printed in *State Tracts . . . in the Reign of Charles II . . .* , pp. 57-61.

[13] *Plato Redivivus* argues for limitations on the power of a Catholic successor, not for his exclusion from the throne.

tance for our purposes is that the polemical counterattack promoted by Shaftesbury restated the old antithesis of "Court" and "Country" in a new form, one based on employment of the civic and republican concept of "corruption," in a version which owed much to Harrington and was at the same time decisive in developing the theory known to us as "the separation of powers." The "Court" which came under attack from this time on was composed no longer of courtiers or of servants of the king's prerogative, so much as of "ministers"—a key term, usually of opprobrium, in Whig ideology—who were seen as employing patronage in the attempt to render parliament compliant with the administration's policies. Opposition politicians hostile to these endeavors sought to represent them as illegitimate, and did so by terming patronage "corruption"—not merely in the sense that it overstepped the proper limits of royal favor and entered the sphere of bribery and venality, but also in the sense that we noted first in Guicciardini: the substitution of private for public authority, of dependence for independence. Patronage, it was argued by the pioneers of the "Country" ideology, rendered representatives of the people, who ought to be as independent as those they represented, dependent upon the Court and the ministers from whom they received it; and dependence was worse, because more lasting, than mere venality—if it was bad that a member should receive a purse of guineas for voting with the Court, it was ten times worse that he should receive a pension, or hold an office, in the Court's gift, since this rendered subservience to the Court his permanent interest. From this there arose two of the most recurrent if never-satisfied demands in the "Country" political program: that for the exclusion of officeholders or "placemen" from the House of Commons, and that for short, i.e., frequently elected, parliaments—triennial if annual could not be secured—on the grounds that to send members regularly back to their constituents for reelection was the best means of ensuring that they did not become dependents of the Court.

It is important to realize that this demand—with its echoes of 1647-1648 and the Good Old Cause—was consciously seen as a Machiavellian *ridurre ai principii*, and by enthusiasts almost as a Savonarolan *rinnovazione*; it was designed to secure the same principle as Harrington had aimed at with his mechanisms of rotation, namely the perpetual renewal of independence, freedom, and virtue. The people were free and independent, as was the role of their representative; the moment of election, then—we should recall the raptures of Harrington's Hermes de Caduceo[14]—was a moment of freedom, nature, and political innocence, in which a basic principle of government was affirmed; and,

[14] Above, ch. XI, n. 98.

as Machiavelli would have agreed, such could not be affirmed too often. But if the freedom of people and representative consisted in their independence, it followed, to men who had read Harrington and to men who had not needed to read him, that freedom and independence consisted in property. The gentry and freeholders of the shires and county boroughs, whom the term "Country" normally comprised, were entitled in these terms to see themselves as a classical *populus*, a community of virtue, and to see their virtue as consisting in their freeholds. But it was at that very point that the menace of "corruption" became actual; place and pension constituted a species of property, or at least of livelihood, one which rendered the recipient dependent upon the donor; Marvell compared such clients with the blue-coated retainer of bastard feudalism; and the patrons on whom the corrupt representative became dependent might not be merely some powerful faction—*setta* or *intelligenza* in the Florentine vocabulary—of dominant "particular men," but the ministers of the royal executive, forming either a new and illegitimate agency of government ("ministers") or an old one ("Court" or "executive") grown corrupt and corrupting through having stepped out of its proper place. The language of "balanced government" and "separation of powers" took on a new meaning—beyond anything to be found in the *Answer to the Nineteen Propositions* or in Harrington's philo-Venetian desire to separate "debate" from "result"—when it presented, as the principal enemy of virtue and liberty, a "corruption" springing from the economic dependence of members of the legislative upon resources controlled by the executive. To this threat any formal weakness in the distribution, or "separation," of powers as between executive and legislative was, at bottom, secondary. The key term is "corruption," which marks a further stage in the assimilation of English constitutional theory to the categories and vocabulary of civic republicanism.

Marvell could see clearly enough that there were not one but two corrupting agencies at work. The opposition politicians who denounced the corruption of ministers might be aiming simply to replace them and continue working with their tools; and in *The Growth of Popery and Arbitrary Government*, he drew an early portrait of parliament along what we know as "Namierite" lines: the Court interest, the opposition factions, and the independent backbenchers or "Country members."[15] But, unlike Sir Lewis Namier, he maximized the role of corruption by attributing it to ministers, faction leaders and their respective followings, in equal and unmitigated

---

[15] 1677 ed., pp. 74-81. Grosart (ed.), *Complete Works of Andrew Marvell* (Fuller Worthies Library, 1875), IV, 322-32. The analogy between factions and retainers is at Grosart, p. 331.

degree; from which it followed that virtue was represented only by the Country members, that their defense of it was static if not passive, and that corruption could be avoided only by those willing both to enjoy no source of income but their estates, and to eschew either the possession or the pursuit of executive power. And it further followed that all power corrupted; that government itself, and parliament considered as a place where power was actually exercised or sought after, could not but be visualized as a mechanism for the corruption of property, independence, and virtue. The ideology that objects to power as such, long established in an England where Country habitually mistrusted Court and property government, was being powerfully reinforced by the adoption of the civic vocabulary; and it was to be the recurrent problem of all Country parties that they could not take office without falsifying their own ostensible values—a problem on which Dr. Johnson was commenting in his dictum that patriotism (a term which had carried "Country" and "commonwealth" connotations since the seventeenth century) was the last refuge of the scoundrel. The problem became inescapable once it was conceded that the executive must win majorities in the legislature, and must win them by means of patronage—a concession implied by Shaftesbury and Marvell alike in their indictments of Danby. There was an ultimate incompatibility between civic republicanism and the facts of legislative sovereignty and king-in-parliament; but for the present the latter provided a vocabulary more flexible and revealing than any other for the conduct, as well as the criticism, of the latter.

In Harrington neither Court, corruption, nor office had been major elements of political analysis; his perspective had been too sanguine and millennial; but it is of significance that the only parliamentary debate in which speakers had employed ideas taken directly from his writings had been the long struggle carried on by the republican group in Richard Cromwell's parliament to avert recognition of the "Other House" established by the *Petition and Advice*. We earlier considered the last-named document as marking the return to the three estates of the *Answer to the Nineteen Propositions* and the Ancient Constitution; but the Harringtonian campaign against the Other House had been waged mainly on the assumption that, since it was impossible to restore the historic peerage, a nonrotatory or "standing" upper chamber must consist largely of major-generals and other military grandees, and only the gathering restorationist backlash had led, contrary to Harringtonian assumptions, to demands for the return of the "old lords" as defenders of the Ancient Constitution. The attack upon army officers as members of an entrenched (if not hereditary) aristocracy had been based in large measure on the assumption that to include them in an upper

house would be to entrench the army, and the taxation that maintained it, in the constitution; they would sit in parliament for life, and
perhaps their heirs after them, and vote themselves the taxes off which
they lived.[16] The debate of 1659 had therefore been an early and special instance of that complaint against placemen and corruption of
which so much was to be heard in later years—military senators would
be dependents of state and means of bringing parliament into dependence on state—but there is a further significance in the circumstance
that it was army placemen who then came under attack. By 1675 the
phrase "a standing army" was among the common coinage of English
political debate, and the Shaftesburean writers were regularly coupling
it with corruption and regularly opposing it to the ideal of the militia.

A *standing Parliament* and a *standing Army* are like those *Twins*
that have their lower parts united, and are divided only above the
Navel; they were born together and cannot long out-live each
other.[17]

The same might be said concerning the only Ancient and true
Strength of the Nation, the *Legal Militia*, and a *standing Army*. The
Militia must, and can never be otherwise than for *English Liberty*,
because else it doth destroy *itself*; but a *standing Force* can be for
nothing but *Prerogative*, by whom it hath its *idle living* and
Subsistence.[18]

The Civil War of 1642 had broken out in a dispute between king
and parliament for control of the county militia, and had, until the regiments were new-modeled, been fought between elements of that armed
force, the only one which England then possessed. Some of the opposition to Cromwell's Protectorate from within the army had come from
New Model idealists who still believed themselves to be a people in
arms and resented being placed under the direct control of the head of
state. The Restoration of 1660—itself in part the work of an army willing to disband itself rather than live at free quarter—had carried with
it an unequivocal declaration vesting control of the militia in the king;
but a necessary counterpoint to this principle had been an unspoken
but no less unequivocal insistence that it should only be the county
militia—the freeholders in arms under the gentry as their natural leaders—over which the king was to exercise command. There are some
manuscript tracts, of Harringtonian inspiration, which recognize that
a monarch logically needs a militia more immediately dependent upon

[16] "James Harrington and the Good Old Cause," above, ch. XI, n. 49.
[17] *Two Seasonable Discourses*, in *State Tracts . . . in the Reign of Charles
II . . .*, p. 68.
[18] *A Letter from a Parliament Man to his Friend, ibid.*, p. 70.

him;[19] and a few stalwarts regretted the abolition of feudal tenures for precisely this reason—a feudal host would be the embodiment of an England where every proprietor's land bound him to direct service and homage.[20] It was then a Restoration understanding that the king should command, but should command only the Country, the proprietors in arms; and any attempt on the part of the Crown to acquire added military strength must touch a very sensitive nerve indeed. "The guards are mercenary, and therefore dangerous," was the observation of an ultra-Cavalier speaker in the House of Commons.[21]

The term "standing army" had been known to Harrington, and he had employed it to denote something politically undesirable: the troops of soldiery kept permanently available to a supreme magistrate, like the guards used by ancient tyrants to establish unlawful power, but briefly permitted to the Lord Archon of Oceana in his capacity as legislator and *pater patriae*, in recognition of his incorruptible and indeed superhuman virtue.[22] Harrington had also employed the term in a more precisely military sense, as the antithesis of "marching army," which meant one taking the field against a real enemy or present danger.[23] A "standing army," then, was one embodied but not in the field, resembling the "standing army in time of peace" made subject to parliamentary consent in the Bill of Rights of 1689. But under the orders of Oceana, standing and marching army alike are composed of citizens, and it is only an improper subjection to the authority of a single magistrate which might render the former politically dangerous. By 1675, however, a change of profound importance was coming over the meaning of the term. It was beginning to be used to denote an army of professional officers and long-service soldiers, commanded, maintained, and above all paid by the state. Such an army differed from the *condottieri* of the Italian writers in being no band of free companions available for hire by any ruler, and from Machiavelli's *sudditi* and *creati*, or Harrington's janissaries and vassals, in not being personally dependent on any prince or overlord. They were (or might be) Englishmen serving a lawful and public authority, but doing so as full-time professionals practicing what Machiavelli had called an *arte*, for which they were paid, on a permanent basis, out of no private purse but from monies raised by public authority and disbursed by public officials. This was something new in the world; the mercenaries of the

---

[19] E.g., British Museum, Lansdowne MSS. 805, fols. 75-82.

[20] The best-known proponent of this view (not in a directly Harringtonian form) was Fabian Philipps; see *The Ancient Constitution*, pp. 215-17.

[21] Colonel Strangways, 29 April 1675; *Parliamentary History*, IV, 696. Cf., *ibid.*, pp. 461, 467, 604-608.

[22] Toland, *op.cit.*, pp. 200, 203-204.   [23] Toland, pp. 77, 101, 114, 190, 207.

Thirty Years War had been *condottieri* more often than not, and, even where they were embryo national armies, had soon exhausted their governments' power to maintain them, bankrupting their princes and devastating countrysides wherever they went, in an incessant secondary war against the peasantry, brought on by their search for food and specie. What was new was, at bottom, the strengthened financial structures which were enabling states to maintain them permanently; and how new this capacity was is indicated by the fact that Harrington, twenty years earlier, had flatly declared it impossible. An army could never be maintained by direct taxation, he said, because of the bitter resistance of the taxpayers;[24] and "a bank never paid an army, or, paying an army, soon became no bank."[25] If he conceded that Holland and Genoa might be exceptions—it is not certain that he did—he covered himself with the remark that "where there is a bank, ten to one it is a commonwealth";[26] and there were good reasons for doubting if even these great consortia could meet the costs of a seventeenth-century land army for ever. It is crucial to Harrington's whole theory that warriors can be maintained, in the last analysis, only by settling them on the land, and that the question is whether this will be done in ways that establish an Asian slave-monarchy, a feudal aristocracy, or a republican citizenry.[27] The ideas that a mercantile society can maintain a permanent (as distinct from recurrent) professional army, or that a monarchy could rule such a society with the aid of a military bureaucracy, were rejected.

But by the later seventies, such possibilities were becoming apparent. The guards and other regiments maintained by the English Crown were not numerous compared with what was to come, but they were beginning to resemble a permanent establishment.[28] Bureaucracies existed at court to pay and equip them, and among the miscellaneous (and suspect) sources from which the monies came there figured grants which parliament had been prevailed upon to make. To those who believed or professed to believe that ministers like Danby were corrupting the two houses with patronage, this presented a double threat: the grants which increased the numbers of serving officers and civilian bureaucrats at the same moment increased the numbers of place-holders who might come to sit in parliament and vote grants and taxes to maintain them as dependents of the executive; and since the process was self-multiplying and cancerous, parliament was being brought to fur-

[24] Toland, p. 67.   [25] Toland, p. 227.
[26] Toland, p. 230.   [27] Toland, p. 65.
[28] For a recent study of their character, see J. R. Western, *Monarchy and Revolution: the English State in the 1680s* (London: Routledge and Kegan Paul, 1972).

ther its own corruption and subjugation. It was the complaint of 1659 in new and graver tones: instead of a military aristocracy entrenched in an Other House, a military and civilian dependency was now being engrafted upon the commons, and instead of the New Model army—which had indeed never been a "standing army" in the new sense—incessantly searching for an executive capable of maintaining it, the restored Crown was proving to be an executive capable of building up its military force by manipulating and disturbing the traditional constitutional relationships.

In his speech of October 1675, Shaftesbury remarked in part:

> The King governing and administering Justice by his House of Lords, and advising with both his Houses of Parliament in all important matters, is the Government I own, am born under, and am obliged to. If ever there should happen in future Ages (which God forbid) a King governing by an Army, without his Parliament, 'tis a Government I own not, am not obliged to, nor was born under.[29]

This vaguely ominous language invokes the balance of three estates described in the *Answer to the Nineteen Propositions*; but the threat to legitimacy is not simply that of military dictatorship. Shaftesbury's hearers (his fellow-peers) are perhaps expected to remember Charles I demanding the Five Members or Cromwell expelling the Rump; but the underlying menace is that of corruption rather than coercion. The "King governing by an Army" is no Cromwell, but a Continental potentate who does not depend upon his estates to supply his standing troops,[30] and the rhetorical setting to which Shaftesbury's speech belongs plainly indicates that in England this is to be achieved through the corruption of parliament. The professional officer is the cause as well as the effect of this corruption, and his capacity to act in this baneful way arises from the fact that his decision to become a professional has rendered him the lifelong dependent of the state that can employ him. Harrington—however limited his understanding of contemporary trends in military organization—had argued that a main reason for the survival of "Gothic monarchy" in France was that the French *noblesses* had now become dependent on the king for their careers, those of the sword expecting to serve him in his armies, those of the robe in his courts and administration.[31] The English freeholders could not be transformed into a service nobility, but they might be corrupted through too much exposure to the pursuit of place. We recall what Lodovico Alamanni might have said of such a process, but in England

---

[29] *State Tracts . . . in the Reign of Charles II . . .*, p. 60.
[30] *Politics, Language and Time*, pp. 121-23.
[31] Toland, pp. 252-56.

the nightmare possibility now existed that parliament, the traditional defender of the freeholders' liberties, was becoming the means of corrupting and transforming their natures. This was the setting in which the myth of the English militia became potent, and did so in a recognizably Harringtonian form. The pamphleteer who declared that the militia could never act against liberty unless willing to destroy itself meant that it was the property and independence of the people in arms. To Harrington this had been the precondition which rendered a republic inescapable; to men of 1675 it was the guarantee of freedom, virtue, and stability in a restored mixed government of king, lords, and commons, operating to prevent corruption in the *materia*—the mass of propertied individuals—to which the constitution, traditional and balanced, ultimately gave form. New modes of corruption had become threatening, but the militia, like the frequent elections of parliament which were beginning to be demanded, could be seen as a means to the reactivation of virtue. Whatever brought government face to face with the mass of propertied individuals could be said *ridurre ai principii*.

The third circumstance mentioned earlier as crucial to the Harringtonian revival of 1675 was its taking place in the context of the continued existence of the House of Lords—and, as regards Shaftesbury's oration, in the physical setting of the house itself. Harrington, it will be recalled, had assumed that the peerage had ceased to be a feudal aristocracy; that England must now be governed as a republic in which the role of the few was no longer played by those on whom the many were dependent, or by any class exercising a hereditary right to powers denied others, but by an aristocracy of talent and function, chosen in rapid rotation by their fellow citizens for their conspicuous leisure and experience, and exercising only the power of debate—or proposing courses of action—rigorously separated from that of result, or choosing among the courses proposed. This carefully specified definition of "natural aristocracy" (as it was to be called) long remained authoritative. The debate in Richard Cromwell's parliament, as we have seen, turned on the proposed establishment of an entrenched if not hereditary aristocracy of Cromwellians (not to mention contemporaneous proposals by Vane, Milton, and others for an aristocracy of saints), but produced a backlash of opinion in favor of the old peerage, on the grounds both that their authority in parliament was part of the traditional constitution and that it discharged the intermediary and balancing function ascribed to it by the *Answer to the Nineteen Propositions*. Harrington himself remained convinced that since the lords could not be restored as a feudal baronage, there was no place for them in the existing distribution of property; and indeed it remains unclear whether, in the era following 1660, they exercised a social power commensurate with their constitutional functions. But we have now to speak of a period in which a hereditary but not feudal aristocracy was paradoxically defended as part of the apparatus of a constitution viewed in neo-Harringtonian terms. To his fellow peers in October 1675, Shaftesbury declared:

> My Lords, 'tis not only your Interest, but the interest of the Nation, that you maintain your Rights; for let the *House of Commons*, and *Gentry of England*, think what they please, there is no Prince that ever *Governed* without *Nobility* or an *Army*. If you will not have one, you must have t'other, or the Monarchy cannot long support, or keep itself from tumbling into a *Democraticall Republique*. Your *Lordships* and the *People* have the same cause, and the same Enemies. My Lords, would you be in favour with the King? 'Tis a very ill way to it, to put yourselves out of a future capacity, to be considerable in his Service. . . .[32]

The language is unmistakably Harringtonian, being a direct allusion to that passage in *Oceana*[33] where it is explained that the decay of feudal aristocracy brought about the Civil War—the king, because he could no longer depend on the peers to keep the people in subjection, being forced to attempt military government, since "a monarchy divested of its nobility hath no refuge under heaven but an army"— and yet the sense is strangely reversed. The lords are not presented as the people's feudal superiors, and it is in the latter's interest that they stand between them and military rule. The danger of government by an army is not the consequence—as it had been for Harrington—of the peerage's collapse, but is a conspiracy promoted by the enemies of peerage, people, and even king; these enemies, then, are working against the traditional mixed constitution and are obviously promoting the new corruption and the new standing army. We find similar thoughts expressed in the contemporaneous *Letter from a Person of Quality to his Friend in the Country*:

> it must be a great mistake in Counsels, or worse, that there should be so much pains taken by the Court to debase and bring low the House of Peers, if a Military Government be not intended by some. For the power of *Peerage* and a *Standing-Army* are like two Buckets, the proportion that one goes down, the other exactly goes up, and I refer you to the consideration of all the Histories of ours, or any of our neighbour Northern Monarchies, whether standing forces, Military, and Arbitrary Government came not plainly in by

[32] *State Tracts . . . in the Reign of Charles II . . .* , p. 59.
[33] Toland, p. 65.

the same steps, that the Nobility were lessened; and whether, whenever they were in Power and Greatness, they permitted the least shadow of any of them. . . .[34]

The same shift in emphasis, from historical to normative, is evident here. To Harrington the point had been that once the nobility lost their feudal power the people were free, and the king could govern them only by military coercion—an enterprise in which he would probably fail for want of soldiers. To the men of 1675 the nobility are the historical precursors of standing-army rule, but they are also the sole guarantee against it; and since it has been established upon the ruins of their power in all "neighbour Northern Monarchies," the need is all the greater to preserve the nobility in England. But the nobility's greatness and the people's freedom are not antithetical, as they had been for Harrington; they are inseparable, and the House of Lords is a necessary part of that mixed constitution of which the *Answer to the Nineteen Propositions* had spoken and whose existence Harrington had denied, condemning it as Gothic instability and "modern prudence." The word "Northern," as here used, is moreover a common synonym for "Gothic"—the Germanic invaders, or "Goths," were held to have come from the Scandinavian north, that *officina gentium*—and "Gothic" government is presented as a mode of rule, once widespread but now surviving only in England, the opposite of "Military and Arbitrary Government," and capable of existing only where a nobility has not given place to its necessary antithesis the standing army. The House of Lords, frequent parliaments, and the militia are being enlisted on the same side, that of the mixed and ancient constitution, whose enemy is something Harrington never thought of, the corruption of parliament by patronage and military professionalization, and the militia, to Harrington a new and revolutionary force, is being made ancient, Gothic, and compatible with a hereditary aristocracy—all things he had denied it could ever have been.

What is called the neo-Harringtonian interpretation, then, involved a complete reversal of the historical order found in Harrington's own account of English government, the reconciliation of his norms—the relation of citizenship to arms and of arms to land—with the *Answer to the Nineteen Propositions* and the Ancient Constitution. Harringtonian freedom was made to exist in the Gothic and English past instead of being founded on its ruins. This reversal of time-sequence was the necessary consequence of two things: the decision to accept a world in which Crown and peerage had retained both existence and legiti-

[34] *State Tracts . . . in the Reign of Charles II . . .*, p. 55.

macy, and the gathering belief that the Court's reviving powers of patronage and military employment presented the main threat to the country's parliamentary independence. Corruption had not been a prominent term in Harrington's vocabulary;[35] he had been interested mainly in emancipation from dependence in its feudal form; but the republican and Machiavellian language of which he was the chief English exponent was the appropriate vehicle for expounding a theory of corruption, and we are seeing something of the reasons why Shaftesbury and the country thinkers of the 1670s found such a theory attractive. A close friend of Harrington's, who survived him for many years,[36] was now at work upon a restatement of his theory, intended to supply a historical context for the transition from old feudalism to modern corruption.

Henry Neville had been close enough to the author of *Oceana* to make Thomas Hobbes suspect he had taken part in its composition,[37] and had been an active member of the republican rearguard in 1659. During the debates in Richard Cromwell's parliament he had heard, and opposed, much argument designed to present the traditional peerage as part of the liberty of the Ancient Constitution, but only twenty years later did he employ doctrine of this kind for his own purposes. His *Plato Redivivus*, a political dialogue published in 1680, accepts the premise that the present troubles of England are due to the decay of the Ancient Constitution,[38] which cannot therefore have been the anarchic wrestling-match which it had appeared during the Interregnum. He affirms, however, that it was founded upon the feudal ascendancy of the peerage, and that its decay is the result of a shift in the balance of property which has emancipated the commons from their control. But if the feudal period was one of constitutional freedom, not of oscillation between anarchy and absolute monarchy, something must be said of the position of the non-noble subject during all that time. The year 1680 was one in which the antiquity of the House of Commons, denied in the posthumously republished works of Filmer, had been angrily affirmed by the Whig writers Petyt and Atwood, and

[35] Toland, p. 68.

[36] Harrington died in 1677, having apparently been incapacitated for a considerable time. Neville lived until 1694. For as much biographical information as is available on the latter, see Caroline Robbins's introduction, pp. 5-20, to her *Two English Republican Tracts* (Cambridge University Press, 1969), in which the full text of *Plato Redivivus* is given; and my "James Harrington and the Good Old Cause," for his role in the 1659 debates.

[37] John Aubrey, *Brief Lives*, ed. Oliver Lawson Dick (London: Secker and Warburg), p. 124.

[38] Robbins, *Republican Tracts*, pp. 76, 81-82, 132-35, 144-50.

was now in process of refutation by the adepts of feudal scholarship headed by Robert Brady.[39] Neville, from his own Harringtonian or neo-Harringtonian perspective, is ambivalent on this score. On the one hand he writes (very much in his manner of 1659):

> In our ancestors' times, most of the members of our house of commons thought it an honour to retain to some great lord, and to wear his blue coat: and when they had made up their lord's train, and waited upon him from his own house to the lords' house, and made a lane for him to enter, and departed to sit themselves in the lower house of parliament, as it was then (and very justly) called; can you think that anything could pass in such a parliament, that was not ordered by the lords?[40]

But a few pages earlier we read:

> And I must confess I was inclined to believe, that before that time [i.e., the reign of Henry III], our yeomanry or commonalty had not formally assembled in parliament, but been virtually included and represented by the peers, upon whom they depended: but I am fully convinced that it was otherwise, by the learned discourses lately published by Mr Petyt of the Temple, and Mr Atwood of Grays-Inn; being gentlemen whom I mention, *honoris causa*.[41]

Neville had to maintain the antiquity of the commons, both because a Tory counterattack was denying it in order to show that all liberties were of the king's gift, and in order to uphold his neo-Harringtonian position that the ascendancy of the baronage had been part of a regime of ancient freedom which must be reformed and preserved. But his closeness to Harrington underlines the paradoxical role he was now playing. The revolutionary of 1656, insisting that there had been no liberty until the commons were free of lords and king alike, was in reality closer to the Tory Brady, who argued on the same grounds that the commons had had no liberty until the king had given it to them; and Neville's attempt to make Harringtonian liberty seem ancient would have been better argued if he could have joined Atwood and Algernon Sidney in scouting the element of vassalage in feudal society and contending that words like *baro* had applied to all freemen, noble and non-noble alike.[42] But his equivocation left him on stronger ground when he sought to argue that the decay of baronage had been

[39] *Ancient Constitution*, pp. 187-95.   [40] *Republican Tracts*, p. 134.
[41] *Ibid.*, p. 120.
[42] Atwood argued this case at length in *Jus Anglorum ab Antiquo* (1681) and *The Lord Holles his Remains* (1682). Sidney, *Discourses on Government* (3d ed., London, 1751), p. 387.

part of the decay of the Ancient Constitution. When the king had had only the barons to deal with, they had brought the commons into line for him; but as their power had decayed, he had been confronted by an increasingly independent landowning commonalty over whom he had no means of influence, and the House of Lords was therefore failing—this at least survived from the Harringtonian interpretation proper—to act as that *pouvoir intermèdiaire* which the theory of mixed government prescribed that they should be.[43] Neville had no intention of restoring them to that role; he proposed setting up a series of councils in which king and parliament should administer the executive power jointly; but it is clear from his treatment that a nobility deprived of feudal power, but retaining a hereditary right of summons, might continue to act as titular and honorary leaders of a landowning class from which nothing now differentiated them—as Giannotti might have put it, all were now *mediocri*. His essential contention, however, is that the decay of the baronage has left the royal executive and its prerogatives face to face with a parliamentary commonalty over whom it has no control; and until a constitutional solution, like that he is concerned to propose, has redistributed power, the relations of Crown and commons are doomed to instability. In the deadlocks which arise, cunning but incompetent ministers and courtiers will gull the king with ingenious proposals, whose effect if carried out might well be to corrupt the people; but Neville, more sanguine than Shaftesbury or Marvell, considers these devices likely to fail.[44] In particular, his Harringtonian training and his New Model memories combine to make him think that no standing army capable of enforcing the royal power can be recruited from the English commonalty.[45] But if Neville himself has no highly developed theory of corruption, he has provided the historical context in which one might be situated. It could now be argued that corruption was a necessary expedient to which kings had been driven by the decay of baronial power over the people; the history of peerage might, at the cost of some inconsistency, be assimilated to the myth of a constitution both ancient and uncorrupted; and if a militia of freemen, independent in arms and in tenure, could be made part of that myth, the new phenomenon of military bureaucracy would fit into place as its corrupting opposite.

The formal restatement of Harringtonian doctrine, in what we have referred to as its neo-Harringtonian form, was now complete. Its two essential characteristics were the acceptance of a House of Lords which was not a feudal baronage and was no longer condemned as an entrenched aristocracy, but might be thought of as an almost natural

[43] *Republican Tracts*, pp. 135, 145-48.   [44] *Ibid.*, pp. 178-82, 198-200.
[45] *Ibid.*, p. 180.

intermediary between Crown and commons,[46] and the relegation to the past of that commonwealth of armed proprietors which Harrington had located in the present. To Neville, Harrington's friend and literary heir apparent, whose experience of the doctrine in action had begun in 1659, it may well have seemed necessary to restate it if its essentials were to survive under the restored Ancient Constitution; and to those in the Shaftesbury circle, as well as Marvell and Neville, who now saw patronage, placemen, and standing army as the chief threat to the political order, an equation of the historic structure of parliament with the classical (as well as historical) militia may have seemed what was chiefly required. But the consequences of reversing the Harringtonian sequence were of moment. The political norm now lay in the past, and the movement of history, which Harrington had seen as a *rinnovazione*, resumed its common pattern of decline. The motive of the neo-Harringtonians was to denounce corruption; they paid the price of obliging themselves to regard all change as corruption (we recall that they had denied themselves recourse to a millennium). Furthermore, that which was exposed to corruption and degeneration was now the Ancient Constitution, and this must accordingly be envisaged in the form of a balance (as since 1642 it had been normal to do). But since the crucial disturbance was no longer that taking place in the relation of lords to commons, the balance being disturbed might better be seen as one of powers rather than estates; it was the executive that threatened to encroach upon the legislature, and the problem of patronage led to a century and more of debate concerning the separation and interdependence of the powers of the constitution. To qualify as corruption, however, the encroachments of the executive must be seen as more than an infringement of the sphere of legislative action. They must be seen as tending to bring the individual members, as well as the corporate body, of the legislature into dependence upon the executive, a dependence which must be termed corruption since it existed where independence should obtain. The importation of the classical concept of corruption necessitated considerable restatement of a theory of the English constitution itself little known before *The King's Answer to the Nineteen Propositions*. That an ideology so founded received so rapidly such widespread acceptance indicates the importance which the issues raised by Shaftesbury's attack on Danby possessed for the English political public.

No important response to *Plato Redivivus* appeared from the Tory side,[47] a fact which indicates the ideological confusion of the last years

[46] *Ibid.*, pp. 192-94.
[47] W. W., *Antidotum Britannicum*, and Thomas Goddard, *Plato's Demon*, neither of much significance, appeared in 1682.

of Charles II's reign. In 1675, when the neo-Harringtonian attack began, the publication of a work of feudal scholarship had fired the train which led to the Brady controversy. In 1679, the republication of the posthumous works of Filmer had had three consequences: the beginnings of the composition of Locke's *Treatises on Government*, of Tyrrell's *Patriarcha non Monarcha*,[48] and of other works which argued for consensual authority against the patriarchal thesis; the continuation by Petyt and Atwood of the antifeudal polemic begun in 1675, now intended as a riposte to those of Filmer's works which denied the antiquity of the commons, and the counterattack of Brady and his allies; and the apparently independent composition by Algernon Sidney of those *Discourses on Government* which were to contribute to his death in 1683. *Plato Redivivus*, essentially a continuation of the neo-Harringtonian polemic of 1675, was caught up in the battle between Petyt and Brady through Neville's decision to accept the former's thesis concerning the House of Commons, and the Tory writers took notice of it only on that score. Brady and his friends were old Royalists rather than new Tories, interested in the defense of prerogative and hereditary succession rather than of patronage and standing armies, and they made no response to Neville's theses linking the decline of feudalism to the rise of patronage. In the next generation, however, such a response developed, and took the form of a blunt assertion that since feudalism had declined patronage was indeed necessary, and not corrupting.[49] Such a version of history might have been arrived at by quoting Harrington against the neo-Harringtonians, but more usually rested upon an acceptance of Brady's theses concerning the feudal past. In the changing patterns of Revolution politics, this argument came to serve the interests of the Whigs, and Whig bishops were carrying on the work of Spelman and Brady by 1698.[50]

Down to 1688, while the Whigs were still a near-rebellious opposition, the statement of the neo-Harringtonian polemic of Country against Court had to coexist with the more pressing need to repudiate Filmer, hold out against the last offensive of the old prerogative and nonresistant school, and finally to justify the Revolution. Generally speaking, these were not operations best conducted in semi-republican or neo-Harringtonian terms, though it is important to bear in mind

---

[48] The complicated story of Locke's and Tyrrell's writings at this time is pursued by Peter Laslett in the introduction to his edition of Locke's *Two Treatises* (Cambridge University Press, 1960 and 1963), ch. III.

[49] See below, pp. 481-82, 494-95.

[50] Edmund Gibson, later Bishop of London, completed editing Spelman's works in 1698 (*Ancient Constitution*, p. 243). See G. V. Bennett, *White Kennet, 1660-1728: Bishop of Peterborough* (London: S.P.C.K., 1957).

that Sidney's *Discourses*, a voice from the past, recalling the Good Old Cause of the fifties and even the Tacitism of an earlier generation still, condemn absolute monarchy for corrupting the subject and equate virtue with a framework of mixed government so austerely defined as to be virtually an aristocratic republic.[51] Canonized for the next century by their author's martyrdom, they were not published until the crucial year 1698, by which time, paradoxically enough, they appeared less anachronistic than they might have fifteen years earlier. The polemic against patronage and corruption was an attack upon modern government, that against prerogative and patriarchalism was an attempt to bury the past; yet it was the former that entailed the language of classical republicanism, the latter that enlisted the services of Locke. The amalgam which was Whig ideology in the eighties disintegrated during the decade following the Revolution;[52] and the neo-Harringtonian thesis became an instrument of radical reaction in an era of devastating economic change.

[51] *Discourses*, II, sections 11-30; III, sections 1-10.

[52] Caroline Robbins, *The Eighteenth-Century Commonwealthman: Studies in the Transmission, Development and Circumstance of English Liberal Thought from the Restoration of Charles II until the War with the Thirteen Colonies* (Cambridge, Mass.: Harvard University Press, 1959), chs. II and III in particular. See the Advertisement to vol. II of *A Collection of State Tracts Published on Occasion of the Late Revolution in 1688 and during the Reign of King William III* (London, 1706), for comment on the disruption of Whig solidarity as revealed in pamphlets.

CHAPTER XIII

NEO-MACHIAVELLIAN POLITICAL ECONOMY

The Augustan Debate over Land, Trade and Credit

[1]

THE HALF-CENTURY FOLLOWING the Revolution of 1688 is a period till recently little studied, but nevertheless of great importance, in the history of English political thought—not least because, strictly speaking, it witnesses the latter's transformation from "English" to "British" in the year 1707. Between the Englishman John Locke at the beginning of the period so designated, and the Scot David Hume commencing his work as it closed, no political theorist or philosopher to be ranked among the giants emerged in Anglophone culture; and yet the period was one of change and development in some ways more radical and significant even than those of the Civil War and Interregnum. Specifically it can be shown that this was the era in which political thought became engrossed with the conscious recognition of change in the economic and social foundations of politics and the political personality, so that the *zōon politikon* took on his modern character of participant observer in processes of material and historical change fundamentally affecting his nature; and it can be shown that these changes in perception came about through the development of a neo-Machiavellian, as well as neo-Harringtonian, style in the theory of political economy, in response to England's emergence as Britain, a major commercial, military, and imperial power. The processes observed, and the changes in language consequent upon the observation, were in a material and secular sense more revolutionary than anything to be detected in the generation of radical Puritanism; and among the phenomena will be found the appearance of Machiavellian thought as a criticism of modernity.

In studying this development in the history of thought, we shall allot a crucial role to neither the justification of the Revolution of 1688 itself, nor the political writings of Locke. The deposition of James II could of its nature give rise to little more than a reexamination of the conditionality of political authority, which in the Machiavellian tradition had always appeared as a feature of the contingent world, and a countervailing emphasis upon the relation of tradition and custom to consent;[1] nor did James—possibly the most unsubtle figure in the history of English political interpretation—ever appear as one of those archetypes of corruption, like Shaftesbury's Danby or Bolingbroke's Walpole, out of whom the mythology of English neo-Machiavellism was to be built. As for Locke, it has to be admitted that the present is an unfortunate moment for including him in syntheses. Among the revolutionary effects of the reevaluation of his historical role initiated by Laslett and continued by Dunn[2] has been a shattering demolition of his myth: not that he was other than a great and authoritative thinker, but that his greatness and authority have been wildly distorted by a habit of taking them unhistorically for granted. Since he was no kind of classical or Machiavellian republican, he does not contribute directly to the formation of the tradition we are to study; it seems possible rather to allot him a place, and debate its magnitude, among that tradition's adversaries.[3] But the deemphasizing of Locke is for the present a tactical necessity. The historical context must be reconstructed without him before he can be fitted back into it.

The acceptance of William III as king proved to mean something not fully foreseen or desired by those who invited him over: the commitment of England—of English troops and money—to a sequence of major continental wars. This involved a quasi-permanent enlargement of that standing army whose sinister role in the public imagination of the seventies had lost nothing in the days of James II and the persecution of the Huguenots; and in addition, by the end of the Nine Years War of 1688-1697 (King William's War in the notation of American historiography), two further massive consequences had made their way to recognition. The maritime losses of this war, undertaken in alliance with the Dutch, had made explicit certain facts of the era of the Dutch Wars now ending: that England was now a trading nation—something which Scotland desperately longed to become—and that according to

---

[1] This conclusion emerges from a study of the overall character of the *State Tracts . . . on occasion of the Late Revolution* (see above, ch. XII, n. 52), I (1705). There is one neo-Harringtonian analysis of the fall of James II: *Some Remarks upon Government, and Particularly upon the Establishment of the English Monarchy, Relating to this Present Juncture*, signed N. T. (pp. 149-62); its tone is consciously extra-moral and "Machiavellian."

[2] John Dunn, *The Political Thought of John Locke: An Historical Account of the Argument of the Two Treatises of Government* (Cambridge University Press, 1969), and "The Politics of Locke in England and America in the Eighteenth Century," in John W. Yolton (ed.), *John Locke: Problems and Perspectives* (Cambridge University Press, 1969), pp. 45-80.

[3] See Isaac F. Kramnick, *Bolingbroke and His Circle: The Politics of Nostalgia in the Age of Walpole* (Cambridge, Mass.: Harvard University Press, 1968), pp. 61-63.

the assumptions of the age, commerce was an aggressive action, an acquisition to the trading society's self of something which might have been acquired by another, an end to which war might or might not be an appropriate means. It was a further aspect of this perception that something called national prosperity was an intelligible field of study, and that there existed an art called "political arithmetic," a quantitative means of estimating every individual's contribution to the political good by measuring what he put into or withdrew from the national stock.[4] At a very rapid pace, an entity known as Trade entered the language of politics, and became something which no orator, pamphleteer, or theorist could afford to neglect and which, in an era of war, was intimately connected with the concepts of external relations and national power.

But the second consequence of England's involvement in major war was perceived in terms more far-reaching still. In what has been called the "financial revolution"[5] that began in the nineties, means were found of associating the national prosperity directly with the stability of the regime, the expanding activities of government and—most significant of these—the prosecution of war. The institutions of the new finance, of which the Bank of England and the National Debt came to be the most important, were essentially a series of devices for encouraging the large or small investor to lend capital to the state, investing in its future political stability and strengthening this by the act of investment itself, while deriving a guaranteed income from the return on the sum invested. With the aid of the invested capital, the state was able to maintain larger and more permanent armies and bureaucracies—incidentally increasing the resources at the disposal of political patronage—and as long as its affairs visibly prospered, it was able to attract further investments and conduct larger and longer wars. The era of the *condottiere*—the short-term military contractor—ended, his place being taken by the military administrator as one arm of the bureaucratic state. But as the volume of investment increased, two further consequences followed. The state felt able to accept more credit, and conduct greater activities, than could be paid for by the existing volume of capital, and it guaranteed the repayment of loans on the security of revenues to be collected, and investments to be made, in the future; the National Debt

[4] The founder of this art was held to be Sir William Petty. See E. Strauss, *Sir William Petty: Portrait of a Genius* (London: The Bodley Head, 1954), and William Letwin, *The Origins of Scientific Economics* (New York: Doubleday Anchor Books, 1965).

[5] P.G.M. Dickson, *The Financial Revolution in England: A Study in the Development of Public Credit, 1688-1756* (London: Macmillan, 1967); Dennis Rubini, "Politics and the Battle for the Banks, 1688-1697," *English Historical Review* 85 (1970), 693-714.

had been born and entailed upon posterity. It was noted that this did not save war from being paid for by a rapidly increasing land tax which, unlike those in previous generations, was efficiently collected; the state was too strong and too heavily legitimated to be defied by the non-payment of the early Stuart period. Secondly, the volume of investment meant that the shares, tickets, or tallies entitling the possessor to a share of repayment from the public funds became marketable property, whose value rose and fell as public confidence in the state's political, military, and financial transactions waxed and waned. The fund-holder and the stockjobber, the bull and the bear, had come upon the stage; and the figure around which they were grouped, the concept which they introduced into the language of English politics, was not Trade but Credit.

The rapidly developing style of political economy, which is the dominant mode of Augustan political thought, took shape around the varying relationships which publicists were prepared to allow between land, trade, and credit as sources not merely of public wealth, but of political stability and virtue. The stress laid upon the last-named is so great that we have to recognize that the first chapter in the history of political economy is also a further chapter in the continuing history of civic humanism; and the Augustan debate derives its Harringtonian and Machiavellian character from the circumstance that the critics of the new finance denounced it as a continuation of that alliance between patronage and militarism, corruption and the standing army, which had figured in the debate of 1675 and had already become so far a staple of political polemic that the defenders of the new order were obliged to accept many of its postulates and assumptions. Debate along these lines reaches a series of peaks during the Augustan half-century: first in the "standing army controversy" or "paper war" of approximately 1698-1702,[6] in which John Toland, John Trenchard, Walter Moyle, Andrew Fletcher, and Charles Davenant wrote for the Country party and Daniel Defoe and Jonathan Swift for the Court; second, during the "four last years" of Queen Anne, when Swift for the Tories was opposed by the Whigs Addison and—with some changes of front—Defoe;[7] thirdly, during the storms of the South Sea crisis, domi-

[6] See Robbins, *The Eighteenth-Century Commonwealthman*, pp. 103-105; Frank H. Ellis, introduction to his edition of Swift, *A Discourse of the Contests and Dissensions between the Nobles and the Commons in Athens and Rome* (Oxford: The Clarendon Press, 1967); W. T. Laprade, *Public Opinion and Politics in Eighteenth-Century England to the Fall of Walpole* (New York: Macmillan, 1936).

[7] Michael Foot, *The Pen and the Sword* (London: Macgibbon and Kee, 1957); Richard I. Cook, *Jonathan Swift as a Tory Pamphleteer* (Seattle and London: University of Washington Press, 1967); James O. Richards, *Party Propaganda*

nated in the field of journalism by John Trenchard and Thomas Gordon, conducting *Cato's Letters* and *The Independent Whig*; and lastly, between 1726 and 1734, when Bolingbroke attempted to destroy Walpole by a journalistic campaign in *The Craftsman*, supported by most of the great writers of the age and countered by *The London Journal* and Lord Hervey.[8] The main lines of argument in all these debates are strikingly consistent, to the point where, with Defoe in 1698 and the Walpolean writers thirty-five years later, one can see the lineaments of a "Court" theory of economics, politics, and history, constructed to meet the challenge of what has become known as the "Country" ideology. By the end of the period the way was clear for the great summations of the controversy written by Montesquieu and Hume at mid-century; and the ideological stage was not significantly altered until the era of the French Revolution.

The "paper war" of the last years of William III's reign is also known as the "standing army controversy,"[9] because it turned largely on the Country party's desire to reduce the king's English and foreign forces immediately after the peace treaty of 1697; but it also involved issues of corruption in at least three senses of the term, varying from ancient to very new. Courtiers, including both foreigners and women, were found to have received excessively large grants of Irish land; there was a recrudescent desire to exclude placemen from the House of Commons; and, most innovatory of all, there were the beginnings of what became a very widespread denunciation of the "corruption" of parliament and society by fundholders and stockjobbers, rentiers living off their share (however acquired) of the public debts. The conjunction of eulogy of the militia with jeremiads against corruption by the executive, with which we are already familiar, developed into a new analysis of the relation of war and commerce to virtue, and into a new controversy concerning the course of English and European history, which with its underlying ambiguities reveals the neo-Machiavellian character of thought about and in the new age. Its study can best be initiated by exploring the writings of Andrew Fletcher, Charles Davenant, and Daniel Defoe.

Fletcher[10] was a Scot, one of the first of a long line of percipient

---

under Queen Anne: the General Elections of 1702-13 (Athens: University of Georgia Press, 1972).

[8] Kramnick, *op.cit.*

[9] Lois F. Schwoerer, "The Literature of the Standing Army Controversy," *Huntington Library Quarterly* 28, no. 3 (1964-65), 187-212; Dennis Rubini, *Court and Country, 1688-1702* (London: Rupert Hart-Davis, 1967).

[10] Robbins, *Eighteenth-Century Commonwealthman*, pp. 9-10, 180-84. His *Political Works* were published in 1732 and repeatedly thereafter. See also Lord

North Britons who understood the language of English controversy better, in some respects, than the English themselves. He had been out with Monmouth in 1685, but had left Somerset hurriedly after shooting a Taunton notable in a quarrel over a horse. The impression of archaic truculence which this detail may leave is misleading; the man was a patriot ideologue of high intellectual attainments, who would have made an admirable contemporary of Patrick Henry and Richard H. Lee. In the *Discourse of Government with Relation to Militias*, he developed the neo-Harringtonian version of history further than anyone had yet carried it, and significantly revealed its latent ambivalences.

He argues that from A.D. 400 to 1500 the Gothic mode of government had guaranteed liberty to Europe by keeping the sword in the hands of the landholding subject. The barons had held of the kings and the vassals of the barons, and

> when this was done, there was no longer any Standing Army kept on foot, but every man went to live upon his own Lands; and when the Defence of the Country required an Army, the King summoned the Barons to his Standard, who came attended with their Vassals. Thus were the Armies of Europe composed for about eleven hundred years; and this Constitution of Government put the Sword into the hands of the Subject, because the Vassals depended more immediately on the Barons than on the King, which effectually secured the freedom of those Governments. For the Barons could not make use of their Power to destroy those limited Monarchies, without destroying their own Grandeur; nor could the King invade their Privileges, having no other Forces than the Vassals of his own Demeasnes to rely upon for his support in such an Attempt.
>
> I lay no great stress on any other Limitations of those Monarchies; nor do I think any so essential to the Liberties of the People, as that which placed the Sword in the hands of the Subject. . . .
>
> I do not deny that these limited Monarchies during the greatness of the Barons, had some Defects: I know few Governments free from them. But after all, there was a Balance that kept those Governments steady, and an effectual Provision against the Encroachments of the Crown.[11]

By this typically Whig slurring over of the dependence of tenant upon lord, Fletcher had once more eliminated Harrington's sharp dis-

---

Buchan, *Essays on the Lives and Writings of Fletcher of Saltoun and the Poet Thomson* (London, 1792).

[11] *A Discourse of Government with Relation to Militias* (Edinburgh, 1698), pp. 7-9.

tinction between "ancient prudence" and "ancient constitution," and had located the balanced commonwealth of armed freemen in the era of "modern prudence" which, with its apparatus of king, lords, and commons, Harrington had dismissed as an ill-regulated disequilibrium. Feudal tenure now became a means to balance, because it ensured an equilibrium between king and barons, and to liberty and equality, because it made the commoner-vassals contributors to that balance. Unlike Harrington's vassal, whose land and sword were his master's, Fletcher seems to have seen his vassal—who was after all a Scot—as intractable upon his own plot of ground, helping to keep the sword where it belonged, in the hands of the proprietors of land. The barons of 1215, or any other date, could be shown defending the principles of ancient balance, *virtù* and liberty, even as they defended their feudal privileges.

But this state of affairs had gone and could not be restored. "About the year 1500," there had occurred an "Alteration of Government . . . in most Countries of Europe," which had left nothing of the old constitutions but "the ancient Terms and outward Forms," so that "the generality of all Ranks of Men are cheated by Words and Names."[12] Harrington had assigned the same dating to the end of feudal tenures, but had seen this as a liberating process, initiated by conscious action even if its author, Henry VII, had not understood the power he was setting loose. It had been essentially legal action which emancipated the vassals from military service, though broader social consequences had ensued when the lords took to lives of conspicuous expenditure at court and the liberated "industry" of the people had seized upon the abbey lands sold them by Henry VIII. To Fletcher, the process was unintended,[13] far more broadly social in its origins and profoundly ambivalent in its consequences.

I shall deduce from their Original, the Causes, Occasions, and the Complication of those many unforeseen Accidents; which falling out much about the same time, produced so great a Change. And it will at first sight seem very strange, when I shall name the Restoration of Learning, the Invention of Printing, of the Needle and of Gunpowder, as the chief of them; things in themselves so excellent, and which, the last only excepted, might have proved of infinite Advantage to the World, if their remote Influence upon Govern-

[12] *Discourse*, p. 5.
[13] *Discourse*, p. 6: "And 'tis worth observation, that tho this Change was fatal to their Liberty, yet it was not introduced by the Contrivance of ill-designing Men; nor were the mischievous Consequences perceived, unless perhaps by a few wise Men, who, if they saw it, wanted Power to prevent it."

ment had been obviated by suitable Remedies. Such odd Consequences, and of such a different Nature, accompany extraordinary Inventions of any kind.[14]

Innovation, we observe, is retaining its dangerous and unpredictable character; but, unlike Machiavelli's concern for the effects upon men of stripping them of a framework of custom, Fletcher's attention is directed toward causation, toward the long-term effects of action in the complex web of human society. Of the innovations he names, the restoration of learning and the invention of printing made the diversities of culture available to previously "Gothic" Europeans, and the invention of the compass opened up a world trade. The significance of gunpowder has yet to emerge.

By this means the Luxury of Asia and America was added to that of the Antients; and all Ages, and all Countries concurred to sink Europe into an Abyss of Pleasures; which were rendred the more expensive by a perpetual Change of the Fashions in Clothes, Equipage and Furniture of Houses.

These things brought a total Alteration in the way of living, upon which all Government depends. 'Tis true, Knowledg being mightily increased, and a great Curiosity and Nicety in every thing introduced, Men imagined themselves to be gainers in all points, by changing from their frugal and military way of living, which I must confess had some mixture of Rudeness and Ignorance in it, tho not inseparable from it. But at the same time they did not consider the unspeakable Evils that are altogether inseparable from an expensive way of living.[15]

The danger of luxury, we soon learn, is not that it produces effeminacy of taste or even mutability of fashion, so much as that it leads to choice and consequently to specialization. The Gothic warrior had nothing much to do but till his soil, bear his arms, and assert his freedom; the refined man of the Renaissance might pursue knowledge or luxury, pleasure or fashion, and so lost interest in defending himself. If he was a lord, he got into debt and commuted his vassals' services for rents; if he was a commoner, he was content to be a tenant instead of a vassal. The kings meanwhile found their subjects willing to pay them a revenue out of which to hire mercenaries to defend them; and the invention of gunpowder, turning wars into long and expensive sieges, intensified this process as soon as it had begun. Once armies were paid for by taxes, taxes were collected by armies and the liberties of nearly all Europe were at an end.[16] But rule by professional soldiers

[14] *Discourse*, pp. 9-10.   [15] *Discourse*, pp. 12-13.   [16] *Discourse*, pp. 13-15.

came about only because the subject was able to exercise choice, to prefer alternatives to bearing arms himself. What he did not like, he could pay another to do for him; what he alienated as he bought this immunity, he did not find out until the step was irreversible. "Luxury," then, is shorthand for culture, leisure, and choice; these goods carry their concomitant ill. The most Fletcher can suggest is that rudeness and ignorance are not inseparable from warrior freedom, meaning presumably that the primitive freeman was still educable; but "an expensive way of living," in which he sells the means of freedom to buy the materials of culture, is inseparable from corruption.

Fletcher has elaborated the neo-Harringtonian perspective to the point where it exposed the most difficult of the many problems to perplex eighteenth-century social thought: the apparent incompatibility of liberty and virtue with culture, which, more than commerce itself, opened up the problem of the diversity of human satisfactions. The freeman must desire nothing more than freedom, nothing more than the public good to which he dedicated himself; once he could exchange his freedom for some other commodity, the act became no less corrupting if that other commodity were knowledge itself. The humanist stress on arms and land as the preconditions of individual civic and moral autonomy had heightened the dilemma by presenting it in the form of an irreversible historical process. Virtue, in its paradigmatic social form, was now located in a past; but the era of freedom was also the era of barbarism and superstition, and the term "Gothic" might, with excruciating ambivalence, be applied in both senses. As for commerce, it was, so to speak, the active form of culture itself: if there were many satisfactions a man might choose between them, and if he assigned priorities, postponing a future satisfaction for the sake of a present one, he was already well on the way toward effecting exchanges. There was a morality for the Aristotelian citizen, joining in the determination of priorities; but if there was a morality for the trading man, exchanging one commodity for its equivalent value in another, that morality was conspicuously not linked to the virtue of the citizen—the only secular virtue yet known to Western man— which still demanded of the individual an autonomy he could not alienate without becoming corrupt. It would be wrong to suppose that Fletcher naively desired to restore an agrarian world of self-sufficient farming warriors; he wrote at length about the undeniably urgent problems of inducing some degree of commercial prosperity in the desperate society of Scotland;[17] but his history of liberty, his "discourse of government in its relation to militias," reveals to us a condition of

[17] See the "First" and "Second Discourses on the Affairs of Scotland" in his *Political Works*.

thought about 1700 in which a bourgeois ideology, a civic morality for market man, was ardently desired but apparently not to be found. This is why he goes on—as Toland did in his contemporaneous *The Militia Reformed*[18]—to describe a scheme of military training for all freeholders, which is essentially a means of education in civic virtue.[19] Men are no longer the barons and vassals of the Gothic world; they have choice, commerce, and the opportunity of corruption. To render unnecessary the professional armies which will make corruption irreversible, they must form a militia; but this austere mode of service to the commonwealth will teach them, by actualizing it in arms, the frugality, the surrender of private satisfactions—there is even an equivalent to the militia sermons which had praised poverty in the Florence of 1528-1530[20]—and in short the virtue, which the social order itself no longer guarantees. To set up such a militia will be legislative, educative, and a *ridurre ai principii*; *buone leggi, buona educazione, buone arme.* Education, however, has begun its long career as a perceived mode of counteracting the course of social development.

But the neo-Harringtonian version of English history was singularly liable to attack; with Brady or with Harrington himself on his desk, a critic might argue that the Gothic epoch had been one of such subjection of the commons to the lords that no balance or liberty had existed. Defoe, in his reply to Fletcher and Trenchard,[21] argued as against the former that

> about the time, when this Service by Villenage and Vassalage began to be resented by the People, and by Peace and Trade they grew rich, and the Power of the Barons being too great, frequent Commotions, Civil Wars, and Battels, were the Consequence, nay sometimes without concerning the King in the Quarrel: One Nobleman would Invade another, in which the weakest suffered most, *and the poor Man's Blood was the Price of all*; the People obtain'd Priviledges of their own, and oblig'd the King and the Barons to accept of an *Equilibrium*, this we call a Parliament: And from this the Due Bal-

---

[18] *State Tracts*, II, 594-614.   [19] *Discourse*, pp. 50-62.

[20] *Discourse*, p. 54. These are to be delivered by members of the militia itself, churchmen being excluded from the camp. Cf. p. 52: "Their Drink should be Water, sometimes tempered with a proportion of Brandy, and at other times with Vinegar."

[21] *An Argument Shewing that a Standing Army, with Consent of Parliament, Is Not Inconsistent with a Free Government* (1698); reprinted in J. T. Boulton (ed.), *Daniel Defoe* (New York: Schocken Books, 1965). This was in answer to John Trenchard and Walter Moyle, *An Argument Shewing that a Standing Army Is Inconsistent with a Free Government, and Absolutely Destructive to the Constitution of the English Monarchy* (1697).

lance, we have so much heard of is deduced. I need not lead my Reader to the Times and Circumstances of this, but this Due Ballance is the Foundation on which we now stand . . . and I appeal to all Men to judge if this Ballance be not a much nobler Constitution in all its Points, than the old *Gothick* Model of Government. . . .[22]

But 'tis said, *the Barons growing poor by the Luxury of the Times, and the Common People growing rich, they exchang'd their Vassalage for Leases, Rents, Fines, and the like.* They did so, and so became entituled to the Service of themselves; and so overthrew the Settlement, and from hence came a *House of Commons*: And I hope *England* has reason to value the Alteration. Let them that think not reflect on the Freedoms the Commons enjoy in *Poland*, where the *Gothick* Institution remains, and they will be satisfied.[23]

Liberty and balanced government were modern, not ancient, and based upon an emancipation of the commons from feudal control, dated about where Harrington had located it in time. In his verse satire of two years later, *The True-Born Englishman*, Defoe made the same point in language which might have been that of a Leveller fifty years before:

The great Invading *Norman* let us know
What Conquerors in After-Times might do. . . .
He gave his Legions their Eternal Station
And made them all Freeholders of the Nation. . . .
The Rascals thus enrich'd, he called them *Lords*,
To please their Upstart Pride with new-made Words,
And *Doomsday-Book* his Tyranny records.

And here begins the Ancient Pedigree
That so exalts our Poor Nobility:
'Tis that from some *French* Trooper they derive,
Who with the Norman Bastard did arrive. . . .

Conquest, as by the Moderns 'tis exprest,
May give a Title to the Lands possest:
But that the Longest Sword shou'd be so Civil,
To make a *Frenchman English*, that's the Devil.[24]

To Lilburne or Harrington, however, such delegitimation of the past was a prelude to a millennial restoration of Saxon liberty or ancient prudence. Defoe's expectations are neither restorationist nor apocalyptic; he is a modern, writing to defend the Junto Whigs, the Bank of

---

[22] Boulton, pp. 44-45.   [23] Boulton, p. 45.
[24] *The True-Born Englishman: A Satyr* (1701), lines 195-96, 205-206, 209-15, 229-32 (Boulton, pp. 59-60).

England, and the standing army. He denies the antiquity of either liberty or virtue—as his successors were to deny that the constitution had any principles to return to—in the name of a balance discovered only two hundred years previously, and that by neither reason nor revelation. "By Peace and Trade they grew rich"; it is, with Defoe no less than with Fletcher—but the value-signs have been reversed—the principle of commerce which put an end to the Gothic constitution. Defoe liked to address himself to trading men, but it is unduly naive merely to invoke the apparition of a trading bourgeoisie to provide him with an audience and motive for writing as he did. In the tract of 1698 he remarked:

> I propose to direct this Discourse to the Honest well meaning English-Freeholder, who has a share in the *Terra firma*, and therefore is concern'd to preserve Freedom; to the Inhabitant that loves his Liberty better than his Life, and won't sell it for Money; and this is the Man who has the most reason to fear a Standing Army, for he has something to lose; as he is most concern'd for the Safety of a Ship, who has a Cargo on her Bottom.[25]

The language now might be that of Ireton at Putney, or Swift and Bolingbroke extolling the "landed interest" in 1711 or 1731. The most we can permit Defoe is the clear understanding that once land ceased to be valued in services, there must be trade and a circulation of money to permit of its being valued in "leases, rents and the like"; and to make land a source of rentals is not the same as to make it a marketable commodity. What he is arguing is that when revenue replaces services, the House of Commons can play its due role in a balanced constitution by exercising the power of supply. In *The True-Born Englishman* he launched a devastating blow at the neo-Harringtonian cult of the militia, with the couplet (referring to William I, to whom William III had been invidiously compared):

No Parliament his Army cou'd disband;
He rais'd no Money, for he paid in Land;[26]

and the whole of his *Argument* in 1698 was directed at showing that a professional army was easily controlled so long as parliament commanded the sources of its pay. But this did not of itself meet the Country objection that the very existence of a standing army corrupted parliament and lessened its ability to refuse supply, or that the power of money provided the executive with means of corruption unknown in former ages. Defoe conceded the point that the nature of war and government had changed:

[25] Boulton, pp. 37-38.   [26] Lines 203-204 (Boulton, p. 60).

England now is in sundry Circumstances, different from *England* formerly, with respect to the Manner of Fighting, the Circumstances of our Neighbours, and of our Selves; and there are some Reasons why a Militia are not, and perhaps I might make it out cannot be made fit for the Uses of the present Wars.[27]

What he denied was that there was any need for a return to the precommercial militia, or a precommercial morality such as Fletcher and Toland saw their militias as inculcating. But there is as yet no sign that his modernism involved a shift to any new conception of morality—only to a greater degree of liberty; and as long as that was the case, the emancipation of the commons might entail entry upon a world less morally stabilized than the Gothic world preceding it. Defoe might abuse the latter for its feudal bloodshed and disorder; but it could be defended in terms of an Aristotelian ethic of self-sufficiency and autonomy. If he could furnish no alternative ethic, the move to a commercial polity might entail the search for a new form of Machiavellian *virtù*, but with all the Machiavellian categories at the service of those who would argue that such a *virtù* must be hopelessly corrupt before it could take hold.

At this point it is appropriate to bring in the name of Locke. In the *Two Treatises of Government*, published if not written nine or so years before this debate, he had argued that societies formed by the simple occupation and cultivation of vacant land would be unlikely to become more than patriarchal family groups, in which little or no institutional government was required to administer the natural law.[28] It was the invention of money that had changed this state of affairs. "Fancy and agreement" had assigned a fictitious value to gold and silver; and these, being more durable than the consumer goods of real value to man, could be stored up, used to assign an exchange value to goods and land, and employed as the means of acquiring more than a man required for satisfaction of his natural wants[29] (including, it might reasonably be added, power over other men). Money, therefore, that partly fictitious and partly perdurable entity, was the precondition of societies on a larger scale than the purely patriarchal, which required exchange relations between the natural rulers of families and tribes, governments capable of dealing with problems rather more complex than those arising between Abraham and Lot, and increasingly sophisticated conceptions of the property rights which were the occasion of

---

[27] Boulton, p. 38.

[28] *Second Treatise*, #36-8; Laslett, ed. (Cambridge), pp. 334-38.

[29] #46-50; Laslett, pp. 342-44. "Fancy and agreement" is on p. 342; see also #37, pp. 335-36.

individuals being in society at all. From the presence of these arguments in Locke's writings, some very far-reaching conclusions have been drawn, and vigorously opposed;[30] and if we are to take him as saying that post-patriarchal government exists merely in consequence of the growth of monetary exchange, it is tempting to conclude that he intended also to argue that government in a money-based society had no more to do than to administer exchange relationships, and that the individual took part in such a government merely to see that the exchange value of his property was maintained.[31] It might further follow that Locke intended to dismiss to a nomadic and patriarchal past that participant civic virtue which Aristotle, Machiavelli, Harrington, and Fletcher had grounded on a conception of property increasingly seen as agrarian, and to contend that the individual under government inhabited an exchange-based society in which virtue was private, consisting in relationships which were guaranteed by government but not in participation in government as a self-creating act of citizenship.

For reasons given earlier, the problem of Locke's intentions will not be pursued here, nor shall we find much occasion to consider what Augustan readers may have made of his writings. But we have found reason to believe that the civic or participatory ideal had come to be expressed in terms of an agrarian mode of property acknowledged to exist mainly in the past; that it employed a theory of social personality in which virtue was held to be civic and was grounded on material bases which could not be bartered away without the loss of virtue itself; that it recognized a modernity which looked very like corruption; and that it knew no theory of civic or moral personality which could easily be applied to the new society. We have now to pursue the analysis initiated by the confrontation of Fletcher with Defoe, bearing in mind among the possibilities that of a "liberal" or "bourgeois"— since such are the favored terms—shift toward privatization, toward the admission that in a commercial society the individual's relation to his *res publica* could not be simply civic or virtuous.

[II]

We have already seen that neither Fletcher nor Defoe operated in terms of a simple opposition between land and trade—which should warn us against expecting Augustan politics to look like a simple confrontation between gentleman and merchant—but that each indicates in opposite ways the difficulties of constructing a fully legiti-

[30] Macpherson, *The Political Theory of Possessive Individualism*, ch. v; Dunn, *Political Thought of John Locke*, chs. 15-20.
[31] An interpretation in which the schools of Marx, Strauss, and Voegelin concur.

mized history out of the movement from the one principle to the other. The emergence of the problem of history enjoins a Machiavellian analysis, and the most ambitious neo-Machiavellian thinker of the early Augustan period was the political economist Charles Davenant.[32] His writings span a period from 1695 to about 1710, during which he can be found first accepting the necessity of prosecuting the Nine Years War (then in its last phase), next taking a furious, and at times questionable, part in the "paper war" and the Country attempt to reduce the scale of war, patronage and finance,[33] and then accepting once more the inescapability of English participation in the War of the Spanish Succession. Like most writers of his day—and like the Renaissance humanists from whom they were descended—he changed positions and allegiances for reasons which may not bear very much inspection; but an intellectual scaffolding can be discovered in his thought, a language of assumptions and problems more consistent than his behavior and shared to a considerable degree by writers on both sides of the political divide. It took shape around the ambivalence of his and their attitudes toward the Machiavellian problem of war and the Augustan problem of commerce. Davenant, more than Fletcher, Toland, or (at this time) Trenchard, was engrossed in the problem of war's ability to generate corrupting forms of finance; and while a major significance of his thought to us is that he looked beyond the problem of trade to that of credit, he did so in the context provided by war.

In 1695 and again in 1701, a starting point of his thought is the menace of universal monarchy supposedly pursued by the French king.[34] He argues against this threat in a way which may well recall the contentions of Florentine republicans against Milanese imperialists, or the Etruscan myth pitted against that of Rome. Universal monarchy is a threat to civil and religious liberty, because it draws all authority together into one place; and he further takes issue[35] with the Spanish historian Pedro Mexia, who had contended that the empire of Charles V promoted trade. Universal rulers bring all virtue under their sway, says Davenant, and then destroy it; similarly, they bring all commerce to focus upon their centers of government, and destroy it also, by war,

---

[32] The only study of his career seems to be that of D. Weddell, "Charles Davenant (1656-1714)—a Biographical Sketch," *Economic History Review*, ser. 2, vol. 11 (1958-59), pp. 279-88. See also D.N.B.

[33] See Ellis, *op.cit.*, n. 6.

[34] Sir Charles Whitworth, ed., *The Political and Commercial Works of . . . Charles D'Avenant . . .* (London, 1771), vol. 1: "An Essay upon Ways and Means" (written in 1695), pp. 4-10; vol. IV, "An Essay upon Universal Monarchy" (1701), pp. 1-42.

[35] *Political and Commercial Works*, IV, 29-37.

tyranny, and depopulation.[36] It is better that there should be a number of centers of religion, of liberty, of power, and of trade; the earth's limited stock, whether of virtue or of commerce, should not be concentrated in one spot, but should be dispersed so that its possessors may nourish one another.[37] Commonwealths are trading societies, and it is better that there should be a plurality of trading commonwealths than that there be the single emporium of a world government.

But between these independent commonwealths and their neighbors, as there will be trade, so there will be war; most commonwealths pursue increase rather than preservation;[38] and the more we explore Davenant's thought on the relations between these two, the more consciously ambivalent it becomes. In the greater part of his writings, especially those belonging to the interwar years of 1697-1702, he seems concerned to argue that war is fatal to a trading commonwealth; but the precise meaning of the term "war," as used here, is "war conducted by means of a land army, which has to be supported by public borrowing." Even this is admitted to have entered the world by processes which are now irreversible:

> Whenever this war ceases, it will not be for want of mutual hatred in the opposite parties, nor for want of men to fight the quarrel, but that side must first give out where money is first failing. . . .
>
> For war is quite changed from what it was in the time of our forefathers; when in a hasty expedition, and a pitched field, the matter was decided by courage; but now the whole art of war is in a manner reduced to money; and now-a-days, that prince, who can best find money to feed, cloath, and pay his army, not he that has the most valiant troops, is surest of success and conquest.[39]

Machiavelli had argued at great length against this proposition, but Davenant sees no point in doing so. The reason is less his interest in the theory of battle as such than his conviction—which Machiavelli, beholding Venice from afar with an unfriendly eye, did not share— that wars are fought by trading societies which employ money to keep armies upon foot. But everything he has to say about the maintenance of land armies stresses its fatal consequences, and the reason is always that it increases the burden of public debt. The Dutch, he remarks in terms that recall Harrington, can bear this better than the English; being wholly a trading society, cramped between the sea and their enemies, they can endure to be permanently in debt to one another, and practice a frugality which makes this debt bearable.[40] The English,

---

[36] *Works*, IV, 33-34, 40-41.   [37] *Works*, I, 348-49; IV, 36-39.

[38] *Works*, IV, 4-5.   [39] *Works*, I, 15-16.

[40] *Works*, I, 67, 142, 253-55 (misnumbered), 390-91.

part trading and part landed, find that the debts contracted to maintain armies are borne largely by the landed gentry,[41] and that corruption is at its worst when indebtedness is concentrated where the power
of returning representatives to parliament chiefly lies;[42] while the
merchants, who need to borrow in order to maintain their profitable
enterprises, find that public debt forces up the price of money and
exposes them to the activities of speculators and the fluctuations of
public confidence.[43] Bad as it is in principle that one sector of the people should be in debt to another, in England this has been managed in
the worst way possible. The institution of the public funds has led to
the growth of a class of professional creditors, who have both the
power and the interest to maximize the conditions producing public
indebtedness, maintaining the standing army in time of peace, converting London from an emporium to the whole kingdom into a separate
interest to which the whole kingdom is in debt,[44] and seeking to reduce
the landed gentry to such a state of dependence that parliament may
soon become meaningless and impotent. Faction is the result, but the
managers of credit know how to manipulate this too to their own ends;
the more it injures public confidence—including the public's willingness to trade—the more it renders government dependent upon their
willingness to borrow further money and corrupt more members of
parliament, and they therefore promote faction by all means in their
power. In *The True Picture of a Modern Whig*, Davenant drew a
bloodcurdling caricature of people of this kind, and deliberately set
no limits to their power to destroy the constitution. By the end of the
dialogue, the confederates are discussing plans to stop the exchequer
and close up parliament;[45] and the point is that there is no theoretical
reason why they should not do so, since they are in a fair way to dispose of all wealth and social power. Everything has become dependent
upon public credit, but the public debts have become a form of movable property. Those who own and manage it may own and manage
everything—including, it is beginning to appear, the social perceptions
and the minds of men. For he had earlier written:

> of all beings that have existence only in the minds of men, nothing
> is more fantastical and nice than Credit; it is never to be forced; it
> hangs upon opinion, it depends upon our passions of hope and fear;
> it comes many times unsought for, and often goes away without
> reason, and when once lost, is hardly to be quite recovered.

[41] *Works*, I, 61, 77, 269, 276; II, pp. 296-97.
[42] *Works*, I, 79.   [43] *Works*, I, 155-56, 268-69; III, p. 329.
[44] *Works*, IV, 217-18.
[45] *Works*, IV, 127-80, 183-266. The dialogue is in two parts.

It very much resembles, and, in many instances, is near akin to that fame and reputation which men obtain by wisdom in governing state affairs, or by valour and conduct in the field. An able statesman, and a great captain, may, by some ill accident, slip, or misfortune, be in disgrace, and lose the present vogue and opinion; yet this, in time, will be regained, where there is shining worth, and a real stock of merit. In the same manner, Credit, though it may be for a while obscured, and labour under some difficulties, yet it may, in some measure, recover, where there is a safe and good foundation at the bottom.[46]

Davenant has entered upon sociology of knowledge; he is discussing for us the epistemology of the investing society. Credit, or opinion, is the appropriate form for the ancient faculty of experience to take where money and war have speeded up the operations of society, and men must constantly translate their evaluations of the public good into actions of investment and speculation, so that political behavior is based upon opinion concerning a future rather than memory of a past. Here, writing just after the peace of 1697, he is depicting credit working in a benign and reasonable way; there are conditions under which men can assay one another, and their common affairs, much as they really are, and then

> men's minds will become quiet and appeased; mutual convenience will lead them into a desire of helping one another. They will find, that no trading nation ever did subsist, and carry on its business by real stock; that trust and confidence in each other, are as necessary to link and hold a people together, as obedience, love, friendship, or the intercourse of speech. And when experience has taught each man how weak he is, depending only upon himself, he will be willing to help others, and call upon the assistance of his neighbours, which of course, by degrees, must set credit again afloat.[47]

There are the beginnings here of a civic morality of investment and exchange, and indeed of an equation of the commercial ethic with the Christian. It is when men realize that their well-being depends upon mutual support that credit is converted into confidence, into a mutual trust and a belief in one another; they realize that they cannot stand alone, that they are members one of another, and that—in words once used to allay a great financial panic of the twentieth century—they have nothing to fear but fear itself. They leave, it might be said, a Hobbesian state of nature and enter upon a Lockean. Yet it is the inde-

[46] *Works*, I, 151 ("Discourses on the Public Revenues," 1698).
[47] *Works*, I, 152.

pendent man of virtue, secure in the self-respect that comes of enjoying his real property, who aims at "depending only upon himself" and drawing from that autonomy the strength to be a citizen. In the century following Davenant's writings, Montesquieu and other social theorists were to conclude that Spartan, Roman, or Gothic virtue, based upon the possession of land by austerely independent individuals, was inhumanly harsh, and that it was only with the spread of commerce and the arts that men became socialized into the capacity for trust, friendship, and Christian love. Machiavelli's antithesis between civic and Christian virtue was in fact repeated in the form of a supposed historical progression from a morality founded on real property to one founded on mobile.

But the epistemological foundations of Davenant's new morality are terribly fragile, and he never effects the full transition. Credit "hangs upon opinion" and "depends upon our passions of hope and fear"; and this is because the objects of its knowledge are not altogether real. It is only in part our opinions of men and things which we declare and which shape our actions, for this theory presupposes a society in which gold and paper have become the symbolic medium in which we express our feelings and translate them into actions, so that at the same time they acquire a fictitious value of their own. The language in which we communicate has itself been reified and has become an object of desire, so that the knowledge and messages it conveys have been perverted and rendered less rational. And the institution of funded debt and public stocks have turned the counters of language into marketable commodities, so that the manipulators of their value—like Tom Double, the political agent and stockjobber of *The True Picture of a Modern Whig*—are in a position to control and falsify "the intercourse of speech."

Davenant could envisage a credit solidly founded upon sympathy and opinion, and he had his cures for the situation in which Double flourished. England must abandon, as soon as possible, the prosecution of war by a land army, funded by a public debt; the debts must themselves be paid off and the mortgaging of future generations' revenues brought to an end; the agents and speculators must cease to disturb the balance of the Ancient Constitution by patronage, the promotion of faction and other forms of corruption;[48] and men's confidence in one another and the commonwealth would again be on the "foundation" of a "real stock of merit," fortified by an understanding of the true principles of trade. Given the premise that Davenant's thought is operating upon republican and Machiavellian assumptions, it is interest-

[48] The "Discourse upon Grants and Resumptions" (1699), in *Works*, III, 1-298, was Davenant's major essay upon this theme. For its impact, see Ellis, pp. 16-27.

ing to note that England as a trading nation is plainly a Venice rather than a Rome; war on the *terra firma* and the employment of mercenaries are what must be avoided. If we link his attacks upon the standing army with the encomiums of Trenchard, Toland, and Fletcher upon the militia, it will follow that the function of the latter is not external war and conquest, and that it exists to preserve a civic, not an imperial virtue; the principle that the sword (and all that goes with it) must be in the hands of the subject is what is to be preserved. There was one mode of war, however, which could be presented as appropriate to England's character as a trading commonwealth less oligarchic than Venice and so obliged—as Machiavelli had pointed out—to pursue expansion and develop a concomitant *virtù*. "The sea gives law to the growth of Venice, but the growth of Oceana gives law to the sea." Harrington had been unspecific as to what kind of expansion he had in mind: possibly agrarian plantation beyond seas—and Davenant and others in the neo-Harringtonian tradition were now writing on Roman colonization and its applicability to England, Ireland, and the Americas;[49] but since at least 1621, Country groups in the House of Commons had intermittently pressed for war against Spain or France conducted at sea, as opposed to war on land which cost the country too much in land taxation. Davenant has many hints of the argument which other Country and Tory pamphleteers were to develop: that war should be conducted at sea, because it injures French and Spanish trade and so promotes English, because seamen do not menace the constitution as the officers and men of the standing army do,[50] because it does not require national debt and its consequent corruptions. There was the difficulty that the navy was a service of state and that trade was falling into the hands of great joint-stock companies closely allied with the Bank, the Court, and the credit structure; but an enthusiasm for interlopers in trade and the *guerre de course* at sea were Country attitudes and carry Machiavellian implications.

Whether or not Davenant thought of trade and naval power as a species of expansive *virtù*, his attitude toward trade itself is at bottom as morally ambivalent as Machiavelli's toward *virtù*, and for very similar reasons. Trade is necessary to give land a value; it is as necessary as the virtues of individual men if the commonwealth is to be maintained:

> for all countries have a certain stock with which their tillage, labour, arts, and manufactures are carried on. And it is the radical moisture

---

[49] *Works*, II, 1-76 ("On the Plantation Trade"); Moyle, *Essay on the Roman Government*, in Robbins, *Two Republican Tracts*. See her introduction, pp. 26-27, and "The Excellent Use of Colonies," *William and Mary Quarterly*, 3d ser., vol. 23, no. 4 (1966), pp. 620-26.

[50] *Works*, I, 408.

of the commonwealth, and if it be quite drawn away the body politic becomes consumptive, hectical, and dies at last (being subject to diseases and death itself, like human frames); and as human bodies are not to be kept alive but by receiving in of nourishment, to repair the hourly decays which time produces, so nations cannot subsist long unless they receive from time to time reliefs and refreshments from abroad, which are no way so well to be administered as by the help of a well governed and extended Traffic.[51]

But a little later he wrote:

Trade, without doubt, is in its nature a pernicious thing; it brings in that wealth which introduces luxury; it gives a rise to fraud and avarice, and extinguishes virtue and simplicity of manners; it depraves a people, and makes way for that corruption which never fails to end in slavery, foreign or domestic. Lycurgus, in the most perfect model of government that was ever framed, did banish it from his commonwealth. But, the posture and condition of other countries considered, it is become with us a necessary evil. We shall be continually exposed to insults and invasions, without such a naval force as is not to be had naturally but where there is an extended traffic. However, if trade cannot be made subservient to the nation's safety, it ought to be no more encouraged here than it was in Sparta: And it can never tend to make us safe, unless it be so managed as to make us encrease in shipping and the breed of seamen.[52]

And about the same time, in an essay entitled "That Foreign Trade is beneficial to England," Davenant gave his history of the phenomenon.

We shall hardly be permitted to live in the way our ancestors did, though inclined to it. The power of our neighbours, both by land and by sea, is grown so formidable, that perhaps we must be for some time upon our guard, with fleets too big to be maintained merely by the natural produce and income of our country.

We must therefore have recourse to those artificial helps which industry and a well governed trade may minister. If we could so contrive it, as never to have a foreign war, we might content ourselves with less Foreign Traffic, which not only brings in the money that must pay the men, but breeds up the very men that must defend us.

Mankind subsisted by their labour, and from what the earth produced, till their corruptions had brought in fraud, avarice, and force;

[51] *Works*, II, 75 ("On the Plantation Trade," 1698).
[52] *Works*, II, 275 ("Essay upon the Probable Methods of Making a People Gainers in the Balance of Trade," 1699).

but when the strong began to invade the weaker, and when strength was to be maintained by policy, they built cities, disciplined men, and erected dominions; and when great numbers were thus confined to a narrower space, their necessities could not be all answered by what was near them, and at hand; so that they were compelled to seek for remoter helps, and this gave rise to what we call Trade, which, at first was only permutation of commodities. . . . [a passage on the origin of money follows.]

It is true, in forming very great empires, the concerns of trade seem not to have been much regarded: As force began them, so force maintained them on; and what wealth they had, came from the spoil of conquered nations: War, and its discipline, was the chief object of their thoughts, as knowing that riches always follow power, and that iron brings to it the gold and silver of other places.

Trade was first entertained, cultivated, and put into regular methods, by little states that were surrounded by neighbours, in strength much superior to them; so the original traders we read of, were the Phoenicians, Athenians, Sicilians and Rhodians; and the helps it yielded, did support those commonwealths for a long time, against very potent enemies.[53]

Davenant proceeds to explain how great empires swallowed up the trading republics, so that all the wealth of the world was gathered into one place—like the finite stock of *virtù* in Machiavelli—but is now dispersed, though again threatened by universal monarchy. It is clear, then, that trade, like *virtù*, is an innovative force and a disturber of the natural order—not of the second nature from which we inherit our traditionally shaped personalities, but of the natural economy of a primitive age in which each man's wants are supplied by each man's labor. Its origins are in a chicken-and-egg relationship with those of violence; or rather, if exchange and trade came after robbery and deceit, both stemmed from luxury—the desire to have more than one needed. The relations between trade and corruption are exceedingly complex: trade generates war, and war debt (which is ultimately fatal to trade); luxury generates both robbery/war and exchange/trade, which generates money—the use of a fictitious medium of exchange— which, when extended from the use of gold coin to that of paper credit, generates debt and consequently corruption. Commerce, then, seems radically inseparable from conflict; it is a mode of power-relationships between finite and local commonwealths, both a cause and an effect of their particularity. In generating the little commonwealths, it gen-

[53] *Works*, I, 348-49 ("Discourses on the Public Revenues . . . ," II, I, 1698).

erates liberty and prosperity, but at the same time generates the causes of their decline.

But while Machiavellian *virtù* simultaneously served to define both power within and without the republic and virtue within it, trade—a modality of power without the commonwealth—makes a material but not a moral contribution to its interior existence. The natural virtues are satisfactorily expressed in terms of the primitive economy. There may be a permutative virtue in giving fairly of a surplus of something necessary to sustain life in exchange for a surplus of some other necessary commodity; but trade is here defined in terms of luxury—the desire to have more than one needs, to have something one does not need. It brings power, and in a competitive world the commonwealth may die without it; and it brings corruption—but it does not bring a virtue of its own by which corruption may be resisted. There is a virtue, Davenant repeatedly assures us, which legislators and rulers may encourage as a means against corruption, but this virtue is frugality,[54] the negation of luxury—the willingness to forego having more than one needs, to live by the standards of the natural economy although in the midst of the artificial. The trader should be frugal; but he will be no more frugal because he is a trader. The trading people should be frugal if they wish to wage war without becoming corrupt; but it is too late to expect them to attain such a degree of frugality that they can do without war and trade altogether, and their prospects of evading corruption are therefore limited.

Frugality, it is notorious, was part of the so-called Protestant ethic. By its means the trader escaped the twin reproaches of avarice and prodigality, which Dante had considered derived from a lack of faith in the goodness of fortune. Denying himself more than he needed, he reinvested his surplus in the circulating common stock, to bring fresh goods to himself and others. Augustan political economics mark the moment when the trader—and, still more pressingly, the financier— was challenged to prove that he could display civic virtue in the sense that the landed man could. It was easy to visualize the latter, anxious only to improve his estate for inheritance, engaging in civic actions which related his private to the public good; much harder to ascribe this role to one constantly engaged in increasing his wealth by exchanging quantities of fictitious tokens. Frugality could appear the civic virtue of the trader; assuming the circulation of goods to be a public

[54] E.g., *Works*, I, 389-92. Note the Guicciardinian language on p. 390: "But sometimes there are diseases so deeply fixed, that it is impossible to root them out; and in such a case there is nothing left, but to keep the distemper under, by natural and easy remedies."

benefit, he displayed in frugality and reinvestment his willingness to subordinate private satisfaction to public good, of which he would be rewarded with a further share. It may very well have been the Augustan debaters who discovered, if they did not invent, the "Protestant ethic"; whether or not it was already established in men's minds, they may have been the first to have need of it in public debate. As handled by Davenant, however, it was a morality without a material foundation in any way peculiarly its own. The trader was asked to be frugal in just the way the primeval cultivator (who had needed no asking) had been; he was asked to imitate the natural man in place of his artificial self; and he was asked to do this to limit the negative effects of his own activity. The virtue enjoined on him was not of his own making, and was only contingently peculiar to him.

[III]

The analysis of the Machiavellian economics of Davenant has left us in a position to construct a schema of the attitudes toward land, trade, and credit of the Court and Country, Whig and Tory writers of the reigns of William III, Anne, and George I. These men, it is already clear, belong in the civic humanist succession by reason of their concern with virtue as the moral as well as material foundation of social and personal life, as well as their use of Machiavelli and Harrington to furnish the categories in which it could be discussed and their rapid development of a neoclassical style in British political rhetoric. Like the humanists of the *quattrocento*, they were not constant in their political allegiances. Swift, Davenant, Defoe—to go no further—were found in differing company at different times of their lives; and, again as with their predecessors, these changes of front are best explained not by attempting to assess questions of commitment and consistency, venality and ambition, but by recognizing that they were employing a highly ambivalent rhetoric, replete with alternatives, conflicts, and confusions, of which they were very well aware and in which they were to some extent entrapped. An anatomy of the great debate as between the "landed" and "monied" interests, conducted by the journalists and publicists of Anne's reign, reveals that there were no pure dogmas or simple antitheses, and few assumptions that were not shared, and employed to differing purposes, by the writers on either side.

In the first place, though Country and Tory writers, from Fletcher to Bolingbroke, praised land as the basis of independent and armigerous virtue, and the Harley-St. John Tory party could make a good claim to be the party of the landed interest, no Court or Whig writer, neither Defoe nor Addison, ever dreamed of denying that land was substantially what its partisans said it was. They could indeed argue that land was of no value, even in rendering its proprietor independent, without money and trade, and there was a line of rhetoric which suggested that a society with no wealth but its land—Gothic England, contemporary Poland, or the Scottish Highlands—would lack both liberty (the tenants being subject to their lords) and culture. In contemporary social criticism, these strictures could be applied to the stay-at-home squire and his High Church politics, ignoring the fact that there was a Whig as well as a Tory style available to the discontented Country: Addison indicates how Sir Roger de Coverley of the *Spectator* can degenerate into the Foxhunter of the *Freeholder*,[55] and he in turn is lineal ancestor to Fielding's Squire Western. But in *Tom Jones* a balance is carefully maintained between Western, the foxhunting booby, and Allworthy, the honorable independent; the figure of the country gentleman remains bi-fronted, and it took Macaulay to accept Western as the portrait of a class.[56] No Augustan saw much need to do so, though there were doubtless plenty of Westerns to be met with.

If the agrarian values of independence and virtue remain a constant in this period's social perceptions, we already know that the argument presenting land as dependent upon trade—not to mention credit—was accepted by Fletcher and Davenant, even as it was pressed by Defoe; and the same is true when we come to oppose Swift to Defoe and Addison. The neo-Harringtonians conceded that trade and bullion had come into the world and irrevocably modified the social character of land; they were merely, as we have seen, ambivalent in their feelings as to how far this change had introduced corruption, and how far corruption could ever be checked. Corruption, however, took the form of credit, accompanied by the diabolic trinity of stockjobbing, faction, and standing army; and when Swift, and later Bolingbroke, set up grand antitheses between the "landed" and "monied" interests, they invariably included among their denunciations of Whig war and Whig finance the charge that these had contributed to the neglect and ruin of trade, and they almost invariably defined the "monied interest" in terms designed to include financiers while excluding merchants.[57] Trade, like

---

[55] Edward A. Bloom and Lillian D. Bloom, *Joseph Addison's Sociable Animal: in the Market Place, on the Hustings, in the Pulpit* (Providence: Brown University Press, 1971), *passim*.

[56] Macaulay, *History of England*, ch. III.

[57] Swift's most sustained analysis of the "monied interest" is in *The History of the Four Last Years of the Queen* (ed. Herbert Davis, with an introduction by Harold Williams; Oxford: Basil Blackwell, 1964), pp. 68-78. Note such phrases as "those whose money by the dangers and difficulties of trade lay dead upon their hands" (p. 68), "a monarchy whose wealth ariseth from the rents and improvements of lands, as well as trade and manufactures" (p. 69), "a new estate

land, was a constant value, until it had to be affirmed or denied that trade entailed money and money credit;[58] the Whigs, for obvious tactical reasons, sought to pillory the Tories as enemies of trade, to depict virtuous and benevolent merchants—like Sir Andrew Freeport of the *Spectator*—as emblems of their cause, and to argue that trade entailed credit in a similarly benignant form, all of which things they upheld. But trade, while exposed to theoretical criticisms like those of Davenant, was immune from polemical assault. The Augustan debate did not oppose agrarian to entrepreneurial interests, the manor to the market, and cannot be said to have arisen from a crude awareness of collisions going on between them.

As for credit, the same pattern of partly shared ambivalences can be detected in this most crucial case of all. No writer of either party presumed to defend stockjobbing, the speculative manipulation of the market values of shares in the public debt; it was universally agreed to be evil, and the sole difference on this score between the party publicists of Anne's reign was that Swift, like Davenant before him, attacked the professional creditors as such—this was the true meaning of his term "the monied interest"—as constantly striving to promote, through war, the extent of the public debt and its value to them,[59] while Defoe hit back by accusing high churchmen and crypto-Jacobites of a design to lower the public credit through alarmism and mob violence, for ends of their own, partly superstitious and partly speculative.[60] Tories attacked bulls, in short, and Whigs bears. The crucial issue was not whether stockjobbing, but whether paper credit was more than a nec-

---

and property sprung up in the hands of mortgagees" (p. 70), "extremely injurious to trade and to the true interest of the nation" (p. 71). See also *The Examiner, 1710-11* (ed. Davis, Oxford: Basil Blackwell, 1957), pp. 5-7, 62-63, 124-25, 134-35, 162-67; *The Conduct of the Allies* (in *Political Tracts, 1711-14*, ed. Davis, 1964), pp. 9-10, 16, 18-19, 41, 53-59.

[58] As clear a statement of this theme as any is to be found in Davenant, *Works*, I, 160: "Now, if the product of the land should sink in its value, it must naturally ensue, that the rents of England, and price of land, will fall in the same proportion. For the great stock that was subsisting in credit, and the great sum of money that circulated about the kingdom, did chiefly fix so high a price upon land and all its produce; and if peace should diminish this price (as perhaps it will), land and its rents will hardly recover their former value, till money can be made to circulate, and till credit is revived."

[59] See references given in n. 57 above.

[60] Defoe, *Review* (published for the Facsimile Text Society in 23 facsimile books; New York: Columbia University Press, 1928), vol. VII, no. 26, pp. 97-99; no. 45, p. 175; no. 47, pp. 181-84; no. 48, pp. 186-87; no. 49, pp. 189-91; no. 50, pp. 195-96; no. 51, pp. 197-99; all in facsimile book 17; also *passim*. For a Swiftian attack on Whigs as bears, see *Examiner*, no. 35 (*ed. cit.*, p. 125).

essary evil; and here too straightforward confrontations are hard to find. Defoe argued at length that just as land could not thrive without trade, so trade could not thrive without money, money without credit, or gold without paper;[61] he had no doubt the more coherent case, but when his opponents retorted by continued philippics against stock-jobbing, he could not deny that stockjobbing was corruption.[62] They, for their part, when asserting that funds were raised from the income upon lands,[63] or that public debts were ruinous to trade, plainly admitted the interdependence of land, trade and credit; and generally speaking, it is observable that while the National Debt usually is, the Bank of England usually is not the object of direct Country and Tory attacks. John Toland, editing and republishing the works of Harrington in 1699-1700—itself an ambivalent action, considering the gulf between Harringtonian and neo-Harringtonian views of history—claimed in later years that he had done so as a service to the Country leader Robert Harley;[64] but the edition is dedicated to the Lord Mayor, sheriffs, aldermen and common council of the City of London, and it is explicitly stated that the Bank of England perfectly exemplifies Harrington's system of government.[65] No doubt the obvious explanation is that Toland was hedging his political bets;[66] but for him to do so at all, it must have been the case that, even in 1700, the relation between Bank and Country was not one of simple hostility. What emerges from every point in the analysis is that, even in the years of most embittered factional conflict, there were no simple antitheses between land and trade, or even land and credit; and that we are not invited to think in terms of a politics of crudely distinguished interest groups, but of politicians, publicists, and their followings maneuvering in a world of common perceptions and symbols and seeking to interpret it for their competitive advantage by means of a common value system. It is evident also that they were conceptualizing their common experience of a new

[61] See *Review*, facsimile books 17-22, *passim*.

[62] *Review* (facsimile book 19), vol. viii, no. 55, p. 222 (an attack on bulls); no. 56, pp. 225-27; no. 59, pp. 237-40; no. 60, pp. 241-44 (bears); no. 68, pp. 273 (misnumbered)-75.

[63] Swift, *Conduct of the Allies*, in *Political Tracts, 1711-14*, p. 56.

[64] See Pierre Des Maizeaux, *A Collection of Several Pieces of Mr John Toland* (London, 1726), ii, 227; but the claim is made in a letter to Harley written in 1710.

[65] Toland, *op.cit.*, pp. ii-iii, and the dedication generally.

[66] Several writers of the "paper war" puzzled even their enemies to know which side they were on; Ellis, *op.cit.*, p. 38, n. 1. Toland appears in Davenant's *True Picture of a Modern Whig* as "Mr Gospelscorn," a confederate of the wicked Tom Double (who is himself partly a portrait of Defoe); Davenant, *Works*, iv, 240-42.

politics and economics in ways which left them acutely aware that change was going on in both the material and the moral world, and that their means of evaluating such changes led to a profound consciousness of moral ambiguity.

Augustan neo-Machiavellism can be characterized in the following way. The Englishman had begun to envisage himself as civic individual through the use of Aristotelian and civic humanist categories, which required among other things that there be a material foundation, the equivalent of Aristotle's *oikos*, for his independence, leisure and virtue. The nature of this equivalent had been described for him, first by Machiavelli in terms of arms, second by Harrington in terms of property; and the realities of the seventeenth-century social structure had established as paradigmatic the image of the freeholder, founded upon real or landed property which was inheritable rather than marketable, was protected by the ancient sanctions of the common law, and brought with it membership in the related structures of the militia and the parliamentary electorate, thus guaranteeing civic virtue. The advent from about 1675 of parliamentary patronage, a professional army, and a rentier class maintaining the two foregoing for its own profit, posed a threat of corruption to the whole edifice, including the balance between estates or powers of which the Ancient Constitution was now held to consist, pervading it with new social types whose economic substance if not property—pensions, offices, credit, funds—defined them as dependent on the executive power and hence incapable of virtue. All this, however, came to be seen during the Nine Years War and its sequel as inescapably based upon the fact that England was now a war-making power, requiring long-service soldiers and long-term debts, and that involvement in foreign war was in one way or another interconnected with the conduct of an extensive foreign trade.

The problem of trade, however—which Harrington had perceived as of altogether secondary importance in the politics of virtue—was, in one crucial sequence of Augustan thought, the last to be perceived among the causes of the new corruption. There was a dimension of this dilemma in which a threat was seen to be posed to the epistemological foundation of the world of real property. It will be recalled that Locke, defining money as crucial to the transition from natural to political economy, had remarked that "fancy and agreement" were what had originally assigned a value to gold and silver for purposes of exchange. Once it was admitted, then—as in the neo-Harringtonian version of English history it was admitted on both sides of the political fence— that land, which had been valued for the services performed by tenants, was now valued for the rents they paid, it must follow that the real property which defined the citizen to himself was itself defined by a blend of fictions, namely fantasy and convention; so that he was doomed to inhabit a world more unstable in its epistemological foundations than Plato's cave. Locke, however, just as he had anchored the fragility of consent in the solid reality of inherited land, had countered the fantastic character of precious metals by alluding to their durability; they could be laid up in the earth and not corrode. It might remain true, for most gentle readers, that the best foundation for personality was still land; it passed from generation to generation by inheritance, carrying with it arms that might be hung up on the wall till needed. Goods possessing a real value to men might pass from hand to hand by exchange, and there was the objection to mobile property as a foundation for civic personality, that what had come might go in the same way; but the difference between real and mobile property was not yet that the latter was unreal. Money, the symbolic representation of value, was in part unreal; but its ability to outlast the things which it symbolized made it still a worthy medium for human existence. Locke—who helped recoin English money in 1696 and was one of the first stockholders of the Bank of England—could argue in 1691 that a man had a property in money he had lent the state in expectation of profit, without compromising the principle that property was what established civilized conditions among men.[67]

It is not clear that Locke meant to attack the neo-Harringtonian critics of society, and there is little sign that they felt the need to assail him. Within ten years of the Revolution, however, the subversion of real by mobile property had entered a phase in which reality was seen as endangered by fiction and fantasy. We have already studied that passage in which Davenant confesses that the ultimate determinant of national prosperity is now credit, which "has existence only in the minds of men," than which "nothing is more fantastical and nice," which "hangs upon opinion and depends upon our passions," which "comes unsought for and goes away without reason."[68] He is alluding to the perceived truth that in an economy dependent upon public finance, everything—including the value of land itself—depends upon the rate at which capital can be got; he is saying that this in turn depends upon men's confidence in one another, and that this again, while in the long run it depends upon their perception of moral and material realities, is in the short run determined by opinion and passion, hope and fear, which render it peculiarly exposed to manipulation by corrupt speculators in the paper tokens to which it has been reduced. Paper, while produced by the same forces and serving the same functions as gold, is less durable in its physical form and there-

[67] Kramnick (above, n. 3), pp. 42, 61-63.
[68] Above, n. 46.

fore infinitely more liable to subjectivity. There is a danger that all men, and all sublunary things, will now become things of paper, which is worse even than to become things of gold.

Credit, to observers of the new economics, symbolized and made actual the power of opinion, passion, and fantasy in human affairs, where the perception of land (until it too was completely eroded by speculation) might still appear the perception of real property and human relations as they really and naturally were. The personification of Credit as an inconstant female figure, it is startling to discover, is a device of Whig rather than Tory writers, and in particular of Defoe and Addison at the time when they were undergoing the assaults which Swift, in the *Examiner*, had launched against all forms of property except land as "only what is transient or imaginary."[69] Personified Credit appears in Defoe's *Review* as early as 1706, and in no very sedate shape:

> Money has a younger Sister, a very useful and officious Servant in Trade, which in the absence of her senior Relation, but with her Consent, and on the Supposition of her Confederacy, is very assistant to her; frequently supplies her place for a Time, answers all the Ends of Trade perfectly, and to all Intents and Purposes, as well as Money herself; only with one Proviso, That her Sister constantly and punctually relieves her, keeps Time with her, and preserves her good Humour: but if she be never so little disappointed, she grows sullen, sick, and ill-natur'd, and will be gone for a great while together: Her Name in our Language is call'd CREDIT, in some Countries Honour, and in others, I know not what.
>
> This is a coy Lass, and wonderful chary of her self; yet a most necessary, useful, industrious Creature: she has some Qualification so peculiar, and is so very nice in her Conduct, that a World of good People lose her Favour, before they well know her Name; others are courting her all their days to no purpose, and can never come into her Books.
>
> If once she be disoblig'd, she's the most difficult to be Friends again with us, of anything in the World; and yet she will court those most, that have no occasion for her; and will stand at their Doors neglected and ill-us'd, scorn'd, and rejected, like a Beggar, and never leave them: But let such have a Care of themselves, and be sure they never come to want her; for, if they do, they may depend upon it, she will pay them home, and never be reconcil'd to them, but upon

[69] *Examiner*, no. 34; *ed. cit.*, p. 119. This passage is a defense of the Qualification Act, intended to exclude all but proprietors of land from the Commons.

a World of Entreaties, and the severe Penance of some years Prosperity.

'Tis a strange thing to think, how absolute this Lady is; how despotickly she governs all her Actions: If you court her, you lose her, or must buy her at unreasonable Rates; and if you do, she is always jealous of you, and Suspicious; and if you don't discharge her to a Title of your Agreement, she is gone, and perhaps may never come again as long as you live; and if she does, 'tis with long Entreaty and abundance of Difficulty.[70]

The student of Renaissance humanism has no hesitation whatever in identifying the rhetoric of this passage. Defoe is describing Credit in precisely the idiom employed by Machiavelli to describe *fortuna* and *occasione*, and we may also appropriately recall that *fantasia* of whose supremacy Giovanni Cavalcanti had been convinced by the triumph of manipulative politics at Florence a hundred years earlier still.[71] Like all these goddesses, Credit typifies the instability of secular things, brought about by the interactions of particular human wills, appetites and passions, and it comes as no surprise to find other passages written in 1706, in which she is shown operating malignantly and irrationally.

Some give Men no Rest till they are in their Debt, and then give them no Rest till they are out again; some will credit no body, and some again are for crediting every body; some get Credit till they can pay nothing, and some break tho' they could pay all. No Nation in the World can show such mad Doings in Trade, as we do.

Debtors abuse Creditors, and Creditors starve and murther their Debtors; Compassion flies from human Nature in the Course of universal Commerce; and *Englishmen*, who in all other Cases are Men of Generosity, Tenderness, and more than common Compassion, are to their Debtors meer Lunaticks, Mad-men and Tyrants.[72]

Is it a Mystery, that Nations should grow rich by War? that *England* can lose so many Ships by pyrating, and yet encrease? Why is War a greater Mystery than Trade, and why should Trade itself be more mysterious than in [*sic*] War? Why do *East India* Company's Stock rise, when Ships are taken? Mine Adventures raise Annuities, when Funds fall; lose their Vein of Oar in the Mine, and yet find it in the Shares; let no Man wonder at these Paradoxes, since such strange things are practised every Day among us?

---

[70] Defoe, *Review* (facsimile book 6), vol. III, no. 5, pp. 17-18; see also pp. 19-20, and no. 6, pp. 21-24; no. 7, pp. 25-27.
[71] Above, ch. IV, n. 22.
[72] *Review* (facsimile book 7), vol. III, no. 92, p. 365.

If any Man requires an Answer to such things as these, they may find it in this Ejaculation—Great is the Power of Imagination!

Trade is a Mystery, which will never be compleatly discover'd or understood; it has its Critical Junctures and Seasons, when acted by no visible Causes, it suffers Convulsion Fitts, hysterical Disorders, and most unaccountable Emotions—Sometimes it is acted by the evil Spirit of general Vogue, and like a meer Possession 'tis hurry'd out of all common Measures; today it obeys the Course of things, and submits to Causes and Consequences; tomorrow it suffers Violence from the Storms and Vapours of Human Fancy, operated by exotick Projects, and then all runs counter, the Motions are excentrick, unnatural and unaccountable—A Sort of Lunacy in Trade attends all its Circumstances, and no Man can give a rational Account of it.[73]

But the unbridled power of fantasy, which to the Whig and promoter of trade Defoe here seems the main importation of early capitalism into human affairs, is not simply the wheel of fortune running eccentrically about its unmoving axis; as he very well knows, it is part of a huge new force in human affairs, creating new modes of war and prosperity, a new balance of power in Europe, a new conquest of the planet. In this respect Credit resembled less *fortuna* than *virtù*, the innovative conquering force which, in the most dynamic moments of Machiavelli's vision, created the disorder, symbolized as *fortuna*, which it then set out to dominate by means so far irrational and amoral that they could be seen as part of the anarchy they pretended to cure. It is arguable that not since Machiavelli himself have we met with language as evocative of his innermost ways of thinking as that of Davenant and Defoe.

But if Machiavelli may have supplied the language which Defoe found appropriate for depicting volcanic and irrational social innovation, he had at the same time supplied by way of Harrington—and in a form recognizable to contemporaries—the language and parameters by which what Credit was doing could be denounced as corruption. In 1710 Defoe, who by the next year would be facing fire from Swift's *Examiner*, had to find means of depicting Credit as a stabilizing, virtuous, and intelligent agency; and here she appears as the daughter of Probity and Prudence, as volatile and temperamental as ever, but capable of recognizing what Davenant had called "the stock of real merit." Among her characteristics is an extreme timorousness; she is thrown into fits at the mere sight of a Sacheverell mob and a panic among the Whigs is all but fatal to her.[74] Only as the public peace is restored and

[73] *Review* (facsimile book 8), vol. III, no. 126, pp. 502-503.
[74] *Review* (facsimile book 17), vol. VII, no. 55, pp. 213-15; no. 57, pp. 221-23; no. 58, pp. 225-28; no. 59, pp. 229-31.

the public nerve is recovered, does she begin to revive, and Defoe is at pains to show that she is a public being, who can exist only where men have confidence in one another and in the kingdom. This confidence—the substance of which Credit is the volatile reflection—can only be publicly expressed.

> The Diseases of Credit are as peculiar to *Parliaments*, as the Disease call'd the *Evil*, is to the Sovereign; none can cure them but themselves—The Royal Touch has no Healing Virtue in it for this Distemper; Queen and Parliament United may do it, but neither by themselves can.
> Credit was not so short-sighted a Politician, *as not to know this*—The Thing is certain, *Parliaments* are the Foundation of our Funds; the Honour and Justice of *Parliaments* in preserving the Publick *on one Hand*, and a firm adherence to the great Principle of making good former Engagements, and supplying the Deficiency of *Parliamentary Security*, *on the other*, these are the great Channels of Credit. . . . *Credit* is not dependant on the Person of the Sovereign, upon a Ministry, or upon this or that Management; but upon the Honour of the Publick Administration in *General*, and the Justice of *Parliaments in Particular*, in keeping whole the Interest of those that have ventured their Estates upon the Publick Faith—Nor must any *Intervention of Parties* be of Notice in this Case—For if one Party being uppermost shall refuse to make good the Deficiencies of the Ministry *that went before them*, because another Party then had the Management, *Parliamentary Credit* would not be worth a Farthing. . . .
> *Credit* is too wary, too Coy a Lady to stay with any People upon such mean Conditions; if you will entertain this Virgin, you must act upon the nice Principles of Honour, and Justice; you must preserve Sacred all the Foundations, and build regular Structures upon them; you must answer all Demands, with a respect to the Solemnity, and Value of the Engagement; with respect to Justice, and Honour; and without any respect to Parties—If this is not observ'd, Credit will not come; No, tho' the Queen should call; tho' the Parliament shou'd call, or tho' the whole Nation should call.[75]

Addison took up the theme in number 3 of the *Spectator*. Credit appears seated in the Bank, beneath the emblems of the Ancient Constitution and the Revolution Settlement, and surrounded by heaps of gold and bags of money.

> She appeared indeed infinitely timorous in all her Behaviour; And,

[75] *Review* (facsimile book 18), vol. VII, no. 116, p. 463.

whether it was from the Delicacy of her Constitution, or that she was troubled with Vapours, as I was afterwards told by one who I found was none of her Well-wishers, she changed Colour, and startled at everything she heard. She was likewise (as I afterwards found) a greater Valetudinarian than any I had ever met with, even in her own Sex, and subject to such Momentary Consumptions, that in the twinkling of an Eye, she would fall away from the most florid Complexion, and the most healthful State of Body, and wither into a Skeleton. Her Recoveries were often as sudden as her Decays, insomuch that she would revive in a Moment out of a wasting Distemper, into a Habit of the highest Health and Vigour.[76]

When the spirits of popery, tyranny, and republicanism appear before her, Credit collapses; the moneybags become filled with wind, and the gold is transformed into piles of paper and notched tallies; but with the entrance of the spirits of liberty, moderation, and the Protestant succession, all is restored.

Credit is now being translated into virtue, in the entirely moral and societal sense of that word. The precondition of her health is the health of all society and the practice of all the moral activities which society entails; and she is being endowed with a faculty of perception sufficient to inform her whether these conditions are being met. Show her real merit and real goods, and the goods which she returns to you will be real also. The wealth created by Credit is described in terms of real bullion, and it is characteristic of Addison that he depicted the Royal Exchange not as a place of dealing in stocks and funds, but as a concourse of solid merchants exchanging real commodities through the medium of money.[77] The ideological thrust was constantly toward the absorption of stockjobber into merchant: the rentier, who frightened social theorists, into the entrepreneur, who did not. Virtue was now the cognition of social, moral and commercial reality, and everything possible had been done to eliminate the element of fantasy and fiction which had seemed so subversive of property and personality.

But the restoration of virtue was subject to a single sharp limitation, one of singular relevance to the epistemological structure of this book. Imagination—the subversive, creative, and destructive power depicted in the boomtime of 1706—is replaced in the Whig literature of 1710-1711 by nothing more than opinion; in Locke's terminology, the emphasis is switched from "fancy" to "agreement." The latter, of course, is social where the former is arbitrary and egocentric, and this

[76] *The Spectator*, ed. Smith (London: J. M. Dent and Sons, Everyman Library, 1961), p. 11.

[77] *Spectator*, no. 69; *ed. cit.*, pp. 212-15. Note the neo-Harringtonian finale.

makes it more rational and virtuous. But the rationality is only that of opinion and experience; and none of the rhetoric about the transformation of Credit into confidence by supplying her judgment with real and concrete data serves to eliminate the volatility with which she oscillates between the extremes of hope and fear. Opinion, it was common form to assert, was the slave of these two passions; and in the case of Credit, not only were the data on which opinion was formed at least partly imaginary, but even those well founded in concrete reality figured to the imagination—in which opinion was shaped—as features of a mobile, somewhat Hobbesian, universe in which every object was potentially a source of either profit or loss, a subject of both hope and fear.

Hobbes had laid it down that the observation of covenants—to be exact, the establishment of a law of nature that covenants must be observed—was the only cure for the insecurity produced by the fears and fantasies of men, but had left it uncertain just how fearful and fantastic man arrived at the discovery of this law. Defoe and Addison, operating in a speculative society where the performance of one commercial covenant was the occasion—as with Machiavelli's "innovation"—of the immediate embarking upon another, had greater need still to show how covenant might keep pace with fantasy but even greater difficulty in doing so; in their world reason was indeed the slave of the passions.

Nor was Credit a mere observer and reflector of this universe; she helped to shape it. As her hopes and fears overreacted to every stimulus, the objects concerning which she formed them gained or lost both value and reality; the universe of commerce and investment was, inescapably, to some degree fantastic and nonrational. Given all the resources of a virtuous society, Credit could coordinate them on a greater scale than ever before in history; but she contributed nothing beyond fantasy, opinion, and passion to making society virtuous in the first place. Virtue must involve the cognition of things as they really were; the power of Credit was irredeemably subjective and it would take all the authority of society to prevent her from breaking loose to submerge the world in a flood of fantasy. It seems possible that she is part of Pope's Great Anarch.

At this point, much of the conventional wisdom in modern historiography of social thought encourages us to take up the theme of a labor theory of value. If Locke's experimenting with such a theory had been intended or understood as a contribution to the Augustan debate, it might indeed have served as the powerful instrument of reification which Marx was to declare it had been. If men created by their labor the values of the goods they exchanged, the reality of a world of commodity and commerce would be assured; and it is conceivable that Adam Smith, three generations later, was engaged in such a venture of validation. But until more is known of the history of labor theory during the eighteenth century, we shall not have the evidence for asserting that Locke was used in the way described. Defoe and Addison do not seem to have reified the world of speculation and exchange by alluding to the labor that gave it value, and the substitution of *homo faber* for *homo politicus* was not effected. They sought instead to validate the commercial world by appeal to conceptions of public virtue, but found themselves confronted by the paradigm of a citizen whose virtue did not rest upon a capacity for exchange.

From this point there were two directions in which the Augustan mind might go. It might assert that the foundations of government were, as they had always been, in virtue, which presupposed both an individual capable of ruling and knowing himself, and a social structure which he could know clearly enough to rule his own part in it. The appropriate material foundation for this was land: real property cognizable as stable enough to link successive generations in social relationships belonging to, or founded in, the order of nature. Such a government would tend to be a commonwealth (with monarch) of independent proprietors with a balanced and ancient constitution, fortified by immemorial customs which helped keep the parts independent and in place; it would be patriotic in defense, but would avoid war and empire. But the ambivalences of the neo-Harringtonian posture reveal that those who took this direction could no longer present history in terms of an uninterrupted continuity of values. Change had occurred; they were looking to a past, and seeking to defend virtue against innovative forces, symbolized as trading empire,[78] standing armies, and credit. The second stood for specialization and the alienation of one's capacities; the last for fantasy, fiction, and social madness, the menace of a false consciousness which would engulf men in a sort of political Dunciad; both stood for corruption, and minds of this persuasion shared to the full the humanist tendency to see corruption as irreversible. Their attitude toward change was therefore negative, but they recognized it even as they repudiated it. Their thought was Machiavellian in its recognition that society was being cut loose from natural order, in its definition of the natural order that was being left behind, and in its affirmation that there were basic virtues, *ordini* and *principii*, to which a return might be made by means of moral legislation. When they set up frugality, the militia, or the independence of the parts of

[78] See Bloom and Bloom, *Joseph Addison's Sociable Animal*, pp. 67-83 (ch. 4, "The War of Economic Right"), for an interesting study of Addison conceding that commerce breeds war and must justify it.

the balanced constitution, as ideals to which a patriot parliament or a patriot king might bring about a return by means of legislation or educative example, they revealed their acceptance of a disjunction between the moral and material components of society, and between value and history.[79] They were conceding that social change was no longer guaranteeing virtue, but claiming that virtue might be reaffirmed independently of social conditions and might even change them.

The alternative was to admit that government was an affair of managing the passions. If money and credit had indeed dissolved the social frame into a shifting mobility of objects that were desired and fictions that were fantasized about, then passion, opinion, and imagination were indeed the motors of human behavior and the sources of human cognition. It is clear, however, from what we have seen that this was strong meat even for the tough-minded Defoe; he busied himself, especially when challenged by Swift, to show how opinion and passion might be grounded upon experience rather than imagination, and become the means of recognizing the real goods of society and the real sociability of men. As we saw, however, this did not eliminate the hysterical volatility of Credit, and all the resources of social stability must be mobilized by crown, parliament, and public, to satisfy the hypersensitive nervous system with which society was now endowed and to control the impulses of human hope and fear. So mobile a human universe, moreover, was unlikely to contain institutional orderings of values, located in a past to which return might be made; an eternal morality there was, but it consisted in the virtues of sociability themselves and not in any set of legislative constructs by which virtue was guaranteed.

The Court Whig version of history, therefore, was not directly legitimatory; it agreed with that of the neo-Harringtonians in finding a society of agrarian warriors in the past, but denied both that this could be restored and that it had embodied principles which could be reasserted in the present. The corresponding version of politics, as we shall see in a further section, denies that there is a formulaically balanced constitution whose principles are fundamental to government. For this to be so there must be a classically cognizable history and a classically cognizable society, neither of which is to be expected in a universe of mobile credit and expectation, concerning which and in which there can only be opinion and passion. The government of the Court Whigs reigns over a mobile society and has sovereign managerial powers, if only because there are no cognizable principles to which its authority can be reduced. It exists in a history of change and flux, and must pragmatically do what must be done by operating upon human pas-

---

[79] Kramnick, pp. 166-69, discusses this point with reference to Bolingbroke.

sions in the ways demanded by the moment. Man remaining sociable—except when driven lunatic by cupidity and imagination—there are real virtues, real passions of sympathy and honesty, to secure the edifice of government in an actual moral universe. But the question is always pragmatic: is credit in harmony with confidence, are men's opinions, hopes, and fears concerning each other operating to stabilize society and increase prosperity? Government's business—the voice of Guicciardini's Bernardo distantly assures us—is to act so that this happens, not to be constantly relegislating some formalized framework in which alone, it is assumed, virtue can flourish. And if there is no such framework, the individual as *zōon politikon* cannot be forever formally reasserting his own civic being, or renewing its principles. His business is to get on with his social life, practice its virtues, and make his contribution to the credit and confidence which men repose in one another;[80] but his world will be primarily conventional and subjective, and only experience (and the state of the market) will tell him how far his opinions concerning reality are founded upon truth. We have perhaps reached the point of defining that "privatization" which modern historians are fond of detecting in the philosophies of commercial society.

This analysis of the language of Augustan social awareness has revealed it to be Machiavellian in a number of ways, which we could never have found it to be had we based the analysis on an explanation of Locke. We have found that Machiavellian and Harringtonian paradigms were exploited by late seventeenth-century minds in setting up an image of a free and uncorrupt society, and that something close to the Machiavellian vocabulary of *virtù* and *fortuna* was employed to express a sense of innovation, loss of legitimacy, and flux at the rapid movement of social change away from that ideal. We have found that a new version of the classical theory of corruption was necessitated by an awareness of the growing relations between government, war, and finance, and that mercantilist warfare caused a revival of interest in the external relationships of commonwealths with other commonwealths and with empires. We have found that it was through the image of the rentier, the officer, and the speculator in public funds, not through that of the merchant or dealer upon a market, that capitalism imparted its first shock and became involved in its first major controversy in the history of English-language political theory. We have found that a "bourgeois ideology," a paradigm for capitalist man as *zōon politikon*, was immensely hampered in its development by the omnipresence of

[80] Addison's *The Freeholder* (1715-16) adjures the individual to limit both the intensity and the range of his participation in government. See nos. 5, 16, 24, 25, 29, 48, and especially nos. 51 (whose modernism should be compared with Hobbes on the political consequences of reading ancient politics) and 52-55.

Aristotelian and civic humanist values which virtually defined rentier and entrepreneur as corrupt, and that if indeed capitalist thought ended by privatizing the individual, this may have been because it was unable to find an appropriate way of presenting him as citizen. "Bourgeois ideology," which old-fashioned Marxism depicted as appearing with historic inevitability, had, it seems, to wage a struggle for existence and may never have fully won it.

Finally, the conflict between real and mobile property, seen by Augustans as the material foundations of social existence, proved to entail a conflict—or more properly, an ambivalence—between modes of social epistemology; the cognition of society through money and credit being unequivocally presented by all concerned in terms of opinion and passion, fantasy and false consciousness. The deep concern felt by eighteenth-century philosophers with the relations between reason and the passions would seem to have something to do with the conflict between the landed and monied interests; but it may be worth emphasizing that this conclusion has not been arrived at through formal or informal Marxist analysis. A Marxist would probably assert that the conflict between real and mobile property is a sole and sufficient explanation of the philosophers' concern with reason and passion, but no need has been found to make that assertion here. It is normal Marxist procedure to arrive at connections between social perception and property relations through a process of "demystification," but that too has not been necessary; Davenant and Defoe were thoroughly and explicitly aware of what they meant to say. Rather than performing an exercise in Marxist analysis, it would seem, we have been studying the historical beginnings of the sort of thought found in Marx. The Augustan journalists and critics were the first intellectuals on record to express an entirely secular awareness of social and economic changes going on in their society, and to say specifically that these changes affected both their values and their modes of perceiving social reality. They used largely Machiavellian paradigms to articulate and express this awareness.

CHAPTER XIV

THE EIGHTEENTH-CENTURY DEBATE

Virtue, Passion and Commerce

[1]

THE DEBATE WE HAVE UNCOVERED—that between virtue and passion, land and commerce, republic and empire, value and history—underlay a great part of the social thinking of the eighteenth century. In the two remaining chapters an attempt will be made to display its role in the American Revolution and the formation of American values, and to depict this part of the story in a wider context of the development of European thought, so that Jefferson and Hamilton may emerge in a broadly discernible relationship to Rousseau and Marx. It can be shown both that the American Revolution and Constitution in some sense form the last act of the civic Renaissance, and that the ideas of the civic humanist tradition—the blend of Aristotelian and Machiavellian thought concerning the *zōon politikon*—provide an important key to the paradoxes of modern tensions between individual self-awareness on the one hand and consciousness of society, property, and history on the other. The American founders occupied a "Machiavellian moment"—a crisis in the relations between personality and society, virtue and corruption—but at the same time stood at a moment in history when that problem was being either left behind or admitted insoluble; it depended on the point of view. Our task in the present chapter is to understand as fully as possible the reasons why the inherited complex of ideas concerning republican virtue and its place in social time was transmitted into the eighteenth century in a form at once so adamant and so vulnerable, so little changed and yet so radically challenged.

The story as we have traced it is, first, that of how the Athenian assertion that man was *zōon politikon*, by nature a citizen, was revived in a paradoxical though not a directly challenging relation with the Christian assertion that man was *homo religiosus*, formed to live in a transcendent and eternal communion, known, however, by the ominously political name of *civitas Dei*; second, that of how the ensuing debate merged with some consequences of the Protestant assertion that all believers were priests, and society, rather than church, the true *ecclesia.* As Puritanism, followed in this respect by rational deism, denied more and more systematically the separateness of the religious organization of society, it became increasingly necessary to affirm that civic was one with religious liberty, and virtue—in the civic sense— one with salvation. The terms in which such claims were made might be evangelical and millenarian; at another extreme they might be post- Christian and utopian; but in either case they reflected the seculariza- tion of personality, its increasing involvement with a projection of society that was historical whether or not it was soterial. Since aware- ness of what transcendental Christianity meant did not die out, it was not forgotten that this affirmation was paradoxical and subversive: Montesquieu could reiterate Machiavelli's acknowledgment that civic virtue was self-contained and secular, identical neither with the Chris- tian communion nor with a social morality founded on purely Christian values.[1] But as the citizen became less like the saint, his civic personality required a *virtù* less like his soul's capacity for redemption and more like the autonomy of Aristotle's megalopsychic man or—in the period that concerns us—the *amour de soi-même* of Rousseau; and this moral- ity required a foundation less spiritual and more social and even material.

We have seen how this foundation was supplied, first by arms and then by property—of which real, inheritable, and, so to speak, natural property in land[2] was the paradigmatic case; for since the function of property was to affirm and maintain the reality of personal autonomy, liberty, and virtue, it must if possible display a reality (one is tempted to say a realty) capable of spanning the generations and permitting the living to succeed the dead in a real and natural order.[3] Inheritance, therefore, appeared more than ever before the mode of economic trans- mission proper to a society's existence in time. Land and inheritance remained essential to virtue, and virtue to the ego's reality in its own sight; there is an element of existential fear about the dread of corrup- tion so prominent in eighteenth-century social values. For the ideal of personality-sustaining property was no sooner formulated than it was seen to be threatened—Locke helping to give expression to ambiguities

[1] In the "Avertissement de l'Auteur" prefixed to the *Esprit des Lois*; quoted below, n. 78.

[2] Property is technically always artificial (*vide* the words of Ireton, above, p. 375); but property in land was thought to arise when men and their families moved freely, and in this sense "naturally," on the face of the earth. It could also be argued that property in flocks and herds had preceded it and was more "natural" still.

[3] See the language of Burke's *Reflections*, discussed in *Politics, Language and Time*, pp. 210-12, in which it is argued that societies where property and rights are envisaged as inheritances are most like families and so most natural.

that had meant nothing to Harrington. Forms of property were seen to arise which conveyed the notion of inherent dependence: salaried office, reliance on private or political patronage, on public credit. For these the appropriate term in the republican lexicon was corruption—the substitution of private dependencies for public authority—and the threat to individual integrity and self-knowledge which corruption had always implied was reinforced by the rise of forms of property seeming to rest on fantasy and false consciousness. Once property was seen to have a symbolic value, expressed in coin or in credit, the foundations of personality themselves appeared imaginary or at best consensual: the individual could exist, even in his own sight, only at the fluctuating value imposed upon him by his fellows, and these evaluations, though constant and public, were too irrationally performed to be seen as acts of political decision or virtue. The threat posed by corruption cut deep; we have next to consider why, and with what effects, there was no consoling or satisfactory answer to it.

The counter-ethics and counter-politics we have watched beginning to arise were based on a series of mitigations of the concept of fantasy or imagination: passion, opinion, interest. To the extent to which the credit economy could be convincingly presented as based on the exchange of real goods and the perception of real values, it could be divorced from the threat of false consciousness and endowed with concepts of the public good and personal virtue. In what scholars have called a "Protestant ethic" of frugality, self-denial, and reinvestment, trading society could even be permitted its own version of that classical virtue which consisted in placing the common good (in this case the circulation of trade) above one's personal profit. But to a very high degree indeed, the ethic of frugality was compelled to take second place to the ethic of self-interest. The landed man, successor to the master of the classical *oikos*, was permitted the leisure and autonomy to consider what was to others' good as well as his own; but the individual engaged in exchange could discern only particular values—that of the commodity which was his, that of the commodity for which he exchanged it. His activity did not oblige or even permit him to contemplate the universal good as he acted upon it, and he consequently continued to lack classical rationality. It followed that he was not conscious master of himself, and that in the last analysis he must be thought of as activated by nonrational forces—those governing the universe of credit rather than the universe of trade. Techniques certainly existed—of which Addison was a literary master—of elevating his motivation to at least the lower forms of rationality and morality: opinion, prudence, confidence, sympathy, even charity; but behind all this lay the ancient problem of showing how society might operate rationally and beneficially when the individuals composing it were denied full rationality and virtue.

Solutions were of course to be found in seeking to depict society as an economic mechanism, in which the exchange of goods and the division of labor operated to turn universal selfishness to universal benefit. In Addison, Mandeville, and Montesquieu we find variously presented[4] the image of the woman who wants a new gown for thoroughly selfish and whimsical reasons—woman as capricious consumer is a recurrent feature of the rather prominent sexism found in Augustan social criticism—and instantly sets tradesmen and artisans to work in ways whose benefit to society is in no way commensurate with the triviality of her motivation. The reason as Montesquieu gives it is that "self-interest is the strongest monarch in the world."[5] But there was an important sense in which all this was either beside the point or the admission of a necessary evil: social morality was becoming divorced from personal morality, and from the ego's confidence in its own integrity and reality. Mandeville, whose principal works appeared between 1714 and 1732, won a reputation in his own time akin to those of Machiavelli and Hobbes in theirs, by proclaiming that "private vices" were "public benefits." He argued that the mainspring of social behavior was not self-love—based on knowledge of one's self as one was; Rousseau's *amour de soi-même*—but what he called self-liking and Rousseau was to call *amour-propre*: based on the figure one cut in one's own eyes and those of others.[6] On this basis he built up a complex social psychology based on the ideas of custom—by which he meant manners rather than usages, fantasy rather than experience—and honor, by which was meant no feudal ethos of heroic pride and shame, but the other-directed intersubjectivity that had led Defoe to use honor as a synonym for credit. At bottom he was saying that the real world of economy and polity rested on a myriad fantasy worlds maintained by private egos; and he deeply disturbed his contemporaries, less by telling them that they were greedy and selfish than by telling them that they were

---

[4] Addison, *Spectator*, no. 69 (see Bloom and Bloom, pp. 38-39); Mandeville, *Fable of the Bees*, Remark G (ed. Harth, Harmondsworth: Penguin Books, 1970, p. 120); Montesquieu, *Lettres Persanes*, cvi.

[5] ". . . l'interêt est le plus grande monarque de la Terre." *Oeuvres Complètes* (Paris: Gallimard, 1949), p. 288.

[6] See *An Enquiry into the Origin of Honour and the Usefulness of Christianity in War*, ed. and intro. M. M. Goldsmith (London: Frank Cass, 1971), pp. xiii, xxiii. Rousseau's distinction is in the *Discours sur l'inegalité* (Vaughan, ed.), *The Political Writings of Jean-Jacques Rousseau* (Oxford: Basil Blackwell, 1962), I, 217. It is interesting that Mandeville was aware of the etymology and history of the word *virtus* and its origins in a warrior ethos; see his preface to the *Enquiry*, pp. iii-vii.

unreal, and must remain so if society was to persist. The specter of false consciousness had arisen, and was proving more frightening than that of Machiavellian *realpolitik*.

In the civic humanist ethos, then, the individual knew himself to be rational and virtuous, and possessed what we can now call *amour de soi-même*, inasmuch as he knew himself to be a citizen and knew how to play his role and take decisions within the *politeia* or *modo di vivere* of a republic. Given the spatio-temporal finitude and instability of any republic, this had always been a precarious and threatened mode of self-affirmation, requiring heroic virtue if not a special grace; and the great Florentine theorists had worked out the implications of this paradox. In Puritan England and Augustan Britain, there had emerged a theory of freehold and real property as the foundations of personality, autonomy, and commonwealth; but the challenge posed to this by the emergence of new forms of property and political economy restated in a new form the problem of individuality and temporal instability—in other words, that of value and history. The universe of real property and personal autonomy now seemed to belong to a historic past; new and dynamic forces, of government, commerce, and war, presented a universe which was effectively superseding the old but condemned the individual to inhabit a realm of fantasy, passion, and *amour-propre*. He could explain this realm, in the sense that he could identify the forces of change that were producing it; he could identify and pursue the goals proposed to him by his passions and fantasies; but he could not explain himself by locating himself as a real and rational being within it. The worlds of history and value therefore extruded one another, and what would later be described as the alienation of man from his history had begun to be felt; but, far from seeing himself as a mere product of historical forces, the civic and propertied individual was endowed with an ethic that clearly and massively depicted him as a citizen of classical virtue, the inhabitant of a classical republic, but exacted the price of obliging him to regard all the changes transforming the world of government, commerce, and war as corruption—corruption essentially the same as that which had transformed Rome from republic into empire. Hence the age's intense and nervous neoclassicism. The dominant paradigm for the individual inhabiting the world of value was that of civic man; but the dominant paradigm for the individual as engaged in historic actuality was that of economic and intersubjective man, and it was peculiarly hard to bring the two together.

We therefore find that all that sociology of liberty which had developed from Aristotle through Machiavelli and Harrington was accessible to British (and to French anglomanic) thought in the form of the "Country" or "Old Whig" ideology, which expressed in great detail the values of civic liberty, the moral and political conditions under which they flourished or decayed, and the interpretation of European and English history in which they were seen as developing and as increasingly exposed to threats of corruption; but that this was obliged by its postulates to attack as corruptive a number of important trends which it isolated as those of a "modern" world. In opposition to it can be found, less eloquently rhetorical because less morally normative, a "Court" ideology—prefigured in such writings as Defoe's—which accurately identified the forces making for historical change and explained how government must and did work on its new foundations, but which supplied neither polity nor personality with a coherent moral structure. Its attitude to historical change was one of pragmatic acceptance; it denied that government was based on principles to which there could be a return; and its moral and philosophical theory affirmed that the mainsprings of both motivation and perception in human beings were pride and passion, fantasy and self-interest, which it tended to describe in Mandevillean and Hobbesian terms. Hard as it was to reconcile the philosophies of value and history, virtue and passion, property and credit, self-love and self-liking, the conditions of British politics in the eighteenth century, with their sharply prescribed interdependence between Court and Country, commanded that some such attempt be made and that neither thesis could be expounded without making some concessions to the other. But in the American colonies—the present state of research strongly suggests—the ideology that presented virtue as ever threatened by corruption was little mitigated by any sense that it was possible to live with the forces of history and contain them. This circumstance helped bring about the division of the Atlantic world in the great civil war of the American Revolution; it presented the civic humanist intellect with an unparalleled opportunity of applying the sociology of liberty to legislation in the sense of actual state-founding; but since the forces of change and modernity had crossed the Atlantic somewhat in advance of the governmental imperative that compelled their recognition, it further ensured that the attempt at classical legislation would encounter its crises and display its paradoxes.

[II]

Cato's Letters, which were originally published in the *London Journal* between 1720 and 1724, were written by John Trenchard—a veteran of the "paper war" of 1698—and his protégé Thomas Gordon, and with the far more anticlerical *The Independent Whig*, appearing from the same pens about the same time, formed some of the most widely distributed political reading of the contemporary American colonists.[7] Cato was mainly bent on diagnosing and proposing to remedy the state of national corruption revealed by the failure of the South Sea Company—much, it should be noted, as Montesquieu's *Lettres Persanes* (1721) were concerned with the similar state of affairs precipitated in France by the failure of John Law's Mississippi schemes;[8] but in Britain the themes it appeared necessary to Cato to take up had been the matter of debate for a quarter of a century. It was neither accidental nor surprising that an old adversary of the standing army should find himself denouncing a gigantic job of the "monied interest," since the two were taken to be at bottom one and the same phenomenon. Cato—Trenchard was the senior partner, though Gordon's contributions were numerous—develops an unmistakably Machiavellian and neo-Harringtonian critique of corruption and of the republic which is its opposite; and he specifically declares that England (or Britain) is a republic, of that peculiarly happy kind which has a king as its chief magistrate.[9] This republic instantly begins to display Machiavellian characteristics: it must be inexorably revengeful against those (the South Sea Directors) who have wronged it,[10] and its freedom cannot long continue without an equality in the distribution of property and consequently of power.[11] Machiavelli had discussed the necessity of an *equalità* of this order, but like him Cato had in mind not so much a leveling of property as "an agrarian law, or something like it" to ensure that no individual or group became so rich as to reduce others to dependence.[12] The words "or something like it" reveal that we are no longer in a purely landed commonwealth; what is to be dreaded is not vassalage, but indebtedness and the corruption through dependence that it brings. Peculation is the worst of crimes against the public,[13] the freeholders should never let themselves be represented in parliament by "men whose estates are embarked in companies";[14] exclusive trading companies, like those designed for the East Indies and the

[7] Robbins, *The Eighteenth-Century Commonwealthman*, pp. 115-25; Clinton Rossiter, *Seedtime of the Republic: the Origin of the American Tradition of Political Liberty* (New York: Harcourt Brace, 1953), pp. 141, 492; Bernard Bailyn, *The Ideological Origins of the American Revolution* (Cambridge, Mass.: The Belknap Press, 1967), pp. 35-37, and *The Origins of American Politics* (New York: Vintage Books, 1970), pp. 40-44; David L. Jacobson, *The English Libertarian Heritage* (Indianapolis: Bobbs Merrill, 1965), introduction (the text consists wholly of selections from Cato).

[8] *Lettres Persanes*, XXIV, XCVIII, CXXXII, CXXXVIII, CXLII, CXLVI.

[9] *Cato's Letters: or, Essays on Liberty, Civil and Religious, and Other Important Subjects*; 3d ed., London, 1723, II, 28.

[10] *Cato's Letters*, I, 6-7, and *passim*.   [11] *Cato's Letters*, I, 11.

[12] *Cato's Letters*, II, 16, 71-74, 85-90.   [13] *Cato's Letters*, I, 134-35.

[14] *Cato's Letters*, III, 24.

South Seas, reduce the landowner to debt, bring about the destruction of trade and corrupt government by introducing inequality.[15] Spurius Melius, who sought to bring the people into dependence by monopolizing the corn supply, was heroic Rome's chief enemy within,[16] whereas to Harrington he was no more than the subject of a remark in passing about the minor dangers to liberty presented by trade.[17] Cato has fully accepted the fact, if also the danger, of such a society; something more than an agrarian law will be needed to ensure that equality which means that all men are equally free and equally subject to public authority—equal in their opportunity of virtue, for if they are not there can be no virtue.

But equality in this sense tends to preclude the discovery of any precise equivalent to an agrarian law, and apart from the undesirability of exclusive companies and a heavy burden of public debt, Cato does not tell us what specific measures should be taken to ensure equality in a trading society. If "equality" means no more than an equal subjection to the *res publica*, no more need (or can) be done to ensure it than to reassert the public authority—Machiavelli's *ridurre ai principii*, which turned out to have little more concrete content than that; but (to approach the problem from its other aspect) since where the public authority is impeded by inequality there is corruption, and where there is corruption there is no virtue, the reassertion of the *res publica* in its uncorrupt form is readily identifiable with the reassertion of virtue. Cato's call for equality therefore makes up in moral fervor for what it lacks by way of a specific program; and though for much of the time he is merely calling for uprightness and independence in the people and their representatives and magistrates, the summons need not have been limited to a purely moral content. The crucial evil of corruption was, to many a theorist, that it disturbed the balance of the constitution; that of the growth of a monied interest that it perverted the relationships between executive, parliament, and propertied people; and a call for virtue and the restitution of the *res publica* might have been a program for restoration of constitutional relationships in what was supposed to have been their properly balanced form.

Cato, however, was not primarily a constitutional theorist, and to the extent that he was not the concept of virtue dictated a politics of

---

[15] *Cato's Letters*, III, 199-213.   [16] *Cato's Letters*, I, 69-70.

[17] Toland, *Works*, p. 28: "As for dominion personal or in mony, it may now and then stir up a Melius or a Manlius, which, if the commonwealth be not provided with some kind of dictatorian power, may be dangerous, though it has bin seldom or never successful: because to property producing empire, it is requir'd that it should have som certain root or foot-hold, which, except in land, it cannot have, being otherwise as it were upon the wing."

personal morality. As we follow out the explorations of this theme, we find it repeatedly conceded that a trading society possesses a psychology of its own, and that this complicates the pursuit and preservation of virtue. Cato's vision presupposes no agrarian utopia, although Gordon tells us of Trenchard in an obituary preface that "though he was careful to preserve his Estate, he was no ways anxious to increase it";[18] the reader is left in no doubt that a society founded in land alone entails the barbarism and vassalage of Poland or the Scottish Highlands and that trade must be added to husbandry if the darker aspects of Gothic society are to be overcome.[19] It is true that

in the first Rise and Beginning of States, a rough and unhewn Virtue, a rude and savage Fierceness, and an unpolished Passion for Liberty, are the Qualities chiefly in Repute: To these succeed military Accomplishments, domestick Arts and Sciences, and such political Knowledge and Acquirements, as are necessary to make States great and formidable Abroad, and to preserve Equality and domestick Happiness and Security at Home; and lastly, when these are attained, follow Politeness, speculative Knowledge, moral and experimental Philosophy, with other Branches of Learning, and the whole Train of the Muses.[20]

But the transition from unpolished virtue to politeness must be made, and made with the assistance of commerce; and we are assured that maritime trade not only can flourish only where there is civil liberty, but can present no possible danger to it. Sailors do not menace the commonwealth as standing armies do. Virtue and liberty protect commerce, and commerce ensures liberty and politeness.[21] But a complex formula has been required in order to bring virtue and commerce together, and we discover the reason when we find, once again, that considerable intellectual effort has been exerted to make the transition from commerce as fantasy to commerce as enriched and ordered reality.

Nothing is more certain than that Trade cannot be forced; she is a coy and humorous Dame, who must be won by Flattery and Allurements, and always flies Force and Power; she is not confined to Nations, Sects, or Climates, but travels and wanders about the Earth, till she fixes her Residence where she finds the best Welcome and kindest Reception; her Contexture is so nice and delicate, that she cannot breathe in a tyrannical Air; Will and Pleasure are so opposite to her Nature, that but touch her with the Sword and she dies:

[18] *Cato's Letters*, I, lvii.   [19] *Cato's Letters*, II, 305.
[20] *Cato's Letters*, III, 27-28.   [21] *Cato's Letters*, II, 272-77.

But if you give her gentle and kind Entertainment, she is a grateful and beneficent Mistress; she will turn Desarts into fruitful Fields, Villages into great Cities, Cottages into Palaces, Beggars into Princes, convert Cowards into Heroes, Blockheads into Philosophers; will change the Coverings of little Worms into the richest Brocades, the Fleeces of harmless Sheep into the Pride and Ornaments of Kings, and by a farther Metamorphosis will transmute them again into armed Hosts and haughty Fleets.[22]

But this is Circe's island; marriage to this enchantress means that we must live in a world of magic and transformation; and the price to be paid is admission that we are governed by our fantasies and passions. Cato explains at length that men are governed by passion, not principle,[23] and that the objects of our hopes and fears are for the most part illusory and fantastic;[24] it is through the sound of words that men are deceived and misled,[25] and stockjobbers form only one class of villains who manipulate and corrupt men through images of false goods and false honor.[26] Nor is this possible merely because human nature has its weaker side; it is essentially "chimerical" and the good man as well as the bad must govern by knowing the passions of men.[27] The language of the *Letters* grows Hobbesian:

When we say, that if such a Thing happened, we would be easie; we can only mean, or ought only to mean, that we would be more easie than we are: And in that too we are often mistaken; for new Acquisitions bring new Wants, and imaginary Wants are as pungent as real ones. So that there is the same End of Wishing as of Living, and Death only can still the Appetites.[28]

But the ideal of civic virtue is not abandoned. Though we are told that to serve the public good is itself a passion, and that passions are called good when they serve the public and bad when they do not, it is no less unequivocally stated:

There is scarce any one of the Passions but what is truly laudable, when it centers in the Publick, and makes that its Object. Ambition, Avarice, Revenge, are all so many Virtues, when they aim at the general Welfare. I know that it is exceeding hard and rare, for any Man to separate his Passions from his own Person and Interest; but it is certain that there have been such Men. *Brutus, Cato, Regulus, Timoleon, Dion,* and *Epaminondas,* were such, as were many more ancient

[22] *Cato's Letters,* II, 267.
[23] *Cato's Letters,* II, 77-84.
[24] *Cato's Letters,* II, 51.
[25] *Cato's Letters,* I, 82-83.
[26] *Cato's Letters,* II, 192-201.
[27] *Cato's Letters,* I, 124-27; II, 50-52.
[28] *Cato's Letters,* II, 51.

Greeks and Romans; and, I hope, *England* has still some such. And though in pursuing publick Views, Men regard themselves and their own Advantages; yet if they regard the Publick more, or their own in Subserviency to the Publick, they may justly be esteemed virtuous and good.[29]

It is a Machiavellian *virtù*, in the sense that civic does not always accord with personal morality; but it is a real and classical virtue nonetheless. The passions now appear as the pursuits of private and particular goods, familiar to us from the whole tradition of Aristotelian politics and ethics; virtue is the passion for pursuing the public good, with which the lesser passions may compete, but into which they may equally be transformed. And corruption is the failure, or the consequences of the failure, to effect this transformation. The "Publick" (*res publica*) is then, to a certain extent, what government was soon to appear in the political theory of Hume: a device or mechanism for requiring men to take long views instead of short, to identify their private interests with the general good, to erect an edifice of reason and virtue on a foundation of passion; but rather more unequivocally than with Hume is it also a device for bringing men out of the cave into the sunlight, from a realm of fantasy into one of reality. And the heroes of the ancient polities are not the mere products of the socializing machine; their virtue is active and authentic, and may be invoked as a principal means of ensuring virtue in others. As well as the moral example of the virtuous hero, other means of preventing corruption are named which are startlingly classical and humanist. There is the people as *guardia della libertà*; though the limitations of their public experience render them liable to be deceived by the sound of words and unreal objects, the fact that they do not seek power for themselves means that they have no interest in multiplying fantasies for the corruption of others, and for this reason they may be trusted to undeceive themselves given time.[30] In a free society, where the danger of deception is in any case less, even their fantasies may tend to the public good: for,

as *Machiavel* well observes, *When the People are dissatisfied, and have taken a Prejudice against their Governors, there is no Thing nor Person that they ought not to fear.*[31]

There is even a sense in which inequality stands to equality in precisely the relation of *fortuna* to *virtus*, and reveals with particular

[29] *Cato's Letters*, II, 48-49. [30] *Cato's Letters*, I, 153-56, 177-83.
[31] *Cato's Letters*, I, 180-81. The thought is authentically Machiavellian, though it is not quite clear to what text this passage alludes.

clarity that the "equality" which is necessary to republics is strictly speaking an *isonomia*. Men are equal by nature, in the sense that all men are born equipped with the same capacities; but fortune unjustly and capriciously distributes the circumstantial advantages of this world, so that some have more of them than others. This makes for emulation, envy, and acquisitiveness, which are not without their utility to society; it also makes for the existence of a ruling class, whose authority checks the tendency of emulation to run to excess. The more and the less fortunate, it seems probable, act as checks on one another, and oblige each other's passions to turn toward service to the common good; and the arbitrariness of fortune constantly challenges me to affirm my virtue, in remembering that it at least is not fortune's gift.

We cannot bring more natural Advantages into the World, than other Men do; but we can acquire more Virtue in it than we generally acquire. To be great, is not in every Man's Power; but to be good, is in the Power of all: Thus far every Man may be upon a Level with another, the lowest with the highest; and Men might thus come to be morally as well as naturally equal.[32]

These forces, and others like them, operate to maintain virtue in free societies. It is clear that the classical republic, with its distribution of powers and rotation of offices, is the paradigm case of the free society, and that the Ancient Constitution of England resembled the republic in most respects—including the rotation of magistracies,[33] by which the authors seem to have meant frequent parliaments (though nothing is said of the fact that Trenchard had supported the Septennial Act in 1717). But an important modification appears at a later stage in the argument.[34] England, it is affirmed, is in its present condition capable of no other form of government than a limited monarchy, because the distribution of property is such that there exists a powerful nobility and a beneficed clergy, both of whom depend upon the patronage of the crown for the wealth and influence which bring other men into dependence on them. There is not, therefore, that equality of property necessary for the existence of a pure republic (even, presumably, a republic of the kind whose head may be a king), and the relations of monarchy and nobility display that restless interdependence which characterized the feudal or "Gothic" monarchy of Harrington. Forces usually identified as those of corruption—courtiers, placemen, exclusive trading companies—operate to maintain the present system; but, insists Cato:

[32] *Cato's Letters*, II, 90; see pp. 85-90 for the argument at length.
[33] *Cato's Letters*, II, 234-40.   [34] *Cato's Letters*, III, 159-65.

If this be the true Circumstance of *England* at present, as I conceive it indisputably is, we have nothing left to do, or indeed which we can do, but to make the best of our own Constitution, which, if duly administered, provides excellently well for general Liberty; and to secure the Possession of Property, and to use our best Endeavours to make it answer the other Purposes of private Virtue, as far as the Nature of it is capable of producing that End.[35]

Spartam—or rather *Venetiam*—*nactus es*; after all, it would appear, Englishmen have not inherited an equality of property so perfect as to permit the practice of a public, as opposed to private, virtue in a republic, and must make the most of what they have. Limited monarchy is not a perfectly balanced commonwealth; it is merely a balance between the forces making for liberty and for corruption, between property and dependence, executive and parliament, good enough to ensure liberty and private virtue and prevent the worst ravages of corruption and fantasy. Trenchard is the writer here, and we plainly hear the voice of 1714-1719; Old Whigs who had joined Tories in a "Country" movement had been driven by the latter's High Church excesses to accept a Court Whig regime,[36] which had passed the Septennial Act and was now moving through the South Sea crisis toward the perfection of Walpolean government. To writers of the neo-Harringtonian lineage, this meant acceptance of a rule by patronage and finance which they could never regard as wholly uncorrupt, which could never be restored to the purity of any principle. And the acceptance of facts meant acceptance of the supremacy of passion and interest.

There is another aspect to Trenchard's and Gordon's indictments of the world of corruption and unreality, which should not pass unremarked. From the depiction of the false consciousness of the speculative society,[37] in which men insanely pursue the fairy gold of paper schemes, they move to portray other forms of false honor and false consciousness, the product of excessive authority rather than excessive liberty: the world of absolute monarchy, in which individuals and their values are not merely subject to the autocrat's power, but exist even in their own eyes simply as defined by him and his courtiers;[38] the world of superstition and priestcraft, which is nothing other than that "kingdom of the fairies" described by Hobbes in Book IV of *Leviathan*, where men are kept in subjection by being obliged to live in a dreamworld of unreal essences and entities.[39] The unstated alliance which we

[35] *Cato's Letters*, III, 162-63.
[36] For the decision of the Commonwealth intellectuals to swallow the Septennial Act, see Robbins, pp. 109-10.
[37] *Cato's Letters*, I, 16-17, 25-27.   [38] *Cato's Letters*, I, 88-90.
[39] *Cato's Letters*, II, 105-12.

earlier noted between *Leviathan* and *Oceana* is still operative in these neo-Harringtonians. The authority of the sovereign and the virtue of the citizen both drive away fantasies and depict things and persons as they really are; but where false consciousness for Hobbes was productive of rebellion, in the republican tradition it issues in corruption. Men who live by fantasies are manipulated by other men who rule through them. Autocrats, priests, and stockjobbers form a common enemy, and the structure of the argument as we have traced it suggests that it was the last who served as catalyst in precipitating the theory. In the *Lettres Persanes*, written about the same time as *Cato's Letters* under the shock of the Mississippi failure, Law appears as a northern magician, selling the wind in bags and making people believe that it is gold.[40] He is empowered to do this by the authority of a king whose courtiers live, and compel others to live, in a mental world constructed out of nothing but honor in the sense of reputation, itself determined partly by the autocrat's fiat and partly by the courtiers' mutual self-delusion.[41] The courtier is equated with the priest, monk, and bogus philosopher; and analysts[42] of those of the *Lettres Persanes* which deal at a distance with the tragedy of Usbek's harem have forcibly suggested that the courtier is to be further equated with the eunuch and the corrupt citizen with the alienated woman, so that Montesquieu is carrying the analysis of fantasy and corruption into the sexual basis of the classical *oikos*. If so, he seems to have abandoned the quest for a *virtus* in marriage itself (Mandeville had drawn attention to the root masculinity of the term's derivation from *vir*); the only idyllic relationships in the work are based on brother-sister incest and polyandrous erotics respectively,[43] and we might come to believe that Montesquieu had despaired of exogamy altogether. Be that as it may, it is apparent that the opposition of virtue to false consciousness was capable of supporting a wide range of sociological analysis.

It is perhaps more immediately significant that both Cato and Montesquieu employ it in the cause of a vigorous anticlericalism. The man of virtue is capable of conducting his own worship, and does so in a setting which is civic where it is not private; the cleric, claiming a monopoly over this activity, appears, like the soldier, lawyer, and stockjobber, one who corrupts by interposing himself in a virtue which all men should practice equally, and—like the latter at least—he can do

[40] *Lettres Persanes*, CXLII.   [41] *Lettres Persanes*, LXXXVII-XC.

[42] Marshall Berman, *The Politics of Authenticity* (New York: Atheneum, 1970), and Orest Ranum, "Personality and Politics in the *Persian Letters*," *Political Science Quarterly* 84, no. 4 (1969), 606-27.

[43] "The Story of Apheridon and Astarte," in Letter LXVII, and the tale of Anais and Ibrahim in Letter CXLI.

so only by placing unreal entities before the minds of those he deceives in order to corrupt.[44] Trenchard and Gordon shared this view with Neville's *Plato Redivivus*, and we recall how Harrington's republicanism merged with the Independent tradition in reducing the clergy to civic functionaries. What is noteworthy here is that there is a high degree of correlation in the early eighteenth century between neo-Harringtonian republicanism and deism. Swift and his *Sentiments of a Church of England Man* should indeed not be forgotten; but the republican lineage includes, as well as Cato himself, Toland, Bolingbroke, and in France Henri de Boulainvilliers, an ardent member of the anti-Christian literary underground whose *Essai sur la Noblesse* and *Lettres sur les Parlements* seek to invest the French nobility with an autonomous *virtù* founded in *sang* and *epèe* rather than in freehold property.[45] Franco Venturi has suggested that the republican example, notably in its English variant, made a more important contribution to the early Enlightenment than has been recognized;[46] and in this connection it is interesting to see that republicanism and deism alike carried on the English and Puritan crusade against a clergy enjoying separate or *jure divino* authority.

There is, of course, one entirely crucial breach in continuity between Puritanism and deism. We have seen that Harrington's thought conformed—perhaps a shade mechanically—to an older tradition which required the republic to locate itself in an apocalyptic moment, and in so doing conformed to another tradition of which Puritanism has a great many instances. Now apocalyptic was founded upon prophecy, and Hobbes also was among the students of prophecy; but deism, and the Enlightenment generally, were based on a singularly complete rejection of prophecy, revelation, and the Hebrew mode of thought at large. It would be possible to preserve the continuity of deism with Puritanism in the respect which concerns us, by emphasizing such matters as the self-secularizing tendency inherent in apocalyptic, the emergence of Socinian over millenarian trends in the post-Puritan inheritance—Toland helped mediate both Milton and Harrington to the thought of the eighteenth century—and that transition, explored by

[44] Volume IV of *Cato's Letters*, and the companion series of *The Independent Whig*, are largely devoted to working out this thesis.

[45] Renée Simon, *Henry de Boulainviller; historien, politique, philosophe, astrologue, 1658-1722* (Paris: Boivin, 1941) and *Un révolté du XVIII⁰ siècle, Henry de Boulainviller* (Garches: Editions du nouvel humanisme, 1948); Ira O. Wade, *The Clandestine Organization and Diffusion of Philosophic Ideas in France from 1700 to 1750* (Princeton University Press, 1938).

[46] Franco Venturi, *Utopia and Reform in the Enlightenment* (Cambridge University Press, 1971).

Tuveson, from millennium to utopia. The more successful we are, how-ever, in anchoring English republican deism in its Puritan inheritance, the more we shall be stressing respects in which England was too mod-ern to need an Enlightenment and was already engaged upon the quar-rel with modernity itself. *Cato's Letters* and the *Lettres Persanes* alike denounce autocracy, priestcraft, and speculative corruption; but in lands where absolute monarchy and Tridentine Catholicism were reali-ties and not bogeys, they could not be the rhetorical embellishments of the case against corruption that they were in England. Where the *philosophes* were fighting to liberate secular history from the authority of the sacred books, the postmillenarist Augustan social critics were examining the impact of historical change on a humanist theory of the social personality which was already wholly secular. It was much more than a persistence of medieval and Renaissance theories of *senectus mundi*—far from dead as these were—that made the Augustans brood over a still cyclical vision of the corruption of nations;[47] they were possessed of a thoroughly social and secular theory of the civic person-ality, whose parameters suggested that for some centuries social change had been undermining its foundations. They were proto-Rousseauan beneath their Whig combativeness, closer to the romantics than to the *philosophes* who read them. The Old Whigs who appeared about 1698 were, it may be suggested, the first intellectuals of the Left, denounc-ing their own party's official leadership for betrayal of its own wholly secular principles; and the poets and satirists who followed Bolingbroke in the 1730s—whether we call them Independent Whigs or Tories—erected Sir Robert Walpole into a figure doubly symbolic, to them a monster of corruption but to us the first modern statesman to impress a modern intelligentsia with the belief that his policies and personality were undermining the moral structure of human society.[48] Their lan-guage was humanist, their enemy was modernity, and their posture had something of the sixteenth century about it and something of the twentieth. The still ebullient Enlightenment had some way to go before it could overtake this dualism.

[III]

The Anglo-Atlantic equivalent of the "Machiavellian moment," we have now recognized, had some positive complexities, in terms of eco-nomics and psychology, not to be found in its Florentine original. The most resonant formulation of its constitutional aspects was the work

[47] E.g., *Cato's Letters*, I, 121.
[48] See Kramnick's *Bolingbroke and His Circle*, and the present writer's review in *Journal of Modern History* 42, no. 2 (1970), 251-54.

of Henry St. John, Viscount Bolingbroke, between his first and second exiles—both of which were self-chosen—when he elected to conduct a press and pamphlet campaign against Walpole's administration in language directly continuous with that of 1698-1702 and 1711-1714.[49] The Country program—frequent parliaments, exclusion of placemen, a qualification in landed property for members of the House of Commons—had originated in the attack on Danby's ministry in 1675 and had continued as a campaign against major war and its effects on government and finance. Following the collapse of the Tory party in 1714, a succession of Whig administrations, while not contesting the decision to withdraw from large-scale European campaigning, had set about constructing that political style known as "the growth of oligarchy."[50] Its characteristics were a strong and stable executive representing a guaranteed Protestant monarchy in parliament, and a steady diminution of political competitiveness; its means included compromised elections, a Septennial (replacing a Triennial) Act extending the duration of parliaments, and a system of political management in which patronage played a visible if not an oversignificant part. It further retained that financial structure of banks and funds which had come into being to support war, and whose adversaries, denouncing it as corruption, saw in its continuation as part of the permanent establishment of government the fulfillment of their darkest prophecies—the hysteria of the South Sea Bubble having done nothing to lessen their fears. From standing armies to stockjobbers, therefore, the vocabulary of the Country ideology remained valid after half a century's shaping, and though Walpole's was a resolutely peace-seeking administration, Bolingbroke and Pulteney in their journal *The Craftsman*, supported by writers of the caliber of Pope, Swift, Gay, Arbuthnot, and Fielding, were able to attack it in the language used against the warmaking Juntos of William and Anne's reigns and to represent it as their historical successor and continuation.

The function of every Country ideology was to mobilize country gentlemen and their independent representatives in parliament against the administration of the day, and the rhetoric of virtue employed to this end was invariably as much constitutional as it was moral. This characteristic, of course, kept it well within the classical mainstream. We know that the Aristotelian polity, the ultimate paradigm of all civic humanism, was simultaneously a distribution of political functions and

[49] Kramnick's is the best study of the thought of these controversies; H. T. Dickinson, *Bolingbroke* (London: Constable, 1970), relates them most fully to the pattern of Bolingbroke's career.

[50] The term is of course that of J. H. Plumb, *The Growth of Political Stability in England, 1660-1730* (London: Macmillan, 1967).

powers and a partnership between many kinds of virtue, and that *virtus* and *virtù* had themselves been used to convey the notion of power as well as that of moral quality. Bolingbroke, like all ideologists in the Country tradition, exploited this ambivalence in attempting to solve his basic problem of accepting the constitutional implications of the Glorious Revolution of 1688 while passionately rejecting the allegedly corruptive consequences of the Financial Revolution that had inseparably attended it; and did so by means that in their turn looked back to the central ambivalence of the *King's Answer to the Nineteen Propositions*. That document, authoritatively formulating the doctrine that England enjoyed a balanced constitution, had left it unavoidably unclear whether king, lords, and commons—standing for the classical one, few, and many—formed a partnership and equilibrium within the process of legislation, a partnership of different functions and powers within some more broadly defined process of government, or a partnership of different social virtues within a *politeia* or *res publica*. As we know, it was only when the concept of legislation assumed a high degree of importance that it was really necessary to draw distinctions between these possible meanings.

Ever since Shaftesbury had pioneered the attack on the Crown and its servants for corrupting the House of Commons, this had been capable of rhetorical expression as an attack on "the executive" (or "ministers") for seeking to bring "the legislative" (or "representative") into dependence or subjection, thus disturbing "the balance" with consequences potentially as grave as those of 1642; but the underlying ambiguities had remained. Whenever a conflict had seemed to occur between prerogative and parliament, the language of balance had been used in its functional sense, and the offending party had been denounced for usurping a jurisdiction not properly its own. But whenever—as was increasingly common—patronage and corruption were the issue, the executive had been attacked less for exceeding its constitutional powers than for bringing the individuals composing the legislature into a personal and demoralizing dependence on the Crown and the financial resources it controlled. While this was, in an important sense, to move from the language of function to that of virtue, the two had never been distinct and tended to coalesce. Even the rise of the "monied interest," depicted in sweeping historical terms as that of a "new form of property," was thought of as increasing "the influence of the Crown" by vastly enlarging the number and wealth of its dependents. A corollary, however, was that threats to the balance of the constitution and increases in the power of the executive were thought to entail the terrifying social and moral threats we have considered. To disturb the balance was, as ever, to corrupt virtue.

One of Bolingbroke's more arresting hypotheses about modern history was that the danger from prerogative had been virtually replaced by the danger from corruption[51]—an argument at bottom neo-Harringtonian—but he nevertheless continued to conflate the languages of function and morality in ways which may have affected the thought of Montesquieu and through him, of the American Founding Fathers. This is the famous problem of the "separation of powers."[52] Bolingbroke at times used terminology which seemed to suggest that king, lords, and commons performed separate political functions which could be distinguished as executive, judicial, and legislative, that the balance of the constitution consisted in the ability of any two of these to check the third, and that since it was vital to prevent any one of them from establishing a permanent ascendancy over any other, the "independence" of each of the three must at all costs be preserved. In spite of the many difficulties of this analysis when applied to British government, it may have been at Bolingbroke's persuasion that Montesquieu[53] substituted the triad of executive, judicial, and legislative for that duality of functions proper to a few and a many—Guicciardini's *deliberazione* and *approvazione*, Harrington's "debate" and "result"—which theorists of the philo-Venetian tradition had insisted must be kept apart, thus constituting a "separation of powers" in the strict sense. Bolingbroke was promptly attacked by his journalistic adversaries—obscure men whose ability has been much underrated—for advancing a chimerical theory of the constitution, and he as promptly conceded that British government could not be analyzed into these absolutely distinct powers. He acknowledged that king, lords, and commons joined in a common political activity, which might as well be termed legislation as government, and insisted that by "independence" he had meant not a rigorous separation of function, but the elimination of "any influence, direct or indirect," which one of the three might exercise over any other.[54] Unless the argument were to go round in a circle again—which it often did and still does—Bolingbroke must be interpreted as meaning, not encroachment by one jurisdiction upon another, but corruption occurring when "indirect influence" made the members of one

[51] This is the argument at large of *A Dissertation Upon Parties* (1733-35).

[52] W. B. Gwyn, *The Meaning of the Separation of Powers: an analysis of the doctrine from its origin to the adoption of the United States Constitution* (New Orleans: Tulane Studies in Political Science, 1965), and M.J.C. Vile, *Constitutionalism and the Separation of Powers* (Oxford: The Clarendon Press, 1967), are two thorough if slightly unhistorical treatments of this concept.

[53] Robert Shackleton, "Montesquieu, Bolingbroke and the Separation of Powers," *French Studies* 3 (1949), 25-38, and *Montesquieu: a Critical Biography* (Oxford: The Clarendon Press, 1961).

[54] Dickinson, pp. 202-204, 305-306.

governing body personally dependent upon another; as talking, not the language of function, but that of morality. There is plenty of evidence that his contemporaries so understood him.

But the ambivalence could not be quite so easily dispelled. In arguing that government by three independent powers was absurd, Bolingbroke's critics were not simply returning to the sixteenth- or seventeenth-century debate between sovereignty and mixed government, though they were echoing a line of argument, found at least as early as Swift's *Discourse of the Nobles and the Commons*, in which it was maintained that in every government there must be a final, absolute, and uncontrollable power, but that this could well be exercised by a complex and concurrent body (like king-in-parliament). They were in fact returning to the position of the *Answer to the Nineteen Propositions* or the *Humble Petition and Advice*, according to which the principles of balanced government could be found within the structure of parliamentary mixed monarchy, and against which Harrington had contended that a true republic was necessary. Montesquieu, it should be noted, for all his separation of powers, virtually accepted their position when he declared that Harrington had erected an imaginary government while having before his eyes a real one containing everything he needed.[55] But in addition to this, Bolingbroke's critics were affirming something at which *Plato Redivivus* had at least hinted and which *Cato's Letters* had acknowledged more directly: that parliamentary monarchy, in which king, lords, and commons must work together, could not subsist without a measure of patronage or "indirect influence." The neo-Harringtonian restatement of English history could be used to make this point: in feudal society, homage and tenure had combined to ensure that free men were responsive to the authority of their superiors, but once property carried with it no element of subjection at all, something must take the place of the vanished *liens de dépendance*. Trenchard may have hoped that a true equality of property would some day make even mixed monarchy unnecessary, but there is a group of works of the 1740s[56] concerned with rendering permanent a structure of influence which has come to replace feudal tenure. Such was a recognized implication of the acceptance of the need for parliamentary sovereignty.

Donato Giannotti would have followed this part of the debate with

[55] Montesquieu, *Esprit des Lois*, xi, 6: ". . . il a bâti Chalcédoine, ayant le rivage de Byzance devant les yeux."

[56] *A Letter from a Bystander to a Member of Parliament* (1741); Earl of Egmont, *Faction Detected by the Evidence of Facts* (1743); Bishop Samuel Squire, *An Enquiry into the Foundation of the English Constitution* (1745), and *A Historical Essay upon the Balance of Civil Power in England* (1748).

interest, recalling his own attempts to invest one of the three components of government with *poca dependenza* upon the other two; even Bolingbroke once or twice confessed that a subordination, as well as a balance, of powers was necessary to maintain government in an imperfect world.[57] Under eighteenth-century conditions, however, it was even harder than it had been in Florence to show that dependence and influence could mean anything but corruption. The man who lived in the expectation of reward for his civic actions was a creature of passion, not of virtue, and by definition lacked the quality necessary to resist further degeneration. Bolingbroke, therefore, on weak ground when it came to eliminating patronage altogether from politics, was driven to find more and more devices for the reaffirmation of virtue. Hence his retention of such staples of the Country program as frequent, instead of septennial, parliaments and the abolition of placemen and standing armies. It is plain also that one motive for his stress on the independence of the three parts of government was the desire to affirm the classical balance in as formulaic a way as possible, and so invest the constitution with "principles" to which there might be a "return"— that most Renaissance of means to the reassertion of virtue. Even about this he displayed ambivalence in his later writings,[58] but in the *Craftsman* period he made the historical reality of principles a cardinal doctrine, and drew heavily on the idealization of "Gothic" society in order to discover a structure of balance in the Ancient Constitution. But here too his critics—Cook and Arnall in the *London Journal*, Lord Hervey in *Ancient and Modern Liberty Stated and Compared*—pressed hard upon him, demonstrating in the tradition of Brady and Defoe that there

[57] *Letters on the Spirit of Patriotism, on the Idea of a Patriot King, and on the State of Parties at the Accession of George the First* (London, 1749), p. 45: ". . . powers, necessary to maintain subordination, and to carry on even good government, and therefore necessary to be preserved in the crown, notwithstanding the abuse that is sometimes made of them; for no human institution can arrive at perfection, and the most that human wisdom can do, is to procure the same or greater good, at the expence of less evil." The language, which is Machiavellian, appears to allude to prerogative, not influence as suggested by Dickinson, p. 345. Cf. *Letters*, p. 93: "There must be an absolute, unlimited and uncontroulable power lodged *somewhere* in every government," but this power is legislative, and is lodged in king, lords and commons jointly.

[58] *Letters*, p. 77 (*On the Idea of a Patriot King*): "My intention is not to introduce what I have to say concerning the duties of kings, by any nice inquiry into the *original* of their institution. What is to be known of it will appear plainly enough, to such as are able and can spare time to trace it, in the broken traditions which are come down to us of a few nations. But those, who are not able to trace it there, may trace something better and more worthy to be known, in their own thoughts: I mean what this institution *ought* to have been, whenever it began, according to the rule of *reason*, founded in the common *rights*, and *interests*, of mankind."

had been no ancient liberty in the turbulent world of barons and vassals, and consequently no principles to which to return.[59] For all his superb arrogance of style, Bolingbroke in his lifetime fought a losing battle; and it does not lessen this truth to point out that the Walpolean writers proclaimed a world of kinetic history, without principles or virtue, in which men were governed through the interests and passions that made them what they were at the moment.

The dichotomy of virtue and interest also accounts for Bolingbroke's—and very generally the age's—inability to devise a satisfactory theory of party. To moderns it seems tolerably evident that competitive pressure groups may be made to function to the overall benefit of the political system; but to the still highly Aristotelian Augustans it was far from clear how any group intent upon its private interest could have any sense of the common good at all, and if it had not it would be no more than a faction, driving its members to further and further excesses of greed and frenzy and robbing them of that virtue, or sense of the common good, which only individuals, not groups, could possess. In societies like Machiavellian Rome, where the relations between the orders were improperly worked out, there might with advantage be conflicting parties embodying the virtues, or "principles," of the nobility or the people; and where the commonwealth itself was threatened, there might (in Ciceronian language) be a party of good men who stood for it, a faction of bad men who were against it.[60] Bolingbroke argued that the terms Whig and Tory were now obsolete, and that there was only the Country, or party of virtue, contending against the Court, or faction of corruption; but this was not essentially different from the arguments of Toland and others in 1714, when—after years of denouncing party as an instrument of corruptive rule—they had conceded that there were still Whigs, who upheld the principles of 1688, and Tories, who could not be trusted to do so, and that a strong executive founded upon a Septennial Act was therefore necessary.[61] Party was for most men tolerable only when it embodied

---

[59] Kramnick, pp. 127-37.

[60] There is now a considerable literature on the idea of party in the eighteenth century. See among others, Harvey C. Mansfield, Jr., *Statesmanship and Party Government* (Chicago University Press, 1965); Kurt Kluxen, *Das Problem der Politischen Opposition: Entwicklung und Wesen der englischen Zweiparteienpolitik im 18 Jahrhundert* (Freiburg and Munich, 1956); Richard C. Hofstadter, *The Idea of a Party System: The Rise of Legitimate Opposition in the United States, 1780-1840* (Berkeley and Los Angeles: California University Press, 1969); J.A.W. Gunn, *Factions No More: Attitudes to Party in Government and Opposition in Eighteenth-century England* (London: Frank Cass, 1972).

[61] Compare Toland's *The Art of Governing by Parties* (1701) with his *The State-Anatomy of Great Britain* (1714). The two positions are not irreconcilable:

principle and so was capable of virtue; two parties representing different particular interests would perpetuate the reign of corruption and fantasy.

Bolingbroke once remarked that the relation of stockjobbing to trade was much the same as that of faction to liberty[62] (the obvious Polybian comment would be that the good and bad aspects of any "virtue" were always hard to keep separate). The apophthegm reveals the dominance and the limitations of the ideal of virtue; it remained a public and a personal characteristic, a devotion of the self to the universal good, in one form or another, which only a highly autonomous self could perform. Politics must be reduced to ethics if it was not to reduce itself to corruption; the rhetoric of the classical style commanded this, irrespective of the sincerity with which Bolingbroke or any other employed it. Therefore the Aristotelian, Polybian, Machiavellian, and now Harringtonian "science of virtue," or sociology of civic ethics, had to be restated with paradigmatic force and comprehensiveness for the eighteenth-century West at large. Montesquieu, seen from this angle, is the greatest practitioner of that science, and this is the period during which Machiavelli's reputation as the chief of civic moralists stood at its highest and blanketed most references to his moral ambiguity. But the price to be paid was that every treatise on politics which could not transcend the limitations of this style was likely to end, not only in moral exhortation, but in the suggestion that virtue as a quality of the personality was the only agency likely to cure corruption. Machiavelli had taken this line, while conceding that individual virtue in a corrupt society faced a task so difficult that merely human actors would almost certainly be defeated by it; only the heroic, the quasi-divine or the truly inspired might succeed. Bolingbroke's later writings, especially those written after he failed to wreck Walpole, are mere exhortations to the leaders of society, and finally to the Patriot King, to display heroic virtue and redeem a corrupt world; and John Brown, a highly intelligent if tragically unstable[63] disciple of Machiavelli, Cato, Bolingbroke, and Montesquieu who wrote between 1757 and 1765, reached at the end of his best-known work the unexpected conclusion that the national decadence could be cured only by the moral example

---

in the first it is bad that there should be parties; in the second bad men have formed a party and good men must associate to resist it.

[62] *Remarks on the History of England*, Letter XIV (2d ed., London, 1747, p. 169).

[63] For his life see D.N.B. He ended as a suicide, though, as an ordained clergyman, he had written against that act as a sin.

of "some great minister."[64] Bolingbroke has been criticized for this retreat from Harringtonian empirical materialism to Machiavellian moral idealism;[65] but, in the first place, a civic virtue which was a dedication to universal public good must sooner or later be seen as independent of contingent and particular social causes, and in the second, it was no longer possible to believe with Harrington that an agrarian law might equalize in perpetuity the distribution of the material foundations of virtue. Land could not be freed from its dependence on trade, or trade from its dependence on credit; and the equivalent of an agrarian law for a speculative society was unknown and perhaps unthinkable. Men had therefore to be better than their circumstances; Montesquieu's *Esprit des Lois* is a magnificently paradoxical attempt to discover the circumstances under which this may be possible.

That Bolingbroke was driven to stake his intellectual and rhetorical all on the concept of virtue has consequences of which the most recent interpreters of his thought have perhaps not taken the fullest possible account. Observing that he differed—fairly explicitly—from Locke in holding that there were natural authority and order in society, that a virtuous king or aristocracy might exercise a paternal authority over lesser men, and that a Great Chain of Being formed the unifying structure of the deist's universe, they have concluded that his ultimate allegiance was to the leadership of the landed gentry in a naturally hierarchical society, and that he felt a nostalgia for an older, Elizabethan or Jacobean, social and philosophical world.[66] But we have repeatedly seen that the ideal of virtue was political, and that the polis, based on the *vita activa* and including equality among its principles, was never finally reducible to the hierarchy. Certainly it included an elite, characterized by wisdom and experience, leisure and property, whose virtue was to lead and in that sense to rule; the authority these exercised over citizens not of the elite might be termed both natural and paternal, as the Roman senate had been termed *patres conscripti*; but Guicciardini, the most aristocratically minded of Florentine republican theorists, had made it clear that the few needed the many to save them from corruption, and that when the many accepted the few as their natural leaders they did not cease to display critical judgment or active citizenship. Leadership and deference were both active virtues; virtue, in a more abstract and formal sense, was a relationship between

---

[64] John Brown, *Essay on the Manners and Principles of the Times* (London, 1757), the closing words. The elder Pitt may have been the person intended.

[65] Kramnick, pp. 166-69; Dickinson, pp. 256-65.

[66] Kramnick, pp. 76-83, 88-110, 261-65; Dickinson, pp. 22-24, 162-72, 119, 206-209, 300-302. The term "nostalgia" is taken from Kramnick's subtitle.

two modes of civic activity; and Bolingbroke's nostalgia, if he felt any, might well have been for the open and turbulent world of Country politics in Anne's reign, as compared with the placidly managed oligarchy of George II's. We shall return to this theme in analyzing the problems of deference and equality in revolutionary America, where he was regarded as a second Machiavelli whose authority as a philosopher of morals and politics exceeded his ambiguity.

[IV]

The "Machiavellian moment" of the eighteenth century, like that of the sixteenth, confronted civic virtue with corruption, and saw the latter in terms of a chaos of appetites, productive of dependence and loss of personal autonomy, flourishing in a world of rapid and irrational change. But to sixteenth-century minds the symbol for that which made the appetites hard to coordinate in swiftly moving secular time was *fortuna*, a concept essentially expressing the inadequacies of classical epistemology; whereas those of the eighteenth century were able to define corruption and irrationality in terms far more positive, material, and dynamic, though these still lacked an ethical content to the point where the history they rendered concrete remained essentially a movement away from virtue. What may be termed the ideology of the Country was founded on a presumption of real property and an ethos of the civic life, in which the ego knew and loved itself in its relation to a *patria*, *res publica* or common good, organized as a polity, but was perpetually threatened by corruption operating through private appetites and false consciousness. To save personality, it urged an ideal of virtue which at times reached unreally Stoical heights of moral autonomy, and was based on the maintenance of a propertied independence hard to sustain in a speculative economy; to save polity, it depicted the British constitution as a classical balance of independent yet coordinate elements or powers, to maintain which was to maintain virtue but which only the assertion of personal virtue could in the last analysis maintain. Since its ethics were reducible to an ideal of the wholly self-sustaining personality, it found it terribly easy to see corruption as irreversible by merely human means; and since its economics tended to ground that personality on a form of property held to have existed in a precommercial past, it tended to see history as a movement away from value which only heroic, not social, action could reverse. But though it was increasingly susceptible to elegiac pessimism, it was endowed with all the riches of the complex and articulate vocabulary of civic humanism with which to expound the science and sociology of virtue. Its paradigms therefore tended to dominate discourse.

486

What may be termed the ideology of the Court, on the other hand, was consequently less prominent and had fewer magisterial exponents. We may synthesize it, however, as founded upon an acceptance of credit as a measure of economic value and of a psychology of imagination, passion, and interest as the mainsprings of human behavior. In the place of virtue it stressed the ego's pursuit of satisfaction and self-esteem, and was beginning to explore theories of how the diversities of passionate and self-interested action might be manipulated and coordinated, or might magically or mechanically coordinate themselves, into promoting a common good no longer intimately connected with the inner moral life of the individual. Since it did not regard virtue as politically paradigmatic, it did not regard government as founded upon principles of virtue which needed to be regularly reasserted; it readily accepted that men were factious and interested beings and, instead of regarding these characteristics as fatal if unchecked to virtue and government, proposed to have them policed by a strong central executive, which did not itself need to be disciplined by the principles of virtue, but might without suffering harm appeal to the passions and interests of men. It saw personal morality as private rather than public, a matter of probity in interpersonal dealings which did not require to be expressed in acts of civic morality or statesmanlike virtue, and might contribute only indirectly if at all to the maintenance of a moral climate in politics.

Because of this, its ethical vocabulary was thin and limited by the lack of any theory which presented human virtue as that of a *zōon politikon*. This weakness relegated it to the margins—if at times to the avant-garde—of eighteenth-century moral theory; but the fact that it located no body of principles, or concept of property, in a past to which there might be return, gave it freedom to adapt itself to those social changes which rendered intelligible the new world of credit, professionalism, and empire. At the same time, however, these changes continued to be measured in terms of history's departure from the world and its values depicted by the Country, and the ethics of the new world must be stated in language as intransigent as that of Mandeville. The Country took its republican ethos very largely from Machiavelli; but the Court was the more Machiavellian in its ability to accept that dynamic change might operate independently of values. The dualism of virtue and *virtù* returns to view here, and we recall that, as it was largely war which had opened up this dichotomy for Machiavelli, it was in part war as an aspect of commerce which had compelled the Augustans to recognize the nature of the new world. In the language of Addison's Cato rather than Trenchard's, the Court ideology could show how to command success, the Country how to deserve it; or, as

Alexander Hamilton once put it—in an interesting employment of party terminology that might have been used by Swift—"Cato was the Tory, Caesar the Whig of his day. . . . The former perished with the republic, the latter destroyed it."[67] But if the Court ideology could claim a monopoly of the understanding of power, it must leave its counter-thesis in sole possession of a theory of virtue; and far more than for Machiavelli, to lack virtue was to be prey to *fantasia* and false consciousness. The gap between civic virtue and dynamic *virtù* was by that much the wider, and the charge that the road to power was the road to corruption and self-destruction the more compelling.

In Britain, however, Bolingbroke's ideological campaign was in its author's lifetime a failure. The country gentlemen were not being reduced to hopeless indebtedness; no monopolist of power and patronage succeeded Walpole; the wars of the mid-century, being fought largely beyond sea, produced no revolt against war finance like that which had brought down Godolphin and Marlborough; and over all, it seemed evident enough that Court and Country were in symbiosis rather than in opposition, so that there was much to be said for the view that the constitution was a parliamentary monarchy rather than a balance of separate powers. In such circumstances there was room for political theorists to reinspect the relations of crown and parliament: historians, those of the landed and trading interests; philosophers, those of reason and passion; and all these revaluations may be found in the writings of the most powerful minds which examined British politics about 1750. Montesquieu's *Esprit des Lois*, in spite of its treatment of the separation of powers, may be thought of, in English terms, as somewhat more Whig than the *Lettres Persanes*; and there is, in Book XIX, chapter 27, a striking study of a free nation—obviously Britain—in the terms we have been considering.

Montesquieu tells us that this analysis will be based on *moeurs* and *manières* in their relation to laws, rather than on *les principes de sa constitution*;[68] and this proves to mean that the importance of keeping the legislative and executive powers separate and *visibles* is that, the passions of men being free, hatred, envy, and ambition shall be equally free to attach themselves to the one or the other.[69] Since the executive power has all offices in its gift, it will always be the object of hope

[67] See below, p. 529.

[68] *Esprit des Lois* (Paris, Garnier, ed. Truc, n.d.), I, 335.

[69] *Ibid.*: "Comme il y aurait dans cet État deux pouvoirs visibles: la puissance legislative et l'exècutrice, et que tout citoyen y aurait sa volonté propre, et ferait valoir à son grè son indèpendance, la plupart des gens auraient plus d'affection pour une de ces puissances que pour l'autre, le grand nombre n'ayant pas ordinairement assez d'equité ni de sens pour les affectionner ègalement toutes les deux."

rather than fear; those who are out of office will hope to return to it, and those who are in, though presumably fearing loss of place, know that even in that event they may hope to regain office in the way that they won it. The problem of Machiavellian innovation—that those it offends will react more dynamically than those it pleases—has to this extent been solved, and the executive power resembles the *principe naturale*, whose position is reinforced by the natures of his subjects, rather than the *principe nuovo*, doomed to act contrary to them. There is no doubt, however, that passion, rather than Machiavellian custom, is a mainspring of this kind of government;[70] *caprices* and *fantaisies* will often lead men to change sides as between the two passionately jealous parties (of ins and outs) into which this society will be divided; there will be little loyalty or principle among the independent particulars who compose it, and the monarch will often be driven to disgrace his friends and promote his enemies.[71] But because passions are free, *amour propre* (in Rousseau's phrase, which Montesquieu does not use) will not become corruptive. Fear, and irrational fear at that, now makes a reappearance; the monopoly of patronage by the executive keeps the people in perpetual fear of they know not what, and the leaders of opposition to the Crown will magnify these fears rather than avow their own motives.[72] But the emotion is healthy; Montesquieu is midway between Cato's citation of Machiavelli to the effect that a people mistrusting its government knows no limits to its fears, and Burke's observation of the Americans that "they snuff the approach of tyranny in every tainted breeze."[73] Because they fear unreal dangers to their

[70] *Ibid.*: "Toutes les passions y étant libres, la haine, l'envie, la jalousie, l'ardeur de s'enrichir et de se distinguer, paraîtraient dans toute leur étendue. . . ."

[71] *Esprit*, pp. 335-36: "Comme chaque particulier, toujours indépendant, suivrait beaucoup ses caprices et ses fantaisies, on changerait souvent de parti; on en abandonnerait un où l'on laisserait tous ses amis pour se lier à un autre dans lequel on trouverait tous ses ennemis; et souvent, dans cette nation, on pourrait oublier les lois de l'amitié et celles de la haine.

"Le monarque serait dans le cas des particuliers; et, contre les maximes ordinaires de la prudence, il serait souvent obligé de donner sa confiance à ceux qui l'auraient le plus choqué, et de disgracier ceux qui l'auraient le mieux servi, faisant par nécessité ce que les autres princes font par chois." The allusion could very well be to the reign of William III in England.

[72] P. 336: "On craint de voir échapper un bien que l'on sent, que l'on ne connait guère, et qu'on peut nous déguiser; et la crainte grossit toujours les objets. Le peuple serait inquiet sur sa situation, et croirait être en danger dans les moments même les plus sûrs.

"D'autant mieux que ceux qui s'opposeraient le plus vivement à la puissance éxecutrice, ne pouvant avouer les motifs interessés de leur opposition, ils augmenteraient les terreurs du peuple, qui ne saurait jamais au juste s'il serait en danger ou non."

[73] In the Speech on Conciliation in *Works*, II, 125.

liberty, they are alert to real ones before these arise[74]—to wait until experience has revealed them to be real is to delay until it is too late— and the elected legislature, being calmer than the people and having their confidence,[75] will allay their fears of unreal dangers and antici- pate the rise of real ones; a role, it is worth noting, which only a few can play.

This nation, situated on an island, will engage in commerce rather than conquest; but its trading and colonizing ventures will be fiercely competitive and aggressive, it will engage in enterprises beyond its strength and even contrary to its interests,[76] and in order to do so will mobilize huge and fictitious power by borrowing. But since it borrows from itself, its *crédit* is sure; and though the wealth and power it creates are imaginary, its *confiance* in itself and its free government will con- vert fiction into reality.[77] Nothing could be further from Cato's por- trait of the South Sea mania, or Montesquieu's own portrait of Law. He is now telling us that in a free society, where power is pluralized and distributed, passion itself is free, not merely to change its objects, but actually to recreate the world in accordance with its fantasies. This, however, operates in the domain of external *virtù*, of commerce and power beyond the frontiers and seacoasts; in the domain of civic virtue, fantasy and truth may coexist and reinforce one another, but there comes a point where prudence and wisdom must rigorously distinguish between the real and unreal as threats to liberty. Given liberty, how- ever—which was lacking in the case of Law—passion and fantasy will contribute to this result; they will fuel the fires by whose light states- men discern, and we are not in Plato's cave. Montesquieu is not argu-

---

[74] *Esprit, loc. cit.*: "Ainsi, quand les terreurs imprimées n'auraient point d'objet certain, elles ne produiraient que de vaines clameurs et des injures: et elles auraient même ce bon effet qu'elles tendraient tous les ressorts du gouvernement, et rendraient tous les citoyens attentifs. Mais si elles naissaient à l'occasion du ren- versement des lois fondamentales, elles seraient sourdes, funestes, atroces, et pro- duiraient des catastrophes."

[75] *Ibid.*: ". . . ayant la confiance du peuple, et étant plus eclairé que lui . . ."

[76] *Ibid.*, p. 337: "Cette nation, toujours echauffée, pourrait plus aisément être conduite par ses passions que par la raison, qui ne produit jamais de grands effets sur lesprit des hommes; et il facile à ceux qui la gouverneraient de lui faire faire des entreprises contre ses veritables intérêts.

"Cette nation aimerait prodigieusement sa liberté, parce que cette liberté serait vraie; et il pourrait arriver que, pour la defendre, elle sacrifierait son bien, son aisance, ses intérêts; qu'elle se chargerait des impôts les plus durs, et tels que le prince le plus absolu n'oserait les faire supporter à ses sujets."

[77] *Ibid.*: "Elle aurait un crédit sûr, parce qu'elle emprunterait à elle-même, et se paierait elle-même. Il pourrait arriver qu'elle entreprendrait au-dessus de ses forces naturelles, et ferait valoir contre ses ennemis d'immenses richesses de fiction, que la confiance et la nature de son gouvernement rendraient réelles."

ing here, as Swift, Cato, and Bolingbroke had argued, that a wisdom
not grounded in commerce is needed to prevent the fantasies of speculation from corrupting society. He is saying that a free and fortunate
society can absorb a great deal of false consciousness without suffering
serious harm, and may use it in order to expand. The frenzies of his ins
and outs, his office seekers, speculators, and aggressive merchants, recall
those hatreds of the patricians and plebeians which Machiavelli contended had contributed to Roman liberty and greatness.

There may be found in Montesquieu—standing somewhat apart
from his studies of British politics—a historical conspectus of the ways
in which commerce, and therefore passion, contribute to liberty and
civic values. Virtue, he laid down, was the principle of republics, but
by this he intended a *vertu politique*, not identical (though not incompatible) with a *vertu morale* or a *vertu chrétienne*, and consisting—
true to the Machiavellian tradition—in an equality of subjection to the
republic's laws and of devotion to her good.[78] More clearly than his
English predecessors, Montesquieu knew that virtue in this sense did
not necessarily coincide with private values or personal morality; and
in his treatment of early Sparta, Athens, and Rome he made it clear that
the republic might enforce it with repugnant and inhuman harshness.[79]
Like Machiavelli, he knew that the Christian ethos made demands to
which the civic ethos might refuse to give way, and that the latter
might flourish best in periods close to barbarism, when there was no
need to accord the rights of humanity to those who were not of one's
city. But he also makes it clear that it was because the ethos of the
ancient cities was essentially a warrior ethos, and commerce and even
agriculture were despised, that Plato and Aristotle believed the person-

[78] *Esprit*, p. 4 ("Avertissement de l'Auteur"): ". . . ce que j'appelle la *vertu*
dans la republique est l'amour de la patrie, c'est-à-dire l'amour de l'égalitè. Ce
n'est point une vertu morale, ni une vertu chrétienne, c'est la vertu *politique*; et
celle-ci est le ressort qui fait mouvoir le gouvernement republicain, comme l'hon-
neur est le ressort qui fait mouvoir la monarchie. J'ai donc appelé *vertu politique*
l'amour de la patrie et de l'égalité. J'ai eu des idées nouvelles; il a bien fallu
trouver de nouveaux mots, ou donner aux anciens de nouvelles acceptions. . . .

"Enfin, l'homme de bien dont il est question dans le livre III, chapitre V, n'est
pas l'homme de bien chrétien mais l'homme de bien politique, qui a la vertu
politique dont j'ai parlé. C'est l'homme qui aime les lois de son pays, et qui agit
par l'amour des lois de son pays. J'ai donné un nouveau jour à toutes ces choses
dans cette édition-ci, en fixant encore plus les idées; et, dans la plupart des endroits
ou je me suis servi du mot de *vertu*, j'ai mis *vertu politique*."

[79] E.g., Book IV, ch. 6: Book V, ch. 19: "On est surpris que l'Aréopage ait fait
mourir un enfant qui avait crevé les yeux à son oiseau. Qu'on fasse attention
qu'il s'agit point là d'une condamnation pour crime, mais d'un jugement de moeurs
dans une republique fondé sur les moeurs."

ality could and must be entirely reshaped by music.[80] That is, men who produce and exchange goods become aware of values which are not merely those of the city's laws, and enter into relations with one another that do not consist exclusively in an equality of subjection to them. If they trade outside the city's walls, they enter into human relations and develop codes of humane values over which the republic has only a contingent authority. On the one hand, manners are now softened, art and refinement can be developed, and the ferocity of Lycurgan or Draconian discipline can be mitigated; but on the other, this is the point at which Plato found it necessary to prohibit commerce outside the city and leave the socialization of the personality entirely to music and other modes of education controlled by the guardians. Commerce is the source of all social values save one—we sense that Christianity itself would be possible only in a world of inter-civic contacts, an *oikumenē* rather than a polis—but that one, the *vertu politique*, is that which makes man a *zōon politikon* and consequently human; and there is a radical disjunction between the two categories of value. Commerce, which makes men cultured, entails luxury, which makes them corrupt;[81] there is no economic law which sets limits to the growth of luxury, and virtue is to be preserved only by the discipline of the republic, educating men in frugality—which indeed is conducive to further commercial growth—by means which include both music and the practice of arms.

Machiavelli, defining civic values as ultimately incompatible with Christian, had employed the concept of arms to express both the citizen's total devotion to his republic and the notion of a world too harsh in its treatment of noncitizens to profess any universal humanity. Montesquieu had added to this the concept of commerce, and had restored the conclusion, hinted at by Fletcher and Davenant, that commerce and culture were incompatible with virtue and liberty. Commerce brought with it pleasures more lively, perceptions more refined, and

[80] Book IV, ch. 8.

[81] Book XX, ch. I (Garnier, ed., II, 8): "Le commerce guérit des préjugés destructeurs; et c'est presque une règle générale, que partout où il y a des moeurs douces, il y a du commerce; et que partout où il y a du commerce, il y a des moeurs douces.

"Qu'on ne s'étonne donc point si nos moeurs sont moins féroces qu'elles ne l'étaient autrefois. Le commerce a fait que la connaissance des moeurs de toutes les nations a pénétré partout: on les a comparées entre elles, et il en a résulté de grands biens.

"On peut dire que des lois du commerce perfectionnent les moeurs, par la même raison que ces mêmes lois perdent les moeurs. Le commerce corrompt les moeurs pures: c'était le sujet des plaintes de Platon: il polit et adoucit les moeurs barbares, comme nous le voyons tous les jours."

values more universal than those of the primeval Spartan, Roman, or Gothic citizen-warrior; but because it represented a principle more universal, and of another order, than that of the finite polis, it was ultimately incompatible with virtue in the sense of *vertu politique*, and though laws, education, and manners might be devised that would check the growth of luxury, it could never be less than equally true that luxury corrupted laws, education, and manners. In the intermediate perspective, commerce and the arts could be seen as contributing to sociability and even to liberty and virtue, just as it was possible to establish a positive relationship between passion and reason; but the ultimate incompatibility remained. Commerce had taken the place of fortune; the republic could not control its own history forever or resist its own corruption; the particular and the universal remained at war.

It was possible at this point to restate the vision of history as an *anakuklōsis*, in which republics were transformed into empires by their own *virtù* and then corrupted and destroyed by the subsequent luxury. But to the eighteenth century, highly confident in its own culture, the intermediate perspective could seem of a surpassing importance, more positively fortified than the *saeculum* or historic present of Christian thought, and the moment of corruption more remote than the tribulations of the Christian apocalypse; there was even, contained in theories of progress, the possibility of a utopia in which culture should become self-sustaining. But as long as the ethos of civic virtue persisted, the threat of an apocalypse of self-destruction could not be eliminated; and the relations between personality and society seemed fragile enough to leave it possible that apocalypse by corruption might come swiftly and irresistibly. Such perspectives can be found even in the thought of David Hume.

It might well be imprudent to draw too close a connection—though a connection of some kind must exist—between the concern which Hume felt as a philosopher with the relation of reason to passion and the interest which he displayed as a historian of England in the relations of land to commerce and of executive to legislative.[82] In the latter capacity, however, he appears as a historian predominantly of the Court persuasion. He followed Brady, Defoe, and the apologists for Walpole in rejecting the belief in an Ancient Constitution, and adopted the perspective of Harrington—whom he admired with reservations—against that of the neo-Harringtonians. There had been in England a Gothic government of landed warriors, barons, and their vassals, but this had been an uneasy tension between violent authority and violent

---

[82] For this caution see Duncan Forbes, "Politics and History in David Hume" (review article on Giarrizzo's *Hume politico e storico*), *The Historical Journal* 6, no. 2 (1963), 280-94.

liberty; no legitimizing principles, whether of precedent or balance, were to be found in it. The emancipation of the people from vassalage would have been impossible without the spread of commerce and of learning; but it had brought about a confrontation between a monarchy whose arbitrary and indeed absolute character stood revealed for the first time, and a people whose demand for liberty was fueled in no small measure by the superstition, fanaticism, and hypocrisy which were all Hume could discern in Puritanism. There were therefore connections between the growth of commerce, the release of passion, and the pursuit of liberty, and since the latter was not at bottom a rational but an appetitive demand, it is the easier to understand Hume's dictum that authority and liberty must always confront one another in government and could never be wholly harmonized. Gothic government had stated this opposition in a form exceptionally crude; what had been achieved by 1688 was a synthesis somewhat more stable.[83] It should be stressed, however, that Hume continued to regard the British constitution as a compromise between absolute monarchy and popular republic, and rated high the chances that it would gravitate toward one extreme or the other in the end.[84]

Commerce and learning, he made clear, had effected more than a trivial transition from the superstition of medieval Christians to the fanaticism of the Puritans. They had enlarged men's ideas by giving them more objects to feed upon, more concepts to entertain and more values to express; and in this way what was at bottom an increase in the appetitive and passional activities of the human mind had facilitated a growth in the rational capacities, including—once the frenzy of Puritanism was worked out—the capacities for rational liberty and (if there could be such a thing) rational religion.[85] Passion might inform reason, and help it rearrange the delicate relations between authority and liberty, but just as there could be no final harmony between the one pair, there could be none between the other; and it comes as no surprise to learn that Hume's view of the eighteenth-century constitution was "Court" in the sense that he accepted the necessity of an ultimate repository of power and an executive possessed of the means of influ-

---

[83] The best recent studies of Hume's historical thinking are those of Giuseppe Giarrizzo, *op.cit.* (Turin: Einaudi, 1962) and Duncan Forbes in his introduction to the Pelican Classics edition of *The History of Great Britain, Volume One, containing the Reigns of James I and Charles I,* originally published in 1754 (Harmondsworth: Penguin Books, 1970).

[84] *Essays Moral, Political and Literary of David Hume* (World's Classics edition, London: Grant Richards, 1903), no. 7: "Whether the British Government inclines more to Absolute Monarchy or to a Republic" (pp. 48-53).

[85] *Essays,* Part II, nos. 1 ("Of Commerce") and 2 ("Of Refinement in the Arts").

encing the legislature.[86] Patronage did not alarm him, since he saw men as creatures ruled by, or rather through, their passions, and government as a filtering device which induced them to transform their short-term perceptions of their private interests into long-term understanding of the general identity of interests—and, in that sense, of the public good. Ideally, a perfect commonwealth would consist of a one, few, and many of the classic type; but in reality, and even in ideality, there must be means of bringing the interests of all three into identity, and this involved the presence of a patronage-dispensing authority, which must always be in some degree of tension with the forces making for liberty.[87]

Hume accepted the necessity for patronage and influence in government in the same way that he had accepted commerce as, for the present era in history, a liberating force which enlarged men's minds through the nourishment of their appetites. It is of interest, at this point, to recall Goro Dati and those other writers of the *quattrocento*, who had argued that the Florentines were the more fitted for active citizenship by the fact that they were merchants, who traveled, studied and compared, and filled their minds with more knowledge than they could have inherited through the simple observance of custom.[88] In the hands of Machiavelli and Guicciardini, we realize, the civic ethos had to some extent turned against this original bourgeois ebullience; the citizen was required to subject particular to public goods so rigorously that he had begun to appear a trade-eschewing Spartan, a warrior, citizen, and farmer, and nothing more. In the eighteenth century, engrossed as it was with the problem of virtue and commerce, it was always from the Court perspective that entrepreneurial man was readmitted to the category of virtuous citizen. As Hume was prepared to accept duality and creative tension between reason and passion, authority and liberty, so in his treatment of English history he had begun—anticipating Coleridge and others of the nineteenth century—to accept a similar duality between the men of real property, who inherited liberty in the form of privilege and custom, and the men of mobile property, who affirmed it in the form of enlarged knowledge and expanding capacities; there was beginning to be an element of progress to pit against an element of conservation.[89]

There were soon to appear enthusiasts—as Hume would assuredly have recognized them to be—of progress, who held that the expansion

---

[86] *Essays*, Part I, no. 6, "Of the Independency of Parliament."

[87] *Essays*, Part I, no. 3, "That Politics May be Reduced to a Science"; Part II, no. 16, "Idea of a Perfect Commonwealth."

[88] Above, p. 91.

[89] Forbes, *op.cit.*, pp. 38-39; Giarrizzo, *op.cit.*, chs. II and III.

of trade and travel over the whole world would in due course equip man with all the data, from which he would draw all the conclusions, necessary to a complete understanding of himself and his environment. The stumbling block here was that such knowledge, being based in appetite and passion, must contain an element of fantasy, imagination, and false consciousness, which it was hard to imagine being finally eliminated from the operations of the mind. Hume was certainly under no such delusions; he was no kind of utopian at all; but he had equipped himself better than most men with the skeptic's ability to accept that, if we must live very largely in a world of phantasms, we were capable of recognizing that they were phantasms and of constructing guidelines which would inform us how far, and within what limits, we had succeeded in converting them into true knowledge. Consequently—and it is a consequence—he did not unduly fear the extension of metal currency into paper credit; indeed, he rather maliciously suggested that it was a pity Lycurgus had not employed paper, rather than iron bars, to restrict the circulation of gold and silver at Sparta. He accepted that, under proper management, men in a credit economy trusted one another's solvency rather than the market value of the funds—much as Montesquieu had shown *crédit* merging into *confiance*—and that paper could serve as a medium for the communication of durable, if not real, values.[90]

But there was a point beyond which credit and confidence could not operate, and it is striking to observe Hume's language when he contemplates its being passed. The determining factor was the burden of public debt. If the time ever came when all property and industry were in debt to the nation up to the limit (nineteen shillings in the pound) to which debt could be imposed, and the nation's debt to itself was secured upon its future revenues to all perpetuity, then public confidence could no longer persist. A ruling class of stockjobbers would appear, in all the horror in which Davenant or Bolingbroke had painted them, owning nothing except the debts of the public and yet owning everything, since the value of every object would now be the extent of its indebtedness. Military service and parliamentary representation would become tasks performed for hire, and men would have nothing to protect them against their own fantasies and gullibility, since the value and meaning of everything would have been destroyed. A "natural death" of national bankruptcy, or a "violent death" of foreign conquest, would be the only possible outcome; and this—Hume declared,

---

[90] *Essays*, Part II, nos. 3 ("Of Money"), 4 ("Of Interest"), 5 ("Of the Balance of Trade"). The reference to Lycurgus is on p. 326 of the World's Classics edition. There is a recent edition of *Hume's Economic Writings* by Eugene Rotwein (Madison: University of Wisconsin Press, 1970).

and may have died believing in 1776—was by far the most predictable result of the state of affairs actually existing: "either the nation must destroy public credit, or public credit will destroy the nation."[91]

Hume was by nature as little addicted to jeremiads as any philosopher in history; yet he was driven to adopt a jeremiad tone by the circumstance, now familiar to us, that commercial society did not contain any ultimate check on the forces making for its corruption. Like the *King's Answer to the Nineteen Propositions*, he ended by depicting the social balance as inherently fragile; like Machiavelli—and with as few illusions, perhaps fewer, since he had even less belief that government rested on virtue in the individual—he conceded that only legislative reform could resist the forces undermining virtue, and that there existed a point after which degeneration would swiftly prove irreversible. If, in Montesquieu's language, virtue was the principle of republics, it was the inner meaning of the republican thesis that virtue must sustain the conditions necessary to virtue, and was self-isolated in its own heroism—from which, perhaps, flowed its evident attraction for the post-Puritan mind. This despite the fact that Hume's philosophical, psychological, and economic analyses of society were as subtle and complex as any his age (or most others) had to offer, and did not oblige him to reify "virtue" as a stable entity on which everything else depended. He had a singularly broad understanding of the diversity of social forces going to make up the complex which was usually termed "virtue," but he saw these forces as operating within certain conditions which they might themselves destroy; and once this happened, the established rhetoric of "corruption" was entirely appropriate.

Within this one limitation, however, it is part of what made Hume a great historian in the eighteenth century that he saw commerce and passion as dynamic forces contributing both to the construction of political society and to an active and kinetic history, and he was by no means incapable of taking a sanguine view of the present and future, in which ultimate corruption might be averted for a very long time. The great Scottish school of social philosophers, who are in a complex fashion his immediate heirs, continued the historical dialectic between virtue and commerce, and in doing so were greatly aided by his teachings.[92] In spite of Hume's much-quoted belief that human nature

[91] *Essays*, Part II, no. 9: "Of Public Credit" (pp. 355-61). The words last quoted are on p. 366. See also p. 371: "These seem to be the events, which are not very remote, and which reason foresees as clearly almost as she can do any thing that lies in the womb of time." For Hume's state of mind in the last years of his life, see Giarrizzo, *op.cit.*, p. 110, and John B. Stewart, *The Moral and Political Philosophy of David Hume* (New York: Columbia University Press, 1963).

[92] Gladys Bryson, *Man and Society: The Scottish Enquiry of the Eighteenth*

was in all times and places the same, his argument that reason was dependent on passion and passion on experience could, in conjunction with the increasingly held opinion that commerce enlarged the sphere of human experience, knowledge, and values, be employed to build up an image of men creating and transforming their own "second natures"—based, since Aristotle, on usage and love, or experience and passion—throughout the centuries of their growing economic life. If it were possible to say with certainty that the leaders of the Scottish school were acquainted with Vico's doctrine that men created their own history through the linguistic and poetic imagination, it is easy to see how the link between commerce and imagination could have been made. And since land and commerce were already opposed as principles of conservation and growth, a movement of history from land toward commerce was enlarged, in the thinking of theoretical sociologists or "conjectural historians," into a scheme of social development which passed from hunters to shepherds, farmers, and traders, with manufacturers beginning to make their appearance toward the end of the sequence. In each succeeding phase, men's methods of providing and distributing the goods necessary to life furnished experience with the raw materials on which passion, imagination, and intellect fed, and in each, human personality was seen as constructed upon the configurations appropriate to that stage of culture. A theory of *homo faber*, of labor as the author of values, could now be invoked by Adam Smith. Man could now be described as a cultural animal and culture as a product of economics; and as the goods produced, and the techniques of producing and distributing them, grew in each phase more complex, human culture, imagination, and personality correspondingly increased in complexity. There was now a historical science of tracing and explaining the growth of culture and commerce; and man, becoming more and more a historical animal, was placed at the core of the resultant process.

But the contradiction between culture and liberty was not thereby fully overcome. The Scottish and French conjectural historians continued to employ the language of virtue and corruption—to employ, that is, the language of civic humanism in that English form which since 1698 had been a means of stating the quarrel between value and history—and they did so with results that were not less pessimistic than those found in Machiavelli. They came, by the time of Adam Smith, to see the division and specialization of labor, and the resulting intensification of exchange, as the driving force which had moved society

---

Century (Princeton University Press, 1945), is still the best one-volume study of the Scottish school.

from each phase of its economic history toward the next; and this is not accidentally related to the circumstance that the whole Anglo-Scottish inquiry into the role of commerce in society and history had begun as a protest against the growth of a professionalized army—against what the classical and civic tradition presented as the crucial and disastrous instance of specialization of social function. The citizen who allowed another to be paid to fight for him parted with a vital element of his *virtus*, in every sense of that word; and the priest, the lawyer, and the rentier had been grouped with the soldier as paradigmatic instances of individuals whose specialization made them the servants of others who became servants to them in their turn. Specialization, in short, was a prime cause of corruption; only the citizen as amateur, propertied, independent, and willing to perform in his own person all functions essential to the polis, could be said to practice virtue or live in a city where justice was truly distributed. There was no *arte* that he must not be willing to make his own. But if the arts proved to have been built up through a process of specialization, then culture itself was in contradiction with the ethos of the *zōon politikon*; and if it were further argued—as it clearly could be—that only specialization, commerce, and culture set men free enough to attend to the goods of others as well as their own, then it would follow that the polis was built up by the very forces that must destroy it. Once land and commerce were placed in historical sequence, civic man found himself existing in a historical contradiction.

Adam Ferguson's *Essay on the History of Civil Society* is perhaps the most Machiavellian of the Scottish disquisitions on this theme.[93] He employs less the sequence of modes of production favored by his contemporaries than a movement of history from barbarism to civilization, from a warrior society marked by primitive virtue toward a state of commerce, refinement, and humanity. He stressed that the primitive human group was constantly in conflict with its neighbors, and derived from these conditions of war and struggle an intense passion of solidarity which socialized the individual and reinforced his ego.[94] This aggressive and disciplined passion is visibly Machiavelli's *virtù*—as it is also the *'asabiyah* of the Arab sociologist Ibn Khaldun—and it is the

[93] There is an edition, with introduction, by Duncan Forbes (Edinburgh University Press, 1966). See also David Kettler, *The Social and Political Thought of Adam Ferguson* (Columbus: Ohio State University Press, 1965).

[94] Forbes, ed., p. 18: "It is here"—i.e., in society—"that a man is made to forget his weakness, his cares of safety, and his subsistence; and to act from those passions which make him discover his force. It is here he finds that his arrows fly swifter than the eagle, and his weapons wound deeper than the paw of the lion, or the tooth of the boar"; p. 59: "Athens was necessary to Sparta, in the exercise of her virtue, as steel is to flint in the production of fire"; and pp. 59-61 generally.

source of virtue in the ordinary sense, as the primitive warriors become patriotic citizens. But as war made societies more cohesive, and therefore more capable of refinement, relations between citizens became relations of specialization, interchange, and commerce; and the growth of professional armies marked for Ferguson—as it had for Fletcher— the moment at which men sought to enjoy the material, intellectual, and moral satisfactions of civilization and leave the defense of them to others paid for the purpose.[95] This was the turning point at which it became problematical whether the contingent, secondary, yet in many scales of values higher, goods which civilization brought did not corrupt men by distracting them from the primary good of sociability itself; that primeval 'asabiyah or virtù which could be described in terms predominantly nonmoral—and was now being depicted as unmistakably a passion—and yet was the source of moral personality and moral relationships.

All Aristotelian theorists were in one way or another troubled by this problem of the universal versus the particular good, but few before Ferguson had stated it in so arrestingly primitivist a form, and the Machiavellian language which he uses indicates that his doing so is one more outcome of the humanist experiment of locating the republic in time. The problem had always been that of deciding when the particular or private goods should be seen as contributory to the universal or public good, when as competitive with it. Because the concept of civic virtue staked everything on an immediate relation between personality and republic, the vivere civile had tended to negate the secondary goods rather than to affirm them. Sparta, where the appetites had been repressed, had traditionally been preferred to Athens, where they had been transcended; it was only in nineteenth-century liberal England, when culture finally replaced property as the qualifying characteristic of the civic elite, that the Funeral Oration of Pericles was ranked among the sacred writings of liberal civilization. Once the republic was placed in time, its history tended to become one of the self-corruption of virtue by virtue; and the eighteenth century, to which Athens appeared the type of a commercial and ultimately effeminate empire,[96]

---

[95] Forbes, ed., p. 230: "The subdivision of arts and professions, in certain examples, tends to improve the practice of them, and to promote their ends. By having separated the arts of the clothier and the tanner, we are the better supplied with shoes and with cloth. But to separate the arts which form the citizen and the statesman, the arts of policy and war, is an attempt to dismember the human character, and to destroy those very arts we mean to improve." Pp. 229-32, generally, and Kettler, pp. 88-91, 100-101, and passim.

[96] For a typical indictment of Pericles as belonging in the same class as Caesar and Walpole, see Cato's Letters, II, 73-74.

faced this problem in an especially tormenting form. The paradigm of commerce presented the movement of history as being toward the indefinite multiplication of goods, and brought the whole progress of material, cultural, and moral civilization under this head. But so long as it did not contain any equivalent to the concept of the *zōon politikon*, of the individual as an autonomous, morally and politically choosing being, progress must appear to move away from something essential to human personality. And this corruption was self-generating; society as an engine for the production and multiplication of goods was inherently hostile to society as the moral foundation of personality. The history of commerce revealed once again that the republic had not solved the problem of existing as a universal value in particular and contingent time.

Ferguson may be thought of as stating this paradox by the device of distinguishing between *virtù* on the one hand—the primary value of oneness with the social basis of personality—and virtue, in the sense of the practice of every value derived from the progress of society, on the other. Montesquieu had done something similar when he observed that the *vertu* of a monk was that by which he repressed every human appetite and achieved complete devotion to his order;[97] the philosopher did not regard monastic orders as being of any value to society. But Ferguson is playing this trick on civilization and personality themselves; and the effect, given the terminology of Scottish social science, is that the citizen, the social animal defined solely by his virtue, is pressed steadily back toward the condition usually defined as savagery, in which he acknowledged no value except group solidarity, and the group made possible no other virtue. There are some extraordinary pages in which Ferguson describes the character of the early city-state Greeks in terms which assimilate them as much as possible to the Homeric warriors, who are in turn identified with Lafitau's American Indians and—the implication is very clear—the clansmen of Ferguson's own Highlands.[98] If the citizen was to give up every virtue except *virtù* itself, he must regress more and more toward the condition of the tribesman, and his *virtù* toward what ethologists like to call the "territorial imperative."

He had no alternative, given the premise—which the lack of a commercial ethos forced upon the philosopher—that the progress of civilization was a multiplication of secondary values, to pursue which necessitated the division of labor and the specialization of personalities. As

[97] *Esprit*, Book v, ch. 2 (ed. Truc, I, 46). Montesquieu does not actually say that the monk's devotion is *vertu*, but intimates that it is what *vertu* is in the citizen.

[98] Forbes, ed., pp. 193-202. For Ferguson as Highlander, see introduction, pp. xxxviii-ix.

the individual pursued any civilized value or combination of values, he became more and more the dependent of those with whom he had contracted to perform specialized functions other than his own, less and less a personality immediately related to society in its undifferentiated form; and if here alone were the roots of individuality to be found, he parted with an essential component of self in proportion as he became progressively refined. The personality was impoverished even as it was enriched. We are at the point where the classical concept of corruption merges into the modern concept of alienation, and the humanist roots of early Marxism become visible. Those theorists of the Scottish school who employ a more highly developed economic scheme of the stages of human progress exhibit the same problem. Certainly, in Adam Smith the principle of the division of labor and exchange of goods and services has been at work since the beginning of history; it has led, not merely to the satisfaction of more human needs, but to the development of new human capacities, wants, and aspirations, so that the personality has been progressively diversified and enriched; this is Smith's expansion of the point that an admixture of commerce was necessary before man could become capable of citizenship. But we are aware of an intimation that some kind of optimum moment has been reached and passed. Those whose lives are spent in putting the heads on pins—the precursors of Marx's proletariat and the assembly-line workers of the twentieth century—are not merely being denied the leisure to enjoy the multiplying goods now circulating in society; their actual capacity to do so is being systematically atrophied, and if specialization is producing an overall diversification of the human personality in history, it is having the reverse, one-dimensional effect upon theirs.[99] John Millar, Smith's most striking pupil and immediate successor, wrote a four-volume historical study of the growth of English political society in which the same point is made in terms which reveal the civic humanist origins of the whole perspective. Virtue and corruption are Millar's organizing categories, and he recurs incessantly to the question whether, as society progresses to the point where men become capable of liberty and virtue, they do not become increasingly exposed to corruption;[100] not

[99] The pin-makers occur in *Wealth of Nations*, Book I, ch. v. Cf. *Lectures on Justice, Police, Revenue and Arms (Adam Smith's Moral and Political Philosophy*, ed. Schneider, New York: Hafner, 1948, pp. 320-21): "Another bad effect of commerce is that it sinks the courage of mankind, and tends to extinguish martial spirit. In all commercial countries the division of labour is infinite, and every one's thoughts are employed about one particular thing. . . . The minds of men are contracted, and rendered incapable of elevation. Education is despised, or at least neglected, and heroic spirit is almost utterly extinguished. To remedy these defects would be an object worthy of serious attention."

[100] John Millar, *An Historical View of the English Government, from the Set-*

merely in the sense that, once men are virtuous, they have nothing to fear except corruption, but in the deeper and more alarming sense that the same historical forces which produce virtue produce also the distraction of the personality, less through the temptations of luxury than by the confusions and alienations of the moral identity, which we now intend when we use the word corruption. *Questa ci esalta, questa ci disface.* The virtuous, or socially healthy, personality is unmade even as it is made.

In the Scottish school we may see how the Machiavellian moment became a moment in a dialectical process. There was now a theory of history which showed how virtue was built up and demolished by the growth of society itself, an extension through time of that image of the centaur which Machiavelli had employed to show how, if man was by nature a *zōon politikon*, he never fully became himself; and there is a relation between Machiavelli's belief that republics never became fully stable or fully virtuous, and the fact that political theory based on commerce increasingly showed society polarized into those enriched by progress and those impoverished by it, and justified government as a necessary evil in a world of specialization and class struggle. The moment was dialectical in the sense that, though it was possible to think of an optimum point at which the forces building up and the forces tearing down virtue were in equilibrium, the historical structure of the theory ensured that such a point could only be attained momentarily. When Ferguson analyzed the citizen in such a way as to reduce him to the clansman, he knew perfectly well that the citizen could only be explained in terms of progressive emergence from the world of the clansman. Contradiction was of the essence, and there had been no golden age to which men might return. The conversion of irrational *fortuna* into positive and progressive commerce had not altered the character of the moment at which virtue and fortune were held in confrontation.

But there are two sides to a dialectic, especially one composed of progress and disruption, and it would clearly be possible to write a study of the Scottish school in which nearly all the emphasis lay on those aspects of their thought which were progressive, in the sense that

---

tlement of the Saxons in Britain, to the Revolution in 1688: to which are Subjoined Some Dissertations Connected with the History of the Government from the Revolution to the Present Time ... In four Volumes (4th ed., London, 1818). See in particular vols. III and IV; the incidental dissertations make up the last volume. W. C. Lehmann, *John Millar of Glasgow* (Cambridge University Press, 1960), has selections from Millar's works with a critical introduction; and see Duncan Forbes, "Scientific Whiggism: Adam Smith and John Millar," *Cambridge Journal* 7 (1954), 643-70.

they were concerned with showing how commerce and specialization had built up society and culture; or conservative, in the sense that they sought to show how the progress of society and the alienation of personality might be mitigated or held in an equilibrium not too intolerable for any party. Scottish thought was not as a rule utopian, in the sense that it showed the forces of progress finally overcoming those of decay—it did not have a final answer to the problem of personality and society—but neither was it strongly marked by a tragic sense of historical contradiction. Are there perhaps concealed ironies in the use of the sobriquet "Modern Athens" to describe Edinburgh in its great years, given the opposition between Athens and Sparta or Rome? But if we concluded that Scottish philosophy envisaged a future in which progress and corruption might coexist for a very long period, it would be important to know whether the time-dimension of that future was simply contingent and secular—in the sense that nothing was held to exist but conflicting social forces and no final resolution of their conflict expected—or semi-apocalyptic, in the sense that the dramatic corruption and collapse of any human society was ultimately to be looked for, but that human efforts favored by circumstances might postpone it almost indefinitely. In either case, however, Jean-Jacques Rousseau—whose visit to Scotland, projected by Hume, was psychologically doomed never to take place—would have appeared among his hosts as an accuser of the brethren, paranoiacally proclaiming that the tensions between personality and society did have apocalyptic possibilities, that the apocalypse had arrived in his own person, and that if properly understood it would be seen to have been present since before the beginnings of human society itself.

Rousseau was the Machiavelli of the eighteenth century, in the sense that he dramatically and scandalously pointed out a contradiction that others were trying to live with.[101] If the Scottish school believed that the contradiction between virtue and culture might be managed by men in society with good hopes of reasonable success, it was his role to insist that the contradiction was intolerable precisely at the moment of personal existence, and that this was and had been true at every moment in the history of society. Since by its nature society humanized man and by the same processes distracted and alienated him again, there was no point in past, present, or future time at which this double effect had not been going on. The entire social enterprise was by its nature necessary and self-defeating. The impact of this declaration was in many ways comparable to that of Machiavelli's announcement of the

[101] Judith N. Shklar, *Men and Citizens: A Study of Rousseau's Social Theory* (Cambridge University Press, 1969), is by far the best exposition of his thought as belonging to the civic humanist tradition.

divorce between civic and Christian values; and, as with Machiavelli, it took time to discern the extraordinary strength of intellect which kept Rousseau a major classical theorist in the humanist succession. He exposed the theme of the alienation of personality with such completeness that, it can be argued, no recourse was left short of the adoption of an idealist mode of discourse in which the personality was seen articulating in itself, and seeking to reunite, the contradictions of history—a line of thought which, in Marx, was recombined with the analysis of the social effects of the division of labor begun by the Scottish theorists. That story, however, is not to be told here. The present study of the civic ideal of personality, and the consequences of its articulation, must conclude with its last great pre-modern efflorescence, which took place in the American colonies, and with its effects upon the American sense of personality and history.

CHAPTER XV

THE AMERICANIZATION OF VIRTUE

Corruption, Constitution and Frontier

[1]

DURING THE NINETEEN-SIXTIES, a number of important works of scholarship appeared which have sharply altered our perception of the mind of the Revolutionary generation in America.[1] They have shown, first, that the mental processes which led to revolution involved a drastic rearticulation of the language and outlook of English opposition thought; second, that through this they were, as we already know, anchored in that Aristotelian and Machiavellian tradition which this book has studied; third, that the experience of the War of Independence and the constitution-making which followed it necessitated a further revision of the classical tradition, and in some respects a departure from it. The American Revolution, which to an older school of historians seemed a rationalist or naturalist breach with an old world and its history, now appears to have been involved in a complex relation both with English and Renaissance cultural history and with a tradition of thought which had from its beginnings confronted political man with his own history and was, by the time of the Revolution, being used to express an early form of the quarrel with modernity. It is now possible to explore the history of American consciousness in search of what manifestations of the problems of the republican perspective may be found there.

In the first place, it has been established that a political culture took shape in the eighteenth-century colonies which possessed all the char-

---

[1] In addition to those of Caroline Robbins and Bernard Bailyn, cited above, ch. XII, n. 52 and ch. XIV, n. 7, see Richard M. Gummere, *The American Colonial Mind and the Classical Tradition: Essays in Comparative Culture* (Cambridge, Mass.: Harvard University Press, 1963); H. Trevor Colbourn, *The Lamp of Experience: Whig History and the Beginnings of the American Revolution* (Chapel Hill: University of North Carolina Press, 1965); J. R. Pole, *Political Representation in England and the Origins of the American Republic* (New York: St. Martin's Press, 1966), and those of Gordon S. Wood and Gerald Stourzh, cited extensively below. For an earlier essay on this theme, see my "Virtue and Commerce in the Eighteenth Century," *Journal of Interdisciplinary History* 3, no. 1 (1972), 119-34.

acteristics of neo-Harringtonian civic humanism. Anglophone civilization seems indeed to present the picture of a number of variants of this culture—English, Scottish, Anglo-Irish, New England, Pennsylvanian, and Virginian, to look no further—distributed around the Atlantic shores. The Whig canon and the neo-Harringtonians, Milton, Harrington and Sidney, Trenchard, Gordon and Bolingbroke, together with the Greek, Roman, and Renaissance masters of the tradition as far as Montesquieu, formed the authoritative literature of this culture; and its values and concepts were those with which we have grown familiar—a civic and patriot ideal in which the personality was founded in property, perfected in citizenship but perpetually threatened by corruption; government figuring paradoxically as the principal source of corruption and operating through such means as patronage, faction, standing armies (opposed to the ideal of the militia), established churches (opposed to the Puritan and deist modes of American religion) and the promotion of a monied interest—though the formulation of this last concept was somewhat hindered by the keen desire for readily available paper credit common in colonies of settlement. A neoclassical politics provided both the ethos of the elites and the rhetoric of the upwardly mobile, and accounts for the singular cultural and intellectual homogeneity of the Founding Fathers and their generation. Not all Americans were schooled in this tradition, but there was (it would almost appear) no alternative tradition in which to be schooled.

In consequence, Bailyn and others have argued, the ideology of eighteenth-century opposition acted as a restricting and compulsive force in the approaches to revolution. The Machiavellian assumptions it contained proved to be self-actualizing. Corruption, which threatened the civic bases of personality, was irremediable except by personal virtue itself, and therefore must very soon become irreversible if action was not taken in time. When ministers at Westminster—the rhetoric habitually identified ministers as the source of most evils—began to take actions which seemed to encroach on colonial liberties, the appropriate language in which to denounce them was that in which the Junto Whigs and Walpole had been denounced in their day; the more so as the enemies of Bute and the friends of Wilkes were already employing that language against the ministries of George III. But once Americans began to talk of corruption, the situation rapidly passed out of intellectual control. If corruption was being attempted from the other side of the Atlantic, the government and (it followed) the society attempting it must themselves be hopelessly corrupt. The virtue and personal integrity of every American were therefore threatened by corruption emanating from a source now alien, on which Americans had formerly believed themselves securely dependent. The language began to sound that paranoiac note which is heard when men are forced by the logic of mental restriction to conclude that malign agencies are conspiring against the inner citadels of their personalities; only diabolical conspiracy could account for actions each one of which appeared more blatantly subversive than the last.[2] Virtue, once endangered, was compelled to fall back on itself, and there was no remedy which Americans could seek short of *rinnovazione* and *ridurre ai principii*; a return to the fundamental principles of British government or—once that was seen as containing the seeds of its own corruption—of the constitution of the commonwealth itself; an attempt to reconstitute that form of polity in which virtue would be both free and secure. The Americans thus repeated, but in actuality, the thought-experiments of Nedham and Harrington, repudiating parliamentary monarchy in favor of an English-derived version of *vivere civile*; and down to this point—soon to be surpassed—the Revolution was paradigmatically determined and an essay in Kuhnian "normal science."

But though virtue and corruption, taken by themselves, formed a closed and compulsive scheme, they could only operate as such when no other scheme was known. In Britain, as we have seen, there existed a "Court" ideology, less articulate and prominent than that of the "Country," but capable both of furnishing some effective replies to the philippics of Bolingbroke and of being enlarged by Hume and his successors into a complex and ambivalent historical philosophy. It was based not on a simple antithesis between virtue and commerce, but on an awareness that the two interpenetrated one another as did land and currency, authority and liberty; we have seen that as far back as 1698, the founders of "Country" ideology admitted this truth, while drawing different conclusions from it. In Britain, moreover, Court and Country themselves were in symbiosis, and the country gentlemen never as radically independent as they liked to pretend.[3] The funds, the army, and the patronage-wielding executive were facts of life, just as the property that made men virtuous derived part of its capacity to do so from the mechanisms of trade and the fluctuations of credit; and while it was hard to deny that these things exerted a corrupting influence, it was no less hard to deny that virtue must exist in the world of commerce, value in the world of an ongoing history. The political independence of the gentry consisted in their ability to affect these

[2] For the growth of conspiracy theory, see Bailyn, *Ideological Origins*, pp. 85-93, 95-102, 119-43; *American Politics*, pp. 11-14, 35-38, 136-49; Gordon S. Wood, *Creation of the American Republic*, pp. 16, 22-23, 30-36, 40-43.

[3] Paul Lucas, "A Note on the Comparative Study of the Structure of Politics in Mid-Eighteenth-Century Britain and its American Colonies," *William and Mary Quarterly*, 3d ser., 28 (1971), 301-309.

processes, to mitigate and limit what might otherwise corrupt their independence; and the probability of an ultimate catastrophe was offset by that of its indefinite postponement. The doctrine of parliamentary monarchy, asserting that executive and representative had the means of coexisting while conceding that some measure of patronage was necessary to get things done, was one mode of responding to this perception of politics, as were Hume's teachings that authority and liberty, selfishness and altruism, passion and reason, existed in comparable relations of tension and symbiosis. English and Scottish theorists could not free themselves from the vision of some ultimate corruption, but had for the most part freed themselves from riding upon a wheel where the catastrophe might come at any moment.

If the perception of reality obtaining in the colonies was so much more fragile, part of the explanation may lie in the fact that they constituted a Country without a Court; they were not face to face with modern government as a force they must and could find means of living with, but, while created by it at a distance, were not in a relation of immediate symbiosis. The greater their apparent independence, the greater their sense that their virtue was their own; but the more active a government in which they did not directly participate, the greater their sense that their independence and virtue were threatened by a force they could only call corruption; and, as Machiavelli and Cato had taught them, once they mistrusted government there was nothing they should not fear. Tyranny was indeed to be dreaded "in every tainted breeze." The interpretation put forward by Bailyn and Wood altogether replaces that of Boorstin and Hartz, who seem to have held that there was no ideology in America, because ideology could be produced only by Old World social tensions which had not been transplanted.[4] As we now see it, modern and effective government had transplanted to America the dread of modernity itself, of which the threat to virtue by corruption was the contemporary ideological expression.

America had been established by plantation, but secured by conquest. The steps by British governments which initiated the process of classical revolution were taken in the course of the reorganization which followed the Seven Years War. From this Britain had emerged triumphant in North America and India; there had occurred a huge expansion of her commercial, naval and colonial power, and she was

---

[4] Daniel Boorstin, *The Genius of American Politics* (University of Chicago Press, 1953) and *The Americans: the Colonial Experience* (New York: Random House, 1958); Louis B. Hartz, *The Liberal Tradition in America: An Interpretation of American Political Thought since the Revolution* (New York: Harcourt, Brace, 1955).

recognized as possessing empire on a giant scale. This was the appropriate moment, according to all the conventions of the classical vocabulary, at which to utter warnings against the fate of Rome, transformed from a republic to a despotism by the conquest of an empire whose wealth corrupted the citizenry and could only be distributed by a Caesar; but though such warnings were heard in Britain, they were directed mainly against the supposed activities of Indian and West Indian nabobs, whose movable wealth might cause them to swell a new "monied interest" and buy up parliament through the purchase of boroughs.[5] The conquest of the internal river system of North America aroused fewer such fears, and seems to have been assimilated to that profitable yet not corrupting maritime war which Country politicians had long compared favorably with war by land in Europe; it was involvement on the side of Hanover and Prussia which Chatham had found needed most defending in parliament. For Americans, however, there was an evident paradox in the discovery that imperial conquests, which had rendered them secure against foreign and aboriginal enemies, now faced them with the threat of corruption by their own government. In such circumstances the rhetoric of republic and Caesar was appropriate and was used;[6] yet were not Americans, even in their own eyes, a system of colonies extending an empire, and not a republic at all?

But the term "empire," it is important to note, was capable in the Machiavellian tradition of being used in more than one way. On the one hand, Rome had been corrupted by conquest, and in that sense by empire; and it was and has remained normal usage to distinguish between the republic and "the empire," meaning the rule by *principes* who were also *imperatores* which succeeded it. On the other hand, the Roman people had exercised *imperium* in the sense of power over other peoples, which they had built up as Machiavelli's "commonwealth for expansion" and by the exercise of Machiavellian *virtù*. Must the successful exercise of *virtù* be in the end the cause of its corruption? Machiavelli had on the whole thought that it must, and the neo-Harringtonians had equated the decay of the republic with commercial empire, which had as in their own day led to the growth of monied interests and professional armies. But it was part of the Augustan paradox that this kind of military and financial corruption was thought of as growing through the pursuit of land war in Europe, while war at sea and in the colonies was part of the non-corrupting *virtus* of the Country. Harrington's Oceana had "given laws to the sea," pursuing foreign plantations which made her a "commonwealth for expansion" unthreatened

[5] The climax of such rhetoric is to be found in the debates over Fox's India Bill of 1783, and in the impeachment of Warren Hastings.

[6] Wood, pp. 34-36.

by corruption; and Americans gazing beyond the Appalachians could—with the aid of a little contemplated genocide—share the same vision. Even if empire must ultimately corrupt, there was a historical *anakuklōsis* whereby liberty-loving warriors—Greeks, Romans, and Goths—won empires by their virtue and held them so long as it lasted. This, hinted at in Machiavelli's theory of the exhaustion and revival of *virtù*, had become assimilated to the medieval doctrine of *translatio imperii* and helps explain the freedom with which Americans of the early national period spoke of the "empire" which was to be theirs in the Ohio and Mississippi valleys. An empire compatible with virtue was a concept very necessary to them if they were to accept themselves as what they were by the circumstances of their foundation and prehistory.

The American version of *translatio imperii* was expressed as early as 1725 in the famous last stanza of Berkeley's *Verses on the Prospect of the Arts and Learning in America*:

Westward the course of empire takes its way;
   The four first acts already past
A fifth shall close the drama with the day;
   Time's noblest offspring is the last.

Ernest Tuveson, the author of an illuminating study of the millennial vision of America, denies that these lines are properly millennial, on the grounds that there is insufficient evidence that the fifth act of the drama will partake of the characteristics of a true millennium; he sees in them only a late-Renaissance vision of the decline and revival of the arts, married to the language of the Book of Daniel.[7] But the *translatio studii*, like the *translatio imperii*, is dependent on the transition of *virtus* (as Berkeley himself makes manifest) and we are accustomed to see virtue demand, if it does not substitute itself for, an apocalyptic context of grace acting in history; and Tuveson himself has shown how far the true millennium, of Christ's reign over the saints, had become identified with a future utopia,[8] in which human capacities would have providentially and progressively arrived at their perfection. It is hard to doubt that Berkeley's "fifth act" was sometimes taken to mean a Fifth Monarchy, the more so as Tuveson has extensively demonstrated the existence of an American apocalyptic, in which the *translatio imperii*, ensuring that the westward cycle of world history culminates in America, became one mode of assigning to that imperial republic precisely the millennial-utopian role he has described.

---

[7] Ernest Lee Tuveson, *Redeemer Nation: The Idea of America's Millennial Role* (Chicago University Press, 1968), pp. 92-94.
[8] *Millennium and Utopia*; see above, ch. II, n. 21.

The national apocalyptic pioneered by Elizabethan Protestants possessed an American variant which survived there without undergoing the extensive recession suffered by this mode of thought in England after the Restoration. New England's initial covenant with the Lord could very easily be given a role in the struggle against Antichrist, and this was in no sense minimized by the persistent jeremiad preachings in which the heirs of the covenant were denounced for falling away from it. A covenanted or chosen people may apostasize many times, and the record of the struggle against the Adversary may be the record of its apostasies and regenerations. But we have seen how readily, in late Puritan and even deist thought, the commonwealth in which there is no clergy, and religion is a civic function conducted by an assembly of citizens, can become equated with the priesthood of all believers and the rule of the saints foretold for the millennium; and the more millennium became utopia, and the rule of the saints the perfection of human capacities, the easier it was to equate the commonwealth with the Fifth Monarchy to which it had always tended to become assimilated. And the perfection of human capacities, seen as providentially directed progress rather than a sudden and apocalyptic infusion of grace, was a secular and historical phenomenon which might well take place within the closed circle of the "westward course." America's apocalyptic-utopian role, therefore, was regularly seen as the maintenance of religious liberty—Whiggish tolerance merging into the holy commonwealth—and part of a structure of Gothic freedom and virtue, which survived in the "westward course" to the "close" of the "drama" after corruption had destroyed it in the Old World.

But this was to identify corruption with the work of Antichrist in both hemispheres, and in particular with the ever-present threat of apostasy in the covenanted lands of the New World. It is therefore logical that Tuveson should have traced the existence of what he calls "apocalyptic Whiggism" and found its echoes even in the language of so un-chiliastic a work as John Adams's *Dissertation on the Canon and Feudal Laws.*[9] The city upon a hill became identified with the balanced government, in which neither an established clergy nor any other agency of corruption disturbed the virtue and freedom of the people, and the corruption which threatened the latter was as much the work of Antichrist as the apostasy which threatened the former. As the operations of grace in sacred history became conflated with the providential progress of secular enlightenment, Antichrist in his turn became identified with the historical forces—Roman clericalism, feudal sur-

[9] *Redeemer Nation*, pp. 20-25; Wood, pp. 116-18.

vivals, modern corruptions—operating to delay progress or pervert it. Arbitrary taxation, standing armies, established churches, could still appear the works of the malign agency which had pursued and undermined Roman, Gothic, and now British virtue through the *translatio* and *anakuklōsis* of the world's history. It was of eschatological as well as global importance to determine whether empire would corrupt American virtue or sustain it, and the latter outcome might be hard to distinguish from the millennium or Fifth Monarchy. The jeremiad— that most American of all rhetorical modes—was merged with the language of classical republican theory to the point where one can almost speak of an apocalyptic Machiavellism; and this too heightened the tendency to see that moment at which corruption threatened America as one of unique and universal crisis.

[II]

The apocalyptic dimension, however, while apparent in the rhetoric of the Revolution, is hardly dominant there. Americans of that generation saw themselves as freemen in arms, manifesting a patriot virtue, rather than as covenanted saints. The reasons for emphasizing in these pages that apocalyptic was still an available recourse are analytical and diagnostic; its presence, and continued compatibility with Old Whig civic humanism, illustrates how far American thought and speech still belonged to the Renaissance tradition we have studied, in which the citizen often required for his self-dramatization the apocalyptic context otherwise properly the saint's. But all those who have recently studied the Revolution in terms of the continuity of this tradition— Bailyn, Pole, and Wood—insist that, in the period of the making of the Constitution and the Federalist-Republican debate, the civic tradition underwent a transforming crisis and was never the same again; Wood in particular speaks of an "end of classical politics."[10] To arrive at so massively dialectical a culmination would indeed be satisfying to the hard-pressed architect of a book such as this, and Wood's thesis requires careful investigation; certain reservations will, however, be expressed.

Perceptive students of the American scene, writing earlier than the crisis which led to independence, had observed that the volatility of colonial politics could be explained by reference to the lack of any

[10] Bailyn, *Ideological Origins*, ch. v, "Transformation"; *Political Pamphlets of the American Revolution*, 1 (Cambridge, Mass.: The Belknap Press, 1965), pp. 3-202 ("The Transforming Radicalism of the American Revolution"); Pole, *Political Representation*, pp. 531-32 ("the decline of virtue"); Wood, ch. xv, #5, pp. 606-18 ("The End of Classical Politics").

equivalent to the House of Lords.[11] By this they meant two not very compatible things. In the first place they were alluding to the doctrine that the Lords in the British constitution played the role of a classical Few, exhibiting greater leisure and experience—it was possible to defend their hereditary character on the ground that it guaranteed these qualities—and discharging a conservative and moderating function which could be depicted as that of a *pouvoir intermèdiaire*, a "screen and bank" in the language of 1642, between king and commons, one and many, executive and legislative. Without an aristocracy, it had been argued since at latest 1675, the commons would be restive and turbulent and could be managed only by force or by corruption. The Country tradition of Shaftesbury and Bolingbroke was in no sense hostile to the peerage; it saw hereditary status as a reinforcement of propertied independence and a guard against the machinations of the Court, and the Peerage Bill of 1719 had failed because it was felt that any attempt to legislate further independence for the Upper House must be self-defeating.

In the second place, however, analysts of colonial politics knew that an ancient aristocracy was hard to establish in a new society and a manorial nobility did not seem to thrive under settler conditions (though the Hudson Valley might offer grounds for disputing this). The Harringtonian constitutions devised by Locke, Penn, and others for the Carolinas, New Jersey, and Pennsylvania had all proved abortive,[12] and if an independent aristocracy could not be created under colonial conditions, to propose a reinforced second chamber was to propose a dependent oligarchy, nominated by the governor and precariously holding office at his will, like the Cromwellian Other House of 1657-1659. The republican tradition, as voiced by Machiavelli and Harrington, indeed declared that colonies and provinces should be ruled through insecure oligarchies dependent on the controlling power;[13] like an Italian *dominio*, they were not fully incorporated in the city or realm of justice; but once a colony began thinking of itself as a commonwealth or autonomously just society—a vital change of perspective to which the adoption of classical language powerfully contributed—such an oligarchy appeared inherently corrupt and, since it could not in practice be distinguished from the governor's council, a breach of the separation of powers as well.

[11] Wood, pp. 210-12.

[12] Francis Newton Thorpe, ed., *The Federal and State Constitutions, Colonial Charters, and Other Organic Laws of the States and Territories Now or Heretofore Forming the United States of America* (Washington: Government Printing Office, 1909), vol. v, has texts of all these.

[13] For Harrington see Toland, *Works*, pp. 40-41.

The conditions of colonial politics therefore pointed powerfully if illogically toward that repudiation of hereditary aristocracy as making for corruption rather than for virtue, which had been unheard of in England since the radical movements of the Commonwealth; and in the era—supposedly begun by Thomas Paine's *Common Sense*—when Americans set about repudiating the British constitutional structure, the existence of a hereditary peerage in the latter helped them to take up the option—which they may have learned from *Cato's Letters*—of dismissing parliamentary mixed monarchy as founded upon corruption. To reject parliamentary monarchy was, for minds still as English as theirs, to revert to the Harringtonian tradition in which English political history was restated as leading to a republican culmination; but in Harrington as in every other republican classic, it was unequivocally stated that the alternative to a hereditary, entrenched, or artificial aristocracy was a natural aristocracy—an elite of persons distinguished by natural superiority of talent, but also by contingent material advantages such as property, leisure, and learning, as possessing the qualities of mind required by the classical Few. It was assumed that a supply of such persons was guaranteed by nature, and part of the case against artificially established aristocracies was that the true elite were naturally recognizable by the Many. The democracy could discover the aristocracy by using its own modes of discernment, and there was no need to legislate its choice in advance; a theory of deference was usually invoked in order to democratize the polity.

In most American colonies a patrician elite—distinguished indeed by its visible property and culture—stood ready to play the role of natural aristocracy. The literature of colonial Virginia in particular contains some interesting idealizations of the relationship supposed to exist between the self-evident leaders of society and the respectful but by no means uncritical yeomanry.[14] These illustrate once again that deference was not a hierarchical but a republican characteristic. The Many of ideal Virginia—small white proprietors—are not politically dynamic, but they are not inactive; they exercise their own kind of judgment and exert their own kind of power. All that could be called hierarchical is that they do not expect to discharge the same role as the Few; but they have their virtue as the Few have theirs, and there is a higher virtue whereby the Few and Many respect the virtues exercised by one another. The Few are not above a kind of deference to the judgment of the Many, even when they deem its expression naive; so that

[14] Charles S. Sydnor, *Gentlemen Freeholders: Political Practice in Washington's Virginia* (Chapel Hill: University of North Carolina Press, 1952), republished as *American Revolutionaries in the Making* (New York: Free Press, 1965); Pole, *Political Representation*, pp. 148-65.

there is a point at which deference and virtue become very nearly identical.

In defense of their virtue against a corrupt parliamentary monarchy, then, the Americans set about reconstituting themselves as a confederation of republics; down to this point, their revolution was a *rinnovazione* in exactly the sense intelligible to Savonarola or Machiavelli.[15] But it is Wood's thesis, documented in great detail from the language and experience of the Revolutionaries themselves, that this consciously undertaken classical enterprise failed at precisely the point we have been examining. When there occurred a Lockean "dissolution of government"—in some areas it was so described, with invocations of Locke's name—the people were found not to differentiate themselves into a naturally distinguishable few and many, performing complementary roles and practicing complementary virtues. In Massachusetts, Pennsylvania, and elsewhere, there were deliberately engineered constitutional experiments aimed at identifying the natural aristocracy by applying the Aristotelian criteria of property, as in Massachusetts, or self-selection, as in the unicameral legislature which was tried in Pennsylvania. None of these experiments succeeded, and soon after the end of the War of Independence, the Revolution faced a crisis of confidence born of the realization that the naturally differentiated people, presupposed by every republican theorist from Aristotle to Montesquieu, had simply failed to appear.[16] And this meant far more than that the patrician elites, having led or survived the struggle for independence, now felt threatened in their ideologically justifying role as natural aristocracies; it meant that there was a threat to the concept of virtue itself.

Unless the people were qualitatively dissimilar, each qualitatively defined category having a function and a virtue appropriate to it, they could not join in a polity where the practice of politics obliged each citizen to practice the virtue of respecting his neighbor's virtue; and any political structure in which they might be united would bear no direct relationship to the unique moral personality of the individual, and would consequently corrupt it by subjecting it to power. When Machiavelli and Montesquieu had laid it down that only equality—in the sense of *isonomia*—made possible the practice of virtue, they had also implied that men who were equal must practice virtue or become corrupt. When the neo-Harringtonians had associated the decline of the baron-vassal relationship with the rise of corruption, they had

[15] Hannah Arendt, *On Revolution* (London: Faber and Faber, 1963), should be read on this point.
[16] Wood, *passim*, but particularly pp. 391-425.

added to Harrington's doctrine that equals must be governed freely or by force the perception that they might also be governed by manipulation and false consciousness. If corruption was to be avoided, there must be virtue within equality; and the still largely Christian minds of eighteenth-century civic humanists had sought to ensure this by employing the classical differentiation into one, few, and many to make the people a trinity-in-unity, within which there could be relationship and hence virtue. But this orthodoxy now seemed to be failing. The *materia* was beginning to seem too monophysite and one-dimensional to be given form, and the paradigm of the *zōon politikon* was in danger. There is an audible note of dismay in the American writings of the early 1780s.

Wood traces, through the rich complexity of the utterances of this period—all articulate Americans seem to have been versed in the vocabulary of the sociology of liberty—the emergence of a new paradigm of democratic politics, designed by the masters of Federalist theory to overcome the crisis caused by the failure of natural aristocracy—though whether they intended to replace the last-named, or to restore it, is not always clear. The crucial revision was that of the concept of the people. Instead of being differentiated into diversely qualified and functioning groups, the people was left in so monistic a condition that it mattered little what characteristics it was thought of as possessing; and the various agencies of government—still essentially the legislature, judiciary, and executive of separation theory—were thought of as exercised not immediately, by social groups possessing the relevant capacities, but mediately, by individuals whose title to authority was that they acted as representing the people. All power was entrusted to representatives, and every mode of exercising power was a mode of representing the people. If the people were an undifferentiated mass, possessed of infinitely diverse qualities, they possessed also an infinite capacity for differentiating between diverse modes of power and embodying themselves in correspondingly diverse means of representation. They had come a long way from the Florentine *materia*.

There was a distinction between the exercise of power in government, and the power of designating representatives to exercise it; and it could be argued both that all government was the people's and that the people had withdrawn from government altogether, leaving its exercise to a diversity of representatives who, situated as they were where the art of ruling might be learned from experience, took on the characteristics of the old natural aristocracy or specialized Few. Rousseau, with his insistence that the *volonté générale* should never engage in the taking of particular decisions, might have approved of this distinction between a constituent and a governing people; and he might have joined the Federalists in seeing Machiavelli's *ridurre* ensured in the provision that the power of constitutional revision was always in the people and its exercise always potentially imminent.[17] Here, at least, the people as such were active in a fairly immediate sense. What Rousseau would not have approved—and what is no part of the republican tradition as we have studied it—is the universal intervention in government of the relation between represented and representative; and here certainly the character of Federalist thought is medieval rather than classical and sovereign rather than republican—Hobbesian, it might even be added, rather than Lockean.

English parliamentary monarchy had been built up by the king's commanding the shires and boroughs to elect representatives, with full power to share in the government of the realm by himself and his council, and the power of these representatives had greatly increased over time. However, as the king's command that they be given full power to act in matters to be proposed by him clearly showed, there was a sense in which they were merely admitted to a share in the function of the true representative of the realm—the king himself, who, as all theory of incorporation insisted, represented the realm as the head did the body. Once representation became a means to the creation and establishment of a sovereign, the act of choosing—or acknowledging—a representative became logically almost the reverse of participation; it was rather the act of saying that there existed a person whose acts were so far authoritative that they were to be taken as equivalent to one's own; and Hobbes, spelling out this interpretation with admirable clarity, had pointed out that a sovereign assembly of representatives was no different in this respect from a sovereign and representative individual. The choice of a representative was a surrender, a transfer to another of one's plenitude of power and one's *persona* if not one's individuality; and republican humanism, which was fundamentally concerned with the affirmation of moral personality in civic action, had cause to ask whether the concept of representation did not exclude that of virtue. How could I designate another to be virtuous for me, in my place and wearing my mask? At the core of Hobbes's moral theory is indeed the statement that it is only when I become capable of owning another's actions as my own that I become a being capable of civic morality;[18] but the *zōon politikon*, the being naturally civic, must act immediately and in his own person. Rousseau, an ambiguous master within the classical tradition, had insisted that there was no virtue in

[17] Wood, pp. 613-14.
[18] For Hobbes on personation, see *Leviathan*, chs. 16 and 17.

the mere choice of a representative and that consequently people governed by plenipotentiary representatives of their own choosing were not free.[19]

The Country tradition in English politics—partially descended from Harrington's republicanism, in which rotation ensures that the people take part in government as individuals and by turns, rather than through representatives—had made an important contribution toward redefining England as a commonwealth when it stressed the importance of short parliaments. The implication was that the people, being propertied and independent, were by definition virtuous, but that their representatives were constantly exposed to the temptations of power and corruption; it was therefore necessary that the representation should return regularly to the represented, to have virtue renewed (*ridurre ai principii*) by the choice of new representatives if necessary. Virtue was an active principle, and in the election of a new parliament the people displayed virtue in action and performed more than a Hobbesian role. But it now became hard to decide whether the electors were one estate or order of the commonwealth (a classical Many) and the elected another (a classical Few), the relations between whom must be preserved from corruption; or whether the elected were at bottom mere servants, stewards, or ministers, who must be presumed corruptible virtually by definition. If the latter, then they must be considered delegates, subject to instruction and recall; but there would be the difficulty that the relation between them and their electors would no longer be a virtuous relation between civic equals. During the years of the American crisis, Burke was propounding to the electors of Bristol the view that their representative was chosen by them to act for the good of the whole realm, and thus to play a part which they could not play themselves. He therefore owed them the exercise of his judgment concerning the common good, even when it conflicted with theirs.[20] They would be exercising their judgment with equal propriety if they decided not to reelect him at the close of his term, but they should not seek to impede his judgment by instructing or recalling him. The relationship is classical, that of the Few to the Many, and virtuous in the sense derived from Aristotle. Each has his judgment, his mode of discernment, and respects that of the other.

In Revolutionary America, the tide had been running strongly in favor of the view that elected representatives were highly corruptible delegates, who must be subject to instruction and recall; but Madison

[19] Rousseau, *The Social Contract*, ch. 15; C. E. Vaughan, ed., *The Political Writings of Jean-Jacques Rousseau* (New York: John Wiley and Sons, 1962), II, 95-98.

[20] Burke, *Works*, II, 95-97.

seems to have leaned toward a Burkean position which presented their role as that of a Few, and their ranks as to be filled, if possible, by members of the patrician elites.[21] The crucial question remained, however, that raised by Rousseau. Given that a natural aristocracy had not emerged, and was not expected to emerge, from the electoral process, was the mere act of choosing a representative, the mere relationship between representative and elector, sufficient to ensure virtue? For some Federalists the answer was predetermined. If there was no natural aristocracy, the people could not be virtuous; if none had emerged, the most probable explanation was that the people were already corrupt; government accordingly became a Guicciardinian affair of guiding a people who were not virtuous, or helping them guide themselves, along paths as satisfactory as could be hoped for in these circumstances. This perspective, of course, did not prevent those who adopted it from regarding themselves as members of a virtuous natural aristocracy, Catos of the deserving side. Madison's position, as we shall see, was more complex; but Wood shows that the Federalists talked both as if virtue was to be restored, and as if it had vanished and must be replaced by new paradigms.[22] And it was, as always, difficult to hit upon surrogates for virtue in its classical sense. There was this to be said for Rousseau's critique of representation. Virtue consisted in a particular being's regard for the common good, and was contingent upon his association with other particular beings who regarded the same good through different eyes. The differentiation of Few from Many, of natural aristocracy from natural democracy, was the paradigm case of this association between men of different qualities; and without some theory of qualitative and moral differentiation between individuals, it was hard to see how the relations between citizens that constituted virtue could be established. The act of choosing a person to act for me, one with whom I asserted an artificial identity, could never be the same as that of recognizing a person who acted with me, and with whom I formed a natural association. This was why it was hard to see the relation of representative to represented as one of classical virtue. Neither the Federalists nor their critics employed Rousseau as a tool of analysis,[23] but there are perceptible tensions between their remodeling of the theory of representation and their unwillingness to abandon the paradigm of the republic of virtue.

They sought—so successfully as to bring about something like a

[21] Wood, p. 505.

[22] Wood, pp. 474-75, 507-18, 543-47, 562-64.

[23] Paul M. Sperlin, *Rousseau in America, 1760-1809* (University of Alabama Press, 1969), indicates that *The Social Contract* was not much read or quoted. Noah Webster—for whom see below, pp. 526, 533-35—is an interesting exception.

paradigmatic revolution—to reconcile the two by developing a theory of multiple representation. Instead of a medieval or Hobbesian identity, natural or artificial, between the representative and the represented as simple entities, they asserted that there was a plurality of modes of exercising power and that every one of these—the quasi-classical executive, judiciary, and legislative were the obvious examples—constituted a separate mode in which the people chose to be represented. The people's representatives taken as individuals formed a plurality of functionally differentiated groups, and to that extent might still be looked upon as a natural aristocracy; the plurality of functions which they exercised ensured the existence between and among them of a system of checks and balances, so that it could be said they were prevented from becoming corrupt, or corrupting the people, by any one's acquiring so much power as to bring the rest into dependence.[24] The rhetoric of the classical tradition, from Aristotle to Montesquieu, thus remained appropriate over wide fields of the phenomena presented by the new government; but beneath it—and accounting for the widespread belief that the concept of representation was the only great discovery in theoretical politics made since antiquity—lay that sharply new perspective which leads Wood to speak of an "end of classical politics." The people were still thought of as uncorrupted, but there were important senses in which they need not and could not be said to affirm their virtue in action. They were not differentiated into groups of diverse quality and function, each of which exercised citizenship in its own way and between which there existed the relationships of virtue; nor, since they were not politically active in a diversity of ways functionally differentiated, could it strictly be said that they were directly or immediately engaged in governing at all. They were directly engaged in the choice of representatives, and the multiplicity of the federal structure ensured that this function could be seen as ongoing and perpetual; they were also constituent, directly engaged in the establishment and revision of constitutions, and there are passages of rhetoric which suggest that this too was seen as a continuous activity.[25] Even Machiavelli, the most kinetic of republican theorists, had seen *ridurre* and *ripigliare lo stato* as no more than an affair of exemplary purges at intervals of a few years; even Rousseau had envisaged no more than occasional if frequent assemblies of the sovereign people, for the duration of which any constitution was necessarily suspended. If Federalist theory surpassed tradition at this point too, it is important to understand how.

The decline of virtue had as its logical corollary the rise of interest.[26]

---

[24] See, e.g., Wood, pp. 446-53.   [25] Wood, pp. 532-36, 599-600, 613-14.

[26] There is much semantic confusion on this point. Given that in classical theory each major institution "represented" a distinct "order" in society—e.g., the one,

If men no longer enjoyed the conditions thought necessary to make them capable of perceiving the common good, all that each man was capable of perceiving was his own particular interest; and to the extent that there survived the very ancient presumption that only perception of the common good was truly rational, perception of one's interest was primarily a matter of appetite and passion and only secondarily of profit-and-loss rational calculation which might extend so far as perception of one's interest as interdependent with that of another's. Non-virtuous man was a creature of his passions and fantasies, and when passion was contrasted with virtue its corruptive potential remained high; but we have already seen how in eighteenth-century theory fantasy and commerce could appear an explosive and transforming force, possessing the dynamism if also the limitations of Machiavellian *virtù*, and rather more than the latter's capacity to transform the natures of men. Interest was both a limiting and an expanding force. As Federalist thought took shape, and the people were less and less seen as possessing virtue in the classical sense, it is not surprising to find, in Madison's writings and those of others—the tenth issue of *The Federalist* is the *locus classicus*—an increasing recognition of the importance, and the legitimacy, in human affairs of the faction pursuing a collective but particular interest,[27] which in older Country and republican theory had figured as one of the most deadly means to the corruption of virtue by passion. Interest and faction are the modes in which the decreasingly virtuous people discern and pursue their activities in politics; but in Madison's thought two consequences soon follow. In the first place, the checks, balances, and separations of powers, to be built into the federal structure, ensure as we have seen that interest does not corrupt, so that the full rhetoric of balance and stability can still be invoked in praise of an edifice no longer founded in virtue, and the very fact that it is no longer so founded can easily be masked and forgotten.[28] In the second place, there are passages which strikingly indicate that the capacity of this structure for absorbing and reconciling conflicting interests is without known limits.[29] There is no interest

---

the few, and the many—it was by this time possible to speak of these "orders" as "interests"; and radical democrats, speaking still from within the classical tradition, could argue that in the popular assembly individuals, not relatively elitist interests, were what should be "represented." But in true interest-group theory, which may be the child of radical individualism, the individual needs to perceive only his interests and the group with which they associate him, and need not practice the "virtue" of looking beyond them.

[27] Pole, pp. 374-75; Wood, pp. 501-506, 576.

[28] Wood, pp. 535-47, 559-60.

[29] Wood, pp. 605-10, relying largely on *The Federalist*, no. 51.

which cannot be represented and given its place in the distribution of power—only the most peculiar of institutions, it has seemed to historians in the Federalist tradition, was to prove an exception to this rule—and should the growth and change of the people generate new interests, the federal republic can grow and change to accommodate them.

In this "end of classical politics," Wood detects primarily a partial shift from republicanism to liberalism[30]—from, that is to say, the classical theory of the individual as civic and active being, directly participant in the *res publica* according to his measure, toward (if not fully reaching) a theory in which he appears as conscious chiefly of his interest and takes part in government in order to press for its realization, making only an indirect contribution to that mediating activity whereby government achieves a reconciliation of conflicts which is all the common good there is. In this sense, representative democracy involves a recession, on the part of both individual and "people," from direct participation in government, of which the "decline of virtue" is the measure; but it does not involve political quiescence or a lowering of tensions. It also coincides with a vast expansion of party activity and appeal to a highly responsible electorate. Wood further detects in Madison a dimension of thought which is kinetic and romantic. Because "the people" is now undifferentiated, it is not circumscribed by the definition and distribution of specific qualities. It is of unknown mass and force, and can develop new and unpredicted needs, capacities, and powers. All of these can be received and coordinated within the structure of federalism, so that the classical rhetoric of balance and stability is still appropriate, but this structure can be proclaimed capable of indefinite expansion, since there is no need to insist in advance that the new social elements which will seek representation be those previously conceived as part of the harmonics of virtue. They are not perceived rationally as elements in the architecture of the common good, but as interests conceived and pursued in passion; the federal structure, however, is capable of absorbing new passions and grows by absorbing them. If the people are perpetually constituent, therefore, this is because they and their republic are in perpetual and kinetic growth. The republic of represented interests is a commonwealth for expansion. Something has been lost to virtue, but more has been gained by *virtù*. The liberal structure is not tame or sedate; like archetypal Rome before it, it is at once stable and expansive.

Wood's "end of classical politics" is at bottom predicated upon an abandonment of the closely related paradigms of deference and virtue. Because natural aristocracy failed the Americans in the moment of

[30] Wood, pp. 562, 606-15.

classical *rinnovazione*, they had to abandon any theory of the people as qualitatively differentiated, and therefore either virtuous in the classical sense or participant in government in ways directly related to personality; and at the heart of Federalist thought arose something akin to the paradoxes of Rousseau—all government was the people's, and yet the people never directly governed. This price once paid, the advantages of the great restatement of paradigms which accompanied the conservative revolution of 1787-89 were enormous. It permitted the overcoming of the widely accepted limitation which enjoined republics to be of finite size if they would escape corruption; the new federation could be both republic and empire, continental in its initial dimensions and capable of further expansion by means of simple extensions of the federative principle, greatly surpassing the semimilitary complex of colonies and provinces which had extended the Roman hegemony. It permitted the growth of new modes of association in pursuit of particular ends—political parties which, it has been argued by Chambers,[31] were modern in precisely the sense that they were not based on deference, and which mobilized participant energies on a scale undreamed of in ancient republics. It is not surprising, then, that Wood and Chambers tend to speak of deference as the principle of the classical republic, and that republic itself as a subspecies of the closed and stable social hierarchy;[32] though less cautious proponents of this view are (and long have been) open to the criticism that they confound the natural with the hereditary aristocracy.

But our pursuit of the Machiavellian consequences of the republican principle that virtue is active has led us through realms of consciousness in which deference was not passive and the republic was not a hierarchy. We have grown used to thinking of virtue as active in a world of proportionately equal citizens, and the republic as expanding beyond the confines of that world through the exercise of *virtù*. In the Polybian and Machiavellian tradition, the republic was not simply and naturally finite, and the injunction to remain small must not be misread. It faced the dilemma, born of its finitude, that it could escape neither expansion nor the corruption that followed expansion. The American republic proposed from its inception to offer a fresh solution to this ancient problem; the terms of this solution were in some respects dramatically new, but in others a restatement of old. We have further grown used

[31] William N. Chambers, *Political Parties in a New Nation: the American Experience, 1776-1809* (New York: Oxford University Press, 1963).

[32] E.g., Wood, p. 606; Chambers, pp. 122-24; Pole, pp. 528-31. Wood in particular presents the republic as an ideal essentially hierarchical and at the same time essentially mobile; pp. 478-79.

to the existence in British thought of an alternative or "Court" ideology, which emphasized that men were guided by interest and passion, that factions and parties were necessary rather than illegitimate, and that government must be carried on by a sovereign power, ultimately unchecked but capable of subdivision into self-balancing powers, which ruled men partly by direct authority, partly by appeal to those passions, and partly by conversion of those passions into perception of a common interest. It should be clear by now that important elements of this ideology reappear in Federalist theory at just the points where the latter moves away from virtue and toward interest.

There are, however, some major and obvious differences. Where the Court thesis locates sovereignty in a parliamentary monarchy, self-balanced by the distinction between executive and legislative but held together by the influence which the former wields in the latter, the Federalist thesis locates it in the represented people and maintains the separation of powers with a rigor which is republican rather than merely Country. Once again we are at the point where the full rhetoric of republicanism was entirely appropriate to Federalist purposes, and the extent to which virtue was being abandoned could be masked to speakers as well as audiences. Where the Court thesis appealed to a version of history in which there were pragmatic adjustments and no fundamental principles, the Federalists could and did claim to be founding a republic in an extra-historical and legislative moment—one of *occasione*—in which the principles of nature, including balance and even virtue, were being reaffirmed. Their kinetic and expansive vision was of the future, and carried with it no Machiavellian sense of being part of an already disorderly *saeculum*. Finally, the Court thesis, originating as we have seen in the collisions of war and credit finance with the presumed stability of landed property, entailed a high degree of recognition that credit and commerce formed the expansive principle, the blend of Machiavellian *virtù* and *fortuna*, which doomed men to follow their passions and government to acknowledge and utilize corruption. Whether or not the failure of natural aristocracy in revolutionary America can be attributed to the competition of new merchant and artisan elements with the older patrician elites, there seems little evidence that the thought of the 1780s was responding to a traumatic intrusion of the "monied interest" like that which so dramatically altered English thinking ninety years before. There was no American Court—as yet; the confrontation between virtue and commerce was not absolute, and once again this furnishes reason to believe that the founders of Federalism were not fully aware of the extent to which their thinking involved an abandonment of the paradigm of virtue. In what follows, it will be argued that Wood's "end of classical politics" was an end of one guiding thread in a complex tissue, but not a disappearance of the whole web.

[III]

Wood shows how it came about that John Adams's *Defence of the Constitutions of the United States*, a vindication of the federal republic as a strict classical blend of natural aristocracy and democracy, was rejected as already a historical freak: partly misunderstood as a defense of the aristocratic principle, partly diagnosed correctly, by more acute minds such as John Taylor of Caroline, as a defense of the republic upon principles which the republic itself had abandoned.[33] Such was the ironic—but, given its author's personality, appropriate—fate of perhaps the last major work of political theory written within the unmodified tradition of classical republicanism. Wood also brings to light two Federalists at least, of the middle to late eighties—Noah Webster in 1785, William Vans Murray in 1787—who declared specifically (as did Hamilton and Taylor) that the virtue of the individual was no longer a necessary foundation of free government; and Murray at least declared, following a line laid down by Montesquieu but going beyond him, that the imperative of subjecting private to public good had been invented in a rude and precommercial society and need not be upheld now that the true secret of republican liberty was known.[34] Liberty, then, could dispense with virtue and would not be corrupted by affluence; but whether Murray was pronouncing a conservative or a revolutionary creed, it would be impossible to say without some modification of language.

But even after the wealth of detail with which Wood's, Pole's, and other analyses have explored the thesis of an implicit abandonment of virtue in Federalist theory, we are not faced with a generation who unanimously made this abandonment explicit. In the last few paragraphs reason has been found for suggesting that the rhetoric of balance and separation of powers operated to keep the language of republican tradition alive; and it can now be further argued that the vocabulary of virtue and corruption persisted in American thought, not merely as a survival slowly dying after its tap-root was cut, but with a reality and

[33] Wood, ch. xiv, "The Relevance and Irrelevance of John Adams," pp. 567-92. For other studies of Adams as among the last great classical theorists, see Zoltan Haraszti, *John Adams and the Prophets of Progress* (Cambridge, Mass.: Harvard University Press, 1952); John R. Howe, Jr., *The Changing Political Thought of John Adams* (Princeton University Press, 1966).

[34] Wood, pp. 610-11; for Taylor, pp. 591-92.

relevance to elements in American experience that kept it alive and in tension with the consequences that followed its partial abandonment in so crucial a field as constitutional theory and rhetoric. If Americans had been compelled to abandon a theory of constitutional humanism which related the personality to government directly and according to its diversities, they had not thereby given up the pursuit of a form of political society in which the individual might be free and know himself in his relation to society. The insistent claim that the American is a natural man and America founded on the principles of nature is enough to demonstrate that, and the pursuit of nature and its disappointments can readily be expressed in the rhetoric of virtue and corruption; for this is the rhetoric of citizenship, and a cardinal assertion of Western thought has been that man is naturally a citizen—*kata phusin zōon politikon.* However, American social thought has long employed a paradigm, supposedly Locke's, of government emerging from and highly continuous with a state of natural sociability; and it has been seriously contended that no other paradigm than Locke's has thriven or could have thriven in the unique conditions of American society.[35] In this book we have been concerned with another tradition, reducible to the sequence of Aristotle's thesis that human nature is civic and Machiavelli's thesis that, in the world of secular time where alone the polis can exist, this nature of man may never be more than partially and contradictorily realized. Virtue can develop only in time, but is always threatened with corruption by time. In the special form taken when time and change were identified with commerce, this tradition has been found to have been operative over wide areas of thought in the eighteenth century, and to have provided a powerful impulse to the American Revolution. But so great is the strength of the "Lockean" paradigm among modern scholars that there is a real likelihood that Wood's demonstration of a shift away from classical humanist premises in the making of the Federal Constitution will be interpreted as an "end of classical politics" and a wholesale adoption of the "Lockean" style. It is therefore of some importance, as we conclude this study of the Machiavellian tradition, to review the evidence which suggests that the theses and antitheses of virtue and corruption continued to be of great importance in shaping American thought.

The episode of the Order of the Cincinnati is relevant here. When we read that officers of the former revolutionary army formed themselves into a society, which took its name from that Roman hero who was called from the plough to take the consulship and thankfully returned to it afterwards, but that this society was suspected of a design

[35] Hartz, *The Liberal Tradition in America*; n. 4, above.

to constitute itself as a hereditary aristocracy, there is not much question about the conceptual universe in which the incident occurred. In a similar way, the Second Amendment to the Constitution, apparently drafted to reassure men's minds against the fact that the federal government would maintain something in the nature of a professional army, affirms the relation between a popular militia and popular freedom in language directly descended from that of Machiavelli, which remains a potent ritual utterance in the United States to this day. The new republic feared corruption by a professional army, even while—like England a century before—it saw no alternative to establishing one; and the implications of the rhetoric employed in this context were to be fully worked out in the debates and journalism of the first great conflict between American parties.

Two recent studies[36] have underlined the extent to which Alexander Hamilton appeared to his Republican and Jeffersonian adversaries a figure defined in ominous outline by every tradition in which corruption threatened the republic. He desired to establish a Bank of the United States, and a class of fundholding public creditors who would be directly interested in upholding the government of the republic and the influence of its executive in Congress; and every reader of *Cato's Letters*, Bolingbroke or James Burgh's *Political Disquisitions*—all widely distributed in America—must recognize him as pursuing the tradition of the Junto Whigs, Walpole and George III, which had contributed so powerfully to the belief that Britain was irredeemably corrupt. To the extent—not inconsiderable—to which Hamilton saw government as conducted by a strong executive which could get its way in the legislature, the means he was seen as promoting seemed to make for a reversion to the style of parliamentary monarchy, which all agreed could not get its way without influence, but which Madisonian Federalism—to say nothing of more radically republican schools of thought—had insisted on abandoning as corrupt and unnatural. This was what was meant by the repeated charge that the Federalist party of the nineties desired to restore the English constitution, and the cry that Hamilton's fundholders would in due time become a hereditary aristocracy is simply an index to the American reversion to the style of the Good Old Cause. Lastly, Hamilton's known desire to build up the republic's permanent military strength, and the widespread suspicion that he hoped to head that strength himself, were all that was needed to confirm his critics in their inherited belief that rule by a strong

[36] Gerald Stourzh, *Alexander Hamilton and the Idea of Republican Government* (Stanford University Press, 1970); Lance G. Banning, Ph.D. dissertation, "The Quarrel with Federalism; a study in the origins and character of Republican thought," Washington University, 1972.

executive, wielding influence and supported by a monied interest, led logically to rule, at once corruptive and dictatorial, by a standing army.

This aspect of the Federalist-Republican controversy is therefore to a quite startling extent a replay of the debates of Court and Country as much as a hundred years before. The Jeffersonians spoke the language of the Country and knew that they spoke it; it is less clear that Hamilton consciously repeated the arguments of Defoe or the Walpoleans, a rhetoric never so highly developed in Britain and ill adapted to an American context. But Gerald Stourzh's exploration of Hamilton's thought against the background of republican humanism has left no doubt that he considered himself a "modern Whig" in the context of the neo-Machiavellian contrast between virtuous antiquity and commercial modernity. We have quoted his remark that "Cato was the Tory, Caesar the Whig of his day . . . the former perished with the republic, the latter destroyed it."[37] The tone is clearly one of preference for success over deservingness, *virtù* over virtue; and it was language of this kind which persuaded Jefferson that Hamilton admired Caesar and wished to emulate him. But when Hamilton became convinced of a threat to his own role from Aaron Burr, he denounced Burr as an "embryo Caesar"[38] and a Catiline—a figure one shade darker than Caesar's in the spectrum of republican demonology. Burr was to Hamilton what Hamilton was to Jefferson, and even the sentence about Cato and Caesar was written in the course of a warning against Burr's ambitions; what makes Burr a Catiline rather than a Caesar, it is interesting to note, is that his ambition is devoid of "the love of glory"[39]— *virtus* in a very classical sense indeed. Hamilton's feelings about Caesar, then, are rich in Machiavellian moral ambiguity; but to Machiavelli himself, Caesar had been a thoroughly execrable figure and no hero at all. It is the use of the words "Tory" and "Whig" which gives us the clue to Hamilton's meaning. The connotations are not contemporary, but Augustan; the *imperator* Caesar can be a "Whig" only in the context of Queen Anne's reign, when the Whigs had been the party of war, of Marlborough, and the monied interest. The triumph of Caesar over Cato is the triumph of commerce over virtue, and of empire over republic. It is this historical role which transforms Caesar into an archetype of ambiguous *virtù*.

Stourzh proceeds[40] to show that Hamilton saw America as predestined to become a commercial and military empire, of a sort to which the figure of Caesar was indeed appropriate, but in which his role must be played by "modern Whig" structures of government if it was not to be played by demagogues like Burr. The whole argument

[37] Stourzh, p. 99 and n. 85; p. 239.   [38] Stourzh, p. 98.
[39] Stourzh, pp. 98-102.   [40] Chs. IV and V, *passim*.

is based on the ascendancy of commerce over frugality, empire over virtue; Hamilton can be said to have added a fourth term to the triads of Montesquieu, showing that if virtue is the principle of republics, interest is that of empires, so that a nonclassical federalism is necessary if the republic is to be also an empire. A West Indian turned New Yorker, he saw America as a manufacturing and mercantile economy, trading into the Atlantic in competition with other trading societies, and he placed himself in the company of the great theorists of specialization by affirming—in the tradition of Fletcher of Saltoun—that as societies had become increasingly commercial, they had become increasingly capable of paying soldiers and sailors to defend and extend their trade. It was this process of specialization—rather than any Hobson-Lenin theory of investment—which ensured that competition for trade became a competition for power, empire, and survival; for once military power was committed to the expansion of trade, military power itself must be fought for. Commerce and specialization were the causes of dynamic *virtù*. Government must now become an engine for the protection and expansion of external power; and in the internal relations between citizens, where liberty and justice were its rightful and necessary ends, it could not any longer base itself on the assumption of virtue in the individual citizen, for

> as riches increase and accumulate in few hands; as luxury prevails in society; virtue will be in a greater degree considered as only a graceful appendage of wealth, and the tendency of things will be to depart from the republican standard. This is the real disposition of human nature. . . . It is a common misfortune, that awaits our state constitution as well as all others.[41]

Parliamentary monarchy in Britain, representative democracy in the United States, had alike presented themselves as modes of government appropriate to societies at the commercial stage of development, which was post-virtuous if it was not actually corrupt. Madison, when a colleague of Hamilton's, had helped build up an image of the federal representative structure as one which might go on expanding, with interest being added to interest, and yet never become corrupt. If Madison separated himself passionately from Hamilton within a very few years of constitutional ratification, one reason for his doing so may have been that Hamilton's argument clearly presupposes a higher degree of corruption, and a more brutally open recognition of its existence by government, than Madison thought could possibly be accepted. The central issue came to be Hamilton's banking proposals, which looked unpalata-

[41] Stourzh, p. 71; and generally, pp. 70-75.

bly like a return to parliamentary monarchy in the form denounced by adversaries of Walpole and George III; but Hamilton's stress on empire and military power may well have been an additional cause of Madison's opposition.[42] The passage from virtue to commerce was not, in Hamilton's mind, a serene withdrawal into liberal complacency, into a world where separate interests balanced one another. He was opting for dominion and expansion, not for free trade, and emphatically rejected any argument that the interests of trading nations were peacefully complementary. There would be war, and there must be strong government; and on the other side of the ledger, he suspected that Madison's theory of balancing interests made too little of the dangers of sectional conflict within a union of states.[43] Hamilton's empire was thus a challenge to Madison's federalism, the more so because it was based on the same premise—the movement from virtue to interest—and drew more drastically Machiavellian conclusions. Could the republic shift its base from virtue without becoming in the full sense an empire? Could America be republic and empire at the same time? Hamilton did not answer these questions in the negative; but the terms in which he proposed to construct affirmative answers were unacceptably strong. They were accordingly denounced as corruption.[44]

The Federalist party of the 1790s is not, of course, to be thought of as made up of Hamiltons suspect of Caesarism; far more of its leading members probably saw themselves as Catos rather than Caesars, upholders of the stern unbending virtue of the natural aristocracy. John Adams, whose republicanism has seemed classical to the point of archaism, was of course a Federalist; and John Taylor of Caroline, who had harshly criticized Adams's *Defence* as obsolescent, was a Republican and wrote anti-Hamiltonian polemic in which the ghosts of Swift and Bolingbroke stalk on every page.[45] Nor should the Republicans be thought of as committed to the postclassical liberalism of the Madisonian synthesis. Some of them walked in the footsteps of old-guard Antifederalists like Patrick Henry, whose austere sense of virtue had led them to criticize the Constitution itself as making too many concessions to self-interest and empire;[46] but once again, there were Antifederalists whose concern for virtue carried them into the posture of Catonian Federalism. The ideological spectrum which ran from republic to federal union to empire was like that of debate in Augustan England, which ran from land to trade to credit; there were no fixed partitions, and the same contradictions and perplexities were shared by men at all points. The commitment to virtue, to the Machiavellian moment,

---

[42] Banning, *op.cit.*
[44] Banning, chs. IV-VI.
[46] Stourzh, pp. 128-29; Wood, p. 526.

[43] Stourzh, pp. 158-62.
[45] Banning, pp. 299-311.

had a way of producing this result; it made men aware that they were centaurs.

For many—and the conditions of the early United States left this option open to many—the solution was to admit that they were centaurs, and immerse themselves in the caucusing and brokerage of professional politics.[47] But given the premise that American values were those of men engaged in the search for virtue under conditions admitted to be partly unfavorable, it is interesting to have Tuveson's opinion that Federalists were more likely than Republicans to adopt the perspective of millennialist apocalyptic as one in which the triumph of American virtue might be envisaged.[48] We have grown used to finding that virtue sometimes demands a millennium in which to behold itself as affirmed and justified by grace; but on the face of it, the Republicans should be the party of virtue, the Federalists that of *virtù*. If we suppose, however, that Federalists included men who believed that in them natural aristocracy was making its last stand, as well as men who believed that "the real disposition of human nature" was toward luxury and empire, we shall have defined them as the party which saw virtue as exposed to the greatest threats and pressures, and it will be the less surprising—since this was, after all, an American party—to find millennialists as well as Machiavellians in its ranks. The Jeffersonian persuasion, as we shall next see, had its own ways of affirming the durability of virtue.

The passage just quoted, in which Hamilton affirms that "the real disposition of human nature" is "to depart from the republican standard," must of course be set beside some even more striking and far more fully discussed writings of Thomas Jefferson. Students of American agrarianism have many times explored the meaning, and the ultimate ambiguities, of:

> Those who labour in the earth are the chosen people of God, if ever he had a chosen people, whose breasts he has made his peculiar deposit for substantial and genuine virtue. It is the focus in which he keeps alive that sacred fire, which otherwise might escape from the face of the earth. Corruption of morals in the mass of cultivators is a phaenomenon of which no age nor nation has furnished an example. It is the mark set on those who, not looking up to heaven, to their own soil and industry, as does the husbandman, for their subsistence, depend for it on the casualties and caprice of customers. Dependence begets subservience and venality, suffocates the germ

[47] Chambers, *op.cit.*, studies this development. See also David Hackett Fischer, *The Revolution of American Conservatism: The Federalist Party in the Age of Jeffersonian Democracy* (New York: Harper and Row, 1965).

[48] Tuveson, *Redeemer Nation*, p. 120.

of virtue, and prepares fit tools for the designs of ambition. This, the natural progress and consequence of the arts, has sometimes perhaps been retarded by accidental circumstance: but, generally speaking, the proportion which the aggregate of the other classes of citizens bears in any state to that of its husbandmen is the proportion of its unsound to its healthy parts, and is a good-enough barometer whereby to measure its degree of corruption. . . . The mobs of great cities add just so much to the support of pure government, as sores do to the strength of the human body. It is the manners and spirit of a people which preserve a republic in vigour. A degeneracy in these is a canker which soon eats to the heart of its constitution.[49]

"The natural progress and consequence of the arts . . . sometimes . . . retarded by accidental circumstance." Jefferson is placing himself, and America, at a Rousseauan moment; man can avoid neither becoming civilized nor being corrupted by the process; but the language further reveals that the process is political and the moment Machiavellian. There is even a glimpse of the continuity of commerce and *fortuna*; the words "casualties and caprice" might without much distortion be replaced by "fortune and fantasy"; but it is typical of the eighteenth-century debate that "manners," which had once, in the form of custom and tradition, served to retard the wheel of fortune, have now become progressive and corrupting. We also know by this time in what shapes corruption may be expected to occur. Dependent, subversive, and venal men in a commercial society are "fit tools for the designs," not only of classical demagogues like Burr, but also of architects of military-financial empire like Hamilton. Jefferson wrote this passage in 1785, but it prefigures the rhetoric of the next decade. He was, then, as committed as any classical republican to the ideal of virtue, but saw the preconditions of virtue as agrarian rather than natural; he was not a Cato, seeing the relation of natural aristocracy to natural democracy as the thing essential—unless this thought was in his mind as founder of the University of Virginia—so much as a Tiberius Gracchus, seeing the preservation of a yeoman commonwealth as the secret of virtue's maintenance. At the same time, we see, he doubted whether agrarian virtue could be preserved forever; but neither his faith nor his doubts separate him from the tradition of classical politics, or from the new liberalism of Madisonian Federalism.

A clue to this paradox is found when we note that Noah Webster,

[49] Jefferson, *Notes on the State of Virginia*, "Query XIX"; quoted and discussed at length in Leo Marx, *The Machine in the Garden: Technology and the Pastoral Ideal in America* (New York: Oxford University Press, 1964, repr. 1970), pp. 124-25 and 116-44.

cited by Wood as affirming that the republic was no longer directly based on the virtue of the individual, wrote as follows:

> The system of the great Montesquieu will ever be erroneous, till the words *property or lands in fee simple* are substituted for *virtue*, throughout his *Spirit of Laws*.
>
> *Virtue*, patriotism, or love of country, never was and never will be, till men's natures are changed, a fixed, permanent principle and support of government. But in an agricultural country, a general possession of land in fee simple may be rendered perpetual, and the inequalities introduced by commerce are too fluctuating to endanger government. An equality of property, with a necessity of alienation, constantly operating to destroy combinations of powerful families, is the very *soul of a republic*.[50]

Webster was reverting to a directly Harringtonian position and arguing that a material foundation was necessary to ensure virtue and equality, that freehold land was a more stable foundation than commerce, but that a predominantly agrarian society could absorb commerce without essential loss of virtue. If he indeed recognized that the Constitution rested upon a foundation other than virtue, that will have seemed to him a concession to the nonagrarian elements in the American system, a compromise in fact with commerce; but America could still remain a society rather agricultural than commercial. This, however, would shift emphasis away from the Constitution itself. The institutions of virtue would now lie, not in the political *ordini* where classical theory would have seen the legislative intellect at work, but in the agrarian laws—or rather, as we shall see, in the unlegislated social forces and human energies—which secured the perpetuation of freehold equality. We are on the verge of a theory in which frontier, not constitution, is the "soul of the republic," unless the latter can be restored to centrality as the perfect resolution of the kinetic struggle between commerce and virtue.

Henry Nash Smith[51] has isolated the phrase "the fee-simple empire," as emblematic of the geopolitical and millennialist rhetoric of the farming West which was rife in nineteenth-century America; and, with its echoes of what Webster had to say in 1787, the phrase may explain for us why a purely agrarian republic had to be a commonwealth for expansion. The Revolutionary generation had made profession of virtue

[50] Quoted by Stourzh, p. 230, n. 104.

[51] *Virgin Land: The American West as Symbol and Myth* (New York: Vintage Books, n.d., repr. of 1950 ed., Cambridge, Mass.: Harvard University Press), ch. XII.

and committed their republic to the escape from corruption, yet had not fully detached it from that universe of interest and faction which was taken to be the sign of the corruption that commerce engendered. Harrington, as Webster seems to have recalled, had laid it down that commerce did not corrupt so long as it did not overbalance land; but since his day, commerce had become recognized as a dynamic principle, progressive and at the same time corrupting. A republic which desired to reconcile virtue with commerce must be equally dynamic and expansive in the search for land. "The growth of Oceana" could "give laws to the sea," and escape the fates of both Venice and Rome, only if the sea led to empty or depopulated lands for settlement; but in America the oceanic crossing had been made, and the land awaited occupation by simple popular expansion. Daniel Boone need not be Lycurgus or Romulus and make laws, and part of the hatred later felt for Mormons probably arose because their prophets insisted on being legislators. An infinite supply of land, ready for occupation by an armed and self-directing yeomanry, meant an infinite supply of virtue, and it could even be argued that no agrarian law was necessary; the safety valve was open, and all pressures making for dependence and corruption would right themselves.

In these conditions virtue might seem to be self-guaranteeing, and the kind of intelligence displayed by the legislator as demiurge superfluous. A romanticization of popular energies, akin to the romanticism which Wood detects in Madisonian liberalism, makes its appearance in frontier rhetoric; but, following the paradigms laid down by Machiavelli, virtue in this sense must be as dynamic as popular *virtù*. A dynamism of virtue was being invoked to counter and contain the dynamism of commerce, and must partake of the latter's passionate and fantastic qualities. The primitive and half-comic heroes of frontier legend, however, were insufficiently political to embody virtue in its republican form—Davy Crockett was not imaginable as the congressman he was in real life—and the myth found its personification in Andrew Jackson.[52] Frontier warrior turned patriot statesman, successful adversary of the second attempt to charter the United States Bank, the Jackson of legend has a good claim to be considered the last of the Machiavellian Romans and the warlike, expanding, agrarian democracy he symbolized a Fourth Rome, perpetuating republican *virtus* as the Third Rome of Moscow perpetuated sacred empire.

Jefferson is recorded as commenting on the ill-conceived War of 1812:

[52] John William Ward, *Andrew Jackson: Symbol for an Age* (New York: Oxford University Press, 1955); see also Marx, *op.cit.*, pp. 219-20.

Our enemy has indeed the consolation of Satan on removing our first parents from Paradise: from a peaceable and agricultural nation, he makes us a military and manufacturing one.[53]

But after that rather meaningless conflict had been officially brought to a settlement, it was suddenly escalated into the domain of myth, and transformed from a corrupting and progressive war into a virtuous and archaic one, by the crowning mercy of the Battle of New Orleans, in which frontier riflemen, the legendary "Hunters of Kentucky," in the role of rustic citizen warriors, were supposed to have triumphed over the veterans of a great professional army. John William Ward, in his study of the Jackson myth which grew up over the next two decades, brings out clearly how much of it was based on allusion to the heroes of early Rome—familiar figures of every schoolbook and patriotic oration—and on the traditional contrast between virtuous militia and corrupt standing army. At the same time that Clausewitz was formulating a great idealist theory of war as the instrument of the democratic and bureaucratic state, Americans were propounding a view of it which was civic and archaic, Machiavellian and at the same moment romantic. Ward further shows how significant were the elements of primitivism and dynamism—of democratic anti-intellectualism—which the myth contained. A mysterious and incalculable force was supposed to have flashed from the warriors of Kentucky and confounded the mere skill, experience, and reliance on material power—what Cromwell might have called the mere "carnal reason"—of their foes at New Orleans; and it was much insisted on that this spirit was that of patriotism, and that patriotism was a spirit. Ward rightly stresses that romanticism of this sort is part of an ethos of egalitarianism; the force which places natural and popular energy on a par with training, experience, and intellect must be of the order of spirit as opposed to reason. But at the same time there is an unmistakable kinship with the dynamic and military *virtù* of the Machiavellian *popolo*. The spirit animating the riflemen, when seen as embodied in the person of Jackson himself, is many times termed virtue; but when Jackson is regularly praised as a general who won victories without attending to the formalities of international law, a president who made laws and decisions without attending to constitutional niceties, it is clear that we are dealing with a leader of *virtù* in a highly Machiavellian sense. "Jackson made law," remarked an admirer; "Adams quoted it." He was commenting on a reputed outburst by the hero which ran: "Damn Grotius! damn Pufendorf! damn Vattel! This is a mere matter between Jim Monroe and

[53] Quoted by Marx, p. 144.

536

myself!"[54] Or again: "John Marshall has made his decision; let him enforce it."

Machiavelli might indeed have been appreciative; but he might also have pointed out that this sort of impetuosity was proper in a legislator founding a republic, or a prince operating where there was none, but in a magistrate supposed to uphold the public authority could prove extremely corrupting. Given that classical history was still every man's textbook of politics, one can see that Jackson's adversaries had reason to dread in him the military adventurer turned tyrant, and one may even feel that his virtue must have been real to withstand so much intoxicating praise of its superhuman qualities; he must have been a Furius Camillus, since he did not become a Manlius Capitolinus. But it is anomalous in Machiavellian terms that a republic should have generated, and benefited from, an almost anarchic hero such as this, when it was not new or declining, but in its second generation of normal functioning. A contemporary explanation, of which Ward rightly makes much, was that the Constitution, being founded on the principles of nature, had released the energies of man as he naturally was; Jackson was nature's child, and the republic of the wilderness had nothing to fear from him.[55] Ward, however, draws the orthodox conclusion that the American myth was one of Lockean primitivism—the revolt of nature against history, which is to say against the traditions, conventions, and intellectualisms of an Old World. Expressions of this view were and are exceedingly common; we are concerned, however, to ask whether this escape into nature is to be properly understood outside the complexities and ambiguities of virtue.

Jackson's America was also the America observed by Tocqueville. While the aggressive *virtù* of agrarian warriors throve on the frontiers, there was visible further east the culmination of that popular revolt against the natural aristocracies which we have learned to call the "decline of virtue" and the "end of classical politics"; and we may ask if there was any relation between the two. Tocqueville charted the transition from equality in its Machiavellian or Montesquieuan sense—*isonomia* or equality of subjection to the *res publica*—which had been part of the ideal of virtue, to that *égalité des conditions* which he saw as marking the triumph of democracy in its modern sense, superseding the values of the classical republic. He went altogether beyond the simply republican fear that a Jackson might turn out a Manlius or a Caesar, and pointed out that the real danger of tyranny in the post-virtuous society lay in the dictatorship of majority opinion. When men had been differentiated and had expressed their virtue in the act of

[54] Ward, p. 63. [55] Ward, pp. 30-45.

deferring to one another's virtues, the individual had known himself through the respect shown by his fellows for the qualities publicly recognized in him; but once men were, or it was held that they ought to be, all alike, his only means of self-discovery lay in conforming to everybody else's notions of what he ought to be and was. This produced a despotism of opinion, since nothing but diffused general opinion now defined the ego or its standards of judgment. Madison had feared that the individual might lose all sense of his own significance;[56] and Tocqueville could have observed that Tom Paine, after escaping the English law of treason and the French reign of terror, had been destroyed by the disapproval of his American neighbors.

This critique of *égalité des conditions* is basically Aristotelian: it is pointed out in the *Politics* that when men are treated as all alike, we fail to take account of them in those respects in which they are not alike; and it could have been pointed out further that a society in which every man is subservient to every other man, because dependent on him for any means of judging his own existence, is corrupt within the accepted meaning of the word, in a very special way and to a very high degree. The cult of Jacksonian will and natural energy may turn out to be part of this society, because *virtù* in the romantic sense is a means of undermining the virtue of the natural aristocracies; but it is a characteristic of the Tocquevillian world that false images of men are very easy to produce and exchange, since men have nothing to live by except each other's images. Here it would be proper to reflect that the myths of Jackson and the other frontier heroes were in part consciously manufactured by not invisible image-makers; that Jackson was a planter and not a frontiersman, who won his victory at New Orleans by artillery and not rifle fire; that if he successfully presented himself as hero and Adams as intellectual in 1828, his image met its ape in 1840, when the Whigs succeeded in manufacturing a hero of their own in Harrison, who signalized his essentially unreal character by catching cold at his own inauguration and dying in a month. It was a severe display of the ironies of history, though his admirers might have reflected that Andrew Jackson was not mocked; and it raises once again the question whether the moment of nature is not a means of escape from a conflict between virtue and corruption, felt as inherent in America since its beginnings.

Let us resume exegesis of the text cited from Jefferson's *Notes on Virginia*. Commerce—the progress of the arts—corrupts the virtue of agrarian man; but, Webster had added and Jefferson had agreed, an agrarian society can absorb commerce, and an expanding agrarian

[56] Wood, p. 612.

society can absorb an expanding commerce. America is the world's garden; there is an all but infinite reservoir of free land, and expansion to fill it is the all but infinite expansion of virtue. The rhetoric of Smith's *Virgin Land*, filling the century after Jefferson and Webster, is the rhetoric of this expansion of arms-bearing and liberty-loving husbandmen; the rhetoric, it may be added, of Berkeley's "westward course," helping to explain the archetypal status assumed by that poem in American thought. The justification of frontier expansion is thus Machiavellian, and in the myth of Jackson it is seen to entail a Machiavellian *virtù* which will extend virtue without corrupting it—a process possible in the fee-simple empire. The serpent has entered Eden—once more necessitating *virtù*—in the sense that commerce has formed part of the American scene since before the republic began. But on the premise that expanding land is uncorrupted by expanding commerce, the latter can add its dynamic and progressive qualities to the dynamic expansiveness of agrarian *virtù*, and be seen as contributory to the image of a farmer's empire, at once progressive and pastoral. The synthesis of virtue and *virtù*, achieved by Polybius and Machiavelli in their more sanguine moments, is recreated in the Jeffersonian-Jacksonian tradition at a far higher level of sociological complexity and hence of optimism. The extent to which the Constitution entailed an abandonment of virtue is more than compensated for by the *virtù* of the frontier.

The rhetoric of the yeoman—America as the new Gothic empire—has always room in it for the rhetoric of the steam-engine; we may recall the "march of mind" and the "Steam Intellect Society" satirized by Thomas Love Peacock in contemporary Britain. Since frontier and industry, land and commerce, are both expansive forces, they can both be described in terms of passion and dynamism: the patriotic *virtù* of the warrior yeoman for the former, the passionate and restless pursuit of interest for the latter. So long as the partnership of expansion lasts, the plunge into nature can be described simultaneously in pastoral and industrial terms; for what the American is in search of is not the nature to be contemplated in Arcadian scenery—though this option is never finally closed off—but his own nature as a man, which is civic, military, commercial, and in a word active. If he invokes Lockean paradigms at this point, it is the complex history of the *vita activa* which has defined this as the point at which to do so.[57]

The wilderness, furthermore, is matter to be shaped into form; his nature as yeoman, warrior, and citizen is not fulfilled until after he has formed it. The intention of the frontiersman is ideally to become a

---

[57] Marx, *op.cit.*, *passim*, is an excellent statement of this theme.

yeoman, although this is one point at which a romantic tension is possible; and the intimation we found in Jefferson that virtue is possible only at a Rousseauan moment in the progress of civilization is carried further in the numerous panoramas—pictorial and verbal—at which the agrarian and civic ideal is presented as occupying a "middle landscape" between the extremes of wilderness savagery and metropolitan corruption.[58] The image of the polis is therefore always in part Arcadian, though in markedly lesser part contemplative. A further corollary is that since the moving frontier is at any moment an intermediate zone between savagery and virtue, there is always the problem of those whose *virtù* impels them to go beyond it, preferring unshaped matter to shaped form, potentiality to actuality, until their own natures are left incomplete and may degenerate. Fenimore Cooper depicted the aging Leatherstocking in such a dilemma, hesitant between the worlds of the hunter and the farmer, natural virtue and settled law;[59] and Burke must have had something of the sort in mind when he imagined settlers beyond the Appalachians degenerating into a nomad cavalry and raiding the farming frontier.[60] Experience on the ground, besides, provided as early as Crevecoeur's *Letters*[61] occasion for seeing the frontier squatter as an ignoble savage, squalidly degenerate rather than barbarously natural; the poor white began his career in the conceptual context of eighteenth-century sociology.

But these problems appeared ideally only as offering reasons why the frontier should not cease to expand. So long as the settlement of new land was possible, the partnership between agrarian virtue and commercial industry could be maintained and could perpetuate the illusion that the American "new man" had reentered Eden. The national apocalyptic could be affirmed at this primary level of optimism. There remained, however, the problem prophetically discerned by Berkeley: that of the closed and cyclical nature of world history. America must be the fifth and last act in the *translatio imperii*, because once the "westward course" was complete it was not conceivable in merely agrarian terms that it should begin again. The quest for agrarian virtue was the quest for a static utopia, imaginable only as a *rinnovazione*, a renewal of virtue for those who could find lands on which to renew it. In these terms, Machiavelli had been prophetically (but not Christianly) right: the amount of virtue there could be in the world at any one time was finite, and when it was used up there must be catastrophe before

---

[58] The "middle landscape" is discussed by Marx, pp. 121-22 and *passim*.

[59] Smith, *Virgin Land*, pp. 64-76.

[60] Burke, *Works*, II, 131-32; Smith, pp. 201-208.

[61] Hector St. John de Crevecoeur, *Letters from an American Farmer*, Everyman's Library edition (London: J. M. Dent, 1912-62), pp. 46-47, 51-55.

renewal—a Stoic conflagration rather than a Christian apocalypse. If the Republicans were, as Tuveson suggests, less millennially minded than the Federalists, this could have been because, with Jefferson, they hoped for an almost infinite renewal of virtue in the fee-simple empire; but beyond this expanding utopia could be discerned only a Machiavellian, not a Christian eschatology.• And the end of utopia must be reached. There are passages in Jefferson's writings where he admits that sooner or later the reservoir of land must be exhausted and the expansion of virtue will no longer keep ahead of the progress of commerce.[62] When that point is reached, the process of corruption must be resumed; men will become dependent upon each other in a market economy and dependent on government in great cities. The serpent will have overtaken Adam and Eve, and the dark forces symbolized by Hamilton and Burr, or the more subtle processes described by Tocqueville, will be unchecked by the expansion of husbandry. When manners are corrupt, not even the Constitution can be counted upon. Even in America, the republic faces the problem of its own ultimate finitude, and that of its virtue, in space and time.

There is thus a dimension of historical pessimism in American thought at its most utopian, which stems from the confrontation of virtue and commerce and threatens to reduce all American history to a Machiavellian or Rousseauan moment.[63] It is because Jefferson's husbandmen, when all is said and done, occupy only a moment in the dialectic of progress and corruption that he has no alternative to describing them as the "chosen people" and "peculiar deposit" of God. They are not, after all, guaranteed by nature, and their moment of virtue can be prolonged and sustained only by grace or providence. Jefferson was capable of appealing to providence, but not to millennial prophecy; both his deism and his agrarianism assured that; for civic virtue, as we have repeatedly seen, while occasionally requiring an apocalyptic framework for its self-assertion, has an equally strong tendency to substitute its own moment for any but an immediately expected millennium. It is therefore of interest to take up Tuveson's generalization concerning the association between millennialism and the Federalists. On the one hand, this may have obtained because Federalists, regarding the decline of virtue with Catonian severity, saw men as subject to greater temptations and fewer secular guarantees, and therefore as standing in greater need of grace, than did those of Jefferson's persuasion; but on the other, Tuveson significantly stresses the prominence accorded to Commerce in the millennial poetry of the

---

[62] Smith, pp. 241-44.
[63] Cf. *Politics, Language and Time,* pp. 100-105.

Federalist Timothy Dwight.[64] Commerce is the dynamic power, the *virtù*, which ensures that nature will not sustain the agrarian utopia forever and that the aid of grace must be invoked; but given the partnership of virtue and commerce in westward expansion, it can also be a means of thrusting toward the millennium which grace will afford and taking it by storm. There was even a mood in which it was seen as breaking out of the reservoir of western land, overcoming its finitude, transcending the closed cycle of virtue, and attaining a truly American millennium.

Among the constants in the literature of American mythology brought to light by Henry Nash Smith is the repetition of prophecies that the fee-simple empire would not only perpetuate the virtue of a farming yeomanry, but generate a commerce designed to exceed continental limits and, by opening up the markets of Asia, bring about the liberation of the most ancient of human societies.[65] "There is the east; there is India," declared Thomas Hart Benton, pointing due west before an audience in St. Louis,[66] and the enlightenment of Japan and China through commerce was foretold more frequently still. It was in the context of the fee-simple union of virtue and commerce that America's global role was prophesied; and the global role, it was maintained, would assure the perpetuation of that union even after the Pacific shores had been reached. The liberation of Asia (Whitman's "venerable priestly Asia"), furthermore, is part of the vision of America as "redeemer nation"; and the reason is plainly that it would break the closed circle in which Berkeley had confined America and would transform the closing fifth act of his *translatio* into a truly millennial Fifth Monarchy. "In the beginning," Locke had written—inadvertently earning his place as a prophet of the new apocalypse—"all the world was America";[67] and if in the end all the world should be America again, the mission of a chosen people would have been fulfilled. Virtue and commerce, liberty and culture, republic and history would have rendered their partnership perpetual by the only possible means—that of engaging all mankind perpetually in it; and in so doing would have attained to that blend of millennium and utopia which was the outcome of the early modern secularization of biblical prophecy.

[64] Tuveson, *Redeemer Nation*, pp. 103-12.

[65] Smith, Book I, "Passage to India," pp. 16-53.

[66] William N. Chambers, *Old Bullion Benton: Senator from the New West* (Boston: Little, Brown and Company, 1956), p. 353. Strictly speaking, Benton imagined a statue of Columbus pointing west, but we may feel sure that he pointed too. It is a historical irony that a statue of him in the act was erected in a part of St. Louis which urban decay has made somewhat rarely visited. See also Smith, pp. 23-35.

[67] Locke, *Two Treatises of Government*, II, 49.

●

The American apocalypse is not inherently more absurd than those entertained in other cultures, which present themselves as embodying the last stage of some unified scheme of human history and as about to attain utopia through the working out of that scheme's final dialectic. But because the movement of American history has been spatial rather than dialectical, its apocalypse has been early modern rather than historicist; it has been envisaged in the form of a movement out of history, followed by a regenerative return to it, so that there have been perpetuated in American thinking those patterns of messianic and cyclical thought with which this book has been concerned. For if the liberation of Asia should not come about, the partnership of virtue and commerce would have failed and the cycle of history would be closed again. The chosen people would be imprisoned in time for lack of a theater for further expansion and the pursuing forces of commerce would once more turn corruptive, imposing upon them the imperial government desired by Hamilton in the eighteenth century and described as the "military-industrial complex" by Eisenhower in the twentieth, or the condition of universal dependence feared by Jefferson and analyzed by Tocqueville. When the chosen people failed of their mission, they were by definition apostate, and the jeremiad note so recurrent in American history would be sounded again. It would call for the internal cleansing and regeneration of the "city on a hill," since the politics of sectarian withdrawal and communal renewal form a standing alternative to those of millennial leadership; "come out of her, my people" might be heard again in the form of George McGovern's "come home, America"; but there would simultaneously be heard a variety of neo-Machiavellian voices offering counsel on the proper blend of prudence and audacity to display in a world where virtue was indeed finite. The fate of Rome began to be invoked by the anti-imperialists of 1898, and has been invoked since.

The twentieth-century intellect distrusts metahistory for many reasons, nearly all of them good, but American culture has been sufficiently pervaded by metahistorical ways of thinking to make the ability to reconstruct eschatological scenarios a useful tool in interpreting it. We can see, in the light of the scheme provided here, why it was necessary, both at the beginnings of the Jeffersonian perspective and as it took further shape, to reject Alexander Hamilton as a false prophet and even a kind of Antichrist; he looked east, not west,[68] saw America as commercial empire rather than agrarian republic, and proclaimed that corruption was inescapable, that the cycle was closed and the end

---

[68] He spoke of Canada as on "our left," Florida on "our right" (Stourzh, p. 195). See also Felix Gilbert, *To the Farewell Address: Ideas of Early American Foreign Policy* (Princeton University Press, 1961, 1970).

had come, before the covenant was fairly sealed or the experiment in escaping corruption had begun. We can further see why it was that Frederick Jackson Turner adopted the tones of an American Isaiah when proclaiming the closing of the frontier in 1890; one phase in the prophetic scheme, one revolution of the wheel in the struggle between virtue and corruption, was drawing to an end. It is also intelligible that there is now an interpretation of American history since that era, which proposes that after 1890 the choice lay between internal reformation on the one hand and oceanic empire on the other, leading to the liberation of Asia by trade through an Open Door;[69] and that the apparent rejection of America by Asia in the third quarter of the twentieth century is seen as leading to a profound crisis in self-perception, in which the hope of renewed innocence and recovered virtue is felt (once again) to have gone forever and the national jeremiad is sounded in peculiarly anguished terms. The Machiavellian note is audible when Americans reproach themselves, as they have at intervals since at latest 1898, with exercising the "tyranny of a free people" and imposing the empire of virtue on those who are not to receive full citizenship within it.[70] But it is also significant that the jeremiad has at times taken the form of a quarrel with the Constitution itself, and more recently of a quarrel with a "Lockean consensus," a politics of pragmatic adjustment and a political science of the empirical study of behavior, all of which are seen—however exaggeratedly—as underlying the edifice of the republic since its beginnings and as contributing to that state of affairs which it is the object of the jeremiad to denounce as corruption. The tensions between political practice and the values to which it must answer sometimes grow so great that Americans lose that delight in both the practice and the contemplation of politics in the Madisonian manner which normally characterizes them. The language of practice has not been republican in the classical sense, but the language of myth and metahistory has ensured the repetition of dilemmas first perceived in the eighteenth century; and what is often stated as a quarrel with

[69] E.g., Max Silberschmidt, *The United States and Europe: Rivals and Partners* (New York: Harcourt Brace Jovanovich, 1972). Is it worth remarking that the "open door" of China policy in the West recalls words on the plinth of the Statue of Liberty in the East?

[70] See, for example, William Graham Sumner in 1896: "Our system is unfit for the government of subject provinces. They have no place in it. They would become seats of corruption, which would react on our own body politic. If we admitted the island [Cuba] as a state or a group of states, we should have to let it help govern us." Cited in Lloyd C. Gardner (ed.), *A Different Frontier: selected readings in the foundations of American economic expansion* (Chicago: Quadrangle Books, 1966), p. 87. Also Robert L. Beisner, *Twelve Against Empire: the Anti-Imperialists, 1898-1900* (New York: McGraw Hill, 1968).

Locke is in reality a quarrel with Madison's solution to these dilemmas. American political scientists currently see themselves as passing through a "post-behavioral revolution,"[71] but much of the language of that movement is recognizable as the language of jeremiad; and a post-jeremiad revolution in the field of ideology would in some respects be more drastic still. It would signal the end of the Machiavellian moment in America—the end, that is, of the quarrel with history in its distinctively American form. But what would succeed that perspective is hard to imagine—the indications of the present point inconclusively toward various kinds of conservative anarchism—and its end does not seem to have arrived.

[IV]

It is notorious that American culture is haunted by myths, many of which arise out of the attempt to escape history and then regenerate it. The conventional wisdom among scholars who have studied their growth has been that the Puritan covenant was reborn in the Lockean contract, so that Locke himself has been elevated to the station of a patron saint of American values and the quarrel with history has been seen in terms of a constant attempt to escape into the wilderness and repeat a Lockean experiment in the foundation of a natural society.[72] The interpretation put forward here stresses Machiavelli at the expense of Locke; it suggests that the republic—a concept derived from Renaissance humanism—was the true heir of the covenant and the dread of corruption the true heir of the jeremiad. It suggests that the foundation of independent America was seen, and stated, as taking place at a Machiavellian—even a Rousseauan—moment, at which the fragility of the experiment, and the ambiguity of the republic's position in secular time, was more vividly appreciated than it could have been from a Lockean perspective.

The foundation of the republic, this interpretation suggests, was not seen in terms of a simple return to nature—Crevecoeur to the contrary notwithstanding—but as constituting an ambivalent and contradictory moment within a dialectic of virtue and corruption, familiar to most

71 David C. Easton, "The New Revolution in Political Science" (presidential address to the American Political Science Association), *American Political Science Review* 73, no. 4 (1969), 1051-61. See also Graham and Carey (eds.), *The Post-Behavioral Era: Perspectives on Political Science* (New York: David McKay, 1972).

72 David W. Noble, *Historians Against History: The Frontier Thesis and the National Covenant in American Historical Writing since 1830* (Minneapolis: University of Minnesota Press, 1965).

sophisticated minds of the eighteenth century. There was indeed a flight from history into nature, conceived by many Americans of the revolutionary and early national periods—and with less excuse by a succession of historians lasting to this day—in terms of a flight from the Old World, from the burden of a priestly and feudal past (Adams's "canon and feudal laws"); but the analysis of corruption makes it clear that what was involved was a flight from modernity and a future no less than from antiquity and a past, from commercial and Whiggish Britain—the most aggressively "modern" society of the mid-eighteenth century—no less than from feudal and popish Europe; just as the nature into which Americans precipitated themselves was not simply a Puritan, Lockean, or Arcadian wilderness, but that *vita activa* in which the *zōon politikon* fulfilled his nature, but which since Machiavelli had grown steadily harder to reconcile with existence in secular time. Because the neo-Harringtonian version of the Machiavellian moment was one from which superstition, vassalage, and paper-money speculation could be beheld and condemned at a single glance, the old and new versions of corruption could be telescoped into one; and because the American republic could be seen in terms of *rinnovazione* in a New World, it was natural to see the departure from corruption as a single gesture of departure from a past—which encouraged the illusion that it led toward a nature which was unhistorical because its future was unproblematical. But this entailed much distortion of history, surviving in the determination of American historians writing in this vein, even today, to equate Britain with Europe and the Whig empire with the *ancien régime*.[73] The dialectic of virtue and commerce was a quarrel with modernity, most fully articulated—at least until the advent of Rousseau—within the humanist and neo-Harringtonian vocabularies employed by the English-speaking cultures of the North Atlantic; and it was in those vocabularies and within the ambivalences of those cultures that American self-consciousness originated and acquired its terminology.

The civil war and revolution which disrupted the English-speaking Atlantic after 1774 can be seen as involving a continuation, larger and more irreconcilable, of that Augustan debate which accompanied the Financial Revolution in England and Scotland after 1688 and issued after 1714 in the parliamentary oligarchy of Great Britain. The fear of encroaching corruption helped drive the Americans to the renewal of virtue in a republic and the rejection of the parliamentary monarchy from which, all agreed, some measure of corruption was inseparable; and the confrontation of virtue with corruption constitutes the Machia-

---

[73] Hartz, *op.cit.*, regrettably *passim*, and R. R. Palmer, *The Age of the Democratic Revolution*, vol. 1 (Princeton University Press, 1959), chs. 2, 3, 6, 10.

vellian moment. Britain, on the other hand, adhered to the course marked out by all but the radical dissentients within the Whig tradition. Under the North, Rockingham, and Shelburne ministries, the political classes were in no doubt that parliamentary monarchy was a form of government to be retained; the issue was whether, in order to retain it, the better course was to fight the colonies or let them go.[74] Loud and threatening though the Country voices were in the crisis of 1780-1781,[75] the Court thesis concerning the character of British government was not in real jeopardy. Unlike the Americans, dominated by neo-Harringtonian conceptual structures, the British, inured by the Court ideology to seeing themselves as less committed to the profession of virtue, attempted no revolutionary *rinnovazione*, did not see the loss of an empire as pointing to irretrievable decline, and were able within a few years to embark on another long period of European war, military professionalism, and inflationary banking. If the younger Pitt resembles Hamilton, there is no British Jefferson. Democratization, when it came, arrived by the medieval technique of expanding the king-in-parliament to include new categories of counselors and representatives.

American independence was therefore followed by a fairly rapid divergence of the political languages spoken in the two principal cultures of the now sundered Atlantic. Christopher Wyvill, Richard Price, and John Cartwright, it is true, employed a vocabulary of corruption and renovation little different from that of their American contemporaries,[76] and "Old Corruption" continued to be the target of radical reformers until perhaps the days of the Chartists. But Jeremy Bentham's *Fragment on Government*—conceived, as its assault on Blackstone shows, as a radical rejection of the language of Court and Country alike—was written, as was the Declaration of Independence, in the year when *The Wealth of Nations* was first published and Hume died; and by 1780 Edmund Burke had perceived that eighteenth-century thought about manners and customs could be restated in the seventeenth-century language of prescriptive antiquity and the Ancient Constitution, and used to attack the notion of Machiavellian *ridurre*,

[74] The most trenchant statements of the latter view came from Josiah Tucker; see his *Four Tracts on Political and Commercial Subjects* (1774), *A Letter to Edmund Burke, Esq.* (1775), *The True Interest of Britain* (1776), *A Treatise Concerning Civil Government* (1781).

[75] H. Butterfield, *George III, Lord North and the People, 1779-80* (London: G. Bell, 1949).

[76] Ian R. Christie, *Wilkes, Wyvill and Reform: The Parliamentary Movement in British Politics, 1760-1785* (New York: St. Martin's Press, 1962) and *Myth and Reality in Late Eighteenth-Century British Politics* (Berkeley: University of California Press, 1970); F. D. Cartwright, *The Life and Correspondence of Major Cartwright* (London, 1826).

as later that of the Rights of Man.[77] Prescriptive conservatism and radical utilitarianism—whose antecedents are Court more than they are Country—could both be employed to diminish the influence of the Crown; but both were as far as they could be from the ideal of republican virtue perpetuated by the Americans.

A history could therefore be written—though it cannot be attempted here—of how British thought diverged from American, and from Augustan neoclassicism, in the half-century following the American Revolution. An ironic feature of such a history would surely be the high degree of success with which Victorian parliamentary legislation set about eliminating that corruption and its image which had been to all men, and to Americans remained, such an obsession. In this respect the British could and did feel well rewarded for their adherence, at the price of a disrupted Atlantic and an Anglo-Irish union, to the paradigm of parliamentary sovereignty over that of republican balance; the Americans, having made the republican commitment to the renovation of virtue, remained obsessively concerned by the threat of corruption—with, it must be added, good and increasing reason. Their political drama continues, in ways both crude and subtle, to endorse the judgment of Polybius, Guicciardini, Machiavelli, and Montesquieu in identifying corruption as the disease peculiar to republics: one not to be cured by virtue alone. In the melodrama of 1973, the venality of an Agnew makes this point in one way; an Ehrlichman's more complex and disinterested misunderstanding of the relation between the reality and the morality of power makes it in another.

The Americans, then, inherited rhetorical and conceptual structures which ensured that venality in public officials, the growth of a military-industrial complex in government, other-directedness and one-dimensionality in individuals, could all be identified in terms continuous with those used in the classical analysis of corruption, the successive civic-humanist denunciations of Caesar and Lorenzo de' Medici, Marlborough, Walpole, and Hamilton. This language remains in many ways well suited to the purposes for which it is used; the case against the modern hypertrophy of Madisonian adjustive politics can be, and is, admirably made in terms of the Guicciardinian paradigm of corruption; but the historian notes that it serves at the same time to perpetuate the singular persistence of early modern values and assumptions in American culture. While the cult of Spartan and Roman antiquity among French revolutionaries was helping to generate the vision of a despotism of virtue through terror,[78] while German idealism was restat-

---

[77] See *Politics, Language and Time*, ch. 6, "Burke and the Ancient Constitution: A Problem in the History of Ideas."

[78] Harold T. Parker, *The Cult of Antiquity and the French Revolutionaries: A*

ing the quarrel between value and history in terms of a vision of reason as the working out of history's contradictions within the self,[79] and while the British were developing an ideology of administrative reform which claimed—in the face of a generally triumphant Burkean counterpoint—to reduce history to a science,[80] the unique conditions of the continental republic and its growth were perpetuating the Augustan tension between virtue and commerce, the Puritan tension between election and apostasy, the Machiavellian tension between virtue and expansion, and in general the humanist tension between the active civic life and the secular time-continuum in which it must be lived. Hence the persistence in America of messianic and jeremiad attitudes toward history; hence also, in part, the curious extent to which the most post-modern and post-industrial of societies continues to venerate pre-modern and anti-industrial values, symbols, and constitutional forms, and to suffer from its awareness of the tensions between practice and morality.

Hegel is on record as commenting upon the United States of his time that though a vital and growing political culture, it as yet lacked anything which he could recognize as a "state." He resorted, however, to the proto-Turnerian explanation that the safety valve of the frontier accounted for the absence of class conflicts, and the prognosis that when the land was filled urbanization, a standing army, and class conflicts would begin, a true "state" would be necessitated, and the dialectic of history as he understood it would begin to operate.[81] This prophecy can be very readily transposed into a Marxist key; but it is notorious that it has yet to be fulfilled. Classical Marxist class conflict has been even slower to develop in America than in other advanced industrial societies, and if Herbert Marcuse be accepted as the most significant Marxist theoretician to operate out of an American context, his Marxism is post-industrial, romantic, and pessimistic. The fact is not, as we have seen, that a complacent Lockean liberalism has led American thought to state too narrowly the quarrel of the self with history; it is that this quarrel has been, and has continued to be, expressed in a premodern and pre-industrial form, and has never taken the shape of a rigorous Hegelian or Marxian commitment to a dialectic of historical conflict. The St. Louis Hegelians, it has recently been shown, were

Study in the Development of the Revolutionary Spirit (Chicago University Press, 1937).

[79] George Armstrong Kelly, *Idealism, Politics and History: Sources of Hegelian Thought* (Cambridge University Press, 1969).

[80] Crane Brinton, *English Political Thought in the Nineteenth Century* (New York: Harper and Row, 1962).

[81] G.W.F. Hegel, *Lectures on the Philosophy of History*, tr. J. Sibree (New York: Colonial Press, 1900), pp. 85-87.

romantic ideologues of a consciousness-expanding urban frontier, inheritors of the geopolitical messianism described by Tuveson and Smith;[82] and the more academic Hegelian philosophers who succeeded them were never ideologues at all. American metahistory has remained the rhetoric of a spatial escape and return, and has never been that of a dialectical process.

In terms borrowed from or suggested by the language of Hannah Arendt,[83] this book has told part of the story of the revival in the early modern West of the ancient ideal of *homo politicus* (the *zōon politikon* of Aristotle), who affirms his being and his virtue by the medium of political action, whose closest kinsman is *homo rhetor* and whose antithesis is the *homo credens* of Christian faith. Following this debate into the beginnings of modern historicist sociology, we have been led to study the complex eighteenth-century controversy between *homo politicus* and *homo mercator*, whom we saw to be an offshoot and not a progenitor—at least as regards the history of social perception—of *homo creditor*. The latter figure was defined and to a large degree discredited by his failure to meet the standards set by *homo politicus*, and eighteenth-century attempts to construct a bourgeois ideology contended none too successfully with the primacy already enjoyed by a civic ideology; even in America a liberal work ethic has historically suffered from the guilt imposed on it by its inability to define for itself a virtue that saves it from corruption; the descent from Daniel Boone to Willy Loman is seen as steady and uninterrupted. But one figure from the Arendtian gallery is missing, curiously enough, from the history even of the American work ethic: the *homo faber* of the European idealist and socialist traditions, who served to bridge the gap between the myths of the bourgeoisie and the proletariat. It is not yet as clear as it might be how the emergence of this figure is related to the European debate between virtue and commerce; but because industrial labor in America conquered a wilderness rather than transforming an ancient agrarian landscape, *homo faber* in this continent is seen as conquering space rather than transforming history, and the American work force has been even less willing than the European to see itself as a true proletariat. The ethos of historicist socialism has consequently been an importation of transplanted intellectuals (even the martyr Joe Hill left word that he "had lived as an artist and would die as an

---

[82] William H. Goetzmann, ed., *The American Hegelians: An Intellectual Episode in the History of Western America* (New York: Alfred A. Knopf, 1973).

[83] Hannah Arendt, *The Human Condition* (New York: Viking, 1958), and Peter Fuss, "Hannah Arendt's Conception of Political Community," *Idealistic Studies* 3, no. 3 (1973), 252-65.

artist"), and has remained in many ways subject to the messianic populisms of the westward movement.

The quarrel between civic virtue and secular time has been one of the main sources of the Western awareness of human historicity; but at the same time, the continued conduct of this quarrel—largely because it is anchored in a concern for the moral stability of the human personality—has perpetuated a pre-modern view of history as a movement away from the norms defining that stability, and so as essentially uncreative and entropic where it does not attain to millennium or utopia. When we speak of historicism we mean both an attempt to engage the personality and its integrity in the movement of history, and an attempt to depict history as generating new norms and values. The underlying strength of historicism is—or has been, since the astronauts and ecologists are working to close the circle once more—this sense of the secular creativity of history, its linear capacity to bring about incessant qualitative transformations of human life; but the paradox of American thought—on the other hand, the essence of socialist thought —has been a constant moral polemic against the way in which this happens. On one side of the paradox, the civic ideal of the virtuous personality, uncorrupted by specialization and committed to the social whole in all its diversity, has formed an important ingredient of the Marxian ideal of the same personality as awaiting redemption from the alienating effects of specialization.[84] On another side, however, the socialist and revolutionary thrust has often ended in failure for the reason—one among others—that it threatens to "force men to be free," to involve them in history, or in political and historical action, to a degree beyond their capacity for consent. Conservatism involves a denial of activism, a denial that the sphere of the *vita activa* is coterminous with the sphere of societal life. At this point our study of the quarrel between virtue and commerce has a contribution to offer on the conservative side of the ledger, with which a history being completed at a profoundly counter-revolutionary point in time may be permitted, without prejudice, to conclude.

In the final analysis, the ideal of virtue is highly compulsive; it demands of the individual, under threat to his moral being, that he participate in the *res publica* and, when the republic's existence in time is seen to have grown crucial, in history. We have found areas of eighteenth-century thought in which the partial withdrawal from citizenship to pursue commerce appeared as a rebellion against virtue and its repressive demands; the republic asked too much of the individual in the form of austerity and autonomy, participation and virtue, and

[84] *Politics, Language and Time*, p. 103.

551

the diversification of life by commerce and the arts offered him the world of Pericles in place of that of Lycurgus, a choice worth paying for with a little corruption. The "liberalism" which some now find an impoverishment did not appear so then. It was already known, however, that what was diversification to some was specialization to others, and the socialist tradition has continued to grapple with the confrontation of riches and poverty in this form.

Further back still in time, it is apparent that the primacy of politics—the ideal of virtue, already bearing with it the ancient ambivalences of justice and war, virtue and *virtù*—reappeared in early modern thought in the form of a Christian heresy. In a cosmos shaped by the thought of the Augustinian *civitas Dei*, it affirmed that man's nature was political and could be perfected in a finite historical frame of action; and the ambiguities of the *saeculum*, which it thus revived, are with us still as the ambiguities of action in history. To a Christian it would appear that the primacy of politics was possible only on the blasphemous supposition that some *civitas saecularis* could be the *civitas Dei*. To a Greek it would appear, more simply still, that every human virtue had its excess, and that civic or political virtue was no exception. There is a freedom to decline moral absolutes; even those of the polis and history, even that of freedom when proposed as an absolute.

A) Primary Sources

Addison, Joseph. *The Works*, with notes by Richard Hurd, ed. Henry Bohn (London: G. Bell, 6 vols., 1898-1912).

————. *The Spectator*, ed. Gregory Smith (London: J. M. Dent, 4 vols., 1958-1961).

Alberti, Leon Battista. *Della Famiglia*, trans. Renée Neu Watkins, *The Family in Renaissance Florence* (Columbia: University of South Carolina Press, 1969).

Anon. *A Declaration of the Parliament of England, Expressing the Grounds of Their Late Proceedings, and of Settling the Present Government in the Way of a Free State* (London, 1649).

Anon. *The True Portraiture of the Kings of England* . . . (London, 1650).

Anon. *State Tracts: in Two Parts . . . Several Treatises Relating to the Government, Privately Printed in the Reign of King Charles II . . . [and] from 1660 to 1689* . . . (London, 1693).

Anon. *A Collection of State Tracts Published on Occasion of the Late Revolution in 1688 and during the Reign of King William III* (London, 3 vols., 1706).

Anon. *A Letter from a Bystander to a Member of Parliament* (London, 1741).

Aquinas, St. Thomas. *Summa Theologica* (Cambridge, England: Blackfriars Press, 43 vols., 1964-1972).

Aristotle. *The Works of Aristotle*, ed. W. D. Ross (London: Oxford University Press, 11 vols., 1908-1931).

————. *The Politics*, ed. Sir Ernest Barker (London: Oxford University Press, 1946).

Ascham, Anthony. *A Discourse Wherein Is Examined What Is Particularly Lawfull during the Confusions and Revolutions of Government* (London, 1648).

————. *Of the Confusions and Revolutions of Governments* (London, 1649).

Aubrey, John. *Brief Lives*, ed. Oliver Lawson Dick (London: Secker and Warburg, 1958).

Bacon, Francis. *Works*, ed. J. Spedding, R. L. Ellis and D. D. Heath (London, 14 vols., 1868-1901).

——. *The Reign of King Henry VII*, ed. F. J. Levy (Indianapolis: Bobbs-Merrill, 1972).

Boccalini, Traiano. *Ragguagli da Parnasso* (Venice, 2 vols., 1612-1613).

Boethius. *The Consolation of Philosophy*, trans. V. E. Watts (Harmondsworth: Penguin, 1970).

Bolingbroke, Henry St. John, Viscount. *Works*, ed. David Mallett (London, 5 vols., 1754).

Brown, John. *An Essay on the Manners and Principles of the Times* (London, 1757).

Burke, Edmund. *Works* (London: Bohn, 1877; Boston: Little, Brown and Company, 1899).

Cartwright, F. D. *The Life and Correspondence of Major John Cartwright* (London, 1826).

Cavalcanti, Giovanni. *Istorie Fiorentine* (Florence, 1838).

Cobbett, William, ed. *The Parliamentary History of England, from the Earliest Times to the Year 1803* (London, 1806-1820).

Contarini, Gasparo. *De Magistratibus et Republica Venetorum* (Paris, 1543).

——. *The Commonwealth and Government of Venice. Written by the Cardinall Gasper Contareno and Translated out of Italian into English by Lewes Lewkenor* (London, 1599).

Crevecoeur, Hector St. John. *Letters from an American Farmer* (London: J. M. Dent and Son, 1912, 1962).

Davenant, Charles. *The Political and Commercial Works of Dr. Charles D'Avenant. Edited by Sir Charles Whitworth* (London, 6 vols., 1771).

Defoe, Daniel. *An Argument showing that a Standing Army, with Consent of Parliament, Is not Inconsistent with a Free Government* (London, 1698).

——. *The True-Born Englishman. A Satyr* (London, 1700).

——. *The Review*, Facsimile Text Society (New York: Columbia University Press, 23 vols., 1928).

Egmont, John Perceval, Earl of. *Faction Detected by the Evidence of Facts* (London, 1743).

Ferguson, Adam. *Essay on the History of Civil Society*, ed. Duncan Forbes (Edinburgh University Press, 1966).

Filmer, Sir Robert. *Patriarcha and Other Political Writings*, ed. Peter Laslett (Oxford: Basil Blackwell, 1949).

Fletcher, Andrew. *A Discourse of Government in Relation to Militias* (Edinburgh, 1698).

———. *Political Works* (London, 1737).

Fortescue, Sir John. *De Laudibus Legum Anglie*, ed. S. B. Chrimes (Cambridge University Press, 1949).

Giannotti, Donato. *Opere*, ed. G. Rosini (Pisa, 3 vols., 1819).

Greville, Fulke, Lord Brooke. *The Remains, Being Poems of Monarchy and Religion*, ed. G. A. Wilkes (London: Oxford University Press, 1965).

Guicciardini, Francesco. *Dialogo e Discorsi del Reggimento di Firenze*, ed. Roberto Palmarocchi (Bari: Laterza, 1932).

———. *Ricordi*, ed. R. Spongano (Florence: Sansoni, 1959).

———. *Maxims and Reflections of a Renaissance Statesman*, trans. Mario Domandi (New York: Harper and Row, 1965).

———. *Selected Writings*, ed. and trans. Cecil and Margaret Grayson (London: Oxford University Press, 1965).

———. *The History of Italy*, ed. and trans. Sidney Alexander (New York: Collier, 1969, and Macmillan, 1972).

———. *The History of Florence*, trans. Mario Domandi (New York: Harper and Row, 1970).

Hammond, Henry. *The Works of Dr. Henry Hammond* (London, 4 vols., 1671-1684).

Harrington, James. *Oceana and Other Works*, ed. John Toland (London, 1771).

Hervey, John, Lord. *Ancient and Modern Liberty Stated and Compared* (London, 1734).

Hobbes, Thomas. *The English Works*, ed. Sir William Molesworth (London, 11 vols., 1839-1845).

———. *Leviathan*, ed. Michael Oakeshott (Oxford: Basil Blackwell, n.d.).

———. *Behemoth*, ed. F. Tonnies (London, 1889; reissued, with intro. by M. M. Goldsmith, London: Frank Cass, 1969).

Hume, David. *Essays, Moral, Political and Literary* (London: World's Classics, 1903).

———. *The History of Great Britain, Volume I, Containing the Reigns of James I and Charles I*, ed. Duncan Forbes (Harmondsworth: Penguin, 1970).

———. *Economic Writings*, ed. Eugene Rotwein (Madison: University of Wisconsin Press, 1970).

Hunton, Philip. *A Treatise of Monarchy* (London, 1643).

Jefferson, Thomas. *Notes on the State of Virginia*, ed. W. Peder (Chapel Hill: University of North Carolina Press, 1955).

Landucci, Luca. *A Florentine Diary from 1450 to 1516*, trans. Jarvis (London: J. M. Dent, 1927).

Locke, John. *Two Treatises on Government*, ed. Peter Laslett (Cambridge University Press, 1960, 1963; New York: Mentor, 1965).

Machiavelli, Niccolo. *Tutte le Opere*, ed. F. Flora and C. Cordiè (Rome: Arnaldo Mondadori, 1949).

――――. *Opere*, ed. Mario Bonfantini (*La Letteratura Italiana*, Storia e Testi, vol. 29; Milan and Naples: Riccardo Ricciardi, 1954).

――――. *The History of Florence*, trans. M. Walter Dunne, ed. Felix Gilbert (New York: Harper and Row, 1960).

――――. *The Prince*, ed. and trans. G. Bull (Harmondsworth: Penguin, 1961).

――――. *Lettere*, ed. F. Gaeta (Milan: Feltrinelli, 1961).

――――. *The Art of War*, trans. E. Farnesworth, ed. Neal Wood (Indianapolis: Bobbs-Merrill, 1965).

――――. *The Discourses*, trans. L. Walker, ed. Bernard Crick (Harmondsworth: Penguin, 1970).

Mandeville, Bernard. *The Fable of the Bees*, ed. F. B. Kaye (Oxford: The Clarendon Press, 2 vols., 1924).

――――. *An Enquiry into the Origins of Honour and the Usefulness of Christianity in War*, ed. M. M. Goldsmith (London: Frank Cass, 1971).

Marvell, Andrew. *Complete Works*, ed. A. B. Grosart (London, 1875).

Millar, John. *A Historical View of the English Government*, 4th ed. (London, 4 vols., 1819).

Montesquieu, Charles Secondat, Baron. *Oeuvres Complètes* (Paris: Gallimard, 1949).

Nedham, Marchmont. *Mercurius Politicus* (London, 1650-1660).

――――. *The Case of the Commonwealth of England Stated*, ed. Philip A. Knachel (Charlottesville: University of Virginia Press, 1969).

Neville, Henry. *Plato Redivivus* (London, 1680), ed. Caroline Robbins, in *Two English Republican Tracts* (Cambridge University Press, 1969).

Parker, Henry. *Observations upon Some of His Majesty's Late Answers and Expresses* (London, 1642).

Polybius. *The Histories*, trans. E. S. Shuckburgh, ed. F. W. Walbank (Bloomington: Indiana University Press, 1962).

Ralegh, Sir Walter. *Works*, ed., with lives by W. Oldys and T. Birch (Oxford University Press, 1829).

Rousseau, Jean-Jacques. *The Political Writings of J. J. Rousseau*, ed. C. E. Vaughan (Oxford: Basil Blackwell, 1962).

Rushworth, John, ed. *Historical Collections of Private Passages of State* (London, 1659-1701).

Savonarola, Girolamo. *Prediche italiane ai fiorentini: I, Novembre-Dicembre del 1494*, ed. F. Cognasso (Perugia and Venice: La Nuova Italia Editrice, 1930).

———. *Prediche sopra Aggeo, con il Trattato circa il reggimento e governo della città di Firenze*, ed. Luigi Firpo, *Edizione Nazionale delle Opere di Girolamo Savonarola* (Rome: Belardotti, 1955).

Sidney, Algernon. *Discourses on Government*, 3d ed. (London, 1751).

Smith, Adam. *Moral and Political Philosophy* (New York: Hafner, 1948).

———. *An Inquiry into the Nature and Causes of the Wealth of Nations* (London: J. M. Dent, 1910, 1950).

Squire, Samuel. *An Enquiry into the Foundation of the English Constitution* (London, 1745).

———. *An Historical Essay upon the Balance of Civil Power in England* (London, 1748).

Swift, Jonathan. *The Examiner*, ed. H. Davis (Oxford: Basil Blackwell, 1957).

———. *The History of the Four Last Years of the Queen*, ed. H. Davis (Oxford: Basil Blackwell, 1964).

———. *Political Tracts, 1711-14*, ed. H. Davis (Oxford: Basil Blackwell, 1964).

———. *A Discourse of the Contests and Dissensions between the Nobles and the Commons in Athens and Rome*, ed. Frank H. Ellis (Oxford: The Clarendon Press, 1967).

Toland, John. *The Art of Governing by Parties* (London, 1701).

———. *The State Anatomy of Great Britain* (London, 1714).

———. *A Collection of Several Pieces of Mr. John Toland*, ed. Pierre Des Maizeaux (London, 1726).

Trenchard, John, with Walter Moyle. *An Argument showing that a Standing Army is Inconsistent with a Free Government and Absolutely Destructive to the Constitution of the English Monarchy* (London, 1697).

Trenchard, John, with Thomas Gordon. *Cato's Letters: or Essays on Liberty, Civil and Religious, and Other Important Subjects*, 3d ed. (London, 1723).

Tucker, Josiah. *Four Tracts on Political and Commercial Subjects* (London, 1774).

———. *A Letter to Edmund Burke, Esq.* (London, 1775).

———. *The True Interest of Britain* (London, 1776).

———. *A Treatise Concerning Civil Government* (London, 1781).

Woodhouse, A.S.P., ed. *Puritanism and Liberty* (London: J. M. Dent, 1950).

B) Secondary Literature: Books

Albertini, R. von. *Das florentinische Staatsbewusstsein im übergang von der Republik zum Prinzipat* (Bern: Francke Verlag, 1955).

Arendt, Hannah. *The Human Condition* (New York: Viking, 1958).

———. *On Revolution* (Chicago University Press, 1963).

Baron, Hans. *Humanistic and Political Literature in Florence and Venice at the Beginning of the Quattrocento* (Cambridge, Mass.: Harvard University Press, 1955).

———. *The Crisis of the Early Italian Renaissance*, 2d ed. (Princeton University Press, 1966).

———. *From Petrarch to Leonardo Bruni: Studies in Humanist and Political Literature* (Chicago University Press, 1968).

Bailyn, Bernard. *Political Pamphlets of the American Revolution, I* (Cambridge, Mass.: Belknap Press, 1965).

———. *The Ideological Origins of the American Revolution* (Cambridge, Mass.: Belknap Press, 1967).

———. *The Origins of American Politics* (New York: Vintage Books, 1970).

Bayley, C. C. *War and Society in Renaissance Florence* (University of Toronto Press, 1961).

Berman, Marshall. *The Politics of Authenticity* (New York: Atheneum, 1970).

Blitzer, Charles. *An Immortal Commonwealth: The Political Thought of James Harrington* (New Haven: Yale University Press, 1960).

Bloom, Edward A. and Lillian D. *Joseph Addison's Sociable Animal: in the Market Place, on the Hustings, in the Pulpit* (Providence: Brown University Press, 1971).

Boorstin, Daniel. *The Genius of American Politics* (Chicago University Press, 1953).

———. *The Americans: the Colonial Experience* (New York: Random House, 1958).

Bouwsma, William J. *Venice and the Defense of Republican Liberty: Renaissance Values in the Age of the Counter-Reformation* (Berkeley and Los Angeles: University of California Press, 1968).

Brandt, William J. *The Shape of Medieval History: Studies in Modes of Perception* (New Haven: Yale University Press, 1966).

Bryson, Gladys. *Man and Society: the Scottish Enquiry of the Eighteenth Century* (Princeton University Press, 1945).

Butterfield, Sir Herbert. *The Statecraft of Machiavelli* (London: G. Bell and Son, 1940, 1955).

———. *George III, Lord North and the People* (London: G. Bell and Son, 1949).

Chambers, William N. *Old Bullion Benton: Senator from the New West* (Boston: Little, Brown and Company, 1956).

———. *Political Parties in a New Nation: The American Experience, 1776-1809* (New York: Oxford University Press, 1963).

Christie, Ian R. *Wilkes, Wyvill and Reform: The Parliamentary Reform Movement in British Politics, 1760-85* (New York: St. Martin's Press, 1962).

———. *Myth and Reality in Late Eighteenth-century British Politics* (Berkeley and Los Angeles: University of California Press, 1970).

Cochrane, Charles Norris. *Christianity and Classical Culture* (New York: Oxford University Press, 1957).

Cohn, Norman. *The Pursuit of the Millennium*, 2d ed. (New York: Harper and Row, 1961).

Colbourn, H. Trevor. *The Lamp of Experience: Whig History and the Beginnings of the American Revolution* (Chapel Hill: University of North Carolina Press, 1965).

Conklin, George Newton. *Biblical Criticism and Heresy in Milton* (New York: King's Crown Press, 1949).

Cook, Richard I. *Jonathan Swift as a Tory Pamphleteer* (Seattle and London: University of Washington Press, 1967).

Cosenza, Mario E. *Petrarch's Letters to Classical Authors* (Chicago University Press, 1910).

Cranston, Maurice and Peters, R. S., eds. *Hobbes and Rousseau* (New York: Doubleday Anchor Books, 1972).

Cumming, Robert D. *Human Nature and History* (Chicago University Press, 2 vols., 1969).

De Caprariis, Vittorio. *Francesco Guicciardini: dalla politica alla storia* (Bari: Laterza, 1950).

Dickinson, H. T. *Bolingbroke* (London: Constable, 1970).

Dickson, P.G.M. *The Financial Revolution in England: A Study in the Development of Public Credit* (London: Macmillan, 1967).

Dorey, T. A., ed. *Tacitus* (New York: Basic Books, 1969).

Dunn, John. *The Political Thought of John Locke: An Historical Account of the Argument of the Two Treatises of Government* (Cambridge University Press, 1969).

Earl, D. C. *The Moral and Political Tradition of Rome* (Ithaca: Cornell University Press, 1967).

Ferguson, Arthur B. *The Articulate Citizen and the English Renaissance* (Durham, N.C.: Duke University Press, 1965).

Ferguson, John. *The Religions of the Roman Empire* (Ithaca: Cornell University Press, 1970).

Fink, Z. S. *The Classical Republicans: An Essay in the Recovery of a Pattern of Thought in Seventeenth-Century England* (Evanston: Northwestern University Press, 1945).

Fleisher, Martin, ed. *Machiavelli and the Nature of Political Thought* (New York: Atheneum, 1972).

Foot, Michael. *The Pen and the Sword* (London: Macgibbon and Kee, 1957).

Frank, Joseph. *The Beginnings of the English Newspaper* (Cambridge, Mass.: Harvard University Press, 1961).

Gardner, Lloyd C. *A Different Frontier: Selected Readings in the Foundations of American Economic Expansion* (Chicago: Quadrangle Books, 1966).

Garin, Eugenio. *Italian Humanism: Philosophy and Civic Life in the Renaissance*, trans. Peter Munz (New York: Harper and Row, 1965).

Giarrizzo, Giuseppe. *Hume politico e storico* (Turin: Einaudi, 1962).

Gilbert, Felix. *To the Farewell Address: Ideas of American Foreign Policy* (Princeton University Press, 1961, 1970).

———. *Machiavelli and Guicciardini: Politics and History in Sixteenth-Century Florence* (Princeton University Press, 1965).

Gilmore, Myron P., ed. *Studies in Machiavelli* (Florence: Sansoni, 1972).

Goetzmann, William H., ed. *The American Hegelians: An Episode in the Intellectual History of Western America* (New York: Alfred A. Knopf, 1973).

Gummere, Richard M. *The American Colonial Mind and the Classical Tradition: Essays in Comparative Culture* (Cambridge, Mass.: Harvard University Press, 1963).

Gunn, J.A.W. *Factions No More: Attitudes to Party in Government and Opposition in Eighteenth-Century England* (London: Frank Cass, 1972).

Gwyn, W. B. *The Meaning of the Separation of Powers: An Analysis of the Doctrine from its Origin to the Adoption of the United States Constitution* (New Orleans: Tulane Studies in Political Science, 1965).

Haley, K.H.D. *The First Earl of Shaftesbury* (Oxford: The Clarendon Press, 1968).

Haller, William. *Foxe's Book of Martyrs and the Elect Nation* (London: Jonathan Cape, 1963).

Hanson, Donald W. *From Kingdom to Commonwealth: The Development of Civic Consciousness in English Political Thought* (Cambridge, Mass.: Harvard University Press, 1970).

Haraszti, Zoltan. *John Adams and the Prophets of Progress* (Cambridge, Mass.: Harvard University Press, 1952).

Hartz, Louis B. *The Liberal Tradition in America: An Interpretation of American Political Thought since the Revolution* (New York: Harcourt Brace, 1955).

Hexter, J. H. *The Vision of Politics on the Eve of the Reformation: More, Machiavelli, Seyssel* (New York: Basic Books, 1972).

Hill, Christopher. *Puritanism and Revolution* (London: Secker and Warburg, 1958).

———. *Society and Puritanism in Pre-Revolutionary England* (New York: Schocken Books, 1964).

———. *Antichrist in Seventeenth-century England* (London: Oxford University Press, 1971).

Hofstadter, Richard C. *The Idea of a Party System: The Rise of Legitimate Opposition in the United States, 1780-1840* (Berkeley and Los Angeles: University of California Press, 1969).

Holmes, George. *The Florentine Enlightenment, 1400-1450* (London: Weidenfeld and Nicolson, 1969).

Howe, John R., Jr. *The Changing Political Thought of John Adams* (Princeton University Press, 1966).

Huffman, C. C. *Coriolanus in Context* (Lewisburg: Bucknell University Press, 1972).

Jacob, E. F., ed. *Italian Renaissance Studies* (New York: Barnes and Noble, 1960).

Jacobson, David L., ed. *The English Libertarian Heritage* (Indianapolis: Bobbs Merrill, 1965).

Jordan, W. K. *Men of Substance: A Study of the Political Thought of Two English Revolutionaries, Henry Parker and Henry Robinson* (Chicago University Press, 1942).

Judson, Margaret. *The Political Thought of Sir Henry Vane the Younger* (Philadelphia: University of Pennsylvania Press, 1969).

Kelley, Donald R. *The Foundations of Modern Historical Scholarship: Language, Law and History in the French Renaissance* (New York: Columbia University Press, 1970).

Kenyon, J. P., ed. *The Stuart Constitution, 1603-88* (Cambridge University Press, 1966).

Kettler, David. *The Social and Political Thought of Adam Ferguson* (Columbus: Ohio State University Press, 1965).

Kluxen, Kurt. *Das Problem der Politischen Opposition: Entwicklung und Wesen der englischen Zweiparteienpolitik im 18 Jahrhundert* (Freiburg and Munich, 1956).

Koebner, Richard. *Empire* (Cambridge University Press, 1961).

Kramnick, Isaac F. *Bolingbroke and His Circle: The Politics of Nostalgia in the Age of Walpole* (Cambridge, Mass.: Harvard University Press, 1968).

Ladner, Gerhart B. *The Idea of Reform: Its Impact on Christian Thought and Action in the Age of the Fathers* (Cambridge, Mass.: Harvard University Press, 1959).

Lamont, William M. *Marginal Prynne, 1600-69* (London: Routledge and Kegan Paul, 1963).

———. *Godly Rule: Politics and Religion, 1603-60* (London: Macmillan, 1969).

Laprade, W. T. *Public Opinion and Politics in Eighteenth-century England to the Fall of Walpole* (New York: Macmillan, 1936).

Leff, Gordon. *Heresy in the Later Middle Ages* (Manchester University Press, 2 vols., 1967).

Lefranc, Pierre. *Sir Walter Ralegh Ecrivain* (Paris: Armand Colin, 1968).

Lehmann, W. C. *John Millar of Glasgow* (Cambridge University Press, 1960).

Letwin, William. *The Origin of Scientific Economics* (New York: Doubleday Anchor, 1965).

Levenson, Joseph R. *Liang Ch'i-ch'ao and the Mind of Modern China* (Berkeley and Los Angeles: University of California Press, 1953, 1959).

———. *Confucian China and its Modern Fate* (Berkeley and Los Angeles: University of California Press, 3 vols., 1958-1965).

Levy, F. J. *Tudor Historical Thought* (San Marino: Huntington Library, 1967).

Lewis, C. S. *Selected Literary Essays* (Cambridge University Press, 1969).

Mansfield, Harvey C., Jr. *Statesmanship and Party Government* (Chicago University Press, 1965).

Manuel, Frank E. *Shapes of Philosophical History* (Stanford University Press, 1965).

Markus, R. A. *Saeculum: History and Society in the Theology of St. Augustine* (Cambridge University Press, 1970).

Marx, Leo. *The Machine and the Garden: Technology and the Pastoral Ideal in America* (New York: Oxford University Press, 1964).

Mazzeo, J. A. *Renaissance and Seventeenth-century Studies* (New York: Columbia University Press, 1964).

Molho, Anthony, and Tedeschi, John A., eds. *Renaissance: Studies in Honor of Hans Baron* (Florence: Sansoni, and DeKalb: Northern Illinois University Press, 1971).

Mosse, George L. *The Holy Pretence: A Study in Christianity and Reason of State from William Perkins to John Winthrop* (Oxford: Basil Blackwell, 1957).

McIlwain, C. H. *Constitutionalism Ancient and Modern* (Ithaca: Cornell University Press, Great Seal Books, 1958).

Macpherson, C. B. *The Political Theory of Possessive Individualism: from Hobbes to Locke* (Oxford: The Clarendon Press, 1962).

Nisbet, Robert F. *Social Change and History: Aspects of the Western Theory of Development* (New York: Oxford University Press, 1969).

Noble, David W. *Historians against History: The Frontier Thesis and the National Covenant in American Historical Writing since 1830* (Minneapolis: University of Minnesota Press, 1965).

O'Malley, John W. *Giles of Viterbo on Church and Reform: A Study in Renaissance Thought* (Leiden: E. J. Brill, 1968).

Parker, Harold T. *The Cult of Antiquity and the French Revolutionaries: A Study in the Development of the Revolutionary Spirit* (Chicago University Press, 1937).

Patch, H. R. *The Goddess Fortuna in Medieval Literature* (Cambridge, Mass.: Harvard University Press, 1927).

Plumb, J. H. *The Growth of Political Stability in England, 1660-1730* (London: Macmillan, 1967).

Pocock, J.G.A. *The Ancient Constitution and the Feudal Law: English Historical Thought in the Seventeenth Century* (Cambridge University Press, 1957, and New York: W. W. Norton, 1967).

———. *Politics, Language and Time: Essays in Political Thought and History* (New York: Atheneum, 1971; London: Methuen, 1972).

Pole, J. R. *Political Representation in England and the Origins of the American Republic* (London: Macmillan; New York: St. Martin's Press, 1969).

Raab, Felix. *The English Face of Machiavelli* (London: Routledge and Kegan Paul, and University of Toronto Press, 1964).

Rawson, Elizabeth. *The Spartan Tradition in European Thought* (Oxford: The Clarendon Press, 1969).

Reeves, Marjorie. *The Influence of Prophecy in the Later Middle Ages: A Study in Joachism* (Oxford: The Clarendon Press, 1969).

Richards, James O. *Party Propaganda under Queen Anne: The General Elections of 1702-13* (Athens: University of Georgia Press, 1972).

Ridolfi, Roberto. *Opuscoli di Storia Letteraria e di Erudizione* (Florence: Libr. Bibliopolis, 1942).

———. *Life of Girolamo Savonarola*, trans. C. Grayson (London: Routledge and Kegan Paul, 1959).

———. *Life of Niccolo Machiavelli*, trans. C. Grayson (London: Routledge and Kegan Paul, 1962).

Ridolfi, Roberto. *Life of Francesco Guicciardini*, trans. C. Grayson (London: Routledge and Kegan Paul, 1967).

Robbins, Caroline A. *The Eighteenth-century Commonwealthman: Studies in the Transmission, Development and Circumstances of English Liberal Thought from the Restoration of Charles II until the War with the Thirteen Colonies* (Cambridge, Mass.: Harvard University Press, 1959).

————, ed. *Two English Republican Tracts* (Cambridge University Press, 1969).

Rossiter, Clinton. *Seedtime of the Republic: The Origin of the American Tradition of Political Liberty* (New York: Harcourt Brace, 1953).

Rowe, J. G., and Stockdale, W. H., eds. *Florilegium Historiale: Essays Presented to Wallace K. Ferguson* (University of Toronto Press, 1971).

Rubini, Dennis. *Court and Country, 1688-1702* (London: Rupert Hart-Davis, 1967).

Rubinstein, Nicolai, ed. *Florentine Studies: Politics and Society in Renaissance Florence* (London: Faber and Faber, 1968).

Seigel, Jerrold E. *Rhetoric and Philosophy in Renaissance Humanism: The Union of Eloquence and Wisdom, Petrarch to Valla* (Princeton University Press, 1968).

Shackleton, Robert. *Montesquieu: A Critical Biography* (Oxford: The Clarendon Press, 1961).

Shklar, Judith. *Men and Citizens: A Study of Rousseau's Social Theory* (Cambridge University Press, 1969).

Silberschmidt, Max. *The United States and Europe: Rivals and Partners* (New York: Harcourt Brace Jovanovich, 1972).

Simon, Renée. *Henry de Boulainviller: historien, politique, philosophe, astrologue, 1658-1722* (Paris: Boivin, 1941).

————. *Un revolté du grand siécle: Henry de Boulainviller* (Garches: Editions du nouvel humanisme, 1948).

Smith, Henry Nash. *Virgin Land: The American West as Symbol and Myth* (Cambridge, Mass.: Harvard University Press, 1950; New York: Vintage Books, n.d.).

Sperlin, Paul M. *Rousseau in America, 1760-1809* (University of Alabama Press, 1969).

Starns, Randolph. *Donato Giannotti and His Epistolae* (Geneva: Librairie Droz, 1968).

Starr, Chester G. *The Awakening of the Greek Historical Spirit* (New York: Alfred A. Knopf, 1968).

Stewart, John B. *The Moral and Political Philosophy of David Hume* (New York: Columbia University Press, 1963).

Stourzh, Gerald. *Alexander Hamilton and the Idea of Republican Government* (Stanford University Press, 1970).

Strauss, E. *Sir William Petty: Portrait of a Genius* (London: The Bodley Head, 1954).

Struever, Nancy S. *The Language of History in the Renaissance* (Princeton University Press, 1970).

Sydnor, Charles S. *Gentlemen Freeholders: Political Practice in Washington's Virginia* (Chapel Hill: University of North Carolina Press, 1952).

———. *American Revolutionaries in the Making* (New York: The Free Press, 1965).

Thompson, David, and Nagel, Alan F., eds. *The Three Crowns of Florence: Humanist Assessments of Dante, Petrarch and Boccaccio* (New York: Harper and Row, 1972).

Tuveson, Ernest. *Millennium and Utopia: A Study in the Background of the Idea of Progress* (Berkeley and Los Angeles: University of California Press, 1949).

———. *The Redeemer Nation: The Idea of America's Millennial Role* (University of Chicago Press, 1968).

Ullmann, Walter. *Principles of Government and Politics in the Middle Ages* (London: Methuen, 1961).

———. *History of Political Thought in the Middle Ages* (Harmondsworth: Penguin, 1965).

———. *The Individual and Society in the Middle Ages* (Baltimore: Johns Hopkins University Press, 1966).

Underdown, David. *Pride's Purge: Politics in the Puritan Revolution* (Oxford: The Clarendon Press, 1971).

Varese, Claudio. *Storia e Politica nella Prosa del Quattrocento* (Turin: Einaudi, 1961).

Venturi, Franco. *Utopia and Reform in the Enlightenment* (Cambridge University Press, 1971).

Vile, M.J.C. *Constitutionalism and the Separation of Powers* (Oxford: The Clarendon Press, 1967).

Von Fritz, K. *The Theory of the Mixed Constitution in Antiquity* (New York: Columbia University Press, 1954).

Wade, Ira O. *The Clandestine Organisation and Diffusion of Philosophic Ideas in France from 1700 to 1750* (Princeton University Press, 1938).

Walbank, F. W. *An Historical Commentary on Polybius* (Oxford: The Clarendon Press, 1957).

Wallace, John M. *Destiny His Choice: The Loyalism of Andrew Marvell* (Cambridge University Press, 1968).

Walzer, Michael. *The Revolution of the Saints: A Study in the Origins of Radical Politics* (Cambridge, Mass.: Harvard University Press, 1965).

Ward, John William. *Andrew Jackson: Symbol for an Age* (New York: Oxford University Press, 1955).

Weinstein, Donald. *Savonarola and Florence: Prophecy and Patriotism in the Renaissance* (Princeton University Press, 1970).

Western, J. R. *The English Militia in the Eighteenth Century: The Story of a Political Issue, 1660-1802* (London: Routledge and Kegan Paul, 1965).

——. *Monarchy and Revolution: The English State in the 1680's* (London: Blandford Press, 1972).

Weston, Corinne Comstock. *English Constitutional Theory and the House of Lords* (London: Routledge and Kegan Paul, 1965).

Whitfield, J. H. *Petrarch and the Renascence* (New York: Russell and Russell, 1965).

——. *Discourses on Machiavelli* (Cambridge: W. Heffer and Sons, 1969).

Wilkins, E. H. *The Life of Petrarch* (Chicago University Press, 1961).

Williams, S. H. *The Radical Reformation* (Philadelphia: The Westminster Press, 1962).

Wood, Gordon S. *The Creation of the American Republic* (Chapel Hill: University of North Carolina Press, 1969).

Yolton, John W., ed. *John Locke: Problems and Perspectives* (Cambridge University Press, 1969).

c) Periodical Articles and Dissertations

Banning, Lance G. "The Quarrel with Federalism: A Study in the Origins and Character of Republican Thought," Ph.D. dissertation, Washington University, 1972.

Baron, Hans. "Machiavelli: The Republican Citizen and the Author of *The Prince*," *English Historical Review* 76 (1961), 217-53.

——. "Leonardo Bruni," *Past and Present* 36 (1967), 21-37.

Forbes, Duncan. "Politics and History in David Hume," *The Historical Journal* 6, no. 2 (1963), 280-94.

Fuss, Peter. "Hannah Arendt's Conception of Political Community," *Idealistic Studies* 3, no. 3 (1973), 252-65.

Gilbert, Felix. "Bernardo Rucellai and the Orti Oricellari: A Study in the Origin of Modern Political Thought," *Journal of the Warburg and Courtauld Institutes* 12 (1949), 101-31.

———. "The Composition and Structure of Machiavelli's *Discorsi*," *Journal of the History of Ideas* 14, no. 1 (1953), 136-56.

———. "Florentine Political Assumptions in the Period of Savonarola and Soderini," *Journal of the Warburg and Courtauld Institute* 20 (1957), 187-214.

———. "The Date of the Composition of Contarini's and Giannotti's Books on Venice," *Studies in the Renaissance* 14 (1967), 172-84.

Lamont, William M. "Richard Baxter, the Apocalypse and the Mad Major," *Past and Present* 55 (1972), 68-90.

Maclean, A. H. "George Lawson and John Locke," *Cambridge Historical Journal* 9, no. 1 (1947), 69-77.

Pocock, J.G.A. "The Onely Politician: Machiavelli, Harrington and Felix Raab," *Historical Studies: Australia and New Zealand* 12, no. 46 (1966), 165-96.

———. "James Harrington and the Good Old Cause: A Study of the Ideological Context of His Writings," *Journal of British Studies* 10, no. 1 (1970), 30-48.

———. "Virtue and Commerce in the Eighteenth Century," *Journal of Interdisciplinary History* 3, no. 1 (1972), 119-34.

Ranum, Orest. "Personality and Politics in the *Persian Letters*," *Political Science Quarterly* 84, no. 4 (1969), 606-27.

Riesenberg, Peter. "Civism and Roman Law in Fourteenth-century Italian Society," *Explorations in Economic History* 7, nos. 1-2 (1969), 237-54.

Robey, David. "P. P. Vergerio the Elder: Republicanism and Civic Values in the Work of an Early Humanist," *Past and Present* 58 (1973), 3-37.

Rosenmeier, Jesper. "New England's Perfection: The Image of Adam and the Image of Christ in the Antinomian Crisis, 1634 to 1638," *William and Mary Quarterly*, 3d ser., vol. 27, no. 3 (1970), pp. 435-59.

Rubini, Dennis. "Politics and the Battle for the Banks, 1688-97," *English Historical Review* 85 (1970), 693-714.

Sanesi, G. R., ed. "Un discorso sconosciuto di Donato Giannotti sulla milizia," *Archivio Storico Italiano*, ser. 5, vol. 8 (1891), pp. 2-27.

Schwoerer, Lois F. "The Literature of the Standing Army Controversy," *Huntington Library Quarterly* 28 (1964-1965), 187-212.

Seigel, Jerrold E. "Civic Humanism or Ciceronian Rhetoric?" *Past and Present* 34 (1966), 3-48.

Shackleton, Robert. "Montesquieu, Bolingbroke and the Separation of Powers," *French Studies* 3 (1949), 25-38.

Skinner, Quentin. "Hobbes's Leviathan," *The Historical Journal* 7, no. 2 (1964), 321-32.

Skinner, Quentin. "History and Ideology in the English Revolution," *The Historical Journal* 8, no. 2 (1965), 151-78.

———. "The Ideological Context of Hobbes's Political Thought," *The Historical Journal* 9, no. 3 (1966), 286-317.

Starr, Chester G. "History and the Concept of Time," *History and Theory*, Beiheft 6 (1966), 24-35.

Wallace, John M. "The Engagement Controversy, 1649-52: An Annotated List of Pamphlets," *Bulletin of the New York Public Library* 68 (1964), 384-405.

Walzer, Michael. "Exodus 32 and the Theory of Holy War: The History of a Citation," *Harvard Theological Review* 61, no. 1 (1968), 1-14.

Weddell, D. "Charles Davenant (1656-1714)—a Biographical Sketch," *Economic History Review*, ser. 2, vol. 11 (1958-1959), pp. 279-88.

Weston, Corinne Comstock. "Legal Sovereignty in the Brady Controversy," *The Historical Journal* 15, no. 3 (1972), 409-32.

Williamson, Arthur H. "Antichrist's Career in Scotland: The Imagery of Evil and the Search for a National Past," Ph.D. dissertation, Washington University, 1973.

Zagorin, Perez, ed. "Sir Edward Stanhope's Advice to Thomas Wentworth," *The Historical Journal* 7, no. 2 (1964), 298-320.

philosophy, 9, 41, 42, 44, 45, 58-60, 66, 99, 220, 230, 250; Aristotelian, 10, 14; of citizenship, 115; of custom, 405; deductive, 10; of government, 22, 28, 29, 320; of history, 5; humanist, 63; medieval, 4; Platonic, 20; political, 9, 36; post-Aristotelian, 6
Philosophy (personified), 38-40
physis, 5-7, 77, 78
Pico della Mirandola, 98
Pisa, 213, 273; Pisans, 125
Pitt, William, the younger, 547
places, placemen, 406-8, 410, 413, 420, 427, 473, 478; placeholders, 412
Plato, 20, 22, 37, 65, 67, 69, 135n, 259n, 491-92; the *Laws*, 102n, 327; myth of the cave, 451, 472, 490; the *Republic*, 20-22, 50-51; the *Statesman*, 20; Renaissance Platonism, 63, 65
plebei (Giannotti), 312
poetry, 5, 61
Poland, 433, 447, 470
Pole, J. R., 513
polis, 3, 57, 64, 66-68, 73-76, 78, 84, 85, 99, 126, 164, 183, 203, 329, 334, 340, 348, 390, 397, 485, 492-93, 499, 527, 540, 552
politeia, 64, 70-72, 78, 86, 116, 121, 132, 138, 157, 169, 388, 479
politeness, 470
politeuma, 78, 169
political: action, 345; activity, 348; animal, 40, 58, 62, 74, 114, 184, 292, 299, 335; aristocracy, 101; arithmetic, 425; associates, 98; capacity, 357; community, 65, 102, 348; economy, 423, 426, 450; history, 36; humanism, 61; knowledge, 220; man, 250; process, 533; society, 277; theory, 220, 222, 503
thought: English, 361, 401, 403; Florentine, 316; humanist, 316; Western, 401
politics, 63, 67, 72, 77, 80, 98, 99, 163, 370, 389-90, 401, 450, 459, 484, 486-87, 509, 516, 522, 537, 544, 552; Christian Aristotelian, 323; classical, 521; colonial, 574; end of classical, 513, 523, 526-27, 537; foundations of, 423
polity, 66, 67, 72-79, 90, 91, 102, 108, 111, 112, 128, 139, 184, 185, 211,

253-54, 263, 300, 307, 373, 465, 467, 486, 508, 515, 516; the English, 357; *polizia*, 393 (*and see politeia*)
Polybius, 79, 116, 189, 190, 213, 273, 296-97, 308, 323, 327, 365, 539, 548
Polybius's *Histories*, 77; Book VI of, 102, 296, 300, 327
Polybian: balance, 277, 295, 319, 326, 329; cyclical scheme, 243, 300, 303; equilibrium, 285; structure, 263; theory, 326, 484; theory of cycles, 317; theory of monarchy, 262; thought, 277; tradition, 524; Venetian paradigm, 263
Pompey, 201
Pomponius Atticus, 276
poor, the, 381
poveri, 300, 302
poverty, Christian, 215, 294
pope, the, 51, 106, 343, 396; popery, 456; papacy, Counter-Reformation, 327
popes: Alexander VI, 173-74; Clement VII (Giulio de' Medici), 242; Julius II, 138, 301; Leo X (Giovanni de' Medici), 138, 147, 149, 150, 152, 203, 242
Pope, Alexander, 457, 478
power: absolute, 353; in *Answer to the Nineteen Propositions*, 353; in Aristotle, 71-72; in Bruni, 90; corruption, 409, 516; in courtier life, 350; in Davenant, 438, 444-45; in *de facto* controversy, 378; Federalist theory of, 521; at Florence, 101; in Harrington, 386-87, 390-91; in humanist tradition, 329; in Hunton, 366, 371; judicial, 314-15, 363; legitimacy of, 223; in mixed government, 307; and money, 435, 490; morality of, 548; national, 425, 530; in Nedham, 382-83; in representation, 518; the republic a structure of, 299-300; in Tacitism, 352-53; ultimate and irresponsible, 494; *virtù* as, 307, 327, 479; and virtue, 488 (*and see* balance, distribution, executive, function, government, separation, sovereignty)
precedent(s), 347-48, 494
prediction, 224
prerogative, 361, 407, 410, 419, 421-22, 479-80

Library of Congress Cataloging in Publication Data

Pocock, John Greville Agard.
  The Machiavellian moment.

  Bibliography: p.
    1. Machiavelli, Niccolò, 1469-1527.   2. Political science–
History–Italy.   3. Political science–History–Great Britain.
4. Political science–History–United States.   I. Title.
JC143.M4P6   320.1'092'4   73-2490
ISBN 0-691-07560-3